WORD BIBLICAL COMMENTARY

WORD BIBLICAL COMMENTARY

VOLUME 25

Isaiah 34-66

JOHN D.W. WATTS

WORD BOOKS, PUBLISHER • WACO, TEXAS

Word Biblical Commentary
Isaiah 34–66

Library of Congress Cataloging in Publication Data
Main entry under title:

Word biblical commentary.

Includes bibliographies.
1. Bible—Commentaries—Collected works.
BS491.2.W67 220.7′7 81–71768
ISBN 0–8499–0224–X (vol. 25) AACR2

Printed in the United States of America

12 — 03 02 01 00 99

To
J. Wash Watts (1896–1975)
and
James W. Watts (1960–   )

my father and my son, who have both been inspiration and help in this work beyond my ability to adequately recognize or thank

Contents

Author's Preface **x**
Editorial Preface **xi**
Abbreviations **xii**

INTRODUCTION **xxiii**
BIBLIOGRAPHY **xxvi**

ACT VI: FROM CURSE TO BLESSING (Chaps. 34–39)

The Sixth Generation: Kings Jehoiakim and Zedekiah (*ca.* 605–586 B.C.) **1**
Historical Background **1**
Scene 1: Edom's Curse—Judah's Renewal (34:1–35:10) **2**
Excursus: Edom **10**
Excursus: Lilith **13**
Scene 2: A Reading from History: The Assyrian's Speech (36:1–22) **18**
Excursus: Seedbed for the Vision **23**
Scene 3: A Reading (continued): From Hearsay to Knowledge (37:1–20) **30**
Scene 4: A Reading (continued): Isaiah's Response from Yahweh (37:21–28) **38**
Scene 5: A Reading (continued): Hezekiah's Illness (38:1–8, 21–22) **48**
Scene 6: Hezekiah's Psalm (38:9–20) **53**
Scene 7: A Reading (continued): Hezekiah's Mistake (39:1–8) **62**

ACT VII: GOOD NEWS FOR JERUSALEM (40:1–44:23)

The Seventh Generation: King Jehoiachin (*ca.* 586–540 B.C.) **68**
Excursus: Deutero-Isaiah **69**
Excursus: The Formation of Chapters 40–66 **71**
Excursus: Form-Critical Categories in Chapters 40–66 **72**
Historical Background **73**
Prologue: In the Hall of Voices (40:1–9) **75**
Excursus: Exodus Typology **80**
Scene 1: The Lord Yahweh Comes Like a Shepherd (40:10–31) **83**
Excursus: ברא *"Create"/"Creator"* **93**
Scene 2: Israel Affirmed as Yahweh's Servant (41:1–20) **97**
Excursus: גאל *"Redeem"* **106**
Scene 3: Yahweh Defends His Authority and His Choice of Cyrus (41:21–42:12) **109**
Excursus: Identifying the "Servant of Yahweh" **115**
Excursus: The Former (ראשון) *and the New* (חדש) **120**

Scene 4: Yahweh Sends His Servant to Rescue Israel (42:13–43:21) **121**
Excursus: בחר *"Choose, Elect,"* בחיר *"Chosen, Elect"* **131**
Excursus: צדק/צדקה *"Righteousness, Legitimacy"* **133**
Scene 5: Remember These, Jacob! (43:22–44:23) **136**

ACT VIII: CYRUS, THE LORD'S ANOINTED (44:24–48:22)

The Eighth Generation: Cyrus/Cambyses (539–523 B.C.) **147**
Historical Background **147**
Scene 1: Yahweh Introduces Cyrus (44:24–45:13) **148**
Scene 2: In Yahweh Is Legitimacy and Strength (45:14–25) **158**
Scene 3: Bel Bows . . . My Purpose Stands (46:1–13) **163**
Scene 4: Sit in the Dust, Daughter Babylon (47:1–15) **167**
Scene 5: Move Out from Babylon! (48:1–22) **172**

ACT IX: THE SERVANT OF RULERS (49:1–52:12)

The Ninth Generation: Cambyses/Darius (522–*ca.* 518 B.C.) **180**
Historical Background **180**
Scene 1: A Light to the Nations (49:1–21) **181**
Scene 2: Even the Captive of a Champion (49:22–50:3) **190**
Scene 3: A Student's Tongue (50:4–51:8) **193**
Excursus: Parties in Palestinian Judaism **198**
Excursus: Zerubbabel **201**
Excursus: Law Codes Under the Persians **204**
Scene 4: Awake! Put on Strength! (51:9–52:2) **207**
Scene 5: How Fitting! A Messenger's Feet (52:3–12) **214**

ACT X: RESTORATION PAINS IN JERUSALEM (52:13–57:21)

The Tenth Generation: Darius/Xerxes (518–465 B.C.) **219**
Historical Background **219**
Scene 1: The Punishment for Our Peace (52:13–53:12) **222**
Excursus: The Sufferer/Martyr of 50:4–9 and Chapter 53 **227**
Scene 2: Sing, You Barren One! (54:1–17b) **233**
Excursus: עולם *"An Age"* **237**
Scene 3: A House of Prayer for All Peoples (54:17c–56:8) **240**
Scene 4: The Dark Side of Jerusalem (56:9–57:13) **251**
Scene 5: I Shall Heal Him (57:14–21) **260**

ACT XI: ZION'S LIGHT SHINES (Chaps. 58–61)

The Eleventh Generation: Artaxerxes (465–458 B.C.) **265**
Historical Background **265**
Scene 1: Yahweh's Kind of Fast (58:1–14) **268**
Scene 2: Troubled Times in Judah (59:1–15a) **277**

Scene 3: Yahweh Decides to Act (59:15b–21) **284**
Excursus: Jerusalem—A Persian Temple City **288**
Scene 4: Zion's Day Dawns (60:1–22) **289**
Scene 5: Yahweh's Agents to Bless Jerusalem (61:1–11) **299**

ACT XII: FOR ZION'S SAKE: NEW HEAVENS AND NEW LAND (Chaps. 62–66)

The Twelfth Generation: Artaxerxes (457–438 B.C.) **306**
Historical Background **306**
Scene 1: A New Name for Jerusalem (62:1–7) **309**
Scene 2: Yahweh's Oath and a Disturbing Apparition (62:8–63:6) **314**
Excursus: Megabyzus **318**
Scene 3: Sermon and Prayers (63:7–64:11[12]) **323**
Scene 4: Yahweh's Great Day: A New Jerusalem (65:1–66:24) **337**
Episode A: Yahweh Deals with His Opponents (65:1–16) **339**
Episode B: Yahweh Moves to Finish His New Jerusalem (65:17–66:5) **349**
Episode C: Yahweh Confirms His Servants in His New City (66:6–24) **358**

Appendix: Trito-Isaiah **367**
Indexes **369**

Author's Preface

Beyond the remarks that may be read in the preface to *Isaiah 1–33,* my thanks go to Dr. Leslie Allen and Dr. David Hubbard who read the manuscript in its entirety and made many useful suggestions. I am even more indebted to Pat Wienandt, Word Books' senior academic editor, who has shepherded this volume through the press, as she has the other volumes of this series, with devotion beyond the call of duty and skills seldom found in the trade. Without all this help the pages of these volumes would never have been printed.

Louisville, Kentucky
January 1987

JOHN D. W. WATTS

Editorial Preface

The launching of the *Word Biblical Commentary* brings to fulfillment an enterprise of several years' planning. The publishers and the members of the editorial board met in 1977 to explore the possibility of a new commentary on the books of the Bible that would incorporate several distinctive features. Prospective readers of these volumes are entitled to know what such features were intended to be; whether the aims of the commentary have been fully achieved time alone will tell.

First, we have tried to cast a wide net to include as contributors a number of scholars from around the world who not only share our aims, but are in the main engaged in the ministry of teaching in university, college, and seminary. They represent a rich diversity of denominational allegiance. The broad stance of our contributors can rightly be called evangelical, and this term is to be understood in its positive, historic sense of a commitment to scripture as divine revelation, and to the truth and power of the Christian gospel.

Then, the commentaries in our series are all commissioned and written for the purpose of inclusion in the *Word Biblical Commentary*. Unlike several of our distinguished counterparts in the field of commentary writing, there are no translated works, originally written in a non-English language. Also, our commentators were asked to prepare their own rendering of the original biblical text and to use those languages as the basis of their own comments and exegesis. What may be claimed as distinctive with this series is that it is based on the biblical languages, yet it seeks to make the technical and scholarly approach to a theological understanding of scripture understandable by—and useful to—the fledgling student, the working minister as well as to colleagues in the guild of professional scholars and teachers.

Finally, a word must be said about the format of the series. The layout in clearly defined sections has been consciously devised to assist readers at different levels. Those wishing to learn about the textual witnesses on which the translation is offered are invited to consult the section headed "Notes." If the readers' concern is with the state of modern scholarship on any given portion of scripture, then they should turn to the sections on "Bibliography" and "Form/Structure/Setting." For a clear exposition of the passage's meaning and its relevance to the ongoing biblical revelation, the "Comment" and concluding "Explanation" are designed expressly to meet that need. There is therefore something for everyone who may pick and use these volumes.

If these aims come anywhere near realization, the intention of the editors will have been met, and the labor of our team of contributors rewarded.

General Editors: *David A. Hubbard*
Glenn W. Barker †
Old Testament: *John D. W. Watts*
New Testament: *Ralph P. Martin*

Abbreviations

PERIODICALS, SERIALS, AND REFERENCE WORKS

AAAbo	Acta academiae Aboensis
AAASH	*Acta Antiqua Academicae Scientiarum Hungaricae*
AASOR	*Annual of the American Schools of Oriental Research*
AB	Anchor Bible
AcOr	*Acta Orientalia*
AfO	*Archiv für Orientforschung*
AfOBeiheft	Beihefte zür Archiv für Orientforschung
AIPHOS	*Annuarie de l'Institute de Philologie et d'Histoire Orientales et Slaves*
AJBI	*Annual of the Japanese Biblical Institute*
AJSL	*American Journal of Semitic Languages and Literature*
ALUOS	*Annual of Leeds University Oriental Society*
AnBib	Analecta Biblica
ANEP	*Ancient Near East in Pictures,* ed. J. B. Pritchard (Princeton: Princeton U. P., 1954)
ANET	*Ancient Near Eastern Texts,* ed. J. B. Pritchard (Princeton: Princeton U. P., 1950)
AnOr	Analecta orientalia
Ant	*Antonianum*
ANTJ	Arbeiten zu Neuen Testament und Judentum
ANVAO	*Avhandlingar utgitt av Det Norske Videnskaps-Akademi i Oslo*
AOT	*Altorientalische Texte und Bilder,* ed. H. Gressmann (Tübingen: Mohr, 1909)
APOT	*Apocrypha and Pseudepigrapha of the Old Testament,* ed. R. H. Charles (Oxford: Clarendon, 1913)
ArOr	*Archiv orientálni*
ArTh	Arbeiten zur Theologie
ARW	*Archiv für Religionswissenschaft*
AsSeign	*Assemblées du Seigneur*
ASTI	*Annual of the Swedish Theological Institute*
ATA	Alttestamentliche Abhandlungen
ATANT	Abhandlungen zur Theologie des Alten und Neuen Testaments
ATR	*Anglican Theological Review*
AUS	G. H. Dalmon. *Arbeit und Sitte in Palästina,* 1928 (reprint, Hildesheim: G. Olms, 1964)
AusBR	*Australian Biblical Review*
AUSS	Andrews University Seminary Studies
ÄZ	*Zeitschrift für ägyptische Sprache und Altertumskunde*
BA	*Biblical Archaeologist*

BAG	W. Bauer, W. F. Arndt, and F. W. Gingrich. *Greek-English Lexicon of the New Testament* (Chicago: Chicago U. P., 1957)
BASOR	*Bulletin of the American Schools of Oriental Research*
BAT	Die Botschaft des Alten Testaments
Bauer-Leander	H. Bauer and P. Leander. *Historische Grammatik der hebräischen Sprache des Alten Testaments* (Halle: Niemeyer, 1922; reprint, Hildesheim: Olms, 1962)
BBB	Bonner biblische Beiträge
BBC	*Broadman Bible Commentary*
BDB	F. Brown, S. R. Driver, and C. A. Briggs, *Hebrew and English Lexicon of the Old Testament* (London: Oxford U. P., 1907)
BenM	*Benediktionische Monatschrift*
BeO	*Bibbia e oriente*
BEvT	Beiträge zur evangelischen Theologie
BFCT	Beiträge zur Förderung christlicher Theologie
BHH	*Biblisch-Historisches Handwörterbuch,* ed. B. Reicke and L. Rost, 4 vols. (Göttingen: Vandenhoeck & Ruprecht, 1962–79)
BHK	*Biblia Hebraica,* ed. R. Kittel, 3rd ed. (Stuttgart: Württ. Bibelanstalt, 1937)
BHS	*Biblia Hebraica Stuttgartensia,* ed. K. Elliger and W. Rudolph (Stuttgart: Deutsche Bibelstiftung, 1967)
BHT	Beiträge zur historischen Theologie
Bib	*Biblica*
BibLeb	*Bibel und Leben*
BibOr	Biblica et Orientalia
BibS(N)	Biblische Studien, Neukirchen, 1951–
BJRL	*Bulletin of the John Rylands Library*
BK	*Bibel und Kirche*
BKAT	Biblischer Kommentar Altes Testament
BLE	*Bulletin de litterature ecclésiastique*
BLex	*Bibel-Lexikon,* ed. H. Haag, 2d ed. (Einsiedeln/Zürich: Benziger, 1968)
BLit	*Bibel und Liturgie*
BMik	*Beth Mikra*
BN	*Biblische Notizen*
BPAA	Bibliotheca Pontificii Athenaei Antoniani
BR	*Biblical Research*
BRL	K. Galling, *Biblisches Reallexikon* (Tübingen: Mohr, 1937)
Br. *Synt*	C. Brockelmann, *Hebräische Syntax* (Neukirchen: K. Moers, 1956)
BSac	*Bibliotheca Sacra*
BSO(A)S	*Bulletin of the School of Oriental (and African) Studies*
BT	*The Bible Translator*
BTB	*Biblical Theology Bulletin*
BVC	*Bible et vie chrétienne*

BWANT	Beiträge zur Wissenschaft vom Alten und Neuen Testament
BZ	*Biblische Zeitschrift*
BZAW	Beihefte zur *ZAW*
CAH	*Cambridge Ancient History* (Cambridge: U. P., 1925)
CB	*Cultura biblica*
CBC	Cambridge Biblical Commentary
CBib	The Cambridge Bible
CBQ	*Catholic Biblical Quarterly*
CBQMS	*CBQ* Monograph Series
CDios	*Ciudad de Dios*
CHAL	W. L. Holladay, *Concise Hebrew and Aramaic Lexicon* (Grand Rapids: Eerdmans, 1971)
ColcTFujen	*Collectanea theologica Universitatis Fujen,* Taipei
ConB	Coniectanea biblica
Conc	*Concilium*
CQR	*Church Quarterly Review*
CTM	Calwer Theologische Monographien
CTom	*Ciencia Tomista,* Salamanca
CuadT	*Cuadernos teológicos*
CurTM	*Currents in Theology and Mission*
CV	*Communio Viatorum*
CVC	*Communio Verbum Caro*
DBSup	*Dictionaire de la Bible, Supplément*
DISO	C. F. Jean & J. Hoftijzer, *Dictionnaire des inscriptions sémitiques de l'ouest* (Leiden: E. J. Brill, 1965)
DOTT	*Documents from Old Testament Times,* ed. D. W. Thomas (London: T. Nelson, 1958)
DTT	*Dansk teologisk tidsskrift*
DunRev	*Dunwoodie Review*
EAEHL	*The Encyclopedia of Archaeological Excavations in the Holy Land,* ed. M. Avi-Yonah, 4 vols. (London: Oxford U. P., 1975)
EBib	Études Bibliques
EglT	*Eglise et Theologie*
EncBrit	*Encyclopaedia Britannica*
EncJud	*Encyclopedia judaica*
EnsMikr	אנציקלופדיה מקראית, Jerusalem
EphMar	*Ephemerides Mariologicae*
ErJb	*Eranos-Jahrbuch*
EstBib	*Estudios Biblicos*
EstEcl	*Estudios Eclesiasticos*
ETL	*Ephemerides Theologicae Lovanienses*
ETR	*Etudes theologiques et religieuses*
EvQ	*Evangelical Quarterly*
EvT	*Evangelische Theologie*
ExpTim	*Expository Times*
FRLANT	Forschungen zur Religion und Literature des Alten und Neuen Testaments

FuF	*Forschungen und Fortschritte*
FzB	Forschungen zur Bibel
FZPT	*Freiburger Zeitschrift für Philosophie und Theologie*
GB	*Gesenius' Hebräisches und Aramäisches Handwörterbuch,* ed. F. P. W. Buhl (Berlin: Springer Verlag, 1915)
GerefTT	*Gereformeerd Teologisch Tijdschrift*
GKC	*Gesenius' Hebrew Grammar,* ed. E. Kautzsch; tr. A. E. Cowley; 2d ed. (Oxford: Clarendon, 1910)
GSAT	G. von Rad, *Gesammelte Studien zum Alten Testament,* ThB 8 (Munich: Kaiser, 1958)
GTTOT	J. Simons, *The Geographical and Topographical Texts of the Old Testament* (Leiden: E. J. Brill, 1959)
HALAT	W. Baumgartner, *Hebräisches und aramäisches Lexikon zum Alten Testament,* rev. 3d ed. of KB (Leiden: E. J. Brill, 1969)
HAT	Handbuch zum Alten Testament
HI	J. Bright, *A History of Israel,* 3d ed. (Philadelphia: Westminster, 1981)
HKAT	Handkommentar zum Alten Testament
HSAT	*Die Heilige Schrift des Alten Testaments,* ed. A. Bertholet, 2 vols. (Tübingen: 1909[3])
HSMS	Harvard Semitic Monograph Series
HTR	*Harvard Theological Review*
HUCA	*Hebrew Union College Annual*
IB	*Interpreter's Bible*
IBR	Institute for Biblical Research
IBS	*Irish Biblical Studies*
ICC	International Critical Commentary
IDB	*Interpreter's Dictionary of the Bible,* ed. G. A. Buttrick, 4 vols. (Nashville: Abingdon, 1962)
IDBSup	Supplementary volume to *IDB,* ed. K. Crim (Nashville: Abingdon, 1976)
IEJ	*Israel Exploration Journal*
IER	*Irish Ecclesiastical Record*
IJH	*Israelite and Judean History,* ed. J. H. Hayes and J. M. Miller (Philadelphia: Westminster, 1977)
Int	*Interpretation*
IOTS	B. S. Childs, *Introduction to the Old Testament as Scripture* (Philadelphia: Fortress, 1979)
ISBE	*International Standard Bible Encyclopedia,* ed. G. W. Bromiley, 3 vols. (incomplete) (Grand Rapids: Eerdmans, 1979, 1982, 1985)
JA	*Journal asiatique*
JANESCU	*Journal of the Ancient Near Eastern Society of Columbia University*
Janus	*Janus: Archives Internationales pour l'Histoire de la Medicine*
JAOS	*Journal of the American Oriental Society*
JBL	*Journal of Biblical Literature*
JBR	*Journal of Bible and Religion*

JCS	*Journal of Cuneiform Studies*
JEA	*Journal of Egyptian Archeology*
Jes.Erl.	K. F. R. Budde, *Jesaja's Erleben* (Gotha: L. Klotz, 1928)
JETS	*Journal of the Evangelical Theological Society*
JNES	*Journal of Near Eastern Studies*
JNWSL	*Journal of Northwest Semitic Languages*
Joüon	P. P. Joüon, *Grammaire de l'Hébreu biblique* (Rome: Pontifical Biblical Institute, 1947)
JQR	*Jewish Quarterly of Religion*
JSJ	*Journal for the Study of Judaism*
JSNT	*Journal for the Study of the New Testament*
JSOT	*Journal for the Study of the Old Testament*
JSOTSup	*JSOT* Supplement
JSS	*Journal of Semitic Studies*
JTS	*Journal of Theological Studies*
JTSA	*Journal of Theology for Southern Africa*
Jud	*Judaica*
KAT	Kommentar zum Alten Testament
KB	L. Koehler and W. Baumgartner, *Lexicon in veteris testamenti libros* (Leiden: E. J. Brill, 1951–53)
KD	*Kerygma und Dogma*
KHC	Kurzer Hand-Commentar zum Alten Testament
KS	A. Alt, *Kleine Schriften zur Geschichte des Volkes Israel,* 2 vols. (Munich: C. H. Beck'sche, 1953)
LBBC	Layman's Bible Book Commentary
LD	Lectio divina
Leš	*Lešonénu*
Löw	I. Löw, *Die Flora der Juden,* 4 vols. (Wien/Leipzig: R. Löwit, 1924–34)
LQ	*Lutheran Quarterly*
LR	*Lutherische Rundschau*
LTP	*Laval Theologique et Philosophique*
LUA	Lund universitäts Ärschriften
LW	*Lutheran World*
MBA	Y. Aharoni and M. Avi-Yonah, *Macmillan Bible Atlas,* 2d ed. (New York: Macmillan, 1977)
MCom	Miscelánea Comillas
MGWJ	*Monatschrift für Geschichte und Wissenschaft des Judentums*
MIO	*Mitteilungen des Instituts für Orientforschung*
MTZ	*Münchener theologische Zeitschrift*
Mut. Nom.	Philo, *De mutatione nominum*
MVAG	*Mitteilungen der Vorder-asiatisch-ägyptischen Gesellschaft*
NC	*La Nouvelle Clio*
NCBC	New Century Bible Commentary
NedTTs	*Nederlands theologisch tijdschrift*
NGTT	*Nederduitse Gereformeerde Teologiese Tydskrif*
NICOT	New International Commentary on the Old Testament

NIDNTT	*The New International Dictionary of New Testament Theology,* ed. C. Brown, 3 vols. (Grand Rapids: Zondervan, 1975–78)
NKZ	*Neue kirchliche Zeitschrift*
NorTT	*Norsk Teologisk Tidsskrift*
NRT	*Nouvelle Revue Théologique*
NThSt	*Nieuwe theologische Studien*
NTS	*New Testament Studies*
NTSup	Supplement to *Novum Testamentum*
OLP	*Orientalia Lovaniensia Periodica*
OLZ	*Orientalische Literaturzeitung*
Or	*Orientalia*
OrAnt	*Oriens antiquus*
OTFC	*Old Testament form Criticism,* ed. J. H. Hayes (San Antonio, TX: Trinity U. P., 1974)
OTL	Old Testament Library
OTM	Old Testament Message
OTS	*Oudtestamentische Studien*
OTT	G. von Rad, *Old Testament Theology,* tr. D. M. G. Stalker (New York: Harper, 1962–65)
OTWSAP	*Die Ou Testamentiese Werkgemeenskap in Suid-Afrika,* Pretoria
PalCl	*Palestra del Clero*
ParLi	*Paroisse et Liturgie*
PEQ	*Palestine Exploration Quarterly*
POS	Pretoria Oriental Studies
POTT	*People of Old Testament Times,* ed. D. J. Wiseman (London: Oxford U. P., 1973)
PSB	*The Princeton Seminary Bulletin*
PSV	*Parola Spirito et Vita*
PVi	*Parole di Vita*
PW	*Pauly's Real-encyclopädie der classischen Altertumswissenschaft,* new ed., G. Wissowa (Stuttgart: J. B. Metzler, 1894–)
PWSup	Supplement to PW
RB	*Revue biblique*
RCB	*Revista de cultura biblica*
RechBib	*Recherches bibliques*
REJ	*Revue des études juives*
ResQ	*Restoration Quarterly*
RevDrCan	*Revue de droit canonique*
RevExp	*Review and Expositor*
RevistB	*Revista Biblica Italiana*
RevThom	*Revue thomiste*
RGG[3]	*Die Religion in Geschichte und Gegenwart,* ed. K. Galling, 3d ed., 6 vols. (Tübingen: Mohr, 1957–65)
RHPR	*Revue d'histoire et de philosophie religieuses*
RHR	*Revue de l'histoire des religions*

RicBR	*Ricerche Bibliche e Religiose*
RivB	*Rivista biblica*
RLC	*Revue de littérature comparée*
RocTKan	*Roczniki Teologiczno-Kanoniczne*
RScRel	*Revue des sciences religieuses*
RSR	*Recherches de science religieuse*
RTP	*Revue de théologie et de philosophie*
RTR	*Reformed Theological Review*
Sal	*Salesianum*
SBeT	*Studia Biblica et Theologica*
SBFLA	*Studii biblici franciscani liber annuus*
SBLMS	Society of Biblical Literature Monograph Series
SBS	Stuttgarter Bibelstudien
SBT	Studies in Biblical Theology
ScEs	*Science et esprit*
Scr	*Scripture*
ScrHier	Scripta Hierosolymitana
SEÅ	*Svensk Exegetisk Årsbok*
Sef	*Sefarad*
SeiRon	*Seisho-gaku ronshu*, Tokyo
Sem	*Semitica*
SJT	*Scottish Journal of Theology*
SNVAO	Skrifter utgitt av Det Norske Videnskaps-Akademie i Oslo
SOTSMS	Society for Old Testament Study, Monograph Series
SPCK	Society for the Propagation of Christian Knowledge
Spfdr	*The Springfielder*
ST	*Studia Theologica*
STDJ	Studies on the Texts of the Desert of Judah
StG	Studium Generale
STU	Schweizerische theologische Umschau
StVladTQ	*Saint Vladimir Theological Quarterly*
STZ	*Schweizer Theologische Zeitschrift*
SWJT	*Southwestern Journal of Theology*
TAik	*Teologinen Aikakauskirja*
TBC	Torch Bible Commentaries
TBT	*The Bible Today*
TD	*Theology Digest*
TDNT	*Theological Dictionary of the New Testament,* ed. G. Kittel and G. Friedrich; tr. G. W. Bromiley; 10 vols. (Grand Rapids: Eerdmans, 1964–74)
TDOT	*Theological Dictionary of the Old Testament,* ed. G. J. Botterweck and H. Ringgren; tr. D. E. Green; 4 vols. (incomplete) (Grand Rapids: Eerdmans, 1974–)
TG	*Theologie der Gegenwart in Auswahl*
TGl	*Theologie und Glaube*
THAT	*Theologische Handwörterbuch zum Alten Testament,* ed. E. Jenni and C. Westermann, 2 vols. (Munich/Zürich, 1971)

ThB	Theologische Bücherei
TK	*Texte und Kontexte*
TLZ	*Theologische Literaturzeitung*
TOTC	Tyndale Old Testament Commentaries
TQ	*Theologische Quartalschrift*
TRE	*Theologische Realenzyklopädie,* ed. G. Krause and G. Müller; 13 vols. (incomplete) (Berlin: de Gruyter, 1977–)
TRev	*Theologische Revue*
TRu	*Theologische Rundschau*
TSK	*Theologische Studien und Kritiken*
TT	*Theologisch tijdschrift*
TTS	Trierer theologische Studien
TTZ	*Trierer theologische Zeitschrift*
TViat	*Theologia Viatorum*
TWAT	*Theologisches Wörterbuch zum Alten Testament,* ed. G. J. Botterweck and H. Ringgren, 4 vols. (incomplete) (Stuttgart: Kohlhammer, 1973–)
TynBul	*Tyndale Bulletin*
TZ	*Theologische Zeitschrift*
UF	*Ugaritische Forschungen*
URAM	*Ultimate Reality and Meaning*
UUÄ	Uppsala Universitetsärsskrift
VC	*Vetera Christianorum*
VD	*Verbum domini*
VE	*Vox Evangelica*
VF	*Verkündigung und Forschung*
VG	C. Brockelmann, *Grundriss der vergleichenden Grammatik der semitischen Sprachen,* 2 vols. (Berlin/New York: Lemcke & Buechner, 1908–15)
VSpir	*Vie spirituelle*
VT	*Vetus Testamentum*
VTSup	*VT* Supplements
WB	J. Aistleitner, *Wörterbuch der ugaritischen Sprache* (Berlin: Akademie-Verlag, 1963)
WBC	Word Biblical Commentary
WC	Westminster Commentaries
WMANT	Wissenschaftliche Monographien zum Alten und Neuen Testament
WO	*Die Welt des Orients*
WTJ	*Westminster Theological Journal*
WuD	*Wort und Dienst*
WZKM	*Wiener Zeitschrift für Kunde des Morgenlandes*
ZAW	*Zeitschrift für die alttestamentliche Wissenschaft*
ZBK	Zürcher Bibelkommentare
ZDMG	*Zeitschrift der deutschen morgenländischen Gesellschaft*
ZDPV	*Zeitschrift der deutschen Palastina-Vereins*
ZKT	*Zeitschrift für katholische Theologie*
ZRGG	*Zeitschrift für Religions- und Geistesgeschichte*
ZS	*Zeitschrift für Semistik*

ZTK	*Zeitschrift für Theologie und Kirche*
ZWT	*Zeitschrift für wissenschaftliche Theologie*

HEBREW GRAMMAR

abs	absolute
acc	accusative
act	active
adj	adjective
adv acc	adverbial accusative
aor	aorist
c	common
coh	cohortative
conj	conjunction
consec	consecutive
constr	construct
fem, f	feminine
fut	future
gen	genitive
hiph	hiphil
hithp	hithpael
hoph	hophal
impf	imperfect
impv	imperative
ind	indicative
inf	infinitive
juss	jussive
masc, m	masculine
niph	niphal
obj	object
pass	passive
pf	perfect
pilp	pilpel
pl	plural
prep	preposition
pron	pronoun
pronom	pronominal
ptcp	participle
sg	singular
subj	subject

TEXTUAL NOTES

'A	Aquila
Akk	Akkadian
Amor	Amorite
Arab	Arabic
Aram	Aramaic
B	MT MS, ed. Jacob ben Chayim, Venice (1524/25)
C	MT MS, Cairo Codex of the prophets
Copt	Coptic
DSS^{Isa}	Dead Sea Scroll of Isaiah = $1QIsa^{a}$
Egy	Egyptian
Eth	Ethiopic
Gr.	Greek
Heb.	Hebrew
K	Kethibh
K^{Occ}	Occidental (western) Kethib
K^{Or}	Oriental (eastern) Kethib
L	MT MS, Leningrad Codex
LXX	Septuagint
LXX^{A}	LXX MS, Alexandrian Codex
LXX^{B}	LXX MS, Vatican Codex
LXX^{L}	LXX MSS of the Lucianic recension
LXX^{Q}	LXX MS, Marchalian Codex
LXX^{S*}	LXX MS, Sinai Codex, original reading
LXX^{S^c}	LXX MS, Sinai Codex, corrector
$MS(S)^{G}$	Heb. MS(S) ed. C. D. Ginsburg (1908)
$MS(S)^{K}$	Heb. MS(S) ed. B. Kennicott (1776–80)

MS(S)^{R}	Heb. MS(S) ed. J. B. de Rossi (1784–88)
MT	Masoretic Text
OL	Old Latin
Q	Qere
1QM	*Milhamah,* the War Scroll, from Qumran Cave 1
1QIsa^{a}	The St. Mark's Isaiah Scroll from Qumran Cave 1 = DSS^{Isa}
1QIsa^{b}	The Hebrew University Isaiah Scroll from Qumran Cave 1
4QpIsa^{c}	*Pesher* on Isaiah from Qumran Cave 4
Syh	Syrohexaplaris
Syr	Syriac
Tg	Targum
Ug	Ugaritic
Vg	Vulgate
Θ	Theodotion
Σ	Symmachus

Biblical and Apocryphal Books

Gen	Genesis
Exod	Exodus
Lev	Leviticus
Num	Numbers
Deut	Deuteronomy
Josh	Joshua
Judg	Judges
Ruth	Ruth
1–2 Sam	1–2 Samuel
1–2 Kgs	1–2 Kings
1–2 Chr	1–2 Chronicles
Ezra	Ezra
Neh	Nehemiah
Esth	Esther
Job	Job
Ps(s)	Psalm(s)
Prov	Proverbs
Eccl	Ecclesiastes
Cant	Canticles, Song of Solomon
Isa	Isaiah
Jer	Jeremiah
Lam	Lamentations
Ezek	Ezekiel
Dan	Daniel
Hos	Hosea
Joel	Joel
Amos	Amos
Obad	Obadiah
Jonah	Jonah
Mic	Micah
Nah	Nahum
Hab	Habakkuk
Zeph	Zephaniah
Hag	Haggai
Zech	Zechariah
Mal	Malachi
1–2 Esdr	1–2 Esdras
Wis	Wisdom of Solomon
Sir	Ecclesiasticus or The Wisdom Of Jesus Son of Sirach
1–2–3–4 Macc	1–2–3–4 Maccabees
Matt	Matthew
Mark	Mark
Luke	Luke
John	John
Acts	Acts
Rom	Romans
1–2 Cor	1–2 Corinthians
Phil	Philippians
Heb	Hebrews
Jas	James
1–2 Pet	1–2 Peter
1–2–3 John	1–2–3 John
Rev	Revelation

Miscellaneous

ANE	Ancient Near East
AV	Authorized Version
B.C.	Before Christ
chap(s)	chapter(s)

col(s).	column(s)
diss.	dissertation
DtH	Deuteronomistic History (Joshua–2 Kings)
Dtr	Deuteronomist
E	East
ed(s).	edition; edited by; editor(s)
esp.	especially
ET	English translation
EV(V)	English verse(s)
FS	Festschrift
hap. leg.	*hapax legomenon*
JB	*Jerusalem Bible*
JPSA	Jewish Publication Society of America Version
lit.	literally
LLS	*Los Libros Sagrados*
MS(S)	manuscript(s)
n.	note
NAB	*New American Bible*
NE	Northeast
NEB	*New English Bible*
NIV	*New International Version*
NJV	*New Jewish Version*
NT	New Testament
OT	Old Testament
p(p).	page(s)
RSV	*Revised Standard Version*
S	South
tr.	translated; translator
U. P.	University Press
v(v)	verse(s)
W	West
§ __	section/paragraph
√	root

Introduction

This volume is a continuation of *Isaiah 1–33* (1985). Relevant explanation of the format and methods used are given there (xxiii–xlvii). The modern bibliography is repeated here with a few additions. The first volume dealt with Acts I through V (chaps. 1–33). This volume continues with Acts VI through XII (chaps. 34–66).

Bibliography and references to other approaches to this material are supplied in *Excursus: Deutero-Isaiah; Excursus: The Formation of Chapters 40–66; Excursus: Form-Critical Categories in 40–66,* each of which is inserted at the appropriate point in the commentary; and in *Appendix: Trito-Isaiah.*

Explanation of significant historical background for each act is presented in the introduction to the act.

THE APOLOGETIC NATURE OF THE DRAMA

The basic apologetic character of the Book of Isaiah is particularly clear in the so-called disputation speeches. Adrian Graffy's book (*A Prophet Confronts His People,* AnBib 104 [Rome: Biblical Institute Press, 1984]) came to my attention too late to be used very much. He has defined the disputational speech narrowly and dealt specifically with certain clear examples of the genre. He has also shown how the term does not fit many other examples for which it has been loosely used.

The Book of Isaiah, especially chaps. 40–66, is clearly controversial in tone and purpose. It presents a particular view of God's will for Israel and Jerusalem in the post-exilic period which is obviously different from that espoused by other groups. This accounts for the tension that is evident in its scenes between different groups and between Yahweh and certain of these parties. The book's dramatic structure allows these debates to be heard from both sides. But there is no doubt concerning the implied author's position.

This book sees the Persian empire, particularly the emperors Cyrus, Darius I, and Artaxerxes I, as God's instruments for a restoration of Jerusalem and its Temple. It sees Israel's role in the post-exilic era to be that of a religious people, with Jerusalem as the symbol of its worshiping unity. It sees no political or military role for its people. Nor does it foresee a complete return to Palestine. Yet in all this it sees Yahweh at work to fulfill his purposes with Israel and Jerusalem as expressed in promises to Abraham and David. It sees the possibility of Moses' covenantal law being accepted and obeyed as never before with the promised blessings that should accompany such obedience.

ROLE DEVELOPMENT AND ROLE REVERSAL IN CHAPS. 40–66

The major roles that appeared in chaps. 1–34 continue in chaps. 40–66. But virtually all of them are reversed, evolve, or are substituted.

This can be demonstrated by a few examples of the major roles. Yahweh continues to be the central figure, but his role in administering the strategy of judgment and curses (chap. 1; 6:11–13), is reversed to become that of comforter for Israel (40:1–2) and restorer of Jerusalem.

While Israel was understood first to have a political role as the Northern Kingdom (1:2–7; chaps. 5, 10), in chaps. 40–48 the role has evolved so that she here becomes simply Yahweh's servant people in exile. Finally, in chaps. 65–66, she is composed of the individual "servants" who loyally worship in the restored Temple.

At the beginning Jerusalem appeared as the Davidic capital under judgment (1:9–31, chap. 3) and promise (2:2–4; 4:2–5). Her role has changed, and in chap. 40–57 she appears as the pile of ruins that remain after Nebuchadnezzar's assault. Finally she is pictured as the restored city of Nehemiah's time.

Assyria is replaced by Cyrus's empire with a reversed role. The Babylon of Merodach-Baladan (chaps. 13, 14, 21, and 39) is replaced by the decaying Babylon of Nabunaid (chaps. 46, 47), and the Babylon of Nebuchadnezzar is ignored.

Kings, officials, and the prophet Isaiah play small roles in the first six acts (chaps. 1–39). Similarly, individual persons are implied without being named in the last six acts and occasionally appear in anonymous cameo appearances. The commentary suggests that they be identified as Sheshbazzar (48:16b), Zerubbabel (50:4–9 and chap. 53), Ezra (61:1–3), and Nehemiah (62:6).

OBSTACLES TO RESTORATION OF JERUSALEM IN THE 6TH AND 5TH CENTURIES B.C.

The exiles faced formidable obstacles in their wish to return to Palestine and to rebuild Jerusalem. The first obstacle was the Babylonian Empire which had brought them into exile and destroyed their land. A second obstacle was the people who remained or moved into the land vacated by the exiles, where they became entrenched by the support of Babylonian officials and by ruling factions of neighboring nations. Ezra-Nehemiah provide ample documentation of this situation.

Those who had increased their holdings by staying in the land were obviously not eager for the former owners to claim it again. Jews who had established their families and livelihoods in Babylon were not eager to give up their situations and start over again in Palestine where they would have to face the spectacle of the destruction that had been wrought and must now be cleaned up and rebuilt. And of course the economic problems in getting a devastated territory back into viable operation were also immense.

There also had emerged a number of parties among the Jews. Each of these had its own objectives and expectations. Getting any common goal before them was difficult, if not impossible.

But Persian conquest and policy supported restoration of Jerusalem and its temple on three different occasions. Persian authorities protected against the pressure of neighboring rulers. And in each of those eras Persian emperors appointed Jewish governors to accomplish the task, as Ezra-Nehemiah tells it and as the Vision celebrates it.

THE ROLES OF PERSIAN EMPERORS

Three Persian emperors play major roles in Isaiah 40–66, just as they do in Ezra-Nehemiah. Only the first, Cyrus, with sixty statements in chaps. 41–48, is mentioned by name. References to him occur in 41:25, 42:1–4, 44:28, 45:1–8, 45:13, 45:24, 46:10b–13, and 48:14–15. He liberated Babylon, decreed that Israel could return to build its temple, commissioned Sheshbazzar to lead the first return, and gave him the vessels that had been looted from the temple by the Babylonians.

The second is Darius I, with eighty-seven assertions in chaps. 49–57. He appears or is mentioned in 49:5–8; 51:4–8; 52:1, 6; 13–15; 53:10; 54:11–15, 55:11; 56:1, 8; and 57:1, 11. He confirmed and repeated the decree for restoration, commissioned Zerubbabel, had the temple built, and secured the safety of Palestine by bringing Egypt under control.

The third is Artaxerxes I, about whom over one hundred statements are made in chaps. 58–63. He appears or is mentioned in 58:1–14; 59:4–15; 60:1, 17–21; 61:3b, 7–11; and 63:1–5. He confirmed and repeated the decree to restore the temple, appointed Ezra and then Nehemiah to carry out his instructions, financed the restoration, built the walls and established the city, and recaptured Egypt, securing Palestine's safety again.

The Vision follows the pattern of Ezra-Nehemiah in recognizing the powerful Persian commitment to the restoration. Undoubtedly Persia had ulterior motives in doing this. A loyal and strong Judah was one more element for stability in that frontier region. But the Vision understands these efforts as ways by which Yahweh accomplished his strategy for his people and for the world.

Bibliography

COMMENTARIES

Chapters 1–39

Gray, G. B. (1912). *A Critical and Exegetical Commentary on the Book of Isaiah I–XXVI.* ICC. New York: T. & T. Clark, 1912. **Boutflower, C.** (1930). *The Book of Isaiah Chapters (I–XXXIX) In the Light of the Assyrian Monuments.* London: SPCK, 1930. **Procksch, O.** (1930). *Jesaia I.* Erste Hälfte: Kapitel 1–39. KAT IX. Leipzig: W. Scholl, 1930. **Scott, R. B. Y.** (1956). "The Book of Isaiah." *IB* 5. New York/Nashville: Abingdon Press (1956) 149–381. **Eichrodt, W.** (1960). *Der Heilige in Israel:* Jesaja 1–12. *Der Herr der Geschichte:* Jesaja 13–23, 28–39. BAT 17/1. Stuttgart: Calwer Verlag, 1960, 1967. **Kaiser, O.** (1960). *Isaiah 1–12. Isaiah 13–39.* Tr. R. A. Wilson. OTL. Philadelphia: Westminster, 1972; 2nd ed., 1983. **Wildberger, H.** (1965–82). *Jesaja 1–12. Jesaja 13–27. Jesaja 28–39.* BKAT 10. Neukirchen-Vluyn: Neukirchener Verlag, 1972, 1978, 1982. **Auvray, P.** (1972). *Isaïe 1–39.* SB. Paris: J. Gabalda, 1972. **Herbert, A. S.** (1973). *The Book of the Prophet Isaiah. Chapters 1–39.* CBC. Cambridge: University Press, 1973. **Clements, R. E.** (1980). *Isaiah 1–39.* NCBC. Grand Rapids: Eerdmans, 1980. **Oswalt, J. T.** (1986). *The Book of Isaiah 1–39.* NICOT. Grand Rapids: Eerdmans, 1986.

Chapters 40–66:

Budde, K. (1909). "Das Buch Jesaja, Kap. 40–66." *HSAT* I. Tübingen: 1909^3. **Levy, R.** (1925). *Deutero-Isaiah.* London: Oxford U. P., 1925. **Volz, P.** (1932). *Jesaja II.* Zweite Hälfte: 40–66. KAT 10. Leipzig: W. Scholl, 1932. **Muilenburg, J.** (1956). "The Book of Isaiah," *IB* 5. New York/Nashville: Abingdon Press (1956) 382–773. **North, C.** (1964). *The Second Isaiah.* Oxford: Oxford U. P., 1964. **Smart, J. D.** (1965). *History and Theology in Second Isaiah.* A Commentary on Is. 35; 40–66. Philadelphia: Westminster, 1965. **Knight, G. A. F.** (1965). *Deutero-Isaiah:* A Theological Commentary on Isaiah 40–55. New York/Nashville: Abingdon Press, 1965. **Westermann, C.** (1966). *Isaiah 40–66.* Tr. D. M. G. Stalker. Philadelphia: Westminster, 1969. **McKenzie, J. L.** (1968). *Second Isaiah.* AB 20. Garden City, NY: Doubleday, 1968. **Elliger, K.** (1970). *Jesaja II.* (Complete through 45:7.) BKAT 11. Neukirchen-Vluyn: Neukirchener Verlag, 1978. **Bonnard, P. E.** (1972). *Le Second Isaïe, son disciple et leurs éditeurs.* SB. Paris: J. Gabalda, 1972. **Whybray, R. N.** (1975). *Isaiah 40–66.* NCBC. Grand Rapids: Eerdmans, 1975. **Herbert, A. S.** (1975). *The Book of the Prophet Isaiah 40–66.* CBC. Cambridge: U. P., 1975. **Scullion, J.** (1982). *Isaiah 40–66.* OTM. Wilmington, Del.: Glazier, 1982.

Only a few in this period have written on the entire book of Isaiah: **Kissane, E. J.** (1941–43). *The Book of Isaiah.* 2 vols. Rev. ed. Dublin: Browne and Nolan, 1960. **Steinmann, J.** (1949–55). *Le Prophéte Isaïe.* Paris: Cerf, 1949–55. **Fohrer, G.** (1960–64). *Das Buch Jesaja.* 3 vols. ZBK. Zürich: Zwingli Verlag, 1960–64. **Leslie, E. A.** (1963). *Isaiah.* New York: Abingdon, 1963. **Young, E. J.** (1965–72). *The Book of Isaiah.* 3 vols. NICOT. Grand Rapids: Eerdmans, 1965–72. **Kelley, P. H.** (1971). "Isaiah." *BBC.* Nashville: Broadman, 1971. 149–374. **Butler, T. C.** (1982). *Isaiah.* LBBC 10. Nashville: Broadman, 1982. **Ridderboss, J.** (1985). *Isaiah.* (Dutch original, 1955). Tr. J. Vriend. Grand Rapids: Zondervan, 1985.

Selected Articles and Monographs

Adams, L. "Selection of Appropriate Methods for Style Analysis in Relation to the Isaiah Problem." *Hebrew Computational Linguistics* 7 (1973) 73–88. **Ahuviah, A.** "ביטויים מן השדה הסימנטי של הבריתות בלשונו של ישעיהו שני." *BMik* 22 (1977) 370–74. **Akpunonu, P.** *Salvation in Deutero-Isaiah: A Philological Exegetical Study.* Diss. Pont. Univ. Urbanianae, Rome, 1972. **Altmann, P.** *Erwählungstheologie und Universalismus im Alten Testament.* BZAW 92. Berlin: de Gruyter, 1964. **Amir, Y.** "המימד האסכטולוגי בנבואת ישעיהו השני" [Dimensions eschatologiques dans la prophétie d'Isaïe II]. FS Z. Shazar. Ed. B. Z. Luria. Jerusalem: 1973. 173–90. **Amirtham, S.** "Das Heil nach Deuterojesaja." *Das Heil der Welt heute.* World Missions Conference, Bangkok. Ed. P. A. Potter. Stuttgart/Berlin: Kreuz-Verlag, 1973. 59–63. **Amsler, S.** "Prophétie et typologie." *RTP* 3 (1953) 139–48. **Arragon, G. J. van.** "Reminiscenties aan Deuteronomium in Jesaja 40–55." *De Knecht.* FS J. Koole. Kampen: Kok, 1978. **Baltzer, K.** "Zur Formbestimmung der Texte vom Gottesknecht im Deuterojesaja-Buch." *Probleme biblischer Theologie.* FS G. von Rad. Munich: Kaiser, 1971. 27–43. **Bardtke, H.** "Der Erweckungsgedanke in der exilisch-nachexilischen Literatur des AT." FS O. Eissfeldt. BZAW 77. Giessen: Töpelmann, 1958. 9–24. **Barrois, G.** "Critical Exegesis and Traditional Hermeneutics: A Methodological Inquiry on the Basis of the Book of Isaiah." *StVlad TQ* 16 (1972) 107–27. **Barstad, H. M.** "Lebte Deuterojesaja in Judaia?" *NorTT* 83 (1982) 77–87. **Bedenbough, B.** "The Doctrine of God in Deutero-Isaiah." *LQ* 11 (1959) 154–58. **Behr, J. W.** *The Writings of Deutero-Isaiah and the Neo-Babylonian Royal Inscriptions.* Pretoria, S.A.: Rubinstein, 1937. **Bjornard, R. B.** "The Evangelist of the Exile." *TBT* 96 (1978) 1614–21. **Blank, S. H.** "The Theology of Jewish Survival According to Biblical Sources (. . . Second Isaiah . . .)." *Prophetic Thought.* Cincinnati: HUC Press, 1977. 45–54. **Blenkinsopp, J.** "The Unknown Prophet of the Exile." *Scr* 14 (1962) 81–90, 109–18. **Boer, P. A. H. de.** *Second Isaiah's Message.* OTS 11. Leiden: E. J. Brill, 1956. **Briggs, C. A.** "An Analysis of Isaiah 40–62." *OT and Semitic Studies.* FS W. R. Harper. Vol. 1. Chicago: U. P., 1908. **Bright, J.** "Faith and Destiny: The Meaning of History in Deutero-Isaiah." *Int* 5 (1951) 3–26. **Carmignac, J.** "Six passages d'Isaïe éclairés par Qumran." *Bibel und Qumran.* Ed. S. Wagner. Berlin: Evangelische Haupt-Bibelgesellschaft, 1968. 37–46. **Carroll, R. P.** "Second Isaiah and the Failure of Prophecy." *ST* 32 (1978) 119–31. **Cassuto, U.** "On the Formal and Stylistic Relationship between Dt-Is and Other Biblical Writings (Jer; Ez; Nah; Zeph)." *Biblical and Oriental Studies.* Jerusalem: Magnes, 1973. 1:141–77. **Causse, A.** *Du group ethnique à la communauté religieuse.* Paris: F. Alcan, 1937. ———. "Le Mythe de la nouvelle Jerusalem du Deutero-Esaie a la IIIe Sibylle." *RHPR* (1938) 377–414. **Chary, T.** *Les Prophètes et le Culte a Partir de l'Exil.* BT 3. Tournai: Desclee, 1955. **Chiesa, B.** "Ritorno dell'Esilio e Conversione a Dio." *BibOr* 14 (1972) 167–80. **Cobb, W. C.** "On Integrating the Book of Isaiah." *JBL* 20 (1901) 77–100. ———. "Where Was Isaiah xl–lxvi Written in?" *JBL* 27 (1908) 48–64. **Conrad, E. W.** *Patriarchal Traditions in Second Isaiah.* Diss. Princeton Theol. Sem., 1974. **Constantinescu, A. N.** "Isaia si Ieremia." *Glasul Bisericii. . . .* Sf. Mitropoliei a Ungrovlahiei 32 (1973) 389–402. **Cross, F. M.** "The Council of Yahweh in Second Isaiah." *JNES* 12 (1953) 274–77. **Crüsemann, F.** *Studien zur Formgeschichte von Hymnus und Danklied in Israel.* WMANT 32. Neukirchen-Vluyn: Neukirchener Verlag, 1969. **Dahl, G.** "Some Recent Interpretations of Second Isaiah." *JBL* 48 (1929) 362–77. **Dahood, M. J.** "Some Ambiguous Texts in Isaiah." *CBQ* 20 (1958) 41–49. ———. "Textual Problems in Isaiah." *CBQ* 22 (1960) 400–409. **Davidson, R.** "Universalism in Second Isaiah." *SJT* 16 (1963) 166–85. **Deming, L.** *Hymnic Language in Deutero-Isaiah: The Calls to Praise and Their Function in the Book.* Diss. Emory, 1978. **Dietrich, E. K.** *Die Umkehr im AT und im Judentum.* Stuttgart: Kohlhammer, 1936. **Dijkstra, M.** *Gods voorstelling: Predika-*

tieve expressie van zelfopenbaring in oudoosterse teksten en Deutero-Jesaja. Kampen: Kok, 1980. xii–478. **Dion, H. M.** "The Patriarchal Traditions and the Literary Form of the 'Oracle of Salvation.'" *CBQ* 29 (1967) 198–206. ———. "Le genre littéraire sumérien de l' 'Hymne à soi-même' et quelques passages du Deutéro-Isaïe." *RB* 74 (1967) 215–34. **Dion, P. E.** "The 'Fear Not' Formula and Holy War." *CBQ* 32 (1970) 365–570. ———. "Les chants du Serviteur de Jahweh et quelques passages apparentés d'Is 40–55." *Bib* 51 (1970) 17–38. ———. "L'universalism religieux dans les différentes couches rédactionelles d'Isaïe 40–55." *Bib* 51 (1970) 161–82. **Driver, G. R.** "Linguistic and Textual Problems: Isaiah xl–lxvi." *JTS* 36 (1935) 396–406. ———. "Hebrew Notes." *JBL* 68 (1949) 57–59. ———. "Hebrew Notes." *VT* 1 (1951) 241–50. ———. "Notes on Isaiah." *Von Ugarit nach Qumran.* FS O. Eissfeldt. BZAW 77. Berlin: Töpelmann, 1958. 42–48. ———. "Isaianic Problems." FS W. Eilers. Wiesbaden: Harassowitz, 1967. 43–57. **Dubshani, M.** "Die Bilder von Frau und Kindern in den Büchern Jesaja und Jeremia." *BMik* 12 (1966/67) 83–93. **Dünner, A.** *Die Gerechtigkeit nach dem AT.* Bonn: H. Bouvier, 1963. **Eakins, J.** "Anthropomorphisms in Isaiah 40–55." *Hebrew Studies* 20 (1970) 47–50. **Eaton, J. H.** "Commentaries on the Book of Isaiah." *Theology* 60 (1957) 451–55. ———. "The Origin of the Book of Isaiah." *VT* 9 (1959) 138–55. ———. *Festal Drama in Deutero-Isaiah.* London: SPCK, 1979. **Ehrlich, A. B.** *Randglossen zur hebräischen Bibel.* Textkritisches, Sprachliches und Sechliches. Vol. 4: Jesaja und Jeremia. Leipzig, 1908. **Eichrodt, W.** *Die Hoffnung des ewigen Friedens im alten Israel.* Zürich: Zwingli Verlag, 1920. **Eisenbeis, W.** *Die Wurzel* שלם *im Alten Testament.* BZAW 113. Berlin: de Gruyter, 1969. **Eissfeldt, O.** "Jahwe als König." *ZAW* 46 (1928) 81–105. **Eitz, A.** *Studien zum Verhältnis von Priesterschrift und Deuterojesaja.* Diss. Heidelberg, 1969. **Eldridge, V.** *The Influence of Jeremiah on Isaiah 40–55.* Diss. Southern Baptist Theological Seminary, 1978. **Elliger, K.** "Der Begriff 'Geschichte' bei Deuterojesaja." *Verbum Dei manet in aeternum.* FS O. Schmitz. Witten: 1953. 26–36 = *Kleine Schriften zum Alten Testament.* TB 32. Munich: Kaiser, 1966. 199–211. ———. "Ich bin der Herr—euer Gott." *Theologie als Glaubenswagnis.* FS K. Heim. Hamburg: Furcheverlag, 1954. 9–34. = *Kleine Schriften zum Alten Testament. 211–31.* ———. "Textkritisches zu Deuterojesaja." *Near Eastern Studies.* FS W. F. Albright. Baltimore: Johns Hopkins, 1971. 113–19. **Engnell, I.** "The ʿEbed-Yahweh Songs and the Suffering Messiah in Deutero-Isaiah." *BJRL* 31 (1948) 54–73. **Feuillet, A.** "L'origine de la seconde partie du livre d'Isaïe et les caractéristiques littéraires et doctrinales d'Is XL–LV (abstraction faite des Poèmes du Serviteur)." *Études d'exégèse et de théologie biblique.* Paris: Gabalda, 1975. 97–117. **Fohrer, G.** "Neuere Literatur zur alttestamentlichen Prophetie, III, 2: Deutero- und Trito-Jesaja." *TR* 19 (1951) 298–305; *TR* 20 (1952). ———. "Zehn Jahre Literatur zur alttestamentlichen Prophetie, VI: Deutero- und Trito-Jesaja." *TR* 28 (1962) 235–49. ———. "Neue Literatur zur alttestamentlichen Prophetie, VI: Deutero- und Trito-Jesaja." *TR* 45 (1980) 23–39. **Franco, E.** "Gerusalemme in Is. 40–66: Archetipo materno e simbolismo sponsale nel contesto dell'alleanza eterna." *Gerusalemme.* FS C. M. Martini. Ed. M. Borrmans et al. Brescia: Paideia, 1982. 143–52. **Galling, K.** "Von Nabune zu Darius." *ZDPV* 69 (1953) 42–64; 70 (1964) 4–32. ———. "Politische Wandlungen in der Zeit zwischen Nabunaid und Darius." *Studien zur Geschichte Israels in Persischer Zeitalter.* Tübingen: Mohr, 1964. 1–60. **Gamper, A.** 'Deutero-Isaias und die heutige katholische Exegese." *TG* 8 (1965) 196–200. ———. "Der Verkündigungsauftrag Israels nach Deutero-Jesaja." *ZKT* 91 (1969) 417–29. **Garofalo, S.** "Preparare la strada al Signore." *RivB* 6 (1958) 131–34. **Gelston, A.** "The Missionary Message of Second Isaiah." *SJT* 18 (1965) 308–18. ———. "A Note on יהוה מלך." *VT* 16 (1966) 507–12. ———. "Some Notes on Second Isaiah." *VT* 21 (1971) 517–27. **Gerleman, G.** "Die Wurzel slm." *ZAW* 85 (1973) 1–14. **Geyer, J.** "קצות הארץ—Hellenistic?" *VT* 20 (1970) 87–90. **Ginsberg, H. L.** "The Arm of JHWH in Is 51–63 and the Text of Is 53:10–11." *JBL* 77 (1958) 152–56. **Gitay, Y.** *Prophecy and Persuasion: A Study of Isaiah 40–48.* Forum Theol. Ling. 14. Bonn: LingBib, 1981.

———. *Rhetorical Analysis of Isaiah 40–48: A Study of the Art of Prophetic Persuasion.* Diss. Emory, 1978. **Glahn, L.** *Hjemkomst Profeten, Endheden af Jesajabogens Kp. 40–66.* Diss. Kopenhagen, 1929. ———. "Quelques remarques sur la question du Trito-Esaïe et son état actuel." *RHPR* 12 (1932) 34–46. ———. *Der Prophet der Heimkehr.* Vol. I. Giessen: Töpelmann, 1934. **Gozzo, S.** "De catholicorum sententia circa authenticitatem Is 40–66 inde ab anno 1908." *Ant* 32 (1957) 369–410. ———. *La dottrina theologica del libra di Isaia. Studio critico-exegetico.* BPAA 11. Rome: Pont. Athenaeum Antonianum, 1962. **Grimm, W.** *'Weil ich dich liebe': die Verkündigung Jesu und Deuterojesaja.* ANTJ 1. Bern: Herbert Lang, 1976. **Gross, H.** *Die Idee das ewigen und allgemeinen Weltfriedens im Alten Orient und im Alten Testament.* BBB. Bonn: Peter Hanstein, 1956. **Guillet, J.** "Le thème de la marche au désert dans l'Ancien et le Nouveau Testament." *RSR* 36 (1949) 161–81. ———. "La polémique contre les idoles et le Serviteur de Yahweh." *Bib* 40 (1959) 428–34. **Gunn, D. M.** "Deutero-Isaiah and the Flood." *JBL* 94 (1975) 493–508. **Hamel, J. A. van.** "Een irenische puzzle: Van de wolf en het lam." *Hermeneus* 35 (1964) 270–73. **Hamlin, E. J.** *Comfort My People: A Guide to Isaiah 40–66.* Atlanta: John Knox Press, 1980. **Hänel, J.** *Das Erkennen Gottes bei den Schriftpropheten.* BWANT 4. Stuttgart: Kohlhammer, 1923. **Haran, M.** *Between Richonot and Hadashot* (Is 40–66). Jerusalem, 1963 (Hebrew). **Harvey, J.** *Le plaidoyer prophétique contre Israël après la rupture de l'alliance.* Studie 22. Paris: de Brouwer, 1967. **Hermisson, H. J.** "Deuterojesaja Probleme: ein aritiacher Literaturbericht." *VF* 31 (1986) 53–84. **Herrmann, S.** *Die Prophetische Heilserwartung im Alten Testament.* BWANT 85. Stuttgart: Kohlhammer, 1965. ———. *Prophetie und Wirklichkeit in der Epoche des babylonischen Exils.* ArTh 1 32. Stuttgart: J. C. B. Mohr, 1967. **Hessler, E.** "Die Struktur der Bilder bei Deuterojesaja." *EvT* 25 (1965) 349–69. **Hillyer, N.** "The Servant of God." *EvQ* 41 (1969) 143–60. **Hoffmann, H. W.** "Form—Function—Intention." *ZAW* 82 (1970) 341–46. **Hofheinz, W. C.** *An Analysis of the Usage and Influence of Isaiah Ch. 40–66 in the NT.* Diss. Columbia U., 1964. DissAbstr 26:1 (1965) 513. **Holladay, W. L.** *Isaiah: Scroll of Prophetic Heritage.* Grand Rapids: Eerdmans, 1978. **Hollenberg, D. E.** "Nationalism and 'the Nations' in Isaiah xl–lv." *VT* 19 (1969) 23–36. **Huey, F. B., Jr.** "Great Themes in Is 40–66." *SWJT* 11 (1968) 45–58. **Humbert, P.** "Laetari et exultare dans le vocabulaire religieux de l'Ancien Testament." *Opuscules d'un hébraisant.* Neuchatel: U. P., 1958. 119–45. **Hurst, J. C.** "Guidelines for Interpreting OT Prophecy Applied to Isaiah 40–66." *SWJT* 11 (1968) 29–44. **Jackson, R. S.** "The Prophetic Vision: The Nature of the Utterance in Isaiah 40–55." *Int* 16 (1962) 65–75. **Jenni, E.** "Die Rolle des Kyros bei Deuterojesaja." *TZ* 10 (1954) 241–56. ———. "Die Präposition *min* in zeitlicher Verwendung bei Deuterojesaja." *Werden und Wirken des Alten Testaments.* FS C. Westermann. Göttingen: Vanderhoeck & Ruprecht, 1980. 288–301. **Jeppesen, K.** "The Cornerstone (Isa. 28:16) in Deutero-Isaianic Rereading of the Message of Isaiah." *ST* 38 (1984) 93–99. **Jepson, A.** "Die Begriffe des 'Erlösens' im Alten Testament." *Solange es 'Heute' heisst.* FS R. Herrmann. Berlin: de Gruyter, 1957. 153–63. ———. "Berith: Ein Beitrag zur Theologie der Exilszeit." *Verbannung und Heimkehr.* FS W. Rudolph. Ed. A. Kuschke. Tübingen: J. C. B. Mohr, 1961. **Junker, H.** "Der Sinn der sogenannten Ebed-Jahwe-Stück." *TTS* 79 (1970) 1–12. **Kahmann, J.** "Die Heilszukunft in ihrer Beziehung zur Heilsgeschichte nach Isaias 40–55." *Bib* 32 (1951) 141–72. **Kaminka, A.** "Le développement des idées du prophète Isaïe et l'unité de son livre." *REJ* 80 (1925) 42–59, 131–69; 81 (1925) 27–48. **Kapelrud, A. S.** "Second Isaiah and the Suffering Servant." FS A. Dupont-Sommer. Paris: Adrien-Maissonneuve, 1971. 297–303. ———. "The Main Concern of Second Isaiah." *VT* 32 (1982) 50–58. **Kaufmann, Y.** *The Babylonian Captivity and Deutero-Isaiah.* New York: U.A.H.C., 1970. **Kennett, R. H.** *The Composition of the Book of Isaiah in the Light of History and Archaeology.* The Schweich Lectures, 1909. London: H. Frowde, 1910. **Kiesow, K.** *Exodustexte im Jesajabuch (bes. Dt.-Jes).* Orbis Biblicus et Orientalis 24. Göttingen, 1979. **Kim, J. C.** *Das Verhältnis Jahwes zu den anderen Göttern in Deuterojesaja.* Diss. Heidelberg,

1963. **Klien, H.** "Der Beweis der Einzigkeit Jahwes bei Deuterojesaja." *VT* 35 (1985) 267–73. **Koch, K.** "Die Stellung des Kyros im Geschichtsbild Deuterojesajas und ihre überlieferungsgeschichtliche Verankerung." *ZAW* 84 (1972) 352–56. **Koch, R.** "Die Theologie des Deutero-Isaias." *TG* 9 (1966) 20–30. **Koole, J. L.** "De beeldenstorm van Deuterojesaja." *Loven en Geloven.* FS N. H. Ridderbos. Amsterdam: Ton Bolland, 1975. 77–93. **Kosters, W. H. A.** "Deutero- en Trito-jesaja." *TT* 30 (1896) 577–623. **Kraus, H. J.** *Die Königsherrschaft Gottes im AT.* BHT 13. Tübingen: J. C. B. Mohr, 1951. **Krupp, K.** *Das Verhältnis Jahwe-Israel im Sinne eines Ehebundes.* Diss. Freiburg im Breisgau, 1972. **Kutsch, E.** *Verheissung und Gesetz. Untersuchungen zum sogenannten "Bund" im Alten Testament.* BZAW 131. Berlin: de Gruyter, 1973. **Kutscher, E. Y.** *The Language and Linguistic Background of the Isaiah Scroll (1QISa), with an Obituary by H. B. Rosén (p. ix–xi).* STDJ 6. Leiden: E. J. Brill, 1974. **Labuschagne, C. J.** *The Incomparability of Yahweh in the Old Testament.* POS 5. Leiden: E. J. Brill, 1966. **Lauha, A.** " 'Der Bund des Volkes.' Ein Aspekt der deuterojesajanischen Missions-theologie." *Beiträge sur Alttestamentlichen Theologie.* FS W. Zimmerli. Göttingen: Vandenhoeck & Ruprecht, 1977. 257–61. **Ley, J.** *Historische Erklärung des zweiten Teils des Jesaia.* Cp. 40 bis Cp. 66, nach den Ergebnissen aus den babylonischen Keilinschriften. Marburg, 1893. 133–56. **Lind, M. C.** "Monotheism, Power, and Justice: A Study in Isaiah 40–55." *CBQ* 46 (1984) 432–46. **Lindblom, J.** *Die literarische Gattungen der prophetischen Literatur.* UUA, Theologi 1, 1924. ———. "The Character of the Prophetic Literature." *ExpTim* 52 (1940/41) 126–31. ———. *Prophecy in Ancient Israel.* Philadelphia: Muilenburg, 1962. ———. *The Servant Songs in Deutero-Isaiah: A New Attempt to Solve an Old Problem.* LUA 47/5. Lund: Gleerup, 1951. ———. "Profetisk bildsprak." FS R. Pipping. AAbo 18. 1950. 208–23. **Ludwig, T. M.** "The Traditions of the Establishing of the Earth in Deutero-Isaiah." *JBL* 92 (1973) 345–57. **Margalioth, R.** *The Indivisible Isaiah.* New York: Yeshiva University, 1964. **Mauch, T. M.** *The Participial Ascriptions to Yahweh in Isaiah 40–55.* Diss. Union Theological Seminary, 1958. **Mayer, R.** "Zur Bildsprache der alttestamentlichen Propheten." *MTZ* (1950) 55–65. **Mendenhall, G. E.** "Echoes from the Teaching of Hosea in Is 40–55." *OTWSA* (1966) 20–29. **Merendino, R. P.** *Der Erste und der Letzte: Eine Untersuchung von Jes 40–48.* VTSup 31. Leiden: E. J. Brill, 1981. **Merwe, B. J. van der.** *Pentateuchtradisies in die prediking van Deutero-Jesaja.* Diss. Groningen, 1955. ———. " 'Actualizing Eschatology' in Is 40–55." *Theologia Evangelica* 1 (1968) 16–19. **Michel, D.** "Das Rätsel Deuterojesaja." *TViat* 13 (1975). ———. "Deuterojesaja." *TRE* 8:510–30. **Mihelic, J. L.** "The Concept of God in Deutero Isaiah." *BR* 11 (1966) 29–41. **Miller, J. M.** *The Concept of Covenant in Deutero-Isaiah: Its Forms and Sources.* Diss. Boston University, 1972. **Miller, J. W.** "Prophetic Conflict in Second Isaiah: The Servant Songs in the Light of Their Context." *Wort-Gebot-Glaube.* FS W. Eichrodt. ATANT 59. Zürich: Zwingli Verlag, 1970. 77–85. **Morgenstern, J.** "The Message of Deutero-Isaiah in Its Sequential Unfolding." *HUCA* 29 (1958) 1–67; 30 (1959) 1–102. ———. "The Suffering Servant—A New Solution." *VT* 9 (1959) 292–329, 406–31. ———. "Isaiah 49–55." *HUCA* 36 (1965) 1–35. ———. "Further Light from the Book of Isaiah upon the Catastrophe of 485 B.C." *HUCA* 37 (1966) 1–28. **Mowinckel, S.** "Neuere Forschung zu Deuterojesaja, Tritojesaja und dem Aebäd-Jahwe-Problem." *AcOr* 16 (1938) 1–40. ———. *Prophecy and Tradition.* Oslo: J. Dybwad, 1946. ———. *He That Cometh.* ET G. W. Anderson. Oxford: B. Blackwell, 1956. **Moye, J. E. M.** *Israel and the Nations in Is 40–66.* Diss. Southern Baptist Theological Seminary, 1972. **Müller, H. P.** *Ursprünge und Strukturen alttestamentlicher Eschatologie.* BZAW 109. Berlin: de Gruyter, 1969. **Murphy, R. T.** "Second Isaiah: The Literary Problem." *CBQ* 9 (1947) 170–78. **Naidoff, B. D.** *Israel and the Nations in Deutero-Isaiah: The Political Terminology in Form-Critical Perspective.* Diss. Vanderbilt, 1980. **Nielsen, E.** "Deuterojesaja: Erwägungen zur Formkritik, Traditions- und Redaktionsgeschichte." *VT* 20 (1970) 190–205. **North, C. R.** *Isaiah 40–55: The Suffering Servant of God.* 5th ed. London: SCM, 1966. **Odendaal, D. H.** *The Eschatological Expectation of*

Is 40–66 with Special Reference to Israel and the Nations. Diss. Westminster Theological Sem., 1966. **Ogden, G. S.** "Moses and Cyrus: Literary Affinities between the Priestly Presentation of Moses in Exodus vi–viii and the Cyrus Song in Isaiah xliv 24–xlv 13." *VT* 28 (1978) 195–203. **Orlinsky, H. M. and Snaith, N. H.** *Studies in the Second Part of the Book of Isaiah.* VTSup 14. Leiden: E. J. Brill, 1967. 2d ed. 1977. **Payne, D. F.** "Characteristic Word-Play in 'Second Isaiah': A Reappraisal." *JSS* 12 (1967) 207–29. **Payne, J. B.** "Eighth Century Israelitish Background of Isaiah 40–66." *WTJ* 29 (1967) 179–90; 30 (1968) 50–58, 185–203. **Penna, A.** "Il libro della Consolazione (Is 40–66)." *PVi* 17 (1972) 405–17. **Perlitt, L.** "Die Verborgenheit Gottes." *Probleme biblischer Theologie.* FS G. von Rad. Munich: Kaiser, 1971. 367–82. **Peterson, D. L.** *Babylonian Literary Influence on Deutero-Isaiah.* A Bibliographic and Critical Study. Diss. Vanderbilt, 1975. **Phillips, M. L.** *The Significance of the Divine Self-Predication Formula for the Structure and Content of the Thought of Dt-Is.* Diss. Drew U., 1969. ———. "Divine Self-Predication in Deutero-Isaiah." *BR* 16 (1971) 32–51. **Plamondon, P.-H.** "Sur le chemin du salut avec le IIe Isaïe." *NRT* 104 (1982) 241–66. **Porubcan, S.** *Il patto nuovo in Is 40–66.* AnBib 8. Rome: Biblical Institute Press, 1964. **Preuss, H. D.** *Deuterojesaja: Eine Einführung in seine Botschaft.* Neukirchen: Neukirchener Verlag, 1976. ———. *Jahweglaube und Zukunftserwartung.* BWANT 87. Stuttgart: Kohlhammer, 1968. ———. *Verspottung fremder Religionen im Alten Testament.* BWANT 92. Stuttgart: Kohlhammer, 1971. **Rad, G. von.** "Die Stadt auf die Berge." *EvT* 8 (1948/49) 439–47 = *GSAT* 214–24. ———. *Old Testament Theology.* Tr. D. M. G. Stalker. Vol. 2. New York: Harper Bro., 1965. **Rendtorff, R.** *Die theologische Stellung des Schöpfungsglaubens bei Deuterojesaja.* ThB 57. Munich: Kaiser, 1975. **Richter, A.** *Hauptlinien der Deuterojesaja-Forschung von 1964.* CTM 11. Stuttgart: Calwer Verlag, 1981. **Rignell, L. G.** *A Study of Isaiah Ch. 40–55.* Lund: Gleerup, 1956. **Ringgren, H.** "Deuterojesaja och Kultspräket." *TAik* 72 (1967) 166–76. **Roodenburg, P. C.** *Israel, de knecht en de knechten, een onderzoek naar de beteknis en de functie van het nomen in Jesaja 40–66.* Diss. Amsterdam-Meppel, 1974. **Ruiz, G.** "Ambivalencía de las preposiciónes en Is 40–66." FS J. Alonso Diaz. MCom 41 (1983) 87–99. **Ruprecht, E.** *Die Auslegungsgeschichte zu den sogenannten Gottesknechtsliedern im Buche Deuterojesaja unter methodischen Gesichtspunkten bis zu Bernhard Duhm.* Diss. Heidelberg, 1972. **Saggs, H. W. F.** "A Lexical Consideration for the Date of Deutero-Isaiah." *JTS* 10 (1959) 84–87. **Sauer, G.** "Deuterojesaja und die Lieder vom Gottesknecht: Geschichtsmächtigkeit und Geduld." FS Ev. Fakultät Wien. Ed. G. Fitzer. Munich: Kaiser, 1972. 58–66. **Saydon, P. P.** "The Use of Tenses in Deutero-Isaiah." *Bib* 40 (1959) 290–301. **Scheiber, A.** "Der Zeitpunkt des Auftretens von Deuterojesaja." *ZAW* 84 (1972) 242–43. **Schmidt, J. J.** *Isaiah and His Interpreters.* New York: Paulist Press, 1986. **Schmidt, K. L.** "Jerusalem als Urbild und Abbild." *ErJb* (1950) 207. **Schmitt, H. C.** "Prophetie und Schultheologie im Deuterojesajabuch. Beobachtungen zur Redaktionsgeschichte von Jes 40–55." *ZAW* 91 (1979) 43–61. **Schnutenhaus, F.** "Das Kommen und Erscheinen im Alten Testament." *ZAW* 76 (1964) 1–22. **Schoors, A.** *De literaire en doctrinele eenheid van Deutero-Isaias: een exegetische analyse.* Diss. Leuven, 1963. ———. "L'eschatologie dans les prophéties du Deutéro-Isaïe." *RechBib* 8 (1967) 107–28. ———. "שבי and גלות in Isa. 40–55." *Historical Background.* Proceedings of the World Congress of Jewish Studies. Jerusalem, 1969. 90–101. ———. "Arrière-fonds historique et critique d'authenticité des textes deutéro-isaïens." *OLP* 2 (1971) 105–35. **Schreiner, J.** *Sion-Jerusalem, Jahwes Königssitz: Theologie der heiligen Stadt im Alten Testament.* Munich: Kösel, 1963. ———. "Das Buch jesajanischer Schule." *Wort und Botschaft.* Ed. J. Schreiner. Würzburg: Echter, 1967. 143–62. **Schroten, E. N. P.** "He Gerundium in Deutero-Jesaja." *NorTT* 17 (1962) 54–58. **Schunck, K. D.** "Die Eschatologie der Propheten des AT und ihre Wandlung in exilisch-nachexilischer Zeit." *Studies on Prophecy.* VTSup 27. Leiden: E. J. Brill, 1974. **Scoggin, E. B.** *Application of Hebrew Verb States to a Translation of Isaiah 40–55.* Diss. Southern Baptist Theological Seminary, 1955. **Seeligmann, I. L.** *The Septuagint Version of Isaiah: A Discus-*

sion of Its Problems. Leiden: E. J. Brill, 1948. **Sellin, E.** "Tritojesaja, Deuterojesaja, und das Gottesknechtsproblem." *NKZ* 41 (1930) 73–93, 145–73. ———. "Die Lösung des deuterojesajanischen Gottesknechtsrätsels." *ZAW* 55 (1937) 177–217. **Seybold, K.** "Thesen zur Entstehung der Lieder vom Gottesknecht." *BN* 3 (1977) 33–34. **Shargel, D.** "אמונת הייחוד והמיתוס בנבואתו של ישעיהו השני" [Monotheism and myth in Deutero-Isaiah]. קטיף[9] (1972) 196–213. **Sicre, J. L.** "La mediación de Ciro y la del Siervo de Dios en Deuteroisaias." *EstEcl* 50 (1975) 193–94. **Sievi, J.** "Der unbekannte Prophet: Buch und Botschaft des Deuterojesajas." *BK* 24 (1969) 122–26. **Simian-Yofre, H.** "La teología del Deuteroisaias." *Bib* 62 (1981) 55–72. **Simon, U.** "König Cyrus und die Typologie." *Jud* 11 (1955) 83–89. **Skehan, P. W.** "Some Textual Problems in Isaiah." *CBQ* 22 (1960) 47–55. **Sklba, R. J.** "The Redeemer of Israel." *CBQ* 34 (1972) 1–18. **Smith, M.** "II Isaiah and the Persians." *JAOS* 83 (1963) 415–21. **Smith, S.** *Isaiah 40–55. Literary Criticism and History.* Schweich Lectures, 1940. London: Humphrey Milford, 1944. **Snaith, N. H.** "The Servant of the Lord in Deutero-Isaiah." *Studies in Old Testament Prophecy.* FS T. H. Robinson. Ed. H. H. Rowley. Edinburgh: T. & T. Clark, 1957. 187–200. ———. "Isaiah 40–66. A Study of the Teaching of Second Isaiah and Its Consequences." *Studies on the Second Part of the Book of Isaiah.* VTSup 14. Leiden: E. J. Brill, 1967. 137–264. **Squillaci, D.** "La conversione delle Isole predetta da Isaia." *PalCl* 41 (1962) 603–7. **Staerk, W.** *Die Ebed-Jahwe-Lieder in Jesaja 40ff: Ein Beitrag zu Deuterojesaja Kritik.* BWAT 14. Leipzig: Hinrichs, 1913. **Steck, O. H.** "Deuterojesaja als theologischer Denker." *KD* 15 (1969) 280–93. ———. "Aspekte des Gottesknechts in Jes 52:13–53:12." *ZAW* 97 (1985) 36–57. **Steinmann, J.** *Le livre de la consolation d'Israël et les prophètes du retour de l'exil.* LD 28. Paris: 1960. **Stramare, P. T.** "Creazione e Redenzione." *BeO* 10 (1968) 101–11. **Stuhlmacher, P.** "Behold I Make All Things New." *LW* 15 (1968) 3–15. **Stuhlmueller, C.** "The Theology of Creation in Second Isaiah." *CBQ* 21 (1959) 429–67. ———. " 'First and Last' and 'Yahweh-Creator' in Deutero-Isaiah." *CBQ* 29 (1967) 295–511. ———. "Yahweh-King and Deutero-Isaiah." *BR* 15 (1970) 32–45. ———. *Creative Redemption in Deutero-Isaiah.* AnBib 43. Rome: Pontifical Biblical Institute, 1970. **Stummer, F.** "Einige keilschriftliche Parallelen zu Jes. 40–66." *JBL* 45 (1926) 171–89. **Swartzentruber, A. O.** *The Servant Songs in Relation to Their Context in Dt.-Is: Critique of Contemporary Methodologies.* Diss. Princeton, 1970. **Talstra, E.** *Deuterojesaja, Proeve van een automatische tekstverwerking ten dienste van de exegese.* 2d ed. Amsterdam: Free University, 1981. **Tannert, W.** *Jeremia und Deuterojesaja: Eine Untersuchung zur Frage ihres literarischen und theologischen Zusammenhanges.* Diss. Leipzig, 1956. **Terrien, S.** "Quelques remarques sur les affinités de Job avec le Deutéro-Isaïe." *Congress Volume, Geneva, 1961.* VTSup 15. Leiden: E. J. Brill, 1966. 295–310. **Torrey, C. C.** "The Influence of Second Isaiah in the Gospels and Acts." *JBL* 48 (1929) 24–36. ———. "Some Important Editorial Operations in the Book of Isaiah." *JBL* 57 (1938) 109–39. **Trembelas, P.** *Ἰπομνημα εις την προφητην Ἡσαιαν.* Athens, 1968. **Uffenheimer, B.** "Aspects of the Spiritual Image of Deutero-Isaiah." *Immanuel* 12 (1981) 9–20. **Vincent, J. M.** *Studien zur literarischen Eigenart und zur geistigen Heimat von Jes, Kap. 40–55.* Diss. Bochum, 1973. **Vogt, E.** "Die Ebed-Jahwe-Lieder und ihre Ergänzungen." *EstEcl* 34 (1960) 775–88. ———. "Einige hebräische Wortbedeutungen: I. 'Voraussagen' in Is 40–48." *Bib* 48 (1967) 57–63. **Volz, P.** *Der Geist Gottes und die verwandten Erscheinungen im AT und im anschliessenden Judentum.* Tübingen: J. C. B. Mohr, 1910. **Waldow, H. E. von.** *Anlass und Hintergrund der Verkündigung des Deuterojesaja.* Diss. Bonn, 1953. ———. "The Message of Deutero-Isaiah." *Int* 22 (1968) 259–87. **Wallis, G.** *Die Gemeinde des Tritojesajabuches: eine traditionsgeschichtliche Untersuchung.* 1957. **Ward, J. M.** "The Servant Songs in Isaiah." *RevExp* 65 (1968) 433–46. ———. "The Servant's Knowledge in Isaiah 40–50." *Israelite Wisdom.* FS S. Terrien. Missoula, MT: Scholars Press, 1978. **Watson, W. G. R.** "Fixed Pairs in Ugarit and Israel." *VT* 22 (1972) 460–67. **Watts, J. W.** *A Distinctive Translation of Isaiah with an Interpretative Outline.* Louisville: Jameson Press, 1979. **Weinfeld, M.**

"God the Creator in Gen. 1 and in the Prophecy of Second Isaiah." *Tarbiz* 37 (1967/68) 105–32. (Heb.). **Weippert, M. H. E.** "De herkomst van het heilsorakel voor Israel bij Deutero-Jesaja." *NorTT* 36 (1982) 1–11. **Wells, R. D.** *The Statements of Well-Being in Isaiah 60–62: Implications of Form Criticism and the History of Tradition for the Interpretation of Isaiah 56–65.* Diss. Vanderbilt, 1968. **Westermann, C.** "Sprache und Struktur der Prophetie Deuterojesajas." *Forschung am Alten Testament.* ThB 24. Munich: Kaiser, 1964. 92–170. ———. "Das Reden von Schöpfer und Schöpfung im Alten Testament." *Das ferne und nahe Wort.* FS L. Rost. BZAW 105. Berlin: de Gruyter, 1967. 238–44. **Whitley, C. F.** "Textual Notes on Deutero-Isaiah." *VT* 11 (1961) 259–61. ———. "Further Notes on the Text of Deutero-Isaiah." *VT* 25 (1975) 683–87. **Wildberger, H.** "Der Monotheismus Deuterojesajas." *Beiträge zur Alttestamentlichen Theologie.* FS W. Zimmerli. Göttingen: Vandenhoeck & Ruprecht, 1977. 506–30. **Williams, D. L.** "The Message of Exilic Isaiah." *RevExp* 65 (1968) 423–32. **Williams, P.** "The Poems about Incomparable Jahweh's Servant." *SWJT* 12 (1968) 73–88. **Wilshire, L. E.** "The Servant City: A New Interpretation of the Servant of the Lord in the Servant Songs of Deutero-Isaiah." *JBL* 94 (1975) 356–67. **Wodecki, B.** "Der Heilsuniversalismus bei Trito-Jesaja." *VT* 32 (1982) 248–52. **Woude, A. S. van der.** "De liederen van de Knecht des Heren." *Homiletica en Biblica* 24 (1965) 1–6, 25–31, 49–51. **Ziegler, J.** *Untersuchungen zur Septuaginta des Buches Isaias. ATA* xii 3. Münster: Aschendorffschen Verlagsbuchhandlung, 1934. **Zillessen, A.** "Bemerkungen sur Alex: Uebersetzung des Jesaja 40–66." *ZAW* 22 (1902) 238–63. ———. "Tritojesaja und Deuterojesaja: Eine literarische Untersuchung zu Jes 56–66." *ZAW* 26 (1906) 231–76. **Zimmerli, W.** "Das Wort des göttlichen Selbsterweises." *Mélanges bibliques.* FS A. Robert. Paris: Bloud & Gay, 1956. 154–64. = *Gottes Offenbarung.* ThB 19. 2d ed. Munich: Kaiser, 1969. 120–32. ———. "Der Wahrheitserweis Jahwes nach der Botschaft der beiden Exilspropheten." *Tradition und Situation.* FS A. Weiser. Göttingen: Vandenhoeck & Ruprecht, 1963. 133–51 = *Studien zur alttestamentlichen Theologie und Prophetie.* ThB 51. Munich: Kaiser, 1974. 192–212. ———. "Ich bin Jahwe." *Geschichte und Altes Testament.* FS A. Alt. Tübingen: J. C. B. Mohr, 1953. 179–209. = *Gottes Offenbarung.* ThB 19. 2d ed. Munich: Kaiser, 1969. 192–204. ———. "Jahwes Wort bei Deuterojesaja." *VT* 32 (1982) 104–24. **Zurro Rodrigues, E.** "Filología y critica textual en Is 40–55." *Burgense* 11 (1970) 81–116.

Isaiah 34-66

Act VI: From Curse to Blessing (Chaps. 34–39)

The Sixth Generation
Kings Jehoiakim and Zedekiah (*ca.* 605–586 B.C.)

The Assyrian empire is no more. Nebuchadnezzar's Babylon rules Mesopotamia and Palestine. He dominates the entire act. Yet the mood of the scenes suggests catharsis and a turning point in history. The scenes do not address the situation directly. Obliquely they suggest the mood, while the audience unconsciously thinks of the terrible times in the invasions that ended Jehoiakim's reign, took Jehoiachin into exile, and finally brought Zedekiah down with the fall of Jerusalem.

Scene 1: Edom's Curse—Judah's Renewal (34:1–35:10)
Scene 2: A Reading from History: The Assyrian's Speech (36:1–22)
Scene 3: A Reading (cont.): From Hearsay to Knowledge (37:1–20)
Scene 4: A Reading (cont.): Isaiah's Response from Yahweh (37:21–38)
Scene 5: A Reading (cont.): Hezekiah's Illness (38:1–8, 21–22)
Scene 6: Hezekiah's Psalm (38:9–20)
Scene 7: A Reading (cont.): Hezekiah's Mistake (39:1–8)

A scene of total judgment on Edom is followed by a beautiful idyllic picture of Judah. The Vision then invites the reader/audience to hear a reading of the account from 1 Kgs 18–20 of Sennacherib's siege of Hezekiah's capital in 701 B.C. The issues of the Babylonian period are treated indirectly through these narratives about Isaiah and Hezekiah. Hezekiah is somehow parallel to Zedekiah. Both led rebellions against a Mesopotamian empire. God saved Hezekiah's Jerusalem, but he did not do the same for Zedekiah, partly, the reading suggests, because of Zedekiah's lack of caution.

Exilic Israel read the stories about Hezekiah while caught up in their own experiences that turned out so differently. In 701 B.C. the royal house survived in Jerusalem. In 586 B.C. the only survivor was Jehoiachin, a prisoner in Babylon. In 701 B.C. the villagers and townsfolk were released to go to their homes. In 586 B.C. they began the long march into exile. Near 701 B.C. the portent of Babylonian peril was enunciated by Isaiah. In 586 B.C. it became grim reality.

Through the reading, the Vision hints at the reverse image from that portrayed in the history. Without a direct word, the entire terrible period is brought vividly to mind.

Historical Background

After a brief interlude when Egypt dominated Palestine during Assyria's last years, Nebuchadnezzar succeeded to Babylon's throne and immediately reasserted Mesopotamian control of the region. The change caught Jehoiakim (609–598 B.C.) in a very bad position. He owed his throne to Egyptian intervention (2 Kgs 23:34–35).

Nebuchadnezzar first campaigned in Syria/Palestine in 605 B.C. Jehoiakim faced the inevitable and paid him tribute (2 Kgs 24:1). For three years (605–602 B.C.) he was Babylon's vassal. But then he refused further tribute, undoubtedly expecting Egyptian support. This did not happen (2 Kgs 24:7). With Nebuchadnezzar in complete control of Palestine, Jehoiakim died, leaving the throne to his son Jehoiachin just before Nebuchadnezzar's attack on Jerusalem in 598 B.C. Jehoiachin was taken to Babylon as prisoner to live in royal exile through most of this period. Many Jews continued to recognize him as the true ruler of Judah.

Jehoiachin was succeeded by his uncle, Zedekiah (2 Kgs 24:17). He continued the series of intrigues with Egypt which finally led to the siege and destruction of Jerusalem in 587 B.C. and the consequent major deportation of many of the inhabitants to regions near Babylon. With this deportation Judah was left desolate and sparsely inhabited. The history of the nation had ended.

Act VI makes no mention of the siege of Jerusalem or the subsequent exile. It apparently presumes that this is too well known to need another description. Instead, it offers a first scene in "Day of the Lord" style that brings punishment on Edom, Babylon's ally in the siege. Edom's destruction prepares the way for the renaissance of Judah's southern Arabah (chaps. 34–35).

The rest of the act is occupied with a reading from Israel's great history in which God rescued Judah from an earlier siege in Hezekiah's time. The Deuteronomistic History (DtH) was current during the period portrayed and was undoubtedly well known when the Vision was produced. The narrative history is read as a commentary on the later period which the readers or hearers were supposed to understand and apply.

Scene 1: Edom's Curse—Judah's Renewal (34:1–35:10)

Bibliography

Caspari, W. "Jesaja 34 und 35." *ZAW* 49 (1931) 67–86. **Elliger, K.** *Deuterojesaja in seinem Verhältnis zu Tritojesaja.* BWANT 63. Stuttgart: Kohlhammer, 1933. 272–78. **Emerton, J. A.** "A Note on Isaiah XXXV 9–10." *VT* 27 (1977) 488–89. **Grätz, H.** "Isaiah xxxiv and xxxv." *JQR* 4 (1891) 1–8. **Hubmann, F. D.** "Der 'Weg' zum Zion. Literar- und Stilkritische Beobachtungen zu Jes 35:8–10." FS F. Sauer. Ed. J. B. Bauer. Graz (1977) 29–41. **Kraus, H-J.** "Jes 35:3–10." *Hören und Fragen* 5 (1976) 495–500. **Mailland, A.** *La "petite apocalypse" d'Isaie. Étude sur les chapîtres xxxiv et xxxv du livre d'Isaie.* Diss. Lyon (1955/56). **Morgenstern, J.** "Further Light from the Book of Isaiah upon the Catastrophe of 485 B.C." *HUCA* 37 (1966) 4–13. **Muilenberg, J.**

"The Literary Character of Isaiah 34." *JBL* 59 (1940) 339–65. **Pope, M.** "Isaiah 34 in Relation to Isaiah 35, 40–66." *JBL* 71 (1952) 235–43. **Scott, M.** "Isaiah xxxv 7." *ExpTim* 37 (1925/26) 122. **Scott, R. B. Y.** "The Relation of Chapter 35 to Deutero-Isaiah." *AJSL* 52 (1935) 178–91. **Torrey, C. C.** *The Second Isaiah.* New York: Scribner's, 1928. 279–301. **Wernberg-Møller, P.** "Isa 35:4." *ZAW* (1957) 71–73. **Young, E. J.** "Isaiah 34 and its Position in the Prophecy." *WTJ* 27 (1964/65) 93–114.

Translation

Herald: 34:1 *Draw near,*[a] *O* [b]*nations, to listen!* 3+2
Pay attention, O peoples!
Let the land and its fullness listen, 3+2
the world and all[b] *that comes from it.*
Earth: 2 *Surely*[a] *Yahweh (has a right)*[b] *to wrath on all nations* 4+2
and fury on all[c] *their armies.*
When he applies the ban to them, gives them over
to slaughter,[d] 3+3+3
3 *their slain are thrown out*
and the stench[a] *of their (unburied) corpses rises,*
mountains are soaked with their blood, 3+3+3
4 *the whole* [a]*army of heaven*[a] *is infected,*[b]
and the sky is rolled up like a scroll.
Their whole army falls 2+3+2
like falling leaves from a vine,[c]
and like falling fig leaves.
Yahweh: 5 *When my sword*[a] *is seen*[b] *in the heavens,* 3+3+3
see it descend on Edom,
on the people of my ban,[a] *for judgment.*
Heavens: 6 *Yahweh (has the right) to a sword* 2+2+2
made full of blood,
gorged[a] *with fat*[b]
from the blood of lambs and goats, 3+3
from the fat of the intestines of rams.
Earth: *Surely Yahweh (has a right) to a sacrifice in Bozrah,* 4+4
a great slaughter in the land of Edom.
7 *Wild oxen go down with them*[a] 3+2
and bull calves with the bulls.
Their land is drunk[b] *with blood,* 3+3
and their ground gorged with fat.
Heavens: 8 *Surely Yahweh (has the right) to a vengeance day,* 4+4
a year of retributions to sue on Zion's behalf![a]
9 *Her streams overflow with pitch,* 3+2
her dust becomes burning sulfur,
and her land becomes 2+2
burning pitch.
10 *Day and night it is not extinguished.*[a] 4+3
For an age its smoke rises.
From generation to generation it will be desolate. 3+2+3

For a forever of forevers[b]
no one will be passing through it.

Earth: 11 *Desert owl and screech owl possess it.* 3+3
Great owl and raven dwell in it.
He[a] *stretches out over it* 2+1+1
a measuring line of desolation
and a plumb line of confusion.

Heavens: 12 *(What has become of) its nobles?*[a] 1+3+3
Nothing there can be called a kingdom.
All her princes are wiped out.
13 *Thorns grow up over her fortresses,* 3+3
nettles and brambles inside her strongholds.
She becomes a den for jackals, 3+3
an enclosure[a] *for ostriches.*

Earth: 14 *Demons*[a] *meet with phantoms,*[ab] 3+3
and a wild goat calls[c] *to his companion.*
Lilith[ad] *also lives there* 3+3
and rests herself.
15 *There*[a] *the arrow-snake*[b] *goes to nest and lay eggs,* 4+3
to hatch and care (for them) in its shade.[c]
Vultures[d] *are also gathered there,* 3+2
each (with) its mate.

Court Scribe: 16 *Examine Yahweh's scroll and read aloud.*[a] 4+4+4
Let nothing be left out.
[b]*Let (no line) miss*[b] *its parallel line.*
For [c]*Yahweh's mouth*[c] *commanded (them)* 3+3
and his Spirit gathered them.
17 *He himself made the decision*[a] *concerning them.*[b] 3+4
and his own hand measured (judgment) to them.[b]
It is their inheritance forever! 2+3
For generation after generation, they must live with it.

Judean Chorus: 35:1 *Wilderness and dry land rouse themselves in gladness!*[a] 3+3
The Arabah rejoices and blooms!
Like crocus,[b] 2 *it blooms suddenly* 3+4
and rejoices with joy[a] *and shout.*
Lebanon's glory is assigned to her[b] 3+3
with Carmel's and Sharon's splendor.
They[c] *see Yahweh's glory, themselves,* 3+2
the splendor of our God.

Pilgrim Chorus: 3 *Strengthen the hands of the feeble!*[a] 3+3
Steady faltering knees!
4 *Speak to fearful hearts:* 2+2
"Be strong! Do not fear!"

Judean Chorus: *See our God!* 2+2+2
[a]*Vengeance comes!*[a]
Divine retribution![b]

He himself comes and is your Savior![c] 3

Pilgrim Chorus: 5 *Then blind eyes are opened* 4+3
and a deaf ear is cleared.
6 *Then lame (persons) leap like deer* 4+3
and (even) a dumb tongue shouts for joy.
For waters break out in the wilderness 3+2
and streams in the Arabah.[a]
7 *Burning sands become a pool* 3+3
and parched land springs of water.
Where jackals lounged[a] 3+3
is an enclosure[b] *for reeds and papyrus.*

Judean Chorus: 8 *A highway*[a] *and a way*[b] *is there.*[c] 3+4
It[d] *is called "The Holy Road."*
No unclean (person) may travel on it. 3+4+3
It is for the one who walks The Way.[e]
Fools may not wander about (on it).

Pilgrim Chorus: 9 *No lion may be there.* 3+3
No[a] *fearful beast may mount up on it.*
[b]*Such may not be found*[b] *there* 3+2
where the redeemed walk.

Judean Chorus: 10 *Yahweh's ransomed ones return* 3+3
and enter Zion with singing.
May everlasting rejoicing be on their heads! 3+3+3
May gladness and joy overtake (them)[a]
while sorrow and sighing flee[b] *from them!*

Notes

1.a. DSS^{Isa} קרובו adds the *holem* in the second syllable. Kutscher, *Isaiah Scroll,* 341, notes that Qumran MSS often change impf with *a* into impf with *o*.

1.b-b. DSS^{Isa} writes plene spellings for גוים "nations," לשמע "to listen," לאמים "peoples," מלאה "its fullness," and כל "all." This is typical of orthography in this MS (Wildberger, 1326).

2.a. כי "surely" is assertative.

2.b. MT ליהוה "Yahweh has" expresses possession. The setting of an imperial court scene makes it the claim of a royal prerogative. Cf. vv 6a, 6c, and 8.

2.c. LXX omits "all."

2.d. DSS^{Isa} inserts a ו, making this an inf לטבוח "to slaughter." MT לטבח should be kept.

3.a. DSS^{Isa} באושמה appears to be the fem sg qal act ptcp from אשם "offend, be guilty" with prep ב "in, on." LXX ἡ ὀσμή "the odor" supports MT.

4.a-a. *BHS* conjectures that instead of "the army of heaven" one should read הגבעות "the hills" to parallel "mountains" in the previous line. The suggestion goes back to Bickel and Duhm. The problem arises from trying to make parallel bistich lines from the tristich lines in vv 2, 3, and 4.

4.b. MT's נמקו "infected" appears in DSS^{Isa} as והעמקים יתבקעו ו "and the valleys will break open and." Wildberger (1326) suggests that it has expanded the text using Mic 1:4.

4.c. DSS^{Isa} גופן "Gophna." A place named Gophna appears in Josephus and the Midrash.

5.a. The 1st pers suff has concerned interpreters, who suggest changing to 3d pers. This is unnecessary if the text is understood as a brief Yahweh speech. On the text of this verse, see L. Levonian, "Isaiah xxxiv 5," *ExpTim* 24 (1913) 45–46.

5.b. LXX ἐμεθύσθη "is drunk" and Vg *inebriatus est* "is drunk" support MT's consonants, but read as a qal: רָוְתָה. Tg תתגלי and DSS^{Isa} תראה "will be seen" may be more nearly correct. Cf. G. R. Driver, *JSS* 13 (1968) 55, and Mailland, *Petite Apocalypse,* 18. See v 7 below.

6.a. הדשנה "gorged" is a hothpaal pf. Cf. GKC § 54*h*.

6.b. חלב is "fat of the human body." Cf. BDB, 316.

7.a. MT עמם "with them." Who or what is the antecedent of the pronoun? The question has led to emendations. Duhm's מרים "fatling" is followed by many, including Wildberger (1325). It is better to keep the MT despite the problem.

7.b. MT וְרִוְּתָה "be drunk." LXX *καὶ μεθυσθήσεται* "is drunk" is followed by Syr Tg Vg. To change to a qal reading with *BHS*, "be sated," results in a weaker figure.

8.a. לְרִיב "to plead for" is a form which many have thought needed to be changed. Syr reads *ldyn*ʾ to judge." Ehrlich (23) reads לְרִיב, i.e., לִירִיב from יריב "opponent, enemy," citing Ps 35:1 and Isa 49:25. Procksch reads רָב ציון "Zion fighter" or רַב ציור "Zion's master" = "Lord of Zion." Driver (55) reads ריב as a noun of agent like ציר "messenger" and קים "opponent" and translates "for the advocate of Zion." Wildberger (1327) notes that all of these look for a parallel to Yahweh. He prefers רָב "one who fights for Zion's rights." MT is difficult but as good as any of these (cf. BDB, 936).

10.a. DSS[Isa] תכובה makes the form a pual pass, "be extinguished." This does not change the meaning.

10.b. לנצח נצחים "for a forever of forevers" has seemed superfluous repetition to many. LXX translates *εἰς χρόνον πολύν* "for a long time," apparently omitting the second word.

11.a. No subject is named. Wildberger (1328) translates an impersonal "one," which apparently picks up "Yahweh" from v 6 and v 8 above.

12.a. MT חריה "her nobles" stands alone, lacking a verb. LXX reads *οἱ ἄρχοντες αὐτῆς οὐκ ἔσονται* (3 pl fut ind) "its rulers will not exist."

13.a. *BHS* suggests חָצֵר "an enclosure" (BDB, 346–47) following DSS[Isa] חצר; LXX reads *αὐλή* "a courtyard," and Tg מדור "a court."

14.a. All these are rare words, traditionally understood as desert creatures. Wildberger (1328) suggests that here the list has changed to demonic beings thought to inhabit waste places: ציים are desert demons (cf. 13:21; see LXX *δαιμόνια* "demons") as are also the איים "phantoms" (cf. KB). לילית "Lilith" is not otherwise known, but must be related to Akk *lilitu*.

14.b. DSS[Isa] אייאמים (cf. Kutscher, *Isaiah Scroll,* 217) is not yet explained.

14.c. MT יִקְרָא "will call." *BHS,* following Procksch, suggests יִקָּרֵא "will meet." This meaning may also fit the qal (cf. BDB, 896, II).

14.d. DSS[Isa] ליליות is pl with other pl forms in this line. But this is unnecessary. MT is correct.

15.a. The change suggested by *BHS* (שמה to שם, both "there") is unnecessary. Cf. Wildberger (1329). On the text of this verse, see F. Hommel, "Isaiah xxxiv 15," *ExpTim* 12 (1900) 336; and W. van Koeverden, "Isaie, XXXIV, 15," *RB* 9 (1912) 542–43.

15.b. קפוז is a *hap. leg.* GB, BDB (891), and KB translate "arrow snake." Torrey (292) thought of a bird, since it related nesting and a Sem. root word meaning to leap (BDB, 891) and suggested "owl," followed by NIV. LXX *ἐχῖνος* means "hedgehog."

15.c. A number of scholars, unsatisfied with "shadow," have suggested emending to ביציה "its eggs" (cf. *BHS;* BDB, 101). But "shadow" makes good sense and should be sustained.

15.d. MT דיות is another difficult word. 'A reads *ἴκτινες* "kite, chicken-hawk," Vg *milvis* "beaked animal." LXX translates דאה in Lev 11:14 as a "kite"; hence, NIV "falcons." A kite or vulture fits the context.

16.a. *BHS* follows LXX in recommending deletion.

16.b-b. Missing in DSS[Isa].

16.c-c. MT פי הוא "my mouth, it." DSS[Isa] פיהו "his mouth," followed as in MT by הוא "it." Several MSS drop הוא with Syr and Tg. Others read יהוה "Yahweh" for הוא, and LXX reads *κύριος* "Lord." Wildberger (1329) notes the frequent use of כי פי יהוה דבר "for the mouth of Yahweh has spoken" (1:20; 40:5; 58:14) and recommends reading יהוה for הוא. J. Morgenstern's suggestion (*JBL* 62 [1943] 278) that הוא is itself a designation for God is then unnecessary.

17.a. Lit., "cast a lot."

17.b. The masc להם "to them" following the fem להן "to them" is confusing. The fem conforms to references in v 16. *BHS* suggests dropping להם. Others change it to להן to conform.

35:1.a. MT יְשֻׂשׂוּם "will be glad in them." The pronom suff must refer to chap. 34, which Wildberger (1353) finds unlikely, or be a reflexive pronoun. But why not? It would make good sense and serve to tie the chapters together. He and others contend that the verb does not take an obj, that the versions do not translate a suff, and that the ם is dittogr for the following letter מ. Ibn Ezra and Kimchi explained the ם as a *nun paragogicum* which has adapted itself to the following מ.

1.b. The verse division is disrupted. Most would end the verse one word earlier. The meaning of חבצלה is uncertain. Various types of flowers have been suggested. Cf. G. Gerleman, *Ruth/Hoheslied,* 116.

2.a. On MT גילת "joy," see GKC § 130*b*.

2.b. The antecedent is probably "Arabah" in v 1 (cf. Wildberger, 1353).

2.c. MT הֵמָּה "they," LXX ὁ λαός μου "my people." But isn't the antecedent the three places mentioned in v 1?

3.a. Note the use of the pl adj with a dual noun. Cf. Joüon § 148*a*. Who is addressed? Those of the Arabah?

4.a. נקם יבוא "vengeance comes" has been variously emended to fit views of its meaning. Most have tried to make Yahweh the subj. Wildberger's suggestion (1353) is convincing that נקם "vengeance" is the subj.

4.d. Following NIV.

4.c. וְיֹשַׁעֲכֶם is a strange form. *BHS* suggests the expected verb form וְיֹשִׁעֲכֶם "and he will save you." Feldmann suggested reading it as a jussive. Ehrlich (*Randglossen* 4:26) reads וְיִשְׁעֲכֶם as a noun: "and your help." Wernberg-Møller (73) keeps MT but understands it to come from a noun יֵשַׁע. It is a verb and its meaning is clear, even if its form is unusual.

6.a. DSS[Isa] adds ילכו "will flow."

7.a. MT רִבְצָהּ "her repose." DSS[Isa] רבץ "he will repose." *BHS* follows several MSS with רבצה "she will lie down." MT may be sustained. A contrast in condition is needed to parallel the first two lines. Wildberger (1352, 1354) reads this as a relative clause: "On the places where jackals camped."

7.b. חציר normally means "grass," but that meaning is difficult here. Note its use in 34:13 where it was translated "an enclosure" (BDB, 346); LXX ἔπαυλις "a cottage."

8.a. MT מסלול "a highway" (a *hap. leg.*); DSS[Isa] מסולל is to be understood as a simple shift of vowel for the same word.

8.b. MT ודרך "and a way" is omitted by DSS[Isa]. LXX reads καθαρά "clean, pure," for which *BHS* suggests טהור "clean, pure," or possibly בָּרוּר. This reading parallels the two words with the following "Way of Holiness." Wildberger (1354–55) follows DSS[Isa] in suggesting that ודרך is a gl intended to explain the little-known מסלול "highway" that preceded it.

8.c. DSS[Isa] שמה. Wildberger (1329, 1354) notes that in later times שם and שמה were interchangeable, both meaning "there," and cites Kutscher, *Isaiah Scroll,* 413.

8.d. לה is fem referring to "way."

8.e. The *athnaḥ* breaks a stich. *BHS* is correct in dividing differently.

9.a. DSS[Isa] adds לוא "not," which is redundant.

9.b-b. Wildberger (1355) and others find the phrase superfluous and omit. It is attested by other texts and versions and should be kept.

10.a. DSS[Isa] adds בה "in her," a meaning which must be understood in any case (cf. also 51:11). LXX καταλήμψεται αὐτούς "take hold of them" adds the pl pron which led Duhm to suggest adding final *mem* to read ישיגום "overtake them." The pl is more appropriate than DSS[Isa]'s sg.

10.b. DSS[Isa] reads a sg which does not change the meaning.

Form/Structure/Setting

These chapters are clearly set off from the preceding and following sections. They are also bound into a unity by a basic theme of God's vengeance or retribution against Edom (34:8 and 35:4) which is to be recorded as a perpetual decision (34:16–17). The outline is concentric:

A Yahweh's Day of Wrath on all nations (34:1–4)
  B Vengeance and ban upon Edom for Zion's sake (34:5–8)
    C Edom to be burned and deserted (34:9–15)
KEYSTONE Yahweh's decision, recorded and perpetual—fate and inheritance for the land of Edom (34:16–17)

C′ Wilderness and Arabah—glad and rejuvenated (35:1–2)
B′ Yahweh's vengeance—salvation and encouragement for Israel (35:3–4)
A′ Festival in Zion again open to pilgrims (35:5–10).

Judah's strife with Edom had a long history (see *Excursus*). But it apparently came to a climax when Edom supported Babylon's siege of Jerusalem in 587 B.C. and participated in the sack of the city. Neither 2 Kings nor 2 Chronicles records this, but Obadiah and related passages clearly state it.

Edom's position allowed her to control the heavily traveled trade route that ran north/south just east of the Dead Sea. These chapters imply that in the sixth century she was thus also able to impede the travel of pilgrims to Jerusalem. Throughout history the boundaries between Edom and southern Judah fluctuated according to their relative strengths. This, too, is reflected in these chapters.

Chap. 34 portrays a day of Yahweh's judgment over the nations. Its structure is clear.

The summons to attend (v 1).
The agenda: in four parts, each introduced with כי "for" and each claiming Yahweh's right.
A. For Yahweh (has a right to) anger/fury toward the nations, to ban (חרם) those who displease him (vv 2–4).
B. For behold, Yahweh's sword will descend on Edom to accomplish justice. They are the people of his ban (חרם). Yahweh (has a right to) the use of a sword (vv 5–6b).
C. For Yahweh (has the right to) a sacrifice in Bozrah (vv 6c–7).
D. For Yahweh (has a right to) a day of retribution for the cause of Zion. Edom will be destroyed and desolate forever (vv 8–15).
Concluding orders for the record to be reviewed and recorded as Yahweh's direct command. He alone has the right to determine such things. This stands as a perpetual deed (vv 16–17).

The four substantive sentences beginning with כי each name something which belongs to Yahweh: קצף "anger," חרב "sword" זבח "sacrifice," and יום נקם "a day of vengeance." His rights are first claimed over all nations in a terrible assertion that the exercise of this right will involve the mountains, the host of heaven, and the skies. Then the focus is upon Edom for the next three items. In a way typical of the artistry of the Vision, these verses play on three words with similar letters: חרם "ban" (vv 2, 5), חרב "sword" (vv 5–6), and חלב "human fat" (vv 6 [twice], 7).

The motifs in A/A′ and in the central pronouncement of 34:16–17 are related to cultic themes. These include the Lord's day of wrath on all nations, the judgment which settles the fate of nations and peoples, and the joyful festival of Zion.

Chap. 35 portrays the response to Yahweh's judgment on Edom by Judean residents and by pilgrims on their way to Jerusalem. Southern and southeastern Judah regains access to more favored lands occupied by Edom and to water from which she has been cut off. The pilgrims receive rights of passage to Jerusalem.

Comment

1 The command to attend Yahweh's court is issued to *nations* and *peoples*. The word pair is inclusive of all forms of social order and government and is common to Jerusalem's liturgies in which they are summoned to Jerusalem to pledge fidelity to Yahweh. *The land* is understood in the Vision to include the entire area of Palestine/Syria which David's rule related to Yahweh's kingship (cf. *Excursus: The Land* in *Isaiah 1–33*). *The world* (תבל) includes all the "known world" and could be understood as the universe. Yahweh's rights there were based on his role as creator (cf. Pss 93:1b–4; 94:3–5; 95:10–13; 98:7–9).

2–4 The first item on the agenda asserts Yahweh's right to *wrath* and *fury* over *all nations* and their *armies*. The announcement is not applied nor are specific charges made. The statement stands starkly alone as the assertion of an imperial right. It is continued by reference to his right to apply *the ban* to any one of them. This term comes from the language of holy war (cf. G. von Rad, *Der Heilige Krieg im alten Israel,* 13; F. M. Cross, "The Divine Warrior," *Biblical Motifs,* ed. A. Altmann [Boston: Harvard University Press, 1966] 11–30; N. Gottwald, "Holy War," *IDBSup,* 942–44). It was used of Israel's occupation of Canaan (cf. Josh 10:1, 28, 35; 1 Sam 15:3, 8, 9). Yahweh claims here, as for Joshua's occupation, the right to have any or all the nations "devoted" to him. Nothing from them can be claimed as booty (cf. Josh 6:18). This principle will be consistently maintained when the ban is applied to Edom. No part of Edom itself will fall into Israel's possession.

The normal application of the ban reads, "I will give them into your hands." But the formula here says *he gives them over to slaughter.* The judgment does not have the purpose of making the land ready for another people, as was the case in Canaan, but of simple destruction and devastation. The dead are to be left unburied as a sign of special disrespect. (Cf. 14:19; Jer 36:30; Ezek 16:5; 1 Kgs 13:24, 25, 28.) Yahweh's fury is intense and highly motivated.

The slaughter has its effect on the *mountains* which are blood-soaked and on *the army of the heavens. Infected* (נמקו) means "to fester, rot away" (cf. BDB, 596). The horrible picture includes the fixed elements of the universe, the mountains and the heavens, who are often summoned as Yahweh's witnesses to judgment. The *army of heaven* usually refers to the stars. The *sky* is the same Hebrew word as *heaven,* שמים, but now is used in a different sense. It is likened to a sheet of paper or parchment, as in 40:22; Ps 104:2; Zech 12:1. But the idea of its rolling up like a scroll in unique here (though repeated in Rev 6:14). The figure is parallel to that of the falling of dried leaves in the next verse. The idea of falling stars in relation to the great judgment is also found in 13:10 and in Mark 13:25. All creation is affected by the sins of nations and the necessary divine reaction. It is a terrible and horrifying picture. But it is only a background for the announcement that follows.

5 The specific announcement for this assembly is like that made to the banquet for all peoples in 25:6–8. In chaps. 24 and 25, the issue also relates to blood guilt and the curse that comes from it. Yahweh's reaction is such that the sun and the moon are affected (24:23). The nations are summoned to hear God's announcement of an amnesty that banishes death (25:6–8).

Here the parallel is closer to the announcement of the fate of powers in the heights and kings on the lowlands (24:21–23). Yahweh himself makes the announcement. His *sword* will *descend on Edom. Descend* implies that Yahweh lives in heaven. Earlier theophanies used the words "go out," "rise up," and "show himself." Mic 1:3 used the terms "come" and "come down" together. Yahweh appears here as a warrior ready for battle as he had in chap. 13. Isa 63:19–64:1 [64:1–2] will pray for his appearance in this manner.

Yahweh is exercising his right of *ban* on the *people* of *Edom*. An important phrase follows. It is the first of two that explain the reasons for the ban. *For judgment* is the equivalent of "for good cause" or "for reasons of justice." The ban and Yahweh's fury through the sword have not been applied arbitrarily. The Vision assumes that its audience/readers would need no explanation of Edom's sins. Everyone in fifth-century Jerusalem would know that. That same fifth-century audience would be aware of Edom's recent devastation (*ca.* 475 B.C.). But this scene is set a century earlier. The specific details of the judgment will be mentioned in v 8. Yahweh's right to wrath and ban had been stated in general terms in vv 2–4. Now the announcement applies them to one people, Edom.

Excursus: Edom

Bibliography

Bartlett, J. R. "The Brotherhood of Edom." *JSOT* 4 (1977) 2–27. ———. "The Moabites and Edomites." *POTT* 229–58. ———. "Yahweh and Qaus: A Response to Martin Rose." *JSOT* 5 (1978) 29–38. **Kellermann, U.** *Israel und Edom, Studien zum Edomhass Israels in 6.–4. Jahrhundert v. Chr.* Habilitationsschrift Münster, 1975. **Rose, M.** "Yahweh in Israel—Qaus in Edom?" *JSOT* 4 (1977) 28–34. **Watts, J. D. W.** *Obadiah, A Commentary.* Grand Rapids: Eerdmans, 1968. 11–19. **Weippert, M.** *Studien und Materialien zur Geschichte der Edomiter auf Grund schriftlicher und archäologischer Quellen.* Diss.: Tübingen, 1971.

The history of Edom parallels that of Israel and Judah, and in many ways they pursued common goals. But, as Wildberger notes (1335), there were two areas of competition and conflict between them. One involved the copper mines in the southern Arabah and access to the port of Elath on the Gulf of Aqabah, which provided entry to the Red Sea. The other problem involved the occupation of the territory called the Arabah, the steppe south of the Dead Sea. The boundaries were not, and could not, be well defined. Throughout the history they shifted back and forth according to the relative strength of the peoples.

Under the Assyrian Empire, Judah and Edom were both victims who had more reason to stand together than to oppose each other. When the Babylonians fell heir to the Empire, they pursued different policies in the region, actively urging the small countries to work for advantages over their neighbors by pleasing the emperor. Syr reads "Edom" for MT's "Aram" in 2 Kgs 24:2, which is fitting since Ammon and Moab are the other allies that Babylon called up against Jehoiakim. Weippert (*Geschichte der Edomiter,* 380) cites a potsherd found in Arad (#6005/1) which records the plea of an army officer in Ramoth-Negeb for reinforcements to prevent Edom's advance there. The potsherd is dated to the closing years of the kingdom of Judah. Babylon's pressure on Judah provided an opportunity for Edom to expand its territory in the Arabah.

Jeremiah 27 reports a delegation in Jerusalem in the fourth year of Zedekiah (*ca.* 594 B.C.) which included Edomites with Moabites, Ammonites, Tyrians, and Sidonians. Their agenda must have included plans for common action against Babylon. But apparently nothing came of the plans. When Babylon stormed Jerusalem's walls in 587 B.C., no allies supported Judah. Obadiah 11 implies that Edom actively supported the sack of the city and took booty from it. Josephus (*Ant.* X.9,7) reports that Moab and Ammon fell to Babylon five years later. Edom is not mentioned which suggests that it was a full ally. Lam 4:21 pictures Edom as a pleased spectator at the fall. Ps 137:7 pictures the Edomites' encouraging cheers for the destroying army. Ezek 35 is a prophecy against Edom. It supports the judgment by reference to its ancient enmity (v 5) but accuses her of active compliance in the final destruction of Jerusalem. She is also accused of ambition to occupy the lands of both Judah and Israel after their fall (v 10). The number of prophecies against Edom in the OT is surprisingly high. Wildberger (1338) lists, in addition to Isa 34:1–17: Num 24:18; Isa 11:14; Jer 9:25; 25:15–25; 49:7–22; Ezek 25: 12–14; 35:1–15; 36:5; Joel 4:19; Amos 1:11–12; Obad 8–15; Mal 1:4; and Lam 4:21–22.

Undoubtedly Edom had its own pressures during this period. Desert tribes of Arabs applied pressure from the east, gradually taking over parts of its territory. Eventually Edom shifted its position toward the west. After 587 B.C. its border ran just south of Bethlehem, very near Jerusalem. When Arabs succeeded the Edomites in that region, they inherited this part of Edomite territory as well (cf. Neh 2:19; 6:1). In a later period the Nabateans would occupy the territory.

6a-b Yahweh's action against Edom is supported by the assertion of his right to the use of deadly force, *the sword.* This is clear from the supporting phrase describing the sword in use. *Blood* is common to both humankind and the animals that face slaughter. The same is true of *fat* which may refer to human or animal body-fat. *Gorged* is literally "fattened" or "nourished." This phrase is repeated in v 7.

6c–7 The terrible action is further described as a *sacrifice* (זבח) to which Yahweh claims the right. A great gathering for sacrifice may be called for many reasons. Samuel announced such a sacrifice when he visited Bethlehem (1 Sam 16:1–5). Jer 46:10 associates Yahweh's sacrifice with a day of vengeance and with the use of his sword as this passage does. Zeph 1:7 also speaks of Yahweh's great day as a day of sacrifice.

The *sacrifice* announced here is enormous. Not only lambs, goats, bull calves, and bulls are to be sacrificed, but also *wild oxen* (ראמים) which are otherwise never mentioned for sacrifice. They are usually symbols of power (cf. Job 39:9; Num 23:22; Deut 33:17; Ps 22:22). Wildberger (1343) understands the passage to picture a sacrifice greater than any that has ever been offered. The sacrifice of these great symbols of power serves to make the point.

Bozrah was thought of as the capital of Edom. It means "impenetrable" (cf. *Note* 22:10.c). Towns with similar names appear for Moab (Jer 48:24; 1 Macc 5:26). This town in Edom was located south and east of the southern tip of the Dead Sea but eleven miles north of Petra at a height of 3,000 feet above sea level. It was placed on a mountain spur with steep cliffs on both sides. Its fortress apparently controlled access to the copper mines in the region (Abel, *Géographie de la Palestine,* vol. 2 [Paris: J. Gabalda, 1938] 287). Bozrah is mentioned in Gen 36:33, Jer 49:13, 22, and Amos 1:12.

Ground translates עפר "dust." This is a fine, loose soil which absorbs moisture easily and is also easily moved by the wind.

8 A fourth right is claimed for Yahweh, the right to *a vengeance day, a year of retribution.* It is the royal prerogative, even responsibility, to bring retributive justice within his kingdom. *Vengeance* in the OT is a term used for justice which must be done to level a situation that has become unequal because a violent crime has been committed (cf. G. Sauer, "נקם *nqm* rächen," *THAT* 2:107). Vengeance is not understood as satisfying an emotional need but reestablishing a social and judicial balance (cf. Wildberger 1344). The parallel to שלומים "retributions" supports this understanding (cf. W. Eisenbeis, *Die Würzel* שלם *im Alten Testament,* BZAW 113 [Berlin: De Gruyter, 1969] 350, 353–58).

The great slaughter/sacrifice takes on historical meaning in the description of *retribution.* This monstrous event is recompense for Edom's decisions, attitudes, and actions. *To sue* (לריב) *on Zion's behalf* sharpens the focus even more. P. Höffken (*Untersuchungen zu Begrundungselementen der Völkerorakel des Alten Testaments* [Diss., Bonn, 1977] 90) states that this is the basic thought behind all the prophetic speeches against the nations. Zion stands under the special patronage of Yahweh. Edom's actions against the city made his intervention necessary (cf. *Excursus: Edom*).

9–10 The effects of the ban bring an end to Edom's existence as a country and as a people. The resulting desolation is pictured in three ways which may remind a modern reader of the anticipated results of nuclear bombing. The countryside will smell of *burning pitch* and *sulfur. Pitch* (זפת) occurs in the OT only one other time (in Exod 2:3 with a very different connotation), but *sulfur* (גפרית) was rained down on Sodom and Gomorrah (Gen 19:24) in a place very near to Edom. Israel is threatened with such a judgment in Deut 29:22 [23] where the word מהפכה "overthrow" is used. The same root word הפך "overflow" appears here at the beginning of v 9. In Ezek 38:22 God allows sulfur and fire to fall on Gog and Magog. And in Isa 30:33 the breath of Yahweh is pictured as a stream of sulfur. The desolation is pictured as lasting forever, burning day and night. Other OT passages speak of fires that will not or cannot be put out (cf. 1:31, 66:24; Jer 4:4, 17:27; Ezek 21:4 [20:48]; and in the NT, Mark 9:48).

11–13 In chap. 13 the destruction of Babylon is also compared to that of Sodom and Gomorrah (v 19) and a description of its desolation follows. The same mood prevails here. The fauna and flora of desolate and deserted places take possession of the entire land. They *possess* it by a right of deed which Yahweh himself has assigned them. *Stretch out a measuring line* is a technical term of surveying the land in the process of such claim and assignment. *Desolation* (תהו) and *confusion* (בהו) are the words of Gen 1:2 for the "formless and empty" (NIV) inchoate mass that God's creative power would turn into a beautiful and orderly world.

A question concerning the fate of the nobility, whose genealogy is traced back to Esau in Gen 36:9–43, is used to emphasize the idea that ordered government and exercise of power in Edom is finished. Nothing worthy of the name *kingdom* remains. All those who might claim the crown are *wiped out. Fortresses* and *strongholds* are unused and overgrown ruins; their only inhabitants are creatures of the wild that regularly move in to fill otherwise unoccupied places.

14–15 Wildberger (1347) correctly perceives an intention of pushing the description of Edom's desolation to an extreme beyond any comparable imagery. He is also right in understanding the words ציים, איים, and שעיר, which are here translated as *demons, phantoms, wild goat* (Wildberger: *Bocksgeister* "goat spirits"), to be demonic beings. He acknowledges that the line between exotic inhabitants of haunted places like snakes, owls, and jackals on the one hand, and phantoms, ghosts, and demons on the other, is not clearly drawn. Nor need it be for the purpose of this scene. But one term is unmistakable: *Lilith,* the demoness of the night.

Excursus: Lilith

Bibliography

Contenau, G. *La magie chez les Assyriens et les Babyloniens.* Paris: Payot, 1947. 94. **Gaster, T. H.** *Myth, Legend and Custom in the Old Testament.* New York: Harper & Row, 1969. 578–80, 697–98. **Hurwitz, S.** *Lilith, die erste Eva: Eine Studie über dunkle Aspekte der Weiblichkeit.* Zurich: Daimon Verlag, 1980. **Killen, A. M.** "La légende de Lilith et quelques interprétations modernes de cette figure legendaire." *RLC* 12 (1932) 277–311. **Krebs, W.** "Lilith—Adams erste Frau." *ZRGG* 27 (1975) 141–52. **Langdon, S. H.** "Semitic Mythology." *Mythology of All Races,* vol. 5. Ed. L. H. Gray. Boston: Marshall Jones, 1965. 361–64. **Patai, R.** *The Hebrew Goddess.* New York: Ktav, 1967. 207–45, 318–22. **Ribichini, A.** "Lilith nell' albera ḪULUPPU." *Atti del 1° congegno italiano sul Vicino Oriente antico* (1978) 25–33. **Scholem, G.** "Lilith." *EncJud* 11:245–49.

Isa 34:14 has the only mention of לילית "Lilith" in the OT, unless suggested emendations to Job 18:15 and Isa 2:18 are accepted. The name is very similar to the Hebrew word for night (לילה). However, the demoness was well known in Mesopotamia. The Sumerian word *lil* "wind" was related to the name and she was known as a storm-demon. But the syllable *lil* was associated with the night in Semitic languages (Wildberger, 1347).

Lilith entered Jewish literature at a late date, but her influence continued a long time. Using Isa 34:15 for justification, Lilith became part of the labyrinthine structures of Jewish and then Christian demonology. Targum Pseudo-Jonathan adds a prayer to Aaron's blessing (Num 6:24–26): "May the Lord bless you in all your deeds and protect you from the demons of the night (Aram לילי) and from anything that frightens and from demons of evening and morning, from evil spirits and phantoms. . . ." *Midrash bammidbar rabba* 119A teaches that Lilith devours her own children if she cannot find other newborn babies to eat. Rabbi Hanina is quoted in the Talmud as teaching that Lilith lives in abandoned houses (citing Isa 24:14; *Sabbath* II 151b, *The Babylonian Talmud,* ed. I. E. Epstein [London: Soncino, 1938] 773).

Some sixth-century A.D. Aramaic texts teach that Lilith wanted to devour a newborn baby but was prevented by Elijah (J. A. Montgomery, *Aramaic Incantation Texts from Nippur* [Philadelphia: University of Pennsylvania, 1913] Text 42). Scholem (*EncJud* 11:245–49) reports that later Jewish literature speaks of Lilith as Adam's first wife. Kabbalistic thought came to regard her as the opposite of the *Shekina*. The latter is called the mother of the house of Israel, while the former is called the mother and ruler of all the unclean. M. J. bin Gorion (*Der Born Judas* [Leipzig: Insel-Verlag, 1922] 83) has one of his characters ban a demon to the kingdom of darkness where Lilith lives. Lilith was also known to the Mandeans (cf. M. Lidzbarski, *Das Johannesbuch des Mandäer* [Giessen: A. Töpelmann, 1915] 8, and *Mandäische Liturgien* [Giessen: A. Töpelmann, 1920] 20, 37, 42).

Krebs (*ZRGG* 27 [1975] 141–52) quotes from Goethe to show how widespread the knowledge of Lilith is in Western literature. On "Walpurgisnacht" Faust encounters Lilith and wants to know who she is. Mephistopheles explains:

> Adam's first wife.
> Beware of her beautiful hair,
> of this adornment, above all else she is proud.
> If she snares a young man with it,
> she does not release him easily.
> (W. Goethe, *The Tragedy of Faust* I. *The Works of Goethe.* Vol. 6. Trans. T. Martin. [New York: C. T. Brainard, 1902] 202.)

Wildberger concludes that the mention of Lilith in Isa 34:14 had paved the way unintentionally for a remarkable "career." The passage itself is only trying to present a picture of a ruin more devastating than any before it. Thus the wild and spooky feel of the desolate land is powerfully portrayed. Ostrichs, snakes, and vultures will join the list of wild creatures and demons who possess the region where for generations to come "no one will be passing through."

16–17 The judicial procedure closes with the formal instructions for the transcript, *Yahweh's scroll,* to be read aloud to be sure that no item of the curses that comprise the judgment has been omitted. The procedure emphasizes that they are his express commands. That they are collated and arranged by *his Spirit* stresses his direct participation in their origin. They are not something prepared by his office staff. *Their inheritance forever:* Yahweh's decisions have settled the fate of Edom's inhabitants and the territory permanently.

35:1–2 The effect of Yahweh's judgment over Edom is felt most immediately by those parts of Judah nearest the borders. They are called here *Wilderness* (מדבר), *Dry Land* (ציה) and *Arabah* (ערבה). The three names refer to the rift of Jordan, especially south of the Dead Sea toward the Gulf of Aqabah. This eastern part of the Negev was disputed territory between Edom and Judah during their entire existence. Although dry and forbidding in the eyes of some, it drew shepherds and farmers who hoped for rains that seldom came. The land was essentially fruitful, if only water were available, and was certainly strategically located to control trade routes to the Gulf of Aqabah and to Arabia.

The three words reflect the ambiguous evaluation of the lands. ציה "dry land" seems to fit the barren dry lands. מדבר "wilderness" could also carry that meaning. But it may refer to pasturage for flocks (Joel 2:22) and to districts containing a number of thriving towns (Isa 42:11). Josh 15:61–62 speaks of the Wilderness of Judea with its six cities. "The Wilderness" is used in the Pentateuch to refer to the entire area through which the tribes wandered on their way to Canaan. This included the Wilderness of Moab (Deut 2:8) and the Wilderness of Edom (2 Kgs 3:8). ערבה "Arabah" bears an even broader connotation. The root has many meanings ranging from "mix," to "exchange," "be pleasing," and "be arid." In the latter sense it refers to desert dwellers (Arabs) and to Arabia. Usually in the OT it refers to the steppe lands around the Dead Sea, especially to that west and south, which Judah claimed but which were often occupied by Edom. The Vision of Isaiah uses the term in this latter sense (cf. 7:3; 11:16; 19:23; 33:8; 36:2; 40:3; 49:11; 62:10).

These regions are to be most directly affected by Edom's devastation. They can now develop without the constant threat which Edom has exercised in the area. The *crocus* is a fit symbol for the sudden change of fortunes in the area. *Lebanon's glory* apparently refers to verdant forest cover, while *Carmel* and *Sharon* were coastal areas known for fertile fields and flowers. (Cf. 33:9 where this comparison is reversed: Sharon becomes like the Arabah!) *Yahweh's glory,* the *splendor of our God,* refers to the sudden removal of Edom's pressures. כבוד "glory" and הדר "splendor" are the divine attributes which are revealed in Yahweh's actions. When chaps. 34–35 are properly seen together, it is clear that they refer not primarily to the beauties of nature but to the judgment on Edom. The Arabah's renaissance is the result of that act and it reflects the glory which is attributed to Yahweh because of it.

That Yahweh's *glory* is revealed is a motif that appears in 4:5, 11:10, 40:5, 60:1, and 66:18. Jerusalem, Israel, all flesh, and the non-Israelite pilgrims see the glory. Both *glory* and *splendor* are spoken of kings (Pss 21:6 [5]; 45:4; Dan 4:27,33; 5:18). And both are used in the praise of Yahweh (Pss 96:6; 104:1; 111:3; 145:5,12).

3–7 The second group to be affected by Edom's fall are the pilgrims on their way to Zion. They had to pass through territory around Jerusalem that was controlled by Edom, which cannot have been a pleasant experience. This is no longer necessary. They encourage each other is these verses. *Feeble hands, faltering knees, fearful hearts,* the *blind, deaf* and *lame* all fit the picture of pilgrimage processions on their way to the Holy City which would certainly have included the infirm, the ill, and the impaired. The goal of pilgrimage lay in seeing God in Zion. The vision of his work of retribution on Edom fulfills that aim. V 4 picks up the theme of 34:8 (cf. 61:2, 63:4). Yahweh acts as their *savior* in remedying a very bad situation.

Note the contrast between *blind eyes opened* and the commission given in 6:9. Between the *streams in the Arabah* and the devastation promised in 6:11–13, the time of curse and judgment placed on Israel is drawing to a close. Edom's devastation and its results for Judah are the first signs of that new day. References to *blind* and *deaf* also pick up another motif in the Vision. They are the symbols of a people who cannot understand the call of God to participate in his work. Now God's unmistakable intervention on Zion's behalf gives a sign that even the blind and deaf should understand.

8 The theme of pilgrimage is encountered again with the promise that a *highway is there.* The motif appears in 11:16 and in 62:10 as a means for the return of the remnant from foreign lands. In 40:3 it is a highway through the wilderness that Yahweh will travel. Here in 35:8 that highway is *there,* that is, in the Arabah which was until recently controlled by Edom. This theme fits the broader motif of pilgrimage to Zion which was first presented in 2:2–4. A major barrier to the achievement of the goal of making Zion open to pilgrims has been removed.

The highway is to be called *The Holy Road,* reserved for pilgrims. Wildberger (1364) understands this to exclude the non-Israelites. But this need not stand in contradiction to 2:2; 19:23, and other places that document the Vision's idea that Zion should be open to all peoples. The Vision is written before the reform of Ezra applied the laws of "clean and unclean" so stringently. The meaning here should be sought in distinguishing ordinary commercial and military traffic on the highway and that of pilgrims, *the ones who walk The Way.* These are those of faith who journey to Zion. The contrast is with *fools* who just *wander about,* not between culticly "clean" Jews and the heathen.

9 The pilgrims making their way through the fruitful Arabah (cf. Ps 84:7 [6]) can also be assured of safety from *fearful beasts.* Three times in vv 8–9 the emphatic *there* (שם) appears. These balance the two appearances of *then* (אז) in vv 5–6. *Then,* that is, after God's act of retribution has straightened things out, and *there,* in the place where things were wrong before, the way to Zion will be open and safe. For now the *redeemed walk there.*

גאולים "redeemed" appears here in the Vision for the first time instead of *the remnant* of Israel or Judah. Yahweh is frequently pictured as the גאל "redeemer" in the following chapters (41:14; 43:14; and others including 60:16; 63:16). The use of the term here signals a change in the basic idea of Israel's/Judah's hope. No longer is this hope for a restoration of a part of the old order. From here on to chap. 66 it takes the form God's redeemed elect in his new order. The *then* and the *there* that signal a new and different time and place also envision participants made eligible, not because they are a part of the past people of Israel or Zion, but because they are part of God's new redemption. But this does not lie in some distant future. It is introduced by God's action against Edom which is presented in chap. 34. The new time of redemption is contemporary with that in which the Vision is first read and heard.

גאל "redeem" is a term used of Yahweh's acts toward Israel in Egypt (Exod 6:6; 15:13; Pss 74:2; 77:16; 106:10; and Isa 63:9). It was originally a legal term which pictured the duties of a family member toward relatives (cf. J. J. Stamm, *Erlösen und Vergeben im Alten Testament* [Bern: A. Franke, 1940] 27–30). Wildberger (1365) notes that this ancient meaning still shows in 62:11 where Yahweh's redemption is "buying" and "ransoming." But the term comes to have a religious meaning which suggests that God has freed the redeemed from the consequences of their sins.

10 *Yahweh's ransomed ones* (פדויי) translates a parallel term. This one appears in the following chapters only once (50:2). It was used in 1:27 and in 29:22. It originally was a legal term which entered the cultic area in relation to redemption of the firstborn (Exod 13:13, 15), but then came to be applied to Yahweh's redemption of Israel from Egypt especially in Deuteronomy (7:8; 9:26, etc.). Like *redeem, ransom* (פדה) becomes a fixed religious term, and is so used here, to designate those whom Yahweh has released from the bondage due them for their sins. Jer 31:11 uses the words together and follows them, as here, with a description of rejoicing. Redemption and ransoming in the Vision pictures a salvation from the judgment curse enunciated in 6:9–13, in chap. 24, and in other places, and which has been so amply fulfilled in the six generations portrayed by the Vision up to this time.

The goal for the redeemed and ransomed pilgrims is *Zion*. They can fulfill what for many of them has undoubtedly been a lifelong hope. They can *enter* the Holy City, sing the songs of Zion, and participate in festivals on the holy hill. They will undoubtedly sing the Songs of Ascents (Pss 120–134).

The chapter ends with words which would be appropriate for a blessing on the pilgrims, wishing *joy and gladness* to replace all *sorrow and sighing* and that these may have an *everlasting* effect on them. The blessing seals the pivotal turn in the Vision. Whenever such calls have been made in earlier chapters (such as chap. 12), they have been immediately turned back to the grim business at hand, as generation after generation has failed to recognize Yahweh's new strategy. With this scene the downward curve has reached its nadir. Without being mentioned, the implied destruction of Jerusalem marked a potential turning point in Yahweh's relation to Israel and Zion. The judgment against Edom is the sign that the change has begun. Israelite and Jew alike may hope for a safe and joyful pilgrimage to Zion in the knowledge that redemption and ransom is to be found in their God.

Explanation

The focus of Scene 1 is a surprise. That Yahweh should hold a great judgment against the nations for all that they had done to Judah and Jerusalem is no surprise, although deuteronomic and prophetic preaching insisted that it all happened because of Israel's sins. The surprise comes from the silence concerning Babylon. She was the chief aggressor and instigator of it all. But no word is spoken about her at this point. Instead the divine wrath is directed toward Judah's eastern neighbor, Edom, those traditional descendants of Esau. There is ample evidence in the OT that this reaction to Edom was widespread in this period (see *Excursus: Edom*). Judah could survive, even thrive, under the empire, but not under the oppression of its ambitious and covetous neighbor.

The scene presumes an exilic setting, undoubtedly well-known to early readers, in which Edom and other neighbors persecute helpless Jewish people in many ways. They expropriate the best land from local residents in Palestine. They collect tolls from commerce on the highways. And they make pilgrimage to Jerusalem dangerous if not virtually impossible. Such pressures added to Judah's memory of Edom's perfidy in collaborating with Nebuchadnezzar in the sack of Jerusalem in 587 B.C.

The first part of the scene portrays the nations summoned to a great courtroom in the manner of the emperors. Yahweh is present. His herald and his aides speak for him, but he himself speaks the central message of v 5. He announces the judgment on Edom in the setting of imperial rights that belong to Yahweh, Lord of all nations. He claims the right of ban with wrath and terrible fury on nations and armies that displease him (v 2), the right of the sword (v 6) or of armed retaliation, the right of a sacrifice (v 6c) in Bozrah, Edom's capital, and the right to a day of retribution (v 8). The ban and the sword are to be understood as righteous judgment (v 5). Retribution is announced on behalf of Zion's cause against Edom (v 8).

The actions against Edom apparently include armed incursion and the devastation of her population followed by "natural catastrophes" not unlike those of Sodom and Gomorrah which leave the entire territory desolate and abandoned. Judah is relieved of the border pressure. The border territories can thrive again while pilgrims can travel unhindered to Zion. The judgment on Edom clears the way for fulfillment of the vision of 2:1–4. The fulfillment of "the sword and sacrifice" parts is pictured in 63:1–4. The destruction of Edom becomes the center of God's action against the nations alongside that against Babylon (chap. 47).

Scene 2: A Reading from History: The Assyrian's Speech (36:1–22)

Bibliography

Ackroyd, P. R. "Historians and Prophets." *SEA* 33 (1968) 18–54. **Boecker, H. J.** *Redeformen des Rechtslebens.* WMANT 14. 2d ed. Neukirchen-Vluyn: Neukirchener Verlag, 1970. 106–11. **Burney, C. F.** " 'The Jew's Language': 2 Kings xviii 26 = Isa xxxvi 11." *JTS* 13 (1912) 417–20. **Childs, B. S.** *Isaiah and the Assyrian Crisis,* 69–103. **Clements, R. E.** *Isaiah and the Deliverance of Jerusalem.* Sheffield: JSOT Press, 1980. **Ellul, J.** *The Politics of God and the Politics of Man.* Grand Rapids: Eerdmans, 1977. 143–89. **Fichtner, J.** "Jahwes Plan in der Botschaft des Jesajas." *Gottes Weisheit,* 27–43. **Horn, S. H.** "The Chronology of King Hezekiah's Reign." *AUSS* 2 (1964) 40–52. **Kaiser, O.** "Die Verkündigung des Propheten Jesaja im Jahre 701." *ZAW* 81 (1969) 304–15. **Lambert, W. G.** "Destiny and Divine Intervention in Babylon and Israel." *OTS* 17 (1972) 65–72. **Moyne, J. le.** "Les deux embassades de Sennachérib à Jérusalem." *Mélanges Bibliques.* FS A. Robert. Paris: Blond et Gay, 1956. 149–64. **Orlinsky, H. M.** "The Kings-Isaiah Recensions of the Hezekiah Story." *JQR* 30 (1939–1940) 33–49. **Vaux, R. de.** "Jérusalem et les prophètes." *RB* 73 (1966) 481–509. **Wiener, H. M.** "Isaiah and the Siege of Jerusalem." *JSR* 11 (1927) 195–209. **Wildberger, H.** "Die Rede des Rabsake vor Jerusalem." *TZ* 35 (1979) 35–47. **Zimmerli, W.** "Jesaja und Hiskia." *Wort und Geschichte.* FS K. Elliger. Ed. H. Gese. AOAT 18. Neukirchen: Keuelaer, 1973. 199–208.

Translation

Reader: [1] *Then it happened,*[a] *in the fourteenth year of King Hezekiah's*[b] *reign, when Sennacherib,*[c] *king of Assyria, campaigned against all the fortified cities of Judah and captured them,*[d] [2] *that the*

king of Assyria[a] sent the field commander[bc] from Lachish[d] to
Jerusalem[e] to King Hezekiah with a large[f] contingent of troops.[g]
He took his stand[h] at the aqueduct of the Upper Pool, by the
road to the Washerman's field. 3[a] Eliakim, son of Hilkiah, palace
administrator, Shebna,[b] the scribe, and Joah, son of Asaph, the
recorder, went out to meet him.[c]

4 The field commander said to them:[a] "Please, say[b] to
Hezekiah:[c] Thus says the emperor, king of Assyria: [d]What is
this confidence in which you put your trust?[de] 5 You say,[a] surely
a word of lips (only), 'A strategy and strength for the battle.'
Now—on whom do you really place your trust that you rebel
against me?

6[a] "Look! If you trust[b] in this splintering reed of a staff, in
Egypt, which if a man lean on it will pierce his hand and wound
it,[c] Pharaoh, king of Egypt, is like that to all who are trusting
in him.

7 "And if you[a] say to me, 'We trust facing Yahweh, our God,'
is not he (the one) whose high places and altars Hezekiah removed,
saying to Judah and Jerusalem, 'You must worship (only) before
this altar.'?

8 "Now—please negotiate[a] with my master the king[b] of Assyria.
I will give you two thousand horses if on your part you can put
riders on them. 9 How[a] can you turn aside the presence of the
governor,[b] (even if he is) one of the least of my master's servants,
and go on putting your trust in Egypt for chariotry and horsemen?[c]
10 And[a] now, is it without a vow to Yahweh that I have come
against this land[b] to destroy it?[c] Yahweh said to me: 'Go up to
this land to destroy it!' "

11 Then Eliakim,[a] Shebna, and Joah said[b] to the field
commander, "Please speak Aramaic[c] to your servants, for we
understand it. [d]Do not speak to us[e] in Judean in the hearing
of the people who are on the wall."[d] 12 But the field commander
said:[a] "Is it to[b] your master and to you (alone) that my master
sent me to speak these words? Does it not also concern the persons
who live on the wall whether they eat their own excrement[c] and
drink their own urine[d] with you?"

13 Then the field commander stood and said[a] loudly in Judean,
"Hear the words[b] of the emperor, the king of Assyria. 14 Thus
says the king:[a] Do not support[b] Hezekiah! For he cannot deliver
you![c] 15 Do not let Hezekiah make you trust Yahweh, saying,
'Yahweh will certainly deliver us. This city[a] will not[b] be given[c]
into the power of the king of Assyria.' 16 Do not listen to Hezekiah.
For thus says the king[a] of Assyria, [b]'Make a mutually
advantageous agreement[b] with me and come out to me. Then
each of you may eat (from) [c]his own vine, and [c]fig tree, and
each water from his own cistern, 17 until I come and take you to
a land like your own land, a land of grain and new wine, a
land[a] of bread and vineyards.'[b]

18[a] "Hezekiah[b] misled you, saying, 'Yahweh will deliver us.'

Did the gods of the nations save each his own land from the
power of the king of Assyria? 19 *Where were the gods of Hamath*
or Arpad? Where were the gods of Sepharvaim?[a] *Or*[b] *indeed*
(those) that delivered Samaria from my power? 20 *Who was it of*
all the gods of these[a] *nations that delivered their country from*
my power that now Yahweh can save Jerusalem from my power?"
21 *They were silent*[a] *and answered him not a word, for the*
king himself had commanded them, "Do not respond." 22 *Then*
Eliakim, son of Hilkiah[a] *who was palace administrator, Shebna*
the scribe, and Joah, son of Asaph the recorder, came back to
Hezekiah with torn clothes and reported[b] *to him the words*[c] *of*
the field commander.

Notes

1.a. 2 Kgs 18:13 omits ויהי "and it happened."

1.b. 2 Kgs 18:13 and DSS^{Isa} read the name without the final *šûreq.* "Hezekiah" is written both ways.

1.c. MT סנחריב "Sennacherib." LXX *Σενναχηριμ* "Sennacherim." 'A *σενηριβ* "Senerib." Heroditus (II, 141) *Σαναχάριβος* "Sanacharibos." MT elsewhere writes the name סנחרב "Sennachereb." The Elephantine-Papyri have סנחאריב and שׂנחאריב (Achikar, 3f, 15, 27, 50, 51, 55; see A. Cowley, *Aramaic Papyri of the Fifth Century* B.C. [Oxford: Clarendon, 1923] 204–48). All these are efforts to transcribe the Akk *sin-aḫḫē-erība* or *Sīn-aḫḫī-iriba* "Sin replaces the brothers" (cf. J. J. Stamm, "Die akkadische Namengebung," *MVÄG* 44[1939] 290).

1.d 2 Kgs 18:14–16 are omitted here (cf. *Form/Structure/Setting* below).

2.a. DSS^{Isa} omits ר of MT to read אשו. Cf. Kutscher, *Isaiah Scroll,* 531.

2.b. 2 Kings includes two other officers, the תרתן "general" and the רב סרים "chief prince."

2.c. MT רב שקה "chief officer" or "field commander" is often transliterated "Rabshakah."

2.d. 2 Kgs 18:17 reads מן לכיש, a slightly different form but the same meaning.

2.e. 2 Kgs 18:17 omits the ה-directive and puts the name at the end of the sentence.

2.f. DSS^{Isa} adds מאודה "very."

2.g. 2 Kgs 18:17 includes additional text: "and they went up and came to Jerusalem and they went up and came."

2.h. 2 Kgs 18:17 is pl, "they stood," to fit the added words. See 2.b above.

3.a. 2 Kgs 18:18 includes the additional words ויקראו אל המלך "and they called out to the king."

3.b. MT שבנא "Shebna." 2 Kgs 18:18 spells it שבנה "Shebnah," DSS^{Isa} שובנא "Shubna."

3.c. 2 Kgs 18:18 להם "to them" is pl in keeping with the other pls in the text.

4.a. MT אליהם "to them" is spelled in DSS^{Isa} אליהמה.

4.b. MT אמרו "say" is spelled in DSS^{Isa} אמורו.

4.c. MT חזקיהו "Hezekiah" is spelled in DSS^{Isa} חזקיה.

4.d-d. LXX *Τί πεποιθὼς εἶ* "what confidence do you have?" This is a shorter text than MT.

4.e. MT בטחת "you trust." DSS^{Isa} אתה בטחתה בו "which you have trusted" is a broader statement of the same thing.

5.a. MT אמרתי "I say." DSS^{Isa} אמרתה, Vg *disponis,* and 2 Kgs 18:20 אָמַרְתָּ read "you say." The 2d pers is correct. MT is wrong.

6.a. 2 Kgs 18:21 has עתה "now" before הנה "behold, look" a redundant particle.

6.b. 2 Kgs 18:21 adds לך "for yourself," an unnecessary expansion.

6.c. ונקבה "and wound it" is omitted in LXX.

7.a. DSS^{Isa} LXX Tg and 2 Kgs 18:22 read a pl.

8.a. MT התערב נא "please negotiate" is sg. DSS^{Isa} התערבונא is pl following its earlier use of pls.

8.b. המלך "the king of." The noun must be a constr here, so the article is wrong. 2 Kgs 18:23 compounds the error by adding את, the sign of the accus. Nonetheless, the meaning must still be "the king of" (cf. Wildberger, 1381).

9.a. MT איך "how" is expanded to איכה in DSS^{Isa}. The meaning is the same.

9.b. פני פחת, lit., "the face of a governor of." The constr form does not make sense. Either it is unnecessarily put into the text or is to be read as an abs. The phrase emphasizes the officer's personal appeal to Hezekiah.

9.c. פרשים may refer to "riders" or to "drivers of chariots." "Horsemen" is used here to cover both meanings.

10.a. ו "and" is omitted by 2 Kgs 18:25.

10.b. MT הארץ הזאת "this land." 2 Kgs 18:25 המקום הזה "this place."

10.c. Consistent with the previous variant, MT has a fem while 2 Kgs 18:25 uses a masc.

11.a. 2 Kgs 18:26 adds בן חלקיהו "son of Hilkiah."

11.b. MT ויאמר "and said" is a sg verb with a following pl subj, which is not unusual in Heb. DSS^{Isa} reads ויואמרו אליו "and they said to him."

11.c. LXX Συριστί "Syrian"; Vg *Syra lingua* "the Syrian language."

11.d-d. DSS^{Isa} ואל תדבר את הדברים האלה באוזני האנשים היושבים על החומה "and do not speak these words in the hearing of the men who live on the walls." Wildberger (1382) correctly notes that MT's "in Judean" is necessary to balance the "in Aramaic" of the previous line.

11.e. MT אלינו "to us." 2 Kgs 18:26 עמנו "with us." DSS^{Isa} omits.

12.a. 2 Kgs 18:27 adds אליהם "to them" followed by LXX *πρὸς αὐτούς* and Vg *ad eos.*

12.b. MT האל "is it to?" 2 Kgs 18:27 העל "is it against?"

12.c. K חראיהם "their dung/excrement" is spelled in 2 Kgs 18:27 חריהם and in DSS^{Isa} חריהמה. Q צואתם means lit. "their filth."

12.d. K שיני הם is divided to accommodate the pointing for Q מֵימֵי רַגְלֵיהֶם "water of the feet," "feet" being a euphemism for "penises" (cf. Isa 6:2), although 2 Kgs 18:27 reads one word שיניהם "their urine."

13.a. 2 Kgs 18:28 adds וידבר "then he spoke" before "and he said."

13.b. 2 Kgs 18:28 reads a sg, "the word of."

14.a. DSS^{Isa} adds אשור "of Assyria."

14.b. ישא "support" has a plene pointing in 2 Kgs 18:29, ישיא. The negative particle אל calls for a juss reading: lit., "let not support be yours." Cf. GKC §74*l*.

14.c. 2 Kgs 18:29 adds מידו "from his hand." Wildberger (1382) notes that the context calls for מידי "from my hand," which several MSS and the Versions support.

15.a. 2 Kgs 18:30 adds the accus particle את before העיר "the city."

15.b. 2 Kgs 18:30 adds the conj ו "and."

15.c. The statement does not indicate by whom it will not be given over. For this use of the passive, see GKC §121*a*.

16.a. 2 Kgs 18:31 and DSS^{Isa} omit the article.

16.b-b. עשו אתי ברכה, lit., "make with me a blessing" is an unusual sentence. Wildberger (1382) admits that it is opaque. His review of the different translations says it all. Ehrlich (*Randglossen* 4:132) changes the vowels to בְּרָכָה (cf. Neh 3:16) meaning a "treaty." GB translates "capitulate." BDB (138) gives the meaning of ברך as both "kneel" and "bless," and suggests here "a treaty of peace" (139). *HALAT* offers "capitulation" following the meaning "kneel" in the root. LXX translates Εἰ βούλεσθε εὐλογηθῆναι "be/make willing to bless." J. Scharbert (" 'Fluchen' und 'Segnen' im Alten Testament," *Bib* 39 [1958] 19 and "ברך *brk*," *TDOT* 2:279–308) suggests the meaning "agree to a truce and treat the winner as absolute lord," i.e., that the field commander is offering an official peace treaty. A. Murtonen ("The Usage and Meaning of the Words *l^{e}barek* and *b^{e}raka^{h}* in the Old Testament," *VT* 9 [1959] 173) suggests it means a situation in which the parties bless each other. Note that Tg translates with שלמא "make peace." The translation above is built upon Murtonen's idea.

16.c. DSS^{Isa} adds את the accus particle.

17.a. LXX has only και "and" for MT ארץ "land."

17.b. 2 Kgs 18:32 adds ארץ זית יצהר ודבש וחיו ולא תמתו ואל תשמעו אל חזקיהו ". . . a land of olive trees and honey. Live and do not die! And do not listen to Hezekiah."

18.a. MT פן, lit., "lest." 2 Kgs 18:32 כי "for."

18.b. "Hezekiah" is omitted in 2 Kgs 18:32 after the addition including his name noted in note 17.b.

19.a. 2 Kgs 18:34 adds הנע ועוה "Hena and Ivvah," apparently place-names (cf. 2 Kgs 19:13/Isa 37:13).

19.b. MT וכי "and that" is unclear in meaning. ו is missing in 2 Kgs 18:34. Several LXX[L] MSS add in the text of 2 Kgs 18:34 *και που εισιν οι θεοι της χωρας σαμαρειας* "and where were the gods of the territory of Samaria," prompting *BHS*'s suggestion איה אלהי ארץ שמרון. LXX Syr Vg translate with *μή* "not," which led Cheyne to emend to הֲכִי, adding interrogative ה (cf. *BHS*). The first word in DSS[Isa] וכיא החצילו is unclear, but the added ה is probably an interrogative as in Cheyne's emendation. However, כי may simply be translated as a particle of emphasis.

20.a. האלה "these" is missing in 2 Kgs 18:35.

21.a. 2 Kgs 18:36 and DSS[Isa] have a pf והחרישו, and 2 Kgs 18:36 adds העם "the people" as subj. The text here assumes the subj to be the emissaries.

22.a. 2 Kgs 18:37 spells the name חלקיה.

22.b. 2 Kgs 18:37 uses a short form, ויגדו "reported."

22.c. 2 Kgs 18:37 lacks the particle את before "the words."

Form/Structure/Setting

The narrative of this and successive chapters is generally equivalent to that in 2 Kings: Isa 36:1 = 2 Kgs 18:13; Isa 36:2–22 = 2 Kgs 18:17–37. The rest of the Hezekiah narrative in 2 Kgs 19–20 appears *in toto* in Isa 37–39 with only the major addition of the Prayer of Hezekiah (Isa 38:9–20). K. A. D. Smelik opposed the view that Isa 36–37 was derived from 2 Kings. He suggested that it was original to Isaiah and written in the Persian period (Report of summer meeting of the Society for Old Testament Study, July 1985). This commentary finds the argument unconvincing and continues to hold that these chapters were derived from 2 Kings.

Two issues emerge from this observation. First, why does the Vision of Isaiah incorporate the account from 2 Kings? The Vision has already given its account of the reign of Hezekiah (chaps. 15–22) and particularly of the events in 701 B.C. relating to Sennacherib's siege of Jerusalem (chap. 22). This account, with its implied negative evaluation of Hezekiah's policies of independence and rebellion, stands in sharp contrast to the adulation of Hezekiah found in 2 Kings and in 2 Chronicles. Hezekiah had surely dealt with Sargon in 714 B.C. and declared his loyalty by paying tribute, as 2 Kgs 18:14–15 testifies. The ploy was apparently successful and Sargon passed Jerusalem by. But in assessing Hezekiah's reign, both 2 Kings and 2 Chronicles ignore this period. Both concentrate their assessment of his reign on the brief period of rebellion between 705–701 B.C., ignoring the longer periods of vassalage which preceded and followed that time. The Vision creates an interesting situation when it portrays exilic Israel reading the account in 2 Kgs 18–20 in a setting when Jerusalem has just fallen to its enemies, when the policy of rebellion has just brought disaster, and when the prophecies of chap. 20 are literally fulfilled. What irony it is!

The second issue concerns the portions of those chapters that are omitted. 2 Kgs 18:1–12 tells of Hezekiah's early reign. The Vision has disagreed on a number of details. In chronology, the Vision has pictured Ahaz to be king during the last days of Samaria (see *Comment* on 14:28 and *Excursus: Chronology* in *Isaiah 1–33*) rather than Hezekiah (2 Kgs 18:9–12). It agreed that he had fought against the Philistines (2 Kgs 18:8; cf. Isa 14:28–32). But it disagreed with 2 Kgs 18:5–7 and its complete approval of Hezekiah as the greatest of Judah's kings. That it says that "Hezekiah trusted in the Lord. . . . The Lord was with him; he was successful in whatever he undertook" (NIV) made the contrast to the Vision's view of Hezekiah a little too obvious. With a delicate touch the author of the Vision avoids pointing out the inner inconsistency in the evaluation in 2 Kings, which characterizes his reign entirely in terms of his rebellions, yet also chronicles his abject servility before Sennacherib (18:14–15). Instead he includes the full story, which Dtr has incorporated in his account. Where Dtr was apparently oblivious of the subtleties and ironies in the story, the Vision reveals them by the simple device of having it read in a setting when all talk of Judah's glory or independence is folly. For this purpose the original account is much more useful than Dtr's introduction.

By placing this narrative in the larger context of dramatic speeches, the Vision has determined the setting in which it should be interpreted. One should think of a narrator reading the passage to a gathering of Jews. The place is not defined. It could be in Palestine or it could be in Babylon. The time is defined by its position in the Vision. It is before 540 B.C. when the following chapters are set, and after the fall of Jerusalem in 587 B.C.

Excursus: Seedbed for Vision

Bibliography

Deutsch, R. R. *Die Hiskia-Erzählung: eine formgeschichtliche Untersuchung der Texte Is 36–39 u. 2 Reg 18–20.* Diss. Basel, 1969. **Payne, J. B.** "The Unity of Isaiah: Evidence from Chapters 36–39." *JETS* 6 (1963) 50–56.

The position of chaps. 36–39 (= 2 Kgs 18:13–20:19) in the heart of the Vision of Isaiah is a puzzle for interpreters. The chronological progression of the acts in this commentary heightens the issue. Why should a narrative about 8th-century Jerusalem appear where one would expect a description of the last days of the Kingdom of Judah in the 6th century B.C.?

The author/composer of the Vision has chosen to spare the reader another account of the gory narrative that is so completely chronicled in 2 Kgs 24–25, in Jeremiah, in Ezekiel, and in Lamentations. Instead, he has repeated the narrative of Hezekiah and Isaiah. Can it be that the reading of this narrative was the inspiration that led to the composition of the Vision? If so, one will find in it the seedbed of ideas, vocabulary, and plot that echoes in the chapters preceding and following in the Vision.

This excursus can be no more than suggestive of the "seeds" that blossom elsewhere. The inspiration begins in the Assyrian commander's speech (36:4–10). He speaks of "confidence" and trust, which are one Hebrew word, בטח. That word appears in 8:17 and at least twelve more times in the Vision. The commander speaks of strategy, עצה, a word that also appears repeatedly (see *Isaiah 1–33,* lv–lvi). He asks: "Would I have come to attack . . . unless Yahweh told me to?" (v 10). This is asserted as fact in 7:17–25 and 8:7–8. He asks, "Has any god delivered from the King of Assyria?" The same claim is made in 10:5–19.

In 37:4 and vv 31–32, references are made to the remnant that survives. This is a major theme in chapters 1–33. The names for God in 37:16 are used repeatedly in the Vision. Hezekiah prays for deliverance (v 20) "so that all kingdoms in the land may know that you alone, Yahweh, are God." This is a central theme of chaps. 40–48. 37:23 employs the title "the Holy One of Israel" which is used so often in the Vision that it is almost an identifying mark. 37:35 records God's promise, "I will defend this city and save it," a statement that seems ironic when read by persons who know that in 586 B.C. God allowed the Babylonians to sack the city.

The narrative about the messengers from Merodach-Baladan (chap. 39) finds full development in chaps. 13, 14, and 21 which picture this period of Babylon's history. Babylon also plays an opposite role in chaps. 46 and 47 as the city where the exiles live which is overrun by the Persians. 39:5 announces that some of Hezekiah's descendants will be taken to Babylon. This is a reference to the story that the reader would expect at this point. Hezekiah's descendants play major roles in chaps. 40–53. These include not only Jehoiachin, the exiled king, but Sheshbazzar, the first leader of a return expedition, (chap. 48) and Zerubbabel, who led in rebuilding the temple and who in dying accomplished atonement for God's people (chap. 53) as Hezekiah had not.

Chapters 1–24 of the Vision use no personal names which could not be known from 2 Kings except those of Isaiah's sons. Hezekiah (chaps. 36–39) appears only in 1:1 but his ministers, Eliakim son of Hilkiah and Shebna son of Asaph, appear in 22:15 and 22. Isaiah, son of Amoz, appears in 1:1, 2:1, 7:1–8, and in 20:1–6. Tirhakah, the Cushite king of Egypt (37:9), appears in chapters 18–19. The King of Babylon (Merodach-Baladan) appears in 13–14 and 21.

The "nations of the land (Canaan)" (37:20) appear in the "foreign prophecies" (chaps. 15–23) and as the "coastlands" and the "borderlands" of chaps. 40–48 and 60–66.

Can the structure of the Vision be explained in this way? The 5th-century author uses the story in 2nd Kings about Isaiah and Hezekiah. He projects a drama-Vision to begin before that story but in Isaiah's lifetime. He uses other Isaiah traditions (chaps. 7–8 and 20) and other prophecies, especially 2:2–4 which he claims for Isaiah, although it is also claimed for Micah in Micah 4:1–3.

Then, using the idea of Yahweh's strategy (עצה), which included sending the Assyrian and raising up the Persian, and the idea of trust (בטח), which God expects from kings and exiles alike, he sketches the work of God over three centuries. He shows how God created the new order that the author and his contemporaries experience through the efforts of Artaxerxes, Ezra, and Nehemiah.

If this is correct, the Vision demonstrates how prophetic literature is a commentary on existing Scripture as well as a reinterpretation and redirection of it. As the author wrestles with the promises that Jerusalem will be saved and never fall (37:35), in light of his knowledge of the catastrophe of 586 B.C., he is led to see how destruction has become a tool of redemption. Salvation is recognized as the re-creation of Zion in a totally new form. Hezekiah's city has not been saved. But the city high on Mount Zion where Yahweh is pleased to dwell has been saved and will be kept forever. (Cf. 2:1–4, 4:2–4, 65:17–66:24). M. Fishbane (*Biblical Interpretation in Ancient Israel* [Oxford: Clarendon Press, 1985] 380–407) calls this "Aggadic exegesis," but has apparently overlooked this particular example.

This recognition helps to establish the purpose of the Vision. It was not meant to predict (what Fishbane calls "mantological exegesis"), but to explain and interpret. It demonstrates what God's will is for that time. This genre should be maintained in exegesis. The book should be exegeted for theological insights, not for predictions of the future.

As 2 Kings, especially chapters 18–20, gives source materials for chaps. 1–34, so it will be seen that Ezra-Nehemiah provides the background for chaps. 45–62.

The narrative of chap. 36 is clearly constructed around two remarkable speeches by the Assyrian field commander. The first (vv 4–10) attacks Judah's confidence (בטח) that help will come and invites them to negotiate a settlement. He probes (v 5) the mental foundations (עצה) of their will to resist. He attacks the idea that Egypt may come to their aid and offers to supply arms in amounts that Egypt cannot match and Judah cannot use. He scorns the belief that Yahweh can be trusted (v 7a), noting that Hezekiah's reforms had offended Yahweh-worshipers in the countryside (v 7b). He closes with an insinuation that Yahweh had instigated the invasion in the first place.

The second speech (vv 13–20) appeals to the people to disregard Hezekiah's appeal for trust in Yahweh. It offers the people the prospect of a peaceful future as tillers of the soil—perhaps in some new land somewhere else (vv 16–17). The people addressed are likely to be refugees from villages in Judah who had fled to the walled city to escape the pillaging of the Assyrian invaders. Then the speech suggests that no god can frustrate the emperor's intentions. None has ever done so, and Yahweh will not become the first (vv 18–20). He challenges Yahweh's power to save, implying that only the emperor can deliver and/or grant the right of peaceful village prosperity.

There is much within the first speech that corresponds to the viewpoint of the Vision. It raises the issue of true and false confidence (בטח) and its foundation. It questions the strategic reasoning (עצה) which supports rebellion (cf. 14:24–27). It deprecates Egypt's capacity and will to support a rebellion in Palestine (cf. chaps. 30–31). It suggests that Yahweh is ultimately responsible for the Assyrian invasion (cf. chaps. 7–10).

But the second speech is as provocative to Yahweh and his prophet as the first had been conciliatory. It is a provocation that cannot be tolerated, illustrating the Assyrians' arrogance which eventually forces Yahweh to destroy them. The thrust of this part of the narrative including this speech (36:11–37:13) is anticipated in the Vision (10:5–19, 24–27; 14:24–27). This second speech sets the stage for the deliverance of Jerusalem from the Assyrian siege in chap. 37 and coincides with the views expressed in the oracles of Zion found throughout the Vision.

The form of the speeches is like that of taunting speech before a battle. But the subtleties of diplomacy have also crept in as well as the narrator's shrewd implication of the appeal to siege psychology by the field commander.

The reasons, then, why the author/compiler chose the two speeches are different. The first speech so closely parallels his own thinking that one is forced to ask whether 2 Kgs 18:4–10 was not in fact a great part of the inspiration leading to the formation of the Vision of Isaiah. One hears the field commander expressing the same doubts concerning the independence policies of Hezekiah and the unmovable confidence in an invulnerable Zion that the Vision represents. The Vision has modified this confidence by exalting Zion's continuing place in God's plan (2:1–4; 4:1–6; chap. 66), but also by distinguishing it from a nationalistic view that supports independence and the continuance of the monarchy (chaps. 7–8; 52–53).

Comment

1 *The fourteenth year.* See the discussion of the chronology of Hezekiah's reign in the *Excursus* in *Isaiah 1–33,* 5–7. The date of the siege is clearly

701 B.C. This note assumes that Hezekiah ascended the throne in 715 B.C. *Sennacherib* was crowned in 705 B.C. on the death of Sargon II. The beginning of his reign was marked by the usual rebellions in various parts of the Empire. He first dealt with Merodach Baladan in Babylon (see chaps. 14 and 39) who fled the city in 703 B.C. (see chap. 21).

2 The Vision's version of this siege is found in chap. 22. The hearers of this reading at this point in the drama will have been reminded of a similar siege by Nebuchadnezzer against Zedekiah in 589–87 B.C. (2 Kgs 25:1 = 2 Chr 36:17).

The titles of the official personages on both sides are interesting. The title מלך "king" is applied both to the Emperor, Sennacherib, who is sometimes called "the great king," and to Hezekiah. The title is usually related to a place as "King of Judah." One may be king of several places. The nomenclature is similar to the familiar titles of dukedoms in England.

The title רב־שקה "Rab-shakah" may well have originally designated the chief cup-bearer to the king. But this ceremonial title became much more than that. J. Nelis and W. Rölig (*BLex* 1442) suggest that he was not only the field commander of the army but also the governor of the province of *Šabirēšu*. He was a high and trusted officer.

The aqueduct of the Upper Pool was outside the wall to the east of the city (see *Comment* on 7:3).

3 Hezekiah sent three high officials of his court to meet him. The *palace administrator* (lit., "who is over the house") was the highest official, a kind of prime minister (cf. 22:15 and the description in vv 20–23). The *scribe* had been an important rank in the court hierarchy since the time of David (2 Kgs 12:11 [10]; 22:3,8; Jer 36:12,20; 37:15,20). The *recorder* was a title used also in 2 Sam 8:16; 20:24; 1 Kgs 4:3; 1 Chr 18:15; 2 Chr 34:8.

Considerable discussion has focused on the terms. J. Begrich ("SŌFĒR und MAZKĪR," *ZAW* 58 [1940/41] 1–29 = *Gesammelte Studien zum Alten Testament* 67–98) suggested that the ספר "scribe" was like the Egyptian *sš* and the מזכיר "recorder" like the Egyptian *whmw* "speaker" with broad powers in counsel, consultation and administration (cf. R. de Vaux, *Ancient Israel,* 131–32). But H. Graf Reventlow ("Das Amt des Mazkir," *TZ* 15 [1959] 171) contended that the office goes back to the old twelve-tribe confederacy in Israel and that its bearer was the highest official in the land for legal and judicial matters. He was the minister of justice. But H. J. Boecker ("Erwägungen zum Amt des Mazkir," *TZ* 17 [1961] 216) rejected this view and returned to the use of Egyptian parallels. W. Schottroff (*"Gedenken" im Alten Orient und im Alten Testament,* WMANT 15 [Neukirchen-Vluyn: Neukirchener Verlag, 1964] 270) understood the term מזכיר to mean "speaker, reporter, herald." He has the double task of communicating the king's will to his subjects and in turn reporting to the king the happenings in his realm. He was the press secretary and the royal reporter who briefed the king on current events. Wildberger (1397) suggests that such offices may well have varied in job description and duties over the years in Israel as in Egypt (cf. A. D. Crown, "Messengers and Scribes: The ספר and מזכיר in the Old Testament," *VT* 24 [1974] 366–70).

The reader will note that in 22:15–19 Shebna was palace administrator.

In vv 20–23 Eliakim was promised the position. This reading from 2 Kgs 18 already has their positions reversed. Eliakim is palace administrator and Shebna is the scribe (see *Comment* on 22:15–25). The name Joah means "Yahweh is brother." 2 Chr 34:8 tells of another Joah who was recorder in the reign of Josiah.

4 *The emperor* is literally "the great king." The designation reflects the Assyrian title that appears in Assyrian texts of the period: "Sanherib, the great king, . . . the king of the four world regions." The Akkadian *šarru rabû,* which the Heb המלך הגדול "the great king" translates, became a fixed title, the equivalent of emperor (cf. Hos 5:13). In the Persian period, Darius II uses the phrase "the great king, king of kings, king of Persia, king of lands" in the Behustin inscriptions (Wildberger, 1398). The reading of the title would have made hearers in Persian times aware that the imperial system begun by the Assyrians had continued under Babylon and the Persians.

What is this confidence (הבטחון) *in which you have put your trust* (בטחת)? The field commander asks for an explanation of Hezekiah's stubborn refusal to surrender in face of superior force. He is determined to shake that confidence to achieve his surrender. The root בטח recurs in vv 5, 6, 7, 9. It is the heart of the speech. Wildberger (1398–99) notes that the word derives from cultic language and that two-fifths of all its uses occur in the Psalms. However, the Vision has already used it in 12:2, 14:30; 26:4; 30:15; and 32:9, 10, 11. It conveys the sense of "trust" and the idea of "security" (BDB, 105). The Vision has used the verb in the sense of a false security (30:12; 31:1). Wildberger (1399) notes a remarkable coincidence: the field commander and earlier text of the Vision share a common goal in breaking down this false hope that Jerusalem is invulnerable. He insists that their real aims, however, are totally different. The Vision wants to make room for a genuine faith in Yahweh, while the field commander wants them to transfer it to the Assyrian emperor. But in the perspective of the Vision the two goals have more in common than Wildberger thinks. Yahweh has brought the Assyrian (7:17; 10:5). The coming of imperial suzerainty is the will of God. Resistance to it is not according to that will. The field commander's speech supports the Vision's position and may, in the version of 2 Kgs 18, have been the inspiration for the Vision's basic thesis (see the *Introduction* in *Isaiah 1–33*). This is the irony inherent in having the text of 2 Kgs 18 read at this point in the Vision.

5 The speech presumes a reply that objectively claims military *strategy* and *strength* to be the basis of Hezekiah's policy. *Strategy* (עצה) has been a key word in the Vision. It is a required attribute for a good king (9:5 [6]; 11:2). In those passages, as here, it is paired with גבורה "strength." This is the attribute of skill and strength for war. The Vision has insisted that *strategy* must come from Yahweh alone. Yahweh's strategy since the time of Uzziah has been to turn over military supremacy to the Assyrian Empire.

The Assyrian commander derides the response as nothing but *words of lips.* The modifier is necessary because the Heb דבר usually implies more substance than that. It can even be used for "facts" or deeds." The issue is plainly put. He challenges a *trust* that supports *rebellion.* In this the Vision and the Assyrian agree.

6 The field commander suspects Egyptian encouragement with promises of support. He was probably correct. His scorn for Egypt's record of reliability is scarcely less than that expressed by Yahweh's words in 30:2–5,7; 31:1–3.

7 The Assyrian derides any protestation of trust in Yahweh by bringing up a sore point. Hezekiah is reported in 2 Kgs 18:5 to have *trusted* (בטח) in Yahweh with unparalleled loyalty which was rewarded with complete success in his rebellion against the king of Assyria. That stands in sharp contrast to this description. 2 Chr 29–30 reports a massive cultic reform in Jerusalem under Hezekiah which resulted in removal of many altars outside the Jerusalem Temple (30:14). After a massive celebration of Passover (chap. 30), zealous participants moved through the towns of Judah destroying the high places, altars, sacred stones, and asherah (31:1). The text does not say to whom these sacred places were dedicated. Presumably, at least some may have been dedicated to Yahweh, as the field commander's words suggest. His propagandistic appeal here is to those from the towns of Judah who were inside Jerusalem but who may not have been absolutely loyal to the king.

Again the speech parallels interests of the Vision which have tried to separate commitment to Zion as a cult center from trust in it as a political power. The speech tries to separate loyalty to Yahweh from loyalty to Hezekiah. This, too, the Vision has done, separating loyalty to Zion and to Yahweh from loyalty to a rebelling monarch or leader.

8 The commander urges negotiations, pointing to Judah's weakness. Even if it had had arms (horses), it does not have the personnel to use them.

9–10 He sums up his appeal with a further disparaging reference to Egypt's help and the claim that Yahweh himself had sent him (cf. 10:5).

11 This interlude provides interesting information about languages current at this time. Assyria had adopted Aramaic as its official imperial language, a practice continued by the Babylonians and the Persians. Yet the commander had apparently used Judean, a dialect of Hebrew. The two languages are distinct but related. After the Exile, Jews adopted Aramaic square letters to write their language, a practice that continues today in the printed editions of Hebrew texts. Hezekiah's emissaries preferred to keep the negotiations secret from the people crowding the walls above them.

12 The commander ignores their request and astutely uses the occasion to his advantage in trying to undermine the morale of the people and their confidence in Hezekiah's leadership.

13–17 The theme of the second speech (vv 13–20) turns on נצל "to deliver." The word is used eight times in vv 14–21. While the first speech spoke about Jerusalem's "trust," this one questions whether Yahweh or anyone can save Jerusalem from the Assyrians. Its purpose is to separate the people from their leaders. *Come out to me* means for them to capitulate, to surrender. The Assyrian message offers peace on Assyrian terms. These are spelled out. They include immediate return to their homes and villages with a later determination of where and when they will be sent away to other places. The Assyrian policy of exiling conquered peoples lies behind the sugar-coated offer. But immediate relief from hunger, thirst, and overcrowding in the city certainly has its appeal.

18–20 The "soft sell" of vv 14–17 is followed by the "hard sell" of vv

18–20. The commander attacks their dependence upon Yahweh claiming that no god can deter the Assyrians. He recalls earlier victories including that over Samaria in 721 B.C.

21–22 The emissaries obey the king's command not to respond. They had fulfilled their mission to hear the commander's terms. The *torn clothes* of grief indicate their estimate of their helpless situation.

Explanation

In 2 Kgs 18–20 this narrative forms the epitaph to Hezekiah's reign as it recites events from the last significant part of it, *ca.* 701 B.C. In the Vision (chaps. 36–39), it is the epitaph marking the end of the kingdom of Judah which came in 587 B.C. under the seige of the city by Nebuchadnezzar's Babylonian armies. On that occasion there had been no deliverance for Zedekiah's forces.

The narrative begins at a point in which the Assyrian army had already destroyed all Judean resistance outside Jerusalem. Sennacherib reported that he had "shut up Hezekiah like a bird in a cage" (*ANET,* 288). The blockade had already been in force for some time and Hezekiah's vaunted water system was being severely tested by the overcrowding because of refugees from towns and villages.

The field commander's first speech (vv 4–10) gets directly to the point. It questions the rationale of rebellion. 2 Kgs 18:7b had listed Hezekiah's rebellion against Assyria as his greatest achievement, his unwillingness to serve the Assyrian Emperor as his greatest merit. 2 Chronicles would later portray Hezekiah's greatest achievement to have been his renovation of the Temple and its worship. But it also would credit to him the rebellion and the subsequent survival of Jerusalem with winning acclaim and gifts from "all the nations" (2 Chr 32:23). It also recounts the great preparations made by Hezekiah (presumably between 705 B.C. when Sargon died and 701 B.C. when Sennacherib finally led a campaign into Palestine) in repairing his aqueducts and walls, in rearming, and in preparing the morale of his nation for war (2 Chr 32:5–8).

The field commander's speech challenges this assessment of Hezekiah's strategy and military potential. It astutely demonstrates the weaknesses in Hezekiah's position. First, it points to the demonstrated unreliability of Egypt as an ally (36:6). The Vision had done the same in chaps. 30–31. Second, it notes the inconsistency between a claim that Yahweh will help and Hezekiah's attacks on apostasy (36:7). Judah was in no spiritual shape to claim Yahweh's protection. The Vision has repeatedly shown her sin and unbelief from chap. 1 on. The deuteronomic editor of 2 Kings showed that the apostasy that led to Samaria's fall had also infested Judah and Jerusalem. Third, it supports the invitation to negotiate a peace-treaty by reference to his own position of strength (36:8–9) and by the claim that Yahweh himself had dispatched him on this campaign against Judah (36:10). In this too, the field commander's speech has echoes in the message of Isaiah in the Vision (cf. 5:26 against Israel, 7:17–25 against Judah, and 8:6–8 against Israel and Judah). Indeed, the very emphasis on strategy and rationale mirror the Vision's repeated references to Yahweh's strategy (cf. 8:10, 14:26–27, etc.). This speech is an excellent illustration for the writer of the Vision of the way the Assyrian Empire could play a positive role in God's strategy. It supplies a solid rationale against Hezekiah's policy of rebellion.

The field commander's second speech (36:13–21) changes the tone. It is much more threatening, referring to the privations of a crowded city under siege (36:12) and attempting to speak directly to these refugees over Hezekiah's head. The propagandistic intent is evident. The theme turns from the "trust" of the first speech to the possibility of "deliverance." In trying to break down the people's confidence in Hezekiah and in Yahweh, the commander ridicules the ability of Hezekiah (36:14) and of Yahweh (36:18–20). Instead he suggests that the king of Assyria is the true "deliverer," the only one who can provide peace and prosperity for the city and its refugees (36:16–17).

His argument is cogent. The emperor has the power to provide many elements needed for peace and prosperity. Earlier portions of the Vision supported a policy which would accept fealty to Assyria as the propitious, even God-willed, way for Judah. For this reason Isaiah in the Vision consistently opposed Hezekiah's rebellions (see chap. 20).

However, the field commander overplays his hand. When he asserts that no god can deliver a people from him, not even Yahweh (36:18–20), he has blasphemed the very God that he had claimed to obey (36:10). From this point on, no case could be made for Yahweh's support of the Assyrian in Judah. The Vision had already noted this characteristic of the Assyrians and the way that Yahweh will deal with them (cf. 10:5–19; 14:24–27; 30:31–33; 31:8–9). Yahweh will not tolerate arrogant insubordination and blasphemy from any servant. That had been the case in 7:1–9 when Isaiah first appeared to Ahaz. It was true in 701 B.C. when Isaiah was called to speak to Hezekiah. Undoubtedly it was understood to hold true for the group that is listening to the narrative in its setting of Babylonian oppression. The audience of the Vision who heard it presented as a play must have had questions concerning their own Persian rulers, questions which will be dealt with in the next act.

Scene 3: A Reading (continued): From Hearsay to Knowledge (37:1–20)

Bibliography

See *Bibliography* for chap. 36.

Avaux, M. "La Mention de Tarhaqa en 2 R 19:9; Js 37:9." *AIPHOS* 20 (1973) 31–43. **Fullerton, K.** "Isaiah's Attitude in the Sennacherib Campaign." *AJSL* 42 (1925–26) 1–25. **Kitchen, K. A.** "Late Egyptian Chronology and the Hebrew Monarch (on 2 Kgs 19:9 and Isa 37:9)." *JANESCU* 5 (1973) 225–33. **Talmon, S.** "A Case of Faulty Harmonization (on 37:18)." *VT* 5 (1955) 206–8.

Translation

Reader: 1 *Then it happened, as soon as Hezekiah heard, he tore his*
clothes, dressed himself in sackcloth, and came into the house of
Yahweh. 2 *Then he sent Eliakim administrator of the palace,*
Shebna[a] *the scribe, and the elders of the priests—all wearing*
sackcloth—to Isaiah, [b]*son of Amoz the prophet.*[b] 3 *They said to*
him,[a] *"Thus says Hezekiah: This is a day of distress, rebuke,*
disgrace.[b] *For children have come to the point of birth, but there*
is no strength to give birth. 4 *Perhaps Yahweh, your (sg) God,*
will hear[c] *the words*[a] *of the field commander whom the king of*
Assyria, his master, sent to scorn the Living God, and will rebuke[c]
the words, which Yahweh your (sg) God has heard, if you will
lift[c] *a prayer in behalf of the remnant that is found in this city.*[b]*"*
5 *When King Hezekiah's*[a] *servants came to Isaiah,*[b] 6 *Isaiah*
said to them:[a] *"Thus you shall say to your master, 'Do not be*
afraid of the words which you have heard with which the boys
of the king of Assyria ridiculed me.

7 *See me setting a spirit against*[a] *him.* 4+2
He will hear a rumor (of it)
and return to[b] *his own country.* 2+3
I will fell him by a sword in his own country.' "

8 *When the field commander went back, he found the king of*
Assyria fighting against Libnah. For he had heard that he had
left Lachish.
9 *When he heard (a report) about*[a] *Tirhakah, king of Ethiopia,*
"He has broken camp to attack you," he sent messengers again[b]
to Hezekiah: 10[a] *"Thus you shall say to Hezekiah, king of Judah,*[a]
Do not let your God deceive you, (the God) in whom you are
trusting, thinking, 'Jerusalem will not be given into the hands
of the king of Assyria.' 11 *Look! You have heard what*[a] *the kings*
of Assyria have done to destroy[b] *all the countries. (Do you think)*
you will be delivered? 12 *Did the gods of the (other) nations which*
my forefathers destroyed[a] *deliver them? Gozan, Haran, Rezeph,*[b]
the Edenites who[c] *were in Tel Assar?*[d] 13 *Where*[a] *is the king of*
Hamath (now)? The king of Arpad, or [b]*the king of the city*[b] *of*
Sepharvaim, [c]*of Hena or Ivvah?"*[c]
14 *When Hezekiah took the scrolls*[a] *from the messengers and*
read it, he went up to the House of Yahweh. Hezekiah spread it
out before Yahweh, 15 [a]*and Hezekiah prayed to*[b] *Yahweh:*[ac]

16 *"Yahweh of Hosts,*[a] 2+2+2
God of Israel,
[b]*sitting (above) the cherubim,*[b]
you are God, you alone, 3+3
to all the kingdoms of the land.
You have made the heavens and the earth. 4
17 *Extend your ear, O Yahweh, and listen!* 4+4
Open your eyes, O Yahweh, and see!

Hear all[a] the words of Sennacherib 4+2+3
which he has sent[b]
to blaspheme the Living God!
18 *Truly, Yahweh,* 2
the kings of Assyria have destroyed 3+2+3
all[a] [b]the nations and their land[b]
19 *and have put[a] their gods in the fire.*
For they were not gods 4+4+2
but only wood shaped by human hands
or stone which they worshiped.
20 *Now,[a] Yahweh our God,* 3+2
deliver us[b] from his hand,[c]
and all the kingdoms of the land shall know 3+3
that you are Yahweh,[d] you alone."

Notes

2.a. MT has את, an accus particle not found in 2 Kgs 19:2.
2.b-b. 2 Kgs 19:2 reverses the words and reads "the prophet, son of Amoz."
3.a. The change in conj of *BHS* is unnecessary.
3.b. LXX adds *καὶ ὀργῆς* "and wrath."
4.a. 2 Kgs 19:4 puts כל "all" before "the words."
4.b. MT הנמצאה "found here" (sg.); DSS[Isa] expands to read הנמצאים בעיר הזואת "those found in this city." MT reads "the remnant" as a technical collective term. DSS[Isa] reads it specifically of the people in the city at that time. The translation above follows DSS[Isa].
4.c. The sequence of tenses following the tentative אולי "perhaps" is intrusive. In Hebrew the three verbs are an impf followed by two pfs with *waw,* lit., "perhaps God will hear . . . and rebuke . . . and you will pray." The loose paratactic construction conveys, however, a relation of God's actions to Isaiah's prayer that requires a different treatment in English.
5.a. MT חזקיהו; DSS[Isa] has a shorter spelling: יחזקיה "Hezekiah."
5.b. MT ישעיהו; DSS[Isa] has a shorter spelling: ישעיה "Isaiah" (also v 6).
6.b. MT אליהם; 2 Kgs 19:6 has a shorter form: להם "to them."
7.a. Ehrlich (*Randglossen* 4:133) insisted that בו must be translated "against him" (cf. Lev 26:17 and Ezek 14:8) and refers to Tirhakah's campaign (cf. v 9). Ehrlich wrote that this would need to read בלבו "in his heart" to be translated "in him."
7.b. 2 Kgs 19:7 reads לארצו for אל־ארצו. Both mean "to his country."
9.a. 2 Kgs 19:9 אל "to" for MT על "about." Wildberger (1384) cites Gen 41:15 for a parallel construction with על.
9.b. MT וישמע "when he heard." 2 Kgs 19:9 וישב "and he returned." DSS[Isa] has both "he heard and he returned" supported by LXX *καὶ ἀκούσας ἀπέστρεψε* "when he had heard he turned back" (cf. Talmon, "Textual Transmission in Light of Qumran," *Textus* 4 [1960] 107). Wildberger (1416) joins other interpreters (cf. especially J. Ziegler, "Die Vorlage der Isaias-Septuaginta (LXX)," *JBL* 78 [1959] 56) in preferring the text of 2 Kings and understands וישב וישלח to mean "he sent again."
10.a-a. Missing in LXX except for LXX[B] of 2 Kgs 19:10. But MT is to be kept.
11.a. MT אשר "what." 2 Kgs 19:11 and DSS[Isa] add the particle את before it.
11.b. החרימם "put to the ban" is very similar in form and position to החריבו "destroy" in v 18. Feldmann and Duhm felt both should agree but disagreed on which to use. Wildberger correctly notes, with Feldmann, that the Assyrians did not use the ban and suggests emending to להחריבם to fit 18.
12.a. MT השחיתו hiph "destoyed." 2 Kgs 19:12 שחתו qal "destroyed."
12.b. LXX Ραφες "Raphes."
12.c. LXX[L] of 2 Kgs 19:12 translates ואשר "and what," a reading adopted by Kissane, Kaiser, and Wildberger (1416).

12.d. MT בתלשר; 2 Kgs 19:12 בתלאשר. KB assumes that this renders the Akk *til ašūri.* LXX ἐν χώρᾳ Θελσαδ "in the region Thelsad." Nothing more specific can be ascertained. The translation follows 2 Kgs 19:12.

13.a. MT אית "where." 2 Kgs 19:13 איו "where is he?"

13.b-b. Missing in some LXX MSS of 2 Kgs 19:13. Interpreters have found it strange that "city" should interrupt the list of cities. *BHS* follows Procksch in emending to לַעַשׁ "Laash." A city by this name is found in the Zakir inscription, line 1 (Wildberger 1417; cf. *ANET,* 501).

13.c-c. No cities by these names are known. Tg and Syr treat them as verbs. Ehrlich (*Randglossen* 4:134) has done the same. The identity of these places is lost in antiquity, but Wildberger (1417) is right in insisting that that is no excuse for eliminating them.

14.a. LXX τὸ βιβλίον "the book" (sg); Tg also sg. The pl of MT has raised questions. Wildberger (1417) suggests eliminating it as dittogr, i.e., ים for the following מיד, but this reverses the letters. It is better to keep MT.

15.a-a. Missing in LXX^B of 2 Kgs 19:15.

15.b. MT אל "to." 2 Kgs 19:15 לפני "before."

15.c. MT לאמר "saying" (here rendered by quotation marks.) 2 Kgs 19:15 ויאמר "and he said."

16.a. צבאות "hosts" lacking in 2 Kgs 19:15.

16.b-b. Tg דשכינתיה שריא עיל מן כרוביא "who causes his home to abide higher than the Cherubim."

17.a. כל "all" is missing in 2 Kgs 19:16.

17.b. MT שלח "he sent." So also LXX Syr Vg in 2 Kgs 19:16 but MT there reads שלחו "send him," a grammatically correct insertion of the relative pronoun.

18.a. כל "all" is lacking in 2 Kgs 19:17.

18.b-b. MT repeats ארץ "all the lands and their land." 2 Kgs 19:17 reads הגוים "the nations" for the first. DSS^{Isa} leaves out the second, as does LXX^B of 2 Kgs 19:17. Wildberger (1417) follows DSS^{Isa}. C. J. Bredenkamp (*Der prophet Jesaia,* Erlangen: Deichert, 1887) understands "their" to refer to the Assyrian's land, but this is not necessary. Talmon (*VT* 5 [1955] 206–8) is with the majority, including *BHS,* in following 2 Kgs 19:17. This translation does the same.

19.a. MT points the verb as an inf abs "and putting," a very strange construction. 2 Kgs 19:18 points it as a pf 3d pl "and they have put," which is preferred.

20.a. MT עתה "now." LXX σύ has read אתה "thou."

20.b. 2 Kgs 19:19 adds נא "I pray."

20.c. MT omits the usual *daghesh* in the *yodh.* With some MSS and 2 Kgs 19:19 it is to be inserted.

20.d. DSS^{Isa} and 2 Kgs 19:19 add אלהים "God" making the sentence read "that you, Yahweh, are God." The addition is logical, yet MT is to be kept as the more difficult text. It makes sense as it is.

Form/Structure/Setting

This is a continuation of chap. 36 and is a response to the previous narrative and speeches. The narrative is structured around four speeches. The motif of שמע "hearing" dominates them all.

Narrative	שמע	*Speech*	שמע
1. vv1–2	1	1. Hezekiah for Isaiah, vv 3–4	2
2. vv 5–6	1	2. Isaiah oracle from Yahweh, v 7	1
3. vv 8–9	2	3. Sennacherib's speech, vv 10–13	1
4. vv 14–15	0	4. Hezekiah's prayer, vv 16–20	2

The prayer ends on ידע "knowing" (v 20) rather than "hearing."

Like the motifs of the field commander's speech in 36:4–10 (see *Comment* above), the motifs of this section speak to the needs of the readers/hearers of the Vision. Sennacherib says: "Do not let your God deceive you . . . thinking 'Jerusalem will not be given over' " (v 10). That very issue was a sore point. The Assyrian's words were wrong in 701 B.C. But they had special pungency after 586 B.C. Had God deceived them? Was he deceiving them? (Cf. 29:21b and other references.) Many in post-exilic Judaism were not sure how they should answer that. Job and the Vision answer differently from 2 Kings.

Hezekiah's prayer (vv 16–20) is more in line with the Vision's position in putting it all in the perspective of Yahweh's sovereignty. The Assyrians had proved nothing about the superiority of their gods. True knowledge comes from recognition of what Yahweh has actually done. There is here a tone of realism which pairs faith with history, with which the Vision will agree.

The Isaiah prophecy (v 7) gives Yahweh's response to the Assyrian's direct challenge to his power and reliability. He will start moving, creating a rumor that will send the king home and eventually lead to his death. Yahweh can play the game of power words, too.

Comment

1 *Sackcloth,* the symbol of grief, accurately portrays Hezekiah's sense of futility and helplessness in this situation.

2 Hezekiah sends a delegation to Isaiah (cf. 1 Kgs 22:5, 2 Kgs 22:12 for parallels).

3 Hezekiah's message for Isaiah evaluates the situation. He uses three terms to describe it. יום צרה "a day of distress" (NIV "day of trouble") is well known from the psalms of lament which pray for Yahweh's help (cf. Pss 20:2 [1]; 50:15; 77:3 [2]; 86:7). The term occurs in the Prophets (Jer 16:19; Obad 12, 14; Nah 1:7) and with a slight variation in 33:2. תוכחה "rebuke" is also found in Hos 5:9 (NIV, "Day of reckoning") and Ps 149:7. The verb has a variety of meanings in the hiphil including "judging, deciding, convincing, rebuking." In 2:4 it spoke of Yahweh's "deciding for" the nations; in 11:3 the king will "decide by what he hears"; in 11:4 he will "decide with fairness for the poor of the land." As "rebuke," it is often followed by the preposition ב "by" as in v 4 (and also 29:21). The term here implies that this is a day that calls for Yahweh's intervention. נאצה is translated "disgrace" (BDB, 611). The verb has the meaning "condemn, spurn," and the noun moves toward "contempt" or "blasphemy." The three terms describe three aspects of the day. It is a time of trouble that cries out for the help of God. It is a day for decision, for rebuke by God. For it has been a day of blasphemy against God.

The figure of the time of childbirth is a familiar one (cf. esp. 26:16–18). Hezekiah apparently speaks of his rebellion and the attempt to make his kingdom independent. Now is the time to move to achieve it. But there is no strength to bring it to pass. Hezekiah's frustration was known to Ahaz (chap. 7), to the generation of Manasseh, and surely to Zedekiah. The same figure of childbirth but with the opposite result appears in 66:7–9.

4 Hezekiah's request to Isaiah is tentative. It speaks only of the possibility that Yahweh will *hear* and *rebuke, if* Isaiah *lifts a prayer*. The prayer should be for the refugee remnant that survives in the city. This is the same group that the Assyrian commander had addressed.

6 Isaiah's response is more forceful. It is not clear what Hezekiah expected from Isaiah. The reader of the account in 2 Kgs 19 would be meeting Isaiah for the first time and would have no preconceptions about him. But the reader/hearer of the Vision would have the full picture of the prophet who counseled Ahaz (chap. 7) to be still and do nothing before military pressure and who demonstrated forcefully against Hezekiah's earlier rebellion (chap. 20). But now Isaiah's message is strong: *Do not be afraid!* Isaiah is certain that Yahweh has heard, while Hezekiah had tentatively hoped that he had heard. *The boys* is deliberately derogatory of the Assyrian commanders. J. Gray (*I & II Kings: A Commentary*, OTL [Philadelphia: Westminster, 1963] 615) translates "flunkeys." H-B. Stähli (*Knabe–Jüngling–Knecht* [Frankfurt am Main/Las Vegas: Lang, 1978] 175) notes that in 7:4–9 Isaiah called Ahaz's enemies "smoking fire-brands."

7 הנני נותן בו רוח "see me setting a spirit against him" is the key to the word from God. Like 65:17 God calls attention to something which he is already doing. בו means "in him" or "against him." Ehrlich argued (see *n.* 7.a above) that this would have to read "in his heart" to be understood as "put a spirit in him." The better understanding is "against him." In effect, it means God will motivate someone to fight against Sennacherib. Whether the reference is to the Egyptian pharaoh in v 9, which is apparently intended to show the fulfillment of this word, or to some other opposition (cf. Wildberger 1390) is unclear. ושמע שמועה "hear a rumor" is literally "hear a hearing." Sennacherib is also susceptible to the power of rumor and report. This one sends him home and finally to his death.

8 In the meantime, Lachish has apparently fallen. Sennacherib had moved to eliminate another city, *Libnah,* which could be an obstacle in approaching Jerusalem. The location of this city remains unclear (cf. Wildberger, 1411–12, and the books on geography).

9 For the historical problems related to the mention of *Tirhakah* at this time, see the discussion on 2 Kgs 19:9 by T. R. Hobbs (*2 Kings,* WBC 13 [Waco, TX: Word Books, 1985]). The Egyptian's advance is, however, given here as the reason for Sennacherib's rushed second approach to Hezekiah, and apparently as the fulfillment of the prophecy in v 7. This report made it urgent for Sennacherib to finish this business with Jerusalem so that he could devote his energies to meeting this new threat.

10 These are ordinary messengers, in contrast to the high-level officers of the first delegation (chap. 36). These are the words of a letter (see v 14). They attack the trustworthiness of Yahweh himself and thus the hope of safety for the city. Sennacherib apparently refers to a religious foundation for Hezekiah's rebellion urged on him by prophets and priests (cf. 36:4, 7). But the deeper implications question Yahweh's promises to preserve the Davidic dynasty (2 Sam 7:16) and to uphold Zion (in the Psalms and Prophets).

The exilic listeners would question whether the events of history had indeed sustained the Assyrian's claims.

11–13 Assyrian kings have dealt with many cities and their gods. Why should Jerusalem be different? Some of the city names are known. Some are not. They are intended to list major Assyrian victories.

14–15 Hezekiah's response this time was to take the message to the temple, *spread it out before Yahweh* and pray. This time he himself prays.

16 The address makes six statements about God. *Yahweh of Hosts* is a fixed title usually associated with the ark, which was probably still in Jerusalem. The third statement *sitting* (*above*) *the cherubim* is often associated with the first in the ark traditions (1 Sam 4:4; 2 Sam 6:2; 1 Chr 13:6) and in the Pss (80:2 [1]; 99:1; 18:11 [10] = 2 Sam 22:11). *The cherubim* in the OT were not God's messengers or angels. The cherubim were pictured as a protective guard for God or the ark (Exod 25:18–22; 1 Kgs 6:23–28; 8:6; Ezek 1:4–14; 10:1–2).

God of Israel was also a major title applied to Yahweh in Jerusalem. It is of interest that Zion is not mentioned in the prayer. Attention is focused on the larger political entity rather than on the Temple or the city itself. The God of Israel dwells in Zion. It is important to maintain that priority.

You are God, you alone is not a theme found for the first time in chaps. 40–48. It had appeared in the first commandment and in 2 Kgs 19:15, 19. It is basic to Israel's distinct religious consciousness. *To all the kingdoms of the land* asserts Yahweh total authority over all the governments involved, including Assyria. *You have made the heavens and the earth:* the monotheism of Israel's worship encompassed its doctrine of creation (Pss 74:12–17; 102:26 [25]; 89:9), which in turn was the basis of its doctrine of Yahweh's sovereignty over history. These three confessions lay the foundations for Hezekiah's appeal for divine intervention.

17 The prayer invites God's attention to the messengers and the blasphemy. Here he is called אלהים חי "the Living God." In some contexts this title may stand in contrast to fertility gods who die to rise up again. But here the contrast is with gods whose impotence was demonstrated in their inability to protect their cities.

18–19 Hezekiah acknowledges the truth of the Assyrian claim. They had destroyed cities and burned idols aplenty. But he notes the differences. These were idols, not really gods in any independent sense at all. Created by human hands, they could be destroyed by human hands.

20 The heart of the plea, *deliver us,* lays bare Hezekiah's personal concern. It was not finally the protection of Yahweh's honor that motivated his plea, but the threat to his people and his kingdom. The objective names for God of v 16 are gone. *Yahweh, our God,* makes the personal relation a claim and a confession.

The kingdoms shall know. The passage has stressed the term "to hear." At this point, where it could well have used it again, it changes to ידע "shall know." Hezekiah prays that the deliverance of the city shall become a means of faith for all who come to know of it. They may come to *know that you are Yahweh,* not the impotent idols, but *you alone.*

Explanation

The Assyrian's speeches (chap. 36) have had their effect. He had tried to break down the people's trust in Hezekiah, in the city, and ultimately in Yahweh. He then questioned the possibility for Hezekiah, the city, or Yahweh to save the people from Assyrian power. His propaganda was skilled and effective. He knew the weakness of words—but also the power of words (36:5).

Chap. 37:1–20 portrays their effects and the response they evoked. The word "hear" appears eight times. Hezekiah heard and was overcome by grief and dismay. His reputation as an administrator and military leader was obviously undeserved. It is his piety that shows through here as elsewhere. He turns to the prophet with the cry: "If only Yahweh has heard. Please pray that Yahweh hears."

Isaiah has no doubt about Yahweh's acoustical sense or attention. He admonishes Hezekiah to avoid fear occasioned by the propaganda: "Do not be afraid of words." Consider their source, Sennacherib's boys. His oracle shows Yahweh also knowing how to use motivation and rumor. Yahweh motivates ("sets a spirit against") the Egyptians to move out and sees to it that the Assyrians hear of it. The Assyrian who uses propaganda well is also highly susceptible to it. He will ultimately be killed because of it.

The Assyrian king hears a rumor that the Egyptians are marching. He becomes desperate. Although his propaganda had failed to bring Jerusalem to its knees, he tries one more massive verbal assault. He stresses the illustrious history of his fathers' successes, a kind of "my father can beat your father" approach.

Hezekiah's prayer makes possible the move from rumor to reality. His recognition of the greatness of God (v 16) helps him regain perspective. His call to God to hear begins the process of helping him assess the situation as God would assess it (v 17). He recognizes a partial truth in the Assyrian's words (v 18), but he also recognizes the falsehood of his claims (v 19). Yahweh is not like the idols of the nations and therefore his deliverance is not to be disparaged by their impotence (v 20). When he has acted, then all the kingdoms may know that he alone is God.

This is the immediate and powerful message of this remarkable narrative, a story so great and so well told that it has been preserved by editors both in 2 Kings and in the Vision of Isaiah. But the readers of both these works must look at the story with a double application. They know that Yahweh answered Hezekiah's prayer and that Jerusalem was saved in 701 B.C. But they also know, as 2 Kgs 25 and Isa 32 show, that in a similar situation under Zedekiah in 587 B.C. Jerusalem was not spared nor were its people saved. And the readers of the Vision knew that the situation for Jerusalem had hardly improved over the century and more that had passed since then.

37:1–20 has dealt with how one is to cope with an assault by words used as weapons of power. Words (דברים) and ideas (עצות) are human and may be as empty and meaningless as fallible humans can make them. But they may come from God. He knows how to use them to fight his battles and to accomplish his purposes. The trick lies in the hearing of them so as to distinguish which is which. Israel had proved itself remarkably inept in this. It was still "deaf" and "blind" to God's ways—all too susceptible to human fallacies.

Scene 4: A Reading (continued): Isaiah's Response from Yahweh (37:21–38)

Bibliography

Becker, J. P. "Wurzel und Wurzelspross" (on 37:31). *BZ* 20 (1976) 22–44. **Budde, K.** "The Poem in 2 Kings xix 21–28 (Isaiah xxxvii 22–29)." *JTS* 35 (1934) 307–13. **Cornaly, W. A.** "2 Kings xix (Js. xxxvii. 36) and Herodotus II.141." *ExpTim* 25 (1913/14) 379–80. **Iwry, S.** "והנמצא—a Striking Variant Reading in 1QIs[a]" (on 37:31). *Textus* 5 (1966) 34–43. **Tawil, H.** "2 Kings 19:24: יארי מצור." *JNES* 41 (1982) 195–206.

Translation

Reader: 21 *Then Isaiah son of Amoz sent to Hezekiah, "Thus says Yahweh, God of Israel, to whom*[a] *you have prayed concerning*[b] *Sennacherib,*[c] *king of Assyria:"*[a] 22[a] *(This is the word which Yahweh spoke against him.)*[a]

Isaiah: (to Sennacherib)

She despises you! — 2+2+3
She mocks you!
The virgin daughter Zion.
She tosses her head behind you, — 3+2
the daughter Jerusalem.
23 *Whom have you blasphemed and insulted?* — 3+3
Against whom have you raised a voice[a]
That you lifted your eyes on high — 3+3
toward[b] *the Holy One of Israel?*
24 *Through your servants*[a] — 2+2
you blasphemed my Lord.[b]
When you said, — 1+2
"By the number[c] *of my chariots*
I myself ascended — 2+2+2
the heights of mounts,
the peaks of Lebanon.
I will cut down the tops of cedars — 3+2
some of the choicest[d] *of its heads.*

I will come to the height[e] *of its end,* 3+2
the forest of its Carmel.
25 *I myself have dug*[a] *(wells)* 2+2
and drunk water.[b]
I dry up with the soles of my feet 3+3
all streams (that come) from rocks.[c]"

Yahweh: (to Sennacherib)
26 *Had you not heard* 2+3
from far off I did it?
From days of old,[a] *I planned it* 3+2
and now I have brought it to pass
that you exist[b] *(here)* 1+3+2
to devastate[c] *to piles*[d] *of ruins*[e]
cities by siege.[f]
27 *The inhabitants, short-handed,* 2+2
are dismayed and shamed.[a]
They are a field plant 3+2
or a tender sprout,
sprouting on rooftops 3+2
scorched[b] *before east winds.*[c]
28 *Your rising*[a] *and your sitting down,* 1+3+3
your going out and coming in I know well,
[b]*as well as your raging against me.*[b]
29 [a]*Because your raging against me*[a] 3+3
and your arrogance[b] *has reached my ears,*
I shall put my ring in your nose 3+2
and my bit in your lip,[c]
and I shall turn (you) back into the way 2+2
in which you have come.

Isaiah: (to Hezekiah)
30 *This will be your sign:*
Eating this year whatever grows by itself 3+3
and in the second year what comes from that.[a]
But in the third year, 2+2
[b]*sowing and reaping,*
planting vineyards 2+2
and eating[b] *their fruit.*
31 *The survivors that remain*[a] *of the house of Judah*
will again 5
take root below 2+3
and make fruit above.
32 *For, from Jerusalem*[a] *a remnant will go out* 4+3
and a surviving group from Mount Zion.[a]
The zeal of Yahweh of Hosts[b] *will do this.* 5

33 *Therefore, thus says Yahweh concerning the king of Assyria:*
Yahweh: *He will not come to this city.* 4+3
He will not shoot an arrow here.

He will not confront it (with) a shield. 3+4
He will not raise a siege-ramp against it.[a]
34 *By the way in which he came*[a] *he will return.* 4+4
But to this city he will not come.
Isaiah: *Expression of Yahweh* 2

Yahweh: 35 *I shall put a cover over*[a] *this city to deliver it.* 4+4
For my sake and for the sake of David, my servant.

Reader: 36 [a]*Then the messenger of Yahweh went out and struck down*[b] *a hundred and eighty-five thousand in the Assyrian camp. When they were to get up in the morning, all of them (were) dead bodies.* 37 *So he broke camp and left.*[a] *Sennacherib, king of Assyria, returned and lived in Nineveh.* 38 *Then it happened (while) he was worshiping in the temple of Nisroch his god, his sons Adrammelech and Sharezer cut him down with swords. They escaped to the land of Ararat. Then Esarhaddon, his son, reigned after him.*

Notes

21.a,a. MT reads אלי . . . אשר "which . . . to me," which changes from 3d to 1st person. 2 Kgs 19:20 adds שמעתי "I have heard," followed here by 2 MSS of LXX and Syr. To be consistent, אלי should be read אליו "to him," or better yet, omitted and אשר translated "to whom" (cf. Ehrlich, *Randglossen* 4:134 and Wildberger, 1417).

21.b. אל, lit., "toward." Procksch, Auvray, and Wildberger (1417) suggest emending to על "against." Translating אל as "concerning" takes care of the problem without changing the text.

21.c. MT סנחריב and 2 Kgs 19:20 סנחרב are both "Sennacherib." The difference is only one of variant transliterations of the foreign name.

22.a-a. The introduction appears redundant and is therefore put in parentheses (see Wildberger, 1417, 1420).

23.a. הרימותה "raised" is spelled in 2 Kgs 19:22 הרימות.

23.b. אל "toward." 2 Kgs 19:22 על "against."

24.a. עבדיך "your servants." 2 Kgs 19:23 מלאכיך "your messengers."

24.b. אדני "my Lord." Many MSS of 2 Kgs 19:23 read יהוה "Yahweh."

24.c. K of 2 Kgs 19:23 ברכב "by the drivers of."

24.d. MT מבחר "choicest of;" 2 Kgs 19:23 writes the *plene* form: מבחור.

24.e. מרום "the height." 2 Kgs 19:23 מלון "lodging." LXX *κὰι εἰσῆλθον εἰς ὕψος μέρους τοῦ δρυμοῦ* "and I came to the highest part of the forest." Σ reads *εις υψος του ακρου αυτου* "to the height of its extremity." Read with MT and Σ.

25.a. קרתי, translated here as "dug," is a *hap. leg.* without a sure meaning (BDB, 881).

25.b. 2 Kgs 19:24, DSS[Isa] add זרים "strange" or "alien" (BDB 266).

25.c. Wildberger (1415) translates יארי מצור as "arms of Egypt's Nile." Cf. NIV and BDB, 596. P. S. Calderone ("The Rivers of 'Masor'," *Bib* 42 [1961] 424–26) divides the letters יארים צור "the mountain streams." This sense fits the context. One may also read מצור "from a rock" with essentially the same result.

26.a. MT "and." But DSS[Isa] correctly omits the *waw*. LXX *συνέταξα, νῦν δὲ* "I arranged (it), but now" appears to have read the *waw* with עתה "now," as did Syr and Vg. (See Wildberger, 1418.)

26.b. MT וּתְהִי "that you exist." *BHS* would delete following Procksch. 2 Kgs 29:25 וַתְּהִי (cons impf) is followed by *BHK*.

26.c. להשאות "to devastate." 2 Kgs 19:25 להשות "make (to be) like" (Ehrlich, *Randglossen* 4:136). But Wildberger (1418) sees both as two spellings of the inf constr from שאה "to devastate."

26.d. גלים "ruins" or "stones." LXX *έόῶε* "nations" appears to have read it as גוים.

26.e. נצים "piles of ruin" has raised problems for some commentators who say one cannot devastate what is already in ruins (Wildberger, 1418). But if one reads it as an adverbial accus, "to ruins," there is no problem.

26.f. בצרות "by siege" (BDB, 848). Wildberger (823, 1418) translates "fortified."

27.a. ובשו "are shamed." 2 Kgs 19:26 ויבשו has an impf.

27.b. ושדמה (BDB, 995) means "field" and is otherwise only pl (see M. R. Lehmann, "שדמות," *VT* 3 [1953] 361–71). 2 Kgs 19:26 and some MSS read ושדפה "blighted." DSS[Isa] הנשדף is a niph ptcp from שדף "to scorch," a root which only appears in Gen 41:6, 23, 27 (see Kaiser). Wildberger suggests נִשְׁדָּף "scorched" following DSS[Isa] but without the article. Or DSS[Isa] has the right word but has made a prosaic paraphrase. Read ושדפה "and scorched."

27.c. קמה "is grown." DSS[Isa] קדים "east winds" is preferable (cf. Gen 41:6, 23, 27 and Iwry, "The Qumran Isaiah," *BASOR* 147 [1957] 28). See n. 28.a.

28.a. DSS[Isa] inserts to begin the verse קומכה "your rising up." The addition fills out the verse and makes excellent sense. Apparently MT had taken this word back into v 27 when קדים was lost (see n. 27.c) and adapted it to קמה for a modicum of sense.

28.b-b. Missing in LXX. Note also that את stands here as accus particle but is missing earlier in the verse. Many exegetes suggest deletion as a gl, noting the repetition in the following line.

29.a-a. Missing in DSS[Isa] which has dealt with the duplication by omitting the second member. Wildberger (1419) defends MT by noting that the beginning with יען "because" is in good order.

29.b. MT ושאננך "your ease" or "your security" is a pilpel inf of שאן "be at ease, rest secure." LXX *καὶ ἡ πικρία σου* "and your bitterness" is followed by Syr Vg. Tg reads ואתרגושתך "and your rioting." Wildberger follows Budde, Grätz, Cheyne, *BHK*, and *BHS* in suggesting וּשְׁאוֹנְךָ "your arrogance" or "your uproar" (see BDB, 983).

29.c. MT בשפתיך "in your lips" is dual. DSS[Isa] בשפאותיכה "in your lips" is pl (Kutscher, *Isaiah Scroll,* 389; cf. BDB, 973).

30.a. MT שחיס and 2 Kgs 19:29 סחיש are both *hap. leg.* BDB (695, 1006) considers them the same word. (On DSS[Isa] שעים see Kutscher, *Isaiah Scroll,* 507.) The meaning of the word is obscure. Akkad *suḫuššu* means "young date palms."

30.b-b. MT זרעו וקצרו ונטעו are all impvs: "sow, and reap, and plant." DSS[Isa] נטוע is an inf abs, and K reads the next verb as ואכול "and eating," also an inf abs. Q and 2 Kgs 19:29 read ואכלו to make it fit the pl impvs. Wildberger (1419) correctly follows Buhl, Procksch, and *BHS* in reading them all as inf abs זרוע וקצור ונטוע . . . ואכול "sowing and reaping and planting . . . and eating" and blaming the error on a dittogr of *waw.*

31.a. הנשארה "that remain." DSS[Isa] הנמצא "that is found" (see Iwry, *Textus* 5 [1966] 34–43). Missing in LXX.

32.a,a. MT מירושלם "from Jerusalem." DSS[Isa] מציון "from Zion" but reverses that in the second line.

32.b. צבאות "Hosts" is missing in 2 Kgs 19:31 but is found in DSS[Isa]. Cf. 9:6.

33.a. MT עָלֶיהָ; 2 Kgs 19:32 and several MSS vocalize this as עָלֶיהָ. This does not change the meaning.

34.a. בא "he came," a pf. 2 Kgs 19:33 יבא, an impf. The pf is correct.

35.a. על "over." 2 Kgs 19:34 אל "to."

36.a. 2 Kgs 19:35 inserts ויהי בלילה ההוא "and it happened in that night."

36.b. ויכה "and struck down." 2 Kgs 19:35 and DSS[Isa] have the apocopated form ויך.

37.a. Missing in LXX.

Form/Structure/Setting

Four of Isaiah's eight speeches in chaps. 36–39 occur in this passage. They address the Assyrian threat, the survival of Judeans, the sanctity of Jerusalem, and the deliverance of the city.

1. The First Speech: Yahweh to the Assyrians (*vv 22–29*). This speech establishes the genre used throughout the Vision for Yahweh-speeches. Part of it (vv 22–25) is spoken by someone else who stands near the throne, a spokesman who is privy to Yahweh's intention. Then Yahweh speaks in the first person (vv 26–29).

Vv 22 and 29bc provide the outer frame in terms of Zion's defiance and Yahweh's deterrence. Vv 23–24a and 28–29a turn the siege into an Assyrian challenge to Yahweh which must be met in like terms. Vv 24b–25 and 26c–27 tell of Assyrian conquests. V 26a-b is the pivotal center which turns the Assyrian boast into a Yahwist claim of sovereignty. The concentric structure looks like this:

A Jerusalem despises you (v 22)
  B You have blasphemed Yahweh (vv 23–24a)
    C You said: "I myself ascended" (vv 24b–25)
Keystone I planned it; I brought it to pass (v 26a-b)
    C′ That you devastate cities by siege (vv 26c–27)
  B′ I know your raging against me (vv 28–29a)
A′ I shall turn you back (v 29bc)

The ascending ladder A-C is spoken by Yahweh's spokesman. The pivot and the descending ladder C′-A′ is a direct speech by Yahweh himself.

Within the larger context of chaps. 36–37, the speech answers Sennacherib's ultimatum in vv 37:10–13.

The speech contains major themes used in the Vision. This includes the portrayal of pride and arrogance associated with human power that is seen as blasphemy against Yahweh and of its inevitable consequence (vv 23–24a/28–29a). Cf. 2:11–22; 10:12–19; 13:9–13; 14:4–23; 26:13–14; 30:31–33; 31:8–9. The Vision looks beyond Assyria to a general sin of hubris in humankind and especially in Babylon.

The phrase קדוש ישראל "the Holy One of Israel" (v 23) is picked up as a distinctive description of Yahweh throughout the Vision. The claim that Yahweh's plans (עצה), made and prepared for long ago, are now coming to pass (v 26) echoes throughout the Vision (14:26–27 and chaps. 40–48). These other passages as well as this one (v 26) reflect the speech of the Assyrian field commander (36:8). Yahweh, not the emperors, directs the course of history.

The speech does not deny the list of Assyrian conquests. Rather, it adds to the list. But it claims (with 36:10) that Yahweh's plan and preparation made them possible. Yahweh claims that he monitors the Assyrian's every move and mood. This accounts for his decision to send him home (v 29bc). This, too, appears in the Vision as it relates the larger history of the Assyrian period (cf. 10:13–19; 14:25; 30:31–33; 31:8–9).

2. The Second Speech: Isaiah to Hezekiah (*vv 30–32*). A sign is offered to support confidence that Yahweh will be faithful to his word. Unlike the sign in 38:7–8, it was not an aid to faith in that moment. Like the sign offered in 7:14 it allowed later generations to confirm Yahweh's fulfillment of his word. The sign offered was that Judeans would survive the siege and repopulate their villages, replanting fields and vineyards. In tracing the promise of a remnant to survive the years of judgment, the Vision builds on this oracle and expands it.

Two key words are used here: פליטה "surviving group" and שארית "remnant." They, with other terms, are developed in the Vision into the doctrine of the remnant that is widely identified with Isaiah. The concept was at home in the violent world of that day. War and famine repeatedly took their toll, and in fact, only a few survived. Isaiah's message here is positive. God can and will use the surviving remnant to accomplish his purposes. The Vision uses that hope as a foundation of its structure and message. It is emphasized in the name שאר ישוב "A Remnant Will Return" (7:3). It is spoken of Israel (4:2; 10:20; 11:11,16; 17:6; 46:3), of the inhabitants of Jerusalem (4:3; 37:32), and of survivors of the Diaspora (45:20). God can and will accomplish his work through them (66:19).

The sign-speech looks beyond the apparent hopelessness of the moment to project three years of progress from survival to ordered village harvests for "the survivors that remain of the house of Judah." This apparently refers to the refugees crowded within Jerusalem's walls as the Assyrian messenger spoke (36:11). Succeeding generations would recognize its fulfillment in themselves as the story was read. The exiles had to acknowledge that even the catastrophe of 587 B.C. had not wiped out all Judean presence in Palestine. The readers/hearers of the Vision saw its fulfillment in themselves. The Vision has already documented the sign's fulfillment in the succeeding generations from chap. 22 on.

3. The Third Speech: A Prophetic Yahweh Speech (vv 33–34). The city of Jerusalem is the theme for this speech, whose genre is much more conventional. A messenger formula, "thus says Yahweh," introduces it (v 33a). The usual נאם יהוה "expression of Yahweh" concludes it (v 34c). It assures the king that the Assyrian threat will not be carried out. The city will not be penetrated. Like the speeches that follow (v 35 and 38:6), its structure is common to others in the genre of oracles of salvation for Zion (W. E. March, "The Basic Types of Prophetic Speech," *OTFC* 162–64).

The genre echoes throughout the Vision, but it is brought into tension with other emphases. This is necessary because, unlike the very realistic sign concerning Judean survivors, the readers of this oracle were aware of events that ran counter to its promise, both from its use in 2 Kgs and in the Vision. Hezekiah bought his reprieve from destruction by abject vassalage to Assyria for the rest of his reign and that of his son Manasseh (chaps. 23–28; 2 Kgs 21). Nebuchadnezzar humiliated the city in 598 B.C. and then breached its walls and entered its sacred areas in 587 B.C. along with Edomites and others. The readers/hearers of the Vision in the fifth century B.C. inhabited ruins that could hardly be called a city. With no secure walls, they repeatedly experienced the terror of marauding bands of soldiers and bandits. Isaiah's promise was fulfilled in a sense in 701 B.C. But neither it nor the broader genre of Zion promises had protected the city since that day. The Vision deals with the theme by affirming Yahweh's commitment to Zion but also by recognizing how vulnerable the city was (cf. 2:1–4, and especially chaps. 49–54 and 60–66).

4. The Fourth Speech: Yahweh's Promise to Zion (v 35). This brief statement of Yahweh's commitment to Zion, repeated in substance in 38:6, is unequivocal. It is the heart of the Vision's commitment to Zion's future. The theme of deliverance (ישע) is enunciated here. It, too, has a large role in the Vision. The Vision's central theme could be defined as Yahweh's deliverance/salvation for Israel and Jerusalem which takes shape over three centuries (twelve generations), from the Assyrian invasions through the Persian conquests. The word and the theme are deeply rooted in Zion traditions, so this amounts to a reinterpretation of Zion tradition and of Israelite doctrine for post-exilic Judean existence and faith. For this Isaiah's name, "Yahweh will deliver," was particularly appropriate.

The primary setting for the four speeches is established by the prophetic narrative relating the siege of Jerusalem by Sennacherib in 701 B.C. DtH (2 Kgs 18–19) used the narrative to characterize the entire reign of Hezekiah. It applies the promises to him and implies that the promises were a guarantee of Jerusalem's sanctity and preservation. DtH creates the tension by contrasting this with the account of the fall of the city to Nebuchadnezzar in 587 B.C. (2 Kgs 25). But no effort is made to resolve the tension. The Vision positions the reading of this account in the generation of Babylonian ascendancy. By this the tension between the promise made concerning the city in 701 B.C. and the destruction of the city in 587 B.C. is heightened. No reader or hearer of the Vision could have been unaware of this or fail to ask the question: If not then (701 B.C.), why then (587 B.C.)? The Vision itself is an attempt to answer that question with its deeper implications.

The narrative frame for the speeches (vv 21, 36–38) joins the larger narrative of chaps. 36–37. It recounts the conclusion of events that began when Sennacherib campaigned in Judah (36:1) and sent his field commander to obtain Jerusalem's capitulation (36:2). The overnight death of 185,000 in the Assyrian camp caused the campaign to be abandoned suddenly. This is attributed to the work of Yahweh's messenger (or angel, v 36). The death of Egyptian firstborn (Exod 12:12, 29–30; 13:15) is a parallel. The immediate cause of the sudden mass death is not given. Isaiah's prophecy (v 7a) predicted that uncertainty concerning domestic politics, precipitated by a message from Assyria, would send the Assyrian army back home. However that may be, the disaster is given credit for the lifting of the siege and the termination of the campaign. V 38 completes the chronicle by telling of Sennacherib's assassination by his sons, a fulfillment of Isaiah's prophecy (v 7b).

Comment

21 This word is mediated through Isaiah, but it comes from *Yahweh, God of Israel.* Hezekiah had sent word to Isaiah (v 2). In vv 14–20 he had appealed directly to God in prayer and had addressed him by this same title, *God of Israel* (v 16). Hezekiah's prayer concerning *Sennacherib, king of Assyria* was the occasion for Yahweh's message.

22 The speech encourages an attitude of mockery and disdain for the enemy. Contrast the faint heartedness of Hezekiah's ministers (36:11) and their despair (37:3). The Vision has portrayed the military situation in 22:8–11. Despair was undoubtedly warranted on that basis. When the subject turned, as Hezekiah had hoped it would (37:4,17–20), from military potential to religious desecration and sacrilege, Yahweh's reaction could be expected. Then Zion could turn to mockery and self-assurance.

23 The Assyrian dared to challenge, not Jerusalem as Hezekiah's fortress, but Zion as Yahweh's dwelling-place. His crime changed a simple war to *blasphemy* which evokes holy war in return. Assyria is charged with pride and arrogance against Yahweh (cf. 2:11–12), the *Holy One of Israel.*

24–25 The speeches of the field commander and of Sennacherib (36:4–10,13–20 and 37:10–13) are summarized in poetry to document the charges of blasphemy and pride.

26 Yahweh's response does not dispute the facts. It challenges Assyria's claim to credit for the victories. He says, *"From far off I did it."* למרחוק "to/from far off" could be understood to apply to *had you not heard* as *BHS* places it. But the word order favors reading the phrase with *I did it.* It may refer to distance or to time: "from far away" or "from long ago." A parallel to *days of old* suggests the latter to many interpreters. But the terms may be complementary like "far away and long ago." No matter the distance, Yahweh claims that he did it. He also claims prior knowledge and responsibility for the idea, the plan and the execution of the Assyrian's campaign.

27 The victories are due not so much to Assyrian prowess as to the collapse of the societies they conquered. This implies Yahweh's doing. The description of people in defeat as "short-handed, dismayed and shamed" or demoralized is a common concept in descriptions of Holy War (N. Gottwald, "War, holy," *IDBSup,* 942–44). Yahweh had prepared the mind of their enemies, so that it was easy for the Assyrians to win. This idea applies throughout the Vision. Yahweh controls the course of battles and of power.

Sprouting on rooftops. Sod on the roofs kept houses both cool and dry. It often included grass seeds. After a rain they began to sprout. But the thin layer of sod gave them no depth or moisture for their roots. When the dry desert wind blew, they quickly withered and died. The figure fits the demoralized populations that faced the Assyrian attack.

28 *I know well.* Yahweh had sent the Assyrian commander (36:10; 10:5) and knew his personal habits. *Rising and sitting, going out and coming in* are word pairs with single meanings. They are meant to include all of life. The Assyrian's *raging* against Yahweh was also known. Within the narrative, this contrasts the speech (36:10) that claimed collaboration with Yahweh with the one that boasted that neither Yahweh nor the other gods could stop him (37:10–13).

29 In the face of this insubordination, Yahweh demonstrated his authority. He promised to put *the ring in his nose* as one would for a bull and *a bit in his lip* as one would for a horse and to send him back home. He was no longer useful for the task that he was sent to perform (cf. 10:5).

30 *Your sign.* Some signs are aids to faith, like that in 38:7. But others, like this one, aid later recognition that God was indeed at work. Only after the third year when vineyards bear their fruit again and Judah's population is secure and reasonably prosperous can they look back, remember the crowded city under siege, and know that Isaiah had spoken a true word from God. The sign offered to Ahaz (7:10–17) was like this.

31 *The survivors* foreseen here are only from Judah. The word refers to groups in the besieged city who will be able to return to their fields. *The house of Judah* is the people of Judah. The remnant theme using both שארית "remnant" and פליטה "surviving group" appears repeatedly in the Vision. For those from Zion, 4:3 promises holiness. 6:13 speaks of repeated ravaging even of those who are left from previous attacks. 10:21–22 promises a remnant from Israel to return to their land. 11:12–16 speaks of exiles from Israel and Judah who will return. Although the Vision does not use the same words throughout, the theme continues to the end. The final group which will be saved in the new Jerusalem represents only a minority of the Jews scattered through the Persian Empire (65:13–16; 66:2).

32 Movement in this narrative is *from Jerusalem,* the besieged city, out to their villages and fields. In the Vision the principal movement is toward Jerusalem (2:2–3; 66:18, 20 *et passim*) in pilgrimage. *The Zeal of Yahweh of Hosts will do this.* The power source for salvation lies in Yahweh, not Judean arms nor Jerusalem's diplomacy. This is quoted verbatim in 9:6 and the basic idea pervades the Vision.

33–34 The verses pick up the line of thought from v 29. Because Yahweh turns the Assyrian back toward home, his warlike actions against the city cease. *To this city* puts the emphasis on Yahweh's protection of Jerusalem (see *Form/Structure/Setting*).

35 *A cover over this city.* This figure of divine protection is picked up again in chap. 4. There it is combined with a promise for the purification of its inhabitants. The cover is described in 4:5–6 in terms of fire and cloud which form a canopy over the city to protect it from sun and storm. *I will deliver it* is repeated in 38:6 and the verb is an integral part of Isaiah's name. It also forms Hosea's and Joshua's names and comes to form the name of Jesus "because he will save his people from their sins" (Matt 1:21). The promise belongs to Israel's faith in the form of holy war speeches and was strongly identified with Zion theology. Yahweh's implied commitment to the protection of Jerusalem and identification with the city is a strong theme in the Vision (see *Form/Structure/Setting*).

For my sake. Yahweh supports his commitment by reference to his own interests and decisions. His sovereign pleasure should be reason enough. But he adds *for the sake of my servant David.* Yahweh's promises to David in 2 Sam 7:12–16 had not included the continuation or protection of Jerusalem. They mention the royal line and were framed in contrast to the proposed temple (and thus to the city). Isaiah's oracle puts Jerusalem's deliverance in the debt of Davidide claims upon Yahweh. The development of this relation in the Vision will reverse this trend. Jerusalem is a constant in God's plan with a new role for the new age following the Exile. But the monarchy does not survive the catastrophe and has no role *per se* in the new order. Its functions and values are to be absorbed by the city.

The Vision deals at length with the delicate issue of the destiny of the Davidic dynasty. Its ideals and glory are portrayed in chaps. 9 and 11. Its intransigence and stubborn willfulness are portrayed in chaps. 22 and 28–33. Then the Vision extracts the title עבדי "my servant" from its identity with David and has Yahweh offer it to Jews in Mesopotamia (chaps. 40–48), to the vulnerable and suffering survivors in Jerusalem's ruins (chaps. 49–54), and to those of Palestine's population who want to worship Yahweh (chaps. 55–59). Beyond that it is silent concerning the role of the Davidic dynasty among the Jews.

36 Yahweh's messenger turned the tables overnight. Assyrian soldiers died in their camp. The king abandoned the siege and the campaign to return to Nineveh. מלאך "the messenger" is a representative or ambassador. When he represents God, it is customary to call him an angel. The Hebrew word is the same. Biblical narrative tells of God's messenger bringing aid (Gen 19; Exod 14:19; 1 Kgs 19:5,7), warning of danger or bringing someone to help (Judg 6:11). Such a messenger was sent to lead Israel out of Egypt (Num 20:16). But the messenger sometimes brings disaster and death (2 Sam 24:16; Pss 35:5; 78:49). The narrative does not explain how the messenger killed the soldiers. 2 Sam 24:15–16 connects a plague to an angel's visitation, but no hint of that appears here.

Wildberger (1437) remarks on the surprisingly large number of the dead (185,000) in a campaign which would ordinarily have been expected to need only a few thousand. But he notes that Sennacherib wrote on a clay prism that he had taken 200,150 away from Jerusalem (*ANET,* 288). A. Ungnad ("Die Zahl der von Sanherib deportierten Judaer," *ZAW* 59 [1942/43] 199–202) thought that number should read 2,150. But other surprisingly high numbers occur in the OT. Num 1:46 tells of 603,550 Israelite men at arms that left Egypt. 2 Sam 24:9 tells of Israel having 800,000 soldiers and Judah 500,000. Wildberger cautions that one should not question numbers in a miracle account or seek exact information about the means. Let a miracle be a miracle and wonder at its power. But the Vision goes beyond the simple telling of a miraculous story. It teaches throughout that the age in which God chooses to use Assyria and Persia for his purposes demands that Israel and Judah depend on him for direction and protection. They are not needed to play active roles for military or political purposes. This story bears that out.

37 The end of the story is short and abrupt. Sennacherib *broke camp and left.* He returned home and *lived in Nineveh.* That means that he did not return to Palestine. He lived some twenty years but no further campaigns in Palestine are reported.

38 This account of Sennacherib's death is partially supported by Assyrian sources. *Esarhaddon* was Sennacherib's designated heir and did succeed to his father's throne in 681 B.C. He was the youngest son. His brothers conspired against him earlier, forcing him into exile. There he received word of his father's murder. Later sources agree with v 38 in blaming it on the other sons, although these are not named (*ANET,* 289). Ashurbanipal, who succeeded Esarhaddon, reported that he avenged the murder of his grandfather by striking them with the same statues with which they had killed his grandfather (*ANET* 2, 288b). This supports the account of murder in a sanctuary. The name *Nisroch* (נסרך) has no counterpart in the Assyrian texts and is not known as an Assyrian god. He is here identified as Sennacherib's personal divine patron. The names of his sons are also missing in the Assyrian texts. אדרמלך "Adrammelech" is the name of the God of the Sepharvaim in 2 Kgs 17:31. W. F. Albright (*Archaeology and the Religion of Israel* [Baltimore: Johns Hopkins U. P., 1946] 163) emended the name to read אדדמלך "Adad (of Hadad) is king." A Phoenician personal name "Adrammelech" is known (*HALAT* 16). *Sharezer* is thought to be a short form meaning something like "Nergal—Protect the King" (Wildberger 1413). It is cited in Zech 7:2 as the name of a man from Bethel. *Ararat* is in the mountains of northwest Assyria between the Van and Urmi lakes in modern Armenia. It joined Babylon and Elam as rivals for Assyrian power and was a likely place to find sanctuary. For more information concerning Esarhaddon's reign, see the commentary on chaps. 23–27.

Explanation

The reading contains a treasure trove of Isaiah's oracles on the occasion of Jerusalem's moment of dire threat. He delivers the powerful taunt against the Assyrian. In doing so he lays the foundation for every other OT claim to Yahweh's sovereignty over the emperors of the eighth to the second centuries in the Ancient Near East. He spoke words of encouragement for the survival of the embattled Judeans which laid the foundation for the remnant-doctrine that became a basic part of Judaism's hope to still be heirs to Abraham's promise. He gave prophetic support to the doctrine of Yahweh's patronage of Zion and his salvation for the city. Royal liturgy and the Psalms had claimed this. But Isaiah's word confirmed Jerusalem's place in Judaism's hope.

Yet these very speeches give no hint that Isaiah was different from the prophets of comfortable salvation that Jeremiah found so troublesome and untruthful (Jer 23:9–40). These speeches take no stand on Israel's or Jerusalem's sin or the necessity for God's judgment against them. The Vision has placed these speeches in the perspective of a broader time to show how that moment in history was an aberration from Yahweh's announced direction, an aberration caused by Sennacherib's provocation. The longer view of the safety of Jerusalem, of the Davidic dynasty, and of Israel's future had to be seen in light of the God-willed rise of empire, the failure of Israel and Judah to follow God's direction, and the events of 734, 721, 714, 598, and 587 B.C. as well as those of 701 B.C. This longer view given in the Vision, as it had been in the Deuteronomic History, showed the direction of God's plan for history. The events and oracles of 701 B.C. showed that Yahweh was still in control, that he valued Zion as his city, and that he would not be bullied by the emperor. These were lessons that were still needed in fifth century Judaism.

Scene 5:
A Reading (continued): Hezekiah's Illness (38:1–8, 21–22)

Bibliography

Fillerton, K. "The Original Text of 2 K. 20, 7–11 = Isa. 38, 7.8. 21f." *JBL* 44 (1925) 44–62. **Illman, K. J.** *Old Testament Formulas about Death.* Åbo: Research Institute of Åbo Academic Foundation, 1979. 24–25. **Iwry, J.** "The Qumrân Isaiah and the End of the Dial of Ahaz." *BASOR* 147 (1957) 27–33. **Jeremias, C.** "Zu Jes xxxviii 31f." *VT* 21 (1971) 104–11. **Landy, D.,** ed. *Culture, Disease and Healing: Studies in Medical Anthropology.* New York: Macmillan, 1978. 278–85. **Pilch, J. J.** "Biblical Leprosy and Body Symbolism." *BTB* 11 (1981) 108–13. **In der Smitten, W. T.** "Patient und Arzt—

Die Welt des Kranken im Alten Testament." *JANUS* 60 (1973) 110. **Zakowitcz, Y.** "2 Kings 20:7—Isaiah 38:21–22" (Heb. with Eng. summary). *BMik* 50 (1972) 302–5.

Translation

Reader: 1[a]*In those days Hezekiah*[b] *was deathly sick. So Isaiah,*[c] *son of Amoz, the prophet, came in to him and said to him:*
"Thus says Yahweh:
Order[d] *your household,* 2+3+2
for you are dying.
You will not live."
2*But then Hezekiah*[a] *turned his face*[b] *to the wall*[c] *and prayed to Yahweh:*
3[a]*"Now, Yahweh, remember, I pray,* 3+4+3
how I have walked[b] *before you*
in truth and with a whole heart.[c]
That which is good in your eyes I have done." 3
Then Hezekiah wept[d] *with great sobs.*[e]
4*Then*[a] *the word of Yahweh happened to Isaiah:* 5*"Go*[a] *and you shall say to Hezekiah:*[b] *Thus says Yahweh, God of David, your father:*
I have heard your prayer. 2+2
I have seen your tears.
See![c] *I am adding*[d] *to your days* 2+3
fifteen years.
6*From the hand of the Assyrian king I save you* 3+3+3
and this city.
I provide a cover over this city.[a]
7*And*[a] *this is for you the sign from Yahweh that*[b] *Yahweh will do this*[c] *thing which he has spoken:*[d] 8[a]*See me turning back*[a] *the shadow*[b] *on the steps*[c] *of Ahaz*[d]*—descending ten steps." So the sun retreated ten steps of the steps which it had already descended.*[e]
21*Then Isaiah said: "Let them take*[a] *a cake of pressed figs and apply (it)*[b] *on the boil." And it was done,* 22*(after) Hezekiah said: "What sign (is there) that I will again go up to the house of Yahweh?"*[a]

Notes

1.a. LXX adds Ἐγένετο "it happened."
1.b. DSS[Isa] חזקיה has the short form of the name.
1.c. DSS[Isa] ישעיה is also the short form.
1.d. MT צו "command" is an apocopated impv (BDB, 845). DSS[Isa] צוי apparently has the full form (Wildberger, 1441), which is usually written צַוֵּה.
2.a. 2 Kgs 20:2 omits. DSS[Isa] uses the short form.
2.b. 2 Kgs 20:2 inserts the accus particle את.
2.c. Tg לכותל בית מקדשא "to the wall of the holy house," i.e., of the Temple.
3.a. The quotation marks translate ויאמר "and he said." 2 Kgs 20:2 has לאמר "saying" at the end of the previous verse instead.
3.b. DSS[Isa] הלכתי "I came" is a qal form. But its scribe knew of MT's hithp התהלכתי and added תה above the word.

3.c. MT לב "heart." 2 Kgs 20:3 and DSS^{Isa} have לבב, a variant of the same word.

3.d. DSS^{Isa} ויבכא "and he wept" is a longer form with the typical vocalic symbol (cf. Kutscher, *Isaiah Scroll,* 328).

3.e. Lit., "with great weeping."

4.a. 2 Kgs 20:4 includes a longer text here: ישעיהו לא יצא העיר (Q חצר) התיכנה "Isaiah had not yet gone out to the middle court." The phrase heightens the sense of an immediate response to Hezekiah's prayer.

5.a. MT הלוך "go." 2 Kgs 20:5 שוב "return" is in keeping with the additional statement in v 4.

5.b. 2 Kgs 20:5 adds נגיד עמי "leader of my people," a title commonly found in Chronicles.

5.c. 2 Kgs 20:5 includes here: רפא לך ביום השלישי תעלה בית יהוה "Healing (will be) yours. On the third day you will go up to the house of Yahweh." The ideas are included in the Isaiah text by the question that concludes the story (v 22).

5.d. 2 Kgs 20:6 reads והספתי "and I shall add," a grammatical difference made necessary by the additional clause noted in 5.c. MT יוסף (K) is pointed by Q יוֹסִיף. *BHS* follows LXX Vg Syr Syh Tg in suggesting a participial form יוֹסֵף, but see 29:14 for a pointing similar to Q's (Wildberger, 1441).

6.a. 2 Kgs 20:6 and DSS^{Isa} add למעני ולמען דוד עבדי "for my sake and the sake of my servant David" (cf. 37:35). 2 Kgs 20:7–8 then recounts here the incident that is placed at the end of the Vision's story (Isa 38:21).

7.a. 2 Kgs 20:9 adds ויאמר ישעיהו "and Isaiah said" in place of MT's ו "and."

7.b. MT אשר "which." 2 Kgs 20:9 כי "that."

7.c. Missing in 2 Kgs 20:9.

7.d. 2 Kgs 20 adds in vv 9b, 10, 11a: " 'Shall the shadow go forward ten steps, or shall it go back ten steps?' 'It is a simple matter for the shadow to go forward ten steps,' said Hezekiah. 'Rather, have it go back ten steps.' Then the prophet called upon the Lord" (NIV).

8.a-a. The verse is different from 2 Kgs 20:11 and apparently suffers from attempts to change it to fit. Two cases of dittogr need to be recognized (see below). When they are eliminated, the text reads smoothly.

8.b. MT המעלות אשר ירדה "of the steps which she had gone down." The verb is fem while the "shadow," antecedent to אשר "which" is masc. The entire phrase is dittogr for the latter part of the verse and should be omitted.

8.c. DSS^{Isa} adds עלית "of the altar" and is followed by Iwry (*BASOR* 147 [1957] 30) who refers to 2 Kgs 23:12.

8.d. MT בשמש "by the sun" is dittogr for the second half of the verse. LXX inserts ὁ ἥλιος "the sun" earlier to provide a fem subj for "she had gone down." If both are seen as dittogr, neither is needed. The first half of the verse is about the shadow; the second is about the sun.

8.e. LXX *κατέβη ἡ σκιά* "the shadow had gone down" tries to compromise between the two subjects, the sun and the shadow. This is not needed if the dittogr are eliminated.

21.a. ישאו lit., "take up." 2 Kgs 20:7 קחו "take." DSS^{Isa} omits.

21.b. וימרחו lit., "let them rub." 2 Kgs 20:7 ויקחו וישימו "so they took and they placed."

22.a. 2 Kgs 20:8 has the words in a longer form and in a different position in the story.

Form/Structure/Setting

The story of Hezekiah's illness is made a part of this complex narrative by the phrase "in those days" (v 1) and by the position of v 6 which repeats the promise of 37:35 concerning the city and expands it to include the king. In addition to the misery of the painful boil, Hezekiah suffered from a diplomatic illness. This depression was due to his forced capitulation to Sennacherib (see Sennacherib's account in *ANET,* 288), the effects of which were not removed by the happy fact that the city was not sacked. In the setting provided to 2 Kgs 20 (Isa 38) Hezekiah's illness was more than physical and needed more than medicine. The added fifteen years of life came from medicine *and* the respite of not being taken to Nineveh in chains (cf. 39:8).

The story has a simple outline:

Hezekiah's illness is pronounced terminal (v 1)
Hezekiah's prayer (vv 2–3)
Yahweh's gracious answer (vv 4–6)
Yahweh provides a sign for Hezekiah (vv 7–8)
Medicine is prescribed for Hezekiah's boil (vv 21–22)
(The psalm that is inserted after v 8 appears as Scene 6 below.)

The story in 2 Kgs 20 is shorter in omitting the psalm, but longer in the narrative of the sign. The miracle of such an immediate response to prayer and of the sign appears to be more important to the account in Kings. The presentation of Hezekiah's attitude is more important to the Isaiah text.

The narrative is complex. Two oracles, contradictory in content, with a prayer between, are unique. But compare 1 Kgs 21:27–29 where contrition occasions a second oracle. And see Isa 7 for a parallel offer of a sign.

The last verse (v 22) seems to be awkwardly placed. 2 Kgs 20 does not have this problem because its longer form allows the question to be placed earlier in the story.

Comment

1 *In those days* sets the time during the siege (cf. v 6 below). *Deathly sick* is literally "sick to death." V 21 tells of a boil which, though painful, is hardly fatal. The story relates the illness to the time of the siege and directly to its threat (v 6). The illness may well have been as much diplomatic as physical, a death which threatened to come as much from the Assyrian as from the boil. *Order* (צו) is literally "command." It calls for Hezekiah to make arrangements for the royal succession in view of his imminent death. *You are dying* may refer to his illness, or it may point to the usual consequences of rebellion. God's decision is not explained.

2–3 Hezekiah turns away from the prophet to appeal to their common Lord. Cf. his prayer for the city in 37:15–20. He appeals to his record of piety. *How I have walked before you* refers to his conduct. *In truth* (באמת) and *with a whole* (שלם) *heart* refer to attitudes and spirit. Cf. the use of the same words in 39:8. אמת means "what is firm or solid." In this context it means integrity and truth (A. Jepsen, "אמת ʾemeth," *TDOT* 1:309–16). שלם refers to completeness and thus to wholeness, health, and peace. *That which is good* is literally "the good" (הטוב). Aware that definitions of goodness vary, Hezekiah makes it precise, *in your eyes.* So he posits his actions as the third part of his appeal and prays with great emotion.

5 As in 37:21 and in Yahweh's response to Ahab in 1 Kgs 21:29, Yahweh answers the prayer, this time with a reprieve of *fifteen years.* The original judgment stands, but is delayed. God takes account of the prayer and the tears. But he makes no reference to Hezekiah's claim to piety. Humility counts for more than piety. *Fifteen years,* added to the fourteen-year reign that preceded the siege according to 2 Kgs 18:13, completes the twenty-nine years of his reign (2 Kgs 18:2). The chronological problems of this period are discussed in the *Excursus: Chronology* in *Isaiah 1–33.*

6 The promise then takes a different turn. Hezekiah is to be saved, not only from the illness, but also *from the hand of the Assyrian king,* and the city with him. This story is tied to the siege recounted in the previous chapter. The problems connected with that siege were enough to make anyone ill. That Hezekiah would be allowed by the Assyrians to remain king after his rebellion was a greater miracle than even that the city should be spared (after paying a heavy indemnity, 2 Kgs 18:14–16).

7 A *sign* is offered to encourage Hezekiah's confidence that it will be done and that Yahweh was the one responsible for it. This end is achieved in the story by having the prophet predict it (*which he has spoken*) and by the unusual sign.

8 A sign, to be effective, must usually contradict the ordinary or expected course of events. In this instance, the sun's shadow moves backwards, i.e., from east to west instead of the usual west to east, as the sun advances in the opposite direction. This was measured on *the steps of Ahaz,* which were built by Hezekiah's father and on which, by design or accident, on an ordinary day a shadow marked the movement of the sun down the steps. On this day, the shadow would move back up ten steps. This was to be Hezekiah's sign.

These did not necessarily represent hours, nor must this be understood to have been a sundial as the Targum's אבן שעיא "stone of hours" and many interpreters suggest (cf. BDB, 752; L. Borchardt, *Altägyptische Zeitmessung,* Die geschichte der Zeitmessung und der Uhren, IB, ed. E. von Bassermann-Jordan [Berlin: DeGruyter, 1920]; R. W. Sloley, "Primitive Methods of Measuring Time," *JEA* 17 [1931] 166–78; J. Iwry, *BASOR* 147 [1957] 27–33; Y. Yadin, "The Dial of Ahaz," *Eretz Israel* 5 [1959] 91–96; P. Welten, "Sonnenuhr," *BLex* 1616; and discussion by Wildberger, 1453). There is no word in ancient Hebrew for "hour." Herodotus (ii, 109) attributes the discovery of the sundial and the division of the day into hours to the Babylonians. Palestinian archaeologists have found a sundial in Egyptian Gezer (Welton, *BLex,* 1616b–1617a). But Israel certainly had steps (מעלות, ἀναβάθμοι) which provided convenient measuring points for the sun's shadow whether it was made by a pole or a protruding corner of the house.

The setting back of the shadow was understood by Hitzig to parallel the delay in the time of death. If that were the conscious intention of the sign, the number should have been fifteen instead of ten. The sign must be understood simply for what it is: a means of encouraging Hezekiah. It is remarkable and unexplained, not even as pragmatic as Joshua's extended daylight (Josh 10:12–14). The interpreter does well to leave it, as the text does, without further speculation as to how it was accomplished.

21 Now that the weighty matters that pressed upon the king's mind and heart have been dealt with, a simple medical procedure can deal with the boil. Figs were used as medicine throughout the ANE, in Ugarit with horses (C. F. A. Schaeffer, *Cuneiform Texts of Ras Shamra* [London: Oxford U. P., 1939] 41), in Mesopotamia for human toothache and lung problems (R. C. Thompson, *Assyrian Medical Texts* [Oxford: U. P., 1923] 554), in Old Egypt for constipation, in Arabia for the plague, and in Turkey even in modern times (Gesenius; Wildberger, 1454). The application of a fig paste appears to have been a very ordinary and usual medical procedure in contrast to the unusual sign.

22 Hezekiah's request for the sign is tacked onto the end of the story.

The course of the story in 2 Kgs 20:8–11 also puts this question after the application of the figs, but the entire section about the sign comes with it. In Isaiah it is integrated into the story above. The result is that the sentence contributes only the reference to Hezekiah again being able to go to the Temple for worship. Again, his piety is brought to the fore.

Explanation

The story appears to have originally been a simple account of prolonged life as an answer to prayer. The psalm (Scene 6, Isa 38:9–20) fits this intention. But by placing the story after chaps. 36–37 (= 2 Kgs 18–19) and by connecting it with that setting through the opening phrase and the connecting promise (v 6), a political perspective has been added. Hezekiah's life and reign had been threatened by the Assyrian siege and by his illness. One would have expected that he would have died either from the infection or because of the policies of rebellion that provoked the Assyrian invasion. God's initial judgment supports that expectation which, as far as the political aspect is concerned, the Vision had developed concerning Hezekiah's ministers in chap. 22.

But the remarkable fact was that Hezekiah reigned for fifteen more years and gained a reputation in history (2 Kgs 18–20) for being a pious and brave king. The story accounts for this by telling of his plea to Yahweh which cited his piety. History agreed with that evaluation. Yahweh hears his prayer, is moved by his emotion, and grants a reprieve of fifteen more years of life. But Yahweh's response through the prophet Isaiah does not grant grace because of the king's piety. He saves Hezekiah and the city. Their fate hung by the same thread. 2 Kgs 20:6 in a phrase not included in Isaiah makes it explicit: "for my sake and the sake of David your father." Grace is motivated by Yahweh's own purposes and by his promise to David.

Hezekiah needed a sign. That, too, was granted although the events called for no further act of faith from Hezekiah. After the assurance met his spiritual and mental needs, medicine brought healing to his boil. Hezekiah would go to worship again and relative order would gradually return to his poor beleaguered country.

Scene 6: Hezekiah's Psalm (38:9–20)

Bibliography

Airoldi, N. "Nota a Is. 38:16." *BeO* 15 (1973) 255–59. **Begrich, J.** *Der Psalm des Hiskia.* FRLANT 25. Göttingen: Vandenhoeck & Ruprecht, 1926. **Boer, P. A. H. de.** "Notes on Text and Meanings of Isaiah xxxviii 9–20." *OS* 9 (1951) 170–86. **Calderone, J.** "HDL–II in Poetic Texts." *CBQ* 23 (1961) 451–60. ———. "Supplementary Note in HDL–II." *CBQ* 24 (1962) 412–19. **Castellino, G. R.** "Lamentazioni individuali Accadiche ed Ebraiche." *Sal* 10 (1948) 145–61. **Dahood, M.** "חדל 'Cessation' in Isaiah

38:11." *Bib* 52 (1971) 215–16. **Hallo, W. W.** "The Royal Correspondence of Larsa I: A Sumerian Prototype for the Prayer of Hezekiah." *AOAT* 25 (1976) 209–24. **Nyberg, H. S.** "Hiskias Danklied Jes 38:9–21." FS H. Kosmala. *ASTI* 9 (1974) 85–97. **Seybold, K.** *Das Gebet des Kranken im Alten Testament.* BWANT 99. Stuttgart: Kohlhammer, 1973. 147–53. **Soggin, J. A.** "Il 'Salmo di Ezechia' in Isaia 38:9–20." *BeO* 16 (1974) 177–81. **Weiss, R.** "Textual Notes." *Textus* 6 (1968) 127–29.

Translation

Reader: 9 *A psalm*[a] *belonging to Hezekiah, king of Judah, when he was sick,*[b] *but survived his sickness.*

(Hezekiah): 10 *I myself said:* 2+3
In the noontide[a] *of my days I must go.*[b]
In the gates of Sheol 2+3
I am destined (for) the rest of my years.
11 *I said: I shall not see Yahweh*[a] 3+3
in the land of the living.
I shall not look on mankind anymore 3+2
with the inhabitants of non-being.[b]
12 *My generation*[a] *will be plucked up* 2+2+2
and removed[b] *from me*
like my shepherd's[c] *tent.*
I shall roll up[d] *my life like a woven cloth*[e] 3+2+3
(when) one shall cut me off[f] *from the loom.*[g]
From (one) day to (its) night you will finish[h] *me.*
13 *I shall be ravaged*[a] *by morning as (by) a lion.* 3+3+3
So he[b] *will break all my bones.*
[c]*From (one) day to (its) night you will finish me.*[c]
14 *Like a swallow,*[a] *a crane,*[b] 2+2
I shall chirp.
I shall moan like a dove. 2+3
My eyes will be cast down,[c] *no longer looking up.*
My Lord! 1+1+1
I am oppressed![d]
Bail me out!
15 *What can I say?* 2+2+2
He has spoken[a] *to me*[b]
and he himself did (it).
Should I walk slowly[c] *all my years* 2+2
because of the bitterness of my (past) life?
16 *My Lord has hidden me.*[a] 2+3
Let there be life[b] *to you,*[c] *my heart.*[d]
Yahweh[e] *has given rest,*[f] *my spirit.* 3+2
You make me well[g] *and I am kept alive.*[g]
17 *See! For wholeness* 2+2
I had great[a] *bitterness.*

But as for you, you kept back[b] *my life*[c] 3+2
from the pit of extinction.[d]
For you threw 2+2+2
all my sins
behind your back.
18 *Indeed Sheol cannot thank you.* 4+2
Death cannot praise you.
Those who go down to the pit cannot hope[a] 2+1
for your faithfulness.[b]
19 *The living! (Only) the living!* 2+2+2
He it is who thanks you
as I do today.
[a]*A father makes known* 2+2+2
to his children your faithfulness,[a]
20 *Yahweh,*[a] *to save me.*[b]
Let us[b] *play our*[b] *stringed instruments* 2+2+2
all the days of our[b] *lives*
at the house of Yahweh!

Notes

9.a. MT מכתב "a writing." LXX προσευχή "a prayer." *BHS* suggests מכתם "a psalm" (cf. the superscriptions to Pss 16, 56–60), which is used here.

9.b. DSS[Isa] בחוליותיו has all the essential elements of MT but adds superfluous vowel letters. Cf. de Boer (*OS* 9 [1951] 171) and Kutscher (*Isaiah Scroll,* 321). It seems to be a fem pl qal ptcp "in his illnesses" rather than MT's inf constr. MT is the better reading.

10.a. בדמי is translated "in the noontide of" by RSV and "in the prime of" by NIV. BDB (198) derives the noun from דמה II and translates "cessation, rest." G. R. Driver (*JTS* 38 [1937] 46) is followed by Wildberger in translating "the half of, the middle of." LXX ἐν τῷ ὕψει "in the height of" led Bredenkamp to emend to ברם ימי "when my days reach their height." *BHK* suggests דומה "underworld" with reference to Ps 115:17. In Pss 62:6, 7 and 83:2 it appears to mean "the quiet of my days," as an elderly person would say it. Wildberger (1442) makes a case for the traditional meaning of "middle" with reference to חצי ימי in Jer 17:11 and Pss 55:24; 102:25 (also Syr *bplgwt ywmy* and Vg *in dimidio dierum meorum*). *BHS* follows Cheyne, Duhm, and Marti in trying to improve the word order by placing the verb first: אלכה בדמי ימי. But this is neither necessary nor helpful.

10.b. אלכה is a cohortative form which is usually translated "let me go." But the context does not support that affirmative consent. GKC § 108g calls this "a resolution formed under compulsion," hence the translation "must go."

11.a. MT has יה "Yah" twice. Two MSS and Syr read יהוה "Yahweh" once. LXX τὸ σωτήριον τοῦ θεοῦ "the salvation of God" makes no attempt at a literal translation. DSS[Isa] has יה once only. The double usage is remarkable, but adds no meaning here. Read as יהוה.

11.b. חדל is a *hap. leg.* as a noun from the verb meaning "to cease." Thus it should mean "cessation" (cf. BDB, 293). Calderone (*CBQ* 23 [1961] 451–60) derives the noun from a second root meaning "to be wealthy, prosperous" and translates "fruitful land." Dahood (*Bib* 52 [1971] 215) considers it "an authentic poetic name" for the underworld, a synonym for Sheol. Begrich (*Der Psalm,* 24) demonstrates an early tendency to translate it as "world." But this is too bland for a word that points to "non-being," "cessation of life," "non-life." It is omitted by LXX.

12.a. דורי "my generation" (BDB, 189), LXX ἐκ τῆς συγγενείας μου "from my kinsmen," Vg *generatio* "generation." Nyberg (*ASTI* 9 [1974] 90) supports the usual meaning of the word arguing that it is not used in Heb. or other Semitic languages with the meaning "dwelling." But most translators have insisted that in this one case the context requires the meaning of "dwelling" and by a *tour de force* keep it (cf. Wildberger, 1442). This translation prefers the usual meaning of the word even if it is awkward.

12.b. ונגלה "removed," a niph pf (BDB, 162). Vg *et convoluta est* "is rolled up" has led Begrich and others to emend to ונגל from the root גלל "roll." In Heb. the ideas are close together, as in "removing a tent by rolling it up."

12.c. MT רעי "my shepherd" (BDB, 945; cf. 44:28 of Cyrus). Σ *ποιμενων* (also Tg Syr Vg) reads a pl: רעים. Some have objected that the רעי seems to be a constr pl but is not followed by a noun. Wildberger (1443) holds it to be an abs sg. But the form may certainly by a ptcp sg with a 1st pers suff.

12.d. קפדתי is also a *hap. leg.* (BDB, 891) which apparently means something like "roll up." DSS[Isa] has ספרתי "I count" (cf. Weiss, *Textus* 6 [1968] 127). Translators have had trouble with the change of persons, leading *BHS* to make this second person.

12.e. Tg and Syr read MT ארג as אריג with the same meaning. *HALAT* follows Begrich in this emendation.

12.f. יבצעני "he cuts me off." *BHS* would change this also to 2d pers to conform to תשלימני "you will finish me" that follows.

12.g. מדלה "from the loom" postulates a third root meaning for דלל to provide a technical term in weaving (cf. C. H. Johl, *Webestühle und Brettchenweberei in Altägypten* [Leipzig: Hinrichs, 1924] 48 and Begrich, *Der Psalm,* 30).

12.h. תשלימני "you will finish me" (BDB, 1022). LXX *παρεδόθην* "I am delivered up" (v 13c). Wildberger (1443) explains the LXX translation in terms of the common Aramaic meaning of the word.

13.a. שִׁוִּיתִי "I shall be smooth/quiet" (שוה BDB, 1000). Ps 131:2 adds נפשי, thus "I quiet my soul." DSS[Isa] has שפותי which Driver (*JSS* 13 [1968] 56) points as שַׁפּוֹתִי and translates "I am racked with pain." De Boer (*OS* 9 [1951] 172) follows 2 Sam 17:29 to read שְׁפוֹתִי "to be quiet/smooth." Houbigant was the first to emend the Heb to read שִׁוַּעְתִּי "I cry out" (שוע BDB, 1002) following Tg. Nyberg (*ASTI* 9 [1974] 92) derives MT from a denominative verb from שׁוא "devastation" (BDB, 996) to translate "I shall be devastated."

13.b. *BHS* would add יהוה "Yahweh" to make the subj explicit. But this is not necessary.

13.c-c. As in v 12, lit., "from day to night you finish me" could mean "all day from morning to night" or "in one day from morning to night." This translation has chosen the latter meaning.

14.a. K[Or] כסיס (cf. Q of Jer 8:7; BDB, 692). KB would read סיס in both places as the name of a bird, *Apus apus L.* (cf. Köhler, *Kleine Lichter,* 35). Everyone is agreed that סוס in this case does not mean "horse" as it usually does.

14.b. עגור "crane" appears in Jer 8:7 paired with סוס. KB (and Köhler, "Hebräische Vokabeln I," *ZAW* 54 [1934] 288) suggests a technical identification as the bulbul, *Pycnonotus Reichenovi.*

14.c. דלו "are cast down" (BDB, 195) and LXX *ἐξέλιπον . . . τοῦ βλέπειν* "cease to look." *BHS* follows Bredenkamp who reads דלפו "are sleepless" like Job 16:20. Driver (*JTS* 38 [1937] 47) follows the Aramaic to translate "my eyes are lifted up" or "strained toward heaven." Begrich and Ehrlich pointed to parallels in Jer 14:6; Pss 69:4[3];119:82, 123; Job 11:20; 17:5; Lam 2:11; 4:17 to suggest reading כלו "are worn out"; thus NIV "grow weak" and Wildberger (1440) "verzehren sich" (cf. כלה, BDB, 447). But MT's meaning is fitting and should be kept.

14.d. 1QIsa[b] reads חשקה "love" (BDB, 365–66). *BHS* suggests עשׂקה "contention" (BDB, 796), changing *shin* to *sin.* But MT עשקה "oppression" is better than all of these (cf. BDB, 798).

15.a. וְאָמַר "when he has spoken." The change of person has bothered interpreters. Tg read וְאָמַר "and I said" and DSS[Isa] ואומר moves in a similar fashion. *BHS* follows them. But MT makes good sense and should be kept.

15.b. Tg and Θ read a 3d pers, thus turning the speech from MT's "he to me" to "I to him."

15.c. אדדה "walk slowly" (BDB, 186; GKC § 55g; cf. Ps 42:5), ʼA *προβιβασω* "I will go forward," Θ *καθοδηγησιν* "he will guide from above." But DSS[Isa] has אדודה "flee" (from נדד BDB, 622). Nyberg (*ASTI* 9 [1974] 93) follows DSS[Isa] but suggests it comes from דודה (from דוה "sad": BDB, 188). Again, MT may be kept.

16. Wildberger (1445) calls this verse "a nightmare for exegetes." He lists six different rearrangements of the text, but agrees with none of them and omits the first two parts in his translation. There seems no way but to work with the mangled text to get some sense. Cf. *BHS.*

16.a. עליהם "upon them" has no antecedent. But if the letter *heh* is moved and the *yodh* joined on the end, it reads העלימי "he hides me." It makes a good stich: "My Lord has hidden me."

16.b. יחיו "they will live" has the same penchant for the pl with no antecedent. But if the two *waws* are read together as *heh,* the form is good: יחיה "life will be" or "it will be life."

16.c. לכל is a problem, but if divided differently, separating the final letter, what remains is לְךָ "to you."

16.d. If the *lamedh* is then attached to the following letter, לב "heart" results. To balance רוחי "my spirit" a *yodh* should be added: לבי "my heart."

16.e. The remaining יי is a common abbreviation for יהוה "Yahweh." The emended Hebrew text compared to MT reads:

(MT) אדני עליהם יחיו ולכל בהן חיי רוחי
(Emend.) אדני העלימי יחיה לך לבי הנח יהוה רוחי

16.f. בהן חיי has now already lost *beth* to the preceding word. The next three letters הנח make sense as a hiph impv from נוח "give rest."

16.g. The two verbs are different person and in MT do not fit well together: "you restored me to health and make (impv) me live." We keep the first as it is and change the *nun* to *taw* in the second, reading והחיתי "I am kept alive."

17.a. MT has מר "bitterness" a second time. DSS[Isa] מאודה suggests the emendation of מר to מאד "very" (*BHS*). LXX leaves out the entire stich. Wildberger (1445) follows Cheyne in omitting the first מר. This translation follows *BHS.*

17.b. MT חשקת means "you loved" (BDB, 365 I). LXX εἵλου "you took" and Vg *eruisti* "you have drawn out" point to Heb. חשכת "you kept back" (BDB, 362). Bredenkamp writes that Maimonides had already suggested the change. Nyberg (*ASTI* 9 [1974] 95) keeps the form of MT but sees the meaning to be "hold fast." The translation reads חשכת "you kept."

17.c. נפשי "my life" is literally "my soul."

17.d. בלי "extinction" or "nothingness" (BDB, 115). Cf. Driver, *JTS* 38 (1937) 46.

18.a. ישברו "hope" (BDB, 960 II) is an Aramaism. Cf. M. Wagner, *Die lexicalischen und grammatikalischen Aramaismen im Alttestamentlichen Hebräisch* (Berlin: Töpelmann, 1966) 108.

18.b. אמתך "your faithfulness." LXX τὴν ἐλεημοσύνην σου "your mercy." Wildberger (1445) wonders if LXX's Heb text read חסדך.

19.a-a. Marti explains the construction: יודיע with ל of the person and אל for the subject matter, and calls it all a late construction.

20.a. The subj followed by an inf with *lamedh* implies something left out. Tg supplies אמר "said." LXX reads the inf as a noun: κύριε τῆς σωτηρίας μου "the Lord my salvation." This translation reads יהוה "Yahweh" as vocative.

20.b. The verse has a problem in persons and numbers. There is a 1st sg on "instruments" but the rest are pl. We read 20a with v 19 as sg and v 20b–d as pl.

Form/Structure/Setting

The psalm is entitled a מכתם "miktam," a familiar technical term for a psalm, but one that remains largely unclear in meaning. The whole is marked by cohortative verbs at the beginning (v 10a "I must go") and the end (v 20 "let us play"). It is constructed in two distinct parts. The first is introduced by "I said" (vv 10a, 11; cf. Jonah 2:5 [4]; Pss 31:23; 41:5 [4]; 116:11), speaks the constraint to go (v 10b), and in six verbs in pf tense describes his plights: "I am destined" (v 10c), "will be plucked up, removed, rolled up" (v 12), "I shall be ravaged" (v 13a), and "will be cast down" (v 14b). The section is filled out with impf verbs in vv 11, 12, and 13. It closes with an impv, "bail me out" (14c).

The second part (vv 15–20) reflects a new perspective. A question asks what his attitude should be since Yahweh "has spoken" and acted (v 15). These verbs are pf, as are "has hidden . . . has given rest" (v 16) and "you kept . . . you threw" (v 17). Again impf verbs are used to fill out the psalm's assurances of what Hezekiah's acts of worship will be (vv 18–20).

The contrast is a familiar phenomenon in the Psalms, in a "before" and "after" confession of God's mercy and salvation. If the psalm is understood to be spoken before the answer to prayer is heard, it is called a psalm of petition or lament. If it is understood to be sung after the prayer has already been answered, it is called a thanksgiving psalm.

The psalm's inclusion at this point (it is not found in 2 Kgs 20) heightens the impression of Hezekiah's meekness, humility and piety. The Vision is careful to protect Hezekiah from blame for the 701 B.C. embarrassment. Chap. 22 put the blame on his ministers, Shebna and Hilkiah. With the prayer and psalm of this chapter, he is made a prime example of the meekness and humility that Yahweh demands from his new city and from his servants of the latter day (cf. 57:15; 66:2).

For more on the form and structure of the psalm see J. Begrich, *Der Psalm,* and K. Seybold, *Das Gebet,* 153.

The psalm may be outlined as follows:

I. I said/thought (vv 10–14).
  A. I am destined to death (vv 10–11).
     In Sheol I would not see,
       I would not look (v 11).
  B. My generation is plucked up and removed
     like my shepherd's tent (v 12a).
  C. I roll up my life
     like a weaver cutting his finished cloth (v 12b).
  D. I am ravaged
     by a lion who would break my bones (v 13).
  E. My eyes are cast down,
     like a bird I would chirp (14a–b).
  F. Bail me out, my Lord! (14c)

II. What can I say now? (15–17)
  A. (After) he has spoken to me?
     (After) he himself has done (it)?
     Shamed, I walk slowly all my years (15b–c).
  B. (After) my Lord has hidden me,
     let there be life to you, my heart (16a).
  C. (After) Yahweh has given my spirit rest,
     you make me well and I am kept alive (v 16b).
  D. In order to be whole, I had great bitterness.
     But you kept my life from extinction (v 17a–b).
  E. You threw all my sins behind your back (v 17c).

Conclusion (vv 18–20):
  Sheol cannot thank you.
  Only the living person can thank you.
  Let us play our instruments.

Comment

9 The superscription gives the setting within which the psalm is to be understood, i.e., the story of Hezekiah's illness and his recovery. This also reminds us that Hezekiah has been told that he is to die. But the psalm is not simply a cry for help. It looks at his attitude of despair on the prospect of death as a prior response, which has now been superseded by new assurance of life. The placement of the psalm after the announcement that his prayer has been heard and after the giving of a sign fits this perspective.

The poem is called a מכתם "psalm" (see n. 9.a above). This is a technical designation used several times in the Book of Psalms. But like a number of other such terms there, we do not know what it means.

10 *I said* in Heb. often has the sense "I thought." *In the noontide of my days* means something like "in the prime of life" (NEB). *The gates of Sheol* speaks of the realm of death and implies that they are closed like the gates of a prison. Homer spoke of death being like a prison (*Iliad* 9:312, 23:71). The OT does not use this phrase again, although Pss 107:18 and Job 38:17 speak of the gates of death or deep shadow. Later Jewish literature will use the term πύλαι ᾅδου "the gates of Hades" (Wis 16:13; 3 Macc 5:51). See the article by Colin Brown in the forthcoming Bromiley Festschrift (Grand Rapids: Eerdmans, 1987).

I am destined (פקדתי) uses a term that is familiar to the Vision but which usually refers to fixing the destiny of nations or cities (see *Excursus: Decide One's Fate* in *Isaiah 1–33*). Fixing the destiny of anyone is a function that only Yahweh does. It is a sovereign act which may imply judgment for sins but may also imply an act of mercy.

11 *See Yahweh in the land of the living* describes an essential distinction between living existence and that of being dead. Although the OT constantly reminds us that no one has seen God and lived, it also makes frequent references to experiences of the presence of God (cf. Gen 16:13; 32:31). Ps 27:4 speaks of seeing the beauty of Yahweh and of seeking his presence as the privileges of worship. "Seeing the face of God" is used as a formula for the experience of cultic worship in the Temple. It is this which will not be possible once one is in Sheol, where contact with God is cut off.

Look on humankind expresses another characteristic of death. The dead are cut off from human contact. *Inhabitants of non-being* is a literal translation of יושבי חדל (see n. 11.b). While Sheol can be thought of in terms of the place of the dead, it can also, as here, simply be thought of in the negation of all that life is. Death eliminates the two relationships that give meaning to life, those with God and those with human persons.

12 *My generation* (דורי) continues the idea of human contacts to focus attention on the psalmist's contemporaries, his family and friends. For this the figure of a *shepherd's tent* is used. Small and easily portable, the one-man tent can be struck in a moment, rolled up and carried away as the shepherd moves with his flock.

A *weaver's* work provides a second metaphor for the imminent death envisioned by the psalmist. The figure pictures a loom on which the woven cloth is carried along by the strong vertical threads (דלה). The finished woven cloth (ארג) is rolled up (קפד, see n. 12.d above) at the end and is cut loose (בצע) from the threads still on the loom (Wildberger, 1461). This technical language of the weaving trade is used to describe the sudden end of life. *From one day to its night* (the time needed for a weaver to complete a job) *you will finish me.*

13 *Ravaged by morning as by a lion.* The figure changes to picture the ravages of the body. This may be the result of illness (cf. Wildberger, 1462) or more likely is another picture of death. *Break all my bones* continues the lion imagery, but also brings up connotations of decay and death (cf. Num 24:8; Ps 141:7; Jer 50:17; Mic 3:3; Lam 3:4). Again the process is completed in a day.

14 Death also brings the loss of voice, the ability to speak. The psalm pictures it in terms of *chirping* or *moaning* like a bird. Only moans or groans are possible there. Parallels to this are found in 8:19, 10:14, and 29:4, each time in connection with the ghosts of the dead. (Cf. also 59:11.) The figure illustrates the deep humiliation that death would bring: *My eyes will be cast down, no longer looking up.*

My Lord introduces the cry for help. *Oppression* (עשקה) is a technical legal term for the pressure a debtor may feel from his creditor (cf. Jesus' picture of the oppressive creditor in Matt 18:28–30). Jeremiah charges Jerusalem with the practice of oppression (Jer 6:6; 22:17). It implies a form of pressure which the receiver cannot withstand. *Bail me out* (ערבני) is another legal term which speaks of someone who takes responsibility for the debt so as to relieve the pressure on the debtor. It is one who co-signs the note, who puts up bail for the debtor's freedom (cf. Prov 11:15; 20:16; 27:13; Ps 119:122). Wildberger (1463) notes the delicate nature of the situation in which the creditor (Yahweh) is asked to intervene by posting bail for the very debtor who is delinquent in a debt to him (cf. Job 17:3 for a parallel).

15 The rest of the psalm assumes that God *has spoken* and God *did it,* i.e., has answered the psalmist's prayer and posted the bail to gain his freedom from the destined death of v 10 (and for Hezekiah of v 1). Given God's gracious response, *what can* the psalmist *say?* What should be the life-style of the one who has been granted a divine reprieve from destined death? *Should I walk slowly?* Hezekiah first entertains the idea that the rest of his days should be spent in pious mourning, a living, somber example of the bitterness of his prior life. But the idea is immediately swept aside.

16 The psalmist's salvation is pictured in four terms: being *hidden, given rest,* made *well,* and *kept alive.* The gift of vitality is emphasized in *let there be life.* He calls on his *heart* (mind) and *spirit* to respond with signs of the granted life.

17 *For wholeness* (לשלום) sums up the gift of life and health which has now been granted. *I had great bitterness* is literally "bitterness was bitter to me" (see n. 17.a. above). The allusion is to v 15; both vv 15 and 17 refer to illness and undoubtedly in Hezekiah's case to political and military defeats. The great patriot and freedom fighter must swallow the bitter pill of total subjection to the Assyrian Empire for the rest of his life. But from his new perspective where God has saved his life he can testify that all this works together for a life of wholeness and health for body and spirit.

But as for you. The psalmist turns from speaking about his experience to giving testimony about God. This is pictured in two figures. The first portrays his predicament as being on the slippery edge of *the pit of extinction* (בלי). This is a cogent example of OT's lack of a general positive view of life beyond death. Death at best is lifeless existence among the shades in dust and darkness. At worst it is *extinction.* From falling into this condition, God's word and action had *kept back my life.* (The MT reads "you loved my life back from the pit"; see n. 17.b above.) *My life* (נפשי) may be translated "soul," but in either case it is to be understood as the entire being or personality.

All my sins. With this sentence a new perspective on the entire episode appears. There had been no hint in the first part of the psalm (or in Hezekiah's story) that sin and judgment had anything to do with the illness or the announcement of imminent death. Yet the OT recognizes the relation between sin and death from Gen 2:17; 3:4 onward. The story does not blame Hezekiah with the events that led to the Assyrian siege, although chap. 22 does pass judgment on his ministers for the disaster. The psalm speaks of sin in general, all of it. The same perspective will play a part in Israel's experience of a reprieve from the *extinction* that exile threatened. The issue of her sin, which DtH stressed so strongly, must be dealt with (cf. 40:2). *Threw . . . behind your back* is not a frequent expression of forgiveness or atonement. It portrays God taking those things that must occupy his attention and determine his relations when they are before him and throwing them behind him where he does not have to see them or take notice of them. He wiped the record clean. *Your back* is one of the expressions of anthropomorphism in the OT that help to make God personable. Moses was not allowed to see God's face, but only his back (Exod 33:23).

18 This last part of the psalm contrasts death and life in terms of the potential for faith and worship. *Death*—that is, the dead—and *Sheol*—that is, those who are in Sheol—are cut off from God and from participation in his worship. (Note the contrast to the NT hope for the believer of life with God and in the worship of God that is portrayed in Rev 7:9–17 *et passim.*) *Thank you, praise you,* and *hope for your faithfulness* together picture the life of faith and worship for the Israelite which is no longer possible in death.

19 On the other hand, those who compose the congregation at worship in the temple are *the living* (חי). They give thanks and testify to God's *faithfulness* and salvation as the psalmist (the king) and every worshiper do. The psalm implies that God gains no advantage by the death of his worshipers. Rather his will would be that they live and worship him. The OT consistently pictures Yahweh as the God of life, the living God, and avoids portraying him as God of death. This phrase draws on that understanding.

20 *To save me* closes the circle begun in v 15 with "he has spoken to me." Yahweh's sovereign word of grace became a deed, a fact in the believer's life. He will instruct his children concerning it. And this becomes a link in the chain of testimony to God's saving acts.

The psalm closes with an exhortation to fellow worshipers in the Temple to use all the opportunities of their lives to sing and play praises to God at the Temple. This is the answer to the question of 15b. The proper life-style for the one who has been sentenced to death but then given a divine reprieve is not continual grief but joyous worship.

Explanation

The psalm is the testimony of one who felt himself sentenced to death, who looked realistically at that stark possibility, appealed to God for divine intervention, received it, and now evaluates the meaning of life in terms of his opportunity to worship God.

The psalm fits the setting of Hezekiah's circumstances when the prophet had announced that he would die. In this setting it helps to change the perceived image of Judah's famous king from that of an incurable rebel and fighter for freedom to that of a man who has learned his lesson and found a greater meaning for life in pious humility, acceptance, and worship. The Vision reminds a later generation that might be tempted to revive the spirit of rebellion that had spurred Merodach-Baladan and Hezekiah (and which would dominate the Maccabees and the Zealots of later centuries) that Hezekiah's true reputation was built on his humble piety (2 Kgs 18:3–6; 2 Chr 29:2–31:21).

The psalm is also fitting to be sung by the post-exilic audience of the Vision. Their fathers at the fateful moments of the Babylonian conquest, destruction, and deportation must have thought: "In the gates of Sheol I am destined for the rest of my years. I shall not see Yahweh in the land of the living" (vv 10, 11). Yet at the point in which the Vision is experienced they, too, must testify, "He has spoken to me and he himself did it" (v 15). They, too, have to question what is the proper life-style for a people after the bitterness of their past history (v 15b). The psalm invited them to confess God's salvation, recognize that they are alive at that time because of it, and join in joyous pilgrimage to the new city of God to worship him.

The Vision will recognize how valid the plea, "Lord, bail me out!" (v 14) is for Israel (cf. 40:1–12). Thus the Vision calls upon all Jews to put the bad times behind them in view of the ways Yahweh has spared them and saved them. It, like the psalm, is a call to turn from sad remembrance of pain to joyous life in worshiping God.

The Christian reader will empathize with the thrust of the psalm, for the whole of Christian experience turns on the theme "from death to life" seen in the Crucifixion and Resurrection (Phil 2:6–9) and symbolized by baptism (Rom 6:4). Equally, the emphasis on the purpose of the redeemed life being worship and testimony fits the NT pattern.

Scene 7:
A Reading (continued): Hezekiah's Mistake (39:1–8)

Bibliography

(See the *Excursus: Babylon and the King of Babylon* in *Isaiah 1–33*)

Ackroyd, P. R. "An Interpretation of the Babylonian Exile: 2 Kings 20, Isaiah 38–39." *SJT* 27 (1974) 329–52. **Allen, L. C.** "Cuckoos in the Textual Nest at 2 Kings xx 13, Isa xlii 10, xlix 24, Ps xxii 17, and 2 Chron v 9." *JTS* 22 (1971) 143–150. **Mitchell, H. G.** "Isaiah on the Fate of His People and the Capital." *JBL* 37 (1918) 149–62. **Moriarty, F. L.** "Hezekiah, Isaiah, and Imperial Politics." *TBT* 19 (1965) 1270–76.

Translation

Reader: 1 *In that*[a] *time Merodach*[b]*-Baladan,*[c] *son of Baladan,*[c] *king*
of Babylon, sent letters[d] *and a present to Hezekiah when he*
heard[e] *that he had been ill but then was strong*[f] *again.* 2 *Hezekiah*
was glad[a] *about them and let them see his treasure rooms,*[b] *the*
silver and gold, the spices and the fine oil, his entire[c] *armory*[d]
and everything found in his warehouses. There was nothing in
his house or in all his kingdom that Hezekiah did not show them.
3 *Then Isaiah the prophet approached King Hezekiah and said*
to him: "What did these men say? And where did they come
from to you?" Then Hezekiah said: "They have come from a
distant land to me,[a] *from Babylon."* 4 *And he*[a] *said: "What did*
they see in your house?" Hezekiah replied: "They saw everything
in my house. There was nothing which I did not show them in
my warehouses."
5 *Then Isaiah said to Hezekiah: "Hear the word of Yahweh*
of Hosts.[a] 6 *'See! Days are coming when all of your house and*
whatever your fathers have stored up until this day will be
transported[a] *to Babylon.*[bc] *Nothing will be left over,' says Yahweh.*
7 *And some of your children that will be descended from you,*[a]
whom you beget, will be taken. And they will become eunuchs
in the palace of the king of Babylon."
8 *Then Hezekiah said to Isaiah: "Yahweh's word which you*
have spoken is good." Then he said: "If[a] *(only) there be peace*
and security[b] *in my days."*

Notes

1.a. K has ההוא "that" but many MSS and Q read the usual ההיא.

1.b. 2 Kgs 20:12 has בראדך "Berodach," but DSS[Isa] מרודך agrees with MT. The Akk name is *Markduk-apla-iddin(a)*. G. Rinaldi (*BeO* 16 [1974] 138) thinks the Heb vocalization of the name imitated the vowels of מְאָרָר "cursed be."

1.c. MT בַּלְאֲדָן "Baladan." DSS[Isa] בלאדין "Baladin" or בלאדון "Baladon." Baumgartner ("Zum hebräischen Lexikon," *Von Ugarit nach Qumran,* FS O. Eissfeldt, BZAW 77 [Berlin: Töpelmann, 1958] 27) reads the former and thinks it fits the Akk better than MT. Wildberger (1469) thinks the latter is more likely and was influenced by אָדוֹן *adhon* "lord."

1.d. MT סְפָרִים "letters." LXX *ἐπιστολὰς καὶ πρέσβεις καὶ δῶρα* "letters and ambassadors and gifts" perceives the need to list the emissaries since the rest of the story speaks of them, not of the letters or the gifts. A different vocalization of the Heb. could give סֹפְרִים "scribes," a position which included representation of the monarch in 36:3 and 37:2 (cf. Ehrlich, *Randglossen* 4:141, and KB). Kennicott knew of one MS that read סופרים, according to A. D. Crown ("Messengers and Scribes," *VT* 24 [1974] 368). The story presumes that letters and gifts must be delivered by messengers. It loses nothing by failing to mention them at this point.

1.e. 2 Kgs 20:12 has כי שמע "because he had heard," a variation in the syntax that is somewhat more precise.

1.f. DSS[Isa] ויחיה "but survived" matches the wording of Isaiah's oracle in 38:1. 2 Kgs 20:12 חזקיהו "Hezekiah" says nothing of his recovery and implies that the visit is one to the sick-bed. MT is correct.

2.a. MT וישמח "and he was glad." 2 Kgs 20:13 וישמע "and he heard." LXX *καὶ ἐχάρη . . . χαρὰν μεγάλην*, lit., "and he rejoiced a great joy." MT is to be kept.

2.b. DSS[Isa], some MSS, and 2 Kgs 20:13 insert כל "all."

2.c. כל "entire" is missing in 2 Kgs 20:13.

2.d. Dahood ("The Value of Ugaritic for Textual Criticism," *Bib* 40 [1959] 162) thinks this should mean "wine cellar." Wildberger (1470) disputes the strange interpretation.

3.a. MT אלי "to me" is missing in 2 Kgs 20:10.

4.a. LXX inserts Ἠσαίας "Isaiah."

5.a. צבאות "Hosts" is lacking in 2 Kgs 20:16 (cf. also n. 37:16.a).

6.a. MT ונשא "transported" is sg. DSS[Isa] has ונשאו, a pl. The change also seems to change a passive form into an impersonal active (see Kutscher, *Isaiah Scroll,* 44). But in Heb, the verb may often be sg at the beginning of a sentence when a pl follows (GKC § 145o).

6.b. MT בבל "Babylon" is accus of direction. 2 Kgs 20:17 בבלה "to Babylon" has a *heh*-directive. Wildberger (1470) notes that Jeremiah uses בבל frequently in this way (Jer 20:6; 24:1; 28:3).

6.c. DSS[Isa] inserts יביאו ו "they will come and"; Tg reads ויתובלו לבבל "and they will be carried to Babylon."

7.a. MT ממך "from you." DSS[Isa] ממעיכה "from your belly" (BDB, 588) is accepted by Kaiser. But Wildberger (1470) correctly defends MT by reference to Gen 10:14; 17:6; and 1 Chr 1:12.

8.a. 2 Kgs 20:19 reads הלוא אם "is it not (so), if" (cf. Delitzsch; BDB, 50) for MT's כי "if" and transposes יהיה "there be" to a position after "security," which hardly changes the sense. LXX δή "indeed, doubtless" reads כי as an assertative.

8.b. LXX translates δικαιοσύνη "righteousness."

Form/Structure/Setting

This story from 2 Kings fits the Vision's thematic purposes admirably (see *Explanation* below) despite the chronological problems in relating it to Hezekiah's illness after the 701 B.C. siege (see Wildberger, 1474–75, and the commentaries on Kings). "When he heard that he was ill and then was strong again" relates it to a time shortly after his illness, perhaps the same time as is depicted in chap. 22.

Yet the story does not develop as a formal visit to a sick friend. Isaiah's response reflects suspicion that a great deal more was taking place. Is it possible that the illness is here a metaphor for Hezekiah's vassalage to Assyria and that his recovery of strength refers to his announcement that he was throwing off that yoke at the time of Sargon's death? A visit from a major leader of rebellion in the east to one who was potentially a leader for rebellion in the west would make political sense. Josephus understood the action in those terms (*Antiq.* X.ii.2). In that case, the date for these events was between 705 and 703 B.C., some three to five years before the siege, a period when Hezekiah still had treasures to show, and the story is out of chronological order. Furthermore, the illness referred to is not that of 701 B.C., told about in the previous chapter. The sequence of stories ignores these historical niceties to make its thematic point concerning the exile of the royal house. Hezekiah's divine reprieve is temporary. His descendants will not be so privileged.

Merodach-Baladan was a cunning chieftain of the Yakin tribe from a territory east of the mouth of the Euphrates river. He conquered and ruled Babylon from 722–711B.C. and reconquered it for two years from 705–703 B.C. The Vision has drawn on this account to portray his earlier reign in chap. 13. He is the terrible king of Babylon pictured in chap. 14. News of his fall in 711 B.C. is presented in chap. 21. (See *Comment* on these chapters and the *Excursus: Babylon and the King of Babylon* in *Isaiah 1–33.*) In each of these chapters, Merodach-Baladan is a basic symbol of the incalcitrant rebel who never gives up, exactly the model the Vision is urging Israel and Judah not to emulate.

This story with its reference to Merodach-Baladan and to Babylon, which the author/composer of the Vision found in 2 Kgs 18–20, had a tremendous influence on the Vision.

The comment about Hezekiah's descendants (v 7) refers to Jehoiachin's removal to Babylon in 598 B.C. with his household and to his services in behalf of the Babylonian emperor Amel-Marduk, who is known in the OT as Evil-Merodach. The comment sets the stage for references to Babylonian captivity in the following act and for the fall of Babylon in chap. 47.

The story has a simple outline:

V 1: Stage setting—letters, a gift and delegates from Merodach-Baladan
V 2: Hezekiah's joy and openness with apparent agreement
Vv 3–4: Isaiah's questions
Vv 5–7: Isaiah's oracle from Yahweh: "All your house—to Babylon to serve the King of Babylon"
V 8: Hezekiah accepts the judgment

The outline is common to the genre of a judgment story. Cf. the story of Naboth's vineyard (1 Kgs 21:1–27) with its account of what happened, a prophet's questions, an oracle, and a response.

The narrative is built around the word בית "house" which occurs in v 2 (three times), v 4 (twice) and in v 6 (once, but has אבתיך "of your fathers" and in v 7 בניך "of your children," both of which are close in sound and spelling to בית "house"). When the narrative speaks of the palace of the king of Babylon (v 7), it uses a very different word. So the story tells how Hezekiah gained "peace and security" for himself at the expense of his "house" both in the sense of riches and strength and the sense of family and progeny. Hezekiah's rebellion put his dynasty, his family, and his descendants at risk. Both he and they would lose by it.

So this story, like the preceding one, has built into it a delayed judgment. Hezekiah would not experience deportation, but his descendants would be exiled to Babylon. The readers/hearers of the Vision would have been keenly aware of the irony inherent in its fulfillment when Jehoiachin and his family were taken to spend the rest of their lives in Babylon (2 Kgs 24:10–16).

Comment

1 *At that time* sets the story-time by the passage that precedes it. Both the Vision and 2 Kings 20 tell these stories in the same order, which creates a historical problem since the dates of Merodach-Baladan's power in Babylon do not coincide with this time period. The story is told here, not because of chronology, but because it is thematically appropriate. The mention of *Merodach-Baladan,* king of Babylon from 722–711 B.C. and 705–703 B.C. and a major rebel against Assyrian authority in the east, suggests some communication concerning collaboration against Assyria. Hezekiah's illness was either an excuse for the expedition or a veiled reference to Hezekiah's forced vassalage under Sargon II from 714–705 B.C.

2 *Hezekiah was glad.* The message was welcome and undoubtedly encouraged Hezekiah to accelerate his moves toward rearmament and independence. He wanted to impress his potential ally with his readiness to go to war. He showed his treasures and his armory—everything. Babylon was too far away for Hezekiah to consider it a threat to Jerusalem. And Merodach-Baladan's resistance would probably keep Sennacherib busy in Mesopotamia for a long time. That second front would be of great benefit to Judah as it worked to build up its own capacity to withstand the inevitable Assyrian assault to come.

3 *Isaiah* was suspicious. The Vision knows of traditions (chaps. 7–8 and 20) that establish the prophet's consistent stand against rebellion and his support for policies of loyal service to Assyria, although Dtr did not include these in his history. Isaiah's questions imply disapproval of this diplomacy. Hezekiah's reply confirms his worst fears.

5–7 The *word from Yahweh* "makes the punishment fit the crime." Whereas Hezekiah had shown *everything in his house* to the emissaries, *all his house* and all his inheritance would in time be *transported to Babylon.* Some of his descendants would become servants in *the palace of the king of Babylon.* This is a remarkable prediction of the Babylonian captivity, especially the events of 598 B.C. when Jehoiachin and his family were taken away by Nebuchadnezzar with everything else of value from Jerusalem's palace.

8 Hezekiah's piety is demonstrated in his acceptance of Yahweh's word. His weakness is implied when no political decisions to reverse his course are recorded. Chap. 22, as well as chaps. 36–37, show the immediate results in the Assyrian siege of 701 B.C. On reading this a century and a half later, the exiles' response must have been bitter: "That is all right for him to say. But what about us?" The effect of that resignation without regard to those who were to follow him is heightened by the last line: *if only there be peace and security in my days.* אמת, here translated *security,* is "that which is firm, is true, has integrity." The Vision has built on that idea in recording the scene of Isaiah's meeting with Ahaz (chap. 7). Here it is used in the simple sense of "security."

Explanation

Merodach-Baladan's message to Hezekiah is a story that was heard on at least three levels. First, it was read as a story joined to other prophet-king stories. It undoubtedly reflected a judgment on Hezekiah for failure to consult Yahweh about his foreign policy and for dependence on a heathen foreign ally (Merodach-Baladan).

On a second level it was incorporated into DtH with the other Isaiah/Hezekiah stories as illustrations of God's judgment on the Kingdom of Judah. DtH is a work completed in the Babylonian period (after 605 B.C.) and would already have been very interested in relating the story to the Babylon of Nebuchadnezzar. By that time Babylon had succeeded Assyria to imperial authority and become a genuine threat to Judah greater than any threat from Assyria had been. DtH was well aware that the delayed judgment expressed in v 8 was in process of being fulfilled.

On a third level, the Vision has placed this story with the others in chaps. 36–39. There they represent that Babylonian period when all these delayed judgments were so thoroughly fulfilled. Like the other stories, this one supplied themes that were to be used throughout the Vision: "Babylon" in chaps. 13–14, 19, and 47; the error of dependence on foreign help in chaps. 18, 23, and 30–33; and the depiction of the rebellious spirit's shallow self-interest which shows little concern for the future of the dynasty or its institutions.

Hezekiah had become so engrossed in his dream of freedom that he reacted with naïve, almost childish, joy to the idea of a new adventure suggested by Merodach-Baladan's letters. His failure to assess carefully the situation compromised his throne, his palace, the Temple, all his possessions, his capital city, and even the future generations of his own family. All this he surrendered for the impossible dream of freedom and independence. It was fantasy because it was not based on God's strategy and God's leading. Hezekiah was satisfied to have things go well for the moment: the temporary relief of Jerusalem (chap. 37), fifteen additional years of life (chap. 38), and peaceful security for his moment in time (chap. 39). He lacked the longer view and the patient character to work for it. His piety was the prayer of the moment. The Vision calls for a faith that relates to the ongoing purposes of God which have a glorious past and an assured future. Hezekiah's piety was not of that sort.

Act VII: Good News for Jerusalem (40:1–44:23)

THE SEVENTH GENERATION:
KING JEHOIACHIN (*ca.* 586–540 B.C.)

The turbulence of the fighting and deportation is past. The exiles settle in various parts of Mesopotamia. Groups in Palestine survive in woeful and desperate straits. In Egypt others struggle to survive. But those in Mesopotamia adapt more easily and establish stable communities. They are addressed in this act.

This act records pivotal changes for the Vision. Instead of the judgment/curse announced in 6:9–13, it announces a policy of blessing/salvation (40: 1–2, 9–11). It also announces that Jerusalem's "warfare is at an end" (40:2). Israel's history from Joshua to the end of the kingdoms was marked by warfare. God's new era shifts the burden of war to others. Israel and Jerusalem no longer have to fill that role. They receive another calling.

Major problems remain. The people are scattered in exile. Jerusalem is in ruins. And no one has emerged as Yahweh's leader and champion for his people.

In this act Yahweh's plan takes shape. Cyrus will become the political and military ruler for Yahweh. Israel is called to be servant, messenger, and witness for him. Jerusalem will be restored. So Yahweh calls upon Israel in exile to comfort Jerusalem with news of help, to bear witness to Yahweh's majesty and power to save, and to witness to his announced plan to use Cyrus. Yahweh will give him Babylon and has promised him Egypt as well.

But Israel proves reluctant to commit herself to this task (40:3–8, 27; 42:18–25; 43:22–24). Yahweh encourages her to recognize this as a new day of hope.

The act has a prologue and five scenes.

Prologue:	The Hall of Voices (40:1–9)
Scene 1:	Like a Shepherd (40:10–31)
Scene 2:	Israel Affirmed as Yahweh's Servant (41:1–20)
Scene 3:	Yahweh Defends His Authority and His Choice of Israel (41:21–42:12)
Scene 4:	Hear, You Deaf! (42:13–43:21)
Scene 5:	Remember These, Jacob! (43:22–44:23)

Chapters 40–48 are usually treated as a unit. But R. F. Melugin (*The Formation of Isaiah 40–55*, BZAW 141 [Berlin: DeGruyter, 1976] 90, 123) has shown good reasons to treat 40:1–43:23 separately. Both Acts VII and VIII are addressed to "Jacob/Israel" in Babylonian exile. In Act VII they are called to be Yahweh's "servant," while in Act VIII Cyrus is the called "servant."

Excursus: Deutero-Isaiah

Bibliography

COMMENTARIES

See *Isaiah 1–33,* pp. xxxviii–xli, for commentaries on the entire book. Commentaries on chapters 40–55 (or 66) are repeated here.

Bonnard, P. E. *Le Second Isaïe, son disciple et leurs éditeurs.* EB. Paris: J. Gabalda, 1972. **Elliger, K.** *Jesaja II* (complete through 45:7). BKAT 11. Neukirchen-Vluyn: Neukirchener Verlag, 1978. **Herbert, A. S.** *The Book of the Prophet Isaiah 40–66.* CBC. Cambridge: The University Press, 1975. **Knight, G. A. F.** *Deutero-Isaiah.* A Theological Commentary on Isaiah 40–55. New York/Nashville: Abingdon Press, 1965 = *Servant Theology:* A Commentary on the Book of Isaiah 40–55. ITC. Grand Rapids: Eerdmans, 1984. **McKenzie, J. L.** *Second Isaiah.* AB 20. Garden City, NY: Doubleday, 1968. **Muilenburg, J.** "The Book of Isaiah." *IB* 5. New York/Nashville: Abingdon Press, 1956. 382–773. **North, C. R.** *The Second Isaiah.* Oxford: Clarendon Press, 1964. **Smart, J. D.** *History and Theology in Second Isaiah: A Commentary on Isaiah 35, 40–66.* Philadelphia: Westminster Press, 1965. **Volz, P.** *Jesaja II.* Zweite Hälfte: 40–66. KAT 10. Leipzig: W. Scholl, 1932. **Westermann, C.** *Das Buch Jesaia 40–66.* ATD 19. Göttingen: Vandenhoeck & Ruprecht, 1966 = ET *Isaiah 40–66: A Commentary.* OTL. Tr. D. M. G. Stalker. Philadelphia: Westminster Press, 1969. **Whybray, R. W.** *Isaiah 40–66.* NCBC. Grand Rapids: Eerdmans, 1975.

MONOGRAPHS AND ARTICLES (recent and selected)

Balzer, D. *Ezechiel und Deuterojesaja.* BZAW 121. Berlin: Walter de Gruyter, 1971. **Banwell, B. O.** "A Suggested Analysis of Isaiah 40–66." *EvT* 76 (1964/65) 166. **Boer, P. A. H. de.** *Second Isaiah's Message.* OTS 40. Leiden: E. J. Brill, 1956. **Bonnard, P. E.** "Relire Isaïe 40–66." *ETR* 50 (1975) 351–59. ———. "Second Isaïe: Nature de la Réalité suprême et sens d'une Conception de Base." *URAM* 4 (1981) 103–21. **Canellas, G.** "El universalismo en el Deuteroisaias." *CuB* 35 (1978) 3–20. **Conrad, E. W.** "Second Isaiah and the Priestly Oracle of Salvation." *ZAW* 93 (1981) 234–46. **Gamper, A.** "Der Verkündigungsauftrag Israels nach Deutero-Jesaja." *ZKT* 91 (1969) 411–29. **Gitay, Y.** "Deutero-Isaiah: Oral or Written?" *JBL* 99 (1980) 185–97. ———. *Prophecy and Persuasion: A Study of Isaiah 40–48.* Forum Theologiae Linguisticae 14. Bonn: Linguistica Biblica, 1981. **Haran, M.** "The Literary Structure and Chronological Framework of the Prophecies in Is. XL–XLVIII." *Congress Volume Bonn.* VTSup 9. Leiden: E. J. Brill, 1963. 127–55. **Holmgren, F.** *With Wings of Eagles: An Interpretation.* Chappaqua, NY: Biblical Scholars Press, 1973. **Kapelrud, A. S.** "The Main Concern of Second Isaiah." *VT* 32 (1982) 50–58. **Klein, R. W.** "Going Home—A Theology of Second Isaiah." *CurTM* 5 (1978) 198–210. **Koch, R.** "Die Theologie des Deutero-Isaias." *TGl* 9 (1966) 20–30. **Melugin, R. F.** "Deutero-Isaiah and Form Criticism." *VT* 21 (1971) 326–37. ———. *The Formation of Isaiah 40–55.* BZAW 141. Berlin: de Gruyter, 1976. **Mowinckel, S.** "Die Komposition des deuterojesanischen Buches." *ZAW* 49 (1931) 87–112, 242–60. **Nielsen, E.** "Deuterojesaja. Erwägungen zur Formkritik, Traditions und Redaktionsgeschichte." *VT* 20 (1970) 190–205. **Odendaal, D. H.** "The 'Former' and the 'New Things' in Isaiah 40–48." *OTWSA 1967* (1971) 64–75. **Paul, S.** "Literary and Ideological Echoes of

Jeremiah in Deutero-Isaiah." *Proceedings of the Fifth World Congress of Jewish Studies* 1969 (Jerusalem, 1971) 102–20. **Radai, Y. T.** "Identity of the Second Isaiah According to Y. D. Brach" (Heb. with Eng. Summary). *BMik* 52 (1972) 74–76. **Rignell, L. G.** *A Study of Isaiah ch. 40–55.* Lund: C. W. K. Gleerup, 1956. **Scheiber, A.** "Der Zeitpunkt des Auftretens von Deuterojesaja." *ZAW* 84 (1972) 242–43. **Schmitt, H.-C.** "Prophetie und Schultheologie in Deuterojesajabuch." *ZAW* 91 (1979) 43–61. **Schoors, A.** "Die Anklagen verurteilt." *Schrift* 34 (1974) 123–58. **Spykerboer, H. C.** *The Structure and Composition of Deutero-Isaiah.* Diss. Groningen, 1976. **Stuhlmueller, C.** "Deutero-Isaiah: Major Transitions in the Prophet's Theology and in Contemporary Scholarship." *CBQ* 42 (1980) 1–29. **Torrey, C. C.** *The Second Isaiah.* Edinburgh: T. & T. Clark, 1928. **Vasholz, R.** "Isaiah versus 'the Gods': A Case for Unity" (48–49). *WTJ* 42 (1980) 389–94. **Westermann, C.** *Sprache und Struktur der Prophetie Deuterojesajas.* Calwer Theol. Monographien 11. Calwer, 1981.

Ibn Ezra (A.D. 1167) questioned the 8th-century Isaiah's authorship of chaps. 40–66. But Eichhorn (*Einleitung in das Alte Testament* [Leipzig, 1783] 3:76–97) and Döderlein (*Esaias* [1775] xii–xv) first developed the question into a suggestion that the chapters should be treated as a separate literary work (see O. Eissfeldt, *The Old Testament: An Introduction,* tr. P. R. Ackroyd [New York: Harper and Row, 1965] 304). Later many interpreters would restrict this work to chaps. 40–55, treating the rest as a third unit (see *Excursus: Trito-Isaiah*).

The date suggested for these chapters was based on references to Cyrus, the first Persian emperor, in chaps. 44–45. He rose to power in the decade before 540 B.C. and entered Babylon in 539 B.C. A second basis for thinking of the material as having been written within this time-frame was the presentation of Babylon, not Assyria, as Israel's principal enemy. Assyria was destroyed as a power between 617 and 609 B.C. Babylon was responsible for the final destruction of Jerusalem in 598 and 587 B.C.

Chaps. 40–55 have usually been interpreted as a compositional unit written by one author who lived in Babylon as a part of the Babylonian exilic community. He is sometimes called "the great prophet of the Exile." However, some think of the "servant poems" (42:1–4; 49:1–6; 50:4–9; 52:13–53:12) as separate compositions that were inserted into the larger text. (See *Excursus: Identifying the "Servant of Yahweh."*)

Some conservative scholars have opposed the division, maintaining the unity of the entire book, the authorship by Isaiah in the 8th century B.C., and these chapters as predictive prophecy (see O. T. Allis, *The Unity of Isaiah* [Philadelphia: Reformed Publ. Co., 1950]; E. J. Young, *Studies in Isaiah* [London: Tyndale Press, 1955], and *Who Wrote Isaiah?* [Grand Rapids: Eerdmans, 1958]).

But the arguments for a 6th-century date have proved decisive for most interpreters. These chapters have thus become the major source for understanding the attitudes of exilic and post-exilic Jews (J. Blenkinsopp, *A History of Prophecy in Israel* [Philadelphia: Westminster, 1983] 207–24). R. N. Whybray (20–30) even provides a biography and analysis of the supposed 6th-century prophet who wrote these chapters. Of course, the only evidence for the existence of such a person and all data for the biography had to be extrapolated from these chapters. There are no external data about him, nor is he even named or mentioned here.

The isolation of these chapters has proved extraordinarily fruitful. The message to the exiles contains some of the best theological thinking and writing in the OT. Its insistence on pure monotheism ("I alone am God"), on developing the Exodus and Creation paradigms theologically (see *Excursus: Exodus Typology* and *Excursus:* ברא *"Create"/"Creator"*), and the presentation of the Servant of Yahweh passages (see *Excursus: Identifying the "Servant of Yahweh"*) have proved to be theological mines well worth excavating repeatedly.

This commentary agrees that the unique quality of chaps. 40–54 sets them apart from those before and after. But it also notes many features that relate them closely to chaps. 55–66 and others that bind them to chapters that precede them. It views them as compositional features, created to present the succeeding generations that they represent rather than clues to a separate authorship and a different date. It thinks of these chapters, like the rest of the book, as being a product of the late fifth century. Their extraordinary ability to evoke the mood and situation of the exile are a tribute to the creative power that fashioned them.

Excursus: The Formation of Chapters 40–66

Bibliography

Begrich, J. *Studien zu Deuterojesaja.* BWANT 77. Stuttgart: Kohlhammer, 1938 = TB 20. Munich: Kaiser, 1969.[2] **Clark, K. C.** *An Analysis of Is 40 (:1)–44:23 Utilizing the Creation-Redemption of the Creator King and Process Theology.* Diss. Claremont, 1977. **Elliger, K.** *Deuterojesaja in seinem Verhältnis zu Tritojesaja.* BWANT 11. Stuttgart: Kohlhammer, 1933. **Gileadi, A.** *A Holistic Structure of the Book of Isaiah.* Diss. Brigham Young, 1981. **Goldingay, J.** "The Arrangement of Isaiah xl–xlv." *VT* 29 (1979) 289–99. **Gressman, H.** "Die literarische Analyse Deuterojasaja." *ZAW* 35 (1914) 254–97. **Haran, M.** "The Literary Structure and Chronological Framework of the Prophecies in Isaiah xl–xlviii." *Congress Volume, Bonn, 1962.* VTSup 9. Leiden: E. J. Brill, 1963. 127–55. **Hessler, E.** *Gott der Schöpfer. Ein Beitrag zur Komposition und Theologie Deuterojesajas.* Diss. Greifswald, 1961. **Köhler, L.** *Deuterojesaja (Jes 40–55) stilkritisch untersucht.* BZAW 37. Giessen: Töpelmann, 1923. **Lack, R.** "La strutturazione de Isaia 40–55." *La Scuola Cattolica* 101 (1975) 43–58. **Liebreich, L. J.** "The Compilation of the Book of Isaiah." *JQR* 46 (1955/56) 259–77; 47 (1956/57) 114–138. **Melugin, R.** *The Formation of Isaiah 40–55.* BZAW 141. Berlin: de Gruyter, 1976. **Mowinckel, S.** "Die Komposition des deuterojesajanischen Buches." *ZAW* 49 (1931) 87–112, 242–60. ———. "Neuere Forschung zu Deuterojesaja, Tritojesaja, und dem 'Ebad-Jahwe-Problem." *AcOr* 16 (1937) 1–40. **Spykerboer, H. C.** *The Structure and Composition of Deutero-Isaiah.* Diss. Groningen, 1976. **Waldow, H. E. von.** *Anlass und Hintergrund der Verkündigung des Deuterojesajas.* Diss. Bonn, 1953. **Westermann, C.** "Sprache und Structur des Prophetie Deuterojesajas." *Forschung am Altentestament.* TB 24. Munich: Kaiser, 1964. 92–170.

Since the decision was made to treat Isaiah as two books and subsequently to divide the second part into two books, discussion of the formation and organization of these chapters has been lively, as the *Bibliography* above testifies.

The present commentary treats the book (all 66 chapters) as a single literary whole (see my *Isaiah 1–33,* xli–l). The book is presented as a kind of drama, divided into acts and scenes, each of which relates to a generation of Israel's life from the mid-eighth century to the mid-fifth century B.C.

Chaps. 34–66 contain several signs that mark the breaks. Chaps. 36–39 are an insertion from 2 Kings. Their narrative prose style sets them off from material on both sides. They stand with chaps. 34–35 to form Act VI of the Vision of Isaiah.

Chap. 40 begins a distinctive style emphasizing lengthy Yahweh speeches which continues to the end of chap. 66. Three times within those chapters a strange theme breaks the flow. Twice it appears in identical words: "There is no peace, says Yahweh, for the adversaries" (48:22; 57:21; and 66:24).

These mark the main divisions: 40–48, 49–57, and 58–66. Further analysis suggests that each of these has been divided in two, yielding the following divisions: 40:1–44:23; 44:24–48:22; 49:1–52:12; 52:13–57:21; 58:1–61:11; 62:1–66:24. Internal consistency and relevance to the historical setting support this division (see the historical introduction to each act).

The first six acts of the Vision (chaps. 1–39) are dominated by the curse (see chap. 6). The last six (chaps. 40–66) stand under the gracious promise of comfort and blessing (40:1–9). The first five acts (chaps. 1–33) are set against the background of Assyria's rise and rule. The sixth (chaps. 34–39) depicts Babylon's dominance. The seventh (40:1–44:23) is set in the last years of Babylon's rule, already under the influence of Cyrus's approach. The eighth to the twelfth acts are set against a Persian background in which the books of Ezra-Nehemiah are a welcome companion and aid to understanding.

In a remarkable way, chaps. 65–66 echo themes of chaps. 1–4 to tie the entire Vision into one whole. The promise in 2:1–4 of Zion being raised to the top of the mountains with peoples streaming to it is fulfilled in 66:1–24 as restored Zion becomes the centerpiece of Yahweh's new heavens and new earth.

Excursus: Form-Critical Categories in Chapters 40–66

Bibliography

Alonso-Schökel, L. "Genera litteraria prophetica (ad librum recentum C. Westermann)." *VD* 39 (1961) 185–92. **Begrich, J.** "Das priesterliche Heilsorakel." *ZAW* 52 (1934) 81–92 = *Gesammelte Studien zum Alten Testament.* ThB 21. Munich: Kaiser, 1964. 217–31. **Bonnard, P.-E.** *Le Second Isaïe,* 28–36. **Caspari, W.** *Lieder und Gottessprüche der Rückwanderer* (Jes 40–55). BZAW 65. Giessen: Topelmann, 1934. **Gressmann, H.** "Die literarische Analyse Deuterojesajas." *ZAW* 34 (1914) 254–97. **Harner, P. B.** "The Salvation Oracle in Second Isaiah." *JBL* 88 (1969) 418–34. **Hermisson, H. J.** "Discussionsworte bei Deuterojesaja." *EvT* 31 (1971) 665–80. **Irons, L.** *A Form-Critical Study of the Trial Speeches in Deutero-Isaiah.* Diss. Vanderbilt, 1976. **Köhler, L.** *Deuterojesaja stilkritisch untersucht.* BZAW 37. Giessen: Töpelmann, 1923. **Melugin, R. F.** "Deutero-Isaiah and Form Criticism. *VT* 21 (1971) 326–37. **Schoors, A.** "The *Riv* Pattern in Is 40–55." *Bijdragen* 30 (1969) 25–31. ———. *I am God Your Saviour: A Form-Critical Study of the Main Genres in Isaiah xl–lv.* VTSup 24. Leiden: E. J. Brill, 1973. **Schüpphaus, J.** "Stellung und Funktion der sogenannten Heilsankündigung bei Deuterojesaja. *TZ* 27 (1971) 161–81. **Stuhlmueller, C.** *Creative Redemption.* 264–67. **Waldow, H. E. von.** *Anlass und Hintergrund der Verkündigung des Deuterojesajas.* Diss. Bonn, 1933, especially "Die Gattungen bei Dtjes," 11–61. **Westermann, C.** "Das Heilswort bei Deuterojesaja." *EvT* 24 (1964) 355–73.
See also the commentaries of Muilenberg and Westermann, and the monograph by R. P. Merendino, *Der Erste und der Letzte, passim.*

Gressmann began the form-critical analysis of speeches in Deutero-Isaiah when he called for abandonment of analyses that viewed the book as an essential unit in favor of analyses of small units. Köhler, Mowinckel, Caspari, Elliger, Begrich, von Waldow, and Westermann have led the parade of those who accepted his challenge.

Schoors summarized the stand of form-critical studies in 1973 by grouping genre in two types: words of salvation including oracles and proclamations, and polemic genres including trial speeches and disputations. Studies since that time have hardly moved beyond this point.

While this commentary acknowledges the great advances in recognition of form and style which this movement has achieved, its essential stance has moved back to a position *ante quo* Gressmann. It looks at the book of Isaiah's Vision as a whole, searching for the signs of composition and unity that define it, and seeing the smaller units as elements of that whole single composition. The book is not seen as a collection of pre-existing small units, but as a single great drama built up of speeches that are created for their own place within the book. The unit from prophetic tradition or from prophetic history (chaps. 36–39) is seen as the exception, not the rule.

This approach preserves the gains made by form criticism while remaining free of its limitations. The work of isolating separate speeches and identifying their genres is essential to understanding the Vision as drama. But the dramatic form allows the speeches to be read within the larger context of the book without endangering their individual distinctiveness. As in form-criticism, the question of setting is crucial, although it is posed differently: instead of determining the life-setting of each speech, this commentary tries to identify its stage-setting.

Historical Background

Bibliography

Ackroyd, P. R. *Exile and Restoration.* Philadelphia: Westminster, 1968. 17–38. **Aharoni and Avi-Yonah.** *MBA,* 146, 161, 168. **Bright.** *HI,* 343–59. **Frye, R. N.** *The History of Ancient Iran.* Munich: C. H. Beck'sche, 1984. **Herodotus.** (Gr and Eng). Tr. A. D. Godley. 4 vols. New York: Putnam's, 1921–24. **König, F. W.** *Die Persika des Ktesias von Knidos.* Graz: Weidner, 1972. **Oded, B.** "Judah and Exile." *IJH,* 476–88. **Smith, S.** *Isaiah Chapters XL–LV.* London: British Academy, 1944. 24–48. **Soggin, J. A.** *A History of Ancient Israel.* Tr. J. Bowden. Philadelphia: Westminster, 1984. 248–57.

Events of the late seventh century B.C. and the first half of the sixth, from a Palestinian perspective, were dominated by rivalry between Babylon and Egypt. A broader perspective reveals that four powers were rivals for Assyria's vacant throne. They were Lydia, Media, Babylon, and Egypt. Media and Babylon collaborated in the defeat of Nineveh and then signed a treaty of peace. This freed Babylon to turn her attention westward toward Palestine and Egypt, while Media concentrated on campaigns to the north and north-west.

Media's Cyaxares was hampered by an invasion of Scythians from the north, but used twenty-eight years of vassalage to them to strengthen his hold on Armenia, Cappadocia, and Parthia. His attempt to push beyond the Halys river into Lydia failed. Lydia under Croesus consolidated her hold on the Ionian Greek cities of the Aegean coast and on the western half of Asia Minor. The trade from the Black Sea and Mediterranean areas made her rich. The influx of Greek culture made her strong.

Nebuchadnezzar rebuilt Babylon and returned some of the lost luster to that ancient city. Meanwhile, Pharaoh Necho consolidated his territory in a bid to succeed Assyria. Although Babylon defeated Egypt handily, it is clear that the Neo-Babylonian Empire lived under the shadow of powerful empires to the north. Babylon's power lay in Nebuchadnezzar, who died in 562 B.C. He was succeeded by Amel-Marduk, who released Jehoiachin from prison (2 Kgs 25:27–30) and may have entertained thoughts of returning him to Jerusalem. In 556 B.C. Nabunaid (the Greeks call him Nabonidus) of Haran displaced him. He was more interested in reforming religious institutions than in building the empire. He weakened the position of the priests and temples of Marduk in Babylon. Then he withdrew to the oasis of Tema, leaving administration in Babylon to Belsharazur, known in Dan 8:1 as Belshazzar. Babylon's power barely outlived Nebuchadnezzar. Its moment in the sun was in fact a brief interim between the rules of Assyria and Media-Persia.

In 559 B.C. Cyrus II became the ruler of one Persian tribe in Parsagarda and a vassal to King Anshan. Through a series of fortuitous circumstances he quickly united all Persia under his flag. In 555 B.C. Nabunaid sought an ally against Media and found him in Cyrus. Cyrus promptly rebelled against Media, allowing Nabunaid to recapture Haran, his birthplace, from the Medes. Two Median armies decided in the field to join Cyrus. With their addition to his forces he quickly made himself master of Media, ruling from Ecbatana. This was the Media-Persian alliance that was to become the greatest empire the world had seen.

At Nebuchadnezzar's death in 562 B.C., no one could have forseen the turn of events which in the next twelve years would make the prince of an obscure Persian tribe a threat before which Babylon trembled. Babylon at mid-century was ruled by a surrogate, Belshazzar. Corruption, economic failure, military weakness and religious confusion characterized its life. Although Nabunaid had credited Babylon's god, Marduk, for his own rise to power, now the Marduk temples were neglected. Nabunaid was committed to Sin, the moon god in Tema. As pressure grew on his borders, he protected the idols from town temples by transporting them to Babylon, until the city was refuge for dozens of these sacred objects.

It was a hopeless time in which dreams and oracles shaped history and events. Nabunaid dreamed that Marduk called him to Babylon in the first place. He dreamed of the rise of Cyrus, and promptly made him his ally. When Cyrus faced Croesus at Sardis, Apollo at Delphi predicted victory for Croesus. The oracle had to be hastily revised when Cyrus won.

Yet the gods and their cult personnel were considered an important part of life. A conqueror or ruler ignored them at his own risk because of their influence on the people. Nebuchadnezzar had faithfully "taken the hand of Marduk" in the annual festival and had spent huge sums to build and restore his temples in Babylon. When Nabunaid failed to do either after 550 B.C., he lost support both from priests and people. Cyrus learned early on the value of appeasing the gods (and their priests). It was useful to arrange for a good oracle well before he arrived. He developed a reputation for restoring local cults and their temples. This pleased both priests and people wherever he went. This also fit in perfectly with Yahweh's announced plans for the restoration of his Temple in Jerusalem.

Secure in his treaty with Babylon, Cyrus had turned his attention to other rivals. By 546 B.C. he had defeated Croesus, king of Lydia, adding that kingdom to his growing empire. He was ready to turn his attention to the south and west into Mesopotamia and toward Egypt. Whereas in 612 B.C. four militant nations vied for Assyria's empire, by mid-century only one was still expansive and growing. Cyrus II was its ruler.

Prologue: In the Hall of Voices (40:1–9)

Bibliography

Botterweck, G. J. "Die Frohbotschaft vom Kommen Jahwes (Jes 40:1–11)." *BibLeb* 15 (1974) 227–34. **Chiesa, B.** "Consolate, consolate il mio popolo . . ." (Isa 40:1–5, 9–11). *BeO* 14 (1972) 265–73. **Conrad, E. W.** "The 'Fear Not' Oracles in Second Isaiah." *VT* 44 (1984) 129–52. **Dijk, H. J. van.** "Consolamini, consolamini, popule meus?" *VD* 45 (1967) 342–46. **Ettore, F.** "Is. 40:1–11: una lettura strutturale." *RevistB* 28 (1980) 285–304. **Fischer, G.** "Die Redewendung דבר על לב im AT. Ein Beitrag zum Verständnis von Jes 40,2." *Bib* 65 (1984) 244–50. **Fisher, R. W.** "The Herald of the Good News in Second Isaiah (40:9; 41:27; 52:7)." *PTMS* 1 (1974) 117–32. **Fokkelman, J. P.** "Stylistic analysis of Isaiah 40:1–11." *OTS* 21 (1981) 68–90. **Galbiati, G.** " 'Nel deserto preparate la via . . .' (Isaia 40,3 e le sue citazioni)." *RicBR* 15 (1981) 7–46. **Garofalo, S.** "Prepare la strada al Signore." *RevistB* 6 (1958) 131–34. **Grindel, J. A.** *The Gospel's Use of Is 40:3 and Qumran.* Vincentian Studies 1. New York: St. John's University, 1968. **Hergesel, A. T.** *Preparare la via del Signore, Is 40:3–5.* La sua reinterpretazione giudaica e neotestamentaria con speciale riferimento alla missione di Geovanni Battista. Diss. Pont. Univ. Gregoriana. Rome, 1975. **Holmes, I. V.** "Study on the translation of Is 40:6–8." *ExpTim* 75 (1963) 317–18. **Kilian, R.** " 'Baut eine Strasse für unseren Gott!' Ueberlegungen zu Jes 40:3–5." *Künder des Wortes.* FS J. Schreiner. Würzburg: Echter, 1982. 53–60. **Koole, J. L.,** and **J. H. van der Lann.** "Jesaja 40:1–11." *GerefTT* 78 (1978) 221–30. ———. "Zu Jesaja 40:3." *Van Kanaan bis Kerala.* FS J. P. M. van der Ploeg. 137–42. **Krinetski, L.** "Zur Stilistik von Jes 40:1–8." *BZ* 16 (1972) 54–69. **Kuyper, L. J.** "The Meaning of חסד Isa xl 6." *VT* 13 (1963) 489–92. **Leeuwen, C. van.** "De openbaring van de *k^{e}bod* JHWH in Jesaja 40:5." *De Knecht.* FS J. L. Koole. Kampen: Kok, 1978. **Limburg, J.** "An Exposition of Isaiah 40:1–11." *Int* 29 (1975) 406–8. **Long, B. O.** "Prophetic Call Traditions and Reports of Visions." *ZAW* 84 (1972) 496–500. **Loretz, O.** "Die Sprecher der Götterversammlung in Is 40:1–8." *UF* 6 (1974) 489–91. ———. "Die Gattung des Prologs zum Buch Deuterojesaja (Jes 40:1–11)." *ZAW* 96 (1984) 210–20. ———. "Mesopotamische und ugaritische-kanannäische Elemente im Prolog des Buches Deuterojesaja (Jes 40:1–11)." *Orientalia* 53 (1984) 284–96. **McCarthy, D. J.** "Vox *bsr* praeparat vocem evangelium." *VD* 42 (1964) 26–33. **Merendino, R. P.** *Corso esegetico-teologico su Isaia 40. I. Parte: 40:1–11.* Rome: Pontifical Biblical Institute, 1970. ———. *Der Erste und der Letzte: Jes 40–48.* VTSup 31 (Leiden: E. J. Brill, 1981) 13–61. **Miegge, G.** "Autour d'une exégèse orthodoxe d'Isaïe 40, 6." *Maqqél shâqédh. Homage a W. Vischer.* Montpellier: Causse et al. (1960) 165–70. **Phillips, A.** " 'Double for All Her Sins.' " *ZAW* 94 (1982) 130–32. **Rad, G. von.** "כפלים in Jes 40:2 = Äquivalent?" *ZAW* 79 (1967) 80–82. **Sacon, K. K.** "Is 40:1–11—A Rhetorical Critical Study." *Pittsburgh Theological Monograph Series.* 1 (1974) 99–116. **Seters, J. van.** "Isaiah 40:1–11." *Int* 35 (1981) 401–4.

Snaith, N. H. "The Exegesis of Isaiah xl 5,6." *ExpTim* 52 (1940/41) 394–96. **Snodgrass, K. R.** "Streams of Tradition Emerging from Isaiah 40:1–5 and their Adaptation in the NT." *JSNT* 8 (1980) 24–45. **Stachowiak, L.** "Die Sendung des Deuterojesaja im Lichte von Jes 40:1–11 und der späteren Text-Tradition." *Dein Wort beachten.* Ed. J. Reindl. Leipzig: St. Benno, 1981. 102–15. **Stendahl, K.** "Judgment and Mercy" (Isa 40:1–8, Paul and Joel 2:12–17). *Paul among Jews and Gentiles.* Philadelphia: Fortress, 1976/77. 97–108. **Stoebe, H. J.** "Zu Jesaja 40, 6." *WuD* 2 (1950) 122–28. ———. "Überlegungen zu Jesaja 40:1–11." *TZ* 40 (1984) 104–13. **Stummer, F.** "Einige keilschriftliche Parallele zu Jes 40–66. 1) Jes 40:3–5." *JBL* 45 (1926) 172–73. **Tidwell, N.** "The Cultic Background of Is 40:1–11." *JTSA* 3 (1973) 41–54. **Tom, W.** "Welches ist der Sinn des 'doppelt empfangen' in Isaias 40:2?" *GerefTT* 59 (1959) 122–23. **Waldman, N. M.** "A Biblical Echo of Mesopotamian Royal Rhetoric (Is 40:3)." *Dropsie Anniversary Volume.* Ed. A. Katsch. Philadelphia: Dropsie U., 1979. 449–55.

Translation

Chorus:	1 *Comfort, comfort my people,*[a]	3+2
(from Yahweh's court)	*says your God.*[b]	
	2 *Speak to Jerusalem's heart*	3+2
	and call out to her	
	that her warfare is at an end,[a]	3+3
	that her iniquity is pardoned.	
	Indeed,[b] *she has taken from Yahweh's hand*	4+3
	double for all[c] *her sins.*	
Herald:	3 *A voice is*[a] *calling:*	2
A Voice:	*Prepare in the wilderness*[b]	2+2
	Yahweh's[c] *way.*	
	[d]*Straighten in the Arabah*	2+2
	a highway[e] *for our God.*[c]	
	4 *Every valley*[a] *will be filled in*	2+3
	and every mountain and hill leveled off.	
	Then uneven[b] *ground will become smooth*	3+2
	and rough places[c] *a plain.*	
	5 *Yahweh's glory will be revealed.*[a]	3+3+3
	All flesh will see it together[b]	
	for the very mouth[c] *of Yahweh has spoken it.*	
A Voice from Israel:	6 *A voice*[a] *is saying, Cry!*	3+3
	But I say[b]*: What shall I cry?*	
	All flesh[c] *is grass,*	2+2+2
	and all its loyalty[d]	
	like a wild flower.	
	7 *Grass withers,*	2+2
	a flower fades	
	[a]*when the spirit of Yahweh*	3+2
	blows against it.	
	[b]*Surely the people are grass.*[b]	3
First Voice:	8 *Grass does wither.*	2+2
	A flower does fade.[a]	
	But the word of our God	2+2
	stands firm for (its) term!	

Chorus: 9 *Up on a high mountain,* 2+2+2
get you[a] *up,*
Messenger[b] *Zion!*
Lift up your voice with strength, 3+2+2
Messenger[b] *Jerusalem.*
Lift it up! Do not fear!
Say to the towns of Judah, 3+2
[c]*See! Your God!*[c]

Notes

1.a. The syntax of עמי "my people" has been variously understood. Vg *popule meus* is vocative, and Jerome (*Commentary*) took נחמו "comfort" to be a piel impv: the people should comfort Jerusalem (so also Snaith, "Isaiah 40–66," *Studies in the Second Part of the Book of Isaiah,* VTSup 14 [Leiden: E. J. Brill, 1967] 177–78, and Elliger, p. 1). Kissane thinks the form is niph impv and thus reflexive: "be comforted" (cf. GKC § 51cde). Merendino (*Der Erste und der Letzte,* 13) argues correctly that עמי is the obj of the verb, thus "comfort my people."

1.b. MT אלהיכם "your God." DSS^{Isa} אלוהיכמה is an expanded spelling. LXX λέγει ὁ θεός. ἱερεῖς, λαλήσατε "says God. Priests, speak" = Heb אל: הכ(הני)ם (cf. J. Ziegler, *Untersuchungen,* 71). Tg introduces the prophet as the one addressed.

2.a. מלאה "be full." Is this to be translated with צבא "warfare, term of conscription" as subj or obj, transitive or intransitive? Volz, Rignell (*Isaiah ch. 40–55* [Lund: Gleerup, 1956] 10), and North suggest transitive: "she has fulfilled her term of service"; so Marti and *BHS* suggest pointing מִלְּאָה. DSS^{Isa} מלא makes it masc to fit this since צבא is usually masc. Elliger (2) supports MT, pointing to the Versions and the parallel in the following stich, and translates as passive.

2.b. כי "that" or "indeed." Is the line a parallel to the two stichs that precede it and thus like them—"that" (with de Boer [*Second Isaiah's Message,* Leiden: Brill, 1956], Muilenburg, North, Westermann)—or is it a new sentence (and thus "indeed") as Elliger (2) and others contend? Tg expands to read "and prophesy to it (Jerusalem) that it will soon be filled by the people who were deported" and continues by translating כי "because" in the first two cases but "as if" in the third. This translation follows Elliger.

2.c. Missing in LXX.

3.a. The Versions understand קול as constr, "the voice of." Elliger (2) insists it is not and should be translated "a voice (is) crying out."

3.b. LXX φωνὴ βοῶντος ἐν τῇ ἐρήμῳ "a voice of one crying in the wilderness" (cf. Matt 3:3; Syr Vg). H. Kosmala ("Form and Structure in Ancient Hebrew Poetry," *VT* 14 [1964] 441–43; 16 [1966] 152; and FS L. Rost, BZAW 105 [Berlin: Töpelmann, 1967] 59) has argued for the originality of LXX. However, MT is clear and should be kept.

3.c. Tg interprets these as "the people of Yahweh" and "the congregation of our God."

3.d. DSS^{Isa} adds ו "and."

3.e. Elliger (2) notes that the Versions translate a pl, "highways," and says they think of the needs of the many peoples of the Diaspora living in many lands.

4.a. MT גֶּיא "valley" is supported by DSS^{Isa} גי. *BHS* גַּיְא shows the more usual form (GKC § 93u).

4.b. LXX Tg Vg translate "crooked." Only Syr "uneven" preserves MT's synonymous parallelism (Elliger, 2).

4.c. MT הרכסים is apparently a *hap. leg.* from a root meaning "to bind." DSS^{Isa} והרוכסים apparently points the word to relate it to another *hap. leg.* from Ps 31:21, which has been variously translated (cf. BDB, 940). Ravenna ("Is 40,4 e Ps 31,21," *RivB* 1 [1953] 69) follows DSS^{Isa} and translates "hindrances."

5.a. MT ונגלה "be revealed." LXX καὶ ὀφθήσεται usually translates ונראה "and is seen."

5.b. LXX τὸ σωτήριον τοῦ θεοῦ "the salvation of God" (cf. 52:10). DSS^{Isa} יחדיו is understood by Dahood on the basis of Ugaritic to be from the root חדה meaning "check," test," which as a noun would mean "a vision" ("Ambiguous Texts in Isaias," *CBQ* 20 [1958] 46–49). But Elliger (3) correctly notes that ראה does not always need an obj (cf. 41:5, 23; 49:7, 18).

5.c. Missing in LXX. Tg has מימרא "the word of."

6.a. The Versions read "the voice of one saying." See n. 3.a.

6.b. MT וְאָמַר "and he said" is supported by Syr. But DSS[Isa] LXX and Vg read a 1st sg, "I said." Tg and 31 Heb MSS read a ptcp. This translation makes it 1st sg, as do *BHS*, Elliger, and most others.

6.c. Tg translates "the godless."

6.d. MT חסדו "its loyalty." DSS[Isa] חסדיו is pl. LXX *δόξα ἀνθρώπου* "glory of man" (1 Pet 1:24, "its glory"), Syr *y'ywṯh* "its beauty," Vg *gloria eius* "its glory." חסד usually means "devotion or loyalty" to covenant. But Kuyper (*VT* 13 [1963] 489–92) argues that here it must mean "power, might" (Tg תוקפהון; cf. 2 Chr 32:32; 35:26) and Elliger (24) points to Pss 59:17 [16] and 62:12–13 [11–12] where חסד is parallel to עז "strength." Perhaps here it denotes a capacity for loyalty.

7.a–8.a. Missing in a number of medieval MSS, LXX (except in LXX[L] and some texts of the Hexaplaric recension), and in 1 Pet 1:24. DSS[Isa] shows them to be inserted by a later hand between the lines and in the margin. The loss in a Syr MS was explained by G. Diettrich (*Ein apparatus criticus zur Pešitto zum propheten Jesaja,* BZAW 8 [Giessen: Töpelmann, 1905] 134) as due to homoiotel. Elliger (4) notes that Syr Tg Vg support MT, although Tg again speaks of "the people" as "the godless of the people."

7.b-b. Usually seen as an interpretive gl. However, the fact that it is an interpretation is no reason to eliminate it.

9.a. On לך "you" (DSS[Isa] לכי) see GKC § 119s.

9.b-b. מבשרת ציון "messenger (of) Zion" is a constr form, a genitive, that has puzzled interpreters. The question is: who are the recipients and who are the messengers? Vg *tu qui evangelizas Sion* "you who evangelize Zion" makes it an objective genitive. LXX changes the fem form to masc, but 'A Σ Θ keep the fem. Tg נבייא דמבסרין לציון "prophet of the heraldry to Zion" has made it a collective related to prophecy. Elliger (31) thinks of a simple appositional relation, not a construct, like that in בת ציון "daughter Zion" and אדני יהוה "Lord Yahweh." The same effect can be achieved by the genitive (cf. GKC § 128k).

9.c-c. Tg paraphrases, "the dominion of your God is revealed."

Form/Structure/Setting

The passage is clearly set off from what follows and what precedes by its very nature. Melugin (*Formation,* 82–86) has correctly seen that vv 1–8 are a tight unity and their relation to v 9 mirrors the structure of chaps. 40–55 as a whole. The scene is a prologue composed of four well-defined speeches: vv 1–2, 3–5, 6–7 (+8), and 9.

The setting of the speeches is similar to that of chap. 1 and has occurred repeatedly throughout the Vision. Yahweh and the members of his court are present and speak sometimes among themselves and sometimes to Judah and/or Jerusalem below them. (Cf. the descriptions in 1 Kgs 22:19–22; Jer 23:18, 22; Job 1:6–12; and H. W. Robinson, "The Council of Yahweh," *JTS* 45 [1944] 151–57.) Efforts to place the scene in a New Year's setting (E. C. Kingsbury, "Prophets and the Council of Yahweh," *JBL* 83 [1964] 279–86) or to see this as a prophetic call for an assumed "Deutero-Isaiah" (F. M. Cross, "The Council of Yahweh in Second Isaiah," *JNES* 12 [1953] 274–77; and Muilenburg, *2 Isaiah*) have individualized a role that is clearly addressed in the plural in vv 1–3 and in a collective sense in v 9.

In Yahweh's great hall three groups are discernible. One group is composed of the usual members of Yahweh's court (Heavens and Earth in 1:2; seraphim in 6:2; sons of God in Job 1:6; spirits in 1 Kgs 22:19–22) who are allowed to speak in Yahweh's behalf in vv 1–2 and 9. A solo voice from this group, perhaps viewed as an official of the court, speaks vv 3–5 and 8.

J. Begrich ("Sofer und Mazkir," *ZAW* 58 (1940–41) 1–29 = *Gesammelte Studien* 67–98) pictures him as an officer of the court, perhaps the recorder (מזכיר) who reports God's decisions to the group.

Two other groups are silent addressees for the speeches. They also were present in earlier acts. But the situation has changed with the movement of time. Israel is in Mesopotamian captivity. Jerusalem is no longer a proud, though embattled, city. Now she is a heap of rubble with a few ragged and poor survivors, no king, no significant commercial or political significance, and no active temple service or annual pilgrims. The speeches in vv 1–3 are addressed in the plural. The imagery of the highway through the wilderness and the theme of Yahweh's revealed glory appear repeatedly in chaps. 40–48 (Melugin *Formation* 85). Is it not likely that those addressed here are the same as those addressed in 40:12–44:12, i.e., Jacob/Israel of the captivity? The second group is addressed by a collective term, Jerusalem/Zion, in v 9. A representative of the first group protests their call to service (vv 6–7) only to be answered by the solo voice from the heavenly court.

While the personalities of prophet and king dominated chaps. 36–39 (and chap. 7), they have not done so otherwise in the Vision. They are clearly missing from 40–66. Solo voices appear, but in the role of neither prophet nor king.

The speeches are urgent calls for messengers to represent Yahweh and the heavenly court in spreading the word of Yahweh's decisions and coming actions. They partake of the character of prophetic tasks. The first two speeches (vv 1–2, 3–5) urge that a mission go to Jerusalem to encourage her with the good news that Yahweh will return to the city very shortly. The group is to prepare a way through the Arabah for his victorious return. Vv 6–7 record a sole skeptical reply which will be echoed in succeeding chapters. The form is that of a lament (cf. Ps 37:2; Job 8:12 for uses of the motif in laments; also Pss 129:6 and 103:15b). The protest is common in the call narratives (cf. Exod 4 of Moses and Jer 1:6). But here the protest not only complains of weakness. It is skeptical of the integrity of humankind.

V 9 addresses Zion/Jerusalem, calling her to encourage the towns of Judah. Melugin (*Formation,* 84–85) has shown how closely this verse is related to chap. 49. Begrich (*Studien zu Deuterojesaja,* 2nd ed., ThB 20 [Munich: Kaiser, 1963] 58–59) recognized its military character and called the genre "instruction to a messenger bringing news of victory" (cf. 2 Sam 18:19–23). Conrad (*VT* 44 [1984] 139) has related this and the following verses to the war oracle in *DtH* which functioned to alleviate fear for an impending battle. But now Jerusalem has no active role in the battle. She is to be a messenger of good tidings only. מבשרת "messenger" is a technical term which has been adapted to this purpose (cf. R. W. Fisher, *A Study of the Semitic Root BSR,* New York: Columbia U. P., 1966). Elliger (33) points to fixed elements in the genre including the impv אמרי "say," the introductory הנה "see" (vv 9 and 10) and perhaps the technical terms for booty, שׂכר and פעלה (v 10). The speech has two parts: instructions to the messenger and the contents of the message to be transmitted. The form is thus continued in Scene 1.

The entire passage serves as a prologue to the sections to follow. Chaps. 1, 6, and 15 each introduced sections in that way. As chap. 6 set the mood and tone for all the sections to this point, 40:1–9 announces the intentions of God that set the tone and mood for the rest of the Vision.

Comment

1 The verbs in vv 1–2a are imperative plurals, calling upon a group of people. It is evident from the following chapters that these as a group may be called Jacob/Israel and that they are the exiles in Mesopotamia. Their task is to *comfort,* to strengthen, to encourage God's people. The message is from *your God.* In that foreign land, people ordinarily worship the gods of the land. But Israelites are being contacted by their own God.

2 *My People* is further defined by *Jerusalem.* The people of Babylon's captivity are called to announce to Jerusalem that *her warfare,* her term of military enlistment, is at an end. This is the most telling description of the change in Jerusalem's status that can be made. The fortress city had served as military headquarters for David's battles and for countless wars since. Warfare was an inescapable part of national existence. Israel and Judah are no longer to be nations. That burden has shifted to the empires. And Jerusalem will be free to fulfill her new role in God's plan (cf. Conrad, *VT* 34 [1984] 139). *Taken from Yahweh's hand* is an acknowledgment that the judgment announced in 1:24–25 and in chap. 3, the travail extending from Pekah's and Rezin's siege (chap. 7) and Sennacherib's siege (chap. 22 and 26–27) to the final unmentioned catastrophes of 598 and 587 B.C., had finally been fulfilled. DtH in Kings had taught that all Israel's and Jerusalem's trouble came about because of their sins. The announcement now is that Jerusalem has received a full, even a *double* portion that atoned for *all her sins.* The time has arrived for Jerusalem to be revived and rebuilt, to be rehabilitated. Babylonian Jewry is called to take a leading part in that recovery. In succeeding centuries they did so with gifts and personnel, including the expeditions of Zerubabbel, Ezra, Nehemiah and their associates.

3 A solo voice calls for monstrous preparation, including a *highway.* One might expect that this would be for pilgrims returning to Jerusalem or for those who would resettle the land. But the highway does not come to Jerusalem from the northeast or from the north (i.e., from Babylon) or even from the south (i.e., from Egypt), where the Diaspora is located. The *wilderness* spoken of here is in the southeast, *the Arabah.* And the one to travel on it is *Yahweh, our God.* Ezekiel had pictured Yahweh abandoning the city (Ezek 9–11). Now he is returning, using the way that was familiar from Temple traditions of Yahweh coming from Sinai or from Edom (cf. chaps. 34 and 63:1–6) through *the Arabah* south of the Dead Sea to approach Jerusalem from the east (cf. *Comment* on 10:27–32). The heart of the announcement, the reason for the messages of good news, is that Yahweh is returning to take up residence in Jerusalem again. This calls for royal preparations.

Excursus: Exodus Typology

Bibliography

Anderson, B. W. "Exodus Typology in Second Isaiah." *Israel's Prophetic Heritage.* Ed. B. W. Anderson and W. Harrelson. New York: Harper and Bros., 1962. 177–

95. **Beaudet, R.** "La typologie de l'Exode dans le Second-Isaie." *LavalTPh* 19 (1963) 12–21. **Blenkinsopp, J.** "Scope and Depth of the Exodus Tradition in Deutero-Isaiah, 40–55." *Concilium* 20 (1966) 41–50. **Daube, E.** *The Exodus Pattern in the Bible.* London: 1963. **Fischer.** "Das Problem des neuen Exodus in Is 40–55." *TübTQ* 110 (1929) 313–24. **Harvey, J.** "La typologie de l'Exode dans les Psaumes." *ScE* 15 (1963) 383–406. **Kiesour, K.** *Exodustexte im Jesajabuch: Literarkritische und motivgeschichtliche Analysen.* Diss. Münster, 1978. Göttingen: Univ. Verlag/Vandenhoech & Ruprecht, 1979. **Lubsczyk, H.** *Der Auszug aus Egypten, seine theologische Bedeutung in prophetischer und priesterlicher Ueberlieferung. ETS* 11. Leipzig: 1963. **Simon-Yofre, H.** "Exodo in Deuteroisaias." *Bib* 61 (1980) 530–53. **Stuhlmacher, C.** *Creative Redemption.* 59–98 (chart on passages and authors), 272. ———. "Yahweh-King and Deutero-Isaiah." *BR* 15 (1970) 32–45. **Zillessen, A.** "Der alte und der neue Exodus." *ARW* 6 (1903) 289–304. **Zimmerli, W.** "Der 'neue Exodus' in der Verkündigung der beiden grossen Exilspropheten." *Gottes Offenbarung.* TB 19. Munich: Kaiser, 1963. 192–204.

The Vision of Isaiah has drawn heavily on the paradigm of the Exodus as other prophetic writings do, notably Jer 2:6–7; 7:22, 25; 11:4, 7; and so on. Hosea (2:16–17 [14–15]; 11:1; 12:10, 14 [9, 13]; 13:4–5), Amos (2:9–10; 3:1–2; 9:7), Micah (6:4), and Isaiah (10:24, 26; 11:16–18) testify to the importance given Exodus imagery in prophetic writing ascribed to the 8th century B.C.

But the intensity and fullness of Exodus symbolism in Isaiah 40–55 is unique. B. W. Anderson (*Israel's Prophetic Heritage,* 181–82) has listed ten key passages in which it appears: 40:3–5; 41:17–20; 42:14–16; 43:1–3; 43:14–21; 48:20–21; 49:8–12; 51:9–10; 52:11–12; 55:12–13. This list does not include references in chapters 56–66 relating to redemption and ransom (see *Excursus:* גאל *"Redeem"/ "Redeemer"*).

The passages are not narrowly concerned with the Exodus itself, but draw on the promises to the patriarchs, the dash to freedom from Egypt, the wilderness journey, and the entry into Canaan (see Anderson, *Israel's Prophetic Heritage,* 182–84).

5 *Yahweh's glory,* the sign of his presence and power, will be visible and experienced in Jerusalem again. *All flesh* announces the universal significance of the event. Not just to Israel and Judah but to all humankind will the revelation take place. The strong claim of Yahweh's universal strategies and goals that will appear in the following chapters is already evident. *Together* may have the sense of "at the same time" or it may mean "in one gathering." Jerusalem's significance for the world at large is recognized, a significance that resides only in the fact that God is there (2:1–4; 65:17–66:24). It is confirmed as Yahweh's own word, spoken by his own *mouth.* This anthropomorphism stresses the reality of Yahweh's decision and his word.

6 A skeptical voice speaks for the group in a tone that will be echoed repeatedly in the following chapters. It questions the content of the announcement to be given as well as its basis. *All flesh* includes all humankind. The term is picked up from v 5. The skepticism is based on a pessimistic view of humanity. *Grass/wildflowers* are figures of its transitory and helpless nature. *Grass* is all that is green and alive. *Wildflowers* are all that glistens and blooms (J. Blau, "Über hononyme Wurzeln," *VT* 6 [1956] 247). חסדו "its loyalty" is a word which is often used to speak of "solidarity" in covenant relations (N. Glueck, *Hesed in the Bible,* tr. A. Gottschalk [Cincinnati: Hebrew Union College,

1967]). The claim is that humans are not capable of preserving loyalty for long (see n. 6.d).

The characteristic of grass and flowers that dominates the comparison is their inability to withstand the *spirit of Yahweh* that *blows against it.* Within the description is the bitter reminder that everything that has happened to Israel has been attributed to Yahweh. It implies that because one is unable to stand against God one also cannot or should not be asked to stand with God. Because *the people* are only *grass* the task is useless or hopeless. העם "the people" in the singular is used in Isaiah to refer to Israel (40:1; 42:22; 43:8,20,21; 47:6; 49:13; 51:7,16,22; 52:4,5,6).

8 The response recognizes the accuracy of the observation concerning human frailty, but counters with the reminder that the call is based on *the word of our God.* This in contrast to grass and flowers *stands firm for (its) term.* קום "stand" appears repeatedly in the following chapters to characterize what stands up or rises up (43:17; 49:7; 51:17; 52:2; 54:17). It will be used about the restitution of destroyed cities (44:26b), of tribes (49:6), and of the land (49:8). Cf. Elliger (26). לעולם "for (its) term" is literally "to the age" and implies continuation for the God-willed length of time. In contrast to grass, God's word remains upright and effective for the time that has been set for it. Neither the word not the temporal concepts of that period dealt with eternity or forever (cf. E. Jenni, "Das Wort *ʿolam* im AT," *ZAW* 64 [1952] 197–248 and *ZAW* 65 [1953] 15–18; S. J. DeVries, *Yesterday, Today, and Tomorrow* [Grand Rapids, MI: Eerdmans, 1975]; J. Barr, *Biblical Words for Time,* SBT 33 [Naperville, IL: Scholar's Press, 1962]).

9 LXX translated *Messenger Zion* as ὁ εὐαγγελιζόμενος Σιων "the one bringing good news to Zion" and thus started a long tradition that led to "you who bring good tidings" in the English versions. The same Greek word stands behind NT usage for "gospel." There is a question about the relation of the two words. Is מבשרת ציון properly "Messenger of (or to) Zion"? Or is Zion the Messenger? (See n. 9.b.) It is here understood that Zion/Jerusalem is the messenger. Note the close relation of themes with those in chap. 49. The message is for *the towns of Judah.* Its content is that Yahweh is coming.

Explanation

The passage marks a major turning point in mood and message. Its exuberant tone contrasts with the dark pessimism of chap. 6. The occasion for the messages is the imminent coming of Yahweh to Zion. (See the parallel in Zeph 3:14–20 and Zech 9:9.)

The turning point in God's plan is the occasion of enlisting Israel, now in Mesopotamian exile, to encourage and support Jerusalem and Zion to, in turn, announce God's coming to the towns of Judah. The great day for a change in their fortunes is at hand.

It is important to notice exactly what the announcement does and does not include, for the rest of the Vision will struggle with differences of expectation on these points. It does include a new day for Jerusalem without the continuing burden of her guilt. And with that change in her status comes the news that Yahweh will mark the occasion by returning to the city (and to the Temple) in all his glory. The world will once again know that God is in his Temple and in his city.

Nothing is said about a return from exile, a restoration of political power, or the royal house of David. Many Jews had thought about God's future and their own future in those terms. Indeed Jeremiah and Ezekiel had done so, although Ezekiel's last great vision had turned to the view of a new temple rather than a new nation. Nonetheless, those expectations will not die easily.

The skeptical response of vv 6–7 does not reflect the disappointment of the zealot but the nihilism of the agnostic. He, like Koheleth, the "preacher" of Ecclesiastes, has learned to look with a cold eye on the happenings of life and expect the least and the worst. The response represents the attitude of exilic Jews who have accommodated themselves to survival. They want only to be left alone, having neither time nor energy to give to dreams or crusades.

The answer given in v 8 puts things in perspective. The foundations of the announcement and the attitudes it calls for do not lie in human capacities but depend solely upon the word of God. He has given it and he will sustain it.

So the good news is that the period in which Yahweh had to act against his people through the Assyrians and Babylonians is over and past. He is now positively related to them. His presence and his grace are turned to their welfare. He is open to their worship and devotion.

Scene 1: The Lord Yahweh Comes Like a Shepherd (40:10–31)

Bibliography

Clifford, R. J. "The Function of Idol Passages in Second Isaiah." *CBQ* 42 (1980) 450–64. **Conrad, E. W.** "The 'Fear Not' Oracles in Second Isaiah." *VT* 44 (1984) 140–43. **Couroyer, B.** "Isaïe xl, 12." *RB* 73 (1966) 186–96. **Dahood, M.** "The Breakup of Two Composite Phrases in Is 40:13." *Bib* 54 (1973) 537–38. **Elliger, K.** "Der Begriff 'Geschichte' bei Deuterojesaja." *Verbum Dei manet in aeternum.* FS O. Schmitz. Ed. W. Foerster. Witten: Luther-Verlag (1953) 26–36 = *Kleine Schriften zum Alten Testament,* ThB 32, Munich: Kaiser (1966) 199–210. **Gordis, R.** "הערות למקרא (Is 44:11; Hab 2:5)." *The Word and the Book.* New York: Ktav (1974) 47–48. **Graffy, A.** "Isaiah 40:27–31." *A Prophet Confronts His People.* AnBib 104. Rome: Biblical Institute Press, 1984. 86–91. **Lupieri, E.** *Il cielo è il mio trono: Isaia 40:12 e 66:1 nella tradizione testimoniaria.* Temi e Testi 28. Rome: Edizioni di storia e letturatura, 1980. **Melugin, R. F.** "Deutero-Isaiah and Form Criticism." *VT* 21 (1971) 326–37. **Merendino, R. P.** *Der Erste und der Letzte,* 61–121. **Mettinger, T. N. D.** "The Elimination of a Crux? A Syntactic and Semantic Study of Isaiah xl 18–20." *Studies on Prophecy.* VTSup 26. Leiden: E. J. Brill, 1974. 77–83. **Millard, A. R.** "Isaiah 40:20: Toward A Solution." *TynBul* 14 (1964) 12–13. **Naidoff, B. D.** "The Rhetoric of Encouragement in Isaiah 40,12–31; a Form-Critical Study," *ZAW* 93 (1981) 62–76. **Schoors, A.** "Two Notes on Isaiah xl 20 and liv 4." *VT* 21 (1971) 501–5. **Snaith, N. H.** "Psalms I 1 and Isaiah XL 31." *VT* 29 (1979) 363–64. **Stummer, F.** "Einige keilschriftliche Parallelen zu Jes 40–66. 2)

Jes 40:12–16." *JBL* 45 (1926) 173–76. **Thomas, D. W.** "A Drop of a Bucket? Some Observations on the Hebrew Text of Isaiah 40:15." *In Memoriam Paul Kahle.* Eds. M. Black and G. Fohrer. BZAW 103. Berlin: Töpelmann (1968) 214–21. **Tidwell, N.** "Isaiah 40:10 (בחזק)." *Semitics* 6 (1978) 15–27. **Trudinger, P.** " 'To whom then will you liken God?' (A Note on the Interpretation of Isaiah xl 18–20)." *VT* 17 (1967) 220–25. **Williamson, H. G. M.** "Isaiah 40:20—A Case of Not Seeing the Wood for the Trees." *Bib* 67 (1986) 1–20. **Whybray, R. N.** *The Heavenly Counsellor in Isaiah xl 13–14: A Study of the Sources of the Theology of Deutero-Isaiah.* SOTSMS 1. Cambridge: U. P., 1971.

Translation

Heavens:	10 *See!* [a]*the Lord Yahweh*[a]	3+2+2
	comes in strength.[b]	
	His arm is ruling for him.	
	See! His reward (is) with him,	3+2
	and his payment[c] *(is) before him.*	
Earth:	11 *As a shepherd, he will feed his flock.*[a]	3+3
	With his arm, he will gather lambs.[b]	
	[c]*He will carry them in his bosom.*[c]	2+2
	He will gently lead ewes giving suck to lambs.[d]	
Heavens:	12 [a]*Who can measure water*[b] *in his hands?*[c]	3+3
	O survey[d] *sky by*[e] *hands-breadths?*	
	Or contain[f] *the dust*[g] *of the*[h] *land in the measure?*	4+3+2
	Or weigh mountains on scales,	
	or hills[i] *in a balance?*	
Earth:	13 *Who can gauge*[a] *Yahweh's spirit?*[b]	3+3
	[c]*Or instruct him*[d] *as his personal*[e] *counselor?*	
	14 *Whom does he consult to make him perceptive?*	3+3
	Or[a] *to teach him in the way of justice?*	
	[b]*Or to teach him knowledge?*[b]	2+3
	Or[a] *to make him know a way of understanding?*	
Heavens:	15 *See! Nations*[a] *(are) like a drop from a bucket*	4+3+4
	and are thought[b] *of as dust on scales.*[c]	
	See! Coastlands[d] *(are) as heavy*[e] *as fine dust.*[f]	
	16 *Lebanon would not suffice for fuel,*	4+4
	nor[a] *its beasts be enough for a burnt offering.*	
	17 [a]*All the nations (are) as nothing over against him!*[b]	3+3
	[c]*Less than nonexistent or unreality*[c] *are they accounted by him.*[b]	
Earth:	18 [a]*To whom would you(pl) liken God?*	3+2
	[b]*Or (with) what likeness would you compare him?*[cb]	
	19 *A workman*[a] *casts*[b] *the*[c] *idol*	3+3+3
	[d]*and a smith beats out*[e] *gold for it,*[d]	
	refining[f] *silver fasteners*[g] *(for it).*	
	20 *The expert*[a] *in such offerings*	2+3
	chooses wood that will not rot,[b]	
	finds[b] *for himself a skilled craftsman*	3+4
	to establish an idol that cannot be moved.	

Heavens: 21 *Do you not know?* 2+2
Do you not hear?
Has it not been made known to you from the beginning? 4+4
Do you not understand the foundations[a] *of the*[b] *land?*
22 *To the One dwelling on the outer rim of the land* 3+2
its inhabitants are like grasshoppers.
(He is) the One stretching out heavens like a curtain[a] 3+3
so that he spreads them like a tent to live in.
Earth: 23 *(He is) the One consigning princes to nothingness,* 3+4
he makes national judges[a] *to be like unreality.*
24 *Scarcely are they planted,* 2+2
scarcely are they sown,
scarcely has their stem 2+2
taken root[a] *in the land,*
but when[b] *he blows*[c] *on them, they wither* 3+3
and the storm carries them away like chaff.
Yahweh: 25 *To whom will you compare me as an equal?* 3+2
Herald: *says the Holy One.*
Heavens: 26 *Life up your eyes on high* 2+3
and see! Who created these?[a]
Bringing out their multitude by number, 3+3
he calls them each by name.
By greatness of might, 2+2+3
and strength[b] *of power,*
not a one is missing.
Earth: 27 *Jacob, why*[a] *do you(sg) say,* 3+2
And Israel, (why)[b] *do you declare,*
"My way is hidden from Yahweh. 3+3
And my justice is disregarded[c] *by*[d] *my God"?*
Heavens: 28 [a] *Do you (sg) not know?* 2+2
Or do you not hear?
Yahweh is a God of the long view, 3+3
Creator of the borderlands.
[b] *He does not faint!* 2+2+2
He does not grow weary![b]
One cannot probe his understanding!
Earth: 29 *(Yet he it is who is) giving*[a] [b] *power to the faint,*[b] 3+4
[c] *and he multiplies strength*[d] *to one with no might.*[c]
30 *Youths may grow faint and be weary.* 3+3
And choice athletes may stumble and collapse.
31 *But*[a] *those waiting*[b] *on Yahweh* 2+2+3
will renew strength.
They will rise (on) wings[c] *like eagles.*
They will run, but not tire. 3+3
They will walk, but not faint.[d]

Notes

10.a-a. LXX and one Syr MS omit "Yahweh." But this is a regular tendency in LXX. MT is consistent in this case.

10.b. MT בְּחָזָק "as a strong one" (BDB, 305), i.e., *beth essentiae* with an adj (GKC § 119i), is supported by *BHS*. DSS[Isa] בחוזק, LXX *μετὰ ἰσχύος* and the other Versions read a noun, בְּחֹזֶק "with strength." The noun is better (so Grätz; Duhm; Elliger, 32; and others).

10.c. DSS[Isa] ופעלתיו is pl "his payments." Tg has "works" and attributes them to the righteous: "See the reward of those who perform his word is with him; for all their works are revealed before him" (Elliger, 32).

11.a. L. Köhler (*Deuterojesaja [Jesaja 40–55] stilkritisch untersucht*, BZAW 37 [Giessen: Töpelmann, 1923], and "Syntactica II," *VT* 3 [1953] 84) reads this as a "naked relative clause" or "contact clause," that is, a relative clause without the particle: "like a shepherd who feeds his flock." LXX and Syr translate in this way.

11.b. The lines are read with MT's accents instead of *BHS*'s line division.

11.c-c. MT ובחיקו "and in his bosom." Several LXX MSS lack "and," and most of the others omit the entire phrase. But MT is supported by Syr Tg Vg.

11.d. MT עלות "ewes giving suck to lambs." DSS[Isa] עולות "unrighteous ones" (BDB, 732 III) or "those giving suck" (BDB, 732 I).

12.a. Tg bridges the verses by paraphrasing, inserting: "Who said that? The Eternal has said it and done it!" (Elliger 41).

12.b. MT מים "water." DSS[Isa] מי ים "water of the sea." Steinmann and McKenzie emend, following DSS[Isa]. Orlinsky ("St. Mark's Isaiah Scroll, VI," *HUCA* 25 [1954] 90–92) defends MT. Fohrer and *BHK* emend to read ימים "seas." MT is to be kept. Elliger notes that Deutero-Isaiah never uses מים for the sea and always uses ים "sea" in the sg (42:10; 43:16; 48:18; [49:12;] 50:2; 51:10, 15).

12.c. בשעלו "in his hand." The pronom suff has been questioned. DSS[Isa] has it but also adds it on בזרתו "in his hands-breadths" in the second stich. Syr has it in all three stichs. Elliger (40) emends *waw* to *yodh* and divides the letters differently to read בַּשְּׁעָלַיִם יָם "with both hands a sea." Duhm and Köhler do the same but read it as pl without an article. LXX Vg omit the suff.

12.d. Missing in LXX.

12.e. DSS[Isa] inserts "his" (see n. 12.c).

12.f. LXX *καὶ πᾶσαν* "and all" has read this as a noun. MT וכל is to be understood as a verb, qal pf 3 masc sg from כול, plus *waw:* "and contain."

12.g. Missing in LXX. *BHS* to the contrary, 'A Σ Θ translate with an inf: *τον χουν* "to heap up."

12.h. The article on הארץ "the land" is strange where other words lack it, but efforts to change it are no better.

12.i. LXX *καὶ τὰς νάπας* "and wooded valleys" is more like MS[R] ובקעות "valleys" than MT's וגבעות "hills." But the MT's parallel to הרים "mountains" is still the best.

13.a. תכן "gauge, survey" repeats the verb of v 12. LXX translates here with *ἔγνω* "understood." Whybray (*Heavenly Counsellor,* 10) has followed it too easily.

13.b. רוח "spirit." LXX *νοῦν* "mind." Whybray (*Heavenly Counsellor,* 11) points to 30:1 and 1 Chr 28:12 to support LXX's reading of MT. But surely *νοῦν* has a much more restricted and passive sense than the dynamic and active רוח, although the latter may include the former.

13.c. LXX Syr Vg repeat the interrogative pronoun "who?" Cf. *BHK* and *BHS*.

13.d. DSS[Isa] "her" refers to "his counsel": "Who can make known his plan?" Tg moves in a similar way, apparently reading Yahweh as subj with איש עצתו "man of his counsel" being a prophet: "the man of his counsel (whom) he has instructed." It interprets "Who ordered the holy spirit into the mouth of all the prophets? Was it not Yahweh? And has he not told the righteous, who perform his word, what pleases him?" (Elliger 41). But the context supports the usual reading of MT.

13.e. איש "personal," lit., "man" of his counsel, is missing in DSS[Isa] but added as a correction over the line.

14.a. LXX inserts *τίς* "who." But this time Syr does not.

14.b-b. is missing in LXX and one MS[K] but is supported by DSS[Isa] and Tg.

15.a. LXX *πάντα τὰ ἔθνη* "all the nations."

15.b. Missing in Syr.

15.c. MT מאזנים "scales" (BDB, 24). Thomas, in *BHS,* suggests that DSS^{Isa} מזנים (omitting *aleph*) means *nubes* "clouds," though he later (*Memoriam P. Kahle,* 217) changes his mind. The word in this spelling does not appear elsewhere, but it could be derived from various roots: זנה (BDB, 275) "commit fornication," though a noun or hiph ptcp from this is not attested; זון (BDB, 266) "feed" (cf. K^{Occ} of Jer 5:8), thus מזון "sustenance"; or יזן (BDB, 402), Q of Jer 5:8, meaning obscure. Elliger (41) is probably right that DSS^{Isa} has the same word as MT, only omitting a letter.

15.d. Missing in LXX.

15.e. MT יִטּוֹל is qal impf 3 masc sg "he takes up." LXX Syr read as pl, יִטְּלוּ "they are lifted up." Missing in Vg. Tg "as chaff (which) flies away." The verb apparently has an intransitive meaning, as it does in Syriac, "be heavy." Elliger (42) suggests that MT has erred in putting *waw* at the beginning of the next word. It should read יטולו "they are heavy" (*BHS*).

15.f. LXX ὡς σίελος "as foam" has apparently read MT's כדק "as dust" as כרק "as spittle" (BDB, 956).

16.a. LXX inserts πάντα "all."

17.a. LXX Syr insert "and."

17.b-b. נגדו "before him" is missing in LXX. Syr repeats the translation of the following "are accounted by him." Tg has עובדיהון "their works." Elliger (40) translates "against him." נגד means what is in front of or opposite to (BDB, 617) and is an excellent word to use in comparisons.

17.c-c. LXX καὶ εἰς οὐθὲν "and to nothing," Syr *lʾbdnʾ wlḥrbʾ* "for downfall and for the sword," Tg גמירא ושיצאה "as riddance and destruction." Vg *et quasi nihilum et inane* "and like nothing and meaninglessness" which is the same as DSS^{Isa} וכאפס. This last reading is followed by a long list of interpreters (see Elliger, 42). However, as a comparative MT also makes sense.

18.a. MT ואל מי "and to whom." LXX Syr omit "and."

18.b-b. Elliger (59) lists the readings of LXX 'Α Σ Θ Syr Tg Vg and summarizes: דמות is apparently taken as abstract, "likeness, comparison," by LXX and Syr, but as concrete, "a picture," by the other Versions. The verb usage is significant in this understanding.

18.c. DSS^{Isa} לי "for me" understands God to be the speaker.

19.a. LXX τέκτων, Syr *ngrʾ*, and Tg נגרא mean "carpenter," a translation that gives them problems with other words. Vg *conflavit faber* "a workman puts together" supports MT.

19.b. MT נסך "casts" (BDB, 650). DSS^{Isa} ויעשה מסך "and he makes a casting" (the latter is a *hap. leg.;* cf. Elliger, 60). LXX ἐποίησε, Syr *(d)ʿbd,* Tg עביד retain the added "he makes."

19.c. MT הפסל "the idol." But LXX and Vg have read the *heh* as an interrogative particle: μή and *numquid* "does not?" Poetry does not ordinarily use an article (cf. n. 12.h above). Tg begins with הא "that." *BLex* § 80g shows that the interrogative particle with *dagesh forte* following is not impossible and points to Lev 10:19. MT, however, may be kept as it is.

19.d-d. LXX ἢ χρυσοχόος χωνεύσας χρυσίον περιεχρύσωσεν αὐτόν "or a goldsmith melts gold and gilds it." Syr Tg speak similarly of overlaying wood with gold.

19.e. DSS^{Isa} וירקענו adds "and," as it also did by adding ויעשה in the previous line. Thus DSS^{Isa} divides the lines and verses differently, but MT is to be prefered (Kutscher, *Isaiah Scroll,* 422–23).

19.f. צורף "refining" (BDB, 864). LXX lacks the entire line. Vg supports MT. *BHS*'s suggestions are unnecessary.

19.g. רתקות is a *hap. leg.* BDB, 958, suggests "chains." But the binding is needed as a means of fastening the beaten-gold forms onto the wood. "Fastener" is a better translation.

20.a. המסכן is usually thought to be related to מְסֻכָּן "poor, needy" (BDB, 698, III) but *BHS* suggests "mulberry tree." See H. G. M. Williamson, *Bib* 67 (1986) 1–20. The Ug root *skn* I means "monument, figure, statue" (Aistleitner, *WB,* n. 1908), and the Heb would then be a hiph ptcp. J. Reider ("Etymological Studies," *VT* 2 [1952] 117) relates Ug *skn* II to Heb סכן with a piel pointing and translates "the administrator of the holy gifts." Trudinger (*VT* 17 [1967] 224) builds upon סכן "dwells with" for the meaning "familiar with, aquainted with." The piel ptcp would mean "the expert" who knows such things. Elliger (62) finds the text hopelessly confused with large gaps. This translation follows Trudinger's suggestion.

20.b-b. DSS^{Isa} switches the second and third radicals in both ירקב "rot" and יבקש "find."

21.a. מוסדות "foundations" (BDB, 414; cf. 28:16) is supported by LXX Syr Vg Tg Rignell and de Boer. But *BHS*, Elliger (62), and others emend to מִיסֻּדַת "from the earth's being founded" to parallel מראש "from the beginning." MT may be kept.

21.b. DSS^{Isa} lacks the article.

22.a. LXX has ὡς καμάραν "like a dome," and Syr *ʾyk kptʾ* "like a bowl." But ʼA Σ Θ ὡς λέπτον and Tg כזעיר mean "like something small." Vg reads *velut nihilum* "like nothing." MT indicates a thin curtain or veil.

23.a. LXX apparently read *yodh* as a *waw* and translates שפט with ἄρχειν "to govern" as part of the first stich and וארץ with τὴν δὲ γῆν "but the earth" as part of the second.

24.a. DSS^{Isa} שרשו makes the verb pl. MT שֹׁרֵשׁ reads it as poel pf 3 masc sg "taken root" or "rooted."

24.b. DSS^{Isa} and one MS^{K} read גם "when," lacking the *waw*. LXX and Syr lack both the particle and the conj (Elliger, 62).

24.c. DSS^{Isa} עשף is a root unknown in biblical Heb. In postbiblical Heb. it refers to metal instruments for plowing (cf. Elliger's [63] references to Levy and Jastrow). A correction is inserted over the letter *ayin*, inserting *nun*, which agrees with MT.

26.a. LXX πάντα ταῦτα "all these." Syr Tg Vg support MT "these."

26.b. MT וְאַמִּיץ "and strong" (BDB, 55) is an adj. *BHS* follows DSS^{Isa} ואמץ, LXX ταὶ ἐν κράτει, Σ Θ και κρατους, and Syr *wbʿwsnh* which read a noun: "and (in) strength." However, other Versions follow MT. See the lengthy discussion by Elliger (63). The issue is whether מרב "greatness" (a noun) and אמיץ should be parallel constructions, both nouns or both adjs. The Versions tend to add "his" before both words. MT does not. The translation reads both as nouns.

27.a. LXX μὴ γὰρ "but do not." Σ Syr Tg Vg support MT.

27.b. LXX καὶ τί "and why?" so *BHS* suggests ולמה. However, MT is supported by the other Versions.

27.c. LXX ἀφεῖλε καὶ ἀπέστη "he removed the judgment and revoked it" apparently missed the preposition before "God" and the suffix on "judgment."

27.d. Lit., "from."

28.a. LXX καὶ νῦν "and now." *BHS* suggests ועתה. Elliger (93) rejects it, correctly referring to the parallel in v 21a.

28.b-b. Tg "not by work and not by tiring," LXX οὐ πεινάσει οὐδὲ κοπιάσει "not by labor nor by exhaustion."

29.a. DSS^{Isa} הנותן "the one giving." MT נתן "one giving."

29.b-b. Tg interprets, "to the righteous who are weary of his word of law, wisdom."

29.c-c. LXX καὶ τοῖς μὴ ὀδυνωμένοις λύπην "and to those who have no pains, trouble" apparently read a disturbed text like ולאין און מעצבה (cf. Elliger, 94). ʼA also translates אונים "might" as λυπαι "pains, troubles" and עצמה "strength" as ὀστέωσιν "to bones." Syr also is influenced by LXX. However, MT is clear and should be kept.

29.d. Tg "riches."

31.a. Tg interprets: "But these who have hoped for salvation in Yahweh will be gathered from their exile, and gain strength and will be renewed in their youth like the growth (of feathers) that rises on the wings of an eagle."

31.b. On the pointing of וְקוֹיֵ "but those waiting," see GKC § 8k.

31.c. LXX πτεροφυήσουσιν "they will grow wings"; Syr *wnwʿwn gpʾ* "and let wings grow"; Vg *assument pennas* "they receive wings." But Tg follows MT. DSS^{Isa} Syr Tg add "and."

31.d. MT ייעפו "they will (not) faint" is qal impf 3 masc pl from יעף (BDB, 419). For the form with unassimilated *yodh*, see GKC § 70a. DSS^{Isa} יעופו "they will (not) fly" is from עוף (BDB, 733).

Form/Structure/Setting

The scene is structured in an arch pattern:

A See, Lord Yahweh comes with power
He tends his flock like a shepherd (vv 10–11)
B Who can gauge Yahweh's spirit or teach him? (vv 12–14)
C Surely nations are like a drop from a bucket (v 15)
D Lebanon is not enough (vv 16–17)

KEYSTONE To whom or what will you liken God?
An idol made by human hands? (vv 18–20)
D′ To the One on the rim of the universe,
people are like grasshoppers (vv 21–22)
C′ He appoints and dismisses princes and judges (vv 23–24)
B′ Look at the stars! Israel, why do you think
Yahweh has failed you? (vv 25–27)
A′ Yahweh is a God of the long view; he does not faint.
One cannot probe his thinking; but he gives power to the faint, to those who wait (vv 28–31)

At the beginning and the end lies the positive message: Yahweh is coming in accordance with his own plan. He is neither discouraged nor weak. He cares for his own who trust him and wait for him.

The keystone of the arch is built on the question: To whom or what will you liken God? The specific reference is to a visible, tangible idol. It ridicules the worship of something made by human hands. But the rest of the structure implies that there are other forms of idolatry (finding comparisons for God) of which Israel may be more guilty than the actual shaping of idols.

B and B′ suggest that Israel's complaint (v 27 and vv 6–7?) presumes to tell God how to run things, thus making a judgment about God's plans and capabilities which is a form of idolatry. C and C′ suggest that Israel's evaluation of the importance of nationhood, nations, and leaders, making them indispensable to God as well as Israel, is a form of idolatry. D and D′ put things in proportion. Not even Lebanon is rich enough in lumber and herds adequately to support a cult worthy of God. Indeed people are infinitesimally small to God (cf. vv 6–7). So the idea that Israel's cult or her people are indispensable to God and his purpose is also idolatrous.

The complex thinking and literary structures that typify the following chapters have their beginning here.

The setting was given in vv 1–5: Yahweh's call for messengers among Mesopotamian refugees to go to strengthen Jerusalem, and their complaining objection (vv 6–7).

Substantial work has been done in analyzing the genre and structures of this section (cf. most recently Melugin, *Formation,* 31–34, 90–93 and *VT* 21 [1971] 326–37; A. Schoors, *I Am God Your Saviour: A Form-Critical Study of the Main Genres in Isaiah XL–LV,* VTSup 24 [Leiden: Brill, 1973] 245–59). These studies have usually related vv 10–11 to the preceding section. The arch structure above shows that they belong here.

An interrogative style dominates the heart of the scene from vv 12–29. But underneath this are several units of a different genre which Melugin calls a disputation speech. Vv 12–17 are a series of rhetorical questions (vv 12–14) concluding with a section introduced by הן "see." This has been compared to forms in "wisdom," e.g., Job 38–42; Prov 30:4 (Melugin, *Formation,* 33; cf. also G. von Rad, "Job xxxviii and Egyptian Wisdom," *The Problem of the Hexateuch and Other Essays,* tr. E. W. T. Dicken [London: SCM, 1984] 287–89; H. E. von Waldow, *Der traditionsgeschichtliche Hintergrund der prophetischen Gerichtsreden,* BZAW 85 [Berlin: Töpelmann, 1963] 48). The closest parallel is in Job 40:25–41:3 [41:1–11] with questions showing man's impotence and a conclusion beginning with הן "see." Melugin (*Formation,* 32) has noted that this disputation form also occurs in Exod 4:11 and 2 Kgs 18:35 = Isa 36:20. The latter is particularly interesting in light of the close connection between the passage and the ideas and forms that have shaped the Vision.

Melugin (*VT* 21 [1971] 333–34; *Formation,* 33) considers vv 18–24 to be parallel to vv 25–26 (and 46:5–11). The outline of all three passages includes the question "To whom will you compare God?"; sometimes a sarcastic description of idols; and an imperative or interrogative appeal to remember cultic instruction, the content of which is then given in participles like those of hymns. This form of disputation speech is unique to the Vision.

Vv 27–31 are identified by Melugin (*Formation,* 35) as a disputation against Jacob's specific complaint (v 27). The complaint is similar to that found in psalms of individual lament. Thus the disputation becomes an argument against the cultic lament. It appeals to something already known and taught to the one praying and then expresses confidence in the manner of the psalms of individual lament (cf, Pss 25:8; 102:13). The content of the argument recalls vv 10–11 above.

Comment

10 Yahweh's return to Jerusalem is pictured as a triumphal procession. שכר "reward" and פעלה "payment" may well be technical terms for booty and tribute carried home by triumphant warriors. As in vv 3–5, it is Yahweh himself who returns. There is no hint of the return of exiles.

11 This beautiful reference to shepherd and flock is similar to Ps 23:1–3. It also carries royal overtones, for *shepherd* is a common figure for the king. *His flock, lambs,* and *ewes* are all part of the larger picture of the people of God. As references to the towns of Judah, they picture the people who for decades have suffered from neglect and worse since their leaders and the majority of the people were taken into exile. God's return promises pastoral, royal concern and care for all of them, particularly for the weak and needy. *His bosom* refers to the fold of the shepherd's robe which can be a natural pocket to shelter a lamb. *Ewes giving suck* are those with newborn lambs who, therefore, need special attention as the flocks move along.

12 The questions present arguments for Yahweh's incomparability (cf. C. J. Labuschagne, *The Incomparability of Yahweh in the Old Testament,* POS 5 [Leiden: Brill, 1966]). תכן "survey" is the same word translated "gauge" in v. 13. *Handsbreadths* refers to a measurement, a half cubit. The inadequacy of human measures or devices for forming any estimation of the larger things in creation is the point here. Modern measures and devices can measure and weigh much larger and greater things than could those of biblical times. But they, too, are limited. One would only have to change the metaphor to show their limits.

13 The questions turn to the infinitely more impossible thought of evaluating God's ways and strategies. No effort is made here to speak of weighing or measuring God himself; that is beyond consideration. Israel had challenged his announcement and his program. Now she is being asked: "Who can 'second guess' God?" *Gauge* is the same word used of the sky in v 12. רוח "spirit" is a literal translation. It includes mind, purpose, and plans, but moves beyond them to include motivation and implementation. איש עצתו "personal counselor" is literally "man of his counsel." Monarchs depend on experts. Presidents have briefings from their intelligence agencies and career bureaucrats. But who could serve as personal counselor to God? (Cf. R. N. Whybray, *The Heavenly Counsellor in Isaiah xl 13–14*.)

14 Insight, *perceptiveness, justice, knowledge,* and *understanding* (one might summarize with "wisdom") are those characteristics which a king needs and which God has. God's spirit might promise these to the king (cf. 11:2–5), but who can impart these to God?

15 *Nations* and nationhood have played an important part in the Vision so far. Israel had been greatly impressed with the trappings and potential of nationalism from the days of Samuel. In exile, when nationalism had progressed to imperialism, she still was consumed with the fear of national power and the ambition to be one, even the greatest of them all. God's view of nations, even empires, is very different. To begin with, he is not awed by them. They are minuscule elements in his creation. The Vision in other places shows how he uses them, and then turns aside their plans. He works in, around, and beyond them.

16 There is an ellipsis of thought between these verses. It was probably more natural and more expected by an ancient hearer/reader than it is by a modern. Implied is the idea: if God is so incomparably great, he must be worshiped. Let us bring a sacrifice that is appropriate to his majesty and authority. To this the verse replies by pointing to the land that Israel and its neighbors thought of as the country with the greatest forests and most luxuriant animal life of all. Even *Lebanon* could not support a sacrifice event that would be worthy of God; there is not enough wood for the fires, and not enough animals for a sacrifice. God is simply too great for sacrifice to be adequate worship of him, even if it is done on a grand scale. This theme is found frequently in the Vision (cf. 1:11–17; 66:1–3).

17 אין "nothing," מאפס "less than nonexistent," and תהו "unreality" are terms used here for God's valuation of nations, *all nations,* even the idea of nationhood. One might have expected this of the idols. Indeed, the same and similar terms will be used of idols (41:24, 29; 44:9–11; 46:1–2). But here the polemic is against nations. Israel's objection (stated in v 27) implied that God showed no sign of using Israel as a nation. The argument here suggests that such nationalism is idolatry which fails to recognize that God has other instruments and ways of doing his work. Nations, like idols, have no ultimate substance in God's eyes.

18 Now to the central idea. Having asked, "Who can gauge Yahweh's spirit?", the question becomes direct and personal: "To whom would you (pl) liken God?" (repeated in v 25 and in 46:5). Human beings think in analogies. We seek comparables within our experience to deal with something outside of our experience. The Bible does this in speaking of God in human terms (anthropomorphism). The fault lies in assuming that one has comprehended, has "gauged" the mind and spirit of God, so that one is in the position to make recommendations to the Deity or correct him in his thinking or acting. This is the human tendency and sin. Israel is doing it here. That is idolatry, as surely as is the building of an image. *What likeness?* Would you prefer the emperor, the general, or the king? These are nationalistic images. We can hardly escape making some comparison. But some are better than others. This passage suggests "shepherd-flock" (v 11) for God's relation to his people, or "creator-sustainer" (vv 28–29). It does not avoid the comparison to king and warrior (v 10). But it does not want that term used as an image that holds God captive or determines the shape of his people or his use of them. For finally God is not human nor is he to be comprehended in any role that humans play.

20 *That cannot be moved* expresses an inherent irony. Of course anything that people can set up they can also remove. Only God cannot be moved.

21 In the same way that school children are reminded of lessons learned before, Israel is reminded of truths imparted in the Temple and through her teachers *from the beginning. The foundations* are those things which are the very origins and structural components that give stability and meaning. The perennial question whether הארץ "the land" is to be understood in terms of territory or in terms of the whole earth is raised again. The word occurs in v 20, parallel to God's stretching out the heavens. This question was faced before in chap. 24 of the Vision (see *Excursus: The Land* in *Isaiah 1–33*). There the sense of the land in its geographic and political terms was chosen. The ambiguity continues here. There are references to the stars and to the heavens (vv 22b and 26), but there are also references to nations and to rulers (vv 15, 17, 22–23). *The foundations of the land* refer to all the social and political structures which make the system work. A particular combination of these had existed in Palestine for well over half a millennium to make the history of Israel possible. They changed with the beginning of empire in the region. Now the foundations of the land are those established by the empire and upheld by it. If one thinks from the perspective of "the foundations of the earth," of course the setting is that of creation faith as expressed in the Psalms. The earth, nature, and the universe are put in their places and kept in their ways by the sovereign will of the Creator. The Vision suggests that these are not two separate ideas. God the Creator and God the Lord of history, political units, and society are one and the same. His *foundations* shape the fabric of nations and societies as surely as they do the heavens and the stars.

22–23 *One dwelling on the outer rim of the land.* Whether this expression looks at the boundaries of Palestine as the political/geographical *outer rim* or thinks vertically of the heavens as the *outer rim,* it is a remarkable concept and stands in contrast to the idea that Yahweh dwells in Zion. God's distance from humankind is accented here. From that distance they appear as insignificant *grasshoppers.* To One who is *stretching out heavens,* individual persons, be they *princes* or *judges,* have no inherent power or relevance. He can make or break them, can establish them in power or determine the *extinction* of them and all their apparent influence and power, and can make them in every sense into *nonentities.* Nothing in human existence is as fragile as power. God can take it away in an instant. The same words used in v 17 (אין "nothing" and תהו "unreality") occur again here. Like the unreality of idols is the unreality of perceived political power in comparison to God's reality and God's existence.

24 The figure of the gardener's plants, helpless before the winds, is applied to the political images.

25 וְאֶשְׁוֶה "as an equal" is literally "that I should be equal." The issue of the incomparability of God is raised again (cf. v 13), but in God's own words this time. It is supported by reference to the creation of the stars.

Excursus: ברא *"Create"/"Creator"*

Bibliography

Albertz, R. *Weltschöpfung und Menschenschöpfung bei Deuterojesaja, Hiob und in den Psalmen.* CTM A3. Stuttgart: Calwer Verlag, 1974. **Bernhardt, K.-H.** "ברא" *TWAT* 1: 769–77. ———. "Zur Bedeutung der Schöpfungs Vorstellung für die Religion Israel's in vorexilischen Zeit." *TLZ* 85 (1960) 821–24. **Böhl, F.** "*br*' Bara, als Terminus der Weltschöpfung im alttestamentlichen Sprachgebrauch." *Alttestamentlichen Studien.* FS R. Kittel, BWANT 13. Stuttgart: Kohlhammer, 1913. 42–60. **Boman, T.** "The Biblical Doctrine of Creation." *CQR* 165 (1964) 140–51. **Fischer, L. R.** "Creation at Ugarit and in the Old Testament." *VT* 15 (1965) 313–24. **Haag, E.** "Der Weg zum Baum des Lebens: Ein Paradiesmotiv im Buch Jesaja." *Künder des Wortes.* FS J. Schreiner. Eds. L. Ruppert et al. Würzburg: Echter Verlag, 1982. 35–52. ———. "Gott als Schöpfer und Erlöser in der Prophetie Deuterojesaja." *TTZ* 85 (1976) 193–213. **Habel, N. C.** "Yahweh, Maker of Heaven and Earth: A Study in Tradition Criticism." *JBL* 91 (1972) 321–37. **Harner, P. B.** "Creation Faith in Deutero-Isaiah." *VT* 17 (1967) 298–306. ———. "He Who Stretches Out the Heavens." *CBQ* 34 (1972) 417–30. **Hessler, E.** *Gott der Schöpfer: Ein Beitrag zur Komposition und Theologie Deuterojesajas.* Diss. Greifswald, 1961. **Humbert, P.** "Emploi du verbe *bara* (créer) dans l'Ancien Testament." *TZ* 3 (1947) 401–22 = *Opuscules d'un Hébraïsant.* Memoirs de l'Université de Neuchâtel 26 (1958) 175–86. **Hyatt, J. P.** "Was Yahweh Originally a Creator Deity?" *JBL* 86 (1967) 369–77. **Keane, D. P.** "Creation Faith in Second Isaiah." *DunRev* 11 (1971) 46–76. **Kirchschläger, W.** "Die Schöpfungstheologie des Deuterojesaja." *BLit* 49 (1976) 407–22. **Kraus, H-J.** "Schöpfung und Weltvollendung." *EvT* 24 (1964) 462–85. **Lambert, G.** "La creation dans la Bible." *NRT* 75 (1953) 252–81. **Legrand, L.** "La creation, triomphe cosmique de Yahvé." *NRT* 83 (1961) 44–70. **Lehmann, H.** "Schöpfergott und Heilsgott im Zeugnis der Bibel. Biblischtheologische Thesen zum problem der 'doppelten Offenbarung.'" *EvT* 11 (1951) 97–112. **Ludwig, T. M.** "The Traditions of the Establishing of the Earth in Deutero-Isaiah." *JBL* 92 (1973) 345–57. **Matthews, A. D.** "The Prophetic Doctrine of Creation." *CQR* 166 (1965) 141–49. **Mauch, T. M.** *The Participial Ascriptions to Yahweh in Isaiah 40–55, as Exemplified in the Participial Ascriptions Concerning Creation.* Diss. Union Theological Seminary, New York. Ann Arbor, Mich.: University Microfilms, 1958. **Napier, B. D.** "On Creation Faith in the Old Testament, A Survey." *Int* 16 (1962) 21–42. **Ploeg, J. S. van der.** "Le sens du verbe hébreu *Bara*', étude sémasiologique." *Muséon* 59 (1946) 143–57. **Raberger, W.** *Schöpfung als Problemfigur: Zur Artikulation einer Sinnprämisse in der Bewältigung ambivalenter Wirklichkeit bei DtJes 45:7.* Diss. Innsbruck, 1974. **Rad, G. von.** "Das theologische Problem des alttestamentlichen Schöpfungsglaubens." *Werden und Wesen des Alten Testaments.* BZAW 66. Giessen: Topelmann, 1936. 138–47 = ET *The Problem of the Hexateuch and Other Essays.* New York: Harper & Row, 1966. 131–43. **Reisel, M.** "The Relation between the Creative Function of the verbs brʾ–ysr–ʿsh in Isaiah 43:7 and 45:7." *Verkenningen in een stroomgebied.* FS M.A. Beek. Ed. M. Boertien, et al. Amsterdam: Huisdrukkerij Universiteit, 1974. 65–79. **Rendtorff, R.** "Die theologischer Stellung des Schöpfungsglaubens bei Deuterojesaja." *ZTK* 51 (1954) 3–13. **Schwabl, H.** "Weltschöpfung." PWSup 9 (1962) 1433–582. **Stuhlmueller, C.** "The Theology of Creation in Second Isaias." *CBQ* 21 (1959) 429–67. ———. *Creative Redemption in Deutero-Isaiah.* AnBib 43. Rome: Biblical Institute (1970) 268–71, *et passim.* **Weinfeld, M.** "God and the Creator in Gen. 1 and in the Prophecy of Second Isaiah." *Tarb* 37 (1967–68) 105–32. **Westermann, C.** "Das Reden vom Schöpfer und Schöpfung im Alten Testament." *Das Ferne und Nahe Wort.* FS L. Rost. BZAW 105. Berlin: Töpelmann, 1967. 238–44.

Yahweh is presented in the Vision as active, exercising initiative. There is no limit to this activity, although it is pictured as focused and intentional. It is portrayed by active participles in Hebrew, following the style of hymnic Psalms which describe the "doer" much more than the "doing."

ברא "create" is a rare word found primarily in Gen 1–2, a few psalms, and Isa 40–66. Yahweh creating the universe is pictured in 40:26, 28; 42:5; and 45:7, 18. He is creator of "peace and violence" in 45:7, of humankind (אדם) in 45:12 and 54:16, of Israel in 43:1, 7, 15, of conditions for the new exodus in 41:20 and 48:7, of a new world order in 65:17, and of salvation and joy in 57:19 and 65:18 (see Bonnard 520).

The concept of "creating" is supported by words that overlap in meaning: יסד "found" (seven times), יסר "form" (fourteen times), עשה "make" (twenty-seven times with God as subject), and כון "stabilize" (three times). These are contrasted with human idolatrous behavior and the inability of idols to do these things. In 45:7 ברא "create," יסר "form," and עשה "make" occur in the same verse. In 45:18 כון "stabilize" takes the place of "make."

All of these portray God as actively creating, forming, shaping, and stabilizing the universe and the historical social order from the beginning on into the present. There is no place for chaos or lack of control, in either sphere. God is in control. And this Creator, Maker, Stabilizer is identical with Israel's Savior and Redeemer who has willed that Jerusalem be restored.

27 Yahweh's antagonist in the disputation is named for the first time. *Jacob/Israel* is a familiar figure in the Vision. She appeared in 1:1–7, was denied a place in the new Temple (2:6–9), and was the vineyard of Yahweh in 5:1–7. She was the one judged in chaps. 5 and 10 by the onslaughts of the Assyrians. Repeatedly recognized in intervening passages is Israel's place in God's affections and plans. But she was always a fractious child. This reference implies that the complaint in vv 6–7 is also to be understood as Israel's complaint. The setting of this act has Jacob/Israel still the heir to election in Abraham but now in Babylonian exile, no longer a nation, and scarcely a people. Yet she still has meaningful existence because she can be and is addressed by the Almighty. She is still disbelieving and complaining.

Her complaint in v 6–7 was that humanity has no real substance or reality when the spirit (רוח) of God blows on it. The intervening disputation has established that in fact humankind is like grass (v 8) and that both nations and their rulers can be destined to extinction and unreality by God (vv 17 and 23). It has asked, who would dare gauge the *spirit* of God (as indeed the speaker in v 7 has done)? What gives humans meaning and reality is precisely the fact that God's spirit includes them in his strategies and that God's word addresses them. Now the complaint turns on *my way* and *my justice.* Jacob/Israel complains that her plans and her rights do not figure as prominently in God's plans as she would like. The words are נסתרה "hidden" and יעבור "disregarded" (lit., "is passed over"). Whether Israel's "way" and "justice/right" are understood in terms of her former life-style, expectations, and assumed rights or in terms of what she considers her just rights, the complaint presumes that she has a right to determine what these are to be and expects God to fit her expectations. This is precisely what the Vision is about. It concerns the question of who steers the ship, who determines the direction of history, and who decides the role for God's people. Jacob/Israel is not open to instruction or to revelation on this point. Yahweh's sovereignty cannot yield on this basic issue. Yet he patiently argues and pleads with Israel to follow his way, rather than trying to force her way on him. In a very real sense, Israel is correct. Her way and her sense of right has been passed over and disregarded because from Samuel to Zedekiah the ways of kingship and kingdom had proved a disaster, as the DtH from Samuel through Kings had adequately shown.

28 The disputation returns to a theme from the complaint in vv 7–8, the frailty and temporary nature of humankind. To counter this complaint the argument looks not to the nature of humanity but to God. First, *Yahweh is a God of the long view* (אלהי עולם is literally "God of an age"). His strategies point to the ages, not to the moment. *Creator of the borderlands,* literally "the ends of the land." His creative task involves the great distances of the land (or the earth), not just the specific locality. Israel is in the process of learning that he has designs on Babylon as well as Palestine. Israel had heard this sung and recited in the Temple, but had never learned the lesson. Her "way" and her "right/justice" still had the narrow scope of Palestine and Samaria in mind. Her sense of time demanded immediate satisfaction. God was prepared for the long haul. *He does not faint* or *grow weary.* He moves on toward his goal through decades, centuries, and millennia. What had been asked as a question in v 14 is now stated as a fact: *One cannot probe his understanding.* Israel was trying to do the impossible.

29 What is available for Jacob/Israel comes from God: *power to the faint* and *strength to one with no might.* The disputation returns to the themes of vv 6–7 where humanity (and presumably Israel) are pictured as wilting flowers and fading grass. The description is apt, but God provides what humanity does not possess: *power* and *strength.* He gives it precisely to those who are weak and faint.

30–31 In circumstances where those in the best condition possible to humans *stumble and collapse* (literally, "stumble stumbling"), a special group runs on with new and greater vigor than before. They are *those waiting* on Yahweh. The word קוה may mean "wait" or "hope." Here the ideas overlap: "waiting hope" or "hopeful waiting." Israel's impatience and insistence on prompt action from God could become her undoing. An attitude which can wait for the God of the ages and his plan will gain *strength* to *rise* above the moment, *not tire* and *not faint,* but go on and on. The figure of the eagle's wings is apt. The soaring eagle is borne aloft not by his powerful wings, but by the wind's currents lifting his rigid pinions. Those *waiting* are those prepared to be lifted up and carried aloft by the spirit of God in his time and his way.

Explanation

This passage is a major response to the protest of vv 6–7. (The call to Jerusalem in v 9 will be dealt with in chap. 49.) It interprets the protest by identifying its source as Jacob/Israel (v 27a) and its thrust as a complaint that Yahweh has been neither open nor fair with Israel (v 27b). The complaint also reveals Jacob/Israel's determination that God must do things her way. The passage then picks up in v 28 the specific themes of "wilting" and "fainting" from v 7, but now in very personal and human terms to promise a solution to her problem, a prescription for her complaint.

God allows her a specific insight into his doings. He is coming to Jerusalem with power. He will win, and he will win in Jerusalem. The promise of his presence and the revelation of his glory there reverses the centuries of struggle for Israel with the kingdoms and the peoples, and even with Jerusalem. It also reveals that he will exercise grace to his flock, i.e., Israel. He will shepherd them (v 11). To such as can "wait" or "hope" for him, he will give power and strength for the glorious days to come and the patience needed before they arrive. The Targums already interpret this as a picture of the return to Jerusalem. See v 31.

But the rest of his strategy remains a shrouded mystery. Israel, who cannot yet see the shape of things to come, is not prepared to listen to the call from God or to think the thoughts of God. Her skepticism is based on the observation that nothing has changed in her very human situation. The empire is still firmly in control. Jews are still totally impotent in all political and military matters. Jerusalem is a pile of ruins. Truly "flesh is grass" with no hope in sight for the weakening of imperial control or for Israelite strength to mount a revolution.

So the people are accused of a lack of trust which is akin to idolatry. It is an idolatry of the mind that demands that God and his word make sense *to them.* They want God to convince them, to listen to their plan which compares him to nations and to governments that they know or that they have known. They expect God to fit his plans to their specifications.

The passage responds by attacking the people's attitude for its lack of perception of God, his greatness, and his strategy for the ages. They have underestimated him and judged him by the moment of their own experience. Judge him rather by star-time or star-space. That is his dimension: the time it takes to set the stars in space; the distances they move and require for their existence. These dwarf all ordinary concepts of human comparison.

If humankind is transitory and helpless like the grass and wild flowers—and in many ways it is—Yahweh is the one who overcomes these weaknesses and gives both meaning and power. But the perspective of God's greatness in size and time requires "waiting on" and "hoping for." God's time is not our time (cf. John 7:6). God's moment is not our moment. Those who can learn to wait on God's time and God's way will renew their strength, will run and not be weary, walk and not faint.

Scene 2: Israel Affirmed as Yahweh's Servant (41:1–20)

Bibliography

Ap-Thomas, D. R. "Two Notes in Isaiah (41:3, 2:22)." *Essays in Honor of G. W. Thatcher.* Sydney: Sydney U. P., 1967. 45–61. **Boadt, L.** "Isaiah 41:8–13: Notes on Poetic Structure and Style." *CBQ* 35 (1973) 20–34. **Conrad, E. W.** "The 'Fear Not' Oracles in Second Isaiah." *VT* 44 (1984) 133–43. ———. *Patriarchal Traditions in Second Isaiah.* (41:8–13; 43:1–4, 5–7; 44:1–5). Diss. Princeton Theological Seminary, 1974. **Elliger, K.** "Der Sinn des hebräischen Wortes שְׁפִי." *ZAW* 83 (1971) 317–29. **Fohrer, G.** "Zum Text von Jes. xli 8–13." *VT* 5 (1955) 239–49. **Goldingay, J.** "The Arrangement of Isaiah 41–45." *VT* 29 (1979) 289–99. **Hamlin, E. J.** "The Meaning of 'Mountains and Hills' in Isa. 41:14–16." *JNES* 13 (1954) 185–90. **Hessler, E.** "Die Struktur der Bilder bei Deuterojesaja." *EvT* 25 (1965) 349–69 (esp. sec. iv). **Joüon, P.** "Le sens du mot hébreu שְׁפִי." *JA* 10/7 (1906) 137–42. **Merendino, R. P.** *Der Erste und der Letzte* 123–90. ———. "Literarkritisches, Gattungskritisches und Exegetisches zu Jes. 41, 8–16." *Bib* 53 (1972) 1–42. **Wypych, S.** *I cosidetti oracoli de salvezza del Deuteroisaia.* Analisi, struttura e tema di Is 41,8–16; 43,1–7; 44,1–8.21.22. Diss. Pont. Univ. S. Tommaso, Rome, 1973.

Translation

Yahweh: 41:1 *Listen to me in silence,*[a] *you coastlands!* 3+3
Let peoples [b]*renew strength!*[b]
Let them approach, then let them speak. 3+3
[c]*Let us assemble for the trial!*[c]
2 *Who has aroused (one) from the east?* 3+3
Whom salvation calls[a] *to its feet?*[b]
(Who) gives up nations before him 3+2
that he beats down[c] *kings?*
(Who) gives up[d] *his*[e] *sword like dust,*[f] 3+3
his bow like driven[g] *chaff?*
3 [a]*He pursues them.*[b] *He passes by (in) peace* 3+4
a path he does not travel[c] *on foot.*
4 *Who has performed and done (this)?*[a] 2+3
calling out the generations from the beginning?
I, Yahweh, (was) with the first 3+2
and with the last I am he.

Heavens: 5 *Coastlands have seen*[a] *and are afraid.*[b] 3+3+2
The borderlands tremble.[c]
They have drawn near and arrived.[d]
6 *Each helps his neighbor* 3+3
and to his brother he says, "Be strong."
7 *Then a craftsman strengthens a goldsmith,*[a] 3+4
a finisher with a hammer,[b] *an anvil striker.*[a]
saying[c] *of the soldering, "It is good."* 3+2+2
Then they strengthen it with nails.
"It cannot be moved."

Yahweh: [8] *But you, Israel, (are) my servant,* 3+3+3
Jacob, whom I have chosen,
Seed of Abraham, my friend,[a]
[9] *Whom I strengthened as far as the borderlands* 4+2
and whom I called from its far corners.
I called you.[a] *You are my servant.* 3+3
I have chosen you! I have not abandoned you!
[10] *Do not be afraid, for I am with you.* 3+3
Do not be anxious[a] *for I am your God.*
I have strengthened you. Indeed, I have helped you. 2+3
Indeed, I have upheld you by the right hand of my salvation.
[11] *See,*[a] *they are shamed and confounded—* 3+3
all who were aroused[b] *against you.*
[c]*They are as nothing*[c] *and they have perished*[d]*—* 3+2
your adversaries in conflict.
[12] [a]*You seek them but do not find them*[a]*—* 3+2
your adversaries in strife.
They are as nothing and as non-entities— 3+2
your adversaries in warfare.
[13] *For I, Yahweh,*[a] *am your God,* 4+2
strengthening your right hand,
who is saying to you: Do not be afraid. 3+2
[b]*I myself have helped you.*[b]

Heavens: [14] [a]*Do not be afraid,* 2+2+2
little worm[a] *Jacob,*
tiny caterpillar[b] *Israel!*
"I myself have helped you" 2+2+3
(is) the expression of Yahweh,
[c]*and your Redeemer (is) the Holy One of Israel!*[c]

Yahweh: [15] *If I had appointed*[a] *you as a sharp threshing*[b] *sled,* 4+3
new, with double rows of teeth,[c]
You would thresh mountains[d] *and crush (them)* 3+3
and[e] *you would make hills*[d] *to be like chaff.*
[16] *You would winnow them and the wind would lift them up.* 3+3
The storm would scatter them.
But you shall rejoice in Yahweh.[a] 3+3
In the Holy One[b] *of Israel you shall sing praises.*
[17] *As for the poor and the needy* 2+3+3
seeking water when there is none,
whose tongue is parched by thirst,
I, Yahweh,[a] *answer them.* 3+4
As God of Israel, [b]*I do not abandon them.*
[18] *I open rivers on the plateaus* 3+3
and fountains in the valleys.
I make the wilderness [a]*a pool of water*[a] 3+4
and a dry land to (be) springs of water.

[19]*I place a cedar in the wilderness,* 3+4
an acacia, a myrtle, and an oil tree.
I put a cypress in the Arabah, 3+3
an elm tree and a pine together.[a]
Earth: [20]*In order that they may see and know,* 3+3
that they may position[a] *and understand (these) together*
that Yahweh's hand has done this[b] 4+3
and that the Holy One of Israel has created it.

Notes

1.a. LXX ἐγκαινίζεσθε "renew yourselves" apparently read החדישו, a *daleth* for a *resh*.

1.b-b. MT's repetition of a phrase from 40:31 is supported by DSS[Isa] and all the Versions. Mowinckel, Muilenburg, and others have demonstrated the deliberate compositional use of repetition in this section (contra *BHK*).

1.c-c. LXX τότε κρίσιν ἀναγγειλάτωσαν "at that time they will announce judgment" apparently has another arrangment of the text.

2.a. Elliger (104) derives יקראהו from a second root (BDB, 896–97) with a meaning like קרה "meet, confront" (BDB, 899). So RSV.

2.b. DSS[Isa] and three MSS[R] read לרגליו "to his feet" (pl); MT is sg. Elliger (105) moves it to the end of the following line.

2.c. MT יַרְדְּ "he beats down" (hiph impf from רדד BDB, 921), DSS[ISA] יוריד "he brings down" (hiph from ירד BDB, 432). LXX ἐκστήσει "will be amazed" apparently read יַחֲרִיד (BDB, 353) as Klostermann pointed out (*BHS*). Syr *ntwrwn* "they are terrified" follows suit. Tg has תבר "they shatter in pieces," Vg *obtinebit* "he will possess." Among these MT does as well as any.

2.d. DSS[Isa] ויתן adds ו "and," supported by LXX. But Syr Tg Vg follow MT. Tg and Vg understand "kings" as the object of the verb. Many (*BHS;* Elliger, 106; and others) think ־ם "them" has fallen out as object and reinsert it. But the parallel to the previous line suggests that Yahweh is subject as Tg and Vg recognized.

2.e. LXX "their."

2.f. LXX εἰς γῆν "to ground, earth" has translated MT literally.

2.g. MT נִדָּף "driven" is a niph ptcp; DSS[Isa] נודף "driven" is a qal act ptcp.

3.a. DSS[Isa] and LXX add "and."

3.b. DSS[Isa] and LXX add "and."

3.c. MT יבוא "he came." DSS[Isa] יבינו "they discerned" (BDB, 106) and Vg *semita in pedibus eius non apparebit* "the path for his feet will not be seen." LXX omits, but Syr and Tg support MT.

4.a. LXX inserts ταῦτα "that."

5.a. The pf tense picks up the relation to v 4 and is continued in 5c. The translation uses a present pf, with a simple present for the Heb impfs.

5.b. DSS[Isa] ויראו "and see" is impv. Translations have had a great deal of trouble with the tenses here. But MT is consistent and should be followed.

5.c. MT יחרדו "tremble" (BDB 353). DSS[Isa] יחדו "together" = LXX ἅμα.

5.d. MT ויאתיון "and come" (BDB 87, GKC § 75u). DSS[Isa] ואתיון appears to read an impv again. Tg has an impf. LXX Syr Vg support MT.

7.a-a. The Versions had trouble distinguishing subj and objs, apparently not yet having את, the sign of the dir obj, in their texts (see Elliger, 107).

7.b. DSS[Isa] פלטיש is without parallel in Heb. Elliger (108) suggests that the doubled middle letter of MT פַּטִּישׁ "hammer" has been released by dissimilation. Cf. Bergstrasser, *Heb. Grammatik* § 20b and M. Mansoor, "Some Linguistic Aspects of the Qumran Texts," *JSS* 3 (1958) 50.

7.c. DSS[Isa] יואמר "he says."

8.a. MT אֹהֲבִי "my lover" or "one loving me." LXX ὃν ἠγάπησα "whom I have loved"; 'A ἀγαπητοῦ μοῦ "my beloved." Σ τοῦ φιλοῦ μοῦ and Vg *amici mei* mean "my friend." The pass ptcp suggested by *BHS,* אֲהֻבִי "one beloved by me," is neither supported nor necessary (cf. Elliger, 132).

9.a. DSS[Isa] ואומרה "and let me call" is cohortative. In 40:6 it has the same form.

10.a. MT תִּשְׁתָּע is usually located as a hithp impf from שעה "gaze about" (BDB, 1043). Elliger (132) refers to recent discoveries of cognates in Phoenician (Jean-Hoftijzer, *DISO,* 322) and in Ug (Aistleitner, *WB,* 2956) pointing to a root שתע meaning "fear." This supports the qal pointing תִּשְׁתַּע found in many MSS.

11.a. Missing in Syr. DSS[Isa] has it added above the line.

11.b. MT הנחרים "aroused" is a niph ptcp from חרה. G. R. Driver (*JTS* 36 [1935] 398) points it as a qal ptcp from נחר "snoring angrily" (BDB, 637; cf. *BHS*).

11.c-c. Missing in DSS[Isa].

11.d. DSS[Isa] and LXX insert "all." 1QIsa[b] has ויבשו "and they are shamed."

12.a-a. Missing in DSS[Isa].

13.a. Missing in LXX (except the hexaplaric MS group oII and MS 403′).

13.b-b. Missing in LXX.

14.a-a. Missing in LXX.

14.b. MT מתי "men of" (BDB, 607). LXX has ὀλιγοστὸς "small number" and Σ αριθμος "a number." But DSS[Isa] ומיתי "you dead ones of," 'A (οι) τεθνεωτες "dead ones," Θ οι νεκροι "the dead," and Vg *qui mortui estis* "who are dead" are followed by W. H. Brownlee (*The Meaning of the Qumrân Scrolls* [New York: Oxford U. P., 1964] 221) and H. E. von Waldow (*Anlass und Hintergrund der Verkündigung des Deuterojesaja,* Diss., Bonn, 1953). Driver (*JTS* 36 [1935] 399) and *BHS* suggest reading מת according to an Akk word, *mutu,* meaning "a small louse" or "cornworm," and suggest that Syr *mnynh* meant not "number" but "cornworm." The latter meaning, though it has no parallel in Heb., fits the context best (cf. Elliger, 147).

14.c-c. LXX ὁ λυτρούμενός σε, Ισραηλ "the one setting you free, Israel."

15.a. The sequence of tenses following הנה suggests subordination: a pf in v 15a introduces six impfs. הנה is taken as a conditional particle "if" (cf. GKC § 159w). The pf tense is understood to represent a condition contrary to fact (GKC § 159lm and Watts, *Syntax,* 136–38). The impfs in the apodosis speak of things that would have been true if the protasis were real, which it is not.

15.b. The lexicons cannot decide whether this is an adj (GB) or a noun (*CHAL;* KB; BDB, 558). The number of words has made some feel that one of these is redundant (cf. *BHS* and Elliger, 147).

15.c. See Ps 149:6.

15.d-d. Tg interprets as "peoples" and "kingdoms."

15.e. LXX puts the "and" after "hills" and thus reads "hills" with "crush," making the Heb. stichs 2 + 2 + 2. MT, however, is followed by Syr Tg Vg.

16.a. Missing in LXX.

16.b. LXX ἐν τοῖς ἁγίοις Ισραήλ "in the saints of Israel." DSS[Isa] adds "and" followed by a number of Heb. and Gr. MSS, Σ Θ and Syr.

17.a. LXX ἐγὼ κύριος ὁ θεός, ἐγὼ "I am the Lord God, I myself." Syr Tg Vg support MT.

17.b. LXX and Syr add "and."

18.a-a. LXX has εἰς ἕλη "into marshes," as do OL and Syh. *BHS* suggests a Heb. original of לַאֲגַמִּים "to pools" for MT's לאגם־מים "to a pool of water" (cf. BDB, 8). The change is minor and of little help.

19.a. MT lists 7 trees; LXX, only 5; Σ, 7; 'A and Θ, 4; Jerome and Vg, 7; Syr, 6; and Tg, 7. See the comparative lists in Elliger, 158.

20.a. DSS[Isa] has ויבינו "and they consider," with וישימו "and position" as a variation above the line.

20.b. LXX ταῦτα πάντα "all this."

Form/Structure/Setting

The setting of 41:1–20 comes from the previous scenes. It lends support to the announcement and call of 40:1–5. It is also a response to Israel's complaint voiced in 40:6–7 and v 27.

V 1 establishes the genre of the scene as a trial speech. The islands and peoples are summoned as witnesses. The purpose is clearly stated: "for the trial." As the trial proceeds it is clear that both Israel and the peoples need to be persuaded by the speeches. Begrich (*Studien zu Deuterojesaja,* 26–48) was the first to study the form of these trial speeches. Substantial work has also been done by von Waldow (*Anlass und Hintergrund,* 37–46, and *Der traditionsgeschichtliche Hintergrund der prophetischen Gerichtsreden,* BZAW 85 [Berlin: Töpelmann, 1963]) and Westermann ("Sprache und Structur der Prophetie Deuterojesajas," *Forschung am Alten Testament,* ThB 24 [Munich: Kaiser, 1964] 134–44). H. J. Boecker's study of legal forms in *Redeformen des Rechtslebens* has contributed to its understanding. The broader study of the covenant lawsuit has been drawn into the discussion. For a full listing of literature, cf. Melugin, *Formation,* 45–46.

The form here is not significantly different from that already established for the Vision from chap. 1 onward. The major change lies in the direct participation by Yahweh himself, who is more active here than he has been since the very first chapter. The pervasive use of "I" speeches for Yahweh has been made the topic of a study by C. E. Crosby (*The Yahweh "I" Speech in Isaiah 40–66* [Diss., Fuller Theological Seminary, 1985]). It is no new thing for Yahweh to speak in the first person. Cf. Gen 15:7, 17:1; Exod 3:6, 20:2/Deut 5:6; and the refrain "I am Yahweh, your God" in the Holiness Code of Leviticus. (See W. Zimmerli, "Ich bin Jahwe," *Geschichte und Altes Testament,* FS A. Alt [Tübingen: Mohr, 1953] 179–209; and "Das Wort des göttlichen Selbsterweises [Erweiswort, eine prophetische Gattung]," *Mélanges bibliques,* FS André Robert [Paris: Bloud et Gay, 1957] 154–64 = *Gottes Offenbarung,* ThB 19 [Munich: Kaiser, 1969] 120–32.) The broader genre, including the Yahweh speeches in Job 38–42, is treated by R. LaPointe ("Divine Monologue as a Channel of Revelation," *CBQ* 32 [1970] 161–81).

The scene has the structure of an arch as so many scenes before it have had:

A The call to trial: islands and peoples (v 1)
  B Who stirred up the eastern conqueror? (vv 2–3)
    C Who calls out the generations from the beginning? (v 4)
      D The islands and ends of the land respond (vv 5–7)
KEYSTONE But you Israel are my servant (vv 8–9)
      D′ Do not be afraid (vv 10–12)
    C′ I, Yahweh, strengthen your right hand (vv 13–14)
  B′ If I had appointed you . . . but you shall rejoice (vv 15–19)
A′ In order that they (the peoples) may know (v 20)

Melugin (*Formation,* 93–98) has divided the speech into four units (vv 1–7, 8–13, 14–16, 17–20) and has summarized the studies of their arrangement and connections. E. W. Conrad (*VT* 44 [1984] 133) has identified the form of the two "fear not" speeches (vv 8–13, 14–16) with oracles found in Deut 3:2/Num 21:34; Josh 8:1–2; 10:8; 11:6. The outline of these is: (a) assurance, (b) object of fear, (c) basis of assurance, (d) result. In 41:8–13 Conrad finds the same pattern: (a) address, vv 8–9; (b) assurance, v 10a; (c) basis of assurance, v 10b; (d) result, v 11–12; (e) basis of assurance, v 13. In vv 14–16 the outline is: (a) assurance, v 14a; (b) address, v 14b; (c) basis of assurance, v 14c–15a; (d) result, v 15b–16. Cf. also Merendino, *Der Erste und der Letzte,* 165, and *Bib* 53 (1972) 25.

The historical setting of Act VII intrudes itself upon the scene for the first time. The conqueror from the east (v 2) will be identified in the next act as Cyrus, the Persian. For a full two decades before he conquered Babylon, he was becoming known in the regions east of Mesopotamia. The mountains of Iran had produced Medes with ambition and power before, but never someone like this. He achieved status over his own tribesmen first. Then he conquered Media before taking control of its allies, the Babylonians. By this time Cyrus had a sizable kingdom extending from the boundaries with Babylon and Elam in the south, to the Aegean Sea across Asia Minor, to the Black Sea in the North, and eastward to the edge of India. His reputation was growing. Yahweh refers to him and claims to be the prime instigator of his ambition and success. He then claims that it has always been so. From the beginning, he has directed the course of such events.

Comment

1 The great judgment scene has witnesses representing the fringe elements of the land, the *coastlands* of Philistia and Phoenicia. This is significant since the primary evidence that is offered concerns an event taking place "offstage" with respect to the normal middle-eastern theater of biblical history.

2 Farther east the political pot is boiling. A bright and fearful new name is being whispered in all the world's seats of power. It is the name of Cyrus the Persian, who already reigns over the combined kingdoms of Media and Persia (cf. 41:21–29; 42:5–9; 44:24–28; 45:1–7, 9–11; 48:12–15). Cyrus II began his rise in 558 B.C. when he was crowned king of Persia in Pasargadae, which lay east-southeast of Babylon in the Iranian mountains. He rebelled against his Median liege lords and conquered their capital, Ecbatana, in 550 B.C. By that act, he became the ruler of the vast Median empire that extended as far north and west as Armenia. This is the "success/salvation" that is referred to here. The verse asks about the power and inspiration behind Cyrus's throne and its power. צדק "salvation" is a word that usually means "righteousness" (BDB, 842). It is often thought now that the context in Isaiah 40–55 requires the meaning of "victory" (cf. Fohrer, Muilenberg, North, and Steinmann). But Elliger (120) makes a convincing case for the more correct meaning "salvation" for all ten cases in Isa 40–55 (41:2, 11; 42:6, 21; 45:8, 13, 19; 51:1, 5, 7). It contains the seed idea of "right," not simply for victory but for success, that is, for "salvation." Yahweh claims to be the one who has made Cyrus's victory march possible.

3 *He passes by (in) peace.* שלום may have the meaning "to be whole, healthy, complete," and many interpreters understand it so in this case. However, it has the special meaning of *peace,* which in this context of warfare, is appropriate. Cyrus gained only part of his kingdom by war. He fell heir to a general discontent against the Median rulers which brought many of their vassals into his camp without struggle. He is pictured as a master diplomat who was skilled in dealing sensitively with the religious and ethnic differences of his subjects. Thus many a campaign trail that brought victory was one he never had personally to travel. One must note here that many interpreters (including Tg, early Jewish scholars [except Ibn Ezra], Luther, Calvin, and among moderns, Torrey and Kissane) have thought this verse referred to Abraham, translating "in righteousness he called him to follow him."

4 Yahweh asks *Who has done this?* and then broadens the question to cover *the generations from the beginning.* In other words, who has controlled the forces of history from the beginning of time? He answers: *I, Yahweh, was with the first,* the ones at the head of the column of marchers in history's generations. ראשון "first" has neither article nor preposition. But את־אחרנים "with the latter" or "last things" (את without an article following is seen as a preposition "with") as a parallel makes the meaning "with" in both cases likely. The context calls for affirmation that he is "with" Cyrus, as he has been with successful rulers from the beginning of time.

The Vision claimed credit for Yahweh in the Assyrian invasions of the eighth century (chaps. 7–10). For the readers of the Vision, then, this is not a new idea. But there is a difference. The earlier chapters were interpreting historical events directly relating to Canaan and to Israel. Now Yahweh's actions deal with the growth of an empire on a distant horizon which, at this stage, seems to have nothing to do with Canaan. And Israel, as a political nation, is no more. Now Yahweh is revealing to Israel, a worshiping community in the foreign country of Babylon, the significance for them of world events beyond their borders. They are being given a glimpse into the complex ways by which God does his will in history.

5 A report is brought that those called to the judgment scene in v 1 are finally stirred into attending. Apparently the course of events has moved them.

Could the *coastlands* and the *borderlands* refer to the extremities of the territory of the old Davidic Empire? איים "coastlands" would then be Philistia and Phoenicia and קצות הארץ "borderlands" the territories that marked the northern and eastern border along the Euphrates River and the desert from Haran and Syria, including Ammon, Moab, Edom, and the territories of Arabian tribes. These are called as witnesses, as were Heavens and Earth in 1:2 and as nations and peoples are called in 34:1. They will be called again in 49:1.

Note the assonance of איים "coastlands" with אין "nothing." The lands that were independent countries in pre-exilic times were treated as such earlier in the Vision: Edom (21:11–12, chap. 34), Moab (chaps. 15–16), Philistia (14:28–32), Aram (17:1–3), Arabia (21:13–17), and Tyre (chap. 23). By this time, however, they are, like Judah, no more than subdivisions of a Persian satrapy.

It is worth noting here and in the following chapters that the leaders of these countries are the very ones that opposed the rebuilding of Jerusalem and its temple on numerous occasions, as Ezra and Nehemiah attest.

6 Their reaction is to bind themselves together, and encourage each other to *be strong* (חזק: this verb is a key motif for the next eight verses). They do this by the futile gestures of building idols. They strengthen each other in the effort. They make the image strong with added supports, as though the "god" must be strengthened. This is the irony of idolatry. Human power supports and strengthens the idol.

7 They say, *it cannot be moved.* Elliger (130) observes, "The stability is only relative, and above all else it is at the same time completely immobile!" The stability is as relative as Dagon's statue in 1 Sam 5:3–4. What a contrast to Yahweh who appears to his people in Babylon and who arouses the next generations of kings to their conquests! The urge for stability corresponds to a real need. But it is Yahweh who cannot be moved and who brings stability out of chaos in his creation. His statutes stand firm (Ps 93:5). His world is firmly established (Pss 93:1; 96:10). His throne is established forever (Ps 93:1). Israel shared humanity's need for stability. But she attained it by faith in God's unshakable order in word, salvation, and creation, not by trying to erect monuments that could not be moved.

8 God's true antagonist in the trial is *Jacob/Israel* and she is addressed now. She is identified clearly as Yahweh's elect by virtue of her descent from *Abraham,* God's friend.

9 But she is also one whom God has *strengthened* and *called,* not simply in Egypt at the beginning nor merely in Canaan. The emphasis here is on God's relation to Israel of the dispersion in *the borderlands* and *its far corners,* the very places from which Abraham was *called* and in which he received strength and faith for his journey to Canaan. This new people, Judaism of the dispersion, is *called, chosen* to be Yahweh's *servant.* This means she is called to worship him, as the Synagogue learned to do in later centuries. It means she is called to support worship in Jerusalem's temple (cf. 40:1–5). But it also carries the meaning of being Yahweh's instrument to perform his will, his messenger to bear his message. Far from being abandoned because they are no longer in Canaan, they are called into the very center of his strategic purposes to serve him.

10 *Do not be afraid.* To be addressed by God, to be called to serve him, is an awesome thing (cf. Judg 6:23). A remarkably similar statement appears in the mouth of Ishtar of Arbela to Asarhaddon: "Do not be afraid, O king, I said to you, I have not overthrown you" (*ANET,* 450). Note that the admonition is lacking from the prophetic call encounters of Moses, Jeremiah, etc. The formula appears repeatedly in this section of the Vision (40:9; 41:10, 13, 14; 43:1, 5; 44:2, 8; 51:7; 54:4; cf. L. Köhler, "Die Offenbarungsformel 'Fürchte dich nicht' im AT," *STZ* 36 [1919] 33–39; J. Becker, *Gottesfurcht im AT,* AnBib 25 [Rome: Pontifical Biblical Institute, 1965] 50–55). But the fear addressed here is not simply the anxiety of being in the presence of God; it is the sense that God has abandoned them. For various reasons, because of their sins or in despair over their usefulness to him, they have been well aware of grounds for abandonment.

But Yahweh insists *I am with you.* The formula has a long history which reaches back to Moses (Exod 3:12) and continues to the NT (Matt 28:20). See H. D. Preuss, "Ich will mit dir sein," *ZAW* 80 (1968) 139–73. Then he adds a second formulaic statement: *I am your God.* This also has ancient roots (cf. Exod 20:2/Deut 5:6) which are connected with Yahweh's appearance at covenant ceremonies (W. Zimmerli, *I am Yahweh, Your God,* tr. D. W. Stott

[Richmond, VA: John Knox Press, 1982]). God announces to Israel that her breech of covenant that led to exile need not mean an absolute and permanent separation. Yahweh is still Israel's God in her exile and in the new age.

Yahweh insists that he *has strengthened, has helped, has upheld* Israel throughout her ordeal. The implication is that she would never have survived if that were not so. *By the right hand of my salvation* (צדקי). The symbol for Divine intervention in human affairs, God's *right hand,* is associated with צדקי, the same word used in v 2 for Cyrus. It carries the meaning of "right," of "success," and of "salvation." God's righteous, successful, saving action in history has benefited Israel.

11–12 God presents proof of his statement. He points to Israel's opponents in all the conflicts of the past. These would include Midianites, Arameans, Assyrians. They were *shamed, confounded,* doomed to extinction. Babylon is in the process of joining the list.

13 This is because Yahweh has *strengthened* and *helped* Israel. The personality and word of Yahweh in the first person is more intrusive in these chapters than anywhere else in the Prophets or in Scripture. *I* (אני) for Yahweh appears in 41:4, 10, 13, 14, 17; 42:6, 8, 9; 43:2, 3, 4, 5, 10, 12, 13, 15; 44:6; 45:2, 3, 5, 6, 7, 8, 12, 18, 19, 21, 22; 46:4; 48:12, 13, 15, 16, 17; 49:18, 23, 26; 52:6. Elliger (140, n. 1) notes that the name of God is used attributively or as predicate in more than half these instances. The longer form אנכי "I" is used by Yahweh in 43:11, 12, 25; 44:24; 45:12, 13; 46:9; 49:15, 25; 51:12, 15; 51:11, 16. The impressive thing about these speeches is the personal appearance and argument of God himself, who addresses Israel directly and personally without intermediary. No prophet stands between. They have been brought into the very courtroom of the Heavenly King. He identifies himself as Yahweh, God of their fathers, and insists that he is and has been their God as well. He promises his personal aid for the tasks he calls them to perform.

14 This verse is an echo. With *little worm* and *tiny caterpillar* Israel is reminded of her own self-deprecation in 40:6–7. But the figure is altered (cf. Ps 22:7 [6]). The change of tone is obvious, but interpreters have differed about its implications. Schmidt thought it flattering. Duhm, Budde, Volz, and Muilenburg found it to be an expression of tenderness. Elliger (149) calls it affirmation of a naked fact. Begrich ("Das priesterliche Heilsorakel," *ZAW* 52 [1934] 87) considered it a motif taken over from the Psalms which was intended to move God to mercy. But it is not spoken by Israel here, nor by God. It is much more understandable as a needling reminder to Israel of her complaint which is used with the admonition *do not be afraid,* even though you are only grass, wildflowers, or a worm. *Yahweh, the Holy One of Israel* has said he has helped you. The name conjures up all the memories of God's acts of salvation on Israel's behalf from the Exodus onward. This great and proven God is showing himself by his public announcement to be Israel's *redeemer* in the present as he has been in the past.

The term גאל "redeemer" had a social and legal meaning in Hebrew, but it also had a religious meaning (Gen 48:16) which is raised to a central and powerful theological place by these chapters. A redeemer is one who has a close relationship with the one being redeemed. This relation of God to Israel is, of course, neither one of blood nor of tribal relation (cf. Elliger, 151). It is formed by the covenant and thus is at least as strong a bond and obligation as that formed by kinship (cf. Hosea's picture of the marriage relation, Hos 1–3). There can be no doubt about the effectiveness of this help. It is *The Holy One of Israel,* Yahweh himself, who has promised it.

Excursus: גאל *"Redeem"*

Bibliography

Bonnard, P. E. *Le Second Isaie* 535–535. **Denton, R. C.** "Redeem." *IDB* 4: 21–22. **Holmgren, F.** *The Concept of Yahweh as Goʾel in Second Isaiah.* Diss. Union Theological Seminary, New York, 1963. **Jepson, A.** "Die Begriffe des 'Erlösens' im AT." *Solange es "Heute heisst."* FS R. Hermann. Berlin: Evangelische Verlagsanstalt, 1957. 153–63. **Johnson, A. R.** "The Primary Meaning of *gʾl. Congress Volume, Copenhagen, 1953.* VTSup 1. Leiden: E. J. Brill, 1953. 67–77. **Procksch, O.** *Der Erlösungsgedanke im Alten Testament.* Göttingen: Vandenhoeck & Ruprecht, 1929. **Snaith, N. H.** "The Hebrew Root *gʾl.*" *ALVOS* 3 (1961–62) 60–67. **Stamm, J. J.** *Erlösen und Vergeben im Alten Testament.* Bern: 1940. **Ringgren, H.** "גאל." *TDOT* 2:350–55. **Stuhlmacher, C.** *Creative Redemption* 99–122, 273–78.

A major feature of chaps. 40–66 is the combining of words describing creation with words describing salvation to picture Yahweh's role and action toward Israel and Jerusalem in the 6th and 5th centuries B.C. (see C. Stuhlmacher, *Creative Redemption in Deutero-Isaiah*).

גאל "redeem"/"redeemer" is a major component of that development, parallel to ישע "save"/"savior." Both words are related to the Exodus (Exod 6:6; 15:13), but are used much more profusely here (גאל, 23 times; ישע, 31 times). גאל "redeem," like its less-used parallel פדה "ransom," is also used with a cultic or sacrificial meaning (see Exod 13; Lev 25 and 27). But in Isa 40–66 they are so closely related to ישע "save" that their meaning is drawn into the realistic political/social/religious world of Jewish survival in the Persian empire. The people are geographically and physically separated from their land. Their social and political structures have been destroyed. Religious institutions, from festivals and shrines to Temple and priesthood, have been disrupted to an extent that they can no longer function as they had in the past. Families and clans have been scattered. Villagers now live in cities. Priests have neither temple nor altar. The kind of relief that is required is similar to that of the Egyptian bondage (see *Excursus: Exodus Typology*).

As "redeemer," God addressed these needs. The Vision relates these salvation-words to strong creator-words (see *Excursus:* ברא "Create"/"Creator") to shape a theological pattern that has dominated biblical thought on salvation from that time on, even when it came to involve spiritual and individual issues widely separated and only metaphorically similar to the need for physical group rescue and restoration evidenced in the Exodus and the Exile.

Redemption addresses the issues of Israel's sin and rebellion, of the effects of judgment on a former generation and age, of problems posed by exile and devastation, and of the need for faith and hope when these were hard to find. Redemption, as the vision of Isaiah portrays it, involves creating an entirely new age, raising up an emperor to provide means and protection, publishing a Torah for the new temple personnel and for pilgrims as well as Jews throughout the empire, and calling out a select group of meek and humble worshipers to share the worship-place with God.

The practical aspects of salvation (restoration of Jerusalem, building highways, restoring land-rights for Judean villages, creating possibilities for pilgrimage), paralleled by social renewal (creating a new Jewish social order and spirit), and leading to spiritual enrichment (sharing the joy of worship in the new Jerusalem) are all part of this redeeming process. The power and determination of Yahweh make it possible. His presence and goals lend a sacramental aspect to the entire project which more than justifies the use of words like "redeem" and "ransom." The practical political and social dimensions of God's work justify the use of terms like "save" and "deliver." For all the strong exhortation in exuberant terms, the project is practical and possible. The city is rebuilt. Judaism becomes a religio-social community that was able to survive and flourish in the social and political setting of empire. All this, along with the development of spiritual aspects of self-identification as Yahweh's people and of trust in him for all they needed, is contained in the picture of salvation/redemption presented in the Vision.

15 Yahweh is again the speaker. What he says is indeed a contrast to the "worm" existence mentioned in the verse before. But the entire picture of Israel's calling is so radically different from anything in the Vision that it is shocking. E. Hessler (*EvT* 25 [1965] 355) considers the impression created by the picture a compositional failure. Her recognition of the abnormal picture is correct. But there is a better way to interpret it. The particle and tense structure fit that used for a conditional sentence based on an "unreal" premise (see n. 15.a). Yahweh is saying that he could have appointed Israel to be his *threshing sled* to do the work that Cyrus is now performing. He could have, and if he had, she would be the glorious victor over all. The *mountains* and the *hills* may well have political meaning in terms of the powers of the earth including Babylon (cf. E. J. Hamlin, *JNES* 13 [1954] 185–90).

16 But Israel's calling is a very different one. Israel is to *rejoice* and *sing praises*. תגיל "rejoice" belongs to the vocabulary of praise in the Psalms. It is a constant element of the Vision's emphasis on worship (25:9; 29:19; 49:13; 61:10; 65:19 [of God]; 66:10). תתהלל "sing praises" also belongs to psalmic language. The familiar "Hallelujah" contains the word with the object "yah," for Yahweh. It appears elsewhere in the Vision only in 45:25. ב "in" is twice prefixed to Yahweh. Praise is not simply directed toward him. He is the basis, the reason for such praise (cf. NT usage of the term "in Christ"). Israel's calling and assigned role for the new age continues that given under Moses: "You are to be to me a kingdom of priests, a holy nation" (Exod 19:6). Hence the call for the Jews of the dispersion to support and encourage Jerusalem in the restoration of the Temple and of worship there (40:2–5).

17–19 In the Vision, praise and honor to God often are mentioned in close relation to God's provision, as here, for the *poor* and the *needy*. Israel's insistence that she is in need is legitimate. Yahweh insists that he does *answer them*. He does *not abandon them*. On the contrary, he provides *water* in abundance in *dry* areas of their existence. He plants luxuriant forests in the *wilderness*. Even if Lebanon's supplies of lumber are limited (40:16), the Arabah can provide amply when God assigns it that responsibility.

20 Israel, wherever she is, is provided for. She survives. She lives, and she is once again addressed by her God. All this *in order that they may see and know.* This is exactly what the Vision has noted that Israel is not capable of doing (cf. 1:3, 6:9, and the many references to blindness and deafness). Yet God continues to try. *That they may position* (ישׂימו) uses a word that often speaks of God "assigning, constituting, placing" things or events. Israel is challenged to put the things she has experienced in proper perspective, to *understand* (them) *together.* If she can think of her remarkable survival along with this new call and the potential in developing world events all in terms of Yahweh's plans and his actions, she will be in position to rejoice and sing praises. She can fulfill her new/old role as Servant of Yahweh.

That Yahweh's hand has done this and that the Holy One of Israel has created it summarizes the basis of the Vision's theology. It looks at the skies and says he made the stars and placed them in space (40:22). It looks at Israel's history from the eighth century onward, the Assyrian invasions, the fall of Samaria, and finally Jerusalem's fall and says, Yahweh planned it and did it (chaps. 1–39). It looks at the rise of Assyria, its fall, and now at the rise of Persia, and says Yahweh did it (chaps. 7–10, *et passim,* and 41:2). In all this the Vision sees Yahweh's plan and purpose and calls upon believers in the dispersion, in Jerusalem, and beyond, in space and history, to do the same.

Explanation

The issue in the great trial scene is the question of strength and success. Israel has complained of human frailty (40:6–7) and of divine neglect (40:27). Now Yahweh parades before her the great political movements of that day, implying that he has Israel's interests in mind as he manipulates the rise and fall of distant kingdoms. The motif of power runs throughout the scene. Where does the energy and strength to change history's structures come from? Yahweh answers, "From me." And where does one gain strength to survive and succeed in such troubled times, when the pagans build more idols to bolster their courage? Again Yahweh answers Israel, "From me."

He points to the futility of self-help and calls her to recognize God's strengthening help. He points to the very fact of her survival through a history in which each of her adversaries, the Philistines, the Arameans, and the Assyrians, has faded from the stage of history. Israel's tiny and insignificant nature is irrelevant. Yahweh's call and Yahweh's help is everything.

If Yahweh had appointed Israel to the task Cyrus is now doing, she could defeat the world. But he did not. Her calling is to worship, rejoice and sing praises to Yahweh. If this leaves Israel "poor and needy," God's miraculous powers can care for her. He who can turn the dry wilderness into a garden and a forest is certainly capable of that.

The entire proceeding has taken place to help the poor and needy Jews of Babylon see and know, so that they can arrange their thinking about world events and about the marvelous powers of their God. They must see that Yahweh has done all of these, from the rise of Cyrus to the arrangement of the stars in space. And they must believe that their election and salvation is also in his hands—a part of his thoughts—while he is doing all the other things.

The NT emphasizes the same theme. Elliger (156) refers to Paul's lesson that God's "power is made perfect in weakness" (2 Cor. 12:9, NIV), to "the enduring city" of Heb 13:14 and the call to be "filled with inexpressible and glorious joy" (1 Pet 1:8, NIV). The ultimate goal of the believer's life is that of joining the heavenly choirs in eternal praise (Rev 14).

Scene 3: Yahweh Defends His Authority and His Choice of Cyrus (41:21–42:12)

Bibliography

Beaucamp, E. " 'Chant nouveau du retour' (Is 42:10–17), un monstre de l'exégèse moderne." *RScRel* 56 (1982) 145–58. **Behler, G. M.** "Le premier chant du Serviteur, Is 42:1–7." *VSpir* 120 (1969) 253–81. **Begrich, J.** "Beilage I: Zur Interpretation von Kap. 42:1–4." *Studien zu Deuterojesaja,* 161–66. **Betram, R. W.** "A Baptismal Crossing, Isaiah 42:1–9." *CurTM* 9 (1982) 344–53. **Beuken, W. A. M.** "Mispat: The First Servant Song and Its Context." *VT* 22 (1972) 1–30. **Coppens, J.** "La mission du Serviteur de Yahvé et son statut eschatologique." *ETL* 48 (1972) 342–71. **Dijkstra, M.** "De koninklijke knecht: Voorstelling en investituur van de Knecht des Heren in Jesaja 42." *De Knecht.* FS J. Koole. Kampen: Kok, 1978. **Freedman, D. N.** "Isaiah 42, 13." *CBQ* 30 (1968) 225–26. **Frezza, F.** "Annotazioni sperimentali su Is. 42, 1–4." *RivB* 19 (1971) 307–30. **Haag, E.** "Bund für das Volk und Licht für die Heiden (Jes 42:6)." *Didaskalia* 7 (1977) 3–14 = *Glaube an Jesus Christus.* Eds. J. Blank, G. Hasenhüttl. Düsseldorf: Patmos Verlag, 1980. 28–41. **Haller, M.** "Die Kyros-Lieder Deuterojesajas." *Eucharisterion.* FS H. Gunkel. FRLANT 19. Göttingen: Vandenhoeck & Ruprecht, 1923. 1:262–65. **Jeremias, J.** "*Mispat* im ersten Gottesknechtslied." *VT* 22 (1972) 31–42. **Koenig, J.** "L'allusion inexpliquée au roseau et à la mèche (Isaie xlii 3)." *VT* 18 (1968) 159–72. **Lauha, A.** "Der Bund des Volkes: Ein Aspekt der deuterojesajanischen Missionstheologie." *Beiträge zur AT Theologie.* FS W. Zimmerli. Göttingen: Vandenhoeck & Ruprecht, 1977. 257–61. **Marcus, R.** "The 'Plain Meaning' of Isaiah 42:1–4." *HTR* 30 (1937) 249–59. **McEleney, N. J.** "The Translation of Isaiah 41:27." *CBQ* 19 (1957) 441–43. **Merendino, R. P.** *Der Erste und der Letzte,* 191–273. **Morgenstern, J.** "Isaiah 42:10–13." *To Do and to Teach.* FS C. L. Pyatt. Lexington: College of the Bible, 1953. 27–38. **Mulder, M. J.** "Filologische kanttekeningen bij Jes. 41, 23b; 42, 19b en 43, 14b." *De Knecht.* FS J. Koole, Kampen: Kok, 1978. **Neyrey, J. H.** "The Thematic Use of Isaiah 42:1–4 in Matthew 12." *Bib* 63 (1982) 457–73. **Oosterhoff, B. J.** "Tot een licht der volken (Is 42:6)." *De Knecht.* FS J. Koole. Kampen: Kok, 1978. **Reiterer, F. V.** "Das geknickte Rohr bricht er nicht: Die Botschaft vom Gottesknecht" (42:1–4). *Heiliger Dienst* 35 (1981) 162–80. **Renkema, J.** "De verkondiging van het eerste lied van de knecht (Jes. 42:1–4)." *De Knecht.* FS J. Koole. Kampen: Kok, 1978. **Saggs, H. W. F.** "A Lexical Consideration for the Date of Deutero-Isaiah." *JTS* 10 (1959) 84–87. **Schoors, A.** "Les choses antérieur et les choses nouvelles dans les oracles Deutero-Isaiens." *ETL* 40 (1964) 19–47. **Schwarz, G.** " '. . . zum Bund des Volkes'? Eine Emendation" (42:6b). *ZAW* 82 (1970) 279–81. **Schweizer, H.** "Prädikationen und Leerstellen im 1. Gottesknechtslied (Jes 42, 1–4)." *BZ* 26 (1982) 251–58. **Sen, F.**

"El texta de Is 41:27a, mejor comprendido." *CB* 31 (1974) 47–48. **Smith, M. S.** *"Berit ʿam/Berit ʿolam:* The Crux of Isa 42:6." *JBL* 100 (1981) 241–43. **Stummer, F.** "Einige keilschriftliche Parallelen zu Jes. 40–55: (5) Jes. 41:22ff." *JBL* 45 (1926) 178–80. **Szczurek, T.** "Trzcina zgnieciona i gasnaca lampa z Iz 42.3" [The bruised reed and the flickering flame in Isa 42:3]. *ACBibCrac* (1972) 30–38, 38–41 (with French trans., 281 f.). **Szlaga, J.** "Analiza filologiczna Iz 42,3b." *RocTKan* 29 (1982) 11–15 (German trans. 16). **Tidwell, N.** "My Servant Jacob, Is XLII 1. A Suggestion." *Studies on Prophecy.* VTSup 26 Leiden: E. J. Brill, 1974. 84–91. **Vasholz, R.** "Isaiah versus 'the Gods': A Case for Unity (Is 42,21)." *WTJ* 42 (1980) 389–94. **Wada, M.** "Reconsideration of *Mispat* in Isaiah 42:1–4." *Seisho-Gaku Ronshu* 16 (1981) 46–79. **Whitley, C. E.** "A Note on Isa. xli 27." *JSS* 2 (1957) 327–388. **Wijngaards, J. N. M.** "The Worldwide Mission of God's Humble Servant." *Jeevadh* 4 (1974) 137–43.

Translation

Heavens: 41:21 *They present*[a] *your* (*pl*) *case,* 2+2
says Yahweh.
Show[a] *your* (*pl*) *proofs,* 2+3
says the King of Jacob.
22 *Let them show*[a] *and set out to us* 3+3
what will happen.
Of previous events, tell us what they (*were*) 4+2
and let us make up our minds.
[b]*And let us know their results.* 2+3
Or let us hear (*about*) *events to come.*[b]
23 *Announce events coming after this*[a] 3+4
that we may know that you (*pl*) *are gods.*
Indeed, do (*pl*) (*something*) *good or do* (*pl*) (*something*) *bad.* 2+3
[b]*Let us be shocked and fear*[b] (*it*) *together.*
24 *See!*[a] *You* (*pl*) *are less than nothing*[b] 2+2+3
and your (*pl*) *action less than non-existent.*[c]
[d]*Anyone who chooses* (*to be*) *among you* (*is*) *an abomination!*[d]

Yahweh: 25 [a]*I stirred up*[b] (*one*) *from the north and he comes.*[c] 3+4
From the rising sun[d] *he is called*[e] *by his*[f] *name.*
And he treads[g] (*upon*) *rulers as on mortar* 3+3
and as a sculptor tramples clay.[h]
26 *Who made it known from* (*the*) *beginning that we may know?* 3+3
And from earlier times that we may say 'He was right'?
In fact, no one announced it! 2+3+3
Indeed, no one made it heard!
In fact, there was no one who heard your (*pl*) *sayings!*
27 *First to Zion: See! See them!*[a] 4+3
and to Jerusalem I appoint[b] *a messenger!*

[28] *When I looked,*[a] *there was no one.* 3+3+3
And of these[b] *there was no counselor*
who, when asked, replied a word (to me).
[29] *See! All of them are nothing.*[a] 3+2+3
Their works are non-existent.[b]
Their images are spirit and un-reality.
[42:1] *See*[a] *my servant whom I confirm!* 3+3
[b]*My chosen in whom my soul delights!*
I have put my spirit on him. 3+3
He extends (the) verdict[c] *to the nations.*
[2] *He does not shout*[a] *nor lift (his voice).* 4+3
He does not let his voice be heard in the street.
[3] *He does not shatter a bruised reed*[a] 4+4+3
nor put out[b] *a flickering wick.*
(Yet) truly[c] *he does extend (the) verdict.*
[4] *He does not fail. Nor is he discouraged*[a] 4+3+3
until he confirms (the) verdict in the land
and coastlands wait for his instruction.

Herald: [5] *Thus says the God, Yahweh,*[a] 3+3+3
the one creating the heavens and stretching them out,
the one hammering out the earth and its produce,
the one giving breath to the people on it 4+3
and spirit to those walking in it!

Yahweh: [6] *I am Yahweh.*[a] 2+2+2
I have called you (sg) in salvation
and I strengthen your hand.
I keep you[b] *and appoint you*[c] 2+2+2
to be a covenant (for) people,
to be a light (for) nations,
[7] *to open blind eyes,* 3+3+4
to release a prisoner from a dungeon,
those who live in darkness from a prison-house.
[8] *I am Yahweh. That is my name.* 4+3+2
My glory I do not assign to anyone else,
nor praise due me to the idols.
[9] [a]*The previous events—see, they have come about!* 3+3
And (now) I am announcing new things.[ab]
Before they happen[c] 2+2
I let you (pl) hear (about them).

Chorus: [10] *Sing (pl) to Yahweh a new song.* 4+3
(Let) his praise (rise) from the borderlands.
Let sea and its fullness glorify him,[a] 3+2
coastlands and their inhabitants.
[11] *Let wilderness and its towns lift up*[a] *(their voices),* 3+3
villages in which Kedar lives.[b]

Sing for joy, you inhabitants of Sela.[c] 3+3
Let them shout[d] *from mountaintops.*[e]
12 *Let them attribute glory to Yahweh* 3+3
and let them declare his praise in the coastlands.

Notes

21.a. קָרְבוּ appears to be qal pf 3 masc pl "they present," but the parallel verb הַגִּישׁוּ is hiph impv 2 masc pl "show!" The first verb's pointing could conceivably be piel impv 2 masc pl (BDB, 897) which would remove the problem, but this form does not appear elsewhere. Or the second verb could be pointed hiph pf 3 masc pl הִגִּישׁוּ "they show." The latter suggestion conforms to the persons of verbs in v 22. But if the addressees of the verbs are the idols or their devotees, and the 3d pers references are to their proofs, the Masoretic pointing may be sustained (see *Comment*).

22.a. MT יַגִּישׁוּ is hiph impf (juss) "let them show" (BDB, 620). LXX ἐγγισάτωσαν presumes a qal יִגְּשׁוּ "let them draw near." The other Versions follow LXX.

22.b-b. The logical relation of these two stichs has bothered interpreters. Many moderns reverse their order (see *BHS* and Elliger, 172). DSS[Isa] placed another או "or" before אחרונות [sic] "results," leaving out the suff, thus placing ונדעה "and let us know" with what precedes. LXX also drops the suffix and substitutes καὶ "and" for או, as does Vg. Syr and Tg support MT.

23.a. MT לאחור, lit., "to afterwards." DSS[Isa] first omitted *lamedh,* then added it over the line.

23.b-b. MT ונשתעה "and be shocked" is a qal impf with coh *heh* (*CHAL* 385; cf. BDB, 1043), with a pausal accentuation (GKC § 29u), perhaps for emphasis. It is synonymous with K ונרא "and let us fear" from ירא (cf. v 10). Q ונראה "and let us see" is from ראה. DSS[Isa] reads the two verbs ונשמעה ונראה "let us hear and see," LXX καὶ θαυμασόμεθα καὶ ὀψόμεθα "and we will admire and see," Vg *et loquamur et videamus* "and let us speak and see." Tg translates the first verb ונסתכל "so we will study it," Syr *wnstᶜh* "we will tell"— or is this simply transcribed? Cf. Elliger, 172.

24.a. MT הן; DSS[Isa] הנה. The meaning is the same.

24.b. MT מאין "less than nothing," lit., "from nothing" (BDB, 34, II). LXX πόθεν "whence?" understood אין to be an interrogative particle (BDB, 32, I).

24.c. Missing in DSS[Isa]. LXX ἐκ γῆς uses the second stich as an answer to the question of the first ("for whence are you and whence your business?") and apparently read מאפע "less than nonexistent" as מארץ "from earth" or מעפר "from dust" (Elliger, 172). Syr has *mn hrbʾ* "from swords." Many interpreters (see *BHS*) would eliminate *mem* on both words. אפע is a *hap. leg.*, best understood as kin to אפס "expressing nonexistence" (BDB, 67).

24.d-d. MT seems grammatically clear. But the shift in subject is strange. The Versions were confused (Elliger, 173): LXX βδέλυγμα ἐξελέξαντο ὑμᾶς "an abomination are they who chose you" (also Syr), Tg "an abomination it is in which you delight," Vg "it is an abomination which has chosen you." It is better to keep MT.

25.a. LXX inserts ἐγὼ δὲ "but I" at the beginning.

25.b. DSS[Isa] omits *yodh* "I" at the end. Keep MT.

25.c. DSS[Isa] ויאתיו is pl, "and they come." Keep MT.

25.d. DSS[Isa] adds *waw* "and."

25.e. Tg אגברניה "I make him strong." LXX κληθήσονται "they will be called" suggests a niph pointing for the Heb. (see *BHS*). The translation follows *BHS.*

25.f. DSS[Isa] "his" (*BHS*). The translation agrees.

25.g. MT ויבא "and he comes," DSS[Isa] ויבואו pl. *BHS* ויבס "and he treads" (BDB, 100) suggests that *samekh* fell out through haplography and later *aleph* was added. The emendation is probably correct.

25.h. LXX οὕτως καταπατηθήσεσθε "so you will be trampled" (see Elliger, 174).

27.a. North thinks DSS[Isa] הנומה is a word from post-biblical Heb, a qal ptcp from נום meaning "speaking, saying." A. Guillaume ("Some Readings in the Dead Sea Scroll of Isaiah," *JBL* 76 [1957] 40) relates it to Arab *namā* "bring news." The Versions apparently had MT's text before them. Modern interpreters have tried all sorts of emendations (cf. Elliger, 174–75, and *BHS*). This translation sticks with MT.

27.b. Missing in LXX.

28.a. Vg *et vidi* "and I looked"; Syr Tg support MT.

28.b. The Versions and modern interpreters have attempted various emendations (cf. Elliger, 175–76).

29.a. MT און means "trouble" (BDB, 19), but all the parallels (40:17; 41:12, 24) and DSS[Isa] Syr Tg read אין "nothing" (BDB, 34).

29.b. DSS[Isa] Syr Tg Vg add "and."

42:1.a. MT הן, DSS[Isa] הנה (cf. 41:24). LXX has Ιακωβ "Jacob" in place of הן. The other Versions as well as a sub-group of hexaplaric LXX MSS oII (including Matt 12:18) support MT.

1.b. LXX inserts Ισραηλ "Israel." See n. 1.a.

1.c. MT משפט "verdict." DSS[Isa] adds *waw* at both ends, "and his verdict." (Trever first read it wrongly as ומשפטי.) LXX Syr Vg support MT. LXX *κρίσιν*, Syr *dynh,* Tg דינה like MT's משפט can mean "judgment" or "justice." Vg chooses *iudicium* "judgment." So also in vv 3 and 4.

2.a. DSS[Isa] has יזעק with no change in meaning.

3.a. A sub-group of LXX MSS (cI) adds *την* (*των*) Ιουδαιων *ασθενειαν* "of Judah's weakness." Tg interprets "the humble who are like a bruised reed."

3.b. MT יכבנה "he will put it out." DSS[Isa] יכבה omits the suff, parallel to ישבור "shatter" before.

3.c. MT לאמת "for truth, truly." LXX *ἀλλὰ εἰς ἀλήθειαν* "but in truth." Matt 12:20 *εἰς νικος* "to victory." Syr *bqwsṭ*ʾ "surely" = Tg לקושטיה and Vg *in veritate* "in truth."

4.a. MT יָרוּץ is qal impf from רוץ "run" (BDB, 930). *BHS* יֵרוֹץ is niph impf from רצץ "crush." LXX *θραυσθήσεται* "he will be crushed"; Syr *ntptq* "he is extinguished"; Tg ילאי "he will become tired" (though Elliger [198] notes that it had interpreted יכהה "he will fail" as יחלי "he will become ill"); Vg *erit . . . turbulentus* "he will be troubled." Diez-Macho ("A New Fragment of Isaiah with Babylonian Pointing," *Textus* 1 [1960] 132–43) reports a Heb MS fragment pointed qal יֵרוּץ, which must then be understood intransitively (so Levy, *Deutero-Isaiah* [London: Oxford U. P., 1925] and North). Read this or *BHS*'s pointing for the same meaning. But also see GKC § 67q.

5.a. MT האל יהוה "the God, Yahweh" is supported by Syr Tg Vg and probably LXX (see Elliger, 222). DSS[Isa] האל האלהים "the God, the God."

6.a. DSS[Isa] lacks the name of God but has points over the line as a correction. LXX *κύριος ὁ θεὸς* "the Lord God" is identical to v 5 and its common usage.

6.b. MT וְאֶצָּרְךָ "I keep you" is qal impf 1 c sg from נצר "watch, guard, keep" (BDB, 665), which Vg *et servavi te* supports. But LXX *καὶ ἐνισχύσω σε*, Syr *whylṭk* and Tg ואתקנינך all mean "I will strengthen you." Elliger (223) thinks the latter reflect a tradition which derives the word from יצר "to shape, to form" (BDB, 427). MT may be used as is. For similar renderings of אצר/עצר/עזר in LXX, see L. Allen, *Greek Chronicles* (VTSup 25 [1974] 127).

6.c. *BHS* suggests emending to *waw* consecutive on all three verbs. But it is a hazardous business to try to read tenses back into Heb. from the Versions as *BHS* and Elliger (223) have done.

9.a-a. Syr has the stichs in reverse order.

9.b. DSS[Isa] adds the article.

9.c. Lit., "spring up."

10.a. MT יוֹרְדֵי הַיָּם qal ptcp pl "those who go down to the sea," i.e., seafarers (BDB, 432) is followed by the Versions. But this leaves מלאו "its fullness" without meaning. From Lowth to Elliger and *BHS,* interpreters have emended to achieve a finite verb: יִרְעַם "it thunders" or, according to Volz, יַאְדִּירֻהוּ יָם "sea glorifies him," a nominative verb kin to the known noun for "majesty" (BDB, 12). The translation follows this suggestion. See *JTS* 22 (1971) 146 for a rationale for MT's error.

11.a. MT ישאו "lift up" is pl, DSS[Isa] ישא sg. LXX Syr Tg Vg read "be glad, rejoice." Keep MT (cf. v 2).

11.b. MT תשב "live in" is sg. LXX *καὶ οἱ κατοικοῦντες* "and the inhabitants of," Tg "the open places inhabited by Arabs in the wilderness." Elliger (242) follows H. P. Rüger in suggesting a noun מֹשְׁבֵי "the dwellings of." But this is unnecessary. MT may be kept.

11.c. MT סלע means "rock" but is also a place-name in Edom. LXX *πέτραν* is also ambiguous. Vg takes it as a name, Syr Tg do not.

11.d. MT יצוחו "let them shout" (BDB, 846) is a *hap. leg.* DSS[Isa] יצריחו "utter a roar"

(BDB, 863) parallels v 13. Orlinsky (*JNES* 11 [1952] 154–56) has shown the reading of DSS[Isa] to be secondary.

11.e. MT מראש הרים, lit., "from heads of mountains." For הרים, DSS[Isa] has הררים, same meaning.

Form/Structure/Setting

This scene continues the preceding action and thought. The coastlands and borderlands (42:10) remain as witnesses. Yahweh's case against Israel still considers idolatry to be the major reason Israel cannot see and is not willing to assume the role for which she is being prepared and to which she is called.

The division of the text follows Melugin's suggestion (*Formation,* 98). He looks at 41:21–29 as "a trial speech." This designation is good in terms of contents, but it fails to recognize that the text is presented by two speakers. The challenge to the idols is presented by Yahweh's advocate (vv 21–24). Yahweh himself clinches the argument that he alone is God (vv 25–29).

42:1–4 present to the court Yahweh's servant as the one who is to implement among the nations (v 1) and in the land (v 4) the verdict (משפט) that Yahweh has reached, with a broad hint to the witnessing coastlands that they should "wait" patiently for the servant's "instruction." This is the role assigned Cyrus in chaps. 44 and 45. The servant's manner will avoid the ostentation and arrogant violence that others might affect. But he will succeed with patient persistence.

42:6–7 address the servant directly with the details of his role and task as a *covenant* for *people* and *a light* for *nations.* His work is to enlighten and to free those who are blind or imprisoned.

42:8–9 address the court, including the witnesses, dissociating Yahweh from idols and their practitioners and claiming victory in the trial by virtue of the announcements of things to come. The content of that announcement is twofold: the role of Jews to do his work in one sphere and the role of Cyrus to do his work in another.

The scene closes with a choral hymn calling upon the witnesses (coastlands and borderlands) to join in the praise of Yahweh. The hymn is an echo and a renewal of the ideals of Davidic sovereignty over greater Palestine. But its frame of reference is different. It assumes imperial suzerainty over all of them. It sees Israel's role as helping the former citizens of David's kingdom to renew their own worship of Yahweh. This new relation is not political at all, but religious.

This scene balances the major themes of the act more completely than any other: prediction of Cyrus' approach (41:25–27); call of Cyrus (42:1–4, 6–7); Yahweh's claim to be the only God (42:5, 8–9); argument against idolatry (41:21–24, 28–29).

The trial bears an uncanny resemblance to scenes in some Babylonian tablets. In one of these (Abu Habba Cylinder, col. I, 8–32; see Olmstead *History,* 36) Nabunaid has a dream in his accession year (550 B.C.) in which Marduk instructs him to restore the temple in Haran. He protests that it is still controlled by the Medes. Marduk predicts that Cyrus, King of Anshan, will overcome the Medes within three years. The Nabonidus Chronicle (*ANET,*

305–6) records the rise of Cyrus from the sixth year of Nabunaid until he enters Babylon in the seventeenth year. The "verse account of Nabunaid" (*ANET,* 312–15) tells the story from another viewpoint. In another inscription (*ANET,* 315–16) Marduk becomes concerned about the state of his sanctuaries in Sumer and Akkad under Nabunaid. "He looked (through) all the countries for a righteous ruler willing to lead him (i.e., Marduk in the annual procession). (Then) he pronounced the name of Cyrus, King of Anshan, (and) declared him to be the ruler of all the world."

This review of writings contemporary with the events shows that the issues in this scene of the Vision were very real to Babylon and to events in Babylon. Under Nabunaid from Haran, idols had been shuffled from one temple to another. Marduk, the traditional king of gods in Babylon had been slighted, if not actually dethroned. The issue of whether he with his cult would be reinstated was hotly debated. The people were all aware that Cyrus, king of the Persian city of Anshan, had gained control of Media and was extending his power in the east and in the north. Marduk's priests looked hopefully to him for the restoration of their cult. Nabunaid benefited from Cyrus's victory over Media by retaking his hometown, Haran. The vision and prophecy of that victory were credited to Marduk.

Against the background of Nabunaid's years of retreat from public life in Tema, this trial speech disputes the claims of Marduk's followers. The coastlands, as well as Israel in exile, are called to witness that Yahweh, not Marduk, had called the conqueror from the east. Yahweh, not Marduk, had foretold the event ahead of time. Yahweh insists that the idols, including Marduk, Nebo, Bel, and the rest, are incapable of any action. They are simply symbols of the ideals and wishes of their adherents, manipulated by their priests to support their worshipers' desires and ambitions.

Excursus: Identifying the "Servant of Yahweh"

Bibliography

Alonso, N. "The Problem of the Servant Songs." *Scr* 18 (1966) 18–26. **Baltzer, K.** "Zur formgeschichtlichen Bestimmung der Texte vom Gottes-Knecht im Deutero-Jesaja-Buch." *Probleme biblischer Theologie.* FS G. von Rad. Munich: Kaiser, 1971. 27–43. **Barstadt, N. M.** "Tjenersangene hoc Deuterojesaja. Et eksegetisk villspor." *NorTT* 83 (1982) 235–44. **Beecher, W. J.** "The Servant." *The Prophets and the Promise.* Grand Rapids: Baker, 1903. 263–88 = *Classical Evangelical Essays in OT Interpretation.* Ed. W. C. Kaiser. Grand Rapids: Baker, 1973. 187–204. **Behler, G. M.** *Serviteur et Roi.* Quatre chants du Serviteur de Jahweh. Fangeaux: Privately printed, 1976. **Blocher, H.** *Songs of the Servant.* Israel's Good News. Downers Grove, Il.: Inter-Varsity Press, 1975. **Brunot, A.** "Le Poème du Serviteur et ses problèmes (Is XL–LV)." *RevThom* 61 (1961) 7–24. **Canellas, G.** "La figura del Siervo de Yahvé." *CB* 37 (1980) 19–36. **Cazelles, H.** "Le roi Yoyakin et le Serviteur du Seigneur." *Proceedings of the Fifth World Congress of Jewish Studies 1969.* Jerusalem: 1971. 121–25. ———. "Israel et son chef, serviteurs humilies." *Vocation* 299 (1982) 20–30. **Charbel, A.** "Os canticos do Servo de Jave." *RCB* 9 (1972) 147–69. **Coppens, J.** "Mission du Serviteur de Yahve et son statut eschatologique." *ETL* 48 (1972) 343–71. **Feuillet, A.** "Les Poèmes du Serviteur." *Études d'exégèse et de théologie biblique* Paris: Gabalda, 1975. 119–79. **Gerleman, G.** "Der Gottesknecht bei Deuterojesaja." *Studien zur alttestamentlichen Theologie.* Heidelberg: L. Schneider, 1980. 38–60. **Grelot, P.**

Les Poèmes du Serviteur. Paris: Editions du Cerf, 1981. **Haag, H.** "Ebed Jahwe-Forschung 1948–58." *BZ* 3 (1959) 174–104 = *Buch des Bundes.* Düsselforf: Patmos Verlag, 1980. 46–78. ———. *Der Gottesknecht bei Deuterojesaja im Verständnis der alten Kirche.* FZPT 31 (1984) 343–77. **Hermisson, H.-J.** "Der Lohn des Knechts." *Die Botschaft und die Boten.* FS H. W. Wolff. Ed. J. Jeremias, L. Perlitt. Neukirchen-Vluyn: Neukirchener Verlag, 1981. 269–87. ———. "Israel und der Gottesknecht bei Deuterojesaja." *ZTK* 79 (1982) 1–24. ———. "Voreiliger Abschied von den Gottesknechtsliedern." *TR* 49 (1984) 209–22. **Kapelrud, A. S.** "The Identity of the Suffering Servant." *Near Eastern Studies.* FS W. F. Albright. Baltimore: Johns Hopkins, 1971. 307–14. **Keller, B.**, and **Voeltzel, R.** "Les 'serviteurs' dans le livre d'Esaïe." FS E. Jacob. *RHPR* 59 (1979) 413–26. **Kruse, C. G.** "The Servant Songs: Interpretive Trends since C. R. North." *SBeT* 8 (1978) 3–27. **Langdon, R.** *The ʿEbed Yahweh and Jeremiah.* Diss. Southern Baptist Theological Seminary, 1980. **Lau, G.**, and **Marcil, M.** "Shangchu p'ujen shihke." (The Songs of the Servant of Yahweh.) *ColcTFuj* 5, 15 (1973) 17–36. **Lindsey, F. D.** "Isaiah's Songs of the Servant." *BSac* 139 (1982) 12–31, 129–45, 216–29, 312–29. **Ljung, I.** *Tradition and Interpretation: A Study of the Use and Application of Formulaic Language in the So-called ʿEbed YHWH-Psalms.* ConB 12. Lund: Gleerup, 1978. **MacRae, A. A.** "The Servant of the Lord in Isaiah." *BSac* 121 (1964) 125–32, 218–27. **Mesters, C.** *Die Botschaft des leidenden Volkes.* Tr. H. Brandt. Neukirchen: Neukirchener Verlag, 1982. **Mettinger, T. N. D.** *A Farewell to the Servant Songs: A Critical Examination of an Exegetical Axiom.* Lund: Gleerup, 1983. ———. "Die Ebed-Jahwe-Lieder. Ein fragwürdiges Axiom." *ASTI* 9 (1978) 68–76. **Monloubou, L.** "Le Serviteur de Iahve selon Isaïe." *BLE* 83 (1982) 288–93. **Moor, J. C. de.** "Knechten can goden en de Knecht van JHWH." *De Knecht.* FS J. Koole. Kampen: Kok, 1978. **Nakazawa, K.** "Saikin 10-nenkan ni okeru Shimabe no uta no kenkyu." *SeiRon* 3 (1965) 7–38. ———. "The Servant Songs' Review—a Second Decade." (Japanese). FS M. Sekine. Ed. S. Arai and others. Tokyo: Yamamoto Shoten, 1972. 223–37. **Nunez Regodon, J.** *El Universalismo de los cantos del Siervo.* FS J. Alonso Diaz. 67–76. **Phillips, A.** "The Servant—Symbol of Divine Powerlessness." *ExpTim* 90 (1978) 370–74. **Pipal, B.** "The Lord's Ebed in the Exile." *CV* 13 (1970) 177–80. **Plamadeala, A.** "Ebed-Yahve in lumina NT." *Mitropolia Banatului* 20 (1970) 284–304. **Ploeg, J. P. M. van der.** "De Dienaar van JHWH en de Psalmen." *De Knecht.* FS J. Koole. Kampen: Kok, 1978. **Riciardi, A.** "Los cantos del Siervo de Yahve." *CuadT* 4 (1976) 124–28. **Roodenburg, P. C.** *Israel, de knecht en de knechten.* Onderzoek naar de beteknis en de functie van het nomen ('ebed) in Jes 40–66. Meppel, 1975. **Seybold, K.** "Thesen zur Entstehung der Lieder vom Gottesknecht." *BN* 3 (1977) 1–33. **Sicre, J. L.** "Le mediación de Ciro y la del Siervo de Dios en Deuteroisaias." *EstEcl* 50 (1975) 179–210. **Steck, O. H.** "Aspekte des Gottesknechts in Deuterojesajas 'Ebed Jahwe-Liedern.' " *ZAW* 96 (1984) 372–90. **Virgulin, S.** "Il deuteroisaia (. . . carmi del servo . . .)." *Problemi e prospettive di scienze bibliche.* FS R. Fabris. Brescia: Queriniana (1981) 211–31. **Wellens, A.** "Le serviteur defigure (le Christ)." *Christus* 27 (1980) 75–82. **Williams, P.** "The Poems about Incomparable Yahweh's Servant." *SWJT* 11 (1968) 73–88. **Wilshire, L. E.** "The Servant City." *JBL* 94 (1975) 356–67. **Wolff, H. W.** "Wer ist der Gottesknecht in Jes 53?" *EvT* 22 (1962) 338–42.

This massive bibliography includes only a part of literary production that indicates what attention is being paid to the servant theme in Isaiah 40–55. The phrase "servant of Yahweh" appears elsewhere in the OT. But nowhere else is it used with the same concentrated emphasis.

Since Bernhardt Duhm identified four passages as "servant songs" (42:1–4; 49:1–6; 50:4–9; 52:13–53:12), the discussion of "the servant" has centered on these passages. A central question has been: who was the servant? Surely the Ethiopian treasurer (Acts 8:34) was not the first to ask it? Most interpretations have assumed that a single servant is represented in the passages. Jewish interpreters have generally seen the servant as a symbol of Israel. Christian interpreters have tended to think of a single individual, whether that be in a prediction of Jesus' ministry and suffering or of an individual who through his experiences became a symbol of suffering service acceptable to God which foreshadowed the suffering Messiah. When pressed for the identity of the person, some have thought the passages autobiographical for the prophet himself, as the Ethiopian did. Others have suggested Jeremiah. Still others pointed to Zerubabbel.

This commentary treats the so-called "servant songs" as parts of the larger Vision which also speaks in many other passages of "the servant of Yahweh." It finds that the description fits at least three identifiable entities within the Vision, two of which are basic.

Israel is explicitly called "the servant of Yahweh" in 40:1–49:4. The speeches imply that this has been Israel's role and that Yahweh intends to continue to deal with Israel in that way, even while she is scattered in Exile.

A second "servant of Yahweh" is also introduced in those chapters. He first appears in 42:1 (the larger passage is 41:25–42:9). He is the conqueror whom Yahweh has called from the east to accomplish his will. He is named in 44:28 as Cyrus with further titles as Yahweh's "shepherd" and in 45:1 as his "anointed." His successors, Darius and Artaxerxes, though not named, are seen in the same roles. In passages that the commentary identifies as speaking of Darius, "servant of Yahweh" appears in 49:5–6, in 52:13 and 53:11. The role is continued in several passages that fit the times of Artaxerxes, especially in chap. 60, although the phrase itself is lacking. So a second "servant" is the Persian authority in the persons of Cyrus, Darius, and Artaxerxes.

A third identity emerges in chaps. 54:17 and 65:13–16. Here the plural pervades: "servants of Yahweh." These are the believing and obedient worshipers who delight in Yahweh's new city that was built by the Persians for loyal Jews and their God. They are contrasted to the rebels who accept neither Yahweh's vision of a new city nor Persian rule.

It is apparent that at least three "servant" identities appear on these pages. Israel, scattered throughout the diaspora, is the first. The Persian emperors who produced edicts supporting the rebuilding of Jerusalem's temple, Cyrus, Darius, and Artaxerxes, are a second, while loyal worshipers in Judah and Jerusalem are a third.

There are also individual leaders in these chapters. But they are not named. Nor are they called "Yahweh's servant." In 48:16–20a such a person speaks. The commentary suggests that this represents Sheshbazzar leading the first return to Jerusalem from Babylon. In 50:4–9 a persecuted leader speaks (see *Excursus: The Sufferer/Martyr of 50:4–9 and Chap. 53.*). Although the word "servant" never occurs, this passage has consistently been identified as one of the "servant songs" by modern interpreters. 53:1–11 speaks of the death of such a sufferer. The commentary separates the identity of this sufferer from the reference to "the servant of Yahweh in 52:13 and 53:11. It suggests that both suffering passages be identified with someone like Zerubbabel, while the "servant" references are to Darius (see the Commentary). 61:1–3 is spoken by another individual. Jesus saw himself as the fulfillment of its words. The commentary suggests that the original role portrays Ezra. 62:6–12 speaks of setting a guard on Jerusalem's walls and exhorts workmen to complete the highway. The commentary suggests an identification with Nehemiah. These touch important individuals who were known to have contributed to Jewish restoration of Jerusalem. But none of them is called "servant of Yahweh."

In a strict sense עבד יהוה "the servant of Yahweh" is used in Isaiah of Israel in Exile and of Cyrus (and his successors). The plural form עבדי יהוה "servants of Yahweh" applies to that part of the Jewish community in Judah and Jerusalem, both residents and pilgrims, who joyfully and loyally respond to Yahweh's new order. Individuals provide powerful models of determined suffering and spirit-endowed leadership but are not called "the servant of Yahweh."

Comment

21 The change between 3rd pl and 2nd pl can be confusing. But if the 2nd pl are addressed to the idols or their advocates, while the 3rd pl references are understood as their *proofs,* the appeal takes on a recognizable shape. *King of Jacob* appears also in 43:15 and 44:6 in both cases parallel to "your redeemer." It points to a fundamental element in the message of these chapters. The announcement that is to be given to Jerusalem and is here revealed to Israel and the gathered assembly is that Yahweh is prepared to reassert his royal prerogatives relating to his people and his city. In 40:10–11 the announcement is made. It is repeated in 42:13. The title with its implied relation to Israel has a long history in the OT (cf. H. Wildberger, *Jahwes Eigentumsvolk,* ATANT 37 [Zurich: Zwingli, 1960] 83–87). It is to be distinguished from the concept of Yahweh, king over the heavenly council (Ps 82) or that of king over creation (Pss 93, 96, 99; cf. J. H. Eaton, *Kingship and the Psalms* and *Festal Drama,* 47–50). Yahweh's role in the confrontation with the advocates of idolatry is that of Israel's patron and the sponsor of the new conqueror from the east.

22–23 Yahweh's advocate specifically prescribes what proofs are required. The test will turn on their ability to predict events and to bring them about as predicted. V 23 rhetorically addresses the nonexistent gods, challenging them to do something, anything that may *shock* the assemblage, like the appearance of a ghost.

24 The failure to appear or present proofs is taken as a proof of their nonexistence. Those who believe in such gods are themselves abhorrent.

25 Yahweh takes up the challenge which his opponents had declined. He predicts a future event, the coming of a new conqueror *from the north.* Earlier he had said "from the east" (41:2). Both descriptions apply to Cyrus who began in the east but pushed his conquests across Armenia, north of Mesopotamia, before beginning his march on Babylon. Note that the claim is not simply the ability to predict. It also includes the underlying claim to have actually produced the events. MT's "he calls on my name" is an explicit statement that Cyrus is Yahweh's worshiper. However, 45:3–5 says that Yahweh calls Cyrus by name, but that Cyrus does not acknowledge Yahweh. (Note that Marduk's adherents were claiming that he was responding to Marduk's call [*ANET,* 315]). LXX has dealt with this difference by making the verb passive "he is called," while DSS^{Isa} has a 3rd person masculine suffix, "his name." These provide a convenient textual basis for a smoother reading, *he is called by his name,* which fits the needs of this context well. The point here is that Yahweh has called Cyrus, not that Cyrus worships Yahweh. יוצר "sculptor" is literally "one who forms." The figure in both parts of the line pictures Cyrus doing to and with the rulers as he wishes.

26–27 The verse asks which of the gods or their spokesmen had predicted this event before it happened, and answers emphatically, no one. (This disputes the claims of the Babylonian inscriptions. See *Form/Structure/Setting* above.) Then (v 27) Yahweh points to his announcement to *Zion* (40:1–5) and his appointment of a *messenger to Jerusalem* as evidence that he had fulfilled the requirements for such a proof. Jacob/Israel, identified as the Mesopotamian dispersion of Judaism, has previously been designated, chosen, and equipped as a "servant" (41:8–9) to carry Yahweh's message to Jerusalem (40:1–2). History records that the initiatives to restore Jerusalem in the sixth and fifth centuries B.C. did in fact come from Mesopotamia. Sheshbazzar, Zerubbabel, Nehemiah, and Ezra are the known names of leaders of such initiatives.

28 But Yahweh had seen no sign of anyone else offering such a proof. He draws the conclusion (v 29) that the idols *are nothing.*

42:1–4 Yahweh's עבד "servant" was identified as Jacob/Israel in 41:8–10 and was named "messenger to Zion" in 41:7. Now a servant is presented as the messenger of the heavenly court to bring notice of decisions reached there *to the nations* and to establish them as *the verdict in the land.* The verdict that has now emerged from the trial that tested the claims of the idols and those who believed in them is the verdict announced in 40:1–5, 9–10. משפט "verdict" occurs three times in these verses. The word, without the article, could mean "justice." But the context calls for something much more specific. The legal setting of the trial that preceded this suggests that it means "the decision reached by the heavenly court (i.e., by Yahweh) before witnesses." That verdict is to become the basis for policy, and needs to be known and acknowledged by all concerned. Cyrus has been chosen to be God's agent to put that verdict into effect. God expresses his confidence in his messenger, and *confirms* him. He has *chosen* him and *delights* in him. He has put his own *spirit on him.* The integrity of the servant's manner of service is expressed in vv 2–3. לאמת "for truth, truly" expresses that integrity, while the rest of the verse notes in negative terms the quiet, pervasive, sensitive way that he will go about his task. The verdict must be made known and established for *the nations, the land,* and *the coastlands.* The nations were called as witnesses to the judgment on a previous generation (chap. 34) and had stood under God's judgment in previous centuries (chaps. 14–22). The land that encompassed Palestine-Syria had felt the full fury of Yahweh's judgment and known the condemnation of "death" (chap. 24) but had also heard his decision of "life" (chap. 25). The coastlands are the immediate neighbors of Jerusalem who will be most affected by Yahweh's decision to restore the city. תורה "instruction" later became a technical term, "Torah," for the Pentateuch, which was in fact completed, copied, taught, and given authoritative status in Babylon before being returned to Jerusalem, probably through Ezra.

5 Yahweh is introduced as creator of the world.

6–7 Cyrus is addressed directly. *Called, strengthened, kept,* and *appointed* are all things that come to him as Yahweh's servant. Yahweh is his patron for positive goals (*in salvation*). The role he is to play has two sides. As *covenant* (*for*) *people* and *light* (*for*) *nations,* the emperor is responsible for government, justice, and order for the peoples under his rule. In *opening blind eyes and releasing prisoners,* his role relates to Yahweh's people. Israel is to be released and restored, her temple-city rebuilt.

8 *My glory* refers to credit due to God for these events.

9 *The previous events* are those portrayed in the Vision which were predicted before coming to pass: the coming and victory of the Assyrians, the fall of Merodach-Baladan's Babylon, etc.

Excursus: The Former (ראשון) *and the New* (חדש)

Bibliography

Bentzen, A. "On the Ideas of 'the Old' and 'the New' in Deutero-Isaiah." *ST* 1 (1948) 183–87. **Bonnard, P.-E.** *Le Second Isaïe.* 522. **Cazelles, H.** "Nouvel An (Fête du), IV Le Nouvel An en Israel." *SDB* 6:620–45. **Feldmann, F.** "Das Frühere und das Neue." FS Edouard Sachau. Berlin: 1915. 162–69. **Haran, M.** *Between Ri'shonot (Former Prophecies) and Hodashot (New Prophecies): A Literary-Historical Study in the Group of Prophecies Isaiah xl–xlviii.* Jerusalem, 1963. **Ludwig, T. M.** "Remember Not the Former Things: Disjunction and Transformation in Ancient Israel." FS Kitagawa. *Transitions* (1980) 25–55. **North, C. R.** "The 'Former Things' and the 'New Things' in Deutero-Isaiah." *Studies in Old Testament Prophecy.* FS T. H. Robinson. Ed. H. Rowley. Edinburgh: T. & T. Clark, 1950. 111–26. **North, R.** "חדש chadhash" *TWAT* 2:762–80; *TDOT* 4:225–44. **Odendaal, D. H.** "The 'Former' and the 'New Things' in Isaiah 40–48." *OTWSA* 1967 (1971) 64–75. **Rabban, N.** "The 'Former and Latter Things' in the Prophecies of Deutero-Isaiah." *Tarbiz* 14 (1942) 19–25 (Heb.). **Schoors, A.** "Les choses antérieures et le choses nouvelles dans les oracles Deutero-Isaien." *ETL* 40 (1964) 19–47. **Stuhlmueller, C.** *Creative Redemption.* 135–68, 286. **Watts, J. D. W.** *The Heavenlies of Isaiah.* Diss. Southern Baptist Theological Seminary. Louisville, KY, 1948. 92–120. **Westermann, C.** "חדש hadas neu." *THAT* 1:524–30.

A particular feature of chaps. 40–66 is the emphasis on the newness of God's action. The Hebrew word חדש "new," characteristic of chaps. 40–48 (41:15; 42:9, 10; 43:19; 48:6), is entirely missing from chaps. 49–60 but appears again in 61:4, 62:2, 65:17, and 66:22. It determines in large measure the tone of both sections. "New" is contrasted with ראשון "former" or "first" in both sections (see 41:22; 42:9, 43:9, 18; 46:9; 48:3; and 61:4; 65:7, 16, 17). This refers to a different order than has existed in the past.

Both of these are related to עולם "age" in 42:9–14; 46:9; and 61:4–8 (see *Excursus:* עולם *"An Age"*). In these instances the former age, before the exile, is contrasted with the new age that Yahweh is inaugurating through the empires.

The idea of the "new" is also closely identified with God's abilities as creator (see *Excursus:* ברא *"Create"/"Creator"*). Emphasis on these words supports the Vision's view that the creator of the world is creating a brand new situation for his restored temple-city and its worshipers. That God does a new creative thing is not simply a feature of the time which the Vision pictures, but is a characteristic of Yahweh God as the Vision understands and presents him. This was a major point made by my 1948 dissertation (see *Bibliography* above).

10–12 The chorus calls on all the ethnic groups of greater Palestine, previously enjoined to silence (41:1), now to praise Yahweh for the coming of the Persians and the imperial peace that brings order and prosperity.

In later passages Cyrus' specific role in rebuilding Jerusalem and the Temple will be announced. At this point it is sufficient that he has been chosen to restore order in Palestine and be a liberator for captives.

Explanation

Yahweh challenges the gods to show that they had in fact foretold events. When they cannot do that, he presents his evidence that he has stirred up the new conqueror from the north and that he had asked Israel to send a messenger of good tidings to Jerusalem with this news (cf. 40:1–9). Then Yahweh introduces this conquerer as his own servant who will administer the verdict of the heavenly council to the nations. He will do this gently yet firmly. He will not fail nor be discouraged until it is done in "the land." Yahweh addresses this servant and appoints him to be "a covenant for people, a light for nations." He is to "open blind eyes" and to "release prisoners."

So now a second servant role is revealed. It will be more clearly defined in later scenes. In these verses his scope of action is noted. "In the land" and "the coastlands" (42:3) show that his authority will relate to larger Palestine, as David's had done. He is to be "a covenant for people" and "a light to nations" (42:6), that is, his mandate is political. It is also "to open blind eyes, to release a prisoner from a dungeon," that is, he is to be a liberator.

All this is related in 41:25 to the one that Yahweh has "stirred up" and empowered for conquest, that is, to Cyrus, the Persian. He is being brought to do Yahweh's work in Palestine and to liberate enslaved peoples including exilic Jews. The passage announces God's decision to spread the range of his work in history by using this Persian prince. This passage and those that follow lay the foundation for a doctrine of divine rule through secular rulers that will later be reflected in Paul's dictum: "The authorities that exist have been established by God" (Rom 13:1, NIV).

Scene 4: Yahweh Sends His Servant to Rescue Israel (42:13–43:21)

Bibliography

Beaucamp, E. 'Chant nouveau du retour' (Is 42, 10–17): Un monstre de l'exégèse moderne." *RScRel* 56 (1982) 145–58. **Conrad, E. W.** "The 'Fear Not' Oracles in Second Isaiah." *VT* 34 (1984) 143–51. **Freedman, D. N.** "Isaiah 42:13." *CBQ* 30 (1968) 225–26. **Grimm, W.** *"Weil ich dich liebe"* (*Jes 43,2*). ANTJ 1. Bern: Lang, 1976. **Krasovec, J.** "Sintakticna in teoloska formulacija v Iz 43,1–3a." *Bogoslovni Vestnik* 33 (1973) 288–95. **Leene, H.** "Denkt niet aan het vroegere. Methodologische overwegingen bij de uitleg van Jes 43:18a." *Loven en geloven.* FS N. H. Ridderbos. Amsterdam: Bolland, 1975. 55–76. **Maalstad, K.** "Einige Erwägungen zu Jes xliii 4." *VT* 16 (1960) 512–14. **Merendino, R. P.** *Der Erste und der Letzte.* 275–347. **Nijen, A. J. van.** "Overwegingen voor een preek over Jesaja 43,16–21." *De Knecht.* FS J. L. Koole. Kampen: Kok, 1978. **Ravenna, A.** "Isaiah 43:14." *RivB* 12 (1964) 293–96. **Reisel, M.** "The Relation between the Creative Function and the verbs br᾽—ysr—ʿsh in Isaiah 43:7 and 45:7." *Verkenningen in een stroomgebied.* FS M. A. Beek. Ed. M. Boertien et al. Amsterdam:

Huisdrukkerij Universiteit, 1974. 65–79. **Rubinstein, A.** "Word Substitution in Isaiah xliii 5 and lix 16." *JSS* 8 (1963) 52–55. **Stummer, F.** "Einige Keilschriftliche Parallel zu Jes 40–55. 7) Jes 43:10, 8) Jes 43:11, 9) Jes 43:13." *JBL* 45 (1926) 180–83. **Waldow, H. V. von.** . . . *Denn ich erlöse dich.* BibS(N) 29. Neukirchen: Verlag des Erziehungsvereins, 1960. **Whitley, C. F.** "Further notes on the text of Deutero-Isaiah" (42:25a). *VT* 25 (1975) 683–87. **Williamson, H. G. M.** "Word Order in Isaiah XLIII, 12." *JTS* 30 (1979) 499–502.

Translation

Heavens: 42:13 *Yahweh moves out like a soldier.* 3+4
Like a man of war he arouses fury.
He shouts[a]*—indeed, he roars.*[b] 2+2
He shows his skill and power against his enemies.
Yahweh: 14 *I have been silent*[a] *for an age.*[b] 2+2
I have been quiet. I have restrained myself.
Like a woman in childbirth, I cry out, 2+3
[c]*I gasp and pant*[c] *together.*
15 *I waste*[a] *mountains and hills* 3+2
and I dry up all their vegetation.
And I make rivers into sand-bars[b] 3+2
and pools I dry up.
16 *I lead blind persons* 2+3+3
in a way [a]*they have not known,*[a]
and I guide them in paths they have not known.
I make[b] *darkness*[c] *into light before them*[d] 4+2
and rough places into level ground.[e]
These are the things 2+3
which I have done. And I have not abandoned them.
Earth: 17 *They have turned*[a] *backwards.* 2+2+2
They are totally shamed[b]
who are trusting in the idol,[c]
who are saying to an image[d] 2+2
"You (pl) are our gods."
Yahweh: 18 *You deaf ones, listen!* 2+3
And you blind ones, look in order to see!
(aside) 19 [a]*Who is blind except my servant?*[b] 4+3
[c]*Or deaf like my messenger (that I send)?*[c]
Heavens: *Who is blind as one in covenant?*[d] 3+3
Or blind as Yahweh's servant?[e]
20 *Seeing*[a] *many things, he*[b] *does not keep (them).* 4+3
Ears open,[c] *he does not listen.*[d]
21 *Yahweh was pleased for his righteousness' sake* 4+3
that he magnify instruction[a] *and glorify (it).*[b]
Earth: 22 *But this*[a] *is a robbed and plundered people,* 3+3+3
trapped[b] *in holes,*[c] *all of them,*
and they have been hidden in prisons.

They have become a prey without a deliverer, 4+3
a spoil[d] *with no one saying, "Give it back."*

Heavens: 23 [a] *Who among you can give ear to this?* 4+3
Attend and listen for the future.
24 *Who has given Jacob over to being plundered*[a] 3+2
or Israel to robbers?[b]

Chorus: *Was it not Yahweh* 2+2
whom we sinned[c] *against?*

Earth: *When they were not willing to walk*[d] *in his ways* 3+3
and did not heed his instruction,
25 *he poured out on him* [a]*the heat of his wrath*[a] 4+2
and the violence[b] *of war.*
It set him on fire[c] *all around* 2+2
but he did not know (it).
It burned him[d] 1+2
but he (still) does not put it on his mind.

Herald: 43:1 *So now, thus says Yahweh,* 3+2+2
your creator, Jacob,
and your shaper, Israel:

Yahweh: *Do not be afraid! For I have redeemed you!* 3+3
I have called[a] *your name. You are mine!*
2 *When you pass into the waters, I am with you.* 3+3
Or into the rivers, they do not sweep you away.
When you walk through fire, it does not consume (you), 4+3
nor flame burn you.
3 *For*[a] *I, Yahweh, am your God!* 4+3
The Holy One of Israel is your Savior![b]
I give [c]*Egypt (for) your ransom.*[c] 3+3
Ethiopia and Seba[d] *in exchange for you.*
4 *Because*[a] *you are precious in my eyes,* 3+3
you are valued and I love you,
I give (of) mankind[b] *in exchange for you* 3+3
and (of) peoples in place of your life.[c]
5 *Do not be afraid, for I am with you.*[a] 4+3+2
From the east I bring your descendants,
and from the west I gather you.
6 *I say to the north "Give them up!"* 3+2
and the the south "Don't hold (them) back!"
Bring[a] *my sons from far away* 3+3
and my daughters from the borderlands,[b]
7 *everyone called*[a] *by my name* 3+2+2
and[b] *whom I created for my glory.*
I shaped, indeed I made him.

Heavens: 8 *Bring out*[a] *a people, blind but who have eyes,*[b] 4+3
deaf ones but who have ears!
9 *All the nations have assembled*[a] *together.* 3+2
So let peoples be gathered.

Who among them can announce this to us? 4+2
Or let us hear[b] *of the former things?*
Let them present their witnesses that they may justify. 3+3
Let them hear,[c] *and let them speak truth.*

Yahweh: 10 *You (pl) are my witnesses,* 2+2+3
Herald: *expression of Yahweh*
Yahweh: *and of my servant,*[a] *whom I have chosen,*
in order that you may come to know 2+2+3
and that you may confirm for me[b]
and that you may understand that I am he.
Before me, no god[c] *was formed.* 3+3
and after me[d] *there is*[e] *none.*
11 *I, I myself am Yahweh* 3+3
and apart from me (there is) no savior.
12 *I have announced (it), and I have saved and I have let it be heard.* 4+3
And no one among you (pl) is a stranger (to the facts).
And you, yourselves, are my witnesses. 2+2+2
Herald: *Expression of Yahweh!*[a]
Yahweh: *I (am) God!*
13 *Also from today*[a] *(on) I am he!* 3+3+3
Nothing can snatch[b] *out of my hand.*
I do it and who can prevent it?
Herald: 14 *Thus says Yahweh,* 3+3
your (pl) redeemer, the Holy One of Israel:
Yahweh: *For your sake I have sent (him) toward Babylon*[a] 3+3+3
and I have leveled[b] *barred gates,*[c] *all of them,*[d]
and Chaldeans[e] *(hear) their joyous shouts with lamentations.*[e]
15 *I am Yahweh, your Holy One,* 3+3
Israel's creator, your king.
Heavens: 16 *Thus*[a] *has Yahweh said,* 3+3+3
who is determining a way by sea
and a path on mighty waters,
17 *who sends out horse and rider,* 2+2
army and power.
Together[a] *they lie down. They never get up.* 3+3
They are extinguished like a wick. They are put out.
Yahweh: 18 *Do not remember earlier (times)* 2+2
and do not think about past (things).
19 *See, I am doing a new thing!* 3+2+2
Now it springs up!
Don't you recognize it?[a]
Indeed, I establish a way in the wilderness, 4+2
rivers[b] *in a wasteland.*

[20] *Wild animals honor me,* 3+3
jackals and owls,
Because I have put[a] *water in the wilderness* 3+2+2
and rivers in a wasteland
to provide drink for[b] *my people, my chosen.*
[21] [a]*This people (that) I formed for myself*[a] 3+2
will tell[b] *my praise.*

Notes

13.a. MT יריע "he shouts," DSS[Isa] יודיע "he makes known." The difference is not simply a different word. DSS[Isa] apparently divides the lines differently, drawing קנאה "fury" from the line before to serve as object. (Cf. Freedman, *CBQ* 30 [1968] 225–26, who translates "with passion he shouts.") LXX Syr Vg support MT's division. Tg is closer to DSS[Isa]. Cf. Elliger, 242, 244.

13.b. יצריח "he roars" (BDB, 863) occurs only here and in Zeph 1:14.

14.a. DSS[Isa] אחשיתי is probably an error, at best a mixed form. MT is superior and clear.

14.b. DSS[Isa] inserts אך "truly!" before מעולם "for an age." The Versions' translations of the preposition מן vary. LXX and Syr relate it to the following verb. Vg follows MT.

14.c-c. LXX changes the figure: ἐκαρτέρησα ὡς ἡ τίκτουσα, ἐκστήσω καὶ ξηρανῶ ἅμα "I persevered like a woman giving birth, I will astonish and dry out at the same time." P. Wernberg-Møller ("Defective Spellings in the Isaiah Scroll," *JSS* 9 [1958] 263) reads LXX's active verbs in the middle voice and translates "I will withdraw and dry up," i.e., stop giving birth (but Ziegler and Elliger [254] suggest that LXX read the last two verbs with v 15). He derives אשם from שמם "be desolate, appalled" (BDB, 1030–31), rather than נשם "gasp, pant" (BDB, 675). אשאף is derived from שאף, but has two roots: I, "gasp, pant," II, "crush, trample" (BDB, 983). DSS[Isa] reads אשופה from שוף "crush" (BDB, 1003) and makes both verbs cohortative. The issue is whether they continue the figure or return to the description of Yahweh's action. The Versions vary. This translation follows the former view.

15.a. DSS[Isa] adds coh *he*.

15.b. MT לאיים "to sand-bars" or "to coastlands." The Versions agree. From Lowth onward interpreters have tried emendations: לציים or לציות "dry land" (so *BHS*), or תלאבים "to dryness." MT may be kept.

16.a-a. *BHS* suggests eliminating as an addition. But it makes sense and fits the meter. Keep MT.

16.b. DSS[Isa] again adds coh *he*.

16.c. DSS[Isa] מהשוכים [sic] is pl.

16.d. MT לפניהם "before them." LXX αὐτοῖς seems to read להם "for them." But Syr Tg Vg support MT.

16.e. Morgenstern ("Loss of Words in Biblical Poetry," *HUCA* 25 [1954] 56) would add אֶתֵּן "I make" at the end of the verse. But that is unnecessary. The second stich still depends upon the previous verb.

17.a. MT's pointing as pf is supported by LXX Vg. Syr Tg appear to translate an impf.

17.b. MT יבשו is impf, "they are shamed." Löwinger ("The Variants of DSI," *VT* 4 [1954] 82) finds DSS[Isa] to read ובושו ("and" with pf) which fits Syr and Tg's readings.

17.c. LXX Σ Syr Tg read pl, perhaps taking the sg as collective (cf. Elliger, 255).

17.d. LXX Syr read pl; see 17.c. Tg and Vg support MT's sg.

19.a. LXX inserts καὶ "and."

19.b. MT עבדי "my servant" is supported by Σ Syr Vg. LXX Tg are pl, "my servants." LXX[L] adds ὁ λαός "the people." Köhler, followed by Elliger, sees *yodh* as an abbreviation for יהוה and reads עבד יהוה "servant of Yahweh," keeping the entire verse in 3d pers. However, MT may be kept by changing speakers.

19.c-c. LXX καὶ κωφοὶ ἀλλ' ἢ οἱ κυριεύοντες αὐτῶν "and deaf except those ruling over them?" DSS[Isa] Σ Syr support MT. Vg *et surdus, nisi ad quem nuncios meos misi* "and deaf except (those) to whom I sent my messengers," Tg "and the sinners to whom I have sent my prophet." Elliger (270–71) understands LXX Vg to be reading a second Heb. כי אם "except" and reconstructs the original to be וְחֵרֵשׁ כִּי אִם־מֹשְׁלָיו "and deaf except those ruling over him." MT is the more difficult text, which should be kept.

19.d. MT משלם. Elliger (271) thinks no one has found a satisfactory meaning for this word. It appears elsewhere as a personal name meaning "substitute" (M. Noth, *Personennamen,* 174). The root שלם has the meanings "to be whole" but also "to be in covenant with." A pual ptcp of the former would mean "a repaid one" (BDB, 1022), which is picked up by Vg *venundatus* "sold," or, of the latter, "one in covenant peace" (BDB, 1023). LXX apparently derived the word from משל III "their ruler." That root also has another meaning, II "their proverb, their joke" (BDB, 605). So there are several meanings for the reader/hearer to choose from. Retain MT and keep the options open in interpretation. For a full discussion, see Elliger, 271.

19.e. LXX Tg have a pl. Syr Vg Σ follow MT's sg.

20.a. K ראית pf "you (sg) have seen" is supported by DSS^{Isa} ראיתה. Q ראות inf abs "seeing" is parallel to פקוח "open" and is supported by many Heb. MSS, including two only recently published (see Elliger, 272). LXX translates 2d pl, Syr 1st sg of Yahweh, Vg 2nd sg. Q is correct and used in the translation.

20.b. MT reads 2d sg, perhaps occasioned by the K reading of ראית, though the second stich has 3d sg. V 18 has a 2d pers address, but it is pl. Read 2d sg.

20.c. MT פקוח is inf abs "being open" (BDB, 824). DSS^{Isa} פתחו is pf "are open" (BDB, 834). Syr *wpthṭ* reads 1st sg "I have opened." But keep MT.

20.d. The issue of person continues here. Many MSS have 2d person: most are sg, but some are pl. The Versions are also 2d person: Vg sg, LXX Syr Tg pl. Keep MT's 3d sg.

21.a. MT תורה "instruction." LXX αἴνεσιν "praise" = Heb. תודה. Tg Σ Syr Vg support MT.

21.b. DSS^{Isa} ויאדרהה "and he glorified it." Syr also read a suffix. Vg Tg have none. *BHS* suggests a suffix following DSS^{Isa}. LXX καὶ εἶδον "and saw" misread the word as a derivative of ראה.

22.a. MT והוא "but this." LXX καὶ ἐγένετω read והיה "and it happened."

22.b. MT הָפֵחַ hiph inf abs "trapped" (BDB, 809) is a *hap. leg.* LXX ἡ παγὶς "the trap" (also Syr Vg) apparently read a noun, הַפַּח "the trap." *BHS* follows previous interpreters in suggesting an emendation to הֻפַּחוּ hoph from פחח "they were trapped." MT may be kept.

22.c. MT has an article, but it has no apparent meaning here.

22.d. DSS^{Isa} Syr Tg Vg repeat *lamedh* "to," which has apparently fallen out of MT through haplography.

23.a. Several LXX MSS insert a line from 50:10a: "Who among you fears God and heeds the voice of his servant?"

24.a. *BHS* considers K למשוסה a poel ptcp "being plundered," which is supported by LXX Syr Tg Vg. DSS^{Isa} למשיסה or, as Q of L and other MSS have it, לִמְשִׁסָּה is a noun, "plunder" (BDB, 1042). Stay with K.

24.b. MT לבוזים "robbers." G. R. Driver ("Notes on Isaiah," *Von Ugarit nach Qumran,* BZAW 77 [Berlin: Töpelmann, 1958] 47) thinks this should also be abstract, "to robbing." MT's act ptcp is better.

24.c. MT חטאנו "we sinned." LXX ἡμάρτοσαν "they sinned" (also Tg) = Heb חטאו. But Syr and Vg support MT.

24.d. MT הלוך inf abs "walking." DSS^{Isa} להלוך inf constr "to walk."

25.a-a. MT חמה אפו, lit., "the heat his wrath." The grammatical relation of these two words is not clear. Budde and Levy divided the sentence between the words (see also Orlinsky, *JJS* 2 [1951] 151–54). The best way is probably to read as a constr חמת "heat of" with DSS^{Isa}, one MS^{K}, and Elliger (273).

25.b. MT ועזוז and DSS^{Isa} ועוזז both mean "violence." LXX καὶ κατίσχυσεν αὐτοὺς (πόλεμος) "and (combat) overcomes them."

25.c. MT ותלהטהו is piel impf 3 fem sg with 3 masc sg suff, "it set him ablaze" (BDB, 529). LXX has a ptcp, καὶ οἱ συμφλέγοντες αὐτοὺς "and those burning them." Tg "and they murdered among themselves."

25.d. LXX has no verb, translating simply ἕκαστος αὐτῶν "every one of them," though LXX^{L} adds at the end και ανηφθη εν αυτοις "and it was set on fire in them."

43:1.a. The Versions translate, "I have called you by your name." But Elliger (273) is correct that this does not necessarily presume a change in the Heb. (as *BHS* suggests).

3.a. Missing in DSS^{Isa}.

3.b. DSS^{Isa} apparently omitted and then inserted over the line גואלך "your redeemer."
3.c-c. DSS^{Isa} reverses the order of the words.
3.d. DSS^{Isa} has a pl, וסבאים "and Sabeans." LXX Σοήνην "Soen."
4.a. MT מאשר, lit., "from (the fact) that." Maalstad (*VT* 16 [1960] 512–24) suggests "more than that." The usual translation is "because."
4.b. MT אדם "mankind." DSS^{Isa} האדם "the mankind." LXX ἀνθρώπους πολλοὺς "many human beings." Tg עממיא "peoples." These early attempts at emendation have been continued by modern interpreters. 1QIsa^{b} Syr Vg support MT.
4.c. נפשך, lit., "your soul" or "your person."
5.a. Some LXX MSS (36, cI′, 403′, 770) add μη πλανω εγω γαρ ειμι κυριος ο θεος σου "I do not deceive, for I myself am the Lord your God" (cf. 41:10).
6.a. MT הביאי "bring" is a fem sg impv. 2 MSS^{K} and 8 MSS^{G} (Elliger 274 adds DSS^{Isa} as well) have הביאו, a masc pl impv. Syr *ʾyty* "I bring." Some Tg MSS also have an indicative "brings," but others as well as Vg support MT. Elliger is probably right in using the pl form.
6.b. MT מקצה "from the border of" (BDB, 892) is masc sg constr. DSS^{Isa} changes to a pl constr קצוי from קצו here and in 48:20 and 49:6, to match MT's 26:15 (but cf. 40:28 and 41:9). LXX ἀπ' ἄκρων and Vg *ab extremis* also have a pl, "from extremes," but some LXX MSS read a sg ακρου like MT.
7.a. MT הנקרא niph ptcp with def art "the one called." Syr *dqrʾ* and Vg *qui invocat* are active, "who calls." LXX Tg translate passive like MT.
7.b. MT ולכבודי "and for my glory." 17 MSS^{K,R} and Syr Vg have no conjunction, but it is present in both DSS^{Isa} MSS. The question is whether the second stich is parallel to the first and so a relative clause defining כל "everyone," or a main clause. MT with *waw* suggests the former against Syr and Vg.
8.a. MT הוציא impv sg "bring out." DSS^{Isa} הוציאו pl impv. 1QIsa^{b} אוציא 1 sg impf, also LXX καὶ ἐξήγαγον, "and I brought out." Tg דאפיק "who led out" keeps MT's form but reads it as a pf 3 masc sg. Like MT, Syr *ʾpq* can be either pf or impv. Vg *educ* is 2 sg impv "bring out." *BHS*, Elliger (306) suggest reading as an inf abs. Read as impv.
8.b. LXX adds ὡσαύτως τυφλοί "likewise the blind."
9.a. Syr *ntknswn* and Tg יתכנשון are impf, "they are able to gather." But MT's pf is in order.
9.b. DSS^{Isa} ישמיעו "they announce it" lacks MT's 1 pl suffix. LXX τίς ἀναγγελεῖ ὑμῖν "who will announce to you?" (one MS ημιν "us") while the MSS group C have no pronoun at all (like DSS^{Isa}). Syr *nsmʿ* is sg, and Vg *audire nos faciet* "he makes us hear" led Oort (followed by *BHS*) to suggest יַשְׁמִיעֻנוּ. Σ Θ Tg support MT's יַשְׁמִיעֻנוּ "they let us hear." Cf. Elliger, 307.
9.c. MT וישמעו "and let them hear." DSS^{Isa} וישמיעו "and let them announce it." LXX omits. Other Gr. versions and Syr Tg Vg = MT.
10.a. Syr pl (see *BHS*). However, LXX Tg Vg = MT. So apparently also DSS^{Isa} עבדי. MT is to be kept.
10.b. MT לי "for me" is omitted by LXX but appears in the other Versions.
10.c. LXX ἄλλος θεός "other god."
10.d. MT ואחרי "and after me." 1QIsa^{b} אחריו "after him." *BHS* suggests ואחר אחרי "or another after me" to try to match LXX. But it is unnecessary. Follow MT.
10.e. DSS^{Isa} is pf, היה. (See Orlinsky, *JBL* 69 [1950] 157–60).
12.a. Begrich's opinion was that נאם יהוה "expression of Yahweh" (Westermann includes the previous line as well) was accidentally repeated from v 10. Keep MT. *BHS* suggests the verse division should follow this phrase.
13.a. גם מיום, lit., "also from a day." LXX ἀπ' ἀρχῆς "from ancient times," Syr *mn ywmm qdmyʾ* "from former days on," Vg *ab initio* "from the start," Tg מן עלמא "from eternity." They all translate a text like MT but interpret it in different ways. For the reading of יום as "today," see DeVries, *Yesterday, Today, and Tomorrow.*
13.b. LXX Syr read the ptcp as passive, "is being snatched." MT Tg Vg read active, "is snatching."
14.a. MT בבלה "to Babylon." DSS^{Isa} בבבל "against Babylon." Tg interprets: "because of your sins you were led out to Babylon." MT may be kept.
14.b. MT והורדתי "I caused to go down, I leveled." LXX καὶ ἐπεγερῶ "I will stir up" (Duhm suggested it equals Heb. וְהֵעִירֹתִי from עור; cf. 41:25; BDB, 735), Syr *wʾytyt* "I made to come,"

Tg ואחיתית "I put down," Vg *et detraxi* "I have withdrawn." Elliger (331) is right that these are not testimonies to another reading, but attempts to come to terms with MT. Emendations like that of Volz, הָרַסְתִּי "I break," are unnecessary.

14.c. MT בריחים "bars" or "refugees" (BDB, 138). MT points it to mean "refugees" but the context suggests "barriers" or "barred gates." LXX *φεύγοντας* and Syr *ʿrwqh* mean "refugees." Tg במשוטין "in boats" is influenced by באניות (see n. 14.f) and thinks *beth* is a preposition. But the attempts of Ehrlich and North to find a meaning for ריחים have not borne fruit (see Elliger, 337–38). Vg *vectes* "door lock" follows the alternate meaning. Westermann corrects to בִּרְחִים "as refugees," Kissane and Penna (*Isaia,* La Sacra Bibbia, 2nd ed., Turin: Marietti, 1962) to בַחוּרִים "the young men." G. R. Driver's (*JTS* 34 [1933] 39) בְּרִיחִים "the nobles" appears in *BHS.* But now Ziegler, Muilenburg, Steinmann, Fohrer, McKenzie, and Elliger (331) have correctly chosen the reading of Vg.

14.d. MT כלם "all of them." Köhler emended to בְּרִיחֵי כְלָאִים "the bars of the jail" followed by *BHS,* Ziegler, Steinmann, Fohrer, and McKenzie. The emendation smooths the text's meaning, but the translation here follows MT.

14.e-e. MT באניות רנתם, lit., "in ships their joyous shouts." LXX *ἐν πλοίοις δεθήσονται* "in ships will be bound." *BHS* suggests inserting אַיֵּה before רנתם: "where are their joyous shouts?" and refers to 51:13 for a parallel. Ewald suggested changing vowels to בַּאֲנִיּוֹת "with lamentations" (cf. *BHS*). Fohrer drops the line. Elliger (332) suggests that several words have dropped out. No satisfactory change has been suggested. The three words of MT's line are rendered in the translation, but the line's meaning is unclear.

16.a. MT כה "thus." 'A Σ Θ and some LXX MSS read *ὅτι* "because" (= Heb כי).

17.a. MT's accentuation relates יחדו "together" to the second half of the verse. *BHS* and many commentators prefer to change the break, citing meter as a reason. The translation follows MT.

19.a. DSS[Isa] omits the fem suffix. But LXX Tg Vg support MT. The metrical problems which commentators have felt in a 3+4 line are removed if it is read as a tristich, 3+2+2.

19.b. MT נהרות "rivers." DSS[Isa] נתיבות or נתיבים (the last letter is illegible) "paths" (BDB, 677). All the Versions support MT (cf. Orlinsky, *JBL* 69 [1950] 160–64).

20.a. MT נתתי "I have put," pf, is אתן impf in DSS[Isa].

20.b. Tg adds "the banished ones of."

21.a-a. On LXX *λαόν μου ὃν περιεποιησάμην* "my people which I have reserved for myself," see Ziegler, *Untersuchungen,* 125.

21.b. DSS[Isa] יואמרו "will say" for MT יספרו "will tell."

Form/Structure/Setting

The scene continues the trial in the heavenly judgment hall. Those present, in addition to Yahweh, Heavens and Earth, are a herald, a chorus of Israelites, and silent nations and peoples from the coastlands and borderlands.

The scene has five parts:

A An argument related to Israel and what is happening to her (42:13–25)
  B A salvation speech (43:1–7)
KEYSTONE A trial speech against gods who do not exist and hence cannot be present (43:8–13)
  B′ A salvation speech (43:14–15)
A′ A closing argument (43:16–21)

This is a key section in Act VII, balancing trial speeches and arguments. It is also important in developing the motifs of a new Exodus, of Yahweh as redeemer, and of Yahweh's creative word.

The usual division of verses at the beginning places v 13 with the previous section as part of the hymn (cf. Stuhlmueller, *Creative Redemption,* 267; Melugin,

Formation, 101). But v 12 contains the imperative calls to praise that usually close a hymn. V 13 makes a fresh start by emphatically placing the name Yahweh at the beginning. It is an announcement, not an ascription, and belongs thematically with what follows.

42:14–25 cannot be placed in a specific genre, although its general characteristics in a complex form fit the place in a trial argument. Yahweh admits being silent, restrained for a season, but now announces a period of action. He ends with the argument: "I have not abandoned them" (v 16). This is continued in dialogue noting the confusion of "the gods" and the failure of Israel to recognize these things. It ends (vv 21–25) with a discussion of Yahweh's actions and Israel's plight.

43:1–7 is usually called an oracle of salvation. Stuhlmueller (*Creative Redemption,* 265) shows its full outline: "Salutation (v 1a), Expression of Encouragement (v 1b, 5a), Reason for Encouragement (noun sentence v 3a, 5a, verbal sentence v 1b pf, 3b–4 pf + impf), Results (v 2, v 3b–4 impf), Purpose (v 7 pf 1st per)." Although Begrich (*Studien,* 20) treated the oracle as a unity, von Waldow (*Anlass,* 15) and Westermann (95) have divided it into two separate oracles. Melugin (*Formation,* 104–5) prefers two oracles (vv 1–3a and vv 5–7) with an intervening promise that Egypt, Ethiopia, and Seba will be given up in ransom for Israel.

However complex the inner structure may be, the entire speech is clearly spoken by Yahweh and should be viewed as a unity (cf. Melugin, *Formation,* 105–6). My student Mark Worthing has drawn attention to the arch structure in these verses:

A Yahweh, Israel's creator and shaper (1a-c)
  B I called you by name (1e)
    C Fear not (1d)
      D Nations given in exchange for you (3c-d)
KEYSTONE Because you are precious and he loves you (4a-b)
      D′ People given in exchange for your life (4c-d)
    C′ Fear not (5)
  B′ Everyone called by name (7a)
A′ I created and shaped him (7b-c)

E. W. Conrad (*VT* 34 [1984] 143–51) has identified the two "fear not" speeches (1b–4, 5–7) and classified them with the patriarchal oracles in Gen 15:1, 21:17, 26:24, 46:3. They fit Israel's role of witness to the new thing God is doing. Their structure has four parts:

(a) self-identification of God (1a, 3);
(b) assurance (1b–2, 5a);
(c) basis of assurance (3a, 4);
(d) promise (3b, 4a, 6–7).

The two "fear not" oracles have been shaped into the larger composition (vv 1–7) addressed to Israel who is a witness as well as defendant in the larger trial proceedings.

Vv 8–13 shift into the format of a trial with appropriate dialogue. Stuhlmueller (*Creative Redemption,* 266) shows the typical outline: "Summons v 9a, Trial Proceedings vv 9b–10a, Verdict vv 10b–13." Yahweh's argument (vv 10–13) is addressed to Israel who has just been ordered to be brought before the assembly of nations and peoples. Contrary to many interpreters, the trial is between Yahweh and Israel. Nations, coastlands, and border countries of Palestine are witnesses with Heavens and Earth. But Israel is the one against whom God brings his complaints and from whom he hears complaints. Israel's tendency to fear other gods and to think like pagans makes it necessary for Yahweh to demonstrate the impotence of the gods, even their existence only as sticks and stones, creations of human hands. He calls for Israel to witness to his announcement of the things that happen. Only Israel, not the nations and certainly not the nonexistent gods, can do that. She is called to witness against herself. The style of the passage is typical of these chapters, but the call on Israel to witness is unique (cf. Melugin, *Formation*, 110).

Vv 14–15 is introduced by the messenger formula, which is expanded in hymnic style. Its heart is the confirmation that the events have been set in motion for Israel's benefit. It is closed by Yahweh's self-identification as Israel's creator and her king. The speech is theologically significant because it brings together the great theological supports of this act, Yahweh as redeemer (גאל) and Yahweh as creator (בורא), with both related to Yahweh's claim to kingship over Israel. Stuhlmueller (*Creative Redemption*) has recognized and demonstrated this blending of themes and vocabulary very convincingly

Vv 16–21 present another oracle of salvation as an outline shows: "Salutation (v 16a), Encouragement (noun sentence vv 16c, 17a ptcp, verb sentence v 17b impf + pf), Results (vv 18–20), Purpose (v 21)" (Stuhlmueller, *Creative Redemption*, 265). However, Melugin (*Formation,* 111) sees beneath this structure of salvation oracle a different purpose and direction. Following the messenger formula is an expanded identification in hymnic form referring to the Exodus (vv 16–17). (A parallel in purpose and direction can be found in Ps 77; cf. B. S. Childs, *Memory and Tradition in Israel,* SBT 37 [Naperville, IL: A. R. Allenson, 1962] 60–63.) Then Israel is told to turn away from preoccupation with the past acts of God, such as those included in his introduction, in order to concentrate on what he is doing now (vv 18–19). The Exodus is used here, like Creation in other passages, to identify Yahweh and describe his miraculous power. But attention is drawn to events and acts which are at present in process in which that power will be used in a new way and for a new purpose.

In this scene traditional genre and powerful traditional motifs are creatively blended to demonstrate Yahweh's will and ability to save his people.

Comment

13 The verse pictures Yahweh as a general who leads his troops out, motivates them, opens the battle with a shout, and wins the war. H. Fredriksson (*Jahwe als Krieger* [Lund: Gleerup, 1945]) and others have pictured Yahweh fighting alone. Elliger (251) correctly understands the description as a leader of armies. The passage recognizes Yahweh's support for the rise of Cyrus in the east.

14 חשה "be silent" occurs often in songs of lament complaining that God is silent and does not answer prayer (cf. 64:11; Ps 28:1). חרש "be quiet"

appears in Pss 32:3, 50:21 in a similar sense. אפק "restrain oneself" appears also in Isa 63:15; 64:11; Gen 43:31; Esth 5:10; 1 Sam 13:12 (cf. Elliger, 260). Yahweh has been silent for a season. Now he must speak. He must act. ילד "give birth" appears in 42:14; 45:10; 49:21; 51:18; 54:1; 55:10. The picture is one of strong and emotional action after a period of passivity.

15 The destructive power of God's action *wastes* and *dries up* everything in its path. Westermann (106–7) compares vv 15–16 with 41:18–20 where God turns the desert into fertile land. Here is the reverse action. Ps 107:33–37 portrays these as opposite sides of the same act. God prepares the way for a new era in dealing with his people and with mankind.

16 God's people have repeatedly been called "blind" in the Vision. They have indeed been blind to God's plan for them and for the world. Vv 18–25 will continue that theme. The point here is assurance that God will *lead* them, blind though they be, through the new experiences and places which their calling as his servant will take them. His presence, who himself is *light*, will push back the *darkness*. He will remove the obstacles on the way. דרך "way" is a familiar metaphor in the Vision (cf. 40:3; 42:24; 43:16; 44:27; 45:13; 48:15, 17; 49:9, 11; 51:10; 53:6; 55:8, 9). It is used in the literal sense of a road to travel as well as in its symbolic sense of a way of life. The last lines insist that God has done these for Israel in the past and that he continues to do them. The new age changes many things. But God's commitment to lead his people does not change.

17 A look at the listening Israelites shows them to be unresponsive. In shame, they have turned their backs on Yahweh because they are idolaters. This is not to be understood literally as worship in the temples of idols (cf. Watts, article in the R. K. Harrison FS). It is a commitment to the "ways of this world" which excludes a response to God's new initiative. The goals which they have set for themselves, the agenda which they have adopted, these are their idols. They are totally unprepared to listen to God's new plan.

18–19a Yahweh calls for attention and notes that the deaf and blind are none other than his own servant, his messenger whom he is now sending. The theme runs through the Vision from chap. 6 through 65:12: "you would not listen."

19b–21 These verses develop the theme of the servant's blindness. Yahweh magnifies his Torah ("instruction" or "law"; cf. 2:3) in spite of them.

Excursus: בחר *"Choose," "Elect";* בחיר *"Chosen," "Elect"*

Bibliography

Altmann, P. *Erwählungstheologie und Universalismus im Alten Testament.* BZAW 92. Berlin: De Gruyter, 1964. **Bonnard, P.-E.** *Le Second Isaïe* 523–24. **Galling, K.** *Die Erwählungstraditionen Israels.* BZAW 48. Giessen: Töpelmann, 1928. **Koch, K.** "Zur Geschichte der Erwählungsvorstellung in Israel." *ZAW* 67 (1955) 205–66. **Martin-Achard, R.** "La signification théologique de l'élection d'Israel." *TZ* 16 (1960) 333–41. **Mendenhall, G. E.** "Election." *IDB* 2:76–82. **Rowley, H. H.** *The Biblical Doctrine of Election.* London: Lutterworth Press, 1950. **Seebass, H.** "בחר" *TWAT* 1:592–

608. **Smith, J. M. P.** "The Chosen People." *AJSL* 45 (1928/29) 73–82. **Staerk, W.** "Zum alttestamentlichen Erwählungsglauben." *ZAW* 55 (1937) 1–36. **Stuhlmueller, C.** *Creative Redemption.* 123–34, 283–85. **Vogt, E.** *Der Erwählungsglaube im Alten Testament.* Diss. Pontifical Biblical Institute, Rome, 1939. **Vriezen, T. C.** *Die Erwählung Israels nach dem Alten Testament.* ATANT 24. Zürich: Zwingli Verlag, 1953. **Wildberger, H.** *Yahwehs Eigentumsvolk.* ATANT 37. Zürich: Zwingli Verlag, 1960.

Words relating to God's choice of Israel were conspicuously absent from chaps. 1–39 (exception: 14:1). בחר "choose" and בחיר "chosen" or "elect" are simple words which mean exactly what they say. They are used of human choices which contrast to God's intention (40:20, 30; 56:4; 62:5; 65:12; 66:3, 4, as well as many times in chaps. 1–39).

Chaps. 1–39 have established how God judged the previous age including the part which Israel and the Davidic kings played in it. Chaps. 40–66 stress that God's choice of Israel to be his servant people is continued and renewed (see *Excursus: Identifying the Servant of Yahweh*) in the new age that was being inaugurated (41:8, 9; 43:10; 44:1–2; 48:10). He calls Israel "my chosen" in 43:20 and 45:4. He has also chosen Cyrus who is also called "my chosen" in 42:1. Another "servant," probably Darius I, is "chosen" in 49:7. The divine choice settles on a group of humble believers in 58:5–6; 65:9, 15, 22 and 66:4 (see Bonnard, 523).

God's active choice of persons to serve him is evident throughout his creative redemption and is an integral part of it.

22 The verse is an apology on the people's behalf, noting the extenuating circumstances of their exile.

23–24a In simple style the speaker begins to teach lessons that the people need, seeking someone who can listen and understand. *Who has given Jacob over to being plundered?* The foundation must be the doctrines of the Deuteronomic History (Joshua–2 Kings).

24b The class responds in chorus. They know their catechism. *Was it not Yahweh whom we sinned against?*

24c–25 The lesson continues, but in the third person. *When they were not willing* refers to God's earlier offer (1:19) to which they failed to respond. *Did not heed his instruction* returns to the basic problem. They do not listen or pay attention. They do not want to hear or see. God's judgment followed, but Israel still *does not put it on his mind.*

43:1–2 בראך "your creator" usually applies to the original creation of matter or mankind, but here it is used parallel to יצרך "your shaper" to describe God's relation to Israel. Israel owes her origin and character, her *raison d'être* to Yahweh.

God has a second claim on Israel. He has *redeemed* (גאל) her. The reference is to the Exodus when she was brought out of Egyptian bondage. He *called her name:* perhaps God's address to Israel at Horeb is in view here. These show that Israel belongs to Yahweh.

3 *I give Egypt as your ransom* needs to be seen within the larger historical context. God has summoned Cyrus to facilitate Israel's access to her homeland in Canaan and to Jerusalem. At the time portrayed in this act, Cyrus is busy consolidating his gains in Asia Minor as far west as the Aegean Sea and as far east as India. He had by-passed Babylon because it was too weak under Nabunaid to be a problem. Palestine in itself had little attraction for him.

The Assyrians came to Lebanon/Palestine to get wood and have a port on the Mediterranean. But Cyrus already has these. One thing could lure Cyrus into Palestine: the prospect of conquering *Egypt, Ethiopia,* and North Africa, where *Seba* was also located (not to be confused with Sheba in southern Arabia; cf. Gen 10:7; 1 Chr 1:9). This verse says that God promised these to the Persian in return for his services in restoring Jerusalem. Cyrus did not invade Egypt, but his son Cambyses did. And his successor, Darius I, continued to use Palestine as a stepping stone to Egypt.

4 *You are precious in my eyes* echoes and confirms the classic statement of Israel's election in Exod 19:5. *I give (of) mankind* (אדם) *in exchange for you* is a succinct assertion that God is manipulating historical forces in Persia and Egypt to support the role which he has destined Israel to fulfill, just as he did in bringing them out of Egypt under Moses. The entire passage reflects the Exodus narrative as it also reflects the military and political conditions of the 6th and 5th centuries B.C.

5–6 These verses are a key statement concerning Israel's return to Palestine. They must be read carefully. This return fits the pattern of 2:1–4 and 66:18–21. There is no promise here of a return to political power. The Vision sees God's servant Israel functioning simultaneously and as a complement to his servant Cyrus. Their roles are distinct.

7 The compatibility of God's election (*called by my name*) and of salvation through his active intervention on Israel's behalf (*whom I created, I made him*) is proclaimed here.

8 The very people that 6:9–10 condemned to continued blindness are now to be released. The period of cursed judgment (6:11–13) is past. (Cf. 40:2.)

10–13 In the presence of the gathered nations Israel is summoned to fulfill her servant role: to bear witness that Yahweh is God. The content of that witness required of Israel is that he had *announced* (it) ahead of time, had *saved* her, and now lets it *be heard.* The nations already know the news of Babylon's weakness and the meteoric rise of the Persian. Israel is to testify that Yahweh predicted it and is responsible for it.

Excursus: צדק/צדקה *"Righteousness/Legitimacy"*

Bibliography

Achtemeier, E.R. "Righteousness in the OT." *IDB* 4:80–85. **Bonnard, P.-E.** *Le Second Isaïe.* Paris: J. Gabalda, 1972. 541–42. **Chilton, B. D.** *The Glory of Israel.* JSOTSup 23. Sheffield: U. of Sheffield, 1983. 81–85. **Dünner, A.** *Die Gerechtigkeit nach dem Alten Testament.* Bonn: Bouvier, 1963. **Fahlgren, K. H.** *S^e^dākā, nahestehende und engegengesetzte Begriffe im Alten Testament.* Uppsala: Almquist & Wiksells, 1932. **Fieldner, M. J.** "Δικαιοσύνη in der diaspora-jüdischen und intertestamentarischen Literatur." *JSJ* 1 (1970) 120–43. **Havelock, E. A.** "DIKAIOSUNE: An Essay in Greek Intellectual History." *Phoenix* 23 (1969) 49–70. **Horst, F.** "Gerechtigkeit Gottes. II. Im AT und Judentum." *RGG* 2:1403–6. **Jepsen, A.** "צדק und צדקה im Alten Testament." *Gottes Wort und Gottes Land.* Ed. H. Graf Reventloh. Göttingen: Vandenhoeck & Ruprecht, 1965. 78–99. **Jones, H. J.** "Abraham and Cyrus: Type and Anti-type?" *VT* 22 (1972) 304–19. **Justesen, J. P.** "On the Meaning of ṢĀḎĀQ." *AUSS* 2 (1964) 53–61. **Lofthouse, W. F.** "The Righteousness of Yahweh." *ExpTim* 50 (1938) 341–45. **Olley, J. W.** *"Righteousness" in the Septuagint of Isaiah: A Contextual Study.* Missoula, MT: Scholars Press, 1979. **Reiterer, F. V.** *Gerechtigkeit als Heil.* צדק *bei Deuterojesaja: Aussage und Vergleich mit der alttestamentlichen Tradition.* Graz: Akadem. Druck, 1976. **Reventlow, H. G.** *Rechtfertigung im Horizont des Alten Testament.* Munich: Kaiser, 1971. **Schmid, H. H.** *Gerechtigkeit als Weltordnung: Hintergrund und Geschichte des altestamentlichen Gerechtigkeitsbegriffes.* BHT 40. Tübingen: Mohr, 1968. **Scullion, J. J.** *"Sedeq-sedaqah* in Isaiah cc. 40–66 with Special Reference to the Continuity in Meaning between Second and Third Isaiah." *UF* 3 (1971) 335–48. ———. *Isaiah 40–66.* Wilmington, DE: Glazier, 1982. 138–40, 211–12. **Snaith, N.** *The Distinctive Ideas of the Old Testament.* London: Epworth, 1944. ———. "Isaiah 40–66: A Study of the Teaching of the Second Isaiah and Its Consequences." *Studies on the Second Part of the Book of Isaiah.* VTSup 14. Leiden: E. J. Brill, 1967. 135–264. **Szubin, Z. H. and Jacobs, L.** "Righteousness." *EncJud* 14 (1972) 180–84. **Watson, N. M.** "Some Observations on the use of δικαιοσύνη in the Septuagint." *JBL* 79 (1960) 255–66. **Whitley, C. F.** "Deutero-Isaiah's interpretation of *ṣedeq.*" *VT* 22 (1972) 469–75.

The words צדק and צדקה, elsewhere translated "righteous" and "righteousness," seem to require different translations in Isa 40–66 where they appear frequently. Lists of occurrences in Scullion (*Isaiah 40–66,* 138–39, 211–12) show how RSV and JB have turned sometimes to "victory" or "integrity" or "deliverance" or "vindication" to translate the words when they are related to Yahweh or his work. Bonnard (541–42) has a similar list which he translates *"sa justice"* [his justice].

Scullion points to chap. 32 as a good starting point in understanding the word: "Behold, a king will reign in righteousness (צדקה) and princes will rule in justice (משפט)." He quotes H. H. Schmid: *"sdq* in Second Isaiah then means Yahweh's world order in salvation history, an order that is based on creation and extends over the proclamation of the divine will, the rousing of Cyrus and the 'servant,' right up to the coming of salvation in the future."

This commentary has found the words "legitimate/legitimacy" appropriate since צדק/צדקה are applied to Persian rule in Palestine. Yahweh lends his support to Cyrus, Darius, and Artaxerxes, thereby granting their rule divine legitimacy, especially as it applies to Yahweh's own land, in order that they may provide protection and restoration for Judah and Jerusalem.

The words are often used in close relation to ישעה "salvation" which in this case refers to the protection and rescue which Persian forces and administration can provide against whatever enemies there may be.

Both "legitimacy" and "salvation" in chaps. 40–66 are very practical political terms in contrast to their religious and spiritual meanings in the Psalms, the Targum, and the NT.

14–15 Yahweh's raising up Cyrus is an act of sovereign redemption for Israel's sake. Yahweh continues to identify himself principally with Israel at the very time when he is demonstrating his universal influence and power.

16–17 The verses echo the Exodus motifs of *the sea* and of *horses and riders.* But the 6th century B.C. is also a time when naval power becomes a military factor. In the Aegean and eastern Mediterranean, powerful Athenian and Phoenician fleets serve Egyptian and Persian interests in seeking control of the shipping lanes. Yahweh claims control of forces at sea, as well as those on land. But eventually they will all be *extinguished like a wick.* Military power plays no ultimate role in God's plan.

18–21 The *earlier* and *past* times are those in which Israel struggled to be a nation among the nations (1 Sam 8:5, 20). A new era has dawned, and Israel is instructed to turn her back on the old ways, not to remember them as a pattern for her current life. Yahweh called attention to the real goal for his use of the Persians's political and military power, *the new thing* he is building. The emphasis in these passages on *a way in the wilderness* and *rivers in a wasteland* is in deliberate contrast to the prophesied wasteland (5:5–10; 6:11) and exile (5:13; 6:12) which had become fulfilled reality for Israel in the 6th century B.C. The genuinely *new thing* is to be *this people,* the worshiping congregation at Jerusalem (2:3–4; 65:17–25).

Explanation

Who is on trial here? This is not a court of law in the British or American sense. It is more like an inquiry or a public hearing. The purpose is to convince and vindicate policy, to win acceptance and compliance for decisions already made.

Yahweh has determined the policy that brings Cyrus and the Persians into West Asia to take over the crumbling Babylonian Empire, to set his people free, and to restore Jerusalem and its temple. The nations of greater Palestine are less than enthusiastic about the change and totally opposed to the restoration of Jerusalem. Egypt would like to have been assigned the Persian's role. Others would have preferred another course. But the Vision concentrates on these neighbors and on the reaction of Israelite exiles in Mesopotamia.

These opponents to Yahweh's policies challenge his right and ability to determine these things. This provokes in return an attack on their gods. Of course the gods so addressed are not present. In fact they exist only as idols in temples or in people's minds. Those whom God addresses are people who make and worship idols to embody their own ideals and goals. Israelites who are cool to Yahweh's plan are included in this group.

The goal of the hearings is to get recognition and acceptance of Yahweh's plans for the reign of the Persians and the restoration of Jerusalem. From exilic Israel he asks active cooperation. From the coastlands (Philistia, Phoenicia, and those to the north as far as Antioch) and from the border countries of greater Palestine (Edom, Moab, Ammon, Samaria, Aram, Arab entities and perhaps the northern Egyptian provinces) he demands recognition, acceptance, and cooperation. The central and key group addressed is exilic Israel, and the main subject is Cyrus. These two are assigned the principal tasks as servants of Yahweh. Cyrus assents and performs his role. Israel demurs, continuing her blind, uncomprehending ways.

The scene's ultimate address is to the audience or readers one or more centuries later. They are challenged to break the precedent of generations which have resisted God's call, and vow to hear, believe, and trust. They are called to adjust their lives and their ways to the plan God has for them and trust that he will be with them in "passing through the waters." Beyond them the scene addresses the people of God through the centuries who are called to be God's witnesses to "Jerusalem, Judea, and to the ends of the earth." Paul Gerhardt's beloved hymn "Befiehl du deine Wege" [Commit your ways to him] was inspired by the beautiful promises of 43:1–7.

Scene 5: Remember These, Jacob! (43:22–44:23)

Bibliography

Booij, T. "Negation in Isaiah 43, 22–24." *ZAW* 94 (1982) 390–400. **Gelston, A.** "Some Notes on Second Isaiah: (b) Isaiah xliv 15–16." *VT* 21 (1971) 521. **Kutsch, E.** "Ich will meinen Geist ausgiessen auf deine Kinder." *Das Wort, das weiterwirkt.* FS K. Frör (Munich, 1981) 122–33. **Merendino, R. P.** *Der Erste und der Letzte* 347–401. **Merwe, B. J. van der.** "Onverdiende gnade. ʾn studie oor Jesaja 43:22–28." *Hervormde Teologiese Studies* 10 (1953/54) 167–91. ———. "Die betekenis van m^{e}liceka (woordvoerders) in Jes. 43:27." *Hervormde Teologiese Studies* 11 (1954/55) 169–77. ———. *Pentateuchtradisies in die prediking van Deuterojesaja.* Groningen/Djakarta: J. B. Wolters, 1956. § 33 (on 43:27). **Schoors, A.** "Les choses antérieures et les choses nouvelles dans les oracles Deutéro-Isaïens." *ETL* 40 (1964) 19–47. **Smith, B. L.** "The significance of catchwords in Isaiah 43:22–28." *Colloquium* 15 (1982) 21–30. **Thomas, D. W.** "Isaiah xliv 9–20: A Translation and commentary." *Hommages à André Dupont-Sommer* (1971) 319–30. **Waldow, H. E. von.** ". . . *denn ich erlöse dich.*" BibS(N) 29. Neukirchen: Neukirchener Verlag, 1960. **Whitley, C. F.** "Further Notes on the Text of Dt.-Is." *VT* 25 (1975) 683–87.

Translation

Yahweh: 22 *But* [a]*me you have not called,*[a] *Jacob:* 3+3
[b]*for you have been weary of me,*[b] *Israel.*
23 *You have not brought*[a] *me a sheep for your burnt-offerings,*[b] 4+3
and with your sacrifices[c] *you have not honored me.*
[d]*I have not burdened you*[e] *on account of an offering,*[d] 3+3
and I have not wearied you on account of frankincense.
24 *You have not bought me sweet cane with silver,* 4+4
and with the fat of your sacrifices[a] *you have not filled me up.*[b]
Yet you have burdened[c] *me on account of your sins.* 3+2
You have wearied[c] *me on account of your iniquities.*

25 *I! I am he* 3+3+3
who is blotting out your guilts [a]*for my own sake.*
And your sins[a] *I do not remember.*[b]
26 *Remind me!*[a] *Let us discuss this together.*[b] 3+4
You recount it,[c] *yes you, so that you may be shown*
to be right.
27 [a]*Your first father*[a] *sinned*[b] 3+3
and your mediators[c] *rebelled against me.*
28 *So I profaned*[a] *princes of holiness* 3+3+2
and I gave up Jacob to the ban
and Israel to revilings.
44:1 *But now listen, Jacob my servant,* 4+3
And Israel whom I have chosen.
Herald: 2 *Thus says Yahweh, your maker,* 3+3
and your shaper from the womb, "I help you."[a]
Yahweh: *Do not fear, my servant Jacob,* 3+3
and Jeshurun,[b] *whom I have chosen.*
3 *For I pour water on a thirsty one*[a] 3+2
and streams[b] *on a dry place.*
[c]*I pour my spirit on your seed* 3+2
and my blessing[d] *on your offspring.*
4 *They shall spring up between*[ab] *blades of grass* 3+2
and like willows by streams[c] *of water.*
5 *This one says "I belong to Yahweh,"* 4+3
and this one calls out[a] *"In the name of Jacob,"*
and this one writes on his hand[b] *"Belongs to*
Yahweh," 4+3
and will entitle himself[c] *by the name "Israel."*
Herald: 6 *Thus says Yahweh* 2+2+2
King of Israel and her redeemer,
Yahweh of Hosts.[a]
Yahweh: *I am first and I am last!* 4+3
Apart from me, there is no God!
7 *Who would be like me?* 2+2
Let him speak out[a] *and announce it!*
And let him arrange it[b] *for me—*[c] 2+2
[d]*from my founding an age-old people*
and future things which are to come[d]*—* 3+2
let them announce them to us![e]
8 *Do not fear! Do not be afraid!*[a] 2+3+3
Have I not let you[b] *hear earlier?*
Is there any god apart from me? 3+3
Each witness (in turn): *There is no*[c] *Rock. I know none.*
Heavens: 9 *Ones forming*[a] *an idol, all of them, are emptiness,* 3+2
and their desirable qualities[b] *do not benefit.*[c]
[d]*They*[e] *are their own witnesses.* 2+2+2
They see nothing.[f] *They know nothing.*
[g]*So they are a shame.*[dg]

Earth: 10 [a]Who would form a god — 2+2+2
or cast an idol
for no profit?
Heavens: 11 See,[a] all its fellows[b] are shamed. — 3+5
As for the craftsmen,[c] they are less than human.
Earth: Let them all gather. Let them take a stand. — 3+3
Let them be terrified. Let them be shamed together.[d]
Heavens: 12 The smith[a] [b]cuts out a mold,[b] — 4+2
and he works in the coals.
[c]And with hammers he shapes it,[c] — 2+3
and then[d] he works it with his strong arm.
Even he gets hungry and has no strength left. — 3+3
If he doesn't drink water, [d]he becomes faint.
Earth: 13 [a]The carpenter stretches[b] a line.[a] — 4+2
[c]He marks it with a pencil.
He works[d] it with planes — 2+2
and with a compass he marks it.[c]
So he makes it with the shape of a person — 3+4
to have the appearance [e]of a human to live[e] in a house.
Heavens: 14 [a]To cut[b] for it cedars, — 2+3
he takes a tree or an oak
which grew strong by itself among the trees of the forest.[a] — 3+4
He may plant a cedar,[c] but the rain makes it grow tall.
15 It becomes[a] a human's fuel, — 3+3+3
so he takes some of it and warms himself.
Indeed, he kindles a fire and bakes bread.
Indeed,[b] he makes a god. Then he worships it. — 2+4
He makes it into an idol. Then he falls down to it.
Earth: 16 Half of it he burns with fire. — 3+3+3
Over that half [a]he eats meat.
He roasts[a] a roast and is satisfied.
Indeed, he warms himself and says "Ah! — 3+3
I am warm. I see[b] flame."
17 And the rest of it he makes into his idol[a] to be a god. — 4+2
He falls down[b] to it and worships it.[c]
He prays to it and says: — 3+4
"Save me! For you are my god."
Heavens: 18 They do not know. They do not think — 4+4+2
because it has closed their eyes from seeing,
their minds from reasoning.
19 One does not let it cross his mind. — 4+3
There is no knowledge,[a] no understanding of it, saying,[b]

"Half of it I burned in fire. 3+4+3
Indeed, I baked bread on its coals.
I roasted meat and ate it.
And the rest I made into an abomination.[c] 3+3
I fall down to a block[d] *of wood."*
Earth: 20 *One feeding*[a] *on ashes,* 2+3
a mind deceived has led him away.
[b]*It cannot save his soul*[b] 2+2+3
and cannot say:
"Is this[c] *not a lie in my right hand?"*
Yahweh: 21 *Remember these, Jacob* 3+3
and Israel, that you are my servant!
I formed you. 1+2+3
You are a servant for me.
Israel, you are not forgotten by me.[a]
22 [a]*I have swept away your rebellions like a cloud* 3+2
and your sins like a mist.
Turn back to me! 2+2
For[b] *I have redeemed you.*
Earth: 23 *Sing praises, O Heavens,* 2+2
for Yahweh has done it![a]
Heavens: *Shout out, you depths*[b] *of Earth!*[c] 3+3+3
Break forth, you mountains! Sing!
You forest and all its trees!
For Yahweh has redeemed Jacob 3+2
and in Israel[d] *he will show glory!*

Notes

22.a-a. LXX *οὐ νῦν ἐκάλεσά σε* "now I did not call you." Follow MT.

22.b-b. MT כי "for" is supported by DSS^{Isa} Syr Tg. LXX *οὐδὲ κοπιᾶσαί σε ἐποίησα* "nor did I cause you to be weary" and Vg *nec laborasti in me* "nor have you troubled yourselves about me" read a negative, ולא. MT makes sense and should be kept. The passage is playing on the word יגע "weary, be wearied" in vv 22–24.

23.a. DSS^{Isa} הביאותה is a variant pronunciation of the form in MT.

23.b. MT עלתיך "your burnt offerings" is pl, as are 1QIsa^{b} and Syr. DSS^{Isa} LXX Tg Vg read a sg. MT may be kept.

23.c. MT וזבחיך "and your sacrifices." DSS^{Isa} ובזבחיכה "and with your sacrifices" makes grammatically explicit what the simple accus implies. So also LXX and Syr. Tg agrees with MT, but adds "holy."

23.d-d. Missing in LXX.

23.e. MT העבדתיך "I have caused you to serve, I have burdened you." DSS^{Isa} עשיתה ליא "I have caused you to make to me."

24.a. Tg adds "holy."

24.b. LXX *ἐπεθύμησα* "angered" (cf. 1:11). Follow MT. Perhaps LXX is avoiding an anthropomorphism.

24.c,c. LXX *προέστην* "I stand before (you)" does duty for the two Heb. verbs. Tg has a similar meaning for both verbs (see Elliger 361). The others including Syr and Vg follow MT.

25.a-a. Missing in LXX. DSS^{Isa} Syr Tg Vg follow MT. For suggested emendations see Elliger, 362. Read MT.

25.b. DSS^{Isa} adds עוד "more" at the end of the verse.

26.a. MT is sg. DSS^{Isa} is pl but follows with sg verbs in the second stich as does MT. LXX

Syr translate a qal (i.e., not causative) form. Tg reads "tell now," Vg *reduc me in memoriam* "refresh my memory."

26.b. MT יחד "together." DSS[Isa] יחדיו "together with him." Missing in LXX.

26.c. LXX adds *τὰς ἀνομίας σου πρῶτος* "first your transgressions." Tg adds "if you can" like Vg's *si quid habes* "if you have something." Syr *'mrt* "I have said" misunderstands the word. Follow MT.

27.a-a. LXX *οἱ πατέρες ὑμῶν πρῶτοι* "your first fathers." DSS[Isa] Syr Tg Vg follow MT's sg.

27.b. LXX omits.

27.c. LXX *καὶ οἱ ἄρχοντες αὐτῶν* (*υμων*) "and their (your) rulers." Syr *slytnyk* "your rulers." 'A Σ *και οι επμηνεις σου* = Vg *et interpretes tui* "and your interpreters." Tg ומלפך "and your teachers." Read MT.

28.a. LXX "your rulers profaned my holy (place)." Syr "your nobles defiled the sanctuary." MT Tg Vg have Yahweh as the subject.

44:2.a. DSS[Isa] ועוזרכה "and your helper" is a ptcp like the two that precede. Vg *auxiliator tuus* "your helper"; Syr is similar. LXX Tg follow MT.

2.b. Several MSS[K,R] have וישראל "and Israel" with Syr. LXX Ισραηλ "Israel" preceded by *ὁ ἠγαπημένος* "the beloved" which Elliger (363) notes may translate MT's ישרון "Jeshurun" (see *Comment*), as do *ευθυτατος* or *ευθης* "honest" of the other Gr. versions and Vg's *rectissime* "most virtuous." Most Tg MSS read "Israel." DSS[Isa] = MT.

3.a. MT צָמֵא is an adj, "a thirsty one" (BDB, 854). *BHS* suggests reading צָמָה a noun, "thirst." MT is adequate.

3.b. MT ונזלים "streams" of flowing water (BDB, 633). LXX *τοῖς πορευομένοις* "the one passing by" is perhaps a confusion with אזל (BDB 23; cf. Ziegler, *Untersuchungen* 126; Elliger, 363).

3.c. DSS[Isa] has כן "so" inserted here between the lines. Tg has treated the first half of the verse as a comparison. Syr also begins the first part with "like."

3.d. LXX Syr have a pl. DSS[Isa] 'A Σ Θ Tg Vg have sg like MT.

4.a. DSS[Isa], 17 MSS[K,R,G], LXX, Tg read כ "like" rather than MT's ב "in."

4.b. בין may be a preposition "between," but it may also be understood in other ways (cf. Elliger, 364). J. M. Allegro ("The Meaning of בין in Isaiah xliv 4," *ZAW* 63 [1951] 154–56; "A Possible Mesopotamian Background to the Joseph Blessing of Gen. xlix," *ZAW* 64 [1952] 249–51) draws on cognate Semitic roots to suggest that it refers to a kind of tree. This would suggest that חציר means "green." A. Guillaume ("The Meaning of בין," *JTS* 13 [1962] 110) compares it to an Arab root meaning "a flat place" and translates "like a field of grass." LXX adds *ὕδατος* "water," to complicate the picture further. The translation has chosen to remain with the simple meaning of the preposition.

4.c. DSS[Isa] יובלי reads a ptcp instead of MT's noun. The meaning remains the same.

5.a. LXX supports the active sense, though one MS (239') has *κληθήσεται* passive "will be called." Syr Tg Vg support MT. However, many recent interpreters prefer the passive sense. The translation follows MT as the more difficult reading.

5.b. MT ידו "his hand." DSS[Isa] ידוהי "?." LXX omits. Syr = MT. Vg *manu sua* = Heb בידו "on his hand." Elliger (364) and others presume that in MT the *beth* has dropped out through haplogr. The sense is "on his hand," whether through the preposition or the accus.

5.c. MT יְכַנֶּה "entitles" is active but lacks an obj. Syr *ntknh* is reflexive, "names himself." Vg *assimilabitur* is passive. BDB (487) and *BHS* suggest rendering as pual יְכֻנֶּה and translating in passive sense "be named." Or one may render a niph יִכָּנֶה in a reflexive sense as in the translation.

6.a. DSS[Isa] adds שמו "is his name" and is supported by Syr. LXX Tg Vg support MT. The longer form appears in 47:4; 48:2; 51:15; 54:5. Morgenstern ("Loss of Words in Biblical Poetry," *HUCA* 25 [1954] 60) considered the longer form correct. It is metrically possible, but not necessary.

7.a. LXX adds *στήτω* "let him stand," which Syr *nqwn* reads in place of MT's יקרא "let him speak out." Tg and Vg follow MT. Many recent commentators follow LXX: "let him stand and speak." However, if the line is recognized as a tristich 2+2+2, MT may be read as it is.

7.b. DSS[Isa] ויעריכהה is probably a variant spelling of MT.

7.c. MT לי "to me" is missing in several MSS. DSS[Isa] לוא "to him."

7.d-d. The line has appeared difficult to virtually all modern readers. It reads, lit., "Since I established an ancient people and coming things and which will come." The position of the *athnaḥ* suggests dividing the lines so as to achieve three pairs of 2+2 lines. DSS[Isa] adds יואמר "let him say" in place of the *waw* with אשר "which" but otherwise supports MT in spite of Löwinger's observations (*VT* 4 [1954] 82; cf. Elliger 396). The Versions also support MT, although

Syr reads *ʾtwt* "signs" instead of "things to come." *BHS* and numerous others (listed and discussed by Elliger, 396) emend to מי השמיע מעולם אותיות "who proclaimed from of old future things?" When all is said and done, a direct translation of MT remains the most satisfactory.

7.e. LXX ὑμῖν "to you," though two MSS ἡμῖν "to us." Missing in Syr. Tg לנא "to us." Vg *eis* "to them." Either "to me" or "to us" is required by the context. The emendation לנו "to us" for למו "to him" is commended (cf. Elliger, 397).

8.a. MT תִּרְהוּ is a *hap. leg.* A root רהה is not known (BDB, 923). DSS^{Isa} תיראו "fear" is the most logical expectation. LXX omits, but the recensions have πλανασθε "lead astray." Syr *ttrhbwn* "be shocked" suggests Heb תִּרְהֲבוּ. Tg תיתברון "be broken." Vg *confundamini* "be perplexed." The choices are to follow DSS^{Isa} "be afraid" or Syr "be shocked" or, with Gesenius, Köhler, and *BHS,* to look to a root ירה like Arab *wariha* "be stupified" (cf. BDB, 436). The translation takes the first option.

8.b. MT ךָ "you" sg. LXX Syr "you" pl. Tg and Vg support MT. Who is the antecedent? If this is directed individually at each witness (see v 8d), the sg is appropriate.

8.c. *BHS* suggests emending ואין "and no" to ואם "or" with Ziegler (*Untersuchungen,* 155). However, Syr Tg Vg support MT. Another suggestion by Gordis and Driver (*Von Ugarit nach Qumran,* BZAW 77 [1958] 47) posits the Aram interrogative particle וְאִין "who?" MT makes sense as it is and should be kept (*contra* Elliger, 398).

9.a. MT יצרי "ones forming." DSS^{Isa} יוצר sg. LXX οἱ πλάσσοντες καὶ "the ones forming and" apparently read a *waw*. Syr has an interpretive paraphrase. Tg Vg follow MT.

9.b. MT וחמודיהם "their desirable qualities" (BDB, 326). LXX οἱ ποιοῦντες τὰ καταθύμια αὐτῶν "those making their heart's desires." Syr *ʿbdyhwn drgw lmʿbd* "their products, which they love to make." Elliger (408) suggests correctly that both should be recognized as paraphrases. Tg ופלחיהון "and their worshipers." Vg *et amantissima eorum* "and their most ardent lovers."

9.c. MT בל־יועילו "do not benefit" is translated as a relative clause in LXX Tg, but not in Syr Vg.

9.d-d. Missing in LXX, but generally found in other Versions.

9.e. MT המה "they" has remarkable and unique Masoretic marks above it (cf. Bergstrasser, *Grammatik* I § 51; Bauer-Leander § 6s). Perhaps they indicate some question about it from the copyists. DSS^{Isa} has the word added over the line. It is missing in MSS^{K99,145}. Some have thought it dittography for the suffix before. Elliger (408) correctly sees it as fitting both meter and sense.

9.f. Syr adds "and hear nothing."

9.g-g. Syr connects to the following verse.

10.a. MS^{K487} omits the entire verse. But the Versions support MT.

11.a. MT הן "see." DSS^{Isa} הנה "see." LXX καὶ "and."

11.b. MT חבריו a noun "his fellows" (BDB, 288). DSS^{Isa} חובריו a qal ptcp "those allied to him" or "those bound by a spell" (but the latter is unlikely in light of the Versions). LXX ὅθεν ἐγένοντο "from whom they came." Syr *ʾwmnyhwn* "their craftsmen." Tg פלחיהון "their worshipers." Θ οι κωνωνουντες αυτω and Vg *participes eius* mean "and his partners." Elliger (409) concludes that DSS^{Isa} Θ Tg Vg share a common tradition, but recommends support for MT.

11.c LXX καὶ κωφοὶ "and deaf ones" and Syr *ḥrsyn* "the deaf" both derive חרשים from the second root meaning "deaf" (BDB, 361, II). Tg and Vg follow MT to derive from the first root meaning "craftsmen" (BDB, 360, I). *BHS* חרשיו "his craftsmen," to conform to its parallels, is unnecessary.

11.d. DSS^{Isa} יחדיו "together with him."

12.a. MT חרש ברזל "worker of iron, smith" (BDB, 360, I). LXX inserts ὅτι "that" before the verse and translates ὤξυνε τέκτων σίδηρον "a worker sharpened iron." Delitzsch thought that required Heb. החד חרש ברזל taking the first word from the end of the last line. Others suggest יחד (see *BHS*) "he sharpens" from חדד (BDB, 292). Both are unlikely and unnecessary. Elliger (409) is right that the Versions are translating freely.

12.b-b. מעצד (BDB, 781) occurs in Jer 10:3 as a tool for woodwork. Hence the idea "an axe" (RSV). But the term is otherwise unknown. Muilenburg attempts to use it as a ptcp. Elliger (409–10) objects and suggests that the letters גל have fallen out as haplogr for the previous letters. He reconstructs as גֹּלֶם עָצַד "he cuts out a mould" (cf. BDB, 166). This seems to be the best solution.

12.c-c. LXX καὶ ἐν τερέτρῳ ἔτρησεν αὐτό "and he bored it with the drill" apparently derives MT's מקבות from the verb נקב "pierce" (BDB, 666, I) rather than the related noun used of the instrument for driving nails, from which the name "Maccabee" was later derived. Tg and Vg have caught MT's meaning.

12.d. *BHS* suggests a simple *waw* in both places. MT's *waw* consecutives are clear and should be kept.

13.a-a. LXX varies, apparently influenced by v 12 and 40:20.

13.b. DSS[Isa] is pl.

13.c-c. LXX writes only one line for the three stichs: *καὶ ἐν κόλλῃ ἐρρύθμισεν αὐτό* "and with glue he put it together." The Versions vary.

13.d. *BHS* emends to ישעהו (reversing two letters) "he smeared over" (BDB, 1044), in this context "he smooths it with planes." But the emendation is unnecessary. The sense is already there.

13.e-e. Tg איתתא יתבת "of a woman who sits." Elliger (411) suggests that it read ישבת "she lives" for MT's לשבת "to live." But Vg properly translated *hominem habitantem.*

14.a-a. LXX has a shorter text, but Tg Vg follow MT.

14.b. *BHS* follows LXX in emending. Elliger (411) finds this both risky and unnecessary.

14.c. LXX *κύριος* apparently misread ארז "cedar" for אדן "lord." Tg supports MT.

15.a. DSS[Isa] והגה "and he wept" or "and he removed it" is apparently an error.

15.b. MT אף "indeed." DSS[Isa] או "or."

16.a-a. *BHS* would reverse the order of two words, citing LXX and Syr. DSS[Isa] preserves a very different text. Tg and Vg agree with MT. See the discussion by Elliger (413) and keep MT.

16.b. DSS[Isa] נגד "before." But the Versions support MT.

17.a. DSS[Isa] לבלוי עץ "to blocks of wood" (cf. v 19) in place of MT's לפסלו "to his idol." *BHS* summarizes the argument of many to emend following LXX *γλυπτὸν* to לפסל "to the idol," leaving off the suffix "his." Follow MT.

17.b. K יִסְגוֹד "he falls down." Q יִסְגָּד is an unusual way to write the same form (BDB, 688).

17.c. MT וישתחו "he worships it" is apocopated (BDB, 1105). DSS[Isa] here (though not in v 15) gives the full form וישתחוה, which *BHS* recommends both here and in v 15. This is unnecessary. The apocopated form is common (cf. Gen 18:2; 19:1; etc.).

19.a. *BHK* suggests inserting לו "to it" or "of it," i.e., "it has no knowledge." The question is, to whom does this refer? Is it the idol's or the worshiper's attitude?

19.b. DSS[Isa] has לאמור "saying" twice.

19.c. DSS[Isa] pl.

19.d. DSS[Isa] לבלוי pl.

20.a. רעה usually means "feed" (BDB, 944–45, I). Tg has taken the second meaning "to associate with" (BDB, 945, II). There is still a third, "to take pleasure in, delight in" (BDB, 946, III).

20.b-b. MT לא יציל "it saves not." DSS[Isa] לוא יוכיל "is not able." LXX *καὶ οὐδεὶς δύναται ἐξελέσθαι τὴν ψυχὴν αὐτοῦ* "and no one is able to rescue his soul" combines the two meanings and is followed by 'Α Σ Θ. However, Syr Tg Vg follow MT.

20.c. DSS[Isa] lacks the interrogative particle.

21.a. DSS[Isa] תשאני is identified by Muilenburg, North, and Bonnard as a hiph impf from נשא "you deceived me" (BDB, 674, II). Elliger (442) suggests it be pointed as a qal impf from נשא = נשה "forget" (BDB, 674, II). This is the direction LXX Syr Vg have taken in reading MT's strange form תנשני. *BHS*'s suggestions are hardly useful. MT's niph reading is still the most likely. Although the suffix with dative connotations is unique, Bauer-Leander § 48h finds it possible. GKC § 117x refuses it.

22.a. LXX inserts *ἰδοὺ γὰρ* "for behold!"

22.b. LXX *καὶ* "and," but Syr Tg Vg support MT's כי "for."

23.a. LXX *ἠλέησεν . . . τὸν Ισραηλ* "he has pitied Israel." Note that LXX also strengthens עשה "doing" in v 24 to *συντελῶν* "had compassion." Syr follows MT, Tg adds "redemption," and Vg *misericordiam fecit* "had mercy" follows LXX.

23.b. MT תחתיות "depths" or "underparts." LXX *θεμέλια*, Syr *st'ṣyh,* and Tg יסודי mean "foundations of"; Vg *extrema* "extremes"; the other Gr versions *τα κατωτατα* "the lower parts."

23.c. DSS[Isa] adds the article, "the earth."

23.d. MT "in Israel." LXX Vg MS[R663] have no preposition. DSS[Isa] Syr and Tg support MT.

Form/Structure/Setting

The scene is composed of four Yahweh speeches, a comic dialogue about idol-makers, and a final hymnic call to praise. The first Yahweh speech (43:22–28) is cast in the form of a judgment as virtually everyone, from Begrich to Merendino (*Der Erste und der Letzte,* 356), has recognized. It contains accusations that Israel has directed her worship to other gods, rather than toward Yahweh (vv 22–24). God recounts his services to Israel, including forgiveness of her sins (v 25). He defends himself against the implied charge that he has abandoned Israel during her recent troubles by blaming them on Israel's sins (vv 27–28). The purpose of the speech is to prepare the way for the offer of grace that is to follow.

44:1–5 is a generally recognized unit which used to be called a salvation oracle. But Merendino (367) has shown its structure to be comparable to that found in Jer 28:15–16; 34:4–5; Ezek 21:3–5; Amos 7:16–17; and Zech 3:8–10. These are all announcements of a judicial decision. But only Jer 34:4–5 and Zech 3:8–10 have a positive announcement of salvation like this one. Another parallel is found in Isa 51:21–23. Here in 44:1–5, a decision has been reached in the heavenly council. It is announced with the salvation promises that it implies. This structure contains an imperative with direct personal address, a citation of the facts in the case, the messenger formula, and direct divine address in the first person with verbs describing his actions, and ends with the anticipated results of the decision.

44:6–8 is the third Yahweh speech, introduced by a herald's announcement (v 6a) and closed by the witnesses' confession (v 8d) which Yahweh demands. Melugin (*Formation,* 118) calls this a trial speech, while Merendino suggests that it has been turned into a judgment speech against the idols (*Der Erste und der Letzte,* 380). It is in fact a challenge to Israel in its Babyonian setting to affirm again the First Commandment (Exod 20:3–4). They are challenged to bear witness in that pagan setting that Yahweh alone is God.

44:9–20 is considered an imitation of a legal setting, a disputational form (Melugin, *Formation,* 119). Westermann calls it a taunting song, while Connard calls it a satire against the idols. Like a piece in a drama, it provides a kind of comic interlude as two characters ridicule those who make and worship idols.

44:21–22 is Yahweh's fourth speech, and is an exhortation and affirmation for Israel (Melugin, *Formation,* 121). Merendino (*Der Erste und der Letzte,* 393) fails to find literary parallels to establish a genre. The form is unique, certainly in Isaiah. The structure is made up of two prominent imperatives: "remember" and "turn back." The first is supported by statements of what God has done for Israel. The second is supported by the reminder that God has redeemed her.

44:23 is a hymnic call to praise for God's decision and action to "redeem Jacob." It marks the end of the act and the period it represents.

The scene is set, like the rest of the act, in Babylon. History records an unprecedented rivalry between competing pagan cults there as the emperor brings into the city the idols from cities threatened by the advances of the

Medeo-Persian armies. Israel is just one worshiping group among many in the region. In this scene she is challenged to give as clear a witness to uniqueness and singularity of Yahweh her God as Moses had demanded from her at Sinai and in Canaan (cf. Exod 20 and Deut 6).

The scene is structured in an arch:

A Yahweh: Remember your history (43:22–28)
B Yahweh: Listen, Israel; I help you (44:1–5)
C Yahweh: Who is like me? (44:6–8c)
KEYSTONE Witness: No one is like you! (44:8d)
C′ Dialogue about the foolishness of idolatry (44:9–20)
B′ Yahweh: Remember, Israel; Turn back to me (44:21–22)
A′ Hymn: Yahweh has done it! (44:23)

Comment

43:22–24 Note the contrasts: Yahweh is calling Israel (v 1), but Israel has *not called* on him. Israel is *weary* (יגע) of Yahweh, though Yahweh has *not burdened* (hiph of עבד) or *wearied* (hiph of יגע) the Israelites with demands for sacrifices, but they have *burdened* (hiph of עבד) and *wearied* (hiph of יגע) Yahweh by their sins. The references to cultic offerings and sacrifices are unique in a book that usually emphasizes spiritual attitude and commitment instead. The emphatic opening ולא אתי "but not me," however, sets the tone for all three verses by claiming that Israel's worship was not directed to Yahweh. The underlying issue, then, is not cultic laxity but once again idolatry.

25 Yahweh announces a unilateral decision to forgive and forget their sins. This decision applies to this new age. In the past period he had exacted retribution (v 28) for the sins of their fathers. But the current generation is offered an opportunity for grace which their fathers did not enjoy.

27–28 Israel's past sinners included their progenitors and leaders. *First father* probably refers to Jacob (cf. Hos 12:2–4). *Mediators* could include Moses (Num 20:1–13), Aaron (Exod 32:1–6; Num 12) and their successors. *Princes of holiness* may well refer to kings from whom God withdrew the status of sanctity and divine protection, thus *profaning* or secularizing them and their kingdom.

44:1 But now God announces a period in which he can emphasize the positive aspects of his people from Jacob on. He has *chosen* them. He is their *maker* and *shaper*. He says, *"I will help you."*

2 *Jeshurun* is an endearing name for Israel used otherwise only in Deut 32:15; 33:5, 26.

3–4 Miraculous new life is promised to Israel by the metaphor of the surprising growth of plants in the desert when rains finally come.

5 The result will be a new enthusiasm among Israelites in Babylon and elsewhere to *belong to Yahweh* and to use the name *Jacob*. The exilic process of assimilation had naturally led Jews to suppress their distinct identity, to hide behind Babylonian names and to deny their religious identity. God's new offering of grace will change all that. Many interpreters have understood this to refer to Gentile proselytes. A defense of this interpretation is presented by Stuhlmueller (*Creative Redemption*, 129, n. 448; 130–31). The Vision contains a clear invitation to worshipers from the nations to come to the Temple in Jerusalem in chap. 2 and chap. 66. There is an open invitation to non-Jews in chap. 55–56. But the context here calls for a description of Israelite reaction to God's new announcement. The exilic Jews have been estranged, secularized, and disaffected by their exilic experience. But God's new policy opens a door to them again.

6a The Herald presents God by a double title. He is *King of Israel.* In this empire and especially in its capital city this is easily forgotten. When Israel has lost its Davidic king, one might assume that Yahweh's royal status and authority over Israel has also gone. Daniel's struggles and those of his friends (Dan 1–6) illustrate this. But Yahweh still claims his title and position. He demonstrates his authority and power by bringing a new emperor to restore his city and set his people free. He is revealed in this act as Israel's *redeemer, Yahweh of Hosts* in a new setting. He had redeemed Israel from Egypt at the beginning of their history as a people. Now, with Israel in exile and under imperial bondage again, it will take a new ransom price to get her free. God promised Cyrus the treasures of Egypt as his reward for rebuilding Jerusalem and freeing the Jews (43:3–4).

6b This verse with its counterpart in v 8d states the essential core of Israelite faith. Israel had to listen and assent to this in order to enter into covenant with Yahweh (Exod 20.2–4 and Deut 6). So now she must affirm that Yahweh alone is God; he is unique. There is nothing and no one with which to compare him (see C. J. Labuschagne, *The Incomparability of Yahweh in the Old Testament* [Leiden: E. J. Brill, 1966]). This singularity applies to all time, *first and last.* Idol cults rose and fell, as that period of Babylonian history showed. But Yahweh stands above and beyond the cyclical waves of popular acclaim.

7 *My establishing an ancient people* must refer to early Israel, from Abraham through the kingdoms. The word עולם "ancient" is capable of past ("ancient") as well as future ("for an age") significance (cf. R. J. Wyatt, "Eternal," *ISBE* 2:160; E. Jenni, "Time," *IDB* 4:644; and the references listed in *Comment* on 40:8 above). This establishes a historical context for Yahweh's claim. He then claims the future as well, a reference to anouncements and predictions earlier in this act and the next in which he claims credit for bringing Cyrus into the region and for predicting his coming. God claims that that speech which announces and interprets events is unique evidence of his divinity which he and he alone can produce. Neither idols nor their worshipers can do this.

8 This is the central moment. God's question elicits the required confession: *there is no Rock.* צור "Rock" is a title used for God in the Psalms and elsewhere. It describes God as a sure place of refuge (26:4; Pss 18:3, 47; 19:15; 28:1; 31:3; 63:3, 7; 73:26; 91:1; Deut 32:4). He is the absolute assurance for those who trust him.

9–20 The idolators are ridiculed. Not the idol but the worshipers are the object of laughter. They are *emptiness,* who *see nothing* and *know nothing.* They are *shamed, less than human* (v 11), *a mind deceived.*

21–22 *Redeemed* translates the Heb. word גאל, which is used in law for the family member who steps in when a husband dies, takes the widow as a wife to raise up sons to inherit the dead man's estate (cf. Ruth and Lev 25:25–49). The word is used in Exodus, parallel to פדה "ransom," to describe God's salvation of Israel from Egypt. Here it describes God's new role of active intervention on behalf of his people and his city in contrast to his "giving up Israel to the ban" (43:28) as part of the judgment announced in 6:9–13.

23 All of *Earth*'s aspects are called to participate in the jubilation: *depths* (or inner parts), *mountains,* and *forests.*

Explanation

This scene sums up the message of the act. God announces his decision to turn things around. A new age dawns and, because of it, Israel is redeemed and called to witness and service. God, having called Cyrus to undertake the practical necessities, turns to exhort Israel to recognize him and respond to him.

The ridiculous futility and self-deception of idol worship is portrayed in the comic satire it deserves. A hymnic call to celebration recognizes the solemnity and significance of the new thing that God has announced. This is gospel: *Yahweh has redeemed Jacob.*

Israel's confession, "I know no other Rock," is restrained. But it is the high point of her response to God. The power of the scene and the act lies in the announcement that God has acted. Stuhlmueller (*Creative Redemption,* 129) summarizes the meaning of this "creative redemption" as these chapters present it. Motivated by election in the patriarchs, it was an act done in love and with care. It will gain for them offspring and abundance. And it is seen as occurring in the present and immediate future.

The phrase "creative redemption" is cogent. These chapters portray God's work in terms of political action through Cyrus, a spiritual appeal to Israel, and through the potential of new creative action that turns deserts into fertile ground. It is a potent combination.

Act VIII: Cyrus, the Lord's Anointed (44:24–48:22)

THE EIGHTH GENERATION:
CYRUS/CAMBYSES (539–522 B.C.)

The promise of a deliverer from the east/north has been fulfilled. Cyrus appeared near Babylon (739 B.C.) and the city has been opened to him. Yahweh introduces him to Israel as his servant. Succeeding scenes interpret his role in restoring Jerusalem, building the temple, and freeing the captives. They urge Israel to accept Yahweh's arrangements and insist that they have not been displaced as Yahweh's people because they now have a limited role.

The humiliation of having idols moved through the streets on the way back to their temples and of having Babylon taken over by a foreign power is pictured in detail. A final scene leads up to a send-off for an expedition from Babylon to Jerusalem (48:16–21), which may well be that of Sheshbazzar (Ezra 1:8).

The act has five scenes.

Scene 1: Yahweh Introduces Cyrus (44:24–45:13).
Scene 2: In Yahweh Is Righteousness and Strength (45:14–25).
Scene 3: Bel Bows . . . My Purpose Stands (46:1–13).
Scene 4: Sit in the Dust, Daughter Babylon! (47:1–12).
Scene 5: Move Out from Babylon! (48:1–25).

HISTORICAL BACKGROUND

Bibliography

Breasted, J. H. *A History of Egypt,* 594–95. **Bright, J.** *HI.* 360–68. **Ctesias,** as quoted by Photeus of Constantinople, "Bibliothekae," *Patrologiae cursus completus.* Series Graeca, vols. 103–104. Lutetiae Parisiorum: J. P. Migne, 1864. **Culican, W.** *The Medes and Persians.* New York: Praeger, 1965. 56–63. **Dahlberg, B. T.** "Sheshbazzar." *IDB* 4:325–26. **Frye, R. N.** *The History of Ancient Iran,* 87–98. **Olmstead, A. T.** *History of the Persian Empire,* 34–93. **Smith, S.** *Isaiah Chapters XL–LV* 70–75.

Cyrus's entry into Babylon is fully recorded in ancient sources. The Babylonians were ready for a change in government. The "Nabonidus" chronicle tells the story: "In the month of Tashritu when Cyrus attacked the army of Akkad in Opis on the Tigris, the inhabitants of Akkad revolted, but he (Nabonidus) massacred the confused inhabitants. The fourteenth day Sippar was seized without battle. Nabonidus fled. The sixteenth day Ugbaru, governor of Gutium, and the army of Cyrus entered Babylon without battle. Afterwards Nabonidus was arrested in Babylon when he returned (there). . . . In the month of Arahsammu, the third day (October 29, 539 B.C.) Cyrus entered Babylon; green twigs were spread in front of him—the state of peace was imposed on the city" (*ANET*, 306). Herodotus (I, 189–91) has an account of a long siege, which is generally discounted today. The Cyrus cylinder adds: "All the kings of the entire world from the Upper (Mediterranean) to the Lower (Persian Gulf) Seas, those who are seated in throne rooms . . . all the kings of the West land living in tents, brought their heavy tributes and kissed my feet in Babylon" (*ANET*, 316). So Cyrus fell heir to Babylon's vassals in Syria and Palestine, including what the Vision calls "coastland" and "borderlands," and the Arabian princes from the "edges of the land."

Apparently, Cyrus soon returned to Ecbatana, leaving his son Cambyses as king of Babylon. When Cyrus died on a campaign east of the Caspian Sea in 530 B.C., Cambyses succeeded him to the throne. Plans for a campaign against Egypt, undoubtedly already underway, were accelerated. In 525 B.C. he moved through Palestine to mount a swift and successful campaign that brought the last of the great kingdoms under Persian rule. Then Cambyses stayed in Egypt to consolidate his power there.

Cyrus is credited in Ezra 1:1–4 with issuing an edict in his first year (presumably as king of Babylon, 538 B.C.) allowing the Jews freedom to return to Jerusalem to rebuild the Temple and commanding that Persian vassals along the way provide support. Ezra 1:5–8 reports an expedition being given the Temple vessels that Nebuchadnezzar had taken from Jerusalem. Sheshbazzar, prince of Judah, was named its leader. Persia's increased interest in the region because of the Egyptian campaign of Cambyses could well have provided a propitious moment to launch such an expedition. The Persians wanted to be assured of loyal vassals on their flanks as their army marched into Egypt.

However, the date of this trip is not certain. When Persia inherited Syria-Palestine, she would immediately have shown interest in the port cities and their shipping, but she may have been much slower to take an active interest in the inland areas.

Cyrus and Cambyses have recorded their established policy of returning idols and supporting the rebuilding of temples that Nabunaid had abandoned. The edict that Ezra mentions is in character with those policies.

Scene 1: Yahweh Introduces Cyrus (44:24–45:13)

Bibliography

Auvray, P. "Cyrus, instrument du Dieu unique." *BVC* 50 (1963) 17–23. **Dahood, M. J.** "Some Ambiguous Texts in Isaias (Isa 45:1)." *CBQ* 20 (1958) 41–49. **Dion, H. M.** "Le genre littéraire de l' Hymne à soi-même et quelques passages du Deutero-Isaïe."

RB 74 (1967) 215–34. **Haag, H.** "Ich mache Heil und schaffe Unheil (Jes 45:7)." *Wort, Lied und Gottesspruch.* FzB 2. FS Joseph Ziegler. Ed. J. Schreiner. Stuttgart: Katholisches Bibelwerk, 1972. 2:179–85. **Haller, M.** "Die Kyros-Lieder Deuterojesajas." *Eucharisterion.* FS H. Gunkel. Göttingen: Vandenhoeck & Ruprecht, 1923. 261–77. **Hecht, F.** "Die Interpretasie van Jes 45:7a." *NGTT* 4 (1963) 117–19. **Hermisson, H-J.** "Diskussionasworte bei Deuterojesaja." *EvT* 31 (1971) 665–80. **Hoffmann, A.** "Jahwe schleift Ringmauern—Jes 45:2aB." *Wort, Lied und Gottesspruch.* FzB 2. FS Joseph Ziegler. Ed. J. Schreiner. Stuttgart: Kath. Bibelwerk, 1972. 2:187–95. **Jenni, E.** "Die Rolle des Kyros bei Deuterojesaja." *TZ* 10 (1954) 241–56. **Johns, A. F.** "A Note on Isaiah 45:9." *AUSS* 1 (1963) 62–64. **Koch, K.** "Die Stellung des Kyros im Geschichtsbild Deuterojesajas und ihre überlieferungsgeschichtliche Verankerung." *ZAW* 84 (1972) 352–56. **Koole, J. L.** "Zu Jesaja 45:9ff." *Travels in the World of the Old Testament.* FS M. A. Beek. Assen: van Gorcum, 1974. 170–75. **Lack, R.** "Vocation et mission d'un roi païen (Is 45,1.4–6)." *AsSeign* 60 (1975) 5–9. **Leene, H.** "Universalism or Nationalism? Isaiah XLV 9–13 and Its Context." *Bijdragen* 35 (1974) 309–34. **Manahan, R. E.** "The Cyrus Notations of Deutero-Isaiah." *Grace Journal* 11 (1970) 22–33. **Merendino, R. P.** *Der Erste und der Letzte.* 402–60. **Naidoff, B. D.** "The Two-fold Structure of Isaiah XLV 9–13." *VT* 31 (1981) 180–85. **Ogden, G. S.** "Moses and Cyrus: Literary Affinities between the Priestly Presentation of Moses in Exodus vi–viii and the Cyrus Song in Isaiah xliv 24–xlv 13." *VT* 28 (1978) 195–203. **Raberger, W.** *"Schöpfung" als Problemfigur: Zur Artikulation einer Sinnprämisse in der Bewältigung ambivalenter Wirklichkeit bei Dtjes 45:7.* Diss. Innsbruck, 1974. **Riesel, M.** "The Relation between the Creative Function of the verbs brʾ–ysr–ʿsh in Isaiah 43:7 and 45:7." *Verkenningen in een Stroomgebied.* FS M. A. Beek. Amsterdam: Huisdrukkerij Universiteit, 1974. 65–79. **Schoors, A.** *I am God Your Savior.* 267–73. **Simcox, C. R.** "The Role of Cyrus in Deutero-Isaiah." *JAOS* 57 (1937) 158–71. **Simon, U.** "König Cyrus und die Typologie." *Jud* 11 (1955) 83–9. **Southwood, C. H.** "The Problematic *h*^{a}*durîm* of Isaiah xlv 2." *VT* 25 (1975) 801–2. **Stummer, F.** "Einige keilschriftliche Parallelen zu Jes. 40–66: 10 Jes 44:24." *JBL* 45 (1926) 183. **Torczyner, B.** "The Firmament and the Clouds, *Raqia* and *Shehaqim.*" *ST* 1 (1947) 188–96. **Westermann, C.** "Sprache und Struktur der Prophetie Deuterojesajas." *Forschung am Alten Testament.* ThB 24. Munich: Kaiser, 1964. 92–170. ———. "Das Reden von Schöpfer and Schöpfung im Alten Testament." *Das ferne und nahe Wort.* FS L. Rost. BZAW 105. Berlin: Töpelmann, 1967. 238–44. **Weinfeld, M.** "God the Creator in Gen. 1 and in the Prophecy of Second Isaiah." *Tarbiz* 37 (1967/68) 105–32. **Whitcomb, J. C., Jr.** "Cyrus in the Prophecies of Isaiah." *The Law and the Prophets.* FS O. T. Allis. Ed. J. H. Skilton. Nutley, NJ: Presbyterian & Reformed P. C., 1974. 388–401. **Zimmerli, W.** "Ich bin Yahweh." *Geschichte und Altes Testament.* FS A. Alt. Tübingen: J. C. B. Mohr, 1953. 179–209 = *Gottesoffenbarung.* ThB 19. Munich: Kaiser, 1963. 11–40.

Translation

Herald: 24 *Thus says Yahweh, your redeemer,* 3+2
who was forming you from the womb:[a]
Yahweh: *I am Yahweh doing all (this):* 4+3+4
stretching out heavens by myself,[b]
beating out the earth, from myself,[c] *with myself.*
Chorus: 25 *Frustrating omens of wiseacres,*[a] 3+2
he makes fools of diviners,[b]
making the wise turn backwards 3+2
when he makes their knowledge "wise,"[c]

[26] *confirming the word of his servant*[a] 3+3
and the counsel of his messengers[b] *he performs.*
The one saying to Jerusalem: "Be inhabited!"[c] 3+3+2
[d]*and to the towns of Judah: "Be built up!"*[d]
and to her ruins: "I[e] *will raise them!"*
[27] *The one saying to the ocean deep:*[a] *"Dry up!"* 3+2
and to your rivers: "I shall dry (you) up!"
[28] *The one saying to Cyrus: "My shepherd*[a] 3+2
who will fulfill[b] *all my pleasure,*
by saying[c] *to Jerusalem, Be built!* 3+2
and to (the) Temple,[d] *Be founded!"*
Herald: [45:1] *Thus* [a]*said Yahweh*[a] *to his*[b] *anointed:* 3+3
Yahweh: *To Cyrus whose right hand I have strengthened.*
To subdue[c] *nations before him* 3+3
I ungird the loins of kings.
To open doors[d] *before him* 3+3
gates[e] *are not closed.*
[2] *I myself*[a] *go before you* 3+2
and level[b] *city walls.*[c]
I shatter[d] *brass doors* 3+3
and cut apart iron bars.
[3] *I give you dark treasures* 4+2
and hoarded goods of secret places
in order that you may know 2+2
that I am Yahweh,
who is calling you by name, 2+2
God of Israel.
[4] *For the sake of my servant, Jacob,* 3+2
Israel, my chosen one,
I called you by your[a] *own name.* 3+3
I entitle you[b] *even though you have not known me.*
[5] [a]*I am Yahweh.* 2+2
There is no one else.
Except for me, there is no[b] *god.* 3+3
I sponsor you even though you have not known me
[6] *in order that they may know* 2+2
from the rising sun and from its[a] *setting place*
that there is no one apart from me. 3+2+2
I am Yahweh.
There is no one else.
[7] *Former of light,* 2+2
creator of darkness,
maker of peace,[a] 2+2
creator of violence,
I am Yahweh 2+2
maker of all these.
Chorus: [8] *Shower down from above, O Heavens,* 3+3
and clouds, rain down right.

Open up, O Earth, 2+2
let salvation spring up
and let legitimacy sprout at the same time. 3+3
Yahweh: *I, Yahweh have created it.*
Heavens: 9 [a]*Woe to anyone resisting*[a] *his maker,* 3+3
[b]*an earthen vessel among vessels*[b] *of earth.*
Would clay say to one molding it, "What are you making?" 4+3
[c]*Or "Your work has no handles!"*[c]
Earth: 10 *Woe to anyone saying to a father:*[a] *"What are you begetting?"* 4+2
Or to a woman: "What are you birthing?
Herald: 11 *Thus says Yahweh,* 2+2+2
the Holy One of Israel
and maker for it[a] *of things to come:*[b]
Yahweh: *Will you (pl) question me about my children,* 2+3
and about the product of my hand will you command me?
12 *I myself have made the earth* 3+3
and I have created humankind upon it.
I stretched out the heavens (with) my own hands 4+2
and I commanded all their legions (of stars).
13 *I myself have aroused him within my rights* 3+2
and I make all his ways straight.
He builds my city 2+2
and he sends out my exiles[a]
with neither bribe 2+2+3
nor reward,[b]
Herald: *says Yahweh of Hosts.*

Notes

24.a. Syr adds *w*ʿ*drk* "and your helper."

24.b. Tg adds במימרי "by my word."

24.c. DSS[Isa] מיא אתי implies a pointing of מִי "who" like 31 Heb. MSS, LXX and Vg. MT's מֵי (read as מני with nun dropped out) "from me" is supported by Syr *mny wly* "from me and for me" and Tg בגבורתי "by my power." The translation follows MT although most modern translations and interpreters emend to an interrogative.

25.a. MT בדים "liars" (BDB, 95, III). DSS[Isa] adds the word over the line. LXX *ἐγγαστριμύθων* "ventriloquists," Σ *ψεύδων* "liar," Syr *dzkwr*ʾ "those who communicate with the dead," Tg בדין "lying oracle," Vg *divinorum* "of diviners." בדים usually means "idle talk." Only here and in Jer 50:36 does it refer to persons.

25.b. LXX *μαντείας* "oracles" (cf. also Syr *qṣmyhwn*). Tg and Vg support MT.

25.c. MT ישׂכל "make wise." DSS[Isa] and 1QIsa[b] have יסכל "make foolish," so also LXX Syr Tg Vg (cf. BDB, 698, which lists Isa 44:25 as יסכל). Elliger (454) points out that MT's *sin* is simply an abnormal spelling. However, note that the two Heb. words sound alike but have opposite meanings. This is a solid example of double meaning, or tongue-in-cheek sarcasm, which is difficult to translate.

26.a. MT has "his servant" sg, but "his messengers" pl, and is followed by DSS[Isa] LXX (except for LXX[A]) Syr Vg. Many modern interpreters (see *BHS*) emend to עבדיו "his servants" to make both pl. Textual evidence supports MT.

26.b. One MS[K] has only ועצתו "and his counsel" instead of "the counsel of his messengers." (See the discussion in Elliger, 454.) DSS[Isa] LXX Syr Tg Vg support MT.

26.c. MT תושב "be inhabited" (BDB, 442) occurs only here, 5:8 and Ezek 35:9 in hoph. DSS^{Isa} and 1QIsa^{b} read תשב, apparently qal "she will dwell." *BHS* suggests a niph "she will be inhabited" or "be inhabited." MT is also passive and just as good.

26.d-d. *BHS* would drop this phrase, perhaps because it is a third stich. That is a metrical bias. The stich should be kept.

26.e. LXX reads 3d pers. But some LXX MSS, Syr Tg Vg support MT's first person. Note the continued usage of 1st pers in v 27.

27.a. Tg adds "concerning Babylon." צולה occurs only here and is usually understood as a shortened form of מצולה "depth, deep" (BDB, 846–47).

28.a. MT רֹעִי "my shepherd" is supported by six MSS^{K} רועי, ʾA Σ Θ Syr Vg. DSS^{Isa} רעי may also mean רֵעִי "my friend." LXX φρονεῖν "to understand" apparently sees a word from the root ידע as in v 20 (cf. Ziegler, *Untersuchungen*, 157). G. R. Driver (*JTS* 36 [1935] 82) suggests that it comes from רעה III, like the Aramaic "intent, purpose." Tg interprets "make him the king." *BHS*'s suggestion of רֵעִי "my friend" had support earlier, but does not in recent commentaries (cf. Elliger, 455).

28.b. Vg *complebis* "you will fulfill" makes the address to Cyrus explicit.

28.c. MT לאמר, lit., "to say." The previous three lines begin with האמר "the one saying." One can emend to make this line parallel to the first three. If MT is kept, this becomes the goal of the first three. LXX Vg suggest emendation. DSS^{Isa} 1QIsa^{b} support MT, and Syr Tg change their translation in the fourth line. MT should be kept. See Elliger's defense (455).

28.d. *BHS* להיכל adds the preposition where MT simply uses a dative without preposition to mean "to the Temple." Σ Syr Tg all support MT. Another issue is the gender of היכל which is usually masc. Here the verb is in the fem which implies that היכל is also thought to be fem.

45:1.a-a. *BHS* suggests changing the verb to 1st pers to fit the rest of the verse. But there is no textual evidence to support this.

1.b. LXX τῷ χριστῷ μου "to my anointed" is followed by Vg. Syr Tg and the other Gr. versions support MT. If one has already emended the previous verb with *BHS,* a change to first person here would make sense. A better way is to keep MT in both cases and to note a change in speaker (cf. McKenzie, 75).

1.c. לְרַד is a strange pointing if a qal inf constr from רדד "to subdue, to beat down" is intended. Cf. GKC § 67p. The Versions do not help to settle the grammatical issue: LXX ἐπακοῦσαι "to obey," Syr *nštʿbdwn* "they prostrate themselves," Tg למסר "to give up," Vg *ut subiiciam* "that I subject."

1.d. MT דלתים dual "a pair of doors" or "double doors." DSS^{Isa} דלתות is pl as in v 2.

1.e. LXX καὶ πόλεις "and cities." It appears that a *shin* had fallen out of its Heb text; it read וערים for MT's ושערים.

2.a. Tg "my word."

2.b. K אוֹשִׁר "I make smooth," hiph, is supported by DSS^{Isa} (cf. K of Ps 5:9). Q אֲיַשֵּׁר "I smooth," piel, is supported by 17 MSS^{K} (see v 13 below). Read Q (BDB, 448; GKC § 70b) but note the kinship to the root אשר "go straight" (BDB, 80).

2.c. MT וַהֲדוּרִים is a difficult word. It could mean "and the generations" (BDB, 187) but would need a different pointing. It is pointed to mean "and the honored ones, the adorned ones" (BDB, 213). DSS^{Isa} והררים "and the mountains." Elliger calls 1QIsa^{b} והרורים a crossing of MT with DSS^{Isa}. LXX καὶ ὄρη "and mountains" follows DSS^{Isa}. Vg *et gloriosos terrae* "and the glorious of the earth" follows MT. Tg שוריא "wall, fortress," Syr *ʿrmʾ* "uneven land." Modern scholars have tried their hand: Houbigant added a letter, והדרכים "and the ways." Others keep MT's consonants but read "swellings," i.e., mountains. Hoffmann (*Wort, Lied und Gottesspruch,* 187–95) and Southwood (*VT* 25 [1975] 801–2) derive it from an Akk word *dūru,* meaning "city wall" with the special connotation of the inner ring of defense in Babylon, where the Tg Jonathan was written (cf. Tg). The translation follows this suggestion. See Elliger (482–83) for further discussion.

2.d. MT אֲשַׁבֵּר piel impf "I shatter, I break in pieces." DSS^{Isa} אשבור qal impf "I break, I rupture" (BDB, 990). There is no great difference in meaning.

4.a. LXX τῷ ὀνόματί μου "by my name." Some LXX MSS and all the other Versions support MT. DSS^{Isa} ובשם has no suffix and connects the word with the following verb.

4.b. DSS^{Isa} הכ(י)נכה is hiph pf "he established you" from כון (BDB, 466); but without the *yodh* added above the line and assuming with Elliger (483) the *he* is a mistake for *aleph,* this is a piel from כנה like MT. LXX *καὶ προσδέξομαί σε* "and I will accept you." Syr *wknjtk* "and I gave you a second name." Tg אתקינתך "I prepare you." Vg *assimilavi te* "I have represented you." MT אכנך piel impf "I surname you" (BDB, 487) is to be maintained.

5.a. LXX begins with *ὅτι* "because."

5.b. MT אין "there is no." DSS[Isa] adds "and" with thirteen MSS[KG]. LXX omits.

6.a. MT "from a setting place." Several of the Versions (see *BHS*) suggest the implied "its" which calls only for a *mappiq* in the *he.*

7.a. DSS[Isa] adds טוב "good" which balances רע "evil." Keep MT.

(The massive commentary of Karl Elliger ends here, except for a few miscellaneous textual notes. The frequent references to his work in these notes are evidence of his importance. His untimely death robbed us all of much more useful comment and understanding.)

9.a-a. MT רב qal act ptcp "one resisting" from ריב (BDB, 936). LXX inspired *BHS* to suggest הֲיָרִיב (interrogative + impf) "would one resist?" parallel to the second line, eliminating הוי "woe" which is unique in chaps. 40–66. *BHS* also moves the accent to add חרש to the first stich. The result reads, "would the vessel resist its maker?" Keep MT.

9.b-b. MT חרש את־חרשי "a vessel among vessels of." *BHS* suggests חרשו, reading *shin* for *sin,* a word with four different root meanings (BDB, 360–61): "cut in, engrave, plough, devise" (Isa 28:24); "be silent, dumb, speechless, deaf" (29:18; 35:5; 42:18,19); "wood, wooded heights" (17:9); "magic art, drugs" with the same vowel pointing as MT (cf. 3:3). The most probable translations with meanings attested in the Vision are: MT "an earthen vessel among vessels of earth," LXX "a ploughman, the ploughing of ground," "a magician, spells of the ground," or *BHS*'s mixture את־חרשו חרש אדמה "an earthen vessel with its deviser." MT is as good as any.

את occurs twice in these lines. The first is translated as a sign of the accusative. The second is a preposition meaning "among" (BDB, 84–87). Cf. Stuhlmueller, *Creative Redemption,* 200, n. 651; North, 150; von Waldow, *Anlass,* 37–38, n. 19; C. F. Whitley, *VT* 11 (1961) 458.

9.c-c. LXX *ὅτι οὐκ ἐργάζῃ οὐδὲ ἔχεις χεῖρας* "that you do not work nor do you have hands." *BHS* emends to ופעלו אין־ידים לך "and his work, 'you have no hands'." Cf. Syr.

10.a. So Stuhlmueller, *Creative Redemption,* 201, n. One might think an unborn child speaks here, but this is not so. Cf. Duhm, de Boer (*Second Isaiah's Message,* 18), Kissane, and McKenzie.

11.a. Read the suffix in the dative case. Cf. Stuhlmueller, *Creative Redemption,* 201, n. 654, and M. Bogaert, "Les suffixes verbaux non accusatifs," *Bib* 45 (1964) 238.

11.b. This translation divides the verse in the same way as LXX, moving the *athnaḥ* forward one word. It also emends האתיות שאלוני "question me about the signs!" to האת התשאלוני "things to come. Will you question me?" (dividing the words differently and reading הת for יות, a common transfer). See Elliger (526–27) and *BHS* for a similar suggestion. DSS[Isa] האותות leaves out one letter of MT.

13.a. LXX adds *τοῦ λαοῦ μου* "of my people." Textual evidence is overwhelming in support of MT (cf. Elliger, 528).

13.b. שחד "reward." Cf. 1 Kgs 15:19 and 2 Kgs 16:8 where a king offers money as tribute or to gain help in war (see North).

Form/Structure/Setting

The setting continues to be that of the heavenly court. A herald steps forward with a royal announcement.

The passage is separate from what goes before and after. It introduces a new cycle of themes which continue some of those that went before. But now the center of attention is Cyrus. The passage is to be kept together (cf. Westermann, *Forschung,* 144–51; and Stuhlmueller, *Creative Redemption,* 196–200) in spite of the arguments of Melugin (*Formation,* 39) and Schoors (*Main Genres,* 267).

The passage is formed in hymnic style (cf. Ps 103), but it functions as a disputation (Melugin, *Formation,* 39). It introduces the act, like an overture touching on the themes that will continue to be developed later in the act.

In doing so, it forms a bridge between what has gone before and what is to come. Note the themes of redemption, creation, ridicule of idolatry and necromancy, fulfillment of prophecy, the rehabilitation of Jerusalem, control of nature, and the relation of Cyrus to the main theme of the larger section, the restoration of Jerusalem and the Temple.

The first part (44:24–28) transmits Yahweh's assurances to Israel connecting his election of Israel and his creation of the world with his determination to sustain his own word which specifically calls for Jerusalem to be rebuilt, for restraints to be laid on chaos curses, and for Cyrus to do the work. This is done through use of participles, as a hymn would do (Crüsemann, *Studien,* 91–95, 152–54), but also by prefixing "I . . . Yahweh" to the list, casting them all into the first person (cf. Dion, *RB* 74 [1967] 215–34). This is not a judgment speech (Westermann, *Forschung,* 147), nor a disputation (Begrich, *Studien,* 42–46; von Waldow, *Anlass,* 31, 193, n. 4; Schoors, *I Am God,* 267–73). It serves to identify Yahweh clearly, and the three announcements, with his work in electing Israel and the creation of the world. The choral section in 44:25–28 expands on Yahweh's self-identification to form the setting for the induction of Cyrus into his position as Yahweh's servant. (So Merendino, *Der Erste und der Letzte,* 411.)

The scene's structure demonstrates its unity. Of its three distinct parts, the first and third are parallel and addressed to Israel about Cyrus (Westermann, *Forschung,* 144–51). The center section is addressed to Cyrus, describing the role that Yahweh is assigning to him. All three sections emphasize Yahweh's authority and sovereign acts which demonstrate his right to do this thing. The internal development of themes in the first and third are parallel and follow the same order (rather than the reversed order of an arch structure).

A To Israel
- a. I am Yahweh, your redeemer and creator of all (44:24)
- b. Who fulfills valid prophecy about Jerusalem (44:25–26)
- c. Who controls all nature (44:27)
- d. Who calls Cyrus to rebuild Jerusalem (44:28)

B To Cyrus, my anointed, whose right hand I take (45:1a)
- a. To subdue nations and pacify kings (45:1bc)
- b. I (Yahweh) go before you (Cyrus) to level mountains, break doors, and give you secret treasures (45:2–3a)
- c. So that you and all may know that (45:3b–7)
  - (1) I am Yahweh
  - (2) I bless you for Israel's sake

C To Israel
- a. I am Yahweh, creator, in my own right (45:8)
- b. Woe to those who question my right to do this! (45:9–11)
- c. I created the world (45:12)
- d. I raise up Cyrus to rebuild my city (45:13)

The centerpiece is Yahweh's announcement to Cyrus which ordains him to the task God has anointed for him. His work will be military and political, relating to nations and kings. Yahweh will go before him to provide favorable circumstances for the accomplishment of these tasks and will reward him with rich booty. But it must be clear that Cyrus is Yahweh's tool (not the reverse) and that Yahweh's primary responsibility and attention continues to be to Israel. Cyrus is employed to do what Yahweh wants for Israel.

This announcement fits in this act as 40:1–9 did in Act VII. It confirms Israel's elect status as servant and messenger. It promises support for Yahweh's word concerning Jerusalem given in 40:1–9. Yahweh who creates Heaven and Earth is equally:

he who calls and sends Israel,
who orders Jerusalem to be rebuilt,
whose word controls nature and the weather,
whose word calls Cyrus to do his will.

Whereas Act VII viewed the rise of Cyrus on the distant horizon, this act presents him in person moving against Babylon and establishing his rule across the Euphrates into west Asia and Palestine.

The essential themes of these acts from VII on are continued here. The announcement of God's plan for Israel, Jerusalem, and the land is met by rejection and complaint, and resistance. The struggle to win Israel's acceptance and acquiescence continues.

Comment

24 Israel is addressed. *Your Redeemer* picks up the theme of previous chapters (43:1, 14; 44:6, 22, 23). Exilic Israel found it difficult to see redemption or salvation in the conquering Persian advance on Babylon. They apparently expected God to make Israel the new ruler of the empire. But Yahweh insists on doing it his way. The Persian conquest is his doing and will provide redemption for his people, Israel. The reminder that Yahweh is the creator of *all* (*this*) puts Israel's claims in perspective. God is also responsible for the world beyond Israel.

25–26 The chorus continues the description of Yahweh, but now in the third person (*his servant*). During Babylon's last years Nabunaid had rescued idols from temples across the empire which were threatened by the Persian advance. He brought them to Babylon for safekeeping. (Olmstead, *History of the Persian Empire,* 49). The result was a plethora of priests, prophets, and diviners in Babylon representing a variety of gods. They all issued forecasts about the city's future. Yahweh proclaims that none of these will be allowed to turn him from his course of action. Israel, as Yahweh's *servant* and *messenger,* had been commissioned to bring good news to Jerusalem (40:1–9). He guarantees that *word* and that *counsel* which promised the restoration of Jerusalem.

27 Yahweh's control of the waters is a recurrent motif in the Vision. Usually it speaks of water in the desert. But here it refers to the control of the mystic deep like that which made created order possible (Gen 1:6) or which, when released, produced the Flood (Gen 7:11). More specifically, it may represent the moat protecting Babylon which connected the Euphrates

why water?

in the north and in the south (*ISBE* 1:386), and which several invaders, but apparently not Cyrus, cut off and drained to gain access to the city. In that case this second of three decrees from Yahweh refers to the fall of Babylon.

28 The announcement's climax mentions Cyrus, the Persian emperor who is entering Babylon. By this time every prophet in the city claimed responsibility for his success. But Yahweh yields nothing in the claim that Cyrus belongs to him. He is Yahweh's *shepherd.* The term is frequently used for a king or ruler (cf. 40:11; Zech 10:2–3; 11:3–9, 16–17; 12:7). The emphasis here is on the pronoun *my.* Cyrus is Yahweh's protegé who will *fulfill* his *pleasure.* The words are important: ישלם "fulfill" is the verb from which "peace" comes. חפץ "pleasure" is used to express Yahweh's will (cf. 46:10; 48:14; 53:10; 55:11; 56:4). Jerusalem is the focus of Yahweh's strategy. The call of Cyrus and the fall of Babylon prepare for the restoration of Yahweh's city.

45:1 Cyrus is presented as Yahweh's *anointed,* his messiah. This must have been a shock to Israel, but nothing else could have summarized his intention. The title normally applied to Israel's high priest (Lev 4 and 6) or to Israel's king (1 Sam 24, 26; 2 Sam 1; and repeated uses in the historical books and Psalms). It would become Judaism's term for its expected deliverer, the Messiah. It describes one who is anointed with oil as a sign of being set apart for a special task. David was chosen to subdue nations within the territory assigned to Israel and thus to establish Yahweh's sovereignty over Canaan. Now that task is being assigned to Cyrus. As the Assyrian was summoned to destroy (10:5–6), so now the Persian is called to perform the military and political tasks necessary to rebuild Jerusalem.

Traditionally, the ruler of Babylon took the hand of Bel in the New Year's festival. Assyrian rulers coveted this affirmation of their authority. Here Yahweh claims that he has seized Cyrus by the hand (42:6) and strenghtened his hold on his realm. He had provided the might necessary for his conquest of Media, of Lydia, and now of Babylon and had weakened the authority of his adversaries so that they opened doors for him as in Armenia.

Remarkably this description fits Cyrus's career. He had profited from many circumstances other than his military strength. He had gained the following of all the Persian tribes with singular ease. He gained an ally in Babylon against Media. Two successive Median armies that were sent against him decided to join forces with him instead. His generosity toward the conquered worked in his favor. He marched without opposition into Armenia and won a surprise victory over the Lydians when their horses were frightened by the smell of Persian camels. And now Babylon, the world's most heavily fortified city, opens its gates to him without a fight (Olmstead, *History of the Persian Empire,* 34–51). Truly *doors* and *gates* had been opened for Cyrus. Yahweh claims credit for it. (Note that in similar ways Yahweh will claim credit for the rise of Darius and Artaxerxes in chaps. 49, 52, and 60.)

3 *Dark treasures* apparently refers to those kept in secret vaults. Yahweh assumes no altruistic motives in Cyrus and promises monetary reward and plunder for services rendered (as in 43:3). But these will not come from Jerusalem or from the Jews who have none left to give (cf. v 13c).

3b–8 This remarkable speech builds on three themes: Yahweh's self-introduction as the only God there is, his identification as God of Israel for whom he is calling Cyrus, and the theme of "knowing" (ידע) him. The theological emphasis continues to be that Yahweh is one in creating the world, ruling over history, and redeeming Israel.

6 *From the rising sun and from its setting place* demonstrates the territorial scope of world empire which sets the stage for Yahweh's new activity. Israel is called to function as witness and messenger on that stage. Although she might have been more comfortable in the confines of Canaan, never again would she be allowed that luxury.

7 *Light/darkness; peace/violence.* Persian religion dealt in opposites of light and darkness. Yahweh claims not to be those conditions, but to *create* both, and thus to overcome the inherent dualism in his sovereign rule over them.

8 *Right/legitimacy:* Yahweh's use of the Persian is regularly described in this part of the Vision with these words. They proclaim the legitimacy of Yahweh's choice in terms of his sovereign right as Lord to choose how he will fulfill his promises to Israel. Some in Israel thought Yahweh should use Israelite armies and an Israelite king.

9–10 The "woes" addressed to Israel are an uncomfortable reminder of the "former days" pictured in chaps. 5 and 10. In the new age of redemption and blessing Israel is still blind and rebellious to the will of God. The unthinkable is happening. Clay protests the potter's intentions. Someone protests the parents' conception of a child.

11–13 Yahweh rejects Israel's protests. The Creator of the world will legitimately do what he thinks is right to rebuild his city and free his exiles, no matter what they think of his plan. It is ironic, but typical, that Cyrus obeys without question, while Israel rebels.

Explanation

The outstanding feature of the full scene is the repeated first person pronoun in Yahweh's speech (9 times) and the verbs in 1st person (15 times, participle after the pronoun; 7 times, perfect; 10 times, imperfect). Although the speech is addressed to Israel and Cyrus, it is a powerful self-assertion by Yahweh about himself. He relates himself to Israel, to all the universe, and to Cyrus—and through Cyrus back to Jerusalem and history on a broader scale. The speech is a *tour de force.* Israel is reluctant. Cyrus does not even know God's name. Certainly kings and kingdoms are less than cooperative. But God proclaims his sovereign right and will to make them all work together to produce the results he wants: a restored Jerusalem and a free exilic community. Through this activity he intends that Cyrus will know (45:3) that Yahweh is God, that all his empire will know (45:6) that Yahweh alone is God, and that Israel will acknowledge God as the one who has accomplished this goal (45:11–13).

The first part repeats God's continuing reasons for expecting faith from Israel (election, providence, and creation) while it proclaims his new threefold decree of redemption (restoration for Jerusalem, lifting of the curse on the land, and the choice of Cyrus to accomplish these).

The last part recognizes Israel's unbelief and refusal by arguing that creatures have no right to protest against the decisions of their creator. It closes again with a double threefold claim in the first person: I made the land and all its people. I stretched out the heavens and commanded its stars. I aroused Cyrus and prepared his way with the primary goals of building my city and freeing my exiles, at no price exacted from either of them.

The scene has adapted hymnic form to announce Cyrus and introduce him, but the real intention of this act moves beyond praise and recognition of Yahweh's grandeur. It confronts Israel's refusal to accept Yahweh's choice of Cyrus to have political sovereignty over the land and Jerusalem and their refusal of the role which is now assigned to them. The announcement that God has chosen the Persian rulers to build Jerusalem and free his exiles will be repeated in each succeeding act. And Israel's complaint which began in 40:27 against God's plan will be a continuing element throughout the Vision.

Scene 2: In Yahweh Is Legitimacy and Strength (45:14–25)

Bibliography

Beuken, W. A. M. "The Confession of God's Exclusivity by all Mankind: Is 45, 18–25." *Bijdragen* 35 (1974) 335–56. **Dijkstra, M.** "Zur Deutung von Jesaja 45:15ff." *ZAW* 89 (1977) 215–22. **Dion, H. M.** "The Patriarchal Traditions and the Literary Form of 'the Oracle of Salvation.'" *CBQ* 29 (1967) 198–206. **Heintz, J-G.** "De l'absence de la statue divine au 'Dieu qui se cache' (Esaïe 45,15)." *RHPR* 59 (1979) 427–37. **Merendino, R. P.** *Der Erste und der Letzte.* 425–61. **Olley, J. W.** "Notes on Isaiah xxxii 1, xlv 19, 23 and lxiii 1." *VT* 33 (1983) 446–53. **Stuhlmueller, C.** *Creative Redemption.* 152–57. **Virgulin, S.** "Un vertice dell'Antico Testamento: Isaia 45, 20–25." *Parola e Spirito.* FS S. Cipriani. Brescia: Paideia Editrice, 1982. 1:119–28.

Translation

Herald: (reads Yahweh's writ to Cyrus)

45:14 *Thus says Yahweh:* 3
Egypt's wealth[a] *and Ethiopia's profit*[b] 4+3
and Sabeans, tall men—
they pass over to you 2+2+2
and they become yours.
They walk behind you.
In chains they pass over.[c] 2+2+2
To you they bow down
and to you they plead!
"God is only[d] *with you.* 3+2+2
and there is no other.
There is no (other) God."

Cyrus: 15 *Certainly you*[a] *are a God hiding himself,*[b] 4+3
O God of Israel, Savior!
16 *They are ashamed and humiliated—*[a] *all of them.* 3+3+2
Together[a] *they walk*[b] *in ignomy—*
those carvers of images.
17 *Israel is safe in Yahweh—* 3+2
her salvation is for the ages!
(to Israel) *You are not shamed, not humiliated* 2+2
for ages everlasting.
18 *For thus says Yahweh,* 3+2+2
creator of the heavens
who is the only God,
maker of the earth, one forming it,[a] 3+2
who is its establisher.
He did not create a waste![b] 2+2
He formed it for habitation!
Yahweh: *I am Yahweh!* 2+2
There is no one else!
19 *I have not spoken in secret,* 3+3
in a place that is a dark land.
I did not say 2+2+2
to the offspring of Jacob,
"Seek me in[a] *a wasteland."*
I am Yahweh 2+2+2
speaking what is right,
declaring what is straight![b]
Cyrus: 20 *Gather yourselves and come!* 2+2+2
Approach together,[a]
you refugees of the nations!
Yahweh: *Those lifting up wooden idols* 2+3
have not known,
nor those praying to a god 2+2
who cannot save.
21 *Announce and present,* 2+3
let them even take counsel[a] *together.*
Who has let this be heard long ago? 4+2
From olden times, declared it?
Was it not I, Yahweh? 3+3
And there is no other god apart from me!
A legitimate God and a Savior, 2+2
there is none except for me!
Cyrus: 22 *Turn to me and be saved, all you borderlands!* 3+4
Yahweh: *For I am God. There is no other.*
23 *I have sworn by myself:* 2+3+3
Legitimacy has gone out from my mouth,
a word which will not be taken back.
Cyrus: *For every knee bows to me!* 3+2
Every tongue swears (*by me*)!

24 *Only by Yahweh* 2+2+2
has one said[a] *to me:*
"Legitimacy and power!"
Heavens: *When anyone comes*[b] *to him,* 2+4
all those aroused against him will be shamed.[c]
25 *All the seed of Israel* 3+2
will be vindicated by Yahweh and will lift their praises (to him).

Notes

14.a. *BHS* suggests יֹגְעֵי "laborers of" for MT יְגִיעַ "product, wealth" (BDB, 388). But there is no other example of the ptcp. LXX translates a verb, ἐκοπίασεν "he has labored." Keep MT.
14.b. Syr *tgr*ʾ and Tg תגרי are pl for MT's sg. LXX is also sg.
14.c. Omitted in LXX Syr Eth. *BHS* recommends deletion or simply shifting *athnaḥ* back one word. But MT makes sense and fits the meter as it is. DSS[Isa] יעבורו supports the pointing of MT.
14.d. On אך "only," see N. H. Snaith, "The Meaning of the Hebrew אַךְ," *VT* 14 (1964) 221–23.
15.a. *BHS* suggests אִתָּךְ "with you" for MT אתה "you." But MT is supported by DSS[Isa] and LXX.
15.b. LXX οὐκ ᾔδειμεν "we did not know" is a paraphrase and does not reflect another Heb. text.
16.a-a. *BHS* recommends deletion. But DSS[Isa] and LXX support MT.
16.b. DSS[Isa] has *waw* and impf for MT's pf.
18.a. DSS[Isa] has ועשיה for MT ועשה. The meaning is the same.
18.b. DSS[Isa] לתהו "for a waste" adds intent to the meaning, parallel to לשבת "for habitation."
19.a. MT has no preposition. *BHS* suggests inserting ב "in." But the word alone may be an accus of place. Whether it designates the place of seeking or that of speaking, parallel to the previous lines, is unclear. LXX reads a simple accus, "seek vanity," omitting the pronoun. DSS[Isa] supports MT.
19.b. LXX reads ἀλήθειαν "truth."
20.a. DSS[Isa] ואתיו "and come" (cf. 21:12; BDB, 87). LXX ἅμα and Vg *simul* support MT יחדו "together."
21.a. Syr (*w*)ʾ*tmlkw*, Tg אתמליכו, and Vg *consiliamini* are all impv. So *BHS* suggests reading הִוָּעֲצוּ "take counsel" impv. However, LXX reads "in order that they may know," and DSS[Isa] supports MT's impf.
24.a. MT אמר "said" pf. LXX λέγων "saying," ptcp. DSS[Isa] יאמר "he will say," impf. MT makes sense and may be kept.
24.b. MT is sg. DSS[Isa] LXX Syr Vg are pl, "they come," which fits the second part of the line. But the sg fits the preceding line and should be kept.
24.c. Cf. 41:11a.

Form/Structure/Setting

The scene follows directly on the commissioning of Cyrus (45:1–7). It specifies that the nations to be subdued (45:1) are Egypt and Cush. The *dark treasures* (45:3) are the booty of Egyptian cities as well as the lucrative control of Egyptian trade routes. It further repeats that all of this is *for the sake of Israel.*

The scene is a dialogue between Yahweh and Cyrus:

Through his messenger Yahweh promises to Cyrus' representative success in his projected campaign against Egypt (v 14).

Cyrus, amazed, confesses to surprise at Israel's good fortune and congratulates her (vv 15–18b).

Yahweh repeats his claims and his intention (vv 18c–19).
Cyrus calls the refugees of the nations of Palestine to gather themselves (v 20a).
Yahweh picks up the challenge (vv 20b–21).
Cyrus calls for the borderlands to pay loyal tribute and thus be saved from military action (v 22a).
Yahweh supports this with his affirmation of Cyrus' legitimate sovereignty over the region (vv 22b–23a).
Cyrus proclaims that everyone will have to submit since Yahweh has approved him (vv 23b–24a).
An observer concludes that Cyrus is unstoppable and Israel will be protected (vv 24b–25).

Understood in this way the scene demonstrates the virtual identity of Yahweh's goals and Cyrus's goals for Israel and Judah. In Ezra-Nehemiah the citing of decrees by Cyrus, Darius, and Artaxerxes achieves the same effect.

Comment

14 Egypt had been and still was a major world trader. Greek and Phoenician ships carried its goods throughout the eastern Mediterranean, the Aegean, and the Black seas. Other trade flowed through the Red Sea. A major achievement under Darius was a canal that linked the Nile with the Red Sea to facilitate the flow of shipping. This verse foresees Egypt's fall to Persia which took place when Cambyses invaded the country in 525 B.C. These are the "dark treasures" of v 3 and the payment of Israel's ransom of 43:3.

God is only with you. In the mouths of subdued prisoners of war the sentence means something like "luck or fate is on your side." But the context in a Yahweh-speech indicates that this is a statement of fact. God—that is, Yahweh God of Israel—*is* with Cyrus in a unique sense. That is the reason for his phenomenal success. And that is the essence of the testimony Israel is to bring before the nations.

15 This response is an important text. *A God hiding himself* (*Deus Absconditus*) is a vital concept in Western theology. In Scripture, the Book of Job explores the experience of God's hiding himself. Ps 22 and the cry of dereliction on the Cross declare it in different terms. But here in this context the words are grudging admiration for the surprising ways in which God does his work, undetected. If Cyrus means that God has been hiding himself to this point, it could be read "a God who has been hiding himself" (see Skinner and Buber as cited in *IB*). *God of Israel* has demonstrated that he is indeed Israel's *Savior* in very unexpected ways.

16 Elsewhere in the Vision, Yahweh contrasts himself to the idols. Here, Cyrus confesses his astonished recognition of Yahweh's saving work on Israel's behalf. When Cyrus arrived, Babylon was filled with refugee idols and their priests whom Nabunaid had brought there. Cyrus had to answer dozens of pleas for help to return them to their own temples. It was for them a terrible experience to be so *humiliated, to walk in ignomy.*

17–18 Only Yahweh deals with Cyrus from a position of strength. Cyrus recognizes that *Israel is safe in Yahweh,* even in Babylonian exile, with a safety that lasts (*salvation of the ages*). Israel has no reason for shame or humiliation in front of Cyrus or the idolaters. Her God had created all the world for order and habitation.

19 *Not spoken in secret . . . not in a dark land* contrast Yahweh's open announcements with secret oracles, like those in Delphi. The priests there had first predicted that Cyrus would be beaten by the Lydian armies, but hastily revised the oracle to conform to the course of events when he won the battle. The secrecy of the oracle made such possible. Not *in a wasteland* picks up the emphasis of the previous verse. Palestine had in fact become largely a wasteland. Many fields had been left untended and grown up in weeds and brambles as chaps. 5 and 6:11–13 had predicted. It was a land that suffered under the bloodshed of centuries as chap. 24 has shown. But these are not God's ways, not his goals. This denial implies that renewal for Israel as a people means renewal of the land as well.

Speaking what is right (צדק). Yahweh is defending himself concerning his appointment of Cyrus. Israel's objection is not voiced, but is clearly implied. They think God is using Cyrus in a way that only Israel or an Israelite should be used. See *Comment* on v 21 below. *Right* does not mean only that the word is fulfilled, but that it is just and correct (see Olley, *VT* 33 [1983] 449–50).

20 The *refugees of the nations* are those in Babylon at that time, particularly those representing the lands of Syria-Palestine. They are summoned to attention before Yahweh and Cyrus in the great hall. They are devotees of the idols, many of whom may have brought their idols to Babylon for safekeeping, only to have the city opened to the invaders without a fight.

21 Both Yahweh and Cyrus are seeking recognition in this meeting, which is like "a press conference" of modern times. They want to be identified in the eyes of Israel and the nations with each other and with this project which will extend Cyrus' sovereignty to the west over Palestine and on into Egypt. Their credibility will stand or fall together in the eyes of the nations. *A legitimate God* (אל צדיק): Yahweh presents himself as the only God, the one who predicts the future accurately and claims the right to choose Cyrus for his purpose. That this choice is legitimate will be shown through the salvation achieved for Israel. Yahweh is *Savior* as well as righteous master of history's forces.

22 Cyrus offers salvation to the borderlands of Palestine. The salvation he offers is restoration of a measure of political order and prosperity, protection from vandals and bandits, and a share in the imperial peace in exchange for fealty and tribute. God will, in time, offer to these peoples from the nations more spiritual and religious salvation through Zion (chaps. 55 and 66). But this chapter deals with the values which God is offering through the Persian conqueror. *For I am God:* This joint "press conference" serves to relate Yahweh and Cyrus in the eyes of the nations just as 45:1–7 notified Israel of their relationship.

23–24a Yahweh confirms the appointment of Cyrus in the strongest terms possible. His own *legitimacy* is at stake in this venture. He swears not to *take back* his approval or support of Cyrus. Based on this, Cyrus announces that allegiance is required of everyone in the territory claimed by Persia, the first real world empire. Then he confesses that only through Yahweh has this *legitimacy* (righteousness) and this *power* been granted to him.

24b–25 An impersonal observation follows concerning the effect of *coming to him,* i.e., to Yahweh, but by extension to Cyrus. Both Cyrus and Israel have enemies. They and the nations need Yahweh's protection. The *legitimacy* of this situation is available to Israel. They, unlike Cyrus, can move beyond the political and economic aspects of the relationship to *lift praises* for the special blessings that Yahweh gives.

Explanation

The scene speaks repeatedly of salvation (vv 15, 17, 20, 21, 22) and of right/legitimacy (vv 19, 21, 23, 24, 25) which contrast with humiliation and shame (vv 14, 16, 17, 24). It is a time when empires are rising and falling. Allegiance is being required by each of the antagonists. To choose the wrong liege lord is to lose freedom (v 14), lands, perhaps even life. It is to be humiliated and shamed.

Everyone seeks security and advantage. Everyone wants a sure winner. Some sought this conservatively by allying themselves to Babylon, the recognized power of that day. Some sought it religiously by following the largest, most influential idol of that time, such as Marduk or Bel. But now Babylon opens its doors to the invader without resistance, and the priests of Marduk are forced to rewrite their oracles to favor new political realities.

Israel had lost its political security through Yahweh's judgments carried out by Assyrian and Babylonian armies. His righteousness had been demonstrated in the fact that Israel had rebelled against him (chaps. 1–33). Now his righteousness is being shown in the restoration of Jerusalem and of the freedom of Jews to worship there. Israel is being restored in humility, since the restoration is being accomplished by a foreigner. But it is not a humiliation like that of those who depend upon the oracles of idols. For Yahweh's anointed, Cyrus the Persian, gives orders for Jerusalem to be restored and for Jews to be guaranteed success. Yahweh's right and saving acts toward Israel and Jerusalem are simultaneously legitimacy and salvation through Cyrus.

And remarkably, Cyrus's call for the refugees of the nations to recognize his sovereignty will further the plans of God far beyond the empire's success in Palestine. The Vision will present an open invitation to all, to Jews and Gentiles alike, to worship in Jerusalem, the city of God (chaps. 55 and 66). This, too, is part of what is right in Yahweh's choice of Cyrus; and the Prince of Peace in another time under another empire will bring God's plans a decisive step nearer fulfillment. (See Phil 2:6–11).

Scene 3:
Bel Bows . . . My Purpose Stands (46:1–13)

Bibliography

Leene, H. "Isaiah 46.8—Summons to Be Human?" *JSOT* 30 (1984) 111–21. **Merendino, R. P.** *Der Erste und der Letzte* 461–82. **Rabinowitz, J. J.** "A Note on Is. 46:4 (*sabal*). *JBL* 73 (1954) 327. **Whitley, C. F.** "Textual Notes on Deutero-Isaiah." *VT* 11 (1961)

457–61. ———. "Further notes on the text of Deutero-Isaiah" (46, 8). *VT* 25 (1975) 683–87.

Translation

Heavens: 1 *Bel has bowed.* 2+2
Nebo is prostrate.[a]
[b]*Their idols belong to beasts and to cattle:* 4+4
things for you to carry, things loaded, a burden for a weary beast.[b]
Earth: 2 *They have stooped. They have bowed down together.* 3+4+3
They have not been able to escape (even as) a burden.
They themselves have walked with the captives.
Yahweh: 3 *Listen to me, House of Jacob!* 4+3
And you whole remnant of the House of Israel!
You who have been carried from before you were born! 2+2
You who have been picked up from the womb!
4 *And even to old age, I am the one,* 3+3
until you have gray hair,[a] *I myself bear (you).*
I myself have done[b] *(it) and I myself will bear it.* 4+3
I myself bear (you), and I will deliver you!
5 *To whom do you liken or equate* 3+2
or compare me that we should be alike?
6 *Those spending gold freely from a purse* 3+3
who weigh silver in scales
hire a goldsmith to make them a god. 4+2
They prostrate themselves. Indeed, they worship.
7 *They lift it on a shoulder and carry it.* 3+3+3
They make a pedestal under it[a] *so it stands firm.*
It cannot move from its place.
He even cries out to it, but it does not answer. 4+2
It cannot save him from his trouble.
8 [a]*Remember this, and take hold*[b] *of yourselves!*[a] 2+3
Recall it to mind, you rebels!
9 [a]*Remember things of the former age!*[a] 3
For I am God! 3+2
There is no other!
God! And there is none like me! 3
10 *Announcing end from beginning,* 3+3
from ancient times, what has not yet been done.
One saying "My strategy stands firm! 3+2
Whatever is my will, I accomplish!"[a]
11 *One summoning an eagle from the east,* 3+4
my[a] *strategy from a distant land.*
Indeed, I have spoken. Indeed, I bring it to pass. 2+2
I have planned (it)! Indeed, I do it!

[12] *Listen to me,* 2+2+2
you strong-minded[a]
who distance yourselves from the legitimate (cause).
[13] *I have made my legitimate (cause) come near!* 2+2+3
It is not far away.
And my salvation is not far behind.
I shall put salvation in Zion! 3+2
My majesty for Israel!

Notes

1.a. *BHS* prefers a pf for the ptcp in order to preserve parallelism. MT makes sense and should be kept.

1.b-b. *BHS* suggests a reordering of words and of verse accents meaning "their idols have become a burden, for a beast like the loading of burdens, for a weary animal." C. F. Whitley (*VT* 11 [1961] 457–61) suggests simply omitting "a burden for a weary beast." The changes are ingenious but have no textual support.

4.a. L lacks the mark over ש. Most editions read שׂ.

4.b. *BHS* proposes עמשתי "I have carried a load" as in v 1 (עמס) above, for MT עשיתי "I have made." Since this is one of four verbs in a row, three with emphatic אני "I," in which all the others are synonyms of "carry," it is a cogent suggestion. However, from another point of view, the bistich has two interior verbs meaning carry, while the exterior verbs in MT mean "I have done it" and "I will deliver." Stay with MT.

7.a. Following the suggestions of P. Volz, *BHS* moves ויתאשש "and it is established" from v 8 to here (see *Note* 8.b. below). But the insertion destroys the metric balance and is unnecessary.

8.a-a. *BHS* suggests deletion. That is not necessary.

8.b. MT והתאששו is hithpolel from אשׁשׁ, a root which occurs only here. Vg *confundamini* "be confused" led Lagarde, BDB (84), and many others to emend to התבששו "be embarrassed" (cf. Gen 2:25). LXX *στηνάξατε* "groan" caused Whitley (*VT* 25 [1975] 685) to emend to התחששו "be concerned" from חוש (BDB 301–2 II; cf. Eccl 2:25). And Syr *w'eṯbayanu* presupposes התבננו, apparently the source of RSV's "consider" (so Whitley). But only Tg ואתיקפו, which points to the Semitic root *'šš* "to establish, to found, be strong" (G. R. Driver, *JTS* 36 [1935] 400), explains MT's form, which is supported by DSS[Isa].

9.a-a. *BHS* suggests joining this stich to v 8 above, but in all three of these verses, MT makes sense and should be kept.

10.a. DSS[Isa] reads 3 masc sg, "he will accomplish," which is possible, but no improvement on MT.

11.a. DSS[Isa] and K read עצתו "his strategy." LXX *ὧν βεβούλευμαι* and Vg *voluntatis meae* support Q עצתי "my strategy."

12.a. LXX *οἱ ἀπολωλεκότες τὴν καρδίαν* "ones deprived of mind, ones who had lost heart" suggests Heb. אבדי לב "lose heart" (cf. Jer 4:9). But DSS[Isa] Tg Vg support MT אבירי לב "strong-minded, stubborn-hearted" which also occurs in Ps 76:6 [5].

Form/Structure/Setting

Yahweh speaks throughout most of the scene. He observes the transport of idols in Babylon, comments on it, and repeats his earlier challenge about comparing them to him. He then addresses Israel in three speeches beginning with "Listen to me" and "Remember this."

1. Bel and Nebo bow and are borne (vv 1–2).
2. Jacob, I have upheld and borne you (vv 3–7).

3. Remember, the former things! (vv 8–11).
4. Listen! I shall put my salvation in Zion! (vv 12–13).

This extended disputation with Israel repeats familiar themes about idols (cf. 40:18–20, 25–26; 44:7, 9–20). It then strongly asserts Yahweh's determination to accomplish his purpose for Zion through his chosen instrument. The tone has become more urgent, more strident. Israel is called "rebels" and "strong-minded."

Comment

1–2 Bel and Nebo are the old traditional gods of Babylon, even older than Marduk. They are also idols in nearby temples. The sight of the awesome idols in a horizontal position, being transported just like the other refugees from one place to another to avoid the approaching invader, elicits this thoughtful comment.

3–4 Yahweh calls Israel to note the contrast. Instead of carrying idols, they have been carried by his providence from *before they were born,* i.e., before they were a people. The reference is to the period of Abraham's promise. Now Israel is old, but Yahweh is still carrying them in his mercy. He intends to go right on doing it.

5–7 He returns then to the idols that have to be carried. Why should anyone see any comparison in such contrasts?

8 The people of Israel are called *rebels.* In the former times of chaps. 1–33 the accusation was leveled repeatedly. Exilic Israel is still stubborn and rebellious. In other words, the people want things to be done their way. They are contemptuous of Yahweh's plan to use Cyrus.

9–11 Israel is summoned to *remember* the events recounted in chaps. 1–33. God has announced his patronage of the Assyrian (14:24–27), insisting that his strategy (עצתי) would come to pass. And it had. He predicted the fall of Tyre and the subjugation of Egypt (19:12–17). These too had come to pass. Now he insists the same will happen with his plan to bring *an eagle from the east.* (See *Excursus: Yahweh's Strategy* in *Isaiah 1–33,* 215–16.)

12 A textual discrepancy appears with the appellation for Israel in this verse. MT אבירי לב (lit., "strong of heart") follows a parallel meaning to "rebels" above. LXX *οἱ ἀπολωλεκότες τὴν καρδίαν* (lit., "those deprived of heart") has an exactly opposite meaning. The change of one letter in Hebrew could produce the same meaning (see n. 12.a). Both meanings are fitting in describing the mindless, yet stubborn, insistence on Israel's part that her salvation must be fashioned in the traditional mold to which she is accustomed. She refuses to accept God's plan to have Cyrus do his work, which God calls *the legitimate cause* (lit., "righteousness").

13 Whatever Israel's attitude, God moves ahead with his plan. It deserves the terms *legitimate* (*cause*) and *salvation.* God gladly claims it as his own. Note the distinction: *salvation in Zion,* meaning restoration of the city and the operation of the Temple, and *my majesty for Israel.* The latter phrase lacks guarantees that Palestine will be returned to Israelite sovereignty and ownership. No settlement which lacks that provision will be satisfactory to those ancient Zionists (cf. chaps. 63 and 64). But God's purposes, as revealed and defended in the Vision, are different (cf. chaps. 65–66).

Explanation

Two major contrasts inspire the scene. One is between idols that have to be carried and supported and Yahweh who carries and supports his people. The other is between Yahweh's proposals to have Cyrus restore Jerusalem and Israel's refusal to approve the plan.

Israel is both unrealistic and idolatrous in rejecting Yahweh's choice of Cyrus to conquer Palestine and rebuild Jerusalem. Idolaters can manipulate their idols to do and symbolize their own will. When Israel insists that Yahweh shape the future to fit her beliefs, she is behaving like an idolater. This won't work with Yahweh. What he decides he does, whether his worshipers agree or not. He has already summoned "the eagle from the east" (v 11). Israel holds back now at the risk of missing her chance to be a part of God's great salvation for Zion. Religious persons are often "strong-minded," so faithful to their doctrines that they cannot hear God's call to a new cause or see God's work on a new project. This is exilic Israel's problem. God will not bend to her stubborn and inflexible beliefs. He will go his own way in any case. Only they who hear and see can respond to his invitation to accompany him.

Scene 4:
Sit in the Dust, Daughter Babylon (47:1–15)

Bibliography

Beeston, A. F. L. "Hebrew *sibbolet* and *sobel* (Is 47,2)." *JSS* 24 (1979) 175–77. **Cohen, C.** "The Widowed' City." *JANES* 5 (1973) 69–81. **Freedman, D. N.** "Mistress Forever. A Note on Isaiah 47:7." *Bib* 51 (1970) 538. **Martin-Archard, R.** "Esaïe 47 et la tradition prophétique sur Babylone." *ZAW* 150 (1980) 83–105. **Melugin, R. F.** *Formation*. 135–36. **Merendino, R. P.** *Der Erste und der Letzte* 461–82.

Translation

Yahweh: [1] *Get down! Sit on the dust,* 3+2
you virgin daughter Babylon!
[a]*Return to*[a] *the land* [b]*without a throne,*[b] 2+1
daughter Chaldeans.
For you will never again 3+2+2
be called
tender and delicate.
[2] *Take millstones* 2+2
and grind meal.
Take off your veil,[a] 2+2
strip off (your) robe.
Uncover a leg. 2+2
Ford streams.

3 *Your nakedness is revealed.* 2+3
Even your "shame" is seen.
I take vengeance 2+3
and do not meet[a] *a human.*

Chorus: (of Israelites)
4 *Our Redeemer!*[a] 1+3+2
Yahweh of Hosts is his name!
The Holy One of Israel!
5 *Sit in silence* 2+2+2
and go into darkness,
daughter Chaldeans!
For you are no longer called 4+2
mistress of kingdoms!

Yahweh:
6 *I was angry against my people.* 2+2
I profaned my possession,
So I gave them into your hand. 2+3
You had no compassion for them.
You weighed on elderly persons, 2+2
your yoke very heavily.
7 *You said, "I am Mistress for an age."*[a] 4+4+3
Until[b] *(then) you had not put these things on your mind.*[c]
You had not remembered what comes after that.
8 *So now, hear this, you voluptuous one* 3+2+2
who was dwelling confidently,
saying in her mind,[a]
"I—and there is no other. 3+3+3
I shall never live (as) a widow.
I shall not know bereavement."
9 *These two things came to you* 3+3+2
one day (when you were) at rest:
bereavement and widowhood.
In their full measure they have come[a] *on you,* 3+2+3
with a multitude of sorceries,
with the exceeding power of your enchantments.
10 *Because you trusted in your evil*[a] 2+3
you thought,[b] *"No one sees me."*[c]
Your wisdom and your knowledge 2+2
turned you around.
So you thought in your mind.[d] 2+3
"I—and none other than I."
11 *But evil has come*[a] *on you.* 3+3
You do not know its dawn.[b]
Disaster falls on you. 3+3
You are not able to counter it.
Suddenly there comes on you 3+3
a ruin of which you had no knowledge.
12 *Stand firm, now, with your enchantments* 2+2+2
and your sorceries

[a]with which you have busied yourself from your
youth.[a]
Perhaps you will benefit. 3+2
Perhaps you will inspire terror.
13 *You have worn yourself out with your many schemes.* 3+2
Let them stand up now to save you,
those dividing[a] the heavens 2+2
and gazing at stars.
Those who know about new moons 3+2
from which[b] come[c] (the things that happen) to
you.
14 *Look! They were like straw.* 3+2
Fire has consumed them.
They could not deliver their own life 2+2
from the power of a flame.
It was not a coal for warming[a] oneself by, 2+3
or a light to sit before.
15 *Such have they been to you,* 2+2+2
those with which[a] you labored,
your companions[b] from your youth!
They have left—each to his own way! 3+2
There is no one to save you!

Notes

1.a-a. MT שְׁבִי "sit" should normally be followed by ב or על "on" as in the first stich. Here it is followed by ל "to." The Versions note the anomaly. DSS^{Isa} reads על "on." LXX^{B} reads *κάθισον* "sit" in both stichs and faithfully reflects MT with *ἐπὶ* "on" in the first and *εἰς* "to" in the second. But LXX^{AQS} translate the second stich *εἴσελθε εἰς τὸ σκότος* "enter into the darkness." They sense that the preposition requires שבי to be read שֻׁבִי "turn to, go in," but they have also inserted the stich from v 5 below. Tg תיבי לארעא follows MT, and Vg *sede in terra* "sit in the land" follows MT lit. in noun and verb, but not in the prep. The correct instinct shown by LXX^{AQS} can be achieved in the Heb. by repointing the verb שֻׁבִי and translating "return to the land."

1.b-b. Omitted in LXX^{B}. Vg Tg support MT.

2.a. MT שבל "veil." DDS^{Isa} שוליך "your skirts." LXX *τὸ κατακάλυμμά σου* "your veil, your covering." Tg translates the entire verse metaphorically, "the glory of your kingdom." Vg *turpitudinem tuam* "your disgrace."

3.a. MT ולא אפגע "I do not meet." LXX *μὴ παραδῶ* "I will not deliver to." Σ *ουκ αντιστήσεται μοι* "he will not oppose me." Tg ואשני דיניך "make your judgments different." Vg *et non resistet mihi* "and he does not resist me." The Versions, like modern translators, have not been able to resist the temptation to translate an opaque word with a meaning gained from the context. There is no sign here that the variants reflect a different text. Modern translators have "spare" (RSV, NIV) "protect" (Melugin, *Formation,* 135), "encounter" (Merendino, *Der Erste und der Letzte,* 482).

4.a. Mt גאלנו "our redeemer" is supported by LXX^{BS*L} DSS^{Isa} Tg Vg. LXX$^{AQS^c}$ prefix *εἶπεν* "he said," followed by OL Syh Eth Arab. Read the MT.

7.a. גברת עד "mistress until." MT divides the lines by placing *athnaḥ* on גברת. *BHS* would place it on עד. The Versions support MT. The meter is possible, and the translation follows MT.

7.b. Omitted in LXX Vg. Tg and DSS^{Isa} support MT.

7.c. Lit., "heart."

8.a. Lit., "heart."

9.a. MT באו pf "they have come" is supported by DSS[Isa]. LXX ἥξει fut "she will come" is supported by Syr Syh Tg Arab Eth. Read MT.

10.a. MT ברעתך "in your evil." DSS[Isa] בדעתך "in your knowledge." LXX Tg Vg support MT.

10.b. Lit., "said."

10.c. LXX ἐγώ εἰμι, καὶ οὐκ ἔστιν ἑτέρα "I am and there are no others" (cf. v 8 above). Tg and DSS[Isa] support MT.

10.d. Lit., "said in your heart."

11.a. MT ובא masc "has come." DSS[Isa] has a fem ובאה which conforms with the subj. Follow DSS[Isa].

11.b. MT שחרה "its dawn." LXX omits. Tg paraphrases למבעי עלה "how to pray against it." Vg *ortum eius* "its dawn" translates lit.

12.a-a. Note parallel in v 15b.

13.a. K הָבְרוּ "they divide." Q הֹבְרֵי "dividers of." DSS[Isa] חוברי "those joining" (cf. 44:11). Read Q.

13.b. MT מאשר "from which." LXX Syr Tg "which." *Mem* could have been dittogr with the previous letter at a time before the use of final letters. But DSS[Isa] supports MT.

13.c. DSS[Isa] LXX Syr Tg read a sg.

14.a. MT לחמם inf constr "for warming." DSS[Isa] לחומם ptcp "for one warming himself." LXX paraphrases ἔχεις ἄνθρακας πυρός "for you have coals of fire." Tg has a totally different text. Stay with MT.

15.a. Two MSS, Syr Tg Vg read באשר "with which." Cf. v 12 above.

15.b. סחר is usually rendered "trader, one who trafficks, one who goes about" (BDB, 695; RSV). G. R. Driver (*JTS* 36 [1935] 400) uses Akk *šāḫiru* and Arab *sāḥirun* to translate "your enchanters." Although sorcerers are part of the context, the milder word has been chosen here.

Form/Structure/Setting

Yahweh speaks throughout the scene, with one choral echo in vv 4–5. Israel is present to serve as the echo. Conquered Babylon is addressed.

The tone of the speeches is sarcastic and taunting. This is different from the judgment of chap. 13, much more like the taunt of chap. 14.

It is composed of six parts:

Vv 1–3 A taunt: the princess has become a slave.
Vv 4–5 Israel's acknowledgment of God and echo of judgment.
Vv 6–7 A taunt: reversals in position and status.
Vv 8–9 Invective and judgment: widow bereaved.
Vv 10–11 Oracular style: wisdom turned demonic.
Vv 12–15 A sarcastic, mocking speech.

The position of the scene in the book is intentional (Melugin, *Formation*, 136). It picks up themes from 46:1–2 and 45:20. It sees Babylon claiming to be a god and insists that she, like the idol she claims to be, must fall. Merendino (*Der Erste und der Letzte* 495) understands the chapter to be an integral part of 44:24–47:15. The themes of the unit are unique in the book and are particularly directed to the period of the coming of Cyrus and the fall of Babylon.

Comment

1 A delicate, refined princess must become a slave-girl. With no throne, she must sit on the ground. *Return to the land* fits the picture of the king and nobles who fled Babylon just before Cyrus arrived. They did in fact return shortly afterward to salvage what they could of property and privileges. But now the throne is no longer theirs. The taunt predicts that Babylon will never again enjoy the luxury of her former position.

2 She will have to earn her way as a servant. Servants cannot afford fine veils and skirts. *Ford streams* implies crossing on foot, in contrast to having been carried over in a carriage or in a chair borne by slaves.

3 She is subject to *nakedness,* an indignity of slaves. *I do not meet a human* is unclear. The verb means "to meet or encounter." The object is אדם "a human being" or "mankind." It has been used in 2:9, 11, 17, 22 and at intervals throughout the Vision. The sentence may mean that God does not find a human being in Babylon, only magic and sorcery. It could mean that he does not meet a man in mercy or judgment. The hearers/readers are left to draw their own connotation from it.

4 Like the plagues on Egypt, God's vengeance on Babylon is seen as redemption for the exiles. *Our Redeemer,* they chant in chorus, calling him by his most characteristic name. Not the idols, not even Cyrus deserves this recognition! Yahweh alone is seen as the one who redeemed them!

5 Then the chorus turns to Babylon, repeating a variation of the judgment taunt against the fabled city that had been their prison. The terms and figures are different. The city of sound and light is condemned to silence and darkness. The figure of the dethroned queen reappears: no longer *mistress of Kingdoms.* The structure of Babylon's empire had been essentially feudal with small kingdoms (actually baronies or dukedoms) swearing fealty to their liege lord, the emperor. But now Babylon is a lowly subject, not the mistress.

6–7 Yahweh explains the reason that the people of the Lord of all creation and history have been subject to Babylon for half a century. He had been *angry with* them for a reason (chaps. 1, 3, etc.) and had *profaned* his *possession.* He had revoked the holy and sacrosanct status of their land, thus removing his protection. He had *given them* up to Babylon's dominance. This was a punishment. But Babylon did not recognize that Yahweh had allowed it to happen. She relished her role and was cruel without mercy. She thought it was her own strength that did it, and that it proved that she was herself divine: *I am Mistress for an age!* It is the recurrent fallacy of power to assume that it is permanent. She gave no thought to the judgment of history, much less to that of Yahweh.

8–11 This taunting speech stresses the ego-centered sense of being divinely eternal, beyond the reach of life's disasters. This sense of *security* was fostered by *sorcery* and magic. Babylon's so-called *wisdom* and *knowledge* were only *enchantments.* They constituted her *evil* which became *disaster* and *ruin.* The house of lies came down around her. The great mistress became *childless* and *widowed* at the same time. This figure was more compelling in that society where women depended totally on husbands or sons for protection and upkeep. Babylon had lost all hope of support.

12–15 The taunt goes on. Babylon knows nothing to do in this crisis but more of the same: *sorcery* and *enchantment.* She is taunted to try once more, like a loser at a slot machine. Her *schemes* (lit., "counsels") have lacked sound political or military advice. Like those of Hitler's last days, they were determined by the horoscope. They are compared to straw walls built to contain a fire. (Cf. the taunt against the idols in chap. 46.) In burning, they are of no use, either to *warm* or to give *light.* Babylon is so deeply involved in her magic and astrology that she cannot be saved.

Explanation

This is the fourth time that Babylon has drawn attention in the Vision. Twice she was offstage (chaps. 21 and 39). Two times (here and in chaps. 13–14) she and her king have been center stage. She is characterized in both instances to be the epitomy of a self-centered, power-crazed, worship of success and luxury. She is the symbol of worldly self-deception, fostered by idolatry with its accompanying sorceries, magic, astrology, and oracles that passed for wisdom and sage counsel. Her pride and ambition were known to all as the ultimate symbol of human sin (cf. Gen 11:1–9).

One aspect of this self-deception is the illusion of being eternal and divine (vv 7, 8, 10). Another is the illusion of living above the normal consequences of human behavior: "This cannot happen to me." Another is the failure to recognize that everyone has to render an account of his or her decisions and actions (v 7b, "You did not remember what comes after that").

Babylon is here the symbol of humanity and its capacity for self-delusion, sinful pride, and ambition. The Revelation of John uses it in the same sense (16:19; 17:5; 18:10, 21).

The larger part of the act (44:24–47:15) has developed a consistent theme of Yahweh's struggle against the idols and the powers of Babylon through his champion, Cyrus. His victory, celebrated in this chapter, was not only over Babylon but over all that she stood for. Yahweh is now free to address his own people about their role in the new age that opens before them.

Scene 5: Move Out from Babylon! (48:1–22)

Bibliography

Bergmeier, R. "Das Streben nach Gewinn des Volkes." *ZAW* 81 (1969) 93–97. **Brawer, A. J.** *"kim-'otajw* (Isa 48:18–19)." (Heb) *BMik* 11 (1966) 93–4. **Brongers, H. A.** "Die Wendung *besem jhwh* im Alten Testament." *ZAW* 77 (1965) 1–20. **Leene, H.** "Juda und die Heilige Stadt in Jes. 48:1–2." *Verkenningen in een Stroomgebied.* FS M. A. Beek. Amsterdam: Huisdrukkerij Universiteit, 1974. 80–92. **Merendino.** *Der Erste und der Letzte.* 497–539. **Schmitt, H.-C.** "Prophetie (Is 48, 3.6.12–15) und Schultheologie (Is 48, 2.4.9–10.17–19) im Deuterojesajabuch. Beobachtungen zur Redaktionsgeschichte von Jes 40–55." *ZAW* 91 (1979) 43–61. **Westermann, C.** "Jes 48 und die 'Bezeugung gegen Israel'." *Studia Biblica et Semitica.* FS T. C. Vriezen. Wageningen: Veenman, 1966. 355–73. **Whitley, C. F.** "Further notes on the text of Deutero-Isaiah" (48, 6a). *VT* 25 (1975) 683–87.

Translation

Herald: [1] *Hear this, House of Jacob,* 2+3+3
you who are called by the name Israel,
and who are descended from the loins [a] *of Judah,*
those swearing by Yahweh's name 3+3
and who confess the God of Israel.
Earth: *Not in truth* 2+2
and not in righteousness.
Heavens: [2] *But they have called themselves "from the Holy City."* 3+3+3
And they have supported themselves on the God of Israel
whose name is Yahweh of Hosts.
Yahweh: [3] *The former things I announced* [a] *from of old.* [a] 3+3+3
They went out from my mouth, and I let them be heard. [b]
Suddenly I did (them) and brought them to pass.
[4] *Since I knew that you were stubborn* 4+3+2
and your neck had iron sinews
and your forehead (was) of brass,
[5] *I announced (it) to you long ago.* 3+3
Before they happened, I let you hear (about them).
Lest you say "My idol [a] *did them.* 3+3
My idol and my image commanded them."
[6] *You have heard! Envision* [a] *all this!* 3+3
And you (pl) [b] *—will you (pl)* [b] *not announce* [c] *(it)?*
I made you hear news from that (time) 3+3
and secrets which you had not known.
[7] *Now they have been created, not long ago.* 4+3+3
Before today you had not heard of them,
lest you say, "See! I knew (about) them!"
[8] *You never heard.* 2+2+4
You never knew.
You never opened [a] *your ear even long ago.*
For I knew you would certainly betray (it), 4+4
rebelling (as you have) from birth against him who is calling you.
[9] *For my name's sake I deferred by anger,* 4+2+2
and for my praise [a] *I restrained* [b] *(myself) toward you*
so that I have not cut you off.
[10] *See, I have refined you,* [a] *but not with silver.* 4+3
I have chosen you [b] *in a furnace of affliction.*
[11] *For my sake, for my sake, I do it!* 3+3+3
For why should it be profaned? [a]
I do not give my glory to someone else!
[12] *Listen to me, Jacob,* 3+2
and Israel, whom I am calling.

I am He. 2+2+3
I am first
Indeed, I am last.
13 *Indeed my hand founded earth.* 3+3
And my right hand stretched out heaven.
I call them. 3+2
They stand there together.
Leader: 14 [a]*Gather together, all of you,*[a] *and listen!*[b] 3+4
Who among them[c] *announced these?*
Yahweh has loved him.[d] 2+3+2
He does his pleasure against Babylon,
and his arm[e] *(against) the Chaldeans.*
Yahweh: 15 *I—I myself have spoken. Indeed I have called him.* 4+3
I have brought him and his way shall prosper.[a]
16 *Come near to me! Hear this!* 3+4+3
From the beginning I have not spoken in secret.
From the time it happened I was there.
Leader: *And now,* [a]*Lord Yahweh*[a] 3+2
[b]*has sent me and his spirit!*[b]
17 *Thus Yahweh, your redeemer, has said,* 3+2
the Holy One of Israel:
"I am Yahweh, your god. 3+2+3
the one teaching you to benefit,
the one leading you in the way you should go."
Yahweh: 18 *If only you had attended to my commandments,* 3+3+3
your peace could have become like a river
and your righteousness like waves of the sea.
19 *Your offspring could have been like the sand* 3+3
and your physical[a] *descendants like its grains.*[b]
Their[c] *name would not be cut off* 2+2
nor destroyed before me.
Leader: 20 *Move out from Babylon!* 2+2
Flee from Chaldea!
Announce it in singing tones! 3+2+3
Let this be heard!
Send it out to the border of the land.
Say: "Yahweh has redeemed 3+2
his servant Jacob!"
Heavens: 21 *They did not thirst* 2+2
in deserts (where) he made them walk.
Water from a rock 2+2
he made to flow for them.
When he split a rock, 2+2
Water gushed out.
Earth: 22 *There is no peace,* 2+2+1
said Yahweh,
for the adversaries.

Notes

1.a. MT מִמֵּי "from the waters of" is unusual. LXX ἐξ Ιουδα "from Judah" suggests מיהודה which appears with יצא "descend" in 65:9. DSS[Isa] 'A Σ Θ Vg support MT. *BHS* suggests the similar sounding but more usual מִמְּעֵי "from the loins of" (BDB, 588–89; cf. 49:1) which is used with יצא in v 19; Gen 15:4; 2 Sam 7:12; 16:11. The translation follows this suggestion.

3.a-a. Missing in LXX.

3.b. Because the Versions translate in past tense, *BHS* suggests a *waw* consec for MT's simple *waw* (Whybray). But in Heb. such a close identification of verb aspect (and the role of *waw* consec) with temporal references cannot be sustained (Watts, *Syntax,* 30, 103–8; contra GKC § 111a).

5.a. MT עֲצָבַי is pointed as from עֹצֶב which usually means "pain" (BDB, 780, I) though BDB (781) postulates a second root occurring only here which means "idol." This meaning is supported by all the Versions, but would usually be pointed עֲצַבַּי from עָצָב "idol," which elsewhere is always pl. Adopt a second root with BDB or emend the pointing with *BHS*. The meaning is the same.

6.a. Whybray follows Syr to read a pf, חזיתָ "you have seen," instead of MT's impv, חֲזֵה "see!" LXX omits, but DSS[Isa] Vg support MT.

6.b-b. MT אַתֶּם "you" and תגידו "you announce" are pl, though the context is full of 2d pers sgs. *BHS* suggests וְאֱמֶת "and truly" or אֹתָם "them" and reads תגיד "you announce," sg. Elliger (528) follows Kissane in reading רָאִ(י)תָה "you saw," arguing that *resh* was mistaken for *waw* by a copyist. But the Versions all support MT. Perhaps the change in number is a signal of an aside to different addressees.

6.c. Many interpreters find the close proximity of a human announcement to the divine announcement (v 5) unlikely. Elliger (528) follows Duhm and others in reading תעיד hiph from עוד "return," "repeat." LXX οὐκ ἔγνωτε "do you not understand?" may have read Heb. תדעו which could be a corruption of תעידו. But this seems far-fetched. MT makes good sense and should be kept.

8.a. MT פִּתְּחָה "she opened" breaks the parallelism which is preserved by DSS[Isa] פתחת "you opened" and Tg. A Cairo Geniza fragment, Syr, and Vg read a passive פֻּתְּחָה "was opened." LXX ἤνοιξα "I have opened" suggests פִּתַּחְתִּי or פָּתַחְתִּי (BDB, 835). Follow DSS[Isa].

9.a. MT תהלתי "my praise" fits awkwardly, but DSS[Isa] has it, as do LXX τὰ ἔνδοξά μου "my splendor," Tg תשבחתי "my praise," and Vg *laude mea* "my praise." With all the Versions supporting it, read MT.

9.b. MT אחטם "I restrain" is a *hap. leg.* (BDB, 310). LXX ἐπάξω "you made firm." Tg אקיים "I will establish." Vg *infrenabo* "I will restrain." The dir obj is left unstated. Merendino (*Der Erste und der Letzte,* 499) suggests that אפי "my anger" is to be understood.

10.a. G. R. Driver (*JTS* 36 [1935] 83, 401) understands צרפתיך to mean "I have bought you." But the weight of evidence is against him (cf. BDB, 864).

10.b. MT בחרתיך "I have chosen you" is supported by LXX Vg. DSS[Isa] בחנתיכה "I have examined you" is supported by Tg. Read MT as the more difficult reading.

11.a. DSS[Isa] has איחל "I profane" (supported by Syr OL) for MT's יחל "it be profaned." Tg יתחל "it be profaned," LXX βεβηλοῦται "it be profaned" (adding τὸ ἐμὸν ὄνομα "my name"), Vg *blasphemer* "I am blasphemed." Read MT.

14.a-a. MT הקבצו כלכם "gather together all of you." DSS[Isa] יקבצו כולם "gather all of them." LXX καὶ συναχθήσονται πάντες "and all shall be gathered together." Vg *congregamini omnes vos* "gather, all of you." Tg אתבנשו כולכון "gather yourselves together, all of you."

14.b. MT ושמעו "and listen." DSS[Isa] וישמעו "and they listened." LXX καὶ ἀκούσονται "and they listened." Tg ושמעו "and listen." Vg *et audite* "and listen." Read MT.

14.c. MT בהם "among them." Several Heb. MSS, Syr, some Tg MSS בכם "among you." Other Tg MSS support MT. LXX αὐτοῖς "them," acc, and Vg *de eis* "of them."

14.d. MT אהבו qal pf 3 masc sg "loves him" (BDB, 12; cf. Deut 15:16). DSS[Isa] אוהבי "is loving me." Tg מדרחים ליה לישראל "because he loves Israel." LXX ἀγαπῶν σε "out of love for you." Vg *dilexit eum* "chose him." Read MT.

14.e. MT וּזְרֹעוֹ "and his arm" (BDB, 283). LXX ἆραι σπέρμα "destroy the seed of" suggests וְזֶרַע "and the seed." Tg דרע דבורתיה "mighty arm." Vg *et brachium suum in* "and his arm in." *BHS* and Elliger (528) follow LXX but Merendino (*Der Erste und der Letzte,* 517) correctly prefers MT as the more difficult reading.

15.a. MT והצליח "prosper." Tg ואצלחית "I made prosperous." LXX εὐόδωσα "I made prosperous." Vg *directa est* "is directed." Vg reflects MT the best. LXX and Tg reflect the context.

16.a-a. LXX and Arab omit. But DSS[Isa] Tg Vg support MT.

16.b-b. *BHS* notes suggested emendations which smooth over the sudden change of person. But this is explained by a change of speaker. ורוחו "his spirit" is better understood as a second obj of "sent" (so Fohrer, Westermann, and others) than as another subj parallel to "Lord Yahweh." The Versions all support MT.

19.a. מעיך "your belly," i.e., physical, is omitted by DSS[Isa]. But MT is supported by LXX Vg.

19.b. מעתיו "its grains" is a *hap. leg.* (BDB, 589). LXX ὁ χοῦς τῆς γῆς "the mound of earth." 'A Σ Θ αι κεγχροι "grains." Tg כפרידוהי "its grains." Vg *lappilli* "pebbles."

19.c. MT DSS[Isa] Vg have 3 masc sg, "its." LXX reads 2 masc sg, "your"; Tg "of Israel." Follow MT.

Form/Structure/Setting

Melugin (*Formation,* 137–42) suggests that the imperative beginning words indicate the structure of the passage: a disputation speech beginning "Hear ye" (vv 1–11), a trial speech beginning "Hear" (vv 12–15), a dialogue beginning "Draw near and hear" (v 16; cf. Zech 2:13, 15; 4:9; 6:15), a word from Yahweh introduced by a messenger formula (vv 17–19), a hymn beginning with "Go out" with introductory instructions like Gen 19:15 (vv 20–21; it is similar to 52:11–12), a speech of judgment (v 22; cf. the repetition in 57:21).

The analysis used here is similar but incorporates the possibilities of the Vision's dramatic genre. The heart of the scene lies in two major Yahweh speeches: vv 3–11 and 12–16.

In the first (vv 3–11) Yahweh summarizes his proofs of announcements before events take place. Then he indicts Israel for being deaf, rebellious, and unreliable. She must be refined like a fine metal. In vv 12–16a he takes up again his defense of the choice of Cyrus. In vv 18–19 he makes a powerful "if only" speech of what might have been if Israel's response had been positive.

These speeches are framed by a herald's call to attention (v 1a–b), an inner debate about whether the audience is worthy of the titles (vv 1c–2), and similar reflections of optimism and cynicism in vv 21–22.

Vv 16b–d and v 20 are structurally important elements depicting an expeditionary leader ready to begin a journey from Babylon toward Jerusalem. This element is repeated in 52:11 and 62:10–12. Ezra-Nehemiah tells of four expeditions in three periods led respectively by Sheshbazzar, Zerubabbel, Ezra, and Nehemiah, paired in each case with an imperial edict to rebuild the Temple. This position in the Vision would fit the role of Sheshbazzar in the reigns of Cyrus/Cambyses. The scene suggests that the expedition had poor support from the exilic Jewish community.

Comment

1 The herald calls the gathered group of Israelites to attention. They include two larger groups, one of which is subdivided. There would be considerable overlapping in the designations, but five addresses make sure no one is left out: *House of Jacob* is properly all those descended from the twelve tribes which bore the names of Jacob's sons. The title may also refer to those of the former Northern Kingdom. *Called by the name Israel* is broader, including those who participated in covenant ceremonies. *Who are descended from Judah* picks up the main group of those who came to Babylon in the exile of 587 B.C. and who, presumably, were most concerned with the restoration of Jerusalem and its Temple. But then the address turns from political and ethnic terms to religious affiliation: *those swearing by Yahweh's name* and *who confess the God of Israel.* (Cf. P. A. H. de Boer, *Gedenken und Gedächtnis in der Welt des Alten Testaments* [Stuttgart: Kohlhammer Verlag, 1962]; H. Gross, "Zur Wurzel *zkr,*" *BZ* 4 [1960] 227–37; F. Horst, "Das Eid im Alten Testament," *EvT* 17 [1957] 366–71; G. Rinaldi, *"Zakar," BeO* 7 [1965] 112–14.) The last designation could well include proselytes.

Not in truth introduces a cynical "aside" which indicates that the speaker doubts that all these are genuinely interested. God's accusation that Israel is rebellious (46:12) had prepared for this reaction. *Not in righteousness* also picks up reference to that verse and is explained by 46:13. *Righteousness* relates to acceptance of God's plan to use Cyrus (see *Excursus:* צדק/צדקה *"Righteousness,* Legitimacy" above). This remark documents the scepticism and rejection apparent in the listeners.

2 Another protests that this is unfair. The exiles do refer to themselves as Zionists. They depend in prayer and worship on *the God of Israel whose name is Yahweh of Hosts.* They do profess affiliation and loyalty.

3 Yahweh's speech picks up elements of his claim to credibility in his earlier speeches. He cites the argument that he had predicted the events which had then occurred. Yahweh claims to be the God who speaks and acts.

4–8 But the speech turns bitter when he refers to Israel's *stubbornness* which had been reflected in the disputations that precede. He did not trust Israel to believe the revelations since they were partly idolatrous throughout this time. Nevertheless, he revealed his secrets of what he would do, which had now come to pass. As he expected, they did not even hear them. (Note the "blind and deaf" motif from chap. 6 on.) God's bitterness shows. Israel is called a traitor (*betray*) and a *rebel.* Her present unbelieving mood had been endemic from her youth, a theme familiar in Hosea and Ezekiel.

9 *For my name's sake* is the opposite of the instructions given to Cyrus (45:5). Cyrus is to do his thing and receive his reward "for Israel's sake." But God moves for his own reasons as well, whether these concern his reputation or his own essential character. This is what the NT calls grace! Because of these he had held back deserved judgment. Otherwise they would have been *cut off* and destroyed long before as Ezekiel had recognized (chap. 20).

10 God's alternative to instant judgment was a refining process. The Vision spoke of this in 1:25 in a passage that presaged this and the following section. It is significant that this chapter is the last time that Yahweh addresses Israel by name in the Vision and that the suffering mediator appears on the scene in the next act. There had been divine purpose in the drawn-out tragedy of faltering kingdoms and in the exile. The Vision seeks to clarify that purpose and the goal to which God continues to call his people.

11 *For my sake.* Repeatedly God proclaims it with emotion and passion.

Why should it be profaned? It apparently refers to his name. When God becomes patron for a people, he enters a difficult position. If he supports and protects them, even though he is being betrayed by their affairs with idols and immorality (cf. Hos 1–3; Ezek 16, 23), he risks being laughed at and despised by all the world. If he punishes them, he risks being thought demonic (Exod 32:9–14). God has walked that tight-rope throughout his association with Israel. Now the decision has been made. Judgment is complete. And he refuses to let idols take credit for his beneficent deeds that follow, for his *glory*.

12–13 Yahweh picks up his appeal in presenting himself again, as he has from chap. 40 onward. He is the only God there is. And he is *calling Israel* by name. The eternal mystery of vocation, that the Absolute, the Wholly Other, the Infinite God should stoop to call a human being's name is enough, as youth say, to "blow one's mind." He who *founded the earth* and *stretched out the heavens* (the anthropomorphic figures are hardly adequate, but the inadequacy is in the figure, not in the reality portrayed) summons the entities of the physical universe. And *they stand* at attention. In the next verse he calls Israel, but scarcely gains their notice.

14 A leader calls for attention, challenging Israel to recognize what God has done. *Yahweh has loved* Cyrus who is now doing his will toward Babylon.

15 Yahweh stresses his personal involvement in calling Cyrus and *prospering his way,* just as he was personally involved with the heavens and the earth. A personal God, hearing, speaking, calling, directing history, raising up kings, giving them power and success, creating and sustaining the universe—this is the powerful theological foundation on which to base his request for recognition as Savior and Redeemer of Israel. Because Yahweh *brought him* to this moment, he will *prosper* (הצליח, which also appears in 52:13 and 55:11) and make *his way* succeed.

16b The scene turns to action on an earthly level. Someone, ostensibly a leader, claims that *Yahweh has sent* him and *his spirit.* The Vision has consistently seen the active participation of God's spirit as essential to his work (cf. 11:2; 32:15; 42:1). Ezra 1:2–8 tells of Cyrus's edict to the expedition under Sheshbazzar. This chapter implies the same scene. Yahweh's spirit which was given to Cyrus also empowers and directs this leader.

17 He then quotes his commission from Yahweh, Israel's *Redeemer.* Redemption is a pertinent concept to apply to the opportunity to return from exile. This expedition is a part of that redemption. The restoration of Jerusalem (40:1–9) is finally under way. Yahweh promises to *teach* the leader *to benefit.* (הועיל "benefit" occurs also in 44:9–10; 47:12; and 57:12, always in settings that negate the benefits that idols and magic promise.) The word may well imply successful life based on piety and prayer. It complements "prosper" of v 15 relating to Cyrus. This unnamed leader has Yahweh's promise to *lead him in the way that he should go,* a promise as old as Abraham, but as necessary now as then.

18 Yahweh's soliloquy is a reminder of what Israel's stubborn rebellion and sin had cost. *Attended to commandments* recalls the potential inherent in a valid covenant. *Peace* and *righteousness* mean health and right-being in the will and blessing of God.

19 *Offspring like sand . . . and its grains* refers to the promise made to

Abraham (Gen 15:5, 22:17). If only life could move in a straight line from promise to obedience and to fulfillment . . . ! But human sin, lack of faith, and stubborn ambition introduce so many diversions. For Abraham there were side-trips to Egypt. For Israel there were extended periods in Egypt and in the wilderness, then the long period of a divided kingdom, and now Babylon. *If only*—then Israel in the old name and shape might have survived and prospered. But that was not to be. Israel would survive, but she would be called by another name and have a different structure and role in God's purpose.

20 The leader gives the command to march from Babylon. Word is sent ahead to the first places to be approached in Palestine (*the land*): *Yahweh has redeemed his servant Jacob!* They are on their way home.

21 An ecstatic hymn rejoices in the miracle of grace. God is marching with his people through the desert toward his land as he did before (Exod 17).

22 But the scene ends with a laconic reminder of reality. Israel is still largely in rebellion against God's use of Cyrus. Her people have put themselves in the position of being *adversaries* to both Yahweh and Cyrus. The word רשעים may also mean "wicked." But the context in which צדק "righteous" refers to Cyrus and his legitimate, God-directed mission requires that it be the opposite, i.e., those who oppose God's righteous plan (cf. 57:21).

Explanation

The Persian decision to make Egypt part of the empire led Cambyses to invade it in 525 B.C. The campaign had been planned and prepared since the days of Cyrus. The Vision looks at it all as part of Yahweh's action to gain respect for Jews and restoration for Jerusalem. But Babylonian Jews had not seen it that way.

When Sheshbazzar, prince of Judah, started his journey to Jerusalem, he had only a small group of supporters. But he also had the Emperor's edict and the precious utensils that once had graced Solomon's Temple before being taken to babylon by Nebuchadnezzar's armies. This could be viewed as a little thing (cf. Zech 4:10) or it could be seen as a sign that God who moved heaven and earth was now moving to restore Jerusalem. The Vision views it in the latter sense. A commission from God, creator of heaven and earth, Lord of history and patron of Cyrus, emperor of the world, and Israel's Savior and Redeemer, begins an expedition to Jerusalem's ruins to rebuild and restore the Temple.

The completion of the task would require three Persian emperors, four Jewish leaders, and a century of time. But now God had put down earnest money on the project. Exilic Judaism was sceptical. Jerusalem was afraid. But the "mills" of God "ground slowly on."

Act IX
The Servant of Rulers (49:1–52:12)

The Ninth Generation:
Cambyses/Darius (522–*ca.* 518 b.c.)

Israel, like much of the Empire, finds itself in a period of stagnation and discouragement. The attempt to rebuild the Temple has come to a halt. Undoubtedly the neighboring enemies mentioned in Ezra have impeded progress. But Yahweh announces a new initiative, a surprise in political developments that should be good news to Jerusalem.

The act has five scenes:

Scene 1: A Light to Nations (49:1–21)
Scene 2: Even the Captive of a Champion (49:22–50:3)
Scene 3: A Student's Tongue (50:4–51:8)
Scene 4: Awake! Put on Strength! (51:9–52:2)
Scene 5: How Fitting: A Messenger's Feet (52:3–12)

The act is set throughout in Jerusalem.

Historical Background

Bibliography

Bright, J. *HI.* 366–72. **Ctesias,** *Patriologiae.* Series Graeca, vols. 103–104. **Culican, W.** *The Medes and Persians,* 64–74. **Dahlberg, B. T.** "Zerubbabel." *IDB* 4:955–56. **Frye, R. N.** *The History of Ancient Iran,* 96–102. **Herodotus.** Book III, 61–160. Tr. A. D. Godley. Cambridge, MA: Harvard U. P., 1938. 2:77–195. **Josephus.** *Antiq* XI.iii. **Olmstead, A. T.** *History of the Persian Empire.* 92–3, 107–18. **Smith, M.** "II Isaiah and the Persians." *JAOS* 83 (1963) 415–21.

Cambyses' stay in Egypt from 525–522 b.c. left him far from the centers of power in the east. News of unrest at home caused Cambyses to begin his journey back in 522 b.c. He died at Agatana near Mount Carmel in Palestine on his way back (Herodotus iii.64–65). It may have been a suicide as Herodotus (iii.62 ff.) suggested, but this is not certain.

The rebellion was led by a Magian named Gaumata who called himself by the name of Cambyses' dead brother Bardiya. The rebellion was popular. Most of the Empire quickly followed him, with the significant exceptions of Egypt, Palestine, and Asia Minor.

Darius was a military aide to Cambyses in Egypt and was with him at his death. He was twenty-eight years old, son of Hystaspes, Satrap of Parthia and Hyrcania, and grandson of Arsames, ruler of one of the Persian tribes when Cyrus began his meteoric rise as ruler of a neighboring tribe. Apparently both his father and grandfather were still alive at this time. With six helpers Darius assassinated Gaumata in Media on Sept. 29, 522 B.C. Although there is no reason to think that he was considered next in line for the throne, Darius was able to establish himself on it.

Darius claims in his Behistun inscriptions that Cambyses had murdered his brother secretly at an earlier time. But Herodotus would put the murder during the Egyptian campaign, while Ctesias places it afterward. Turbulent years followed in which Darius had to subdue virtually all of the Persian Empire before his authority was recognized. It took two years of hard fighting. For the second time, a very unlikely candidate had successfully ascended the throne to become a strong ruler for a long period of time.

Ezra 2–6 refers to Zerubbabel as leader of Jews in Jerusalem, to a new initiative to rebuild the temple, to opposition from leaders of neighboring provinces and cities, to the work of Haggai and Zechariah, and to an appeal to Darius with a confirmation of Cyrus' original edict in the 2nd year of Darius (520 B.C.). By this decree Darius become the second Persian emperor to directly support the building of Jerusalem's Temple. The Temple was completed in the 6th year of Darius (520 B.C.).

Strangely, the name of Zerubbabel no longer appears in the record of the completed Temple, not does it appear in any other records of the time. His fate continues to be a mystery. The preaching of Haggai and Zechariah contains material which could be understood to support a rebellion against the empire. Those were days when most of the realm was in revolt. They seemed to be encouraging Zerubbabel to lead Judah to freedom. But there is no evidence that Zerubbabel actually did participate in any such activity.

Scene 1: A Light to Nations (49:1–21)

Bibliography

Beuken, W. A. M. "De vergeefse moeite van de knecht: gedachten over plaats van Jesaja 49,1–6 in de kontext." *De Knecht.* FS J. L. Koole. Kampen: Kok, 1978. **Blythin, I.** "A Note on Isaiah xlix, 16–17." *VT* 16 (1966) 229–30. **Goshen-Gottstein, M. H.** "Bible Exegesis and Textual Criticism; Isaiah 49,11, MT and LXX." *Études bibliques.* FS D. Barthelemy. Göttingen: U. P., 1981. 91–107. **Graffy, A.** "Isaiah 49:14–25." *A Prophet Confronts His People.* 91–98. **Gruber, M. I.** "Will a Woman Forget Her Infant?" (49:14; Heb. with Eng. summary). *Tarbiz* 51 (1982) 491–92. **Lindsey, F. D.** "Isaiah's Songs of the Servant. Part 2: The Commission of the Servant in Isa 49:1–13." *BSac* 139 (1982) 129–45. **Lohfink, N.** "'Israel' in Jes 49, 3." *Wort, Lied und Gottesspruch.* FzB 2. FS J. Ziegler. Stuttgart: Katholisches Bibelwerk, 1972. 217–29. **Merendino, R. P.** "Jes 49, 1–6: ein Gottesknechtslied?" *ZAW* 92 (1980) 236–48. ———. "Jes 49, 7–13: Jahwes Bekenntnis zu Israels Land." *Henoch* 4 (1982) 295–342. ———. "Jes 49, 14–26: Jahwes Bekenntnis zu Sion und die neue Heilszeit." *RB* 89 (1982) 321–69. **Morgenstern, J.** "The Drama of the Suffering Servant." *HUCA* 31 (1960) 20–22.

———. "Isaiah 49–55." *HUCA* 36 (1965) 1–35. **Ringgren, H.** "Zur Komposition von Jesaia 49–55." *Beiträge zur AT Theologie.* FS W. Zimmerli. Göttingen: Vandenhoeck & Ruprecht, 1977. 371–76. **Rosenrauch, H.** "Note on Is 49:16." *JQR* 36 (1945/46) 81. **Snaith, N.** " 'Israel' in Isa. xlix, 3: A Problem in the Methodology of Textual Criticism." *EI* 8 (1967) 42–45. **Stamm, J. J.** "*Berît ʿam* bei Deuterojesaja." *Probleme biblischer Theologie.* FS G. von Rad. Munich: Kaiser, 1971. 510–24. **Widengren, G.** "The Gathering of the Dispersed." *Svensk Exegetisk Årsbok* 41 (1976) 224–34.

Translation

Episode A

Servant Israel: 1 *Listen to me, you coastlands!* 3+3
Pay attention, you distant peoples!
Yahweh called me before I was born. 3+2+2
Since I was in my mother's body,
he has recalled my name.
2 *When he made my mouth to be like a sharp sword,* 4+3
he hid me in the shadow of his hand.
When he made me a polished arrow, 4+2
he hid me in his quiver.
3 *When he said to me, "You are my servant,* 4+3
Israel,[a] *in whom I will glorify myself,"*
4 *on my part, I thought I had labored for nothing* 4+4
that I had spent my strength for waste and to no purpose.[a]
But surely just compensation is with Yahweh. 3+2
And my reward is with my God.

Episode B

Servant Darius: 5 *But now, says Yahweh,* 3+4
who was forming me before I was born to be a servant for himself
to restore Jacob to himself 3+3
that Israel might be gathered[a] *to himself,*[b]
[cd]*I shall be honored in Yahweh's eyes* 3+3
and my God will be my strength.[c]
6 *Then he said: It is not enough that you be my servant* 4+3+3
to establish the tribes of Jacob
and to restore those of Israel who have been protected.[a]
I appoint you a Light to Nations 3+4
to be my salvation to the border of the land.
Herald: (to Darius) 7 *Thus says Yahweh,* 3+3
Redeemer of Israel, his Holy One,
to one despised[a] *of soul,*[b] 2+2+2
to one abhorred[c] *by a nation,*

to a servant of rulers:
Kings will see and rise up. 3+2
Princes will bow down,
for the sake of Yahweh, who has proved faithful, 4+3
the Holy One of Israel, because he chose you.
8 Thus says Yahweh: 3
Yahweh: (to Darius) In a favorable time, I answer you. 3+3
And in a day of salvation, I help you.
I form[a] you and[b] appoint you to be a people's covenant, 4+4+3
to constitute a land,[c]
to reassign abandoned land-rights,
9 to say to prisoners, "Go out," 3+3
to those in darkness, "Appear."
Let them find pasture on all ways[a] 2+2
and let their pasture be on all bare heights.
10 Let them not hunger 2+2+3
nor thirst.
And do not let the hot wind or sun strike them.
For he who has compassion on them leads them 3+3
and guides them beside springs of water.
11 I establish all my mountains[a] to be a way, 3+2
and my highways will be raised up.
12 See! These come from far away. 3+3+3
And look! These from the north and from seaward.
And these from the land of the Syenites.[a]

Episode C

Herald: 13 Rejoice, Heavens! 2+2+3
Be glad, Earth!
Break out[a] in singing, Mountains!
For Yahweh has comforted his people 3+2
and has compassion on his afflicted ones.
14 Then Zion says: 2+2+2
Zion: Yahweh has forsaken me!
My Lord has forgotten me!
Yahweh: (to Zion) 15 Can a woman forget her nursing child? 3+2
Or not have compassion[a] on the child in her womb?
Even if[b] these could forget,[c] 3+3
I myself will certainly not forget you!
16 See! I have engraved you on the palms (of my hands). 3+3
Your walls (are) before me constantly.
17 Your builders[a] move faster than your destroyers[b] 3+3
or your devastators[c] who have now departed from you.
18 Lift up your eyes all around and see! 4+3
All of them are gathered! They have come to you!
As I live, oracle of Yahweh, I swear: 4+4+2

You will put them on like a fine dress,[a]
like a bride's[b] *trousseau.*
19 [a]*Though I struck you, and wasted you, and destroyed you,*[a] *as a land,*[b] 5+4+2
now you have become too small to live in
and those who were swallowing you up are far away.
20 *Again they say in your hearing,* 3+2
these children born during your bereavement:
This place is too small for me! 2+2
Move back and give me room!
21 *And you think in your mind:* 2+3
Who birthed these for me?
while I was bereaved and barren 3+2+3
[a]*exiled and put away*[ab]
who raised these?
If I was left alone 4+3
where did these come from?

Notes

3.a. ישראל "Israel" is missing in one MS[K]. But DSS[Isa] LXX Tg Vg support MT.

4.a. MT והבל "no purpose." DSS[Isa] ולהבל repeats the prep, which is implied in MT.

5.a. MT יאסף "be gathered." Syr Arab suggest לאסף "to gather." LXX *συναχθήσομαι* "I will be gathered" seems to have read אספף and connects it with the next line. DSS[Isa] Tg Vg support MT.

5.b. K לא "not" is followed by Vg. Q לו "to him" is supported by DSS[Isa] LXX Tg.

5.c-c. *BHS* suggests transposing to the end of v 4. Unnecessary.

5.d. Syr *ʾštbht* suggests reading *waw* consec, "so that I. . . ."

6.a. K וּנְצִירֵי adj "and protected" (BDB, 666) is supported by DSS[Isa]. Q וּנְצוּרֵי qal pass ptcp "the protected ones" (BDB, 665). *BHS* follows Syr to read וְנִצְרֵי "and the green shoots of" (BDB, 666). Tg paraphrases, as does LXX *τὴν διασπορὰν* "the *diaspora*/dispersion." Read Q.

7.a. MT לִבְזֹה prep + inf constr "to despise." A Cairo Geniza fragment has לְבֹזֶה prep + ptcp "to the one despising," supported by LXX *τὸν φαυλίζοντα* "one reviling." DSS[Isa] לבזוי qal pass ptcp "to one despised" is followed by ʼA Σ Θ Syr. Cf. Tg לדבסירין pl "to those despised." Follow DSS[Isa].

7.b. LXX Syr add a 3 masc sg suff. Driver (*JTS* 36 [1935] 401) translates "to him who despises his soul" and refers to v 4 above. The parallel is clear, but this reference contrasts the two. The action here is not reflexive but passive. Read as "despised of soul," meaning "as to soul or person," i.e., as to his birth, social standing, or status.

7.c. MT לִמְתָעֵב גּוֹי prep + ptcp can be translated "to one abhorring a nation," "to one regarding a nation as abhorrent," or "to one making a nation to be abhorrent." LXX *τὸν βδελυσσόμενον ὑπὸ τῶν ἐθνῶν* "to one abominated by the nations," Vg *ad abominatam gentem* "to a detested nation," Tg (combining this with the previous phrase) "them that are despised among the nations" all read a pass ptcp, מְתֹעַב (see BDB, 1073; *BHS*). DSS[Isa] למתעבי seems to have a pl constr as does Tg. Follow the Versions in reading a pual ptcp: "to one abhorred by a nation."

8.a. LXX[BL] *καὶ ἔπλασά σε* "and I formed you" and Tg derive MT אצרך from יצר "form," "fashion" (GKC § 71; cf. 44:12), while ʼA Σ Vg and BDB (665) derive it here and in 27:3; 42:6 from נצר "watch," "guard," "keep." (Omitted in other LXX MSS.) The form fits both roots. The parallel to נתן "appoint" suggests reading the first of these. LXX[BL] probably read a *waw* consec.

8.b. LXX suggests reading a *waw* consec.

8.c. *BHS* suggests inserting צִיָּה "dry" for metrical reasons, Not necessary.

9.a. DSS[Isa] כול הרים "all the mountains." LXX *ἐν πάσαις ταῖς ὁδοῖς* "in all roads," but in the next stich reads ἐν πάσαις ταῖς τρίβοις "in all paths." *BHS* suggests reading כל "all" here. All of these are attempts to make the parallelism more exact, which only goes to show the accuracy of MT (so Kutscher, *Isaiah Scroll,* 230–31).

11.a. LXX ὄρος is sg. Syr *ṭwr*ʾ and Tg טוריא are pl, but without the first person gen pronoun. Keep MT.

12.a. MT סינים has sometimes been translated "Chinese" (BDB, 696). DSS[Isa] סוניים (the transcription in Burrows, *Dead Sea Scrolls of St. Mark's Monastery,* plate XLI, is wrong; cf. the facsimile) supports the suggestion of Cheyne and Michaelis (BDB, 692) to read סונים "Syenites," from modern Aswan, a city on the border between Egypt and Ethiopia. Ancient translators also had trouble here: LXX Περσῶν "Persians," Tg דרומא "south." They translated by the context.

13.a. K יפצחו "let them break out." Q ופצחו "and break out" and DSS[Isa] פצחו "break out" are impv. Follow Q.

15.a. MT מֵרַחֵם prep + inf constr "from having compassion." *BHS* suggests מְרַחֵם piel ptcp "having compassion" (BDB, 933; cf. Ps 116:5). Read MT as a negative to parallel the previous stich.

15.b. On גם and concessive clauses, see GKC § 160*b*.

15.c. MT תִּשְׁכַּחְנָה qal impf 3 fem pl "they may forget." Cairo Geniza frag. תִּשָּׁכַחְנָה niph "they may be forgotten." LXX ἐπιλάθοιτο "can forget" and Vg *illa oblita fuerit* "(even if) she could forget" have a sg to match the antecedent אשה "woman." *BHS* suggests תִּשְׁכָּחֶנָּה to explain the form as *nun energicum* (cf. GKC § 58*l*) and therefore sg. Tg supports MT.

17.a. MT בָּנָיִךְ "your sons" is supported by Σ οι υιοι σου. But DSS[Isa] בוניך "your builders" is followed by ʾA οικοδομουντες σε, Θ οι οικοδομουντες and Vg *structores tui.* LXX οἰκοδομηθήσῃ "you will be built" and Tg יבנון "they will build" also point in this direction. Read בֹּנָיִךְ "your builders."

17.b. MT מְהָרְסַיִךְ piel ptcp "your destroyers" (BDB, 248). DSS[Isa] מהורסיך prep + qal act ptcp "from those destroying you." LXX ὑφ' ὧν καθηρέθης "by some of those by whom you were destroyed." Read מֵהֹרְסַיִךְ with DSS[Isa] and *BHS,* "from your destroyers," a comparison with the previous מהר "hurry": "Your builders move faster than your destroyers."

17.c. DSS[Isa] ומחריביך accents MT's pointing with a *hiriq yodh* instead of a simple *hiriq.*

18.a. LXX and Arab omit.

18.b. MT ככלה "like a bride." LXX ὡς κόσμον νύμφης "like a bride's attire" leads *BHS* to suggest reading כעדי כלה together, "like a bride's dress." But Tg Vg preserve MT's phrasing.

19.a-a. MT consists of three noun phrases without a verb: "for your desolation and your devastation and your destruction of land." Torrey suggests pointing the three words as verbs, pf 1 c sg (see *BHS*). The verse must then be seen as a conditional clause (GKC § 159*aa;* Watts, *Syntax,* 134) with perfects in the protasis and imperfects in the apodosis.

19.b. LXX omits.

21.a-a. LXX omits.

21.b. MT וסורה "and put away." DSS[Isa] וטורה could be act, "and one who turned aside," i.e., apostate. Σ Syh Vg may have read ואסורה "and one imprisoned." There is, however, no reason to change MT.

Form/Structure/Setting

There are two major breaks in the passage. The first is marked by ועתה "but now" in v 5 and by a change of speaker. The second is shown by a choral call for celebration in v 13.

The three episodes use different persons in pronouns and verbs. The first uses first and third person, except for the quotation in v 3. The second begins with first and third person verbs and pronouns, but settles into emphasis on second person masculine singular pronouns in vv 6–8 before turning to third person plural in vv 9–12. The third episode is marked by second person feminine singular pronouns addressed to Zion in vv 14–21.

Episode A (vv 1–4) has Servant Israel identify herself, recite her call to servanthood, and then complain that she has not been used in that role. The reader will recognize that she has not understood (or accepted) the call extended in 41:8–10, 43:1–7, and 44:1–5. She still covets or want to usurp the role assigned to Cyrus in 42:1–4, 44:28–45:7 and 45:13.

Melugin (*Formation,* 69) suggests that this be called "a report of the commissioning of a servant." Kaiser, Westermann, and Begrich have attempted form-critical analyses. In context the passage moves beyond a report to register a complaint, in effect a resignation of her commission as servant. Israel does not appear again in the Vision. Her place is taken by Jerusalem and later by the worshiping congregation.

Episode B (vv 5–12) presents another servant. This follows the pattern of Act VIII in which Israel and Cyrus were both called to be servants but with differing roles. Here Cyrus's successor unexpectedly appears to claim the role. This must be Darius (see *Historical Background* above) who was in fact a most unlikely and unexpected successor to Cambyses, the son of Cyrus. Ezra 4:1–2 and 5:1–15 record the role he played, after becoming king, in confirming the edict of Cyrus and ordering that work on Jerusalem's temple be resumed and completed. Most interpreters have failed to distinguish the two servant speeches in this chapter (but see J. Wash Watts, *A Survey of Old Testament Teaching* [Nashville: Broadman Press, 1947] 2:191–93 and *A Distinctive Translation of Isaiah with an Interpretative Outline* [Louisville: Jameson Press, 1979] 100). Almost no one has recognized that the scene has moved in time to a generation later than Cyrus.

The episode is complex. It begins with a mirror image of the commissioning scene (v 5) and then an expansion reflecting 42:1–4 (v 6). V 7 has been called an oracle of salvation which Melugin (143) thought was addressed to Israel. In context, however, it supports the report just given and expands it, reflecting 45:1–6 and applying it to Darius.

Vv 8–12 is a new section that has confounded form-critics (Melugin, *Formation,* 143–44). In context it further defines the servant's role in v 8 to include reconstituting the government and agrarian economy of Palestine and repopulating the land using exiles (vv 9–11).

V 13 is a choral break. Melugin (*Formation,* 144) calls it an eschatological hymn. In context it simply recognizes those who are observing Yahweh's work in this drama of redemption and invites their applause and participation. It is a signal for the readers or audience to recognize the significance of the action and dialogue, and to join in the applause.

Episode C (vv 14–21) breaks the mood by allowing another speaker a word. Zion, the recipient of God's redemptive acts through the Persian, protests that she has been and is being neglected. The tone is petulant, as of one who feels sorry for oneself.

Melugin (*Formation,* 148) recognizes that this begins a Zion-Jerusalem section that continues through 55:13 [sic]. Jacob/Israel does not appear. Melugin notes the "disputational tone." Westermann (*Forschung am alten Testament,* 164) abandons attempts at form-criticism, recognizing the dominance of longer compositions in this section. Begrich (*Studien zu Deuterojesaja,* 14–16, 26) sees three separate speeches (vv 14–21, 22–23, 24–26). This insight is correct. The second and third speech will appear in the next scene. Melugin concludes that this speech should be called a "disputational pronouncement of salvation."

The episode begins with Jerusalem's complaint of being forgotten (v 14), which is answered by a protest that this is impossible (vv 15–16). It points to the building program in progress (v 17) and to returning settlers (v 18b) to argue that the time of judgment is past (v 19a). The number of Zion's children suggests that she is now accepted and favored (vv 19b–21).

The setting for the scene is clearly in Palestine. Note the appeal to coastlands (Phoenicia and Philistia) and distant peoples on the borders of Palestine. This is confirmed by the appearance of Jerusalem in v 14.

Cambyses was in Palestine at the time of his death (see *Historical Background* above) and Darius was apparently present as his aide. A rebellion had broken out in Persia and Gaumata had already been recognized as king by several satrapies. Who at that point could have predicted that Darius would become emperor?

The year 522 B.C. was also a point of low morale among Jews in Babylon and in Jerusalem. Sheshbazzar's expedition had made little progress, perhaps because of opposition from neighboring Persian officials (Ezra 4:5).

Comment

1–4 The *coastlands* and *distant peoples* are in Palestine. They are competitors with Jews for rights in the land and favors from the Persians. Israel based her claim on Yahweh's call and her heritage from Jacob, Joshua and David. Now she feels that her position has been eroded. Yahweh has protected her in exile but has shown no signs of allowing her to reconquer Palestine as Moses, Joshua, and David did. She still yearns for that role. This speech shows no recognition that it has now been assigned to Cyrus. (See the passages about Israel's new role in chaps. 40–48.) Instead she feels neglect and lack of support which seems to make further labor useless. V 4b is not a statement of trust, but a self-serving sigh of pseudo-piety (note the reference to *reward* from 40:10b).

5–6 A second speaker makes a parallel claim to having been called by Yahweh to be his servant. The assigned role to *restore Jacob* echoes that given to Cyrus in 45:4a and 13b. Then the assignment is expanded to include being a *light to the nations*. In context this refers to the other nations of Palestine. Chaos and disorder had reigned there for most of that century. Persia had not established firm control under Cyrus. Cambyses had taken some steps in that direction in order to make Palestine a support area for his conquest of Egypt. But with his death this progress was threatened. Darius is here promised a role as a beacon light to the nations whose fate is now bound up so closely with the Persian Empire. *Salvation* is to be defined in such political and economic terms. Stable rule would in fact restore their economies and social orders. Westermann cites parallels in Psalms to show the theological relation of light to salvation.

7 As the Vision claimed that Yahweh had initiated Cyrus' rise to power in Persia in order to accomplish his purpose (41:25–26), so a generation later the One who has the redemption of Israel in his heart addresses Darius. The Vision with great temerity claims that the God of tiny Israel pulls the strings that makes emperors rise and fall!

Darius, spear-bearer to the previous emperor and only distantly related to royalty, was a most unlikely candidate for the throne. The Vision describes his low status in three phrases: *despised* as regards *soul* (בזה־נבש), referring to his personal status; *abhorred* as regards *nation or nationality* (מתעב גוי), referring either to Israel's attitude to his Persian nationality or to Persia's lack of regard for him at this point; and *servant of rulers* (עבד משלים), describing his low position as an aide to the emperor. This oracle accurately predicts the rapid, if violent, rise of Darius to power in Persia and claims credit for Yahweh who *chose* him for the office.

8 A second Yahweh oracle announces that this is an auspicious time for Darius because Yahweh is supporting him. It defines Darius's role in Palestine, and toward Jerusalem/Judah with three terms. He is to be a ברית עם "a people's covenant." The emperor is personally to be the constitutional basis by which each people will function as a people. The breakdown of authority under the Assyrians in the seventh century B.C. and under the Babylonians in the sixth century could only be brought into some sort of order by imperial authority. In fact Darius would do exactly that by bringing a uniform legal system to the entire empire as Cambyses had done in Egypt (cf. Olmstead, *History of the Persian Empire,* 119–34). In this way he provided the constitutional basis for peoplehood. A second function is to הקים ארץ "constitute a land." The parallel words, עם "people" and ארץ "land" define the elements in the situation without getting into the political details that גוי "nation" would involve. Persia, of course, would dictate the political structures and powers. The third term combines the elements of people and land in terms of the specific problem at hand: להנחיל נחלות שממות "to reassign abandoned land-rights." Two centuries of shifting sovereignties, wars, deportations, and abandonment had made establishing title to land a nightmarish impossibility. Only by the application of a sovereign *fiat de novo* could order be restored to the system of village cultivation in the fields which a healthy economy needed.

9 These steps would mean that released captives and returned exiles would have a place to go and an opportunity for livelihood with legal rights to homestead ancient areas without being harassed by other claimants to the land (cf. Ezra 4:1–4).

10 The metaphor in v 9b pictured the people as a flock of sheep. It follows that Yahweh (and, by appointment, Darius) is pictured as a benevolent and compassionate shepherd (cf. 40:11).

11–12 The metaphor changes to focus more directly on God and his work. He builds *highways* for his people, even over difficult terrain, so that they can return to Zion. These are not necessarily migrants. Increasingly through the Vision they are seen as pilgrims on their way to Zion for festal worship in terms of 2:2–4 and 66:18–21.

Seaward from Palestine means "from the west." *The land of the Syenites* (see n. 12.a) probably stands for Aswan in Egypt. It fits the context in designating the far south.

13 The audience is made aware that the persons on the elevated stage include Yahweh, his spokesmen, Heavens and Earth. These latter spectator-witnesses are called upon to applaud Yahweh's acts on behalf of his people and his city. *Heavens, Earth,* and *Mountains* have been addressed at various times in the Vision from 1:2 on.

14 Attention is now drawn to the earthly scene. Zion speaks. Apparently ignoring the developments of vv 1–13, she complains that *Yahweh has forsaken* her. The figure is that of a wife or lover who feels abandonment. She concentrates on the implied wrongs done here in Nebuchadnezzar's invasions of 598 and 587 B.C. and the intervening decades. The complaint ignores the thrust of the Vision's presentation that Yahweh had called on exiles to be messengers of good news to Zion (40:1–11) some twenty-five years before, that the rise of Cyrus was directly related to Yahweh's plan to rebuild Jerusalem (44:28b; 45:13b), and that Yahweh had inspired the edict of Cyrus and the expedition of Sheshbazzar in the previous decade (48:20 and Ezra 1:1–8). The complaint may have been partly justified in that Sheshbazzar had apparently accomplished very little and that exilic Israel had, by her own admission (49:4), been ineffective in doing her assigned work.

15–16 Yahweh emphasizes his continued concern and *compassion* by using a comparison with a nursing mother and insisting that his regard and intention is even more certain and sure. Jerusalem is *engraved on his palms,* that is, cut into his very flesh, thus constantly, unendingly, on his mind. The particular issue of rebuilding *her walls* (cf. 44:28b and 45:13b) is constantly (תמיד) on his agenda.

17 The practical matter of slow progress in building comes up. Of course, there are opponents to be dealt with. These *destroyers* and *devastators* would include neighboring brigands from Edom (Obad 5) and surrounding areas who regularly pillaged the defenseless city. They include enemies among governors and leaders of neighboring provinces (Ezra 4:1–4). Similar adversaries in succeeding periods are called by name in Ezra and Nehemiah. But Yahweh insists that the builders (Sheshbazzar, Zerubbabel and their helpers) are one step ahead of their opponents. The account in Ezra supports this assessment.

18 Zion is challenged to recognize that some have already returned, presumably with Sheshbazzar. Yahweh swears that Zion will come to see them as a *bride's trousseau,* symbol of her new status and acceptance by God.

19 The judgment that had befallen Jerusalem, summarizing her experiences from the seventh century to her destruction in 587 B.C. is described in three words: *struck, wasted,* and *destroyed.* Yahweh had done each of these himself. The Assyrians and Babylonians were simply instruments of his wrath (cf. 10:5). But these belonged to the former times. Now things have changed in this favorable period of grace. But Jerusalem has failed to notice the difference. The city's growth is cited as an unmistakable sign of Yahweh's grace. This theme continues through v 21. But the figure is changed. She is shown to be Yahweh's beloved wife, no longer abandoned, in that she has borne so many children.

Explanation

This scene develops the servant motifs and shifts attention from the Jews in Babylon to Jerusalem and its people. The claims that Babylonian Jews are to be recognized as the true Israel, heirs to Jacob's heritage, are ended by confessions of frustration and failure (vv 1–4). This servant role will have to be assumed by someone else.

Cyrus's servant role is promised to and assumed by Darius. His task is defined in terms of restoring political and economic order in Palestine in addition to Cyrus's tasks of rebuilding the temple and restoring Jewish rights to return to Jerusalem (vv 5–12).

God's program to comfort and restore Jerusalem (40:1–11) is on schedule in spite of the refusal of Babylonian Jews to accept their role. But Jerusalem complains and Yahweh tries to assuage her feelings of having been abandoned.

Scene 2: Even the Captive of a Champion (49:22–50:3)

Bibliography

Dahood, M. "Textual Problems in Isaiah." *CBQ* 22 (1960) 404–6. **Grether, H. G.** "Translating the Questions in Isaiah 50." *BT* 24 (1973) 240–43.

Translation

Herald: 49:22 *Thus says* [a]*Lord Yahweh:*[a] 3
Yahweh: (to Jerusalem) *See! I raise my hand toward nations* 4+3
and toward peoples I lift my signal
that they bring your (fem) sons in their bosom-fold[b] 3+3
and that your (fem) daughters be carried on a shoulder.
23 *Kings will be your (fem) patrons* 3+2
and their queens your (fem) wet nurses.
Faces to the land,[a] *they will bow to you (fem)* 4+3
and the dust of your (fem) feet they will lick.[b]
And you (fem) will know that I am Yahweh, 3+3
[c]*I in whom those waiting will never be disappointed.*[c]
Jerusalem: 24 *Can booty be taken away from a champion?* 3+3
If a captivity be legitimate,[a] *can one be rescued?*
Herald: 25 *Indeed! Thus says Yahweh:* 3+3+3
Yahweh: *Even the captive of a champion can be taken!*
And the prey of a terrorist can be rescued!
I will personally struggle with the one struggling with you (fem)[a] 3+3
and I will personally save your (fem) children.
26 *And I will make your (fem) oppressors devour their own flesh.* 3+3
And they will be drunk (from) from their own blood as from wine.

And all flesh will know 2+2
that I am Yahweh,
your (fem) Savior and your (fem) redeemer, 2+2
Mighty One of Jacob!
Herald: 50:1 *Thus says Yahweh:* 3
Yahweh: *Where is this writ* 3+2+2
of your (pl) mother's divorce
with which I sent her away?
Or who is the one of my creditors 3+3
to whom I sold you (pl)?
See! You (pl) were sold[a] *because of your (pl)*
transgressions. 3+3
And because of your (pl) own rebellions
your (pl) mother was sent away.
2 *Why, when I came, was there no one there?* 4+3
I called, but no one answered.
Is my hand altogether too short to ransom?[a] 4+3
Or is there in me no power to rescue?
See! By my rebuke I dried up a sea! 4+3
I make rivers become a desert!
Their fish rotted from lack of water, 4+2
and died[b] *because of thirst!*
3 *I clothe heavens with darkness* 3+3
and I make sackcloth their covering.

Notes

22.a-a. DSS^{Isa} LXX omit אדני "Lord." Tg reads יהוה אלהים. Such variants in the divine titles are common. Stay with MT.

22.b. MT חצן is an obscure word (BDB, 346) occurring elsewhere only in Ps 129:7 and Neh 5:13. It is usually translated "bosom" or "fold" in a garment.

23.a. MT אפים ארץ, lit., "faces a land." LXX ἐπὶ πρόσωπον τῆς γῆς "on the face of the earth." Tg על אפיהון על ארעא "with their faces to the ground." The words are not in constr relation. "Faces" and "land" stand side by side with no grammatical signals concerning their relation. Either of the meanings chosen by LXX and Tg may be intended.

23.b. Cf. Ps 72:9; Mic 7:17.

23.c-c. MT אשר לא יבשו קוי, lit., "who they are not ashamed those waiting on me," creates problems for syntax. The antecedent and relative pron for אשר "who" is unclear. The word order is confusing. LXX^{BL} ουκ αισχυνθησονται οι υπομενοντες "those waiting for me will not be shamed." Tg interprets דלא יבהתון צדיקיא דמסברין לפרקני "that the righteous who wait for my salvation shall not be ashamed." Read אני יהוה "I Yahweh," which is picked up in the final pronom suff, as antecedent for אשר "who": "I in whom those waiting will never be disappointed/ashamed."

24.a. צדיק "right" or "legitimate." DSS^{Isa} עריץ "awe-inspiring" (BDB, 792), i.e., "a captive of an awesome one" (see v 25a). Syr and Vg support this reading. LXX ἀδίκως "unjustly." Tg דשבו זכאין "one which the righteous have captured." Read MT.

25.a. MT יריבך "your adversary." Some MSS and Vg יריביך "your adversaries." Other MSS and LXX Syr Tg read ריבך "your dispute," as did DSS^{Isa} originally, which was later corrected to ריביך pl (or רוביך; see Kutscher, *Isaiah Scroll,* 384). Kutscher points out that in the other occurrences of יריב (Ps 35:1; Jer 18:19), the MSS and the Versions also try to read ריב. Stay with MT.

50:1.a. Z. W. Falk ("Hebrew Legal Terms: II," *JSS* 12 [1967] 242–43), followed by Whybray, argues that מכר "sell" can also mean "hand over," "transfer" without money changing hands. This fits the second occurrence of the word, but in the context of "creditors" obviously not the first.

2.a. יָדִי מִפְּדוּת, lit., "my hand for ransom" (noun: BDB, 804). LXX *τοῦ ῥύσασθαι* "to redeem" preceded by a negative interrogative particle, Tg אתקפדת גבורתי מלמפרק "is my might shortened that it cannot save?" and Vg *redimere* "to redeem" lead *BHS* to suggest reading מִפְּדוֹת inf constr "from ransoming." Follow *BHS* and the Versions.

2.b. *BHS* suggests inserting בְּהֶמְתָּם "their cattle," i.e., the sea creatures, presumably for more balanced meter. This is unnecessary.

Form/Structure/Setting

This short dialogue between Yahweh and Jerusalem begins with Yahweh's announcement (vv 22–23). It is interrupted by Jerusalem's incredulous questions (v 24). Yahweh responds in vv 25–26. Then he takes the initiative in 50:1–3 to challenge Jerusalem on the earlier complaint of abandonment (49:14).

Melugin (*Formation,* 151) calls vv 22–23 "an announcement of salvation" followed by a statement of Yahweh's purpose in deliverance. Vv 24–26 continue the disputation. But he has no satisfactory category for 50:2b–3.

The scene is built around three Yahweh speeches:

Vv 22–23 present a salvation statement addressed to Jerusalem as a city in 2nd person feminine singular. It announces a decision to return former inhabitants to the city and its surroundings.

Vv 24–26 present a challenge and response. Jerusalem questions whether the exiles' return is possible. Yahweh assures her that it can and will be accomplished.

Vv 1–3 issue a counter challenge in three questions and answers addressed to Jerusalem's people (2 masc pl). The questions are: where? (v1), why? (v 2), is? (v 2b). Yahweh answers each of his own questions.

Comment

22 In earlier times of judgment (5:26; 7:18; 13:2) Yahweh's signal brought nations to invade with the resultant destruction. Now in a period of favor and blessing, with the Persian emperor as her parton, countries around Jerusalem may be ordered to aid the pilgrimage of Jews and the restoration of the Temple (cf. Ezra 1:4; 3:7).

23 Jerusalem's restoration is not an end in itself. It will serve to spread the knowledge of Yahweh and will witness to the valid form of faith: *waiting* on Yahweh.

24 Jerusalem, however, continues to think in terms of confrontation with Persia. For their own success to be accomplished the Israelites think Persia must be defeated. They wonder how these things can become reality unless someone breaks the empire's hold on them. This is the ultimate question for every unspiritual or unbelieving person for whom strength and power are everything.

25 Yahweh's plans are more subtle. He is using Persia to accomplish his will. He is not confrontational. Thus, for him all these things are possible within the framework of empire. God can accomplish his purposes in many ways. To Zerubbabel Yahweh said, "Not by might nor by power, but by my Spirit" (Zech 4:6). Jesus spoke of faith that moves mountains (Matt 17:20/Luke 17:6).

26 *Devour their own flesh* and *be drunk from their own blood* are metaphors meaning "are reduced to their last extremity" (cf. M. Dahood, *CBQ* 22 [1960] 404–5).

50:1 Yahweh again takes up the complaint that he had abandoned Jerusalem (cf. 49:14). He demands proof, using the metaphor of Zion as his wife. The present generation is seen as her children (cf. 49:18–21). The charge of estrangement or divorce requires proof. Where is it? There was a separation, all right, but it was all due to their sins. *Rebellions* has a dual sense. It refers to rejection of God and of God's way of life. But it also had a political sense in their refusal to accept Assyrian rule during the reigns of Hezekiah and Josiah and more recently in those elements of Judaism that conspired against Persian rule. These were the direct causes of exile and dispersion, says Yahweh.

2–3 Yahweh's charge that they had been unresponsive reflects a major motif through the entire Vision (cf. 29:16; 30:12–18; 63:5; 65:1–5). It is Yahweh's turn to show unbelief. He cannot believe that anyone would think that past events of judgment and exile meant that he was impotent, unable to do anything about them. He cites his mighty acts of old to refute any such suggestion.

Explanation

The scene focuses on Yahweh and Jerusalem. It picks up both Yahweh's determination to move ahead with restoration and Jerusalem's skepticism that this is possible. She shows neither faith nor knowledge—no sign that she has heard or understood anything about God's plan for her redemption.

The Lord of all the earth and all history finds little or no faith among his own people in his own city. Jesus encountered a similar situation centuries later (Luke 18:8).

Scene 3: A Student's Tongue (50:4–51:8)

Bibliography

Beuken, W. A. M. "Jes 50, 10–11: Eine kultische Paränese zur dritten Ebedprophetie." *ZAW* 85 (1973) 168–82. **Corney, R. W.** "Isaiah L, 10." *VT* 26 (1976) 497–98. **Holmgren, F.** "Chiastic Structure in Isaiah LI, 1–11." *VT* 19 (1969) 196–201. **Kuntz, J. K.** "The Contribution of Rhetorical Criticism to Understanding Isaiah 51:1–16." *Art and Meaning.* JSOTSup 19. Sheffield: U. of Sheffield, 1982. 140–71. **Leene, H.** *De stem van de knecht als metafoor: Beschouwingen over de compositie van Jesaia 50.* Kampen: Kok, 1980. **Lindsey, F. D.** "Isaiah's Songs of the Servant, Part 3: The Commitment of the Servant in Isaiah 50:4–11." *BSac* 139 (1982) 216–29. **Lugt, P. van der.** "De strofische structuur van het derde knechtslied (Jes. 50,4–11)." *De Knecht.* FS J. L. Koole. Kampen: Kok, 1978. **Maggioni, B.** "Le troisième chant du Serviteur Yahvé, Is 50,4–9a." *AsSeign* 19 (1971) 28–37. **Morgenstern, J.** "Isaiah 50:4–9a." *HUCA* 31 (1960) 20–22. **Schwarz,**

G. "Jesaja 50,4–5a: Eine Emendation." *ZAW* 85 (1973) 356–57. **Uchelen, N. A. van.** "Abraham als Felsen (Jes. 51:1)." *ZAW* 80 (1968) 183–191. **Yalon, H.** "לדעת לעות את יעף דבר (Isa 50:4)." *Leš* 30 (1966) 248–49.

Translation

Persecuted Expedition Leader: 50:4 *My Lord*[a] *Yahweh has assigned me* 4+2
a student's[b] *tongue*
to know how to sustain[c] *a weary one*[d] *(with) a word.*[e] 4
He wakes up[f] *morning by morning*[g]*—* 3+3+2
he wakes up my ear
to listen as students[b] *do.*
5 [a]*My Lord Yahweh has opened my ear.*[a] 4+3+3
And I, on my part, have not been rebellious.
I have not turned my back (to him).
6 *I gave my back to ones who beat me* 3+2
and my cheeks to those who plucked them bare.[a]
I did not hide[b] *my face* 3+2
from insult and spitting.
7 *And my Lord Yahweh gives me help.* 3+3
Therefore I have not been insulted.
Therefore I have set my face like a flint 4+3
and I know that I shall not be shamed.
8 *My Vindicator is near.* 2+2+2
Who dares contend with me?
Let us stand up together!
Who wants to be master of my case? 3+2
Let him approach me!
9 *See! My Lord Yahweh gives me help.* 4+2
Who would accuse me of wrongdoing?
See! All of them are like a garment that wears out. 4+2
A moth can devour them.

Darius: 10 *Who among you fears Yahweh,* 4+3
heeding[a] *his servant's voice?*
Anyone who has walked (in) dark places 3+3
where there is no light
should trust in Yahweh's name 3+2
and rely on his God.
11 *See! All of you who kindle a fire,* 4+2
tying up[a] *torches,*
walk in the flame[b] *of your fire* 3+2
and in the torches you have kindled.
This will be yours from my hand! 3+2
You lie down for torture!
51:1 *Listen to me,* 2+2+2
you who pursue right,
you seekers of Yahweh!
Look to a rock (from which) you were cut out[a] 3+3

and to the quarry-cut[b] *(from which) you were dug.*[c]
2 *Look to Abraham, your father,* 3+2
and to Sarah who gave you birth.
Yahweh: *For he was only one when I called him.* 3+2
Then I made him fruitful[a] *and multiplied him.*
Heavens: 3 *For Yahweh comforts Zion!* 3+2
He comforts all her desolation!
Earth: *When he makes*[a] *her wilderness to be like Eden* 3+3
and her steps like Yahweh's garden,
joy and gladness will be found in her 4+3
and thanksgiving and the sound of song.
Darius: 4 *Pay attention to me, my people,*[a] 3+3
and give ear to me, my people.[b]
For law goes out from me. 4+4
And I make my justice flash[c] *for light (over) peoples.*
5 *My right*[a] *is near.*[b] 2+2+3
My salvation has gone out.
and my arms judge peoples.
Coastlands look toward me eagerly 3+2
and hope for my arm.
6 *Lift up your eyes to the heavens* 3+3
and look to the land beneath.
For the heavens are grey[a] *like smoke* 3+3+3
and the land wears like a garment
and its inhabitants die [b]*like a gnat.*[b]
But my deliverance is for an age, 3+3
and my right will not set (like the sun).[c]
7 *Listen to me,* 2+2+3
you who know right,
people with my law in their hearts.
Do not fear human reproach 3+2
or be dismayed by their revilings.
8 *For a moth could devour them like a garment* 4+3
or a worm devour them[a] *like wool.*
But my right will be for an age 3+3
and my deliverance for a generation of generations.

Notes

4.a. Those who pronounce "Yahweh" as *Adonai* "Lord" have a problem here and in vv 5, 7, 9, with the repetition. Some LXX MSS repeat *κυριος κυριος* "Lord Lord" as did Luther. Cf. 49:22.

4.b. למודים, lit., "of ones who are taught." Tg "them that teach."

4.c. לעות is a *hap. leg.* BDB (736) calls its meaning "very dubious." There have been many attempts to emend, but none are satisfactory. *BHS* lists לְרְעֹת "to teach" (Klostermann and Cheyne), לְעַוֹּת or לְעַוֵּת "to bend" (BDB, 736). The usual way out is to translate from context as "to help," "to sustain."

4.d. MT יָעֵף adj "a weary one" (BDB, 419; cf. 40:29 and the uses of the verb in 40:28, 30, and 44:12). Cairo Geniza frag. יעוף is the qal inf constr of the verb.

4.e. דבר "a word" stands alone in the sentence without connection. It is best understood as an adverbial usage, "with or by a word." Tg paraphrases, "how to teach wisdom to the righteous who long (lit., faint) for the words of his law." LXX ἡνίκα δεῖ εἰπεῖν λόγον "when it is necessary to speak a word." LXX takes לעות as the denominative verb from עת "time."

4.f. *BHS* recommends deletion because it is repeated in the next line. But if the Masoretic division of the verse is maintained, the repetition for emphasis makes good sense.

4.g. LXX OL Eth omit the second "morning."

5.a-a. *BHS* suggests this is a later addition. But the line fits and should be kept.

6.a. MT למרטים "to those making bare" (BDB, 598). For a violent sense, cf. Ezra 9:3; Neh 13:25. On DSS[Isa] למטלים, see Kutscher, *Isaiah Scroll,* 255–56.

6.b. MT הסתרתי "I hid" (BDB, 711) is supported by Tg. DSS[Isa] הסירותי hiph pf from סור "turn away" (BDB, 694) is supported by LXX ἀπέστρεψα and Syr *ʾpnyt.* Kutscher (*Isaiah Scroll,* 268) points out that LXX and Syr usually translate this way in Isaiah. Stay with MT. See S. E. Balentine, *The Hidden God* (Oxford: Oxford Univ. Press, 1983), 17, who cites Dahood's theory of an infixed ה.

10.a. MT שמע "listening." LXX ἀκουσάτω "let him hear" suggests ישמע. Tg דשמע "to hear" suggests לשמע. DSS[Isa] supports MT. Read MT.

11.a. MT מְאַזְּרֵי piel ptcp constr "girding," "preparing" from אזר (BDB, 25). *BHS* cites Syr in suggesting מְאִרֵי hiph ptcp constr "lighting" from אור. LXX κατισχύετε "you overpower." Tg מתקפי חרב "lay hold of a sword" follows the meaning "to gird" and emends the following word to fit. The translations struggle with two words that do not easily go together, but all attest the same text. Read MT.

11.b. MT בְּאוּר "by the flame of" occurs otherwise only in 31:9; 44:16; 47:14; and Ezek 5:2 (BDB, 22). LXX τῷ φωτὶ "in the light," supported by Syr and Vg, suggests בְּאוֹר (cf. *BHS*) "in the light of." Read MT.

51:1.a. MT חצבתם "you were cut" (BDB, 345) appears only here in pual. LXX ἣν ἐλατομήσατε "which you have cut," active. Tg paraphrases in passive. Read MT.

1.b. Syr omits.

1.c. MT's pual is again unique. LXX is active. See n. 1.a.

2.a. MT ואברכהו "I blessed him." DSS[Isa] ואפרהו "I make him fruitful" (BDB, 826). Either reading is possible. LXX Tg Syr Vg support MT. Both words appear elsewhere with רבה "multiply" (Kutscher, *Isaiah Scroll,* 275–76).

3.a. MT וַיָּשֶׂם "so that he establishes." LXX καὶ θήσω "I will make." Tg וישוי and Vg *et ponet* "and he makes." *BHS* suggests changing ַ to ָ. That is unnecessary.

4.a. Some MSS and Syr read עמים "peoples." But LXX λαός μου "my people" supports MT, as do DSS[Isa] Tg Vg.

4.b. Some MSS and Syr read pl abs for MT's sg constr with suff. LXX οἱ βασιλεῖς "the kings" goes its own way. DSS[Isa] Vg support MT, as does Tg כנשתי "my congregation." *BHS,* Elliger (525), and others follow Syr in both cases because of the pl verbs. But these are explained by the collective sense of the nouns.

4.c. ארגיע may have either of two meanings (BDB, 920–21): I, "disturb" (cf. 51:15); II, "be at rest" (cf. Jer 50:34). Hiph occurs in both words. A related noun refers to a moment in time. The denominative verb would mean "shine for a moment" or "twinkle for a moment." Several interpreters (Marti, Cheyne, Bachmann, Elliger [525–26]; cf. *BHS*) join the word in this sense to the following verse, as apparently LXX ταχὺ "speedily" and Σ do. MT is the more difficult reading. Driver (*JTS* 36 [1935] 401) follows Arab *rgʿ* to suggest a happy translation: "I will make flash for a light of the peoples" (cf. NEB). Despite Elliger's complaints about the meter (526), this seems the best solution.

5.a. LXX[BLS] and others add ὡς (εις) φῶς "as light."

5.b. LXX ἐγγίζει "draws near" suggests a finite verb for MT's adj. *BHS* suggests קָרַב qal pf or אַקְרִיב hiph impf. But MT makes sense with an implied verb "to be."

6.a. G. R. Driver (*JTS* 36 [1935] 401–2) explains מלח as a denominative from מלח "salt" (BDB, 571 III). He uses a secondary sense from Arab *mlḥ* to mean "being grey," the color of evaporated salt from the Dead Sea. He translates "the heavens are murky like smoke."

6.b-b. MT כמו־כן "like a gnat" (BDB, 487) or "like this," i.e., like nothing (BDB, 486 § 3*c*). 1QIsa[b] כמוכן may be related to Arab *makin* (Whybray), so "like a locust." DSS[Isa] supports MT.

6.c. MT תחת is usually derived from חתת "shatter," "break" (BDB, 369). LXX ἐκλίπῃ, Tg תתעכב, and Vg *deficiet* seem to have read תחדל "will fail" (*BHS*). Driver (*JTS* 36 [1935] 402) suggests deriving תחת from נחת "go down," "descend" (BDB, 639), metaphorically of the sun "set."

8.a. MT יאכלם "devour them" appears twice, supported both times by DSS^{Isa} LXX. Tg translates the second as דאחיד "seizes." Vg translates with different synonyms. *BHS* suggests יכלם from כלה "complete," "finish" with reference to Jer 10:25 to eliminate the duplication.

Form/Structure/Setting

The smaller units in this scene have been identified by form-critics (see Melugin, *Formation* 152). They build an arch.

A 50:4–9: A speech by a beleaguered teacher shows his determination to follow Yahwah's course. He expects his vindicator to appear momentarily. He condemns his opponents for their lack of substance and permanence.

B 50:10–11: Darius appears to vindicate him, appealing to all who trust Yahweh that he, Darius, was Yahweh's choice (cf. 49:5–7) and threatening rebels with a dose of their own medicine.

C 51:1–2a: A second speech by Darius appeals to those in Jerusalem who seek a legitimate government at the same time that they seek Yahweh. He calls on them to look to Yahweh.

KEYSTONE 51:2b–3a: Yahweh supports and expands the reference to Abraham. His spokesman applies the word to Zion.

C′ 51:3b-c: Yahweh's spokesmen expand ecstatically on the announcement.

B′ 51:4–6: Darius addresses the people who are loyal to Persian rule and to his claims to the throne, promising them legitimacy, deliverance, and justice based on law. He emphasizes the promise of permanence in a rule of law.

A′ 51:7–8: Darius' fourth speech is addressed to those who recognize him as the legitimate ruler and who are loyal to his law. He calls them to stand firm against opposition which he claims to be transitory while his rule promises permanence.

50:4–9 is one of the so-called "servant songs." (See *Excursus: The Sufferer/Martyr.*) Melugin (*Formation,* 71–73, 152) considers the passage to be "an imitation of a psalm of confidence." Begrich (*Studien* 54–55) called it a lament by an individual with vv 4–6 representing his complaint. O. Kaiser (*Der Königliche Knecht* [Göttingen: Vandenhoeck & Ruprecht, 1959] 67–69), Westermann (183–84), and Elliger (*Deuterojesaja* 34) call it a psalm of confidence. Melugin calls attention to parallels in Jeremiah's confessions.

The passage does not use the word "servant." The speaker is different from the major servant figures in the Vision, such as Israel, Cyrus, or the worshipers in Jerusalem. The speaker is more like the leader heard in 48:16 and in 62:1–3. He is in the same category as the speaker in 48:20; 57:14; 62:6; and, of course, the one described in 53:1–12. If this role is to be thought of as a "servant role," it must be carefully distinguished from the explicit references to Israel and Cyrus. This speaker is Darius's advocate and defender in Jerusalem. He is also to be identified as a leader in the movement to restore the Temple.

50:10–11 is clearly of a different genre. The vindicator appears and speaks in an arrogant and sarcastic tone. He identifies himself as Yahweh's servant and reprimands the people for their lack of faith. He then threatens to punish the rebels.

Melugin (*Formation,* 156) breaks 51:1–8 into three speeches because of the introductory formulas (following Gressmann, "Die literarische Analyse Deuterojesajas," *ZAW* 34 [1914] 264; Begrich, *Studien,* 13, 20, 50; von Waldow, *Anlass und Hintergrund,* 36; but against the arguments for unity by Mowinckel, "Die Komposition des deuterojesanischen Buches," *ZAW* 49 [1931] 108; Köhler, *Deuterojesaja,* 108; and Fohrer, III, 141). 51:1–3 is called a disputation text by Begrich and von Waldow. Melugin (157) recognizes an element of a salvation speech in v 3 and suggests that there is a combination of genres here. 51:4–5 is a new speech. He calls v 5 an announcement of salvation separate from v 6, but the themes of right, salvation, justice and law unite the three verses. 51:7–8 opens, as the previous two speeches have, with calls for attention. Again the genres are mixed. Form criticism is hampered in its attempts to analyze such a passage where dramatic requirements overrule the usual strictures of form. The scene introduces a beleaguered leader in Jerusalem and has Darius appear to support him, to announce his program, and to warn against rebellion.

The historical background is to be found in Jerusalem in 522 B.C. Cambyses is dead. Gaumata has proclaimed himself emperor and been recognized as such in Mesopotamia and the eastern parts of the empire. Darius has taken command of Cambyses' army in Palestine, and he is taking steps to consolidate control of that area and of Egypt, which they had just left. This scene portrays his moves as they apply to Jerusalem and to Judah.

Ezra 3:2 speaks of Zerubbabel as the Jewish leader in Jerusalem. Ezra 2:2 lists him as one of a group returning to Jerusalem, apparently in a later expedition than that of Sheshbazzar. Opposition from neighboring peoples is recorded in Ezra 3:3. Further opposition involving Zerubbabel is recorded in Ezra 4:1–5.

The yearning for order and permanence permeates the scene. The lack of it in the opposition is noted in 50:9b. The reference to "a rock" in 51:1b picks up the theme. It is continued with references to permanence in vv 6 and 8. Darius promises that his program of law and justice will provide the permanence that they long for. History records that one of the great contributions of Darius's long reign was the promulgation of an extensive code of law for the entire empire (cf. Olmstead, *History of the Persian Empire,* 119–34).

Excursus: Parties in Palestinian Judaism

Bibliography

Achtemeier, E. *The Community and Message.* 17–26. **Blenkinsopp, J.** *A History of Prophecy in Israel.* 225–51. **Hanson, P. D.** *The Dawn of Apocalyptic.* 32–279. **Meyers, E. M.** "The Persian Period and the Judean Restoration: From Zerubabbel to Nehemiah." FS F. M. Cross, Jr. **Miller, J. M. and J. H. Hayes.** *A History of Ancient Israel and Judah.* Philadelphia: Westminster, 1986. 437–75. **Peterson, D. L.** *Late*

Israelite Prophecy. Missoula, MT: Scholars Press, 1977. 26–27. **Plöger, O.** *Theocracy and Eschatology*. Tr. S. Rudman. Richmond: John Knox, 1968. **Rofe, A.** "Isaiah 66:1–4: Judean Sects in the Persian Period as Viewed by Trito-Isaiah." *Biblical and Related Studies Presented to Samuel Iwry*. Ed. A. Kort and S. Morschauer. Winona Lake, IN: Eisenbrauns, 1985. 205–18. **Simon, M.** *Jewish Sects at the Time of Jesus*. Trans. J. H. Farley. Philadelphia: Fortress, 1967. **Smith, M.** *Palestinian Parties and Politics That Shaped the Old Testament*. New York: Columbia U. P., 1971. **Steck, O. H.** "Deuterojesaja als theologischer Denker." *KD* 15 (1969) 280–93. **Talmon, S.** "Return to Zion—Consequences for Our Future." *Cathedra* 4 (1977) 29 (Heb.). **Wolff, H. W.** *Joel*. Hermeneia. Philadelphia: Fortress, 1977.

The books cited above show the current tendency to interpret exilic and post-exilic writings against a background of party strife among Jews. The sectarian divisions that Simon catalogs for first-century Jews and that have been endemic to Christian communities throughout their history make this understandable and believable.

Morton Smith sees at least three parties in post-exilic Jerusalem: a local party with a syncretistic cult who had been given land by Nebuchadnezzar, sometimes called the עם הארץ, "the people of the land"; a second Yahweh-only party, adherents of Deuteronomy who sacrificed only in Jerusalem, most of whom had returned from Mesopotamia; and a third group who were priests returned from Mesopotamia. (This group has an economic interest in restoration. Some are Yahweh-only while others are syncretists.) Plöger thinks of two parties—the eschatologists following Daniel, and Deutero-Isaiah—while Hanson's two parties are prophetic visionaries (powerless and eschatological) and the hierocracy (the priests who control the cult and the political community). Rofe thinks of two parties that are fairly clearly delineated in Trito-Isaiah and in Ezra-Nehemiah.

Steck, Wolff, and Peterson think more in terms of theological streams in which certain books of the Old Testament have primary authority. Peterson (97–100) proposes a development in three stages: first, views of prophets who depend on Deuteronomy; second, views of prophets who follow Jeremiah and Ezekiel; and finally, prophets who follow the Chronicler, and Levites like Asaph and Korah and those represented in Isaiah and the Twelve Prophets.

The Vision of Isaiah does not name parties. But it pictures the entire exilic and post-exilic experience as one of polarization and strife. Chaps. 40–44 show the Mesopotamian Jewish community as reluctant to respond to Yahweh's call to "comfort Jerusalem." Chaps. 45–48 show the same reluctance to recognize in Cyrus' ascendancy a new opportunity for the restoration of the city, despite the fact that an expedition under Sheshbazzar did actually leave for Jerusalem (chap. 48). There are many suggestions in these chapters concerning the spiritual state of the exiles, but little that would help to define Jewish parties in Babylon except that a small minority may be assumed to support Yahweh's appeal while the great majority were apathetic or closed to his appeal, being more impressed by the imperial idolatry of the great city. This goal is dismissed in the Vision by their own statement of resignation in 49:1–4.

Then the scene changes to Jerusalem. Here disunity, persecution, and violence are apparent in addition to powerful emotion in the argument from chaps. 49–52. Darius was a controversial leader who had trouble establishing his right to rule. The plans of Zerubbabel around the year 520 B.C. raised emotional and deep feelings. The issues polarized the people. Some approved Zerubbabel's use of partisan Persian politics (support of Darius) for the purpose of gaining Persian patronage for the restoration of the Temple and the Temple cult in Jerusalem.

They would hold Darius to his promise and that of Cyrus to make Jerusalem a Temple city sponsored and protected by imperial funds and power. Opposition is fierce and violent from a group that includes landholders in Jerusalem and neighboring areas who fear that land-grant deeds given by Nebuchadnezzar might be superseded by grants under Darius and who fear that the restoration of the Temple under Persian sponsorship might give control of the Temple cult to priests and Levites returning from Babylon. But these groups, polarized on this issue, probably contain several small "parties" or interest groups on each side.

The polarization becomes clearer in the period that follows the restoration of the Temple cult (chaps. 53–57). One group is strong in its appeal for the growth of Jerusalem (chap. 54) and for open worship in which everyone who "seeks Yahweh" is welcome (54:17c–56:8). But it is opposed by those willing to use violence and terror to keep their privileges and limit access to the cult and to cult-service. The vision does not name the parties concerned. The second group is likely to be Smith's "local party" with its connection with jealous neighbors in Samaria and Ammon. It may also include the entrenched local priests (Zadokite?) who resent the return of priests and Levites from Babylon. These are accused of illegitimacy and paganism (57:3–10), of idolatry and apostasy. The opposing open party includes those who follow Zerubbabel's dream toward a Temple city, open to Yahweh-worshipers from all over the empire.

The division and definition of the opposing groups becomes clearer in chapters 58–61. The period is that of the rise of Artaxerxes and of the returns of Ezra and Nehemiah. Opposing groups are accused of rebellion (58:1), of worship with no regard for justice (58:2–12), and of breaking the Sabbath (58:13). The land-owning groups oppress those not so privileged, which undoubtedly include many who have returned from Babylon. They are further denounced in chap. 59 and the breach between the groups appears to have become deeper. Chaps. 60–61 show the renewed interest that the Persian emperor has in Jerusalem (for political and military reasons, no doubt) and his willingness to renew its status as a Temple city. With this political clout, order is restored to the city, the walls are rebuilt, and the cult is given a legal order. Ezra and Nehemiah establish the position of Levites as well as all qualified priests in the Temple, prohibit marriage to foreigners, and establish a strict rule of Sabbath observance.

The final chapters (62–66) show that the old strife between the parties has not been eliminated. There are those who still will not accept the patronage of the Persian emperor and who yearn for the old days of autonomy (chaps. 63–64). Yahweh (and the party representing the prophetic views of the Vision) will not tolerate this group and move to cut them off from the Temple worship. They are accused of pagan practices (65:2–4, 7, 11–12; 66:3–4), of violence against legitimate worshipers (66:5b–6), and of becoming an abhorrence to all worshipers (66:24). The group that the Vision represents claims control of an open cult with priests coming from many places for anyone "who is humble and contrite in spirit and who trembles at God's word."

The Vision is clearly a partisan book claiming lineage to the Prophets and to the Pentateuch. It approves of Deuteronomy, but moves beyond it. It claims Yahweh's sovereignty over the empires and gladly allows him to use the empire, its treasure, and its power to restore Jerusalem and provide order for it.

The victory which the Vision celebrates is neither as complete in history nor as final as it indicates. Jerusalem will be invaded and sacked numerous times before its final destruction in A.D. 70. Parties would continue to proliferate in Judaism with numerous schisms, like that from which the Samaritans came a few decades after the Vision was written. But the main lines of the Vision were formative for

Judaism and for Christianity, and the lines along which parties could be distinguished as God's chosen, or his enemies, continue to be very much the same.

Comment

4 For the third time in this act someone speaks of a task assigned by Yahweh. In 49:1–4 Israel claimed the title of עבד "servant." In 49:5–7 a second person, which this commentary identifies as Darius, claims that distinction. Now a third speaker claims to have been assigned (נתן, lit., "given") a special task. His qualification is education. He knows how to use words to *sustain a weary one*. The word יעף "weary" appeared in 40:28–29 to describe the particular condition in Israel to which God would minister. In 44:12 the word is used to describe the idolaters. The malady is one that hope can cure. It is particularly appropriate here in v 4 to refer to Israel's confession in 49:4 which did not use the word but which does define its context perfectly.

Who is this speaker? He is not called by name. Perhaps the anonymity is deliberate, as the Vision does this repeatedly. The speaker appears to be an organizer, a leader, a motivator. He has clear convictions and a sense of obligation to represent them to others. Any leader in Jerusalem at this time would have had to make political choices between the contending claimants to the Persian throne (see the *Historical Background* to Act IX). He would have had to stand firm against pressures from neighboring officials (Ezra 4:1–4). He may best be identified as the leader in Jerusalem responsible for rebuilding the Temple, Zerubbabel.

Excursus: Zerubbabel

Events in Judah during the early reign of Darius I are referred to in Ezra-Nehemiah and by Haggai–Zech 1–8. Four important Judeans are known by name from that period: Joshua, the high priest; the prophets Haggai and Zechariah; and Zerubbabel. Acts IX and X, which cover the period in the Vision of Isaiah, have no roles for the first three. But Zerubbabel may well be the individual who speaks in 50:4–9; 52:11–12; and who is spoken of in 52:13–53:12.

Bibliography

Ackroyd, P. R. "Two Historical Problems of the Early Persian Period." *JNES* 17 (1958) 13–27. ———. *Exile and Restoration. A Study of Hebrew Thought of the Sixth Century* B.C. London: SCM Press, 1968. 138–254 *passim.* **Avigad, N.** *Bullae and Seals from a Post-exilic Judaean Archive* (*Qedem 4*). Jerusalem, 1976. **Bright, J.** *HI.* 371–72. **Cook, S. A.** "The Age of Zerubbabel." *Studies in Old Testament Prophecy.* FS T. H. Robinson. Edinburgh: T. & T. Clark, 1950. 19–36. **Dahlberg, B. T.** "Zerubbabel." *IDB* 4:955–56. **Galling, K.** *Studien zur Geschichte Israels in Persischer Zeitalter.* Tübingen: J. C. B. Mohr, 1964. **Japhet, S.** "Sheshbazzar and Zerubbabel—against the Background of Historical and Religious Tendencies of Ezra-Nehemiah." *ZAW* 94 (1982) 66–98. **Hanson, P. D.** *The Dawn of Apocalyptic.* Philadelphia: Fortress Press, 1975. 174–349. **Josephus, F.** *Antiq.* XI.i–iv. **Laperrousaz, E. M.** "Le regime théocratique juïf a-t-il commencé à l'époque perse ou seulement à l'époque hellénistique?" *Sem* 32 (1982) 93–96. **Petersen, D. L.** "Zerubbabel and Jerusalem Temple Reconstruction." *CBQ* 36 (1974) 366–72. **Reyse, K. M.** *Zerubbabel und die Königserwartungen der Propheten Haggai und Zacharja.* Berlin, DDR; Stuttgart: Kohlhammer Verlag, 1972. **Sauer, G.** "Serubbabel in der Sicht Haggais und Sacharjas." *Das ferne und nahe Wort.* FS L. Rost. Ed. F Maass (1967) 199–207. **Schottroff, W.** "Zur Socialgeschichte Israels in der Perserzeit." *VF* 27 (1982) 46–68. **Sellin, E.** *Zerubbabel.* 1898. **Soggin, J. A.** *History.* 264–71. **Stern, E.** *Material Culture in the Land of the Bible in the Persian Period, 538–332 B.C.* Jerusalem and Warminster: Aris & Phillips, 1982. **Widengren, G.** "The Persian Period." *IJH.* 520–23.

Zerubbabel appears in the genealogies of 1 Chr 3:19 as being of the line of David, the son of Pediah, grandson of Jehoiachin. He had two sons and a daughter, Shelomith. It is unusual for a woman to be named. A seal has been found by archeologists with the inscription "Shelomith, maidservant of Elnathan." (See E. M. Meyers, "The Shelomith Seal and the Judean Restoration," *Eretz-Israel* 18 [1985] 33–38, who thinks Elnathan was the governor who succeeded Zerubbabel and that Shelomith was his wife and claimed to be related to the Davidic line.)

Ezra 2:2 lists the name of Zerubbabel among those returning to Jerusalem. In 3:2 he joins Joshua, the priest, in building the altar. In 3:8 he and Joshua appoint Levites to care for the altar and begin the actual work. In 4:2–3 he is the leader who rejects an offer from non-Jewish neighbors to help with the building. In 5:2 he and Joshua with the prophets begin to build the Temple, only to be challenged and ordered to stop by Tattenai, the territorial governor. Neh 7:7 and 12:1 list him among those who return.

Zerubbabel figures prominently in Hag 1:1, 12, 14 and 2:2, 4, 21, 23 in the prophet's encouragements to press on with the building of the Temple. Zech 4 is a vision of a golden lampstand and two olive trees that affirms both Zerubbabel and Joshua as chosen of God for leadership.

1 Esdr 3:13–4:63 narrates the story of three young men, one of whom is Zerubbabel, who are aides of Darius. They engage in a contest in wisdom and speechmaking. Zerubbabel wins and thereby is granted his wish to return to Jerusalem to build the Temple.

Josephus (*Antiq.* III.ii) says that Cambyses had been opposed to the building, but Darius had made a private vow before setting out to take the throne to support the rebuilding if Yahweh gave him the throne. Zerubbabel, now governor in Judea, comes to court as part of a delegation from Jerusalem. He renews an old friendship with Darius. Then Josephus tells another version of the contest story, placing it in this setting.

All of these tell of events close to the time specified by Haggai (the second year of Darius, 520–518 B.C.). Zerubbabel is portrayed as a co-worker with Joshua in rebuilding the Temple. He is the leader or governor of Judah and obviously enjoys the confidence of the Persians, perhaps even having known Darius personally from earlier days in the Persian court. He is also pictured as Judah's leader in one or more confrontations with the territorial governor and petty leaders of neighboring towns and areas. Zerubbabel is also the last of the line of David to have held administrative office in Judah. His official listing beside the priest indicates that they shared in administrative responsibility. The next governor, Elnathan, is a Davidide only by marriage.

There is a strange silence in all these sources about the fate of Zerubbabel. He simply disappears from the narratives. This commentary suggests that the Vision of Isaiah breaks that silence (without using his name, as is the custom in most of the Vision). The interpretation begins by understanding chaps. 49–57 to be set in the reigns of Darius I and Xerxes. Chaps. 49–54 interpret the early reign of Darius (*ca.* 522–515 B.C.).

Twice in these chapters a single leader speaks (50:4–9 and 52:11) and once such a person is described as having been brutally killed (52:14, 53:4–12). This parallels somewhat similar speeches in 48:16b and 20–21 and 61:1–3. The person in 52:11 is a leader for an expedition returning to Judah, like the leader (Sheshbazzar) in 48:20–21. He is one who must face confrontation with oppressive authorities and endure them patiently (50:2–5) as Zerubbabel does in Ezra 4:2–3, 5:2–5. Note that Zerubbabel is not mentioned in Ezra's account when Darius's letter finally arrives.

A useful interpretation of these passages then turns on Zerubbabel, implying that his confrontation with Tattenai and his men was heightened by subsequent visits in which they put pressure on Jerusalem (as shown in Ezra 5:10 by "writing down the names of the leaders.") Zerubbabel would have resisted their pressure, refusing to provide the names. He was threatened and then executed. When Jerusalem still did not given in, they backed off. Darius then supported the Judean building effort and the pressures relaxed, at least temporarily.

If this is correct, the Vision's interpretation of the lasting significance of Zerubbabel's suffering and death becomes a classic picture of the role and effect of substitutionary suffering, and makes a major contribution toward understanding God's attitude toward substitutionary atonement.

The pseudepigraphic "Martyrdom of Isaiah" (*The Old Testament Pseudepigrapha* II, ed. J. H. Charlesworth [Garden City, NY: Doubleday, 1985] 59) transfers this role to Isaiah the prophet during the reign of Manasseh. When he is about to be sawed in half he sends all the other prophets away "because for me alone the Lord has mixed this cup." Throughout his ordeal "he did not cry out or weep."

It is therefore proper to see in 52:13–53:12 a picture of a son of David who, though innocent of conspiracy or rebellion, died and in so doing caused the remaining people in Jerusalem to be spared.

So now the Vision has identified three assignments. They include, first, Israel's role in witness and worship. Then Cyrus and his successors are called to govern, defend, and provide necessary resources for building the Temple and the city. And now this third role of an individual leader, teacher and motivator is assigned to Zerubbabel.

He wakens. A beautiful description of God's inspiration *to listen,* to be taught and to learn. To teach effectively one must first learn. And learning takes motivation and discipline. Yahweh provides them all.

5 *I have not been rebellious* against God's leading or against God's strategy. The Vision has shown how God revealed his strategy which used the empires to accomplish his goals. This made it necessary that Judean rulers and Jewish leaders submit and cooperate with them. But many of them from Hezekiah's time onward refused to do this, but conspired against the empires and participated in rebellious movements. After the Exile, zealous nationalists continued to be active. History records that the leaders who were of genuine help to Jerusalem were those of unquestioned loyalty to Persia. Sheshbazzar and Zerubbabel were of this type as, later, were Ezra and Nehemiah.

6 But, since all were not of one mind in Jerusalem or in Palestine about this or about which claimant to the Persian throne should be recognized, conviction aroused opposition, even violent opposition. The opponents may have belonged to rebellious circles in Judah or from neighboring areas that wanted to force Jerusalem to join in rebellion. This leader accepted such beatings and humiliations as part of his job.

7 But he held firmly to his convictions and to his loyalties to Yahweh and to the one who had been shown (49:5–7) to be Yahweh's choice as the new emperor of Persia.

8–9 The leader defends his position. *My Vindicator* may refer to God. But it may also refer in this context to Darius (see *Excursus:* צדק צדקה *"Righteousness, Legitimacy"*) who he believed to be the one Yahweh had chosen to rule Persia and to restore Jerusalem. Anyone who takes sides in such a political struggle must be prepared to face the consequences when the issue is finally decided. He challenges his opposition to stand up and act openly. He jeers their refusal to do so.

10–11 The tone changes, and apparently the speaker also changes. The verse speaks of Yahweh's *servant.* Which servant is this? At this point Yahweh, Darius, and Zerubabbel are all in position to call for loyalty and action of the same kind. They are practically interchangeable as speakers here. But identifying him as Darius gives the speech particular meaning. He speaks to support the Jewish teacher/leader who has just spoken. He is also asking for Judah's loyalty to his cause by claiming Yahweh's choice of himself to be his servant. Then, in the manner of emperors, he threatens retribution on all rebels.

51:1 Darius continues to speak, calling attention to himself. He appeals to those *who pursue right* (see *Excursus: "Right"*). They long for an orderly rule of law in Israel to replace the arbitrary rule of might. Darius claims that he is the only one capable of restoring such order. He then appeals to *seekers of Yahweh* (מבקשי יהוה). These want free access to the new Temple in order to worship there. The Vision has presented Cyrus as Yahweh's servant, chosen to restore the Temple (44:28; 45:13), and Darius as his heir in that assignment (49:6).

2–3 Darius challenges the Jews to look to their history. Specifically, he calls Jerusalem to look to Abraham and Sarah. Abraham's relation to Jerusalem is told in Gen. 14:18–20. He received a blessing from Melchizedek just as now Jews may be blessed by Darius's support in rebuilding the Temple. Yahweh's brief speech emphasizes how he began with one person to achieve his much larger goal. The lesson of blessing is immediately applied to Zion's needs and the way that God is going to meet them.

4 Darius speaks again, addressing Judah as *my people.* He presents himself as a benevolent monarch. The close identity of God and his chosen king over the empire are especially related in matters of law, justice, and legitimate rule. Darius did in fact bring a measure of common law to the empire beyond anything that had existed before (see *Excursus: Law Codes under the Persians*). The references to *law* (תורה) and *justice* (משפט) are to Persian law and justice. This accounts for their application to *peoples* rather than only to Judah. Darius's position is a fulfillment of the prediction concerning Cyrus in 42:1–4.

Excursus: Law Codes under the Persians

Bibliography

Blenkinsopp, J. *A History of Prophecy in Israel,* 227. *Encyclopedia Britannica* 22:410.
Olmstead, A. T. "Darius as Lawgiver." *AJSL* 51 (1935) 247–49. ———. *History of the Persian Empire,* 119–34.

Persian concern for statute law on the one hand and its tolerance for religious minorities on the other encouraged the publication of law codes for those minority communities which would in turn be recognized by the imperial authorities. These codes became binding on that community in family and religious matters. The communities themselves were then responsible for enforcing their own law.

This began in Egypt when Cambyses required the priests in Memphis to publish their code before he would grant them privileges to collect taxes. (See Olmstead, *History,* 142, 220, 373, 393, 402, 431.) Darius I was in Egypt with Cambyses when this was done. On his accession to the throne he began to prepare a new law for the entire empire based on a code already in effect in Babylon that traced its origin to Hammurabi more than a millennium earlier. He changed the name for "law" to *dat,* an Iranian word that is also found in the Hebrew writings of the Persian period (Ezra 7:26; Esther 1:8, 13–15, 19; 2:8, 12). This replaced the previous name that meant "judgments." This great law code became the Law of the Medes and Persians for the entire empire (Olmstead, *History,* 119–34).

But, as in Egypt, other religious minorities were permitted to publish their own codes to be administered by their priests in and from their temple centers. So it was undoubtedly with Persian approval that Ezra introduced his book of the law (probably, the Pentateuch) in Jerusalem. "The decisive constitutional event of the new community was the covenant subscribed to by its leaders in 444, making the Torah the law of the land: a charter granted by the Persian king Artaxerxes to Ezra—scholar and priest of the Babylonian Exile—empowered him to enforce the Torah as the imperial law for the Jews of the province of Anar-nahra (Beyond the River) in which the district of Jerusalem (now reduced to a small area) was located. The charter required the publication of the Torah and the publication in turn required its final editing—now plausibly ascribed to Ezra and his circle" (*EB* 22:410).

The Jewish religious community was recognized legally within the larger body politic and given authority over family and religious practices as well as over other matters of purely community (inner Jewish) interest. This law was applicable, in Persian eyes, in Judah, but also in all communities who claimed to belong to the Jerusalem cult community of Yahweh, God in Jerusalem. This was probably first true for all those in Palestine (Beyond the River). But it came to apply to all Jewish communities in the empire. When the Jewish community in Elephantine sought Persian recognition for their Temple, they were referred to Jerusalem to fulfill the requirement for a written code (*ANET,* 491–92). The same practice continued in succeeding empires for Jewish and other sectarian communities. The recognition of religious (or communal) law and law enforcement has continued from those imperial times down to the twentieth century in countries with significant religious pluralism, such as Lebanon. It allowed self-government in family, religious, and communal matters. But it called for mutual tolerance to make it function. The increased application of secular civil law to marriage and family law in most modern states as well as the practice of freedom of religion has made the place of communal law and justice obsolete or irrelevant.

The Vision of Isaiah supports the development (in Ezra-Nehemiah) in the 5th century B.C. that granted Judaism legal status for its Temple worship in Jerusalem and for community structure as a religious/ethnic self-governing community in Palestine/Syria. In it the Torah of Yahweh could be heard and obeyed. Yahweh's presence could be experienced in festivals and ceremonies as a guiding, strengthening and unifying force. The Vision says, "Yahweh's Torah will go out from Jerusalem" (2:4).

5 The foundations of Persian justice, as presented repeatedly in the Vision, are three. צדקה "right" speaks of legitimacy in divine appointment. ישע

"salvation" (which BDB, 443, translates as "deliverance, rescue, salvation, safety, or welfare") refers to specific acts, usually military, which bring people under Persian rule and responsibility. For Jerusalem this means protection from predatory bands of brigades and neighbors. The first two provide the right and responsibility for the third: משפט "justice," which is the system and function of bringing justice to the peoples. To do this a published, known, and applied law is needed (v 4b). Darius claims that *the coastlands,* the cities of Phoenicia and Philistia, are partial to him. This may well have been historically true. He had been with Cambyses in Egypt. Their reforms had stimulated trade for all the area of Palestine. Cambyses was in Palestine with his army when he died. There is no record that this area ever recognized Gaumata as emperor, perhaps because of Darius' presence there. When he began his campaign to take over the empire, it is understandable that Palestine and Egypt would support him. Their trade depended on the stability which they believed Darius could bring to the empire.

6–8 Darius uses hyperbole to emphasize the permanence and stability of his reign and of his law. *Not set* is a metaphor referring to the setting of the sun. His legitimacy, determined by Yahweh's mandate, is claimed to be permanent. He appeals to those who *know righteousness,* those who are convinced that he is in fact Yahweh's choice for legitimate ruler, and who have *my law in their hearts,* those who are loyal to Persian law and administration, to hold fast despite *reproach* and *revilings* from opposition parties. In Judah these would be nationalists who want no foreign rulers. In Samaria, Ammon, and Edom opposition would come from envious groups who oppose Judah's restoration of the Temple or the walls of Jerusalem. Darius claims that this opposition is weak and temporary, while his *right* to legitimate rule and his deliverance, the results of his military accomplishments, will be lasting. *For an age,* as in v 6 above, suggests permanence to the end of that historical era. It is parallel in meaning to *a generation of generations.*

Explanation

Yahweh's third appointee is willing to suffer abuse and taunts to hold fast to his assigned task. He is supported in this by God and by the emperor. Darius, sensitive to the legitimacy provided by Yahweh's call and the power inherent in his military position, is also motivated by a vision of a legal system that would span the empire. This fits Yahweh's strategy for Jerusalem and for the exiles.

The abuse which the teacher receives (50:6) and the call to withstand pressure (51:7) imply that this course is controversial in Jerusalem. But a deep yearning for permanence and order is apparent in 50:9b; 51:1b, 6, and 8. Constant agitation and rebellion brings no peace, no order, no justice. Constancy in following God's plan, even if it has no power of its own, can bring legitimate government (צדקה), freedom from oppressors (ישוע), and justice under law (משפט). These are implicit in Yahweh's choice of Darius to be his servant and Judah's sovereign.

Scene 4: Awake! Put on Strength (51:9–52:2)

Bibliography

Bilik, E. "התוא איננו עוף (Isa 51:20)." *BMik* 21 (1977) 458–61. **Dahood, M.** "Isaiah 51, 19b and Sefire III 22." *Bib* 56 (1975) 94–95. **Helberg, J. L.** "Nahum-Jonah-Lamentations—Isaiah 51–53." *OTWSAP* (1969) 46–55. **Martin, W. C.** "An Exegesis of Is 51:9–11." *ResQ* 9 (1966) 151–59. ———. "Storia, mitologia, ed eschatologia in Is 51,9–11." *RicBR* 3 (1968) 231–42. **Morgenstern, J.** "Isaiah 49–55." *HUCA* 36 (1965) 11. ———. " 'The Oppressor' of Is 51,13—Who Was He?" *JBL* 81 (1962) 25–34. **Seidl, T.** "Jahwe der Krieger—Jahwe der Tröster (Jesaja 51,9–16)." *BN* 21 (1983) 116–34.

Translation

Chorus: (to the Arm of Yahweh)	9 *Awake! (fem sg) Awake!*	2+2+2
	Put on strength,	
	Arm (fem) of Yahweh!	
	Awake as in former days,	3+2
	in generations of (past) ages!	
	Are you (fem sg) not she[a]	2+2+2
	who was wounding[b] *Rahab?*	
	who was piercing a dragon?	
	10 *Are you (fem sg) not she*	2+2+3
	who was drying up a sea,	
	the water of the great deep?	
	Who was establishing[a] *the depths of the sea*	2+3
	(to be) a way[b] *for redeemed ones to pass over?*	
Chorus:	11 *Yahweh's ransomed ones*[a] *return*	3+3
	and come to Zion with singing!	
	A once-in-an-age kind of joy will be on their heads.	3+3+3
	Joy and gladness will be theirs.	
	Sorrow and sighing will flee away.[b]	
	12 *I, I am he who comforts you (pl)*[a]*!*	4
Yahweh: (to the people) (to Jerusalem)	*Who are* [b]*you (fem sg) that you (fem sg) are afraid*[b]	2+2+3
	of mortal man,	
	of a human made like grass?	
Heavens:	13 *So that you (fem sg) forgot Yahweh, your (fem sg) maker*	3+2+2
	who is stretching out heavens	
	and founding earth?	
Earth: (to the leader)	*So that you (masc sg)*[a] *fear continually every day*	3+3+3
	before the fury of the oppressor	
	as though he were the one established to destroy?	
	And where is the fury of the oppressor?	3
	14 *He who is subdued hurries to be released.*	3+2+2
	He does not die (going) to the pit.	

His life-force[a] *does not fail.*
Yahweh: (to his leader) 15 *I am Yahweh your (masc sg) God,* 3+2+2
[a]*stirring up*[b] *the sea*
so that its waves roar.
Herald: *Yahweh of Hosts is his name.*[a] 3
Yahweh: 16 *So I have put my words in your (masc sg) mouth.* 3+3
And in the shadow of my hand I hid you (masc sg)
to plant[a] *heavens and found earth* 4+3
and to say to Zion: you (masc sg) are my people.
Heavens: 17 *Rouse yourself (fem sg)!*[a] *Rouse yourself (fem sg)!* 2+2
Stand up (fem sg), Jerusalem!
You who have drunk (fem sg) from the hand of Yahweh 4+2
his cup of wrath.
The bowl of the cup[b] *of staggering* 3+2
you (fem sg) have drunk to the dregs.
Earth: 18 *No one is guiding her*[a] 2+2
of all the sons she has borne.
And no one is taking hold of her hand 3+2
of all the sons she has brought up.
Heavens: 19 *These two things have happened to you (fem sg)* 3+3
Earth: *Who can console you?*
Heavens: *Devastation and destruction,* 2+2+2
and famine and sword.
Earth: *Who can comfort*[a] *you (fem sg)?*
Heavens: 20 *Your (fem sg) sons are faint!* 2+3+2
Earth: *They lie* [a]*at the head of all streets*[a]
like a trapped antelope.
Heavens: *They are full of Yahweh's wrath,* 3+2
the rebuke of your God.
Herald: (to Jerusalem) 21 *Therefore hear (fem sg) this now, you afflicted ones,* 4+2
and drunk, but not from wine.
22 *Thus says your (fem sg) Lord Yahweh*[a] *and*[b] *your (fem sg) God* 4+2
who pleads the case of his people.
Yahweh: *See! I have taken out of your (fem sg) hand* 3+2+3
the cup of staggering,
the bowl of the cup[c] *of my wrath.*
You (fem sg) shall not drink (of it) again! 3+2
23 *for I shall place it in the hand of your (fem sg) tormentors,*[a]
who said to your (fem sg) soul: 2+2
"Bow down and let us pass over."
So you had to make your (fem sg) back like land 3+2
and like a street for those passing over.
Heavenly Chorus: 52:1 *Awake (fem sg)! Awake!* 2+3
Put on your strength, Zion!

Put on your beautiful clothes, 3+3
Zion, City of the Holy One!
For the uncircumcized and unclean 3+2+2
shall not again
come into you (fem sg).
2 *Shake off the dust from yourself.* 2+3
Rise, Jerusalem, and take your seat.[a]
Loose yourself[b] *from the bonds*[c] *of your neck,* 3+2
captive daughter Zion.

Notes

9.a. The fem sg pronouns in vv 9–10 and 12 b refer to "the arm of Yahweh."

9.b. MT המחצבת "the one cutting up" is usually used of quarrying stones (BDB, 345; but cf. Hos 6:5). DSS[Isa] המוחצת "the one wounding" seems to confirm a previously suggested emendation to the more common root מחץ (BDB, 563; cf. Job 26:12). Kutscher (*Isaiah Scroll,* 32–33, 255) points out that both roots appear in parallel three times in Ug, but that חצב is less common in Heb. and therefore more likely original. 'A Σ Θ support MT.

10.a. The accentuation of הַשָּׂמָה suggests qal pf, but the context requires a ptcp הַשָּׂמָה (GKC § 138*k*) as LXX ἡ θεῖσα realized.

10.b. *BHS* suggests transposing ׃ here to change the line division. Read MT.

11.a. MT פדויי "ransomed ones of" (BDB, 804). DSS[Isa] פזורי "the scattered ones of" (BDB, 808), but had first written and then erased פד(ו)יי (Kutscher, *Isaiah Scroll,* 275). LXX Θ Tg Syr Vg support MT. Read MT.

11.b. Many Heb. MSS and Syr insert *waw* "and." DSS[Isa] ונס "and it flees" has *waw,* but the verb is sg; so also Tg ויסוף. 35:10 has a similar couplet with *waw.* LXX Vg have no copulative. Read MT.

12.a. LXX Σ have masc sg for MT's masc pl. The masc pl refers to the people of Jerusalem.

12.b-b. The second person pronouns are now fem sg. *BHS* suggests making both masc, but without textual foundation. Stay with MT throughout the verse.

13.a. The masc sg pronouns in vv 13, 15–16 refer to either Zerubbabel or Darius.

14.a. G. R. Driver (*JTS* 36 [1935] 402–3), reported also by *BHS,* suggests reading MT לַחְמוֹ "his bread" as לֵחוֹ or לֵחֲמוֹ "his natural force"; BDB (535–36) "moisture," "freshness." Cf. Deut 34:7 for a similar usage about Moses.

15.a-a. An identical parallel appears in Jer 31:35.

15.b. *BHS* notes the proposal גער "rebuke" for MT רגע "stir up," but the same usage with ים "sea" appears in Job 26:12 and Jer 31:35. Read MT.

16.a. MT לנטע "to plant." *BHS* follows Syr in suggesting לנטות "to stretch out," which is the usual word with "heavens" (cf. 40:22; 42:5; 44:24; 45:12; 51:13). LXX ἐν ῇ ἔστησα "with which I fixed." Tg paraphrases to make it refer to Israel. Vg follows MT. MT makes sense and should be kept.

17.a. The 2d pers pronouns return to fem sg in 51:17–52:2 and refer to Jerusalem.

17.b. LXX repeats τοῦ θυμοῦ "of his wrath" instead of כוס "cup." Σ may or may not have omitted "cup," depending on which witness one chooses to believe. 'A Θ Tg support MT.

18.a. DSS[Isa] has 2d fem sg, but follows MT for the rest of the verse. LXX has 2d sg throughout. Σ Syr Tg Vg support MT.

19.a. MT is 1st sg, as is Tg. Read with DSS[Isa] MS[K] LXX Σ Syr Vg a 3d masc sg.

20.a-a. *BHS* suggests that this was added from Lam 2:19; 4:1.

22.a. Omitted in one MS[K]. Duhm, Köhler, *BHK,* and Elliger (527) delete on metrical grounds. Stay with MT.

22.b. DSS[Isa] omits "and." 'A Σ Θ Syr Tg Vg support MT.

22.c. Omitted in LXX and Syr. Cf. note 17.b above.

23.a. DSS[Isa] adds ומעניך "those causing you to be afflicted." LXX adds καὶ τῶν ταπεινωσάντων "and of those afflicting you." So *BHS* suggests adding וביד מעניך "in the hand of those afflicting you" for a more balanced meter. Σ Syr Tg Vg support MT. Stay with MT.

52:2.a. MT שְׁבִי. The *dagesh* suggests an impv from ישב "sit," a meaning supported by DSS[Isa]

ושבי (Kutscher, *Isaiah Scroll,* 423) and all the Versions. The contrast with קומי "arise" is perhaps to be explained with reference to 1 Sam 28:23; 2 Sam 19:9 (BDB, 442). But many Heb. MSS omit *dagesh* to allow the meaning "captivity," while Oort, Budde, Duhm, *BHS,* and others suggest שביה "captive" (BDB, 985–86) as in the second half of the verse.

2.b. K and DSS[Isa] התפתחו impv masc pl. Q התפתחי impv fem sg. LXX 'A Σ Θ Syr Vg follow Q. Tg reads K with following pl. The following pronoun in MT is fem sg. Read Q.

2.c. *BHS* suggests adding the prep מן "from." Not necessary.

Form/Structure/Setting

Form critics are not agreed about the units or the genre of the passage (Melugin, *Formation,* 159)

The central admonition and promise to Darius (vv 15–16) place the scene in historical perspective. Darius is still in Palestine and thus shielded from the great events in the empire to the east. While enthusiasts in Jerusalem try to conjure up mythical models for Yahweh's action on Jerusalem's behalf (vv 9–11), a more conventional Israelite approach sees Yahweh's acts in history as part of an orderly process like that in creation (vv 12–14) and encourages Jerusalem to calm its terror and panic. Whether this is unnecessary fear of Darius or of someone else is not clear.

Yahweh introduces himself to Darius (v 15) as the one who has inspired him and protected him (v 16a) in order to have him bring order to his (Yahweh's) world and to restore his people (16b).

The scene returns to encouragement for Jerusalem to believe that Yahweh has ordained a new and different fate for her: blessing rather than curse (v 17). Her lack of leadership after the years of devastation is graphically portrayed (vv 18–20). So now Yahweh personally confirms her new status and condition (vv 21–23).

The scene closes with another choral encouragement for Jerusalem to seize the opportunity to do her part to put off the chains of the past (52:1–2).

The scene's structure is fixed by three stirring calls to awake or rouse oneself. The first is addressed to the Arm of Yahweh as an almost mythical entity who had won primeval battles (vv 9–11) and who is now invoked to work a miraculous victory to bring the age of joy. The second is addressed to Jerusalem in v 17 to rouse herself from her drunken stupor brought on by having to drink Yahweh's "cup of wrath." The third is addressed to Zion, calling for her to get up out of the dust, put off her bonds, and again take her seat in dignity and strength.

Between the first and the second calls, Yahweh addresses first Jerusalem encouraging her not to fear God's strategy of using human instruments (rather than a mythical means) to achieve his goals (vv 12–14), and then Darius to instruct him how he is to order God's world and restore his people (vv 15–16).

Between the second and third calls, note is taken of Jerusalem's lack of manpower and leadership (18–20) and Yahweh draws attention to his personal acts to change her status and condition (vv 21–23).

The whole is cast in an arch-form which serves to call Jerusalemites away from a mythical hope in a dramatic miracle to win their freedom. It calls them to recognize the central role Jerusalem has in God's plan and the way that he is bringing salvation in history through Darius. Jerusalem is challenged to recognize the dignity and worth that this plan gives to her role and to act with becoming grace in filling it.

A A choral challenge to the Arm of Yahweh to bring redemption (vv 9–11)
B Yahweh chides Jerusalem for her fear (vv 12–14)
C Yahweh encourages and instructs Darius (vv 15–16)
KEYSTONE Jerusalem is challenged to stand up and stand firm (v 17)
C′ Jerusalem has no manpower or leadership to help herself (vv 18–21)
B′ Yahweh affirms the change in Jerusalem's fate: from curse to blessing (vv 22–23)
A′ A choral challenge to Zion to seize her God-given opportunity (vv 1–2)

Comment

9 *Arm of Yahweh* is addressed as an independent entity, as though it represents power in itself. The term appears also in Exod 15:16; Deut 4:34; 7:19; 9:29; 11:2; 26:8; 1 Kgs 8:42/2 Chr 6:32; 2 Kgs 17:36; Jer 27:5; 32:17, 21; Ezek 20:33–34; and Ps 136:12. Sometimes it is used metaphorically for Yahweh's power, as support for the weak, as a shepherd (40:11 and Deut 33:27). But it also seems to move beyond metaphor. In this passage it is associated with mythic themes: the *wounding of Rahab* (cf. 30:7; Job 9:13; 26:12; Ps 89:11 [10]) and the piercing of Tanin, the mythical *dragon* of chaos (cf. Deut 32:33; Ps 91:13; and Exod 7:9, 10, 12, of snakes; Jer 51:34 and Neh 2:13, of a dragon; and Gen 1:21; Job 7:12; Ps 74:13; Isa 27:1; Ezek 29:3; 32:2, of a sea monster). The references clearly relate Yahweh to a great victory over these primeval sea monsters in a form that is not included in Scripture and which is probably not acceptable in biblical doctrine. Yet it obviously played a role in popular thought.

10 *The Arm of Yahweh* is further identified with *drying up a sea,* which may mean the crossing of the Reed Sea of Exod 14:21. Or this, too, may be a mythical reference. ים "sea" was one of the gods in Ugaritic myths who played out the mythical drama of the seasons. *The water of the great deep* (תהום) may be an expansion of the same story or another version of Gen 1:2–10. *Establishing the depths of the sea to be a way* clearly returns to the crossing of the Reed Sea. Exod 15:1–15 is an ancient hymnic version of the event in which Yahweh's "right hand" (v 12) and "arm" (v 16) play major roles. The Vision has used imagery from the Exodus repeatedly from chap. 40 onward to depict Yahweh's new act of salvation.

At issue in the Vision is the manner of Yahweh's work. Passages like vv 9–10 (and later 63:7–64:12) picture God's work as a series of sudden dramatic victories and yearn for such magic to be applied again. The Vision, while keeping alive the hope for decisive transformation of nature and human conditions, stresses the ways God works within the historical and natural process. Salvation comes from the Creator who continues the creative process and from the Lord of History whose plan opens the door to rebuilding Zion's Temple and restoring Israel's freedom to worship there. It grows in the potential for spiritual communion with Yahweh and from knowledge gained from his law, not from a flashy repetition of exciting myths.

11 The names for the Israel of the new age are significant: *the ransomed ones* and *the redeemed ones* (v 10). A new hope requires God's action. That action would come and already is in process, but it takes a very different form from that envisioned by many. Nonetheless, the hope for a new *age* of *joy and gladness* is to be kept alive. The return *to Zion with singing* is a key element in that hope. For those who labor to build the Temple it is very important.

12 Yahweh introduces himself with an emphatic *I, I*—not the mythical "Arm" nor any other form, but God himself. The pronoun *you* is masculine plural in Hebrew, addressing the people of Jerusalem. But the question returns to the feminine singular *you,* meaning Jerusalem. Yahweh offers his own presence as comforter and guardian but questions Jerusalem's character in being *afraid.* The question does not ask "Why are you afraid?" but rather *Who are you that you are afraid?* Her inability to experience God's presence in a way that eliminates fear indicates that something basic is lacking in Jerusalem's character. The modifiers for *man* stress his mortality (literally, "who will die") and general humanity (אדם).

13 Fear feeding on itself made Jerusalem *forget* Yahweh, creator of all things. The sermons of Deuteronomy stress the importance of memory for faith and the devastating effect of forgetfulness on God's people. Forgetting makes them *fear continually* in anticipation *of the fury of the oppressor.* Who is this oppressor? Can this be a dread that they may be on the wrong side in Persia's civil war of 522 B.C.? Or that they fear the victor might wreak vengeance for perceived wrongs against himself and the state? So now Yahweh asks: *Where is the fury of the oppressor?* The whole issue is being resolved without the anticipated terror.

14 *He who is subdued* appears to refer to someone who has lost a struggle and been made to submit. In this setting it could well mean the one who has lost the struggle for the throne, and his supporters. He could not be Gaumata who was assassinated in 522 B.C., but the reference might well be to one of the Jews who had supported someone other than Darius or who had struggled for Judah's independence. The verse looks for a speedy *release* that prevents his death or failure of health.

15–16 Yahweh introduces himself again, but this time in terms of his control of the raging *sea.* He addresses the one he is using, putting his *words* in his *mouth* and protecting him very carefully. The purpose of this care is to allow him *to plant heavens and earth.* That makes no sense if it refers to the original creation. A similar phrase in the Vision has become a standard way of describing Yahweh's work in creation. It uses נטה "stretch out" while here the verb is נטע "plant." In the other instances God acts alone, using no agent. Here the one he has hidden in the shadow of his hand is his agent. *Heavens* and *land* here must refer metaphorically to the totality of order in Palestine, *heavens* meaning the broader overarching structure of the Empire, while *land* (ארץ) is the political order in Palestine itself. The assignment is then focused more precisely: *to say to Zion: you are my people.* The two pronouns are challenges for the interpreter. Does *my* refer to God or to the speaker? Throughout this larger section God's work and that of Darius seem fused together. It is often difficult to separate the two, as will be seen in the following verses. Because God has chosen Darius and uses him, loyalty to Darius is viewed as equivalent to loyalty to God. To be Yahweh's obedient people is to be Persia's loyal people, too. Zion is usually referred to with a feminine pronoun. Here it is masculine, apparently because it refers to the people of the city rather than to the city itself. This last clause defines Darius's main task which had so far (49:6, 8) been less precise than it had been for Cyrus (44:28b; 45:13b–c).

17–20 Jerusalem appears to be unaware of what is happening or unable to respond. Whether she is drunk or faint is not clear. These speeches attempt to rouse her from that stupor. Sixty-five years have passed since Nebuchadnezzar razed her walls. The ruins are populated by a generation that has known no other condition. No leadership has emerged among them (v 18). The inhabitants lie about with no resolve and no ambition (v 20). They are consumed by self-pity and self-reproach. They are very conscious of the devastations visited on the city (v 19), reciting them bitterly. They are sure that they came from Yahweh (v 17) and feel that they and the city are cursed by his decree of wrath (6:11–13). Comfort and rehabilitation do not come easily to a people who have fed on bitterness for so long.

21–23 Yahweh speaks to these *afflicted* ones in their stupor, *drunk but not with wine.* Yahweh is simultaneously judge and advocate for their cause. He determines their fate. Though he had once placed an implacable curse on them as judgment for their sins (chap. 6), here called *the cup of my wrath,* he now reverses that judgment. The cup is taken away and given to Jerusalem's *tormentors.* These are not the great powers, but Jerusalem's neighbors who have exploited her weakness to their own advantage and diabolical delight (cf. Obadiah and Ezra 1:1–4). They had figuratively walked over the prostrate Judeans. Yahweh decrees that it shall not happen again.

52:1–2 The chorus takes up the chant, calling on Jerusalem to recognize her new God-given opportunity. She must dress up and *put on her new clothes* without fear that the stranger might attack and ravage her again. *Take your seat* is a difficult word (see n. 52:2.a). It apparently pictures Jerusalem, seated on the ground, now called to take her proper seat on an elevated place of honor. She may put aside her subject status, take off the bonds from *her neck,* and assume her proper place as *the City of the Holy One.*

Explanation

Redemption and restoration are not easy for a person or for a people when they have experienced an extended period of helpless oppression. Bitterness, fear, and despair rob them of even that spark of individual or group vitality which could become either resentment or hope. Apathy becomes the order of the day. Submission to brutality is a means of survival. So Yahweh's announcement of hope and comfort is met with scepticism (49:14, 24) and apathetic stupor. What hope there is finds expression in bizarre mythological projections of Yahweh's magical powers over monsters (vv 9–11).

Yahweh's response calls the people back to a sound doctrinal view of himself.

As creator, he uses the created order to accomplish his will and it responds. As Lord of history, he summons world leaders to do his bidding. And they, like Darius, respond. He calls Jerusalem to recognize this new age of opportunity and to be prepared to use it. Salvation and deliverance require their active participation. It does not come in a flash. It takes time. Twenty years have passed since Cyrus appeared in Babylon. Zechariah (4:10) had it right. It is "a day of small things." Jerusalem is not ready for more. So God acts through Darius for the sake of a rebuilt Temple and calls on Jerusalem to seize the opportunity.

Scene 5: How Fitting: A Messenger's Feet (52:3–12)

Bibliography

Blank, S. "Isaiah 52:5 and the Profanation of the Name." *HUCA* 25 (1984) 1–8. **Fichtner, J.** "Jes. 52:7–10 in der christliche Verkündigung." *Verbannung und Heimkehr.* FS W. Rudolph. Tübingen: J. C. B. Mohr, 1961. 51–66. **Hanson, P. D.** "Isaiah 52:7–10." *Int* 33 (1979) 389–94. **Melugin, R. F.** "Isaiah 52:7–10." *Int* 36 (1982) 176–81.

Translation

First Messenger: 52:3 *Indeed, thus says Yahweh:* 3+2+2
"You (pl) were sold for nothing.
So you (pl) will not be redeemed with money."
Second Messenger: 4 *Indeed, thus says my Lord Yahweh:* 5+5+3
"My people went down to Egypt in the first place
to sojourn there,
but Assyria oppressed them for nothing."
Third Messenger: 5 *"And now, [a]what have I here?"[a]* 2+2
Oracle of Yahweh.
"Indeed my people were seized for nothing. 3+2+2
Its rulers[b] boasted."[c]
Oracle of Yahweh.[d]
"But my name was being despised[e] 2+2
continually, all day.
6 *Therefore my people shall know my name* 4+2+3
[a]in that day
because I am the one who keeps saying 'Behold me!'"
Heavens: 7 *How fitting they are on the mountains,* 2+2+2
those feet of a messenger
proclaiming peace,
a messenger of good things 2+2

proclaiming salvation,
saying to Zion 2+2
"Your (fem sg) God reigns."
Earth: 8 *The voice of your (fem sg) watchmen—* 2+2+2
they lift up their voice.
Together, they sing joyfully.
For they see with their own eyes 4+4
when Yahweh returns to Zion with compassion.[a]
Messengers: 9 *Break (masc pl) into singing together,* 3+2
you waste places of Jerusalem.
For Yahweh comforts his people. 3+2
He redeems Jerusalem.[a]
10 *Yahweh bares his holy arm* 4+2
in the sight of all the nations,
and all the borders of the land see 2+2
the salvation of our God.
Heavens: 11 *Depart (masc pl)! Depart!* 2+2+2
Get out of there!
Do not touch anything unclean!
Earth: 12 *But you (masc pl) will not go out in haste.*[a] 4+3
And do not walk (as) if fleeing.
For Yahweh goes before you 4+3
and the God of Israel is your (masc pl) rear guard.

Notes

5.a-a. K מי־לי, lit., "who to me?" Q and DSS^{Isa} מה־לי "what to me?" Read Q.

5.b. K משלו "its ruler," sg. Q משליו "its rulers," pl. DSS^{Isa} follows K.

5.c. MT יהילילו "they howl" from ילל (BDB, 410, hiph). DSS^{Isa} והוללו "they boast," "they play the fool" from הלל II (BDB, 239, poel). G. R. Driver (*JTS* 36 [1935] 402) suggested this reading thirteen years before DSS^{Isa} was found, and translated "they are gone mad." Tg makes the nations its subject, reading משתבחין "boast themselves" which presupposes a hithp of הלל. It fits the context as a contrast to the following bistich. LXX *θαυμάζετε καὶ ὀλολύζετε* "wonder ye and howl" has read משלו as a verb "speak in proverbs" and והילילו with a *waw* and impv of ילל. Read with DSS^{Isa}. (Cf. Kutscher, *Isaiah Scroll,* 230.)

5.d. "Yahweh" is omitted in DSS^{Isa}.

5.e. MT מְנֹאָץ "was being despised" is identified as hithpoel ptcp (BDB, 611). GKC § 55*b* suggests that this is "probably a *forma mixta* combining the readings מְנֹאָץ and מִתְנֹאֵץ." There are no parallels in this conjugation. DSS^{Isa} מנואץ confirms the *holem* but adds nothing more. Tg seems to read it as a noun. LXX has *βλασφημεῖται* "is blasphemed," then adds "among the nations."

6.a. MT לכן "therefore" is omitted by DSS^{Isa} LXX Syr Vg. ʼA Σ Θ Tg follow MT. Delete.

8.a. DSS^{Isa} adds ברחמים "with compassion." LXX *ἡνίκα ἂν ἐλεήσῃ* "when he has mercy" confirms the usage. Tg Vg support the shorter version of MT. Read DSS^{Isa}.

9.a. Two MSS read ישראל "Israel." DSS^{Isa} LXX Tg Vg support MT.

12.a. חפזון "haste" occurs otherwise only in Exod 12:11 and Deut 16:3, and seems to be a technical term with reference to the Exodus (Whybray).

Form/Structure/Setting

The use of חרבות "waste places" in v 9 completes a circle that began with its usage in 49:19 at the beginning of the act (Melugin, *Formation,* 167).

The setting for the entire act is in Jerusalem, desolate in an empty and wasted countryside. This scene summarizes the hopes aroused by Darius's rise to power. As an officer under Cambyses, he was undoubtedly known in Palestine, which had served as a staging area for the Persian invasion of Egypt.

As in chap. 48, the hope takes a practical turn in vv 11 and 12, as Jews in Babylon are encouraged to go participate in the welcome being prepared in Jerusalem for Yahweh's return.

The messengers address God's people in vv 3–6 in three brief speeches on Yahweh's behalf. Presumably these are members of an expedition to Jerusalem who are in turn addressed in vv 11–12. The themes "for nothing" (vv 3, 4, 5), and "my people" (vv 4, 5, 6), and "my name" (vv 5, 6), dominate explanations of the redemption to come.

Vv 7–9 proclaims the appropriateness of this fulfillment of God's call for messengers of good news (40:1–9). A chorus of these messengers of peace announces God's actions (v 10).

Then vv 11–12 speed the expedition on its way. God who is returning to Zion invites Israelite exiles to join him in the journey. This is the second expedition. The first was acknowledged in 48:20–21. It may well signal the renewed efforts of Zerubbabel recorded in Ezra 5:1–2.

Comment

3 The plain meaning is that Judah had gone into exile through defeat. She had not been sold into slavery. There was no gain, either to God or to her king, in her exile. Therefore God promises that her redemption will be accomplished without paying ransom.

4 Two earlier exiles are cited. Israel went into *Egypt to sojourn* there because of a famine in Canaan (Gen 46–47). This was voluntary and done for practical gain. Assyrian invasions and deportations were carried out at Yahweh's command and accomplished the judgment that he had ordered.

5 But now, the Babylonian captives had *been seized for nothing,* that is, with no profit back to Israel or to God. Judah's rulers had boasted of their prowess even as they allowed Yahweh's *name* to be *despised.* They had been neither respectful nor pious. So judgment had been in order. (Note the parallel in Rom 2:24.)

6 Now God is using the entire historical process of defeat and deportation to make his people aware of himself, to know his name, and to recognize his call for attention. Yahweh's central goal is repeated. He wants a people who know him and his name. He wants them and all peoples to be aware of his presence and of his return to Zion.

7 נאוה "fitting" is used only here and in Cant 1:10 and Ps 93:5. *The feet of a messenger* (מבשר). This is the same word, but now a masculine form, that was used in 40:9. That exhortation to "get up on a high mountain" is here an accomplished reality. The message is an encouraging one, a good one, and most welcome.

The content of the message is defined: *peace, goodness,* and *salvation. Your God reigns!* In historical context this means that Darius, Yahweh's protégé, has firmly grasped the reins of power. Peace has returned to the empire and so to Jerusalem. It also means that the normal functions of government may begin again, including Sheshbazzar's project for restoring Jerusalem and its Temple. But how does this show that Zion's God reigns? The Vision had announced in the first scene of this act (49:5–9) Yahweh's choice of Darius to be his servant, heir to the favor shown to Cyrus and to the tasks assigned to him. Now the last scene announces that Darius has established his authority, thus fulfilling Yahweh's word and demonstrating his control of the empire's throne. Zion's God has shown that he does in fact reign!

8 Jerusalem's watchmen joyously confirm the news. They see the messengers *with their own eyes,* evidently a group of new returnees from Babylon appearing over the crest of the hills to the east. This is hard evidence that Yahweh is returning to Zion.

9 *Waste places* is another tie to the first verses of this act (49:19). Restoration has hardly begun. Yet rejoicing can begin. Yahweh has already made the necessary decisions and taken steps to *comfort* and *redeem* Zion. The mention of *his people* resumes the theme of vv 4, 5, 6. Not just a city or a temple are at the heart of God's action. Yahweh is out to redeem his people! Restoration of the city is a means to that end.

10 *Yahweh bares his holy arm* interprets the rebuilding of the Temple as an act of salvation. *Baring his arm* is not simply a nature miracle like rolling back the sea or stopping the sun. It is not necessarily a great military feat like felling the walls of Jericho. The Vision uses the same term to proclaim God's work through the political processes of history to produce salutary results for his people and his city. The results will be public knowledge. Neighboring cities and peoples will have to take note of *the salvation of our God.* They took note, all right, and sometimes rose up in opposition to it (cf. Ezra 4:1–4).

11–12 This exhortation to *depart* must be addressed to Babylonian Jews preparing another expedition to Jerusalem like the earlier one in 48:20. They are urged to protect their ritual cleanliness because their journey is a pilgrimage. They are going to present themselves in the holy place before God. This is not *fleeing* from an enemy. *Yahweh goes before you and the God of Israel is your rear-guard.* He is their protection and also the reason for their journey. The watchmen at Jerusalem (v 8 above) will see that and know what it means.

Explanation

Christian Advent celebrates God's coming into the world through the baby in Bethlehem. This scene celebrates the signs of God's coming to *the waste places of Jerusalem.* The phrases that say this are repeated six times in the passage: v 6 "say, 'Behold me,' " v 7 "your God reigns," v 8 "Yahweh returns to Zion with compassion," v 9 "Yahweh comforts his people and redeems Zion," v 10 "Yahweh bares his holy arm," and v 12 "Yahweh goes before you" (cf. Zech 8:3–18). The excitement of a great venture by people which mirrors great plans and actions by God—that is what is portrayed here. It is like a vision of world mission because God has redeemed all people in Christ. Here it is encouragement to a group of Babylonian Jews who, after twenty years, determine to carry out the commission of 40:2 to "comfort God's people in Jerusalem."

Ezra (4:1–4 and chaps. 5–6) records a great new surge of work to build the Temple in the time of Zerubbabel and of Haggai-Zechariah. It was accomplished despite severe opposition because of the belated active support of Darius. This scene, indeed this act and that which follows, supplies an account of the color, the emotion, and the personal pain that went into the effort that Ezra presents so factually. Zechariah recognized that it was a day for "small things" (4:10). So it was. But God's history records and depicts the "small things" which turn the tide of events in God's struggle to redeem his people. This time and these people deserve and get recognition for doing this significant "small thing."

Act X: Restoration Pains in Jerusalem (52:13—57:21)

The Tenth Generation:
Darius/Xerxes (518–465 b.c.)

Darius is hailed as the exalted, if unlikely, successor to the throne and then hears a complaint concerning an innocent person who was executed. Jerusalem is exhorted to see a bright future in this new reign. Everyone is invited to the new Temple with the promise that old taboos will be dropped. But with the new worshipers come violent and disruptive persons. Persian discipline slackens and Jerusalem feels itself helpless before the predatory elements.

The act has five scenes:

Scene 1: Punishment for Our Peace (52:13–53:12)
Scene 2: Sing, You Barren One! (54:1–17b)
Scene 3: A House of Prayer for all Peoples (54:17c–56:8)
Scene 4: The Dark Side of Jerusalem (56:9–57:13)
Scene 5: I Shall Heal Him (57:14–21)

The end of the act is marked by the words "there is no peace, says my God, for the wicked," like 48:22.

Historical Background

Bibliography

Ackroyd, P. R. "Two Old Testament Historical Problems of the Early Persian Period." *JNES* 17 (1958) 13–27. **Avigad, A.** *Bullae and Seals from a Post-exilic Judean Archive* (Qedem 4). Jerusalem, 1976. **Avi-Yonah, M.** *The Holy Land from the Persian to the Arab Conquests.* Grand Rapids: Baker, 1966. 13–14. **Bright, J.** *HI.* 373–79. **Cook, J. M.** *The Persian Empire.* London/Toronto: J. M. Dent and Sons, 1983. 58–63. **Cook, S. A.** "The Age of Zerubbabel." *Studies in Old Testament Prophecy.* FS T. H. Robinson. Edinburgh: T. & T. Clark, 1950. 19–36. **Cross, F. M.** "A Reconstruction of the Judaean Restoration." *JBL* 94 (1975) 4–18. **Culican, W.** *The Medes and the Persians.* 75–82. **Frye, R. N.** *The History of Ancient Iran.* 103–27. **Herodotus.** Books III–VIII. **McEvenue, S.** "The Political Structure in Judah from Cyrus to Nehemiah." *CBQ* 43 (1981) 353–64. **Meyers, E. M.** "The Persian Period and the Judean Restoration from Zerubbabel to Nehemiah." Paper read at SBL 1985, to appear in the new FS for F. M. Cross, Jr. ———. "The Shelomith Seal and the Judean Restoration." *Eretz-Israel* 18 (1985, FS A. Avigad) 33–38. **Olmstead, A. T.** *History of the Persian Empire.* 119–301. **Rainey, A.** "The Satrapy 'Beyond the River'." *AJBA* 1 (1969) 51–53. **Soggin, J. A.** *A History of Ancient Israel.* 265–71 (see, *Introduction* bibliography). **Stern, E.** *Material Culture of* *the Land of the Bible in the Persian Period.* Warminster: Aris & Phillips, 1982. 204–5. **Tadmor H.** "The Babylonian Exile and the Restoration." *A History of the Jewish People.* Ed. H. Ben-Sasson. Cambridge: U. P., 1976. 168. **Widengren, G.** "The Persian Period." *IJH.* 509–11.

Darius I established himself as a master of organization and a famous law-giver. His new codes were recognized in Egypt and through most of his realm. His organizational skill increased imperial efficiency in collecting taxes. He built a magnificent capital in Persepolis. He cut a canal in Egypt between the Nile and the Red Sea. He built roads across the empire and established a standard coin for the realm.

But he increasingly turned his attention to wars with Greece. The struggle for dominance of the eastern Mediterranean laid an emphasis on naval power beyond anything known before, which increased the strategic importance of Phoenician fleets and harbors as well as the Palestinian hinterland and highways. The control of Egypt was a central issue throughout the period. The famous battle of Marathon (490 B.C.) marked a turning point in the war, though it still kept Xerxes busy through most of his reign (485–465 B.C.).

Darius I reestablished the lenient religious policies of Cyrus. Xerxes, however, lacked his father's tolerance in religious matters. He was a heavy-handed tyrant in politics as well. His military ventures failed despite his possession of the greatest armies and fleets in the world.

Darius first consolidated his reign in the East, and then he moved to strengthen his hold of the rest of his empire. In the satrapy Beyond the River (i.e., Palestine/Syria) conflict had broken out between Judah's neighbors and Jerusalem even in the reigns of Cyrus and Cambyses over renewed efforts to build the Temple. When Zerubbabel renewed the work in 520–518 B.C. opposition surfaced again (Ezra 4:1–5). The work had to be stopped (Ezra 4:24). The renewal had been led by Zerubbabel, Joshua the High Priest, and the prophets Haggai and Zechariah (Ezra 5:1–2; Hag 1:1–2:23; Zech 3–4).

Tattenai, the governor of the territory, with his aides (Ezra 5:3), intervened. Their investigation gathered names for possible prosecution (Ezra 5:4). An official correspondence with Darius included the ominous phrase "wrote down the names." Jerusalem was vindicated by Darius's response. The decree of Cyrus had been found. But the name of Zerubbabel disappears at this point from the account. Zerubbabel seems to have opposed the participation of neighboring rulers in the rebuilding effort (Ezra 4:1–5). Apparently they were appeased by Zerubbabel's removal and were quieted by the reversal of policy at the emperor's command (Ezra 6:6–10 and 13). The Temple was finally completed with official help in 516–515 B.C. (Ezra 4:1–5).

These issues play a prominent part in this act: the death of a leader (Zerubbabel) when he was recognized as innocent of any culpable crime while others might have beem implicated (chap. 53), encouragement for Jerusalem to build and reach out (chap. 54), open policies toward neighborly participation in Temple worship (chap. 55).

Jerusalem still had its problems when imperial controls were relaxed later in Darius's reign and sharply under Xerxes, who had to concentrate on the wars against the Greeks. New archeological evidence (cf. E. M. Meyers, *Eretz-Israel* 18 [1985] 33–38, and in FS Cross, n. 8) suggests that Elnathan succeeded Zerubbabel as governor and that he was related by marriage to the line of David (Avigad, *Bullae and Seals,* 7, 34). The names of two other governors have been gleaned from jar handles found at Ramat Rahel: Jehoezer and Ahzai. So now Avigad's list of governors may parallel Cross's list (*JBL* 94 [1975] 17) of high priests of this period:

Governors (פחה)	*Priests*
Sheshbazzar, ca. 538 B.C.	Josadaq
Zerubbabel, ca. 520 B.C.	Joshua
Elnathan, late 6th cent.	Jeoyakim
Jehoezer, early 5th cent.	Eliashib
Ahzai, early 5th cent.	Johanan I

The period was one of relative stability. Jewish groups became established in various parts of the empire. Babylon continued to be a hospitable home for them. They rose to leading positions in business and in the government bureaucracy. In Asia Minor and in lower Egypt other groups flourished. A military community of Jews at Elephantine in Egypt is known by the wealth of Aramaic texts found there by archeologists.

Persian authorities undoubtedly expected their largesse for the Temple to be repaid in taxes and loyalty. These put strains on the economy and on the community in general (cf. Neh. 5:15). The strategic importance of Palestine for campaigns in Egypt and for naval activity in the Mediterranean required a strong military presence there throughout the period. Darius passed through in 519–518 B.C. Olmstead (*History of the Persian,* 142) thought that he summoned Zerubbabel and had him executed at this time for the kind of sedition that not he, but the prophets Haggai and Zechariah, had spread. Undoubtedly a military and tax-gathering presence remained in the following years. Darius's new code of law was promulgated in Egypt in 495 B.C. and was probably in force in Palestine at the same time.

When Xerxes ascended the throne in 485 B.C., Egypt rebelled again and there was unrest in Judah (Ezra 4:4–6). In 484 Xerxes passed through Palestine and recovered Egypt. Order was restored at an undoubtedly harsh and expensive price. Xerxes was more sectarian and less tolerant of religions than his father had been. Judah's privileges lapsed. Pressure was felt in Jerusalem from groups in Samaria as well as from Edom where Arabian settlers were now mixed with the older population.

In 482 B.C. the satrapy Beyond the River was detached from Babylon. Its most important subdivision was Phoenicia, which included Sidon, Tyre, and Arvad. By this time Phoenician ships were the core of the Persian navy and had the task of controlling the shipping lanes between Greece and Egypt. Cyprus and Syrian Palestine were also included in the satrapy (cf. Olmstead, *History of the Persian* 482–83).

Scene 1: The Punishment for Our Peace (52:13—53:12)

Darius had successfully established his rule (v 1) and now appears in Jerusalem in 518 B.C.

Zerubbabel had set to work diligently (Ezra 3:1–13). But the governor of the territory and Judah's neighbors did not understand (Ezra 4:1–5). They intervened and stopped the work on the Temple (Ezra 4:24). In the second year of his reign, 520 B.C. (Ezra 4:24 and Hag/Zech), Darius seemed to be firmly in control of the Empire, so Zerubbabel and his helpers set to work immediately (Ezra 5:1–2). Tattenai, governor of the satrapy Over the River, and Shether-Bozenair interfered again (Ezra 5:3–4). But work was allowed to proceed while a report was requested from Persian officials at court.

Before work was resumed with official support, Zerubbabel's name disappears from the account. This scene in the Vision suggests that he was beaten and killed in an encounter with authorities who had no idea that the emperor would support his work. Undoubtedly this brought increased bitterness in Judah toward the empire. Darius, who showed the kind of religious toleration that characterized his predecessor, Cyrus, was also concerned to stabilize his position in Palestine for the coming Egyptian campaign and for the sake of increased naval activity from Phoenician ports. Scene 1 portrays the emperor's intervention to set matters right in Jerusalem, not simply with a letter (as in Ezra 6:1–13) but by a personal appearance there during a military campaign in that region.

Yahweh notes Darius's status and work with satisfaction (v 13). Then Darius hears an inquiry into complaints of Zerubbabel's death.

Bibliography

Ahlström, G. W. "Isaiah 53, 8f." *BZ* 13 (1969) 95–98. **Allen, L. C.** "Isaiah LIII 2 again." *VT* 21 (1971) 490. **Alonso, A.** "Anotaciónes críticas a Is 53, 8." *CDios* 181 (1968) 89–100. ———. "La suerte del Siervo: Is 53, 9–10." *CDios* 181 (1968) 292–305. **Baars, W.** "Een weinig bekende oudlatijnse tekst van Jesaja 53." *NedTTs* 22 (1968) 241–48. **Bachl, G.** *Zur Auslegung der Ebedweissagung (Is 52:13–53:12) in der Literature des späten Judentums und im Neuen Testament.* Rome: Pont. Univ. Gregoriana, 1982. **Battenfield, J. R.** "Isaiah LIII 10: Taking an 'If' out of the Sacrifice of the Servant." *VT* 32 (1982) 485. **Bergmeier, R.** "Das Streben nach Gewinn—des Volkes עון." *ZAW* 81 (1969) 93–97. **Blythin, I.** "Difficulties in the Hebrew Text of Is 53:11." *BT* 17 (1966) 27–31. **Bundy, D. D.** "Isaiah 53 in East and West." *Typus, Symbol, Allegorie.* FS A. Brems. Ed. M. Schmidt, C. F. Geyer. Regensburg: F. Pustet, 1982. 54–74. **Clines, D. J. A.** *I, He, We and They. A Literary Approach to Isaiah 53.* JSOTSup 1. Sheffield: U. of Sheffield, 1976. **Collins, J. J.** "The Suffering Servant: Scapegoat or Example?" *Proceedings of the Irish Biblical Association* 4 (1980) 59–67. **Coppens, J.** "La finale du quatrième chant du Serviteur (Is LIII, 10–12)." *ETL* 39 (1963) 114–21. **Daabe, P. R.** "The Effect of Repetition in the Suffering Servant Song." *JBL* 103 (1984) 77–84. **Dahood, M.** "Isaiah 53:8–12 and Massoretic Misconstructions." *Bib* 63 (1982) 566–70. ———. "Phoenician Elements in Isaiah 52:13–53:12." *Near Eastern Studies.* FS W. F. Albright. Baltimore: Johns Hopkins, 1971. 63–73. **Day, J.** *"da'at* 'humiliation' in Isaiah LIII 11." *VT* 30 (1980) 97–103. **Elliger, K.** "Jes 53,10: alte Crux—neuer Vorschlag." *MIO* 15 (1969) 228–33. **———.** "Nochmals Textkritisches zu Jes 53." *Wort, Lied und Gottesspruch.* FzB 2. FS J. Ziegler. Stuttgart: Katholisches Bibelwerk, 1972. 137–44. **———.** "Textkritisches zu Deuterojesaja." *Near Eastern Studies.* FS W. F. Albright. Baltimore: Johns Hopkins, 1971. 113–19. **Fohrer, G.** "Stellvertretung und Schuldopfer in Jesaja 52,13–53,12 vor dem Hintergrund des Alten Testaments und das Alten Orients." *Das Kreuz Jesu.* Göttingen: Vandenhoeck & Ruprecht, 1969. 7–31. **Galland, C.** "A Short Structural Reading of Isaiah 52:13–53:12." *Introduction à la Journée Biblique.* Centre Protestant d'Études et de Documentation. 88–92 = *Structuralism and Biblical Hermeneutics.* PTMS 22. Ed. and tr. A. M. Johnson, Jr. Pittsburg: Pickwick Press, 1979. 197–206. **Gispen, W. H.** "Jesaja 53,10 und das Schuldopfer." *GerefTT* 72 (1972) 193–204. **Gordon, R. P.** "Isaiah LIII 2." *VT* 21 (1970) 491–92. **Gosker, R.** "Jesaja 53—ein Denklied." *TK* 7 (1980) 5–18. **Haag, H.** "Das Lied vom leidenden Gottesknecht (Is 52,13–53,12)." *BK* 16 (1961) 3–5. **———.** "Das Opfer der Gottesknechts (Jes 53,10)." *TTZ* 86 (1977) 81–98. **Hertzberg, H-P.** "Die 'Abtrünnigen' und die 'Vielen'." *Verbannung und Heimkehr.* FS W. Rudolf. Tübingen: J. C. B. Mohr, 1961. 97–108. **Koch, K.** "Messias und Sündenvergebung in Jesaja 53—Targum." *JSJ* 3 (1972) 117–48. **Komlosh, J.** "The Countenance of the Servant of the Lord: Was It Marred?" *JQR* 65 (1974/75) 217–20. **Lindsey, F. D.** "Isaiah's Songs of the Servant, Parts 4 and 5: The Career of the Servant in Isa 52,13–53,12." *BSac* 139 (1982) 312–29; 140 (1983) 21–39. **Marcheselli-Casale, C.** "Proiezioni di risurrezione corporale nell'AT. Suggerimenti di analisi strutturale su Is 53,8–12; Sal 16,9–11 e Ez 37,1–14." *Asprenas* 31 (1984) 367–82. **Martin-Achard, R.** "Trois études sur Esaïe 53." *RTP* 114 (1982) 159–70. **Müller, H-P.** "Ein Vorschlag zu Jes 53,10f." *ZAW* 81 (1969) 377–80. **Murray, H.** "An Approach to the Fourth Servant Song." *Compass* 13 (1979) 43–46. **Nakazawa, K.** "Emendation of the Text of Isaiah 53,11." *AJBI* 2 (1976) 101–9. **———.** *Kunan no Shimobe.* Tokyo: Yamamoto Shoten, 1975. **Payne, D. F.** "Recent Trends in the Study of Isaiah 53." *IBS* 1 (1979) 3–18. **Reiterer, F. V.** "Stellvertretung—Lied—Jenseitshoffnung." *Heiliger Dienst* 36 (1982) 12–32. **Rembaum, J. E.** "The Development of a Jewish Exegetical Tradition Regarding Isaiah 53." *HTR* 75 (1982) 239–311. **Schwarz, G.** ". . . wie ein Reis vor ihm" (53:2a). *ZAW* 83 (1971) 255–56. **———.** "'. . . sieht er . . . wird er satt . . .'? Eine Emendation." *ZAW* 84 (1972) 356–58. **Soggin, J. A.** "Tod und Auferstehung des leidenden Gottesknechtes. Jesaja 53,8–10." *ZAW* 87 (1975) 346–55. **Steck, O. H.** "Aspekte des Gottesknechts in Jes 52,13–53,12." *ZAW* 97 (1985) 36–57. **Treves, M.** "Isaiah LIII." *VT* 24 (1974) 98–108. **Welshman, H.** "The Atonement Effected by the Servant, Is 52:13–53:12." *BT* 23 (1973) 46–49. **Whybray, R. N.** *Thanksgiving for a Liberated Prophet: An Interpretation of Isaiah Chapter 53.* JSOTSup 4. Sheffield: U. of Sheffield, 1978. **Williamson, H. G. M.** "*DA'AT* in Isaiah LIII 11." *VT* 28 (1978) 118–22. **———.** " 'The Sure Mercies of David': Subjective or Objective Genitive?" *JSS* 23 (1978) 31–49. **Zimmerli, W.** "Zur Vorgeschichte von Jes 53." *Studien zur alttestamentliche Theologie und Prophetie.* Munich: Kaiser, 1974. 213–21.

Translation

Yahweh: (about Darius)	52:13 *See! My servant succeeds!* [a] *He rises up!* [b] *He is exalted and very high!*	3+4
Tattenai: (to Darius about Zerubbabel)	14 *Just as many were astonished about you* [a] *(masc sg),* [b] *so* [c] *marred* [d] *was his appearance—hardly a person,*	4+3+3

and his form—hardly[e] *human.*[b]

Tattenai's men: 15 *So he has startled*[a] *many nations.* 4+4
Because of him, kings shut their mouths.
For they see something which had not been told to them 5+3
and that of which they had heard nothing they understand.

Messengers: (about Zerubbabel) 53:1 *Who believed our report?* 3+4
And to whom is the Arm of Yahweh revealed?

Messengers: (about Darius) 2 *But he grew up before him*[a] *like a plant,* 3+3
and like a vine from dry land.
He had no form 2+3+3
and no beauty that we should look at him.[b]
No attraction that we should desire him.

First Chorus of Jerusalemites: (about Zerubbabel) 3 *He was despised and rejected (by) men,*[a] 3+2+2
a man of pains
who was visited by[b] *sickness.*

Second Chorus: *Like one hiding (his) face from us,* 3+3
he was despised[c] *and we did not value him.*

Third Chorus: 4 *Surely he bore our sickness!* 4+2
and our pains—he[a] *carried them!*
But as for us, we thought him struck down, 3+3
beaten by God and afflicted.

First and Second Choruses: 5 *He was being wounded*[a] *because of our rebellions.* 3+2
He was being bruised because of our wrongs.
The punishment for our wholeness was on him 3+3
and with his stripes comes healing for us.

Entire Chorus: 6 *All of us like sheep stray away.* 3+3
Each of us—we turn to our own way.
But Yahweh laid on him 3+3
the iniquity of us all.

Darius: 7 *He was oppressed and afflicted,* 3+3
yet he did not open his mouth.
Like a lamb he was led to slaughter 3+4+3
and like a ewe before her shearers is silent
he did not open his mouth.
8 *Because of prosecution and judgment, he was taken away.* 3+3
Who thinks of his misfortune?[a]
That he was cut off from the land of living ones 4+4
because of the rebellion of my people[b] *(was this) stroke*[c] *to him.*[d]
9 *And now one has appointed*[a] *his grave with criminals* 3+2
and with a rich one is his grave.[b]
Although he has done no violent act 3+3
and no deceit was in his mouth.

Heavens: 10 *Yahweh willed to bruise him.* 3+1
He caused his sickness.[a]

Earth: *If he (Darius) considers*[b] *his soul a sin offering,* 3+2+2
he (Darius) will see seed.
He will prolong days.

Heavens: *And the will of Yahweh* 2+2
succeeds in his (Darius') hand.

Yahweh: 11 *Because of the travail of his (Zerubbabel's) soul,* 2+2
he (Darius) will see.[a] *He will be satisfied.*[b]
In knowing (about) him (Zerubbabel), he (Darius)
will justify (many). 2+3+3
My servant (Darius) becomes a righteous one[c]
for many
and will forgive their wrongs.

Darius: 12 *Therefore I allot to him (Zerubbabel) a share with*
the many. 3+3
And he will share an allotment with the healthy,
because he poured out his soul even to death 5+2
and was numbered with rebels.
He himself bore the sins of many 3+2.
and interceded for rebels.[a]

Notes

13.a. Budde emends to ישראל "Israel." This is without textual support and is unnecessary.

13.b. LXX omits "and he rises up." DSS^{Isa} adds *waw* "and."

14.a. Two Heb. MSS, Syr Tg read עליו "about him." DSS^{Isa} עליכה, LXX ἐπὶ σέ, Vg *super te* support MT עליך "about you," the more difficult text. Read MT.

14.b-b. *BHS* suggests transposing to the end of 53:2. This is not necessary. Note instead the parallel themes.

14.c. The repetition of כן "thus," "so" in v 15 is unusual, but the use of כ followed by כן is not (BDB, 486 § 2).

14.d MT מִשְׁחַת "marred" (BDB, 1008) is a *hap. leg.*, but is clearly pointed as a noun related to שחת "go to ruin." DSS^{Isa} משחתי is pf from משח "anoint" (BDB, 603; Kutscher, *Isaiah Scroll,* 262). The Babylonian tradition points מָשְׁחַת "spoiled," "ruined," a hoph ptcp from שׁחת, as does one MS מושחת. LXX interprets ἀδοξήσει "he will be without glory," followed by Vg. Tg חשוך "was wretched" may be thinking of the root שׁוח "sink down," "be depressed" (BDB, 1001). ʼA Σ Θ (translated by Chrysostom as *corrupta est*) and Syr *mḥbl* support MT. With so many possible roots, the Heb. word is a teaser. MT's pointing is probably as good as any.

14.e. MT מן may introduce the comparative "more than," "hardly" or it may indicate instrumentality "by." Both of these meanings are applications of the basic idea of separation (GKC §§ 119*w–z;* BDB, 577–83).

15.a. MT יַזֶּה may be from נזה "sprinkle" (BDB, 633, I) or may be a *hap. leg.* from an identical root related to Arab *nazā* "startle," "cause to leap" (BDB, 633, II). LXX θαυμάσονται "they will wonder" may suggest the latter derivation. Tg יבדר "he will scatter" supports the former. *BHS* suggests יַזֶּה/יַזּוּ "he/they will splatter" or ירגזו "they are agitated" (BDB, 919) or יבזהו "they despise" (BDB, 102). DSS^{Isa} supports MT. Read MT with the meaning "startle."

53:2.a. *BHS* notes a proposal to read לפנינו "before us." This has no textual support and is unnecessary.

2.b. *BHS* suggests moving the *athnaḥ* to this point. The translation agrees with this division of the verse. The meter and sense are better.

3.a. אישים "men" is an unusual pl, occurring only in Ps 141:4, Prov 8:4, and here. The usual form is אנשים.

3.b. MT וידוע qal pass ptcp "and known," but GKC § 50*f* considers it a verbal adj denoting an inherent quality, "knowing." DSS^{Isa} ויודע qal act ptcp "and one knowing." 1QIsa^{b} וידע "and he has known." LXX εἰδώς ptcp "knowing." Tg paraphrases. Read MT.

3.c. MT נבזה "despised" is niph ptcp from בזה (BDB, 102). DSS^{Isa} ונבוזהו "and we plundered him" is a qal impf from בזז. LXX Tg support MT. Read MT.

4.a. Several Heb. MSS and Syr Vg insert הוא "he." Not necessary. The pron is understood.

5.a. MT מְחֹלָל is poal ptcp. *BHS* suggests a pual ptcp.

8.a. MT דורו "his generation." But G. R. Driver (*JTS* 36 [1935] 403) compares it to Akk *dūru* and Arab *dauru(n)* to translate "his lasting state," "change of fortune."

8.b. DSS[Isa] עמו "his people." LXX Tg support MT.

8.c. MT נֶגַע "a stroke" is a noun (BDB, 619). DSS[Isa] נוגע inf constr "to strike." LXX paraphrases ἤχθη "he was led." Tg also paraphrases ימטי "he will transfer." MT is the difficult reading. Keep it.

8.d. MT למו, lit., "to them" (BDB, 510), though many argue that here it is identical to לו "to him." 'A Σ Θ Tg "to them"; Vg "him." LXX εἰς θάνατον, "to death" presupposes Heb. למות (*BHS;* GKC § 103 n. 3). DSS[Isa] supports MT. Read MT, meaning "to him."

9.a. MT וַיִּתֵּן "and he appointed." DSS[Isa] ויתנו "and they appointed." LXX δώσω "I shall give." Tg וימסר "he shall deliver." *BHS* suggests וַיֻּתַּן "and he was appointed." Read MT.

9.b. MT בְּמֹתָיו may be translated "in his deaths" from מות (BDB, 560) or be derived from במה "funeral mound" (BDB, 119; on the pl constr, see GKC §§ 87*s*, 95*o*). DSS[Isa] בומתו suggests the latter derivation (Kutscher, *Isaiah Scroll,* 225); LXX Syr Tg Vg support the former. But all read a sg. So *BHS,* following Albright ("The High Place in Ancient Palestine," *Volume du Congrès, Strasbourg,* VTSup 4 [Leiden: E. J. Brill, 1957] 242–58) suggests במתו "his grave."

10.a. MT החלי "he made him sick" (BDB, 317). DSS[Isa] ויחללהו "he profaned him" (BDB, 320; cf. Kutscher, *Isaiah Scroll,* 236–37). LXX Tg paraphrase. Driver (*JTS* 36 [1935] 403–4) draws on the Syr to emend MT החלי אם־ to read והחליאמו "and made him suffer." Vg *in infirmitate* "in sickness." Read MT.

10.b. MT אם תשים "if she/you make(s)." DSS[Isa] agrees. M. Dahood ("Textual Problems in Isaiah," *CBQ* 22 [1960] 406) suggests dividing the letters אמת שם "truly, he made himself." Read MT, the more difficult text. LXX Tg turn the meaning on its head.

11.a. DSS[Isa] and 1QIsa[b] add אור "light," as does LXX δεῖξαι . . . φῶς "to show light." But these intentionally change the meaning (see Kutscher, *Isaiah Scroll,* 543). Read MT with Syr Tg Vg. Cf. Elliger 529.

11.b. יִשְׂבָּע "he is satisfied" has a pausal pointing. Read בדעתו "by knowing him" with what follows (contra *BHS*).

11.c. *BHS* suggests placing צדיק "righteous one" after בדעתו, but DSS[Isa] supports MT's order. Read MT.

12.a. לפשעים "for the rebels." DSS[Isa] and 1QIsa[b] לפשעיהמה "for their sins" emend to parallel the previous line (Kutscher, *Isaiah Scroll,* 383). LXX reverses the meaning καὶ διὰ τὰς ἁμαρτίας αὐτῶν παραδόθη "and on account of their sins he was delivered." 'A Σ Θ Tg Syr Vg support MT. Read MT.

Form/Structure/Setting

This scene contains the culmination of several themes from previous scenes. 52:13 and 15 imply fulfillment of promises made in 49:7, and 53:1 recalls the joy at the approach of messengers in 52:7 and the messengers commissioned in 40:9. But there is also an ominous sense of foreboding concerning one who had been disfigured and mutilated (52:14), pierced, crushed, punished, and wounded (53:5), oppressed and afflicted under judgment (53:7–8), and finally buried (53:9). The theme is complex, recognizing success on one side and agonizing over public humiliation and the execution of an innocent man on the other. The tension is resolved in 53:10–12.

The scene is obtuse because of the very large number of personal pronouns which lack antecedents. The speakers are also not clear. Yahweh must be the speaker when "my servant" is mentioned in 52:13 and 53:11. Perhaps the same could be said for 53:8 "my people," although this could also be spoken by the king. The subject matter of 53:1 relates it to the messengers of 52:7. The entire section from 53:1–6 is spoken in first person plural by a chorus or by several groups of speakers.

A key question is whether the "servant" is also the sufferer. In the previous act, 49:5–9 is spoken by a Cyrus-type servant, Darius, while 50:4–9 presents a sufferer who is obviously a different person. But 50:10 was spoken by the "servant" Darius. The sufferer was identified in the commentary as Zerubbabel.

Can it be that the same is true here? "Righteous" is a term regularly used about Cyrus (cf. *Excursus:* צדק/צדקה *"Righteousness, Legitimacy"*). The *Translation* above understands the "servant" in this scene to be Darius who is therefore the speaker of 53:7–9 and 12.

Excursus: The Sufferer/Martyr of 50:4–9 and Chapter 53

Bibliography

Buri, F. *Vom Sinn des Leidens.* Basel: F. Reinhardt, 1963. **Cazelles, H.** "La destinée du Serviteur, Is 52,13–53,12." *AsSeign* 2 (1969) 6–14. **Chavasse, C.** "The Suffering Servant and Moses." *CQR* 165 (1964) 152–63. **Duarte Lourenco, J.** "A Identificacao do Servo do cap. 53 de Isaias. Perspectivas judaicas e cristas." *Itinerarium* 30 (1984) 169–212. **Homerski, J.** "Cierpiący Mesjasz w starotestamentalnych przepowiedniach prorockich." *RocTKan* 27 (1980) 27–42. ———. "Cierpiący wybawca i oredownik (Iz 52,13–53–12)." *RocTKan* 24 (1977) 75–90. **Kapelrud, A. S.** "Second Isaiah and the Suffering Servant." *God and His Friends in the Old Testament.* Oslo: Universitetsforlaget, 1979. 123–29. **Kida, J.** "Second Isaiah and the Suffering Servant: a New Proposal for a Solution." *AJBI* 5 (1979) 45–66. **Liao Yong-hsiang.** "Shangchuchihp'u: Lun Tierh Yisaiyachung de shouk'uchihp'u." *ColcTFujen* 6 (1974) 317–52, 523–46. **Ruppert, L.** "Le serviteur souffrant." *Conc* (Paris) 119 (1976) 63–72. ———. "Der leidende Gottesknecht." *Conc* (Eins./Mainz) 12 (1976) 571–75. **Sekine, S.** "Die Theosizee des Leidens im Deuterojesajanischen Buch, unter redaktionsgeschichtlichem Gesichtspunkt," *AJBI* 8 (1982) 50–112. **Waldow, H. E. von.** "The Servant of the Lord, the Jews, and the People of God." *Integrini Parietis Septum.* FS M. Barth. Pittsburgh Theological Monograph Series 33. Pittsburgh: Pickwick Press, 1981. 355–69.

See the following for full bibliographies:
Clines, D. J. A. *I, We, They: A Literary Approach to Isaiah 53.* JSOTSup. Sheffield: University of Sheffield, 1976. **North, C. R.** *The Suffering Servant in Deutero-Isaiah.* London: Oxford University Press, 1948. **Whybray, R. N.** *Thanksgiving for a Liberated Prophet.* JSOTSup 4. Sheffield: U. of Sheffield, 1978.

The bibliography on this topic is enormous, indicating the great interest in the subject and the lack of agreement on it. The interpretation of these passages and the discussion of identification (who is the sufferer?) have continued at least from the first century (Acts 8:34) until now. C. R. North has traced the history of the discussion in detail, including possible identification of Zerubbabel as the sufferer (pp. 2 and 42).

In recent times "the sufferer passages" (50:4–9 and chapter 53) have been grouped with "servant of Yahweh" poems by Duhm and those who followed him. The sufferer and the servant have therefore been considered identical.

This commentary will show that "the sufferer passages" are distinct from "the servant passages" and that the sufferer and the servant are not the same person in the Vision. Israel and the Persian emperor (Cyrus or Darius) are called "the anointed" or "the servant of Yahweh" (See *Excursus: Identifying the "Servant of Yahweh"*). But the sufferer in 50:4–9 and the dead sufferer in chap. 53 is more likely to be a leader in Jerusalem (perhaps Zerubbabel) who has been executed before the arrival of authorities sent by Darius.

This identification should take nothing away from the model or symbol of Yahweh's appointed one who patiently bears suffering even to death which means so much for New Testament christology. The importance of chap. 53 lies in showing God's attitude toward and use of an innocent death to accomplish peace and healing for the community. God is prepared to regard the death as vicarious propitiation for the sins of the group, "a guilt offering."

In context this view is shared by the emperor who agrees not to prosecute those who killed him. The decisions of Yahweh and the emperor, his servant, create the possibility for harmony in the district.

The sufferer does not speak because he is already dead. The historical background of this period is described at some length in Ezra 3–6, Haggai, and Zechariah 1–8. A remarkable feature of the accounts is the leadership of Zerubbabel in the early work on the Temple and in the conflict with the territorial governor and leaders of neighboring districts. But his name is totally missing in the accounts of the completion of that work (cf. *Excursus: Zerubbabel*). Perhaps he was a victim of a confrontation with the governor and was summarily executed while the governor thought that the building operation had no official sanction. The issue of succession to the throne had not been finally settled, so that such leadership could be interpreted as preparation for rebellion against the empire or against one of the claimants to the empire. (Is it even possible that Tattenai and the other official had initially supported another candidate for the throne and been surprised and embarrassed by Darius's success, as 52:13–15 implies?) If this is true, it would furnish a very plausible setting for this scene. By the time Darius, with Tattenai the territorial governor in his entourage, appeared in Jerusalem on his way to Egypt to suppress a rebellion there, it had been clearly established that Jerusalem's leaders had had official approval of their project from Cyrus and that Darius fully supported Cyrus's policies in religious matters (Ezra 6:1–12). Darius may have also known Zerubbabel during the days when both served in the Persian capital. So the case is of special interest to the emperor and particularly awkward for the governor. The issue of the murder, however, is pressed upon the emperor at his reception in Jerusalem (see *Excursus: Zerubbabel*).

Critical explanation of the passage has been difficult because it has been assumed that the successful "servant" of 52:13 and 53:11 is also the suffering, dying one of the other verses. The form of the passage has been called "two speeches of salvation" with "a confession" between (Melugin, *Formation,* 167). The nations also have been presumed to be participants in the scene. A careful examination shows this is not true. Recognition of the "servant" is past. The issue at hand is not recognition of Darius as "servant" (and emperor) but the unresolved charge that the governor and his troops executed an innocent man, perhaps even a supporter of Darius's claims to the throne. An outline of the scene should take these into consideration.

The order of events is:

The introduction of Yahweh's servant (Darius) in Jerusalem (52:13)
Excuses by Tattenai related to the execution (52:14–15)
Protests by the messengers that no one listened to them (53:1)
Excuses (among themselves) for failure to rally to Darius earlier (53:2)
The crowd identifies itself with the executed leader (53:3–6)
The facts of the case are established (53:7–9)
Interpretation from a heavenly perspective (53:10–11)
The official disposition of the case (53:12)

The literary presentation assumes an arch structure:

A The servant of Yahweh is the one who has succeeded (52:13)
  B Problem: How could they have known that Darius would win or that the murdered one was innocent? (52:14–15)
    C How could we (the crowd) have known? (53:1–2)
KEYSTONE He died for us (the many in Jerusalem)! (53:3–6)
    C′ The facts are known to Darius (53:7–9)
  B′ Yahweh's strategy for Darius and for the death (53:10–11)
A′ The servant absolves the people of guilt (53:12)

The Solomonic solution (Yahweh's strategy) to the delicate problems posed by the visit of Darius to Jerusalem with the territorial governor soon after the brutal murder of Zerubbabel recognizes that the incident had been followed by confession and humiliation by both the governor and the people. The emperor, in the interest of securing stability and peace for this part of his newly won realm, absolves both the governor and the rebellious people. He rehabilitates the name and family of the deceased. Thus peace and the continuation of the Temple project are secured (Ezra 6:13–15).

Comment

52:13 *My servant succeeds.* This optimistic assertion is typical of ones made in the Vision about the work of emperors chosen to do Yahweh's work, from Tiglath-Pileser through Cyrus. It is especially true of the Persians. God chose unlikely men for the task, those not necessarily in line for the throne. This was true of Cyrus and of Darius, and it will be true of Artaxerxes. They gained the seat of power and then each decreed that the Temple in Jerusalem be built (Ezra 1–6). Thus the unlikely successor who has now established himself on the throne of the Persian Empire is introduced in Jerusalem.

14 *Just as many were astonished about you.* When Cambyses died Gaumata was quickly recognized as his successor in much of the Empire. Although Darius was of royal blood, he was not in direct line to the throne. He had held the fairly humble position of military aide to Cambyses on their campaign in Egypt. So many in the empire, including the officials in the satrapy Beyond the River of which Judah was a part, must have been surprised and even deeply embarrassed by the swift rise of Darius to power. The pungent relevance of this surprise concerned imperial policy toward Jerusalem and the building of the Temple (Ezra 4:6–17). Cyrus, Darius, and Artaxerxes were well-disposed toward the project (and to various other religious enterprises as well). There is no evidence that Cambyses or Xerxes showed any positive interest in it, or that Gaumata would have. Tattenai, the territorial governor, may well have been following approved imperial policy in suppressing the work while Cambyses and Gaumata lived. Through a quick turn of events, it is now Darius who rules and his policies favor Jerusalem (Ezra 6:1–12). An additional embarrassment to Tattenai and to the groups in Jerusalem who allowed him to brutalize Zerubbabel is the clear evidence in this case of their observance of policies belonging to Darius's enemies. The *many* in the satrapy Beyond the River and in Jerusalem are desperately adjusting to the new realities of Darius's regime. Reference to *the many* appears again in the settlement announced in 53:11–12.

14–15 *So marred* implies that the executed body was mutilated. The use of כן . . . כ "as . . . so" suggests that the execution fitted the circumstances. *He had startled many nations* asserts that the diligent work of rebuilding the Temple had deeply disturbed neighboring peoples and their rulers. They interpreted the work to be a sign that Judah was preparing for war, intending to regain supremacy over the area which it had ruled under David centuries before.

For they see something which had not been told to them. What they saw was the rebuilding of the Temple in Jerusalem. What they had not been told was the royal decree that sanctioned it (Ezra 5:8–17). Now that these things are known, the governor and his people are deeply embarrassed. So the state visit of the emperor to Jerusalem is taking place under a cloud of resentment and distrust.

53:1 *Our report.* Messengers who had brought word protest that it was not their fault. No one had believed them. Are these the same messengers who were greeted with such jubilation in 52:7–10 when they brought a message of peace and salvation? *The Arm of Yahweh* was predicted in 52:10. The sign of Yahweh's power and presence had appeared to be conspicuously absent at that time.

2 *He grew up like a plant before him.* Pronouns without antecedents appear throughout these verses. The *waw* consecutive ties this verse closely to v 1. This interpretation understands most of the third person masculine pronouns to refer the "the servant" of 52:13 (Darius). The second pronoun may refer to his patron Cambyses. That is, Darius grew up in the court of Cambyses as an insignificant and unpromising person. *A vine from dry ground* is figurative language for one of parentage not in line for succession to the throne. *No form, no beauty, no attraction* imply that Darius was a most unlikely candidate to gain support for his seizure of the throne. *We:* the speakers are the *many*, the crowd, of 52:14. They are talking among themselves, not addressing the emperor.

3 The verse begins independently with no connection to the previous verse. The theme is the same but is about a different person. This group is less concerned with their earlier lack of support for Darius than about the unresolved issue of the violent execution of a Jewish leader by Tattenai and his troops. *He was despised and rejected* may refer to the challenge to Zerubbabel mentioned in Ezra 3:1–5 or 5:3–4. *A man of pains who was visited by sickness* may speak of his death, but the reference could also reflect his earlier troubles recounted in 50:4–9. *We did not esteem him* implies a recognition that the crowd had not supported Zerubbabel as they should have.

4 The chorus of Jerusalemites continues: *He bore our sickness.* This is a belated expression of solidarity with him. He was executed for something in which they were all involved. The official reaction could have prosecuted all of them. As it was the governor made an example of one man and let it go at that. But it could have been very different. *We thought him struck down, beaten by God and afflicted.* At the time of his death this sense of solidarity had been missing. They had been glad to be rid of the problem and rationalized his death as his fate determined by God. In that way they could simply forget it.

5 But now they confess, even at the risk of being charged by the emperor and the governor, *he was being wounded because of our rebellions. He was being bruised because of our wrongs.* The sense of solidarity and recognition is complete. Then the understanding comes full circle. *The punishment* which made possible their present peaceful *wholeness* had been placed *on him.* Because of the beatings that produced *his stripes* no one else was beaten. They experienced a *healing* of their problems.

6 The people recognize their collective and individual culpability in straying away, whether the sin be against God or the empire. Then Yahweh's fateful use of one person is picked up from v 4 above, but with a much deeper meaning. *Yahweh laid on him the iniquity of us all.* The language has changed from political rebellion to the religious and moral sense of iniquity, and an understanding of substitutionary atonement is born. It had long existed in the sacrificial cult (Lev 16), but in this verse it finds classical expression in a new sense.

7 The speaker and the tone change. The speech is more factual, expressing wonder that the punishment was accepted in silence. Ezra 5:4 tells of Tattenai and his men asking for the names of all those involved in the project. The silence of the sufferer not only avoided a craven plea for mercy but also revealed no information even under torture.

8 The phrase *prosecution and judgment* confirms the official nature of the execution by the governor and his men. *His misfortune* implies a change of status from an enthusiastic builder, acclaimed by prophets (Hag 1:1–2:9, 20–23; Zech 4:1–14) and supported by priests and the community (Zech 4:1–14; Ezra 4:1–3), to a tortured prisoner executed on a baseless charge. *Cut off* means that he was killed. *Because of the rebellion:* there were doubtless zealous rebels among the people. The Jews had such terrorists every time they were under foreign rule. But Zerubbabel was not one of them. *My people* is a term usually spoken by Yahweh. But any ruler could use it. It is fitting here in the mouth of Darius.

9 A formerly respected leader has been dishonored by the placing of *his grave with criminals. With a rich one* remains unexplained. The phrase has been applied to Jesus (cf. *Explanation* and *Excursus: The Sufferer/Martyr*), but it is difficult to find the meaning in its original setting. But the verse leaves no doubt that Darius considers him to have been innocent of any act worthy of death, whether *a violent act* or perjury (*deceit in his mouth*). His execution was clearly unwarranted.

Darius has a problem. The execution is an old issue. He has now received the loyalty of the governor, Tattenai, and of other local administrators in the region, and has announced his support for the rebuilding project (Ezra 6:1–9). Things are going well, but this unfortunate old incident threatens the peace and well-being of all. Since he is on the way to quell a revolt in Egypt, it is even more important that the peace in Palestine be maintained.

10 As is customary in the Vision, the perspective from heaven's balcony adds meaning to the scene. Yahweh's purpose will also be threatened if the old case is reopened in earnest. From this perspective the death was not simply an unfortunate accident. *Yahweh willed to bruise him. He caused him pain.* This does not mean that Yahweh's will, unrelated to the circumstances, was to bring harm or to kill. The biblical view is very practical in these things. All events, even the will of Yahweh in them, must be seen in context. In the confrontation with the governor, Yahweh chose the option of allowing the death of the leader so that the project and the rehabilitation of Jerusalem could continue. *Willed* (literally, "was pleased") is a term used of sovereigns. Their pleasure is equivalent to their will in a matter.

The antecedent for the pronoun changes in the second distich. The subject is Darius and the disposition that he will make of the case. If he comes to see the issue as Yahweh does, all will go well. *If he considers his soul a sin offering,* that is, if Darius will reckon Zerubbabel's death, innocent though he may have been, as sufficient atonement for whatever culpable rebellion there may have been on the part of all concerned and thus wipes the slate clean, then Darius *will see seed and prolong days;* that is, he will have a long and fruitful reign. Yahweh's will, announced long before (44:28), is to have the Temple restored and to have Israelites come to it from all over the empire (2:2–4; 40:9–11; 45:13; 49:8b–9; 52:7–10). *Succeeds* is the term used for the Cyrus-type servant in 52:13 above and means that he will be able to accomplish God's will.

11 The heavenly perspective is accented by Yahweh's words. *The travail of his soul* refers to the suffering and death of Zerubbabel. *He will see; he will be satisfied.* This speaks of Darius. He has a way out of his dilemma if he treats Zerubbabel's death as atonement for the charge of rebellion. *By knowing about him* (Zerubbabel), *he* (Darius) *can justify.* The death of Zerubbabel provides Darius with a legal way to resolve the issue. *My servant* refers to Darius, who by this act proves his legitimacy as Yahweh's servant. He vindicates Jerusalem and its people against the charges brought by the governor and neighboring peoples. *He forgives their wrongs.* This is presented as Yahweh's realistic and practical solution to the problem posed in 52:14–15.

12 This is Darius's announced decision in the case. Presumably, he has dealt with the people of Jerusalem and with the governor and his officials as Yahweh had proposed. Now he turns to the issue of Zerubbabel's innocence. He cannot undo the hurt and death. But he does remove the stigma of a criminal's death and the disabilities imposed on an executed criminal's family. Darius restores the rights of inheritance (*I allot to him*) with the *many* of Jerusalem's population, because he recognizes that the innocent men voluntarily took the place of rebels in death. The point is emphasized: *He himself bore the sins of many and interceded for rebels* although it is clearly recognized that he was in fact not one of them and probably opposed their views and plans.

Explanation

The arrangement adopted by this commentary places this passage in a specific historical setting. But from that specific setting emerges a universal truth about God and his ways that is vital for the faith of Jew and Christian: the principle of substitutionary atonement, not only through animal sacrifice as in the day of atonement, but supremely through a willing person.

This is effective atonement when the recipients of the benefits gained through the sacrifice confess their guilt and recognize that one has died for them (53:4–6) and when the sovereign agrees to recognize the atoning effect (53:10–12). Christians have viewed the crucifixion of Jesus Christ in these terms and used this passage to interpret and appropriate that meaning (cf. Luke 22:37; Mark 10:45 = Matt 20:28; Mark 14:24 = Matt 26:28 = Luke 22:20; and the discussion by R. T. France, *Jesus and the Old Testament* [London: Tyndale Press, 1971] 110–32).

This passage illustrates how past wrongs (the rebellion of Jerusalemites and the death of the sufferer) are hindrances to appropriation of something new and good (the favor of the new emperor). It shows how good can come from something that was wrong. This is only possible when all parties are humbled in recognition of the wrongs and of higher authority and goals. It is further possible because God is prepared to endorse the arrangement. Justice is served, not through vengeance and retribution, but by allowing the death to be a means of atoning reconciliation in order to build a foundation for cooperation, peace, and salvation.

God is shown to be goal-oriented. His justice looks forward, not backward. His drive toward deliverance and salvation, toward restoration and fellowship, can use innocent death to achieve these goals for others.

Scene 2: Sing, You Barren One! (54:1–17b)

Bibliography

Beuken, W. A. M. "Isaiah 54: The Multiple Identity of the Person Addressed." *OTS* 19 (1974) 29–70. **Dahood, M.** "Yiphil Imperative *yaṭṭī* in Isaiah 54,2." *Or* 46 (1977) 383–84. **Gunn, D. M.** "Deutero-Isaiah and the Flood." *JBL* 94 (1975) 498–508. **Martin-Achard, R.** "Esaïe LIV et la nouvelle Jérusalem." *Congress Volume Vienna.* VTSup 32. Leiden: E. J. Brill, 1981. 238–62. **Pavan, V.** "Is 54,1 (Laetare sterilis) nella catechesi dei primi due secoli." *VC* 18 (1981) 341–55. **Schwarz, G.** "Keine Waffe" (54:17a). *BZ* 15 (1971) 254–55.

Translation

Heavens: 54:1 *Sing, barren one who never gave birth!* 4+4
Break into singing![a] *Cry out, you who have not travailed!*

For the children of the desolate are a multitude— 2+2+2
more than the children of a married woman,
says Yahweh.

Earth: 2 *Enlarge the place of your (fem sg) tent,* 3+2+2
and the curtains of your dwelling!
Let them stretch out![a] *Do not hold back!*

Heavens: *Lengthen your cords* 2+2
and strengthen your stakes.

3 *For you (fem sg) spread out to the right and to the left,* 3+3+3
your descendants possess nations
and populate abandoned cities.

Earth: 4 *Do not (fem sg) fear! For you will not be rebuffed!* 3+4
And do not be confounded, for you will not be disappointed.

For you will forget the shame of your youth 4+4
and the shame of your widowhood,[a] *you will no longer remember.*

Heavens: 5 *Indeed, the one married to you*[ab] *is your maker!*[b] 3+3
His name is Yahweh of Hosts.

Your redeemer is the Holy One of Israel 3+3
who is called the God of All the Land.

Earth: 6 *For, like a forsaken wife* 2+2+2
or one grieved of spirit,
Yahweh has called you.

Or a wife of youth 2+2+2
when she is cast off,
[a]*your God says:*

Yahweh: 7 *In a brief moment I abandoned you,* 3+3
but in great compassion I gather you.

8 *In overflowing*[a] *wrath I hid* 3+3
my face from you momentarily.

But in age-long devotion I have compassion on you, 3+3
says Yahweh, your Redeemer.

9 *This is for me* [a]*like the waters*[a] *of Noah!* 4+2+4
which [b]*waters of Noah*[b] *I swore*
(would never) again pass over the land.

So I swear 2+2+2
I shall not be angry with you[c]
or rebuke you (again).

10 *For the mountains may move* 3+2
and the hills be removed,

but my devotion will not move from you 3+4+3
and the covenant of peace will not be removed.

Herald: *Says Yahweh, who has compassion on you.*

Darius: 11 *You afflicted, storm-tossed one* 2+2
who has not been comforted,

	Look at me
	  setting your stones in antimony[a]
	    and your foundations[b] *in sapphires.*
		2+3+2

	12 *I make your towers of agate*
	  and your gates of carbuncle stones
	    and all your border to be of precious stones.
		3+3+2

	13 *All your children are being taught by Yahweh* *and the prosperity of your children*[a] *(will be) great.*	3+3

	14 *In legitimacy you will be established;*
	  be far removed[a] *from oppression,*
	    for you will not fear,
		2+2+3

	nor be in terror, *for it will not come near you.*	1+3
	15 *If someone picks a fight,* *it is not*[a] *from me.*[b]	3+2
	[c]*Whoever picks a fight with you (fem sg)*[c] *will fall*[d] *because of you.*	2+2

Yahweh:	16 *If*[a] *I create a smith,*
	  blowing a coal with fire,
	    producing a weapon for its deed,
		4+3+3

	then I created *a ravager to destroy.*	2+2
Darius:	17ab *No weapon that is formed against you* *will succeed.*	3+2
	[a]*And every tongue raised for legal witness against you* *will prove to be false.*[a]	3+1

Notes

1.a. רנה "singing" is omitted by LXX, followed by *BHS* and others who consider it redundant. But DSS[Isa] and the other Versions support MT.

2.a. MT יַטּוּ "let them stretch out" hiph impf/juss from נטה is omitted in one Heb. MS. 'A Σ Θ εκταθητωσαν presupposes יֻטּוּ hoph (i.e., passive) "let them be stretched out." LXX *πῆξον* and Vg *extende* suggest הַטִּי impv "stretch out." Read MT.

4.a. MT אלמנותיך "your widowhood" is dual. *BHS* suggests reading a sg or pl. But DSS[Isa] confirms MT.

5.a. MT בֹּעֲלַיִךְ ptcp "your married man." DSS[Isa] בעלכי is an Aramaism, as is DSS[Isa] גואלכי for MT גאלך "your redeemer" (Kutscher, *Isaiah Scroll,* 209–11). LXX *κύριος* "Lord" and Tg מריך "your lord" lead *BHS* to suggest the noun בְּעָלַיִךְ "your husband, your lord." But 'A εχει σε, Σ κυριευσει σου, and Vg *dominabitur tui* translate a verb. Read MT.

5.b,b. GKC § 124*k* explains the pl endings on בעליך "the one married to you" and עשׂיך "your maker" as *plurales excellentiae* referring to God, and therefore to be translated sg.

6.a. DSS[Isa] adds יהוה "Yahweh." LXX Syr Tg Vg support MT.

8.a. שׁצף is a *hap. leg.* Its meaning is uncertain. LXX *μικρῷ* "short, brief" and Vg *momento* "moment" translate parallel to v 7. Ewald, Dillmann, and BDB (1009) equate שׁצף with שׁטף "flood." Duhm and others delete as dittogr. *BHS* suggests שׁפץ like Akk *šipṣu* "strength." North and Whybray note rabbinic Heb. שׁצף "to cut, to slash" and suggest "a fragment of time" supported by Σ, but this seems redundant with רגע "momentarily" following. With BDB, translate "in overflowing wrath."

9.a-a. MT כִּי־מֵי, lit., "for waters of." DSS[Isa] כימי "like the seas of." LXX *ἀπὸ τοῦ ὕδατος τοῦ ἐπὶ* "from the waters upon." *BHS* is probably right to read כְּמֵי "like the waters of."

9.b-b. Omitted in LXX. In MT the words are placed later in the verse after "never pass over." They are intended to define the relative particle and should be kept. Cf. DSS^{Isa}.

9.c. DSS^{Isa} adds עוד "again."

11.a. MT בפוך "in antimony" (BDB, 806: "a dark cement setting off precious stones") is supported by DSS^{Isa}. LXX ἄνθρακα "a burning coal" is L. *carbunculus*. Read MT.

11.b. MT וִיסַדְתִּיךְ "and I have laid your foundations" or "I have founded you" (BDB, 413). DSS^{Isa} ויסודותיך "your foundations" (cf. Kutscher, *Isaiah Scroll*, 322). LXX τὰ θεμέλιά σου "your foundations." Tg ואשכלליניך "I will lay your foundations." MT Syr Tg Cairo Geniza ʼA Σ Θ have a verb. DSS^{Isa} and LXX make it a noun. Read DSS^{Isa} because it fits as a parallel to the first stich.

13.a. MT בָּנַיִךְ "your children." DSS^{Isa} בוניכי "your builders." The Versions support MT, though Kutscher (*Isaiah Scroll*, 225) notes rabbinic evidence for DSS^{Isa}'s reading. Since Duhm, many (cf. Elliger, 530, for a list) have substituted בֹּנַיִךְ "your builders" for the first בָּנַיִךְ. MT, however, is well supported and should be kept.

14.a. MT רחקי "be far removed" is impv. *BHS* suggests an impf instead, but GKC § 110*c* and Whybray defend MT as an emphasis on the assurance being offered. Read MT.

15.a. MT אפס "it is not" (BDB, 67). LXX and Syr omit which changes the sense. DSS^{Isa} אכס is described as a "mechanical error" by Kutscher (*Isaiah Scroll*, 218).

15.b. MT מאותי "from me." DSS^{Isa} מאתי, lit., "from with me," was perhaps influenced by אתך "with you" in the next line (Kutscher, *Isaiah Scroll*, 405).

15.c-c. MT מי גר אתך "whoever picks a fight with you." DSS^{Isa} יגר is impf. LXX and Syr omit.

15.d. MT יפול "he will fall." DSS^{Isa} יפולו "they will fall."

16.a. K הן "if." Q and DSS^{Isa} הנה "see, behold." Read K parallel to v 15.

17.a-a. DSS^{Isa} omits the line, leaving a blank space. The Versions support MT. Read MT.

Form/Structure/Setting

The limits of the scene are clear. The beginning is clearly different from chap. 53. V 17c may be viewed as a summary of the preceding section or an introduction to the one following. The latter has been chosen here. See *Form/Structure/Setting* on 54:17c–56:8.

Form-critical analysis has agreed on dividing the chapter into four sections: vv 1–3, 4–6, 7–10, and 11–17. Köhler (*Deuterojesaja*, 108) divides the last part into vv 11–14a and 14b–17. But no agreement on the genre of the sections has been achieved (Melugin, *Formation*, 169–72).

The outline followed here is this:

Vv 1–6: Jerusalem is encouraged by heavenly messengers, by Yahweh himself and by Darius to expand into villages and towns that have long been abandoned.

Vv 7–10: Yahweh pledges Jerusalem lasting devotion in a passage patterned on reconciliation after a lovers' quarrel.

Vv 11–15: Darius promises to rebuild the city and to protect it.

V 16: Yahweh proclaims an end to his hostility toward the city in contrast to chap. 6.

V 17ab: Darius confirms his recognition of Yahweh worship and grants special imperial rights to worshipers of Yahweh in Jerusalem.

Comment

1 *Barren one, who never gave birth* picks up Jerusalem's complaint in 49:14 of being abandoned. In 49:18 she was called to see the children gathered about her. *More are the children* suggests that the growth of population in

Jerusalem that has been desolate so long exceeds the natural growth of such a city.

2 She is challenged to expand on all sides to make room for her enlarged family.

3 Growth will continue as her descendants move out into the villages and towns. When Judah's population went into exile leaving many of these villages and towns abandoned, the vacuum was filled by squatters from neighboring areas. Now the Jews are reclaiming their land.

4–5 Jerusalem is urged to be bold *forgetting* how she had been helpless for such a long time. Now God, *her maker* is also *the one married to her* (בעל), her owner and her cultivator. He protects, supports and nourishes her. He is no other than *Yahweh of Hosts.* The verse piles up titles and words of relation:

Your Maker	Yahweh of Hosts
Your Husband	The Holy One of Israel
Your Redeemer	The God of All the Land

The imagery of *the one married to you* is appropriate to the reestablishment of the people on their own land. The proclamation of redemption is the theme of these acts as Yahweh uses the Persian emperors to rehabilitate Jerusalem and the Jews. The other titles reach back to older Israelite theology. *Yahweh of Hosts* was the title used for worship around the Ark of the Covenant in early Israel which was then transplanted to the Temple in Jerusalem. It recalls the Exodus, the wilderness journey, Joshua's conquest of Canaan, and David's conquest of the larger area of Palestine. *The Holy One of Israel* is the particular title used in Isaiah's Vision. It describes Yahweh as "the wholly other," who links Israel to Abraham by election. *The God of all the land* repeats Yahweh's claim, enforced by David's conquest, that all of Palestine from the Euphrates to the River of Egypt belongs to Yahweh in a unique sense (Gen 15:18; Deut 11:24; Josh 1:4; 1 Kgs 4:21). The Vision has consistently maintained this setting for God's action. The coastlands and the borderlands have frequently been called to witness and recognize Yahweh's new claim to his old land.

6–8 This renewal of Jerusalem after having lain desolate for so long is pictured as the reconciliation of a broken marriage. *Abandonment* and *wrath* are put behind them. *Compassion* and *devotion* describe the Redeemer's attitude and action.

9–10 *Yahweh swears* that it will never happen again. He cites his promise to Noah after the flood (Gen 9:11) and insists on the unshakable nature of his *devotion* (חסד) and his *covenant of peace.*

Excursus: עולם *"An Age"*

Bibliography

Barr, J. *Biblical Words for Time.* SBT 33. Rev. ed. Naperville, IL: Allenson, 1969. 73. See extended annotated bibliography since 1940, 174–84. **Bruce, F. F.** "Age."

ISBE 1:67–68. **DeVries, J.** *Yesterday, Today and Tomorrow: Time and History in the Old Testament.* Grand Rapids: Wm. B. Eerdmans, 1975. 29–54. **Jenni, E.** *Das Wort 'olam im Alten Testament.* Diss. Basel. Berlin: Töpelmann, 1953. **MacRae, A. A.** "עולם." *Theological Wordbook of the Old Testament.* Ed. Harris, Archer, and Waltke. Chicago: Moody Press, 1980. 1631a. **Nandrasky, K.** "Zum Begriff 'Zeit'." *CVv* (1962) 228–33. **Orelli, C. von.** *Die hebräischen Synonyma der Zeit und Ewigkeit genetisch und sprachvergleichend dargestellt.* Leipzig, 1871.

Attempts to understand the Hebrew vocabulary for time have been extensively studied and debated as the works of Barr, von Orelli, and DeVries above will testify. Attempts to translate עולם have been a basic part of the problem. Earlier the word was often understood to mean "eternity." Jenni's study, among others, has clearly shown that its OT usage referred to time, not eternity. But he insisted that it was never used in pre-Christian times to name a limited time period or aeon. But others, including Bruce, MacRae, and Nandrasky have found the meaning of "age" or "epoch" to translate at least some of its uses appropriately.

In the Vision of Isaiah, עולם is used often with "from" or "to" to relate something to the old or the new, to the former or the latter age. It is related to creation on the one hand and to new order that is being brought into existence on the other.

The Vision of Isaiah recognizes a great division between the age of the monarchy and that of colonial Israel under the empires. עולם is used to refer to both of those ages or epochs. Yahweh reminds Israel that he is God "of עולם," of an age that is past when Israel was autonomous, living on its own land. The age reached back as far as Moses (63:11, 12), Abraham (29:22; 41:8; 51:2; 63:16), and even to Noah (54:9), although he is mentioned as one living, as it were, between ages, very much like that current generation. That past age knew Yahweh as God, Lord of Canaan, and Covenant God of Israel. He now proclaims himself still Master of Palestine, Lord of History and its emperors, and God of Israel and Jerusalem in the new age that he is inaugurating.

עולם refers to a long period of time, probably best translated as an "age." It defines not only the time involved but also the total complex of circumstances that could be called "the world of that time." When the Persian is promised a place that will be secure and whole "to that age," it means continuity in power to the end of that epoch. God ranges across the ages to achieve his purpose. But, of course, this is not the sense of "eternity" which a later age would use. Nor does it define the "other-worldly reality" which is inherent in the idea of "eternal." עולם speaks of historical periods of considerable length, either past or future, which have particular characteristics to distinguish them.

The major distinctives of the "ages" with which the Vision deals turn on the absence or presence in Palestine and the world around it of great empires who exercised direct sovereignty over the area. From the Assyrian through the Persian empires (and later the Greek and Roman empires) their presence produced startlingly different conditions from those that had allowed tribes and small city states to flourish in the region for more than a thousand years. The Vision proclaims that Yahweh who had established his position and identity in the previous "age" by placing his people Israel in Canaan and David in Jerusalem had determined to bring that age to an end. He did so by raising up the Assyrian empire. Then he used the Persian empire to redefine the position and status of Israel and Jerusalem in that new "age."

References to עולם, including מעולם "from an age," in descriptions of the creation of the universe may refer to a still earlier "age" as Gen 1–9 do. This would mean that the Vision pictures Yahweh's raising up the Assyrian empire in terms not unlike the Flood to close one "age," and his summons to Cyrus, something like the outreach of the sons of Noah, to inaugurate a new one. In this sense the parallel of Abraham with Zerubbabel and his successors in chap. 54 is very appropriate.

The use of עולם to mean something like "everlasting" or "eternal" comes in 45:17 where it is used in the plural. תשועת עולמים is, literally, "a salvation of ages." And עד עולמי עד is, literally, "to ages onward" or "to ages to come."

The greatest concentration of uses of עולם occurs in 60:15, 19, 20, 21; 61:4, 7, 8; and 63:9, 11, 12, 16, 19; 64:3, 4. In chap. 60 the word stresses the permanence of the new city and its cult. In chap. 61 it emphasizes the way old ruins from another age will be rebuilt and speaks of joy and covenant that will be age-long. Chaps. 63–64 look back with nostalgia to a past age, unwilling to face the reality of the new age that is already about them.

עולם occurs in the Vision before chap. 40 eleven times. In chaps. 40–54 it occurs eleven times. In chaps. 55–66 twenty-one times, thirteen of which come in chaps. 60–64. It can look back to a past era, as when it describes a period that extends back to Moses (chaps. 63–64), or back to Abraham in chaps. 29, 41, 51, and 63, or even as far back as Noah (54:9). Or it can describe the present to future in terms of the full thrust of chaps. 40–66, especially chaps. 60–61. It is the view of this commentary that the concept of "age" in Isaiah is much closer to that of Jewish and Christian writings of the following centuries than some current scholarship thinks.

11–12 *Afflicted* Jerusalem is challenged to recognize that the rebuilding program is of excellent quality.

13–14 Restoration goes beyond walls and buildings. All her *sons are being taught about Yahweh.* One of the most remarkable achievements of ancient Judaism was the education of virtually all their male children in the language and content of the Torah. Education was the reason for the existence of the synagogue and was what made it possible. This was a major goal which God had announced for his new city (2:3b–c). Their *prosperity* (שׁלום) *will be great.* The word may be understood as peace or as well-being. It means much more than simply wealth. The expansion of the city will be matched by spiritual, social and political stability and health.

14 *In legitimacy* (בצדקה) *you will be established.* The word "legitimate" has consistently been used of Cyrus and his successors (cf. *Excursus: צדק/צדקה "Righteousness, Legitimacy"*). It means that Jerusalem's new order will have legitimacy through imperial recognition and support. Since the legitimacy of the empire itself derives from Yahweh, this is simply an extension of Yahweh's own recognition and support. *Oppression* and *terror* had been a constant part of life in Jerusalem for over half a century—longer if one counts the Assyrian oppression before the destruction of the city—but the new age promises order and safety under the *pax Persica.*

15 The assurance that any harassment, if such should come, will not derive from imperial sources stands in contrast to earlier generations when Yahweh used the Assyrians for just that purpose (7:17–25; chap. 13). In this period Jerusalem is assured of imperial favor and protection.

16–17 When *God created a smith,* as he did in Assyria, *to produce a weapon,* the purpose was *to destroy.* Assyria and Babylon had done that very efficiently. But now any weapon so formed will not have God's support and cannot succeed. Imperial recognition will mean that no accusation raised against Jerusalem (as in Ezra 3:1–5 and 5:3–17) will be sustained.

Explanation

The scene celebrates the work of God through Darius to restore Jerusalem. The city is ready again to be the center of Yahweh-worship for villagers in the surrounding countryside and for pilgrims from all over the empire. She must expand her capacity to accommodate immigrants and pilgrims. She must become bold in faith, assured of her status before God and of the revelation of his glory in the Temple.

Jerusalem had to overcome the trauma of her grief and abandonment to be ready for this new visitation of God's grace and mercy. She needed assurance and courage to stand tall in that faith. God's plan used Persia's emperors to provide material resources, legal support, and great moral encouragement. But then Jews and Jerusalem had to look deep within themselves for faith, vision, and spiritual power to match the opportunity which God provided.

Students of modern missions will recognize in v 2b the text used by William Carey to challenge English Baptists to launch the mission enterprise. He answered his own challenge by spending the rest of his life as a missionary in India. From that time on the work of modern missions has helped the Church "lengthen its cords and strengthen its stakes" to move toward a world-wide witness, as Paul and other missionaries like Francis Xavier had done before.

Scene 3: A House of Prayer for All Peoples (54:17c—56:8)

Bibliography

Beek, M. A. "De vreemdeling krijgt toegang (Jessaja 56,1–8)." *De Knecht.* FS J. L. Koole. Kampen: Kok, 1978. **Beuken, W. A. M.** "Isa. 55,3–5: The Reinterpretation of David." *Bijdragen* 35 (1974) 49–64. **Brueggemann, W.** "Is 55 and Deuteronomic Theology," *ZAW* 80 (1968) 191–203. **Caquot, A.** "Les 'grâces de David'. À propos d'Isaïe 55,3b." *Sem* 15 (1965) 45–59. **Chiesa, B.** "Ritorno dall'Esilio e Conversione à Dio." *BeO* 14 (1972) 167–80. **Clifford, R. J.** "Isaiah 55: Invitation to a Fast." *The Word of the Lord Shall Go Forth.* FS D. N. Freedman. Ed. C. L. Meyers and M. O'Conner. Winona Lake, IN: Eisenbrauns, 1983. 27–35. **Dahms, J. V.** "Isaiah 55:11 and the Gospel of John." *EvQ* 53 (1981) 78–88. **Eissfeldt, O.** "The Promises of Grace to David in Isaiah 55,1–5." *Israel's Prophetic Heritage.* FS J. Muilenburg. New York: Harper & Bros., 1962. 196–207. **Golebiewski, M.** "L'alliance éternelle en Is 54–55 en comparaison avec d'autres textes prophétiques." *Collectanea Theologica* 50 (1980) 89–102. ———. "Die Wirksamkeit des Wortes Gottes nach Is 55,8–11." *Studia Theologica Varsaviensia* 20 (1982) 47–67 (Polish); 68–69 (German). **Hanson, P. D.** *Dawn of Apocalyptic.* 388–401. **Komlosch, Y.** ". . . נבואת הישועה. The Prophecy of Salvation, Is 56,1–

8." *Bar-Ilan Annual* 11 (1973) 11–16. **Lipinski, E.** "The Comparison in Isaiah LV 10." *VT* 23 (1973) 246–47. **Morgenstern, J.** "Isaiah 55:1–5." *HUCA* 22 (1949) 365–431. ———. "Isaiah 55:6–13." *HUCA* 24 (1952) 1–74. **Pauritsch, K.** *Die Neue Gemeinde: Gott Sammelt Ausgestossene und Arme* (Jesaia 55–66). AnBib 47. Rome: Biblical Institute Press, 1971. 31–51. **Ravasi, G.** "La parola viva (Is 55,10–11)." *PSV* 5 (1982) 61–74. **Robinson, G.** "The Meaning of *jad* in Isaiah 56,5." *ZAW* 88 (1976) 282–84. **Sanders, J. A.** "Is 55:1–9." *Int* 32 (1978) 291–95. **Troadec, H. G.** "La parole vivante et efficace." *BVC* 11 (1955) 57–67. **Williamson, H. G. M.** " 'The Sure Mercies of David': Subjective or Objective Genitive?" *JSS* 23 (1978) 31–49. **Zenger, E.** " 'Hört auf dass ihr lebt' (Isa 55:3)." Alttestamentliche Hinweise zu einer Theologie des Gotteswortes. *Freude am Gottesdienst.* FS J. G. Plöger. Ed. J. Schreiner. Stuttgart: Verlag Kath. Bibelwerk, 1983. 133–44.

Translation

Yahweh:	54:17c *This is the heritage of Yahweh's servants,*	4+2+2
	their right (given) by me.	
Herald:	*Oracle of Yahweh.*	
Heavens:	55:1 *Hail! Every one who thirsts, come to water!*	4+3
	And whoever has no money,	
	come,[a] *buy,*[b]	2+2+2
	without money and without price,	
	wine and milk.	
Earth:	2 *Why do you spend money without bread (in return)*	3+3
	and your labor without satisfaction?	
Yahweh:	*Listen (masc pl) carefully to me!*	3+2+3
	And eat well.	
	Delight your (masc pl) soul in fatness.	
	3 *Turn your ears and come to me.*	4+3
	Hear that your soul may live.	
	And I will make for you (masc pl) an age-long covenant	4+3
	The devotions of David—which are sure.	
	4 *See! I made him a witness for peoples,*[a]	4+3
	a leader and commander for peoples.	
Heavens: (to Darius)	5 *See! A nation that you (masc sg) do not know you (masc sg) will call*	4+4
	and a nation that does not know you (masc sg) will run to you (masc sg).	
	For the sake of Yahweh, your (masc sg) God.	3+4
(to Jerusalem)	*And for the Holy One of Israel that he may beautify you (fem sg).*	
Earth:	6 *Seek (masc pl) Yahweh while he may be found!*	3+3
	Call (masc pl) him while he is near!	
Heavens:	7 [a] *May the guilty forsake his way*	3+3
	and the troublemaker his convictions.	
	And may he turn to Yahweh that he may have compassion on him	3+3
	and to our God that he may multiply pardon.[b]	

Yahweh: [8] *For my convictions are not your convictions* 3+3+2
and my ways not your ways.
Herald: *Oracle of Yahweh.*
Yahweh: [9a] *For as heavens are higher*[a] *than land* 3+4+2
so my ways are higher than your ways
and my convictions than your convictions.
[10] *For just as the rain and the snow* 3+3+3
descend from heaven
and does not return there
until it water the land, 3+2
and it bear and sprout
and give seed for the sower 3+2
and bread for the eater,
[11] *so it is with my word* 3+3
which goes out[a] *from my mouth.*
It does not return to me empty 3+4+3
unless it has done what I will
and succeeded in what I sent it (to do).
Heavens: [12] *Indeed you* (masc pl) *will go out in joy* 2+2
and be led out[a] *in peace.*
The mountains and the hills break out before you in singing, 5+3
and all the trees of the field clap their hands.
Earth: [13] *Instead of the thorn*[a] *a cypress will grow up.* 4+4
And instead[b] *of the brier*[c] *a myrtle will grow up.*
And this will be a memorial to Yahweh 3+2+2
for an age-long sign
that will not be cut off.
Herald: [56:1] *Thus says Yahweh:* 3+4
Yahweh: *Keep Justice! Do Right!*
For my salvation is about to come 3+2
and my righteousness to be revealed.
Heavens: [2] *Blessed will be the mortal who does this!* 3+3
And the human who holds fast to it!
Earth: *One keeping sabbath—not profaning it.*[a] 3+4
And keeping his hand from doing any wrong.
Heavens: [3] *Let the foreigner not say* 2+3
who has joined himself[a] *to Yahweh:*
"Yahweh will certainly keep me separate from his people." 2+3
Earth: *Let the eunuch not say* 2+4
"See! I am a dried-up tree."
Herald: [4] *For thus says Yahweh:* 3+4
Yahweh: *To the eunuchs who keep my sabbaths*
and who choose what I will 3+2
and who hold fast my covenant:
[5] *I shall give them* 2+2+2

	in my house and within my walls *hand and name.*	
	Better than sons and daughters, *an age-long name I give to them,*[a] *which will not be cut off.*	3+3+3
Heavens:	6 *Foreigners who are joining themselves to Yahweh*[a] *to minister to him*[b] *and worship the name of Yahweh*[c] *to be his*[d] *servants,*	4+4+3
Yahweh:	*everyone keeping*[e] *sabbath—not profaning it*[f]— *and holding fast my covenant,*	3+2
	7 *I bring them to my holy mountain* *and I make them rejoice in my house of prayer.*	3+3
	Their burnt offerings and their sacrifices[a] (*are*) *acceptable on my altar.*	2+2
	For my house *is to be called a house of prayer* *for all peoples.*	2+3+2
Herald:	8 *Oracle of my Lord Yahweh* *who is gathering Israel's outcasts:*	3+3+4
Yahweh:	*I gather more to him than those already gathered to him.*	

Notes

55.1.a. *BHS* suggests moving the *athnaḥ* to לכו "come," as is usual. This divides the verse differently than MT. If one should divide the verse by sense and literary form, one would have to move the *athnaḥ* two words further to ואכלו "and eat." But see n. 1.b. MT makes sense and should be kept.

1.b. MT adds ואכלו ולכו שברו "and eat and come, buy," followed by 'A Σ Θ Vg. DSS^{Isa} and two MSS^{K} (partially supported by LXX and Syr) omit the words. Kutscher (*Isaiah Scroll,* 552) wonders if DSS^{Isa}'s reading is due to homoiotel, and Westermann defends MT's repetition as natural for the words of a street vendor. But DSS^{Isa} has the better meter and considerable support (see Whybray).

4.a. MT לאמים "peoples" (BDB, 522) occurs twice in this verse. Because Syr Tg Vg translate each with a different synonym and Heb. parallelism usually prefers synonyms to repetition, many commentators, including *BHS* and Elliger (525), emend the first to לעמים "to peoples." But DSS^{Isa} 1QIsa^{b} and LXX support MT, and Driver (*JTS* 36 [1935] 404) points to this as "a characteristic mark of the author's style." Read MT. Elliger (117, n. 4) remarks that Deutero-Isaiah uses לאם often, though still not as much as its synonyms גוי and עם.

7.a. Duhm and Westermann regard the verse as a pious interpolation. This is unnecessary. It makes sense where it is. (See Whybray.)

7.b. Or "pardon abundantly"; cf. GKC § 114n^2.

9.a-a. MT כי גבהו "for they are high." LXX ὡς ἀπέχει "as heaven is distant" is supported by Syr and Tg. DSS^{Isa} includes both particles and reads a noun, כי כגובה "for as the height" (so also Σ except MS 86). Kutscher (*Isaiah Scroll,* 321–22) defends MT by suggesting that כי here has the unusual meaning "like," which LXX Syr Tg recognizes but DSS^{Isa} did not. This translation fits the parallel structure with כן "so."

11.a. MT יֵצֵא qal impf "goes out." Syr suggests a past יָצָא "has gone out." Read MT.

12.a. MT תובלון "you will be led out" (BDB, 385) is followed by LXX Σ Θ Tg. DSS^{Isa} תלכו "you will go." Read MT, the less common language (cf. 18:7; 53:7).

13.a. On נעצוץ "thorn" see n. 7:19.b. The word occurs only in these two verses.

13.b. K תחת "under, instead." Q, DSS^{Isa}, some MSS, and the Versions ותחת "and instead." Read Q.

13.c. סרפד "brier" is a *hap. leg.* LXX κονύζης "fleabane"; Σ κνιδης "nettles"; Vg *urtica* "nettle." One must translate from context.

56:2.a. MT מחללו prep + inf constr + 3rd masc sg suffix "from profaning it" (BDB, 320, III). DSS[Isa] מחללה apparently has a fem suffix. שבת "sabbath" is viewed sometimes in the Bible as masc and sometimes as fem (cf. BDB, 992), but in the Mishna and DSS[Isa] it is always fem (Kutscher, *Isaiah Scroll,* 394).

3.a. MT הַנִּלְוָה. The ending is pointed as a qal pf, but then the article is impossible. A niph ptcp would be הַנִּלְוֶה "one joining himself" (BDB, 530; GKC § 138*k*). LXX ὁ προσκείμενος "who attaches himself" (lit., "one leaning on"), Θ Syr and Tg support the change. Read הַנִּלְוֶה.

5.a. MT לו "to him." DSS[Isa] להמה "to them," followed by the Versions, is consistent with the context. Read DSS[Isa].

6.a,b,c,d. *BHS* would emend all four places to make the verse parallel to v. 5. That is not necessary if Yahweh is no longer the speaker.

6.e. MT כל שמר "everyone keeping" as in v 2 above. DSS[Isa] שומרים "those keeping" omitting כל "all." LXX καὶ πάντας τοὺς φυλασσομένους "and all those keeping" has a pl like DSS[Isa] but also "all" like MT. Tg כל דיטר "everyone keeping" supports MT. Read MT.

6.f. DSS[Isa] has a fem suff, as in v 2.

7.a. DSS[Isa] inserts יעלו "they ascend," which Torrey suggested before the scroll was discovered. MT is elliptical with no finite verb. But this is acceptable Heb. DSS[Isa] and the Versions change the inf to a finite verb or supply one. Read MT.

Form/Structure/Setting

54:17c is set off from the context on both sides. זאת "this" may theoretically refer to what has gone before in chap. 54 or to what follows in chap. 55. The translation above has placed it with what follows because two phrases point to themes most relevant to the following section. The first is נחלה "heritage." The scenes that follow are involved with the reactivation of rights to the inheritance of land and to participation in Temple service. The second phrase is עבדי יהוה "servants of Yahweh." Up to this point the term "servant" has been singular, referring either to God's chosen people or to God's chosen ruler. From here to the end of the Vision only the plural is used. A climax will be reached when the true servants are separated from the false in 65:13–16. On one side those who may serve as servants of Yahweh will be expanded in chaps. 55–57. On the other side, some in Israel will eliminate themselves from their ranks by refusing to accept God's plan for this new age (chaps. 63–65). So 54:17c is taken here to be a kind of title beginning this new section.

The address is no longer to Jerusalem (feminine singular), nor to Darius (masculine singular), but to a crowd (masculine plural). Begrich (*Studien,* 59–61) relates vv 1–5 to a Wisdom genre: invitation to a meal. Melugin (*Formation,* 25–26) demurs, calling vv 3b–5 a salvation speech. But he correctly acknowledges that Von Waldow's (*Anlass und Hintergrund,* 22) suggestion that this is an imitation of a street-merchant's speech may also be right.

Melugin (*Formation,* 86–87) sees vv 6–13 as the conclusion of a corpus that began in chap. 40. He thinks the passages correspond to each other in theme and arrangement:

The theme of returning to Yahweh, 55:6–7	= 40:1–2
Promise of exodus from captivity, 55:12–13	= 40:3–5
Radical differences between Yahweh and man, 55:8–9, and reliability of Yahweh's word, 55:10–11	= 40:6–8

Melugin overlooks obvious differences. 40:1–9 is addressed to exiled Israelites in Babylon. 55:6–11 speaks to an unlimited group, not about restoration of the Temple, but about use of the Temple. Melugin divides the book wrongly. Chap. 55 should be related to the following chapters in keeping with the forward thrust of the entire Vision. This commentary's approach views the work as a piece, which opens the door to seeing chap. 55 as an integral part of chaps. 55–57. 56:1–8 continues the same themes and is therefore a part of the scene.

An outline of the scene:

54:17c	Announcement of the heritage of God's people in this new era.
55:1–2	Everyone who wants to worship Yahweh is called to celebrate a feast (cf. chap. 25) in Jerusalem.
55:3	The purpose of the feast: Yahweh is establishing a new relationship with Darius.
55:4	This is compared to his earlier relationship to David in that it provides for sovereignty over peoples.
55:5	Yahweh speaks to Darius and recognizes his restoration of Jerusalem.
55:6–7	Everyone is called to worship Yahweh. Rebels are challenged to abandon their rebellion because Yahweh supports Darius.
55:8–11	Yahweh defends his plan to use the Persian (cf. 40:8, 12–26) and insists that his decisions are final.
55:12–13	Yahweh insists that his goal is using the Persian is Jerusalem's well-being.
56:1–2	Yahweh calls for justice and the keeping of sabbaths because his salvation is near.
56:3–7	The requirements for entry and service are to be intention, keeping of sabbaths, ministry and worship, with no reference to ethnic origin or cultic purity.
56:7–8	The Temple is to be open to all peoples. God is gathering more than just Israelites to Jerusalem.

(For literature and a description of chaps. 55–66 in source-critical terms, see *Appendix: Trito-Isaiah,* p. 367.)

Comment

54:17c The verse points to the content of the following chapters which emphasize the privilege of worship in Yahweh's presence. נחלה "heritage" picks up a theme that has been mentioned several times. The exiles' freedom to return was meaningless unless they could reestablish their right to cultivate the land (cf. 49:8; 54:3). But the Vision's use of "the heritage from Yahweh" also understands this right as a base from which to claim their real birthright of worshiping Yahweh freely and constantly in Jerusalem (cf. Pss 1:2; 23:6b; 84:10). This scene begins the process by which sincere worshipers are distinguished from those with ulterior motives who resist Yahweh's plan.

55:1–2 Like street vendors hawking their wares in an open market, the speakers announce a feast open to everyone. Compare the invitation in 25:6 to a banquet where God will announce his decision to remove the people's disgrace from the land, and that in Matt 22:8–10 and Luke 14:16–24. At the end the host himself calls for attention, even as he urges his guests to *eat well* and enjoy the feast.

3 The address is still to the crowd (shown by the plural pronoun) calling for attention and promising to guarantee security and prosperity *that your soul may live.* Yahweh announces that he is making a *covenant,* an arrangement, an agreement. עולם "age long" indicates its permanence and longevity. Its character and purpose are described by *the devotions of David that are sure.* The covenant with David (cf. 2 Sam 7:12–16) was the basis for Israel's (especially Judah's) hope of salvation. It was unconditioned and *sure* (נאמן) in contrast to the covenant with Moses which was conditioned on obedience (cf. Deuteronomy). This covenant with David was the sure basis for Zion's confidence as demonstrated by Isaiah and Hezekiah in 37:35.

4 Yahweh points to a new leader to assume the mantle and responsibilities of David in such a covenant. His task is to be *a witness* (עד) *to peoples* of Yahweh's sovereignty and providence. He will be *a leader and a commander of peoples* to carry out Yahweh's will to establish peace and order in the realm.

5 Then the implications of the appointment are made clear in a direct speech to Darius. The verbs are second person masculine singular. The addressee in context would be the emperor whose wisdom settled the complex problem of an innocent person's execution in chap. 53 and who encouraged Jerusalem in chap. 54. These speeches demonstrated his fitness for the task. The *nation* that he does not know is not identified. The empire continued to expand under Darius and reached the zenith of its size and power during his long reign. This will happen *for the sake of Yahweh your God.* The claim that Darius's success is due to Yahweh and that he acknowledges Yahweh as his God is consistent with the Vision's presentation in 49:6–9 and his claim to be Yahweh's servant in 50:10. Yahweh's identity is made clear. He is none other than *the Holy One of Israel* whose goal through Darius is to beautify *you.* This pronoun is feminine singular. The speaker has turned to address Jerusalem, the recipient of the emperor's as well as Yahweh's favor.

6 The rest of the chapter addresses the crowd with masculine plural pronouns and verbs. They are exhorted to *seek Yahweh* and *call on him.* The Temple is open and they are urged to avail themselves of the worship opportunities it offers. *While he may be found. While he is near.* The Vision is a massive illustration of times when he is not so readily available to the worshiper, when he is upholding his curse or his ban on his people (chap. 6), with good reason. But now is the acceptable time, a time of openness and grace (cf. 40:1–9, *et passim*). The opening call had excluded no one. Let him or her who wills come to seek Yahweh.

7 A particular group needs a special exhortation to come. *Their way* of life and thought, *their convictions,* stand in the way. They oppose God's plans, resisting his announcement and invitations. This direct clash prevents communion and cooperation. But God's ways are set. They will not be changed. They, *the guilty and the troublemaker,* who have resisted both Yahweh's grace and his invitation, as well as that of the emperor, are implored to change their ways. These are probably the people who were in fact guilty of rebellion in chap. 53 and who had received amnesty because of Zerubbabel's judicial murder. But they have not changed their convictions or their ways. The offer still stands: if they will repent, *turn to Yahweh* and *to our God,* he will receive them in love and *multiply pardon.* The verse is a classic expression of God's open invitation to those who resist his call, determined to live their own way.

8 But Yahweh makes clear that they cannot have the benefits of his presence while they resist the structures of his will. The old truth of Sinai's covenant remains valid (Exod 20 and Deuteronomy).

9 The gap between Yahweh's *convictions* (his plan) and *ways* (his use of Darius) and their *convictions* (insistence on Judah's and Jerusalem's independence and autonomy) is enormous—as far *as heavens are higher than land.* There can be no compromise.

10–11 God's *word* (the announcement of his plan and the appointment of Darius) is as sure of fulfillment as are *the rain and the snow* that *water the land* and make cultivation possible. This word is a comfort to the one who yields to God's will. It will be felt as a threat and a warning to the one who stubbornly resists it.

12 The heavenly messengers recognize the significance of the announcement. God's plan is being put into effect. Glorious results will follow. The Vision has greeted such moments with hymns and joy (cf. 11:1–9; 12:1–6; 35:1–10; 44:23; 48:20–21; 49:13; 52:7–10). Here, also, the crowd is to rejoice and join *mountains, hills,* and *trees of the field* in *joy* and *peace,* in *singing* and *clapping.*

13 The contrasts in vegetation are symbolic of contrasts in God's attitude toward his land. *The thorns* and *the briers* are signs of abandoned fields, symbolizing Yahweh's punishment of exile (cf. 5:6; 6:11–13; 7:22–25; 27:4; 32:13). But trees like a *cypress* or a *myrtle* mark a cultivated and well-watered land such as Yahweh's new age promised for Palestine. They are destined to be a *memorial,* a reminder to Yahweh. עולם "age long" reflects the biblical view that these things are fixed in God's plan for a long period of time, an age. This is not the "forever" of a different world-view. The Vision recognizes that one age ended with Noah's flood (cf. 54:9). It depicts an age in which Israel flowered and floundered as a nation among other small nations (chaps. 1–39) which ended during the eighth to sixth centuries with the rise of Assyria and Babylon. It then proclaims a new age in which Cyrus and his successors in empire will rule in David's stead and in which Israel will have the opportunity to be God's worshiping people in Jerusalem. Reference to the *age* here speaks of the permanence of that system. Judaism continued to function as a recognized religious community under successive empires. This was also the position of the early Christian church under Rome. The distinction between religious community and political dominion continues to be relevant in defining the relation of church and state. This understanding of *the age* leaves open the possibility of an age to come, such as the NT recognizes in the return of Jesus Christ. But Jesus and the kingdom he proclaimed still belong to the age introduced here, the age which sees separate roles for Caesar and the people of God. Yahweh's commitment to this plan is clear: *it will not be cut off.*

It is clear that Jews were (and are) not all agreed in their response to this invitation. Nor are the rest of those to whom the invitation is now addressed. Resistance to the word and plan of God has been constant throughout the Vision. The resisters are chided for spending money and labor for things without substance or satisfaction, that is, for their own ideas and fantasies. These may include idolatry as such. But they may simply be chasing after shadows of pride and ambition, hoping for the return of what they believe were days of glory, or determining to satisfy a hopeless desire for vengeance for long-past wrongs.

They are guilty of resisting God. They are violent people who fancy that holding fast to their convictions is a virtue. But their acts are treasonable offenses against the empire, a disservice to their own people, and rebellious unbelief and blasphemy against God.

God will not change his plan. The Vision has charted the course he has followed since first choosing Tiglath-Pileser as his instrument for demolition. Now he is near to his goal. He will not change. So the rebels are invited to change, to become a part of God's new city and new age. They are offered a warm reception and a full pardon.

56:1 *Keep justice! Do right!* These simple instructions summarize God's law, as does Exod 19:5a, Deut 6:5, or Mic 6:8. Note the balance between the worshiper's "doing right" (צדקה) and God's "righteousness" (צדקתי). The old covenant of mutual responsibilities for right is confirmed. *My salvation* and *my righteousness* in this context refer to accomplishments through the Persian: rebuilding the Temple, restoring Jerusalem, and restitution of land-rights for Jews. These are seen to be very near. There is therefore good reason, from a prophetic point of view, to be attentive to God's justice and God's right.

2 אשרי "blessed is" is the same word as that in Ps 1:1 and in Jesus' Beatitudes (Matt 5:2–12). The two words, אנוש "mortal" and בן אדם "human being" (lit., son of Adam), are generic. They speak of persons in the most basic and universal sense possible. They pick up the broad appeal of 55:1, just as the injunction in v 1 recalls the address in 55:1. What distinguishes one person from another is whether one keeps justice or not, whether one does right or not. It has nothing to do with ethnic origins, economic power, or political status.

Keeping sabbath becomes a specific and symbolic example. The sabbath commandment is one of the Ten (Exod 20:8–11; Deut 5:12–15), but it became central and important only in post-exilic Judaism. The emphasis here parallels that in Ezek 22:8; 23:38; 46:1; and Neh 9:14; 10:31; 13:15–21. *Keeping his hand from doing any wrong* moves back to a broader statement.

3–7 *The foreigner who joined himself to Yahweh* came to be known in Judaism as a proselyte, a member of the synagogue who was not a Jew by birth. The position of the proselyte was a controversial one in Judaism. Not all Jews were prepared to grant them full covenant rights. Such openness to receiving Gentiles who would commit themselves to Yahweh was actively resisted by some (note Zerubbabel's rebuff of an offer to help rebuild the Temple in Ezra 4:1–3 and Ezra's concern and action in Ezra 9–10). In this passage Yahweh assures those who voluntarily seek to join themselves to Yahweh, i.e., to the covenant community of worship, of full acceptance.

A second group, no doubt symbolic of all persons excluded from the worshiping community by the Torah, are eunuchs (cf. Deut 23:1–2 and Lev 21:20 using different terms). Eunuchs were used in eastern courts in many capacities (cf. Esther *passim;* Dan 1:3–18). They were used in Jerusalem and Samaria, as references in 1 and 2 Kings show. An early convert to Christianity was such an Ethiopian official (Acts 8:27–37). Cf. C. U. Wolf, "Eunuch," *IDB* 2:179–80; D. G. Burke, "Eunuch," *ISBE* 2:200–202. They were prominent at court, but forbidden to enter the Temple. That prohibition is now removed on Yahweh's authority. *I am a dried-up tree* was apparently a deprecating remark about their inability to father children.

4 In the new Temple the door should be open wide for proselytes and eunuchs who fulfill God's requirements. What are these requirements? *Keep God's sabbaths, choose what God wills, and hold fast to his covenants.* That which distinguishes persons acceptable to God from those who are unacceptable is their commitment to God's will and to God's ways (cf. 1:19).

5 Yahweh grants access to his *house,* the Temple, and status in his community within its *walls* in Zion. *Better than sons and daughters.* The Vision began by taking note of God's bitter experiences with his children (1:2–3). It has repeatedly documented Israel's and Jerusalem's failures to keep covenant and their unwillingness to do what Yahweh wants. So volunteer worshipers are now promised an *age-long name,* not just a temporary place, in the people of God. *It will not be cut off* could be a real threat as Ezra's order about foreign wives (Ezra 9–10) shows. The Vision, a book which must be roughly contemporary to Ezra, stands in sharp contradiction to Ezra's policies. This passage places Yahweh's promise in an earlier generation. It demonstrates the struggle between different attitudes and viewpoints during that period.

6 *The foreigners* are described in four ways: they *join themselves to Yahweh,* that is, they become proselytes; they *minister to him,* that is, they are prepared to perform services in the Temple (cf. 66:21); they *love the name of Yahweh,* that is, they are devoted to him beyond the acts of worship themselves; and they become *his servants* (cf. 54:17c). This group includes all who *keep sabbath* holy and who *hold fast* his *covenant.* This implies a return to the original understanding of Israel as a worshiping and covenanting congregation, composed of persons who swore fealty to Yahweh in covenant ceremonies (cf. Exod 19:1–20:21; Deuteronomy; Josh 24). The tendency to claim Temple rights as one might claim land rights began early in the kingdom and continued in Judaism, especially among priests and Levites, but also among Jews who wanted to claim their birthrights. The scene does not despise such birthrights, but it insists on the prior necessity of commitment and acceptance of the responsibilities that such a birthright implies. Commitment and acceptance of responsibility are more important than the birthright; cf. the story of Esau and Jacob in Gen 25:29–34. The Vision shows that Israel/Jacob also despised his birthright. Now others, more worthy, are invited to enter into it.

7 The scene culminates in the observation that the new Temple gives God the opportunity to *bring them to his holy mountain* and to *make them rejoice* there. *My house of prayer* is a singular description of the Temple. (See 1 Kgs 8:27–30 where prayer is seen as the purpose of the Temple.) It is not that *sacrifices and offerings* are no longer acceptable, but that the basic understanding of the Temple's function has changed. It is a place of prayer, of communion with God. 2:2–4 had stressed its nature as a gathering place for teaching. Now its accessibility to *all people* who want to pray to Yahweh is stressed. This tendency in understanding the nature of worship influenced the synagogue, the church, and the mosque.

8 The verse stresses the continuity inherent in Yahweh's *gathering Israel's outcasts* even as it emphasizes the new invitation *to gather more to him* to join *those already gathered.* (Cf. Jesus' prayer in John 17:20–21 which has a similar intent.) Yahweh continues his efforts to gain Jewish devotees who will do his will, keep his covenant, and love his name (cf. Paul's emphasis in Rom 9–11, which quotes liberally from Isaiah). But he does not limit himself to those who are "Israel according to the flesh."

Explanation

The scene defines the legacy to which this generation of Yahweh's servants fall heir. It is provided for them without cost by their gracious God. It consists of a permanent contract with the same provisions given to David in the previous age. It provides for political stability, order, and justice. It provides for economic prosperity for the people. It makes possible worship, witness, and service of Yahweh in Zion, his city, and in Palestine, his land. These were God's goals when he led Abraham to Canaan, when Moses led the Israelites through the wilderness so that Joshua could establish them in Canaan, and when David was crowned king. Now they are offered to Jews and anyone else who wants to come take part in that blessing through Yahweh's servant, the Persian emperor, Darius. He has been made Yahweh's witness, his prince and commander of peoples, in order to make this possible for Israel and any others who want to worship Yahweh. There is in the offer promise of satisfaction, joy, peace, and prosperity. There is pardon for rebels if they will turn to God. The new age is beginning with all the potential of joy and fulfillment which that implies. Everyone is invited to participate.

At a later time Jesus would hail the culmination of this age in the coming of God's kingdom (Mark 15; Matt 4:17). He would claim that these prophetic books were speaking of him, his mission and his message (Mark 1:2; Luke 4:17–21). He would lament Jerusalem's failure to believe the prophets in their own times and in his (Matt 23:37–39). He, too, would picture the scene as a great banquet to which Israel is invited, which many in Israel disdained, and which is then opened to all who want to come (Matt 22:1–14; Luke 14:15–24). Preachers of his Gospel would pick up the theme of this great invitation (Acts 10:34–35, 43; 11:38 *et passim*) and of this call to repentance (Acts 20:38–39). They continue it to the present day. The great call to any and all who will come remains the heart of evangelism and mission.

The universal openness apparent in the great invitation of 55:1–8 is real. It is applied in 56:1–8 to the stranger who joins God's people and to eunuchs. Undoubtedly these are intended as examples of all classes of people who had been kept at a distance. In time women and all disabled persons would be included.

The requirements for entrance into the Temple are still strict and high:

commitment to doing God's will, to doing right and justice, to keeping covenant and sabbath. But all who love Yahweh and want to do these are welcome and accepted.

The scene recognizes the argument always raised against such liberal openness. It says it is naïve to open the doors so wide. It implies that persons of evil intent will take advantage of the innocent and do violence and take plunder. It urges that one cannot live like that in this evil world. Realism requires that the doors be kept shut and the walls high.

The same arguments are advanced in NT times and in current churches and synagogues. To open membership to just anyone is to invite trouble. This is at least partially true, yet God prefers the vulnerable openness. He will pay the price of suffering (chap. 53) to gain access for all who would come. (Cf. the struggle among the early Christians about receiving Gentiles.) The same battle has to be fought in each new culture before God's truth is accepted that he truly wants the outcasts to be a part of his people. The spiritual and social dangers inherent in a closed society are far greater than those of an open society, particularly in the community of faith.

But dangers are there, and the probability of imposition and pressure are ubiquitous. (Cf. Jesus' warnings to his disciples of persecution to come, Matt 10:16–23.) There is no reason to change the open nature of the Temple community (or of the church). To change it in order to protect it from such violence would rob it of its essential nature. The Temple (and the church) must remain an open *house of prayer for all peoples* if it is to house the presence of the living, loving God with integrity.

This is not to say that just anyone may enter. Only sincere seekers of Yahweh who want to be in his presence and rejoice to do his will should be admitted. Unfortunately many who were born with this right wanted no part of the Temple on those terms. There is now no place for the power brokers who would use Yahweh and his Temple to further their own purposes or to increase their own wealth. There is no place here for those with a private agenda or a hidden goal, no matter what their birth or station.

Scene 4:
The Dark Side of Jerusalem (56:9—57:13)

Bibliography

Bongers, H. A. "Jes. LVI 10a." *VT* 25 (1975) 791–92. **Fohrer, G.** "Kritik an Tempel, Kultus und Kultusausübung in nachexilischer Zeit (Jes 56,9—57,13; 65,1–7; Hag; Mal)." *Studien zu alttestamentlichen Texten und Themen.* Berlin: De Gruyter, 1981. 81–95. **Greenfield, J. C.** "The preposition *B . . . Taḥat* in Is 57,5." *ZAW* 73 (1961) 226–27. **Hanson, P. D.** *Dawn of Apocalyptic.* 186–202. **Irwin, W. H.** "The Smooth Stones of the Wadi. Isaiah 57:6." *CBQ* 29 (1967) 31–40. **Morgenstern, J.** "Two Prophecies from the Fourth Century B.C. and the Evolution of Yom Kippur. *HUCA* 24 (1952/53) 1–74. ———. "Jerusalem—485 B.C." *HUCA* 27 (1956) 101–79; 28 (1957) 15–47,

31 (1960) 1–29. ———. "Further Light from the Book of Isaiah upon the Catastrophe of 485 B.C." *HUCA* 37 (1966) 1–28. **Pauritsch, K.** *Die Neue Gemeinde.* 51–66. **Renaud, B.** "La mort du juste, entrée dans la paix (Is 57,1–2)." *RScRel* 51 (1977) 3–21. **Weise, M.** "Jesaja 57:5f." *ZAW* 72 (1960) 25–32.

Translation

Observer: 56:9 *Every beast of the field!* 3+2+2
Come to devour,
every beast in the forest!
10 *His watchmen*[a] *are blind.* 2+3
None of them knows[b] *anything.*
All of them (are) dumb dogs 3+3
who cannot bark,
dreamers,[c] *lying down,* 2+2
who love to sleep.
Heavens: 11 *The dogs (are) of strong appetite* 2+3
who never know when they have enough,
[a]*and these are bad ones*[a] 2+3
who know no understanding.
All of them have turned to their own way, 3+3
each [b]*to his own gain from its border.*[b]
Thieves: 12 [a]*Come! let me get wine* 2+2
and let us fill ourselves with liquor,
And may tomorrow be 4+3
immeasurably great.
Heavens: 57:1 *The one in the right perishes*[a] 2+4
but no one takes it to heart.
Loyal men are being taken away 3+2
with no understanding (of what it means).[b]
Indeed, when confronting the evil, 2+2
[c]*the one in the right is taken to prison.*
Earth: 2 *When peace*[a] *comes,*[b] 2+3+2
they[c] *will rest in their beds,*[d]
his[e] *uprightness goes on.*
Heavens: (to rebels) 3 *But as for you (masc pl), come near* 3+2+3
you, sons of a witch,
seed of an adulterer,[a] *and commit fornication.*[b]
4 *Of whom are you making sport?* 2+3+2
Toward whom do you contort your mouth?
Do you stick out your tongue?
Are you (masc pl) not children of rebellion? 4+2
Seed of deceit?
Earth: 5 *You (masc pl) who burn with the gods,*[a] 2+3
under every green tree.
You murderers of children in the valleys 3+3
under clefts of rock.
Heavens: (to Jerusalem) 6 *Among the smooth stones of the wady is your (fem sg) portion.* 3+3

They! They are your (fem sg) your allotted piece
of ground.
Although to them you (fem sg) have poured a drink
offering, 3+2+3
you (fem sg) have offered a cereal offering.
Yahweh: [a]*Shall I comfort*[b] *myself about these?*[a]
Earth: [7]*On a mountain, high and lifted up,* 3+2
(to Jerusalem) *you (fem sg) set your bed.*
You (fem sg) also go up there 2+2
to sacrifice a sacrifice.
Yahweh: [8]*Although behind the door and the doorpost* 3+2
you (fem sg) had set up your memorial,
you (fem sg) left[a] *me* 3+3
when you (fem sg) went up, you (fem sg) opened
your bed.
When you cut yourself off[b] *from them,*[c] 3+2+2
[d]*you loved their bed.*[d]
You envisioned a hand.
[9]*When you (fem sg) roused yourself*[a] *by rubbing*[b]
with oil, 3+2
when you increased your (fem sg) perfumes,
when you sent your envoys to one far away, 3+2
when you sent down even to Sheol,
[10]*although, by the length of your (fem sg) way you*
were tired, 3+3
you did not say "It is hopeless."
You found [a]*life for your strength,*[a] 3+3
so you were not faint.
[11]*Whom did you (fem sg) dread* 2+3
so that you were afraid when you lied?
And you did not remember me 3+2
and did not fix it[a] *on your mind!*
Have I not been silent, and hiding?[b] 4+3
But you did not fear me.
[12]*I myself will announce your (fem sg) rights* 2+2+2
and your deeds,
but they will not help you.
[13]*When you cry out, let your collectibles*[a] *help you,* 3+3
and all of them lift a spirit or take a breath.
But the one who takes refuge in me will possess
land. 4+3
He will inherit my holy mountain.

Notes

56:10.a. K צפו "his watchman." Q and DSS[Isa] צפיו "his watchmen" followed by 'A Σ Θ Vg. LXX omits; Tg paraphrases. The pronoun's antecedent is unclear. Duhm, Marti, *BHS* and others emend to make this a Yahweh speech, but Pauritsch (*Neue Gemeinde,* 54) defends MT as referring to "Israel" in v 8. Read Q and DSS[Isa].

10.b. MT ידעו "they know" is supported by DSS^Isa Σ Tg Vg. LXX^AQS adds φρονῆσαι "to understand" (followed by Eth Arab), influenced by לא ידעו הבין "they know no understanding" in v 11. Read MT.

10.c. MT הזים "dreamers" (BDB, 223), supported by LXX 'A Tg, is a *hap. leg.* DSS^Isa substitutes the more common word חוזים "seers," followed by MSS^K Σ Syr Vg (see Kutscher, *Isaiah Scroll,* 235). Read MT.

11.a-a. MT המה רעים "these are shepherds" (DSS^Isa adds an article, "the shepherds"). LXX καὶ εἰσι πονηροὶ "they are wicked," Σ και εισι κακοι "they are wicked," and Tg ואנון מבאשין "and these do evil" read רעים from רעע "to do evil." The choice is between the possible meanings of רֹעִים from רעה I "pasture, graze," i.e., "shepherds" (BDB, 944, I; so 'A Θ Vg), or רעה II "associated with," i.e., "companions" (BDB, 945, II), or רעע "be evil" and thus point as a noun, רָעִים "evil ones" (BDB, 947–48). Follow LXX Σ Tg and the context.

11.b-b. MT לבצעו מקצהו "to his own gain from his border." LXX omits מקצהו "from his border." MT is the more difficult reading and should be kept.

12.a. LXX omits the verse.

57:1.a. MT אָבָד "perishes," pf. DSS^Isa אובד "is perishing," ptcp.

1.b. LXX καὶ οὐδεὶς κατανοεῖ "and no one considers" is a close parallel to the first bistich. DSS^Isa supports MT. LXX continues the verse with a paraphrase.

1.c–2.b. *BHS*'s suggestion that these be changed to pl has missed the careful literary arrangement in the verses. Read MT.

2.a. MT שלום "peace." LXX interprets ἔσται ἐν εἰρήνῃ ἡ ταφὴ αὐτοῦ "his burial shall be in peace" and continues with a paraphrase. Tg supports MT.

2.c. The antecedent of "they" is "watchmen" in 56:10. The mix of sg and pl has led many commentators to dismiss the entire verse as a series of glosses. But 56:10–57:2 consistently uses sg for the righteous one while usually reserving the pl for the wicked.

2.d. DSS^Isa's sg suffix with a pl verb is unaccountable. LXX paraphrases. Tg 'A Σ Θ support MT.

2.e. DSS^Isa הלוך נוכחה "to go her uprightness" is unclear (cf. Kutscher, *Isaiah Scroll,* 476). MT "his" refers back to הצדיק "the one in the right" in v 1.

3.a. *BHS* suggests a fem form.

3.b. MT ותזנה "and you (sg) commit fornication." DSS^Isa ותזנו is pl. LXX καὶ πόρνης "and a fornicator," a noun. Cf. Σ Syr Vg. *BHS* follows LXX to read וזנה, deleting *taw.* Follow DSS^Isa with simple *waw,* "and you (pl) commit fornication."

5.a. MT אלים is usually translated "oaks, terebinths," though that is more commonly spelled אילים (1:29; BDB, 18). Weise (*ZAW* 72 [1960] 25–32) translates "gods," which is supported by the Versions. Read "gods."

6.a-a. *BHS* suggests moving to the end of v 7. But DSS^Isa LXX support MT's placement.

6.b. MT אנחם "I will comfort myself" or "be sorry" (BDB, 636). LXX οὐκ ὀργισθήσομαι "shall I not be angry?" Tg יתום "shall it turn back?" or "be appeased?"

8.a. MT גִּלִּית, piel, "you uncovered" (BDB, 163). LXX ἀποστῇς "you departed" and 'A Σ Θ απωκισθης "you emigrated" lead *BHS* to point as qal, גָּלִית "you departed." On the other hand, Duhm emended מאתי "from me" to מאתו "from it," thus "you uncovered (yourself) on account of it." But the vowel change is better attested. Follow the Gr. versions.

8.b. MT ותכרת "when you (masc) cut." DSS^Isa ותכרותי fem is more consistent. LXX omits. Tg וגזרת "made a covenant."

8.c. מהם "from them" is often read עמהם "with them" (H. Grätz; cf. BDB, 504), or else תכרת "you cut" is changed to תכרי "you bought" to make the phrase "you bribed some of them" (Duhm, Buhl, *BHS*). But DSS^Isa Tg support MT; LXX omits. MT is unintelligible if כרת is translated "to cut a covenant" (AV, RSV). But if it is read in its basic meaning together with לך "to you" as "cut yourself off from them," it makes good sense and prepares for the next clause. Then "from me" and "from them" are parallel, a deliberate contrast.

8.d-d. *BHS* suggests reading as a generalized inf constr and a pl "loving beds." But this has no MSS support.

9.a. MT ותשרי "you journeyed" (BDB, 1003, I). DSS^Isa supports the form. There is only one other use of the verb with this meaning (Ezek 27:25). A second meaning is "behold, regard." A third root meaning postulated only for some nouns (BDB, 1004) is related to שרר (BDB, 1057), also only postulated for nouns. They mean something like "become raised, excited, be firm." The latter can refer to genitals. LXX ἐπλήθυνας τὴν πορνείαν σου "you increased your prostitution" may presuppose a root related to Arab *ṯarra* "abound" (cf. P. Wernberg-Møller, "Two Notes," *VT* 8 [1958] 307–8; *BHS*). Tg avoids the issue altogether. Thus LXX and the context suggest that the meaning here is related to sexual excitement.

9.b. MT למלך "to the king." *BHS* posits a noun מל "hair" from a hypothetical root מלל. One could also point as a verb from מלל II "rub" (Prov 6:13). Some translations have read "to Molech," a Canaanite god. If the sentence is as erotic as seems possible, it is understandable that translations should tend to soften the sexual imagery.

10.a-a. MT חית ידך "life of your hand." DSS[Isa] agrees. LXX paraphrases. Tg אסגית "riches." "Hand" may mean riches or strength. It may also refer to the sexual implications of v 8. *BHS* suggests reversing the words to די חיתך "a sufficiency of your life" (BDB, 191). But this has no support in the sources.

11.a. DSS[Isa] adds אלה "these things." But LXX Syr Tg support MT.

11.b. MT וּמֵעֹלָם "and an age long" is supported by DSS[Isa] ומעולם. LXX παρορῶ "I overlook," supported by 'A Σ Vg, presupposes Heb. וּמַעְלִים "hiding," hiph ptcp from עלם, which fits the context. Read the emendation.

13.a. MT קבוציך "collectibles" is the only occurrence of this noun from קבץ "gather, collect." Cheyne and others (see BDB, 868) emend to שקיציך "your detestable things," and Torrey suggests an original מקבציך "those who gather you (in their arms)." But there is no need to change MT. M. Dahood (*Bib* 52 [1971] 343–44) suggested "pantheon."

Form/Structure/Setting

Jerusalem's neighbors respond to Yahweh's announcement that Jerusalem is to be an open city with the cynical judgment that she will be easy pickings for raiders and thieves (56:9–12). They may include Jews who have not lived under the law for a long time (like those in Zech 7:1–3). Others may not have been Jews at all, like the mixed population of neighboring districts, such as those who asked to join Zerubbabel in building the Temple (Ezra 4:1–2), or like those to whom Malachi said that they would need instruction (Mal 1:6–9).

The accusations that follow recall the rhetoric of the pre-exilic prophets Hosea, Jeremiah, and Ezekiel. The targets of the attack are pagan rites being performed in Palestine like those in the eighth to the sixth centuries B.C. They are just as abominable to Yahweh now as they were then. The picture of Judah as Yahweh's lewd and unfaithful wife is picked up from Hosea (chaps. 1–3), Jeremiah (2:20–3:18), and Ezekiel (chaps. 16 and 23).

The optimistic tone of chaps. 54–55 has been shattered by the cynical taunts of 56:9–12. This scene takes serious note of those who are not "meek and mild," who seek their own salvation by constant agitation and terror against the empire and by pagan practices that offend Yahweh. Note the contrast between הרעה "the evil" and הצדיק "the one in the right" in 57:1c.

57:1 describes a chaotic situation where the persecution of faithful and law-abiding people is tolerated or ignored.

V 2 affirms Yahweh's support for the well-being of those who are in the right.

Vv 3–13a address the רעים "evildoers." Vv 3–5 revile religious apostates as well as political rebels and liars. The address is masculine plural. Vv 6–13 are addressed to Jerusalem in feminine singular. Yahweh enters the dialogue, speaking bitterly, and in terms of a broken marriage and adultery, accuses Jerusalem of apostasy. The issue is both religious and political. By rejecting Persian rule the people reject Yahweh's patronage of Persia (v 9).

The outcome affects the right to land tenure in Palestine (v 13b), which is assured to those who stay close to Yahweh.

57:1–13 has been called a prophetic liturgy (Kaiser), a lament or a threat (Eissfeldt, *Introduction,* 462), and a prophetic disputation and a judgment speech (Fohrer, 161; cf. Pauritzsch, *Die Neue Gemeinde,* 62–63). It is a carefully composed speech responding to 56:9–12 and is directed to paganized Jews who attempt to enter the open Jerusalem Temple fellowship without changing their ways. They corrupt the system of justice and mock the ways of God by their life-style. The passage opens by taking note of the collapse of the judicial system. Then these interlopers are challenged in an elaborate arch structure.

3 m sg The one in the right dies—but no one notices (v 1)
3 m pl A Peace comes—the upright rest in their beds (v 2)
2 m pl B But you sorcerers and adulterers, come near (v 3)
C Of whom do you make sport? (v 4)
2 f sg D Six acts (two in masc pl; four in fem sg) (vv 5–6)
KEYSTONE While behind the doorpost was your memorial, indeed you left me (vv 7–8b)
D′ Six acts (vv 8c–10)
C′ Whom did you dread? (v 11a–b)
B′ Have I been silent? I will announce your rights. (v 11c–13a)
3 m sg A′ He who takes refuge in me will possess the land (v 13b)

The references in vv 2 and 13b are impersonal, one plural and one singular. Vv 3–5 are consistently addressed in second person masculine plural, apparently to the speakers of 56:9–12. Vv 6–13a are addressed in second person feminine singular. This has usually indicated the city of Jerusalem and should probably be so understood here. The section begins by addressing a particular group of רעים "bad ones" who had spoken so arrogantly in 56:9–12. But then it recognizes that the pagan practices of the city herself have identified Jerusalem with the attitudes toward justice, law, and order held by the bad ones. Participation in pagan practices produces a pagan morality.

Despite building the Temple, the basic population of Judah and Palestine remained as pagan as it ever was. Before the work of Ezra and Nehemiah, this picture of prevalent paganism and of unpunished violence is historically believable (cf. Pauritsch, *Die Neue Gemeinde,* 66). It is not necessary to postulate a pre-exilic background for this section, as Westermann does in comparing 56:9–12 with Ezek 34:1–10.

The situation indicates that the Persian administration has broken down. Persia's extended wars with Greece near the end of the reign of Darius and throughout that of Xerxes could well explain neglect in many areas of the empire. Morgenstern has postulated a period of severe unrest and rebellion in Palestine at this time (*HUCA* 24 [1952/53] 1–74; 27 [1956] 101–79; 28 [1957] 15–47; 31 [1960] 1–29; 37 [1966] 1–28).

Yahweh repeats the list of six actions with parallel statements (each an imperfect with *waw* consecutive) addressed in second person feminine singular to Jerusalem (vv 8b–9). The last two turn from symbolic paganism to political rebellion. Note the artistic balance of שמת "you set up" with "your bed" in v 7 and "your memorial" in v 8a, the use of alliteration (גלית *galith* "you left" parallels עלית *ʿalith* "you go up") and the use of תיראי "you feared" twice in v 11.

Comment

56:9 The change is dramatic. A different speaker observes Jerusalem building a Temple without first building her defenses and thinks her totally vulnerable to vandalism and plunder. *Beast of the field* is a metaphor for the human beasts who live by pillage and plunder.

10 He finds *their watchmen* to be inept, innocuous, inattentive and ineffective.

11 The predators are described. They are insatiable, bad, and as devoid of *understanding* as they claim Jerusalem's guards to be. *Turned to their own way*, i.e., away from right as established by either God or society, is the ultimate description of the unbeliever (cf. the confession in 53:6 and Paul's words in Rom 1:21–32) in contrast to the believer who turns to God. The selfish ego is further emphasized by *his own gain from its border*. The latter phrase suggests that the brigands may enjoy sanctuary and even encouragement from the districts from which they come. This situation is apparently typical of Jerusalem's plight in the latter reign of Darius and that of Xerxes, who were too caught up in their wars with Greece to look after affairs in Judah. Ezra-Nehemiah is filled with references to this banditry against an unwalled and largely defenseless city.

12 The bandits anticipate a great haul tomorrow.

57:1 An observer notes the collapse of order and justice in the city. The situation has come full circle to that described in 1:21–23 and in chap. 3. הצדיק "the one in the right" suggests a person whom a court should recognize to be "in the right." That would be justice. Instead he is condemned. אנשי חסד "loyal men" are accused of treason and convicted. In legal confrontations between the innocent and the guilty, the innocent one is punished with imprisonment.

2 A promise looks beyond the disorder to the return of *peace* (שלום). This does not look merely to a cessation of hostilities, but to the return of a healthy social order and a just application of law.

3 But attention returns to the current bad times. The rebels are called to order by outside observers. Those addressed are the ruffians who spoke in 56:12. They are branded as *sons of a witch, progeny of an adulterer* (i.e., bastards), who *commit fornication*. The insults identify their rough and provocative behavior with their origin in a pagan society.

4 The verse refers again to the speeches in 56:9–12, implying that their disparaging references to Yahweh-worshipers in Jerusalem were in fact against God himself. The insults are resumed in pointed terms. *Children of rebellion* picks up the term from 1:2 and suggests that they are descendants of those northern Israelites who did not go into exile. They have continued the pagan practices of their ancestors and expanded them. *Seed of deceit* = "children of lies" and may also refer to the pagan rites of sacred prostitution. שקר "a lie" is the term Jeremiah (10:14; 51:17) used for an idol that deceived and disappointed (cf. Isa 28:15) and also produced adherents who are as much violence-prone and liars as it is.

5 A list of pagan rites is given. *Who burn among the oaks* refers to sexual orgies in pagan garden shrines. *Murderers of children* refers to participation in rites of child sacrifice like those attributed to Phoenician worshipers of Molech (Lev 18:21; 20:2–5; 1 Kgs 11:7; 2 Kgs 23:10; Jer 32:35).

6 The address changes to second person feminine singular, apparently identifying the same practices with Jerusalem itself. It is a sad commentary on the situation. Very similar judgment had been passed on the city two and a half centuries earlier (1:21–23 and chap. 3). Jerusalem is often hailed for its brightness. But it also had a dark side. At the same time that some in Jerusalem are building a new Temple for Yahweh others reserve places in pagan valleys for *drink* and *cereal offerings,* probably intended to insure fertility in fields, domestic animals, and families. Yahweh asks in sorrow, *Shall I comfort myself about these?* Should he overlook them? Should he expect that they will vanish by themselves?

7 The list continues. In contrast to the *wady* of v 6, the setting here is a high *mountain.* There Jerusalem establishes her *bed.* The reference is again to fertility rites, as vv 8–10 will make clear. The imagery and implications are unmistakable when compared with similar passages in Hosea, Jeremiah, and Ezekiel. To *sacrifice* there is to break covenant with Yahweh. This is compared to infidelity to a marriage contract.

8 The *memorial behind the door* and on *the doorpost* is the *mezuzah* (see *Enc. Jud.* 3:1475–76), a little metal container for a scrap of Scripture (Deut 6:9; 11:20), usually the Ten Commandments and the Great Commandment of Deut 6:4. Every orthodox Jewish home has one of these fastened to the doorpost. But this did not prevent apostasy of the worst kind. The problem of apostasy to pagan cults in the post-exilic community is faced head-on. A prophetic metaphor which had been used for pre-exilic sin is revived. There is here a sense of *déja vu,* a feeling that this has all happened before. The tragedy is that nothing has changed. *When you went up you opened your bed* summarizes the accusation in terms of the Ten Commandments and of the prophets Hosea, Jeremiah, and Ezekiel. The metaphor using sexual language continues. *When you cut yourself off from them* is in conscious parallel to the first half of the verse. מאתי "from me" represents the voluntary separation of apostasy. מהם "from them" speaks of the separation of deportation and exile. Then, far removed from Palestine and the lure of Baʿal religions, she still *loved their bed,* in fantasy she *envisioned a hand,* perhaps that of a lover stroking sensuously.

9 ותשרי למלך is usually translated "then you traveled to the king." The verse stands between a description of apostasy in terms of sexual deviation and political rebellion. It could be seen as a turning point. But the second stich reads, *when you increased your perfumes* which is more like the sexual fantasy than political rebellion. If the first stich is intended to stay within the sexual metaphor it may be translated *when you roused yourself by rubbing with oil,* an apparent reference to masturbation. In exile the attraction to idolatry was less seductive. Participation there was induced by nostalgia for the familiar love of Canaan's Baʿals.

When you sent envoys to one far away. In chap. 7 there is an implication that Ahaz sent a message to Tiglath-Pileser. In chap. 39 the envoys of Merodach-Baladan came to Hezekiah. Is this a reference to those Hezekiah sent in return? Or does this refer to Manasseh's trip to Nineveh? Whatever the specific reference, the words are a reminder of the political aspects of apostasy. Conspiracy against God's chosen ruler is viewed as rebellion against God. *Even to Sheol* may recall chap. 14 with its poem about the death of Babylon's king. Or it may simply use another metaphor for the low estate to which Israel and Jerusalem had fallen before the end came.

10 Jerusalem's ardor for apostasizing paganism, whether in exotic cults or in adventurous politics, did not tire them. They traveled far and long without giving up. *You found the life of your hand* is a strange sentence. Is it a return to the accusation of masturbation? Or is it a figure of finding lively inner resources of strength?

11 Yahweh asks in wonder, *Whom did you dread?* The term carries implications of worshipful commitment. This is the awe, the *dread,* the *fear* that is basic to worship and to faith. It is the fear toward Yahweh recommended in the oft repeated proverb, "the fear of Yahweh is the beginning of wisdom" (Job 28:28; Ps 111:10; Prov 1:7). Here apparently a greater *dread* has replaced it and made apostasy possible. *You lied* describes the participation in pagan worship whose gods can be called "lies" (28:15, 17). *You did not remember me.* Remembering Yahweh is the great virtue of faith that Deuteronomy extols. *Your mind:* the Hebrew word is "heart," but the connotation is that expressed in English by "mind." Sin or apostasy occurs in the mind before it determines actions, and all of these take place after one has transferred allegiance to another god.

As in v 6 above, Yahweh muses: *Have I not been silent* about their sin, and *hiding,* that is, not punishing them on the spot? has usually been read to mean "and from an age." But the translation *hiding* (see n. 11.b) fits this context much better. The final stich of the verse returns to the question raised in the first: *But you did not fear me.* God's exercise of grace and forbearance does not always inspire grateful faith and devotion in response. It had not in this case.

12–13a Yahweh is both judge and witness. But truthful testimony does not help the situation. He suggests sarcastically that Jerusalem should ask for help in the next emergency from those she had served, that is, from the idols that she had collected (her *collectibles*). Let *them lift a spirit* or *take a breath.* This apparently refers to the séances of spiritualism.

13b The scene closes as it began (v 2) with the admonition that *the one who takes refuge* in Yahweh is the only one with a right to *possess the land* or *inherit* his *holy mountain.* This again speaks of the importance of reestablishing land rights in Palestine (49:8c). But it also speaks of the right to meet God in his sanctuary, a right that becomes increasingly central as the Vision moves to its culmination. The admonition clearly suggests a basis for defining who are Jews and as such legitimate heirs to land rights and rights to pilgrimage. They are to be recognized not so much by their ethnic origins as by their religious practice and devotion.

Explanation

An open religious society is in fact very vulnerable. Evil neighbors see it as easy booty. A favorable observer recognizes injustices inherent in having such an open city in a venal and corrupt setting where "one who is in the right may perish."

The scene affirms that final "peace" and ultimate "inheritance" belongs to those "who take refuge" in Yahweh. Others stand, as they have always stood, under God's judgment. The first six acts of the Vision traced the curse of judgment over Israel and Jerusalem through two centuries. Now, in this time of grace, blessing, consolation, and restoration, have the people forgotten those lessons from the past? Yahweh has not forgotten. Nor has he changed. Should he be indulgent to idolaters now when he was so opposed to them in the past? Of course not. The blight and damage of paganism is as abhorrent and repugnant to him as it ever was. Its results are equally disastrous and predictable. The new believing community that is restoring the Temple needed to remember that. Believers in every age must recognize that. "The gates of Hades will not overcome" the people of God (Matt 16:18). Ultimately the world cannot overcome the synagogue or the church just as darkness cannot overcome the light (42:16; 58:10; 59:9; John 1:5; 1 John 1:5; 2:8).

Scene 5: I Shall Heal Him (57:14–21)

Bibliography

Cannon, W. W. "Isaiah 57, 14–21. CC. 60–62." *ZAW* 62 (1934) 75–77. **Hanson, P. D.** *Dawn of Apocalypitc.* 77–78. **Kselman, J. S.** *"w'nhhw* in Isa 57:18." *CBQ* 43 (1981) 539–42. **Pauritsch, K.** *Die Neue Gemeinde* 66–73. **Rubinstein, A.** "Isaiah 57:17—הסתר ואקצף and the DSIa Variant." *VT* 4 (1954) 200–201.

Translation

Yahweh: 14 *And I say:* [a] 1
Build up! Build up! Prepare a way! 4+4
Remove every obstacle from my people's way.
Herald: 15 *For thus says one high and lifted up,* 4+4
Dweller Forever whose name is Holy:
Yahweh: *I dwell in the high and holy* [a] *place* 3+2
with one contrite and lowly of spirit
to revive the spirit of humble ones 3+3
and to revive the heart of those practicing contrition.
16 *Indeed, I will not contend for an age,* 4+3
and I will not always be angry.
For spirit procedes before me 3+3
and life-breath which I have made.
17 *Because of the iniquity* [a] *of his profit from violence* [b]
was I angry 3+3+4

so[c] *that I struck him, hiding (my face) when I was angry.*[d]
But then he continued apostate in the way of his heart.
18 *I have seen his ways, yet will I heal him,* 3+2+3
and I will lead him[a] *and complete*[b]
comforting deeds[c] *for him and for those mourning with him,*
19 [a]*creating the fruit*[b] *of lips:* 3+4
"Peace! Peace![c] *To the distant*[d] *and to the near."*[e]
Herald: *Says Yahweh.* 2+1
Yahweh: *And I shall heal him.*
Heavens: 20 *The adversaries (are) like the tossing*[a] *sea.* 3+4+4
For it is incapable of resting[b]
and its waters put out[c] *mire and dirt.*
Earth: 21 *There can be no peace,* 2+2+1
says my God,
for the adversaries.

Notes

14.a. MT וְאָמַר "and he says," pf with *waw,* implies that Yahweh continues to speak. LXX καὶ ἐροῦσι "and they shall say." Vg *et dicam* "and I say" leads *BHS* to propose a 1st pers impf, וְאֹמַר, which changes only the vowel points. Read the emendation. A new speaker says, "I say."

15.a. MT מרום וקדוש "in the high and holy place" is acc of place (cf. 33:16; GKC §§ 117*bb,* 118*d-h*). According to Kutscher (*Isaiah Scroll,* 383), the construction fell into disuse, which accounts for DSS^{Isa} במרום ובקודש "in the high place and in holiness," LXX ἐν ἁγίοις "in holy places" or "among saints," and Vg *in excelso et in sancto* "in heights and in holiness." Syr Tg support MT. Read MT.

17.a. *BHS* suggests moving "his" to עון "iniquity." MT is a constr and may be kept.

17.b. MT בִּצְעוֹ "his covetousness, his profit from violence" (BDB, 130). DSS^{Isa} Tg 'A Σ Θ Vg agree. LXX βραχύ τι "a brief time" leads *BHS* to translate בצע as "for a little while," but such a translation is dubious (see Whybray). Read MT.

17.c. *BHS* correctly suggests a *waw* consec following the Versions.

17.d. One MS reads וְקָצֹף inf abs "and being angry" parallel to הסתר "hiding." But DSS^{Isa} Tg Vg support MT's 1st pers ind. LXX has 3d pers. Read MT.

18.a. MT וְאַנְחֵהוּ "and I will lead him" from נחה (BDB, 634). *BHS* suggests וַאֲנִחֵהוּ "and I will give him rest" from נוח (BDB, 628). DSS^{Isa} omits; LXX paraphrases; Tg וארחים "I will have compassion"; 'A Vg support MT. Read MT.

18.b. DSS^{Isa} inserts a second לוא "for him" (on DSS^{Isa}'s spelling, see Kutscher, *Isaiah Scroll,* 171–72).

18.c. MT נחמים "comfort" (BDB, 637; cf. Hos 11:8; Zech 1:13). DSS^{Isa} תנחומים "consolations" (BDB, 637) is the more usual form (cf. 66:11; Jer 16:7; Ps 94:19; Job 15:11; 21:2), especially in rabbinic Heb. (Kutscher, *Isaiah Scroll,* 386).

19.a. *BHS* suggests inserting אני "I." But this is already implied.

19.b. K נוב inf constr "bearing" is a *hap. leg.* Q and DSS^{Isa} ניב "fruit" is a noun (BDB, 626) occurring elsewhere only in Mal 1:12, where the text is also uncertain (see R. L. Smith, *Micah-Malachi,* WBC 32 [Waco, TX: Word Books, 1984] 309–10). Tg supports Q but expands. LXX omits the phrase.

19.c. DSS^{Isa} omits the second שלום. But LXX Syr Tg Vg have two (although Tg distributes them interpreting).

19.d. Tg interprets, "for the righteous who have kept my law from of old."

19.e. Tg interprets, "for the repentant who have returned to my law recently."

20.a. MT נגרש niph ptcp "tossing" or niph pf "it is tossed" refers to the sea, and is supported by Tg. DSS[Isa] נגרשו "they are tossed" refers to the adversaries and is followed by LXX.

20.b. MT השקט hiph inf abs "rest, security" (BDB, 1052; cf. 32:17). DSS[Isa] לאשקיט is perhaps a mistake for להשקיט inf constr.

20.c. MT ויגרשו qal "they cast out, toss out," hence "put out" (BDB,176). DSS[Isa] ויתגרשו hithp has the same meaning. There are no parallels in either qal impf or hithp (see Kutscher, *Isaiah Scroll,* 359).

Form/Structure/Setting

This scene brings the act to a close by repeating "There can be no peace for the adversaries" (cf. 48:22 and 66:24). It combines very optimistic encouragement to "build a way" with a clear recognition of the apostasy that is rampant. It summarizes the tension between God's anger over sin and his determination to heal his people and his city. This passage has sometimes been called an oracle of salvation. But the mixture of positive and negative elements hardly fits that genre.

Someone says: "Build up." Is this Haggai or Zechariah after the death of Zerubbabel? Or is this an unknown leader near the end of Darius's reign or during the reign of Xerxes? (Cf. parallel calls in 48:20 and in 52:11–12, although here the object is a highway, as in 40:3–4.) Perhaps the Temple is finished. Preparations are being made for pilgrims to come for festival.

The passage begins with imperatives: "Build up! Prepare!" (v 14). Yahweh, host to Jerusalem's festival, supports this command with three speeches beginning with כי "for, indeed" (vv 15, 16a, 16b). He continues with a complex explanation of his apparent inconsistency (vv 17–18) which makes his invitation and promise possible (vv 19). The scene closes with a disclaimer: this promise does not apply to הרשעים "the adversaries" (vv 20–21). (See Pauritsch, *Neue Gemeinde,* 66–73, for a summary of critical appraisals of the pericope's structure.) The problem of hard opposition from within Jerusalem has not been solved, but Yahweh's plan moves on toward completion anyway.

Comment

14 The work goes on. It does little good to have a Temple if there is no access. *Build! Prepare! Remove every obstacle* so the pilgrims may take the road to Jerusalem. The previous scene suggests that it may still be a dangerous journey for pilgrims beset by thieves and robbers.

15 The great title for Yahweh שכן עד "Dweller Forever" suggests that he is now settled in Zion's Temple, *high and lifted up. Whose name is holy* is reminiscent of Zion language in the Psalms (33:21; 103:1; 145:21).

The invitation is for suitable worshipers to join Yahweh here. Note the contrast of *high and holy* with *contrite and lowly.* This is God's paradox. The place of glory and power belongs not to the proud, ambitious, and strong of humankind, but to the *contrite,* meek, and *lowly of spirit.* The invitation foresees the benefits of worship and pilgrimage. Worship *revives the spirit of humble ones.* It *revives the heart of those practicing contrition.* Whether attendance brings any benefit for the arrogant and powerful is not mentioned.

16 Yahweh recognizes that during the past two centuries and more, the people were under a ban (chap. 6). Their experience of devastating invasions and exile made them more aware of his anger than of his grace. Yahweh admits his anger for just cause. But now he insists that it is past. This is the time of grace, a time of good news (40:1–9). It is a time for the *spirit,* a time to emphasize that the Lord is the source of *life-breath,* that is, every breath of life comes from God. He gives life and it is his spirit that upholds and energizes creation.

17 The explanation begins. God was *angry* because of Israel's (the pronoun is third person masculine singular) *iniquity* which consisted of violent acts for profit, that is, banditry. Yahweh punished him. *Hiding my face when I was angry:* the characteristic grace and blessing were absent during that time. *Hiding* his *face* meant no answer to prayer and no spiritual benefit from worship. God had, in effect, abandoned his Temple. But the sad fact remained that, instead of responding to punishment by repenting and turning back to God, Israel had continued *apostate in the way of his* (Israel's) *heart.* This statement recognizes that a large proportion of Israel in Babylon and in Palestine was still not spiritually inclined to Yahweh or faithful to his covenant.

18 God is fully aware of this fact. *Yet he healed him.* The age of grace has begun, not because Israel is better than before, but because God has determined to show grace in spite of the prevalent iniquity. He offers to *heal, lead, and complete* (which can also mean "providing peace") *comforting deeds* (cf. 40:1–2) to Israel and to *those mourning with him,* that is, those who wish him well, proselytes and others who fear Yahweh.

19 *Creating* (בורא) is usually a word reserved for physical creation. But here the announcement of peace is seen as a divine work of equal proportions. *The fruit of lips* is a literal translation of an elaborate phrase for "the words." The announcement is a benediction of *peace.* Only the creator can speak words which create what they say. But he can and does. When he says "Peace," there is peace. The pilgrimage to Zion's Temple allows one to hear that blessing at first hand. The fulfillment of God's requirements, contrition and humility, opens the ear to hear his blessing and experience his peace.

The blessing is offered to those who are *distant* and to those who are *near.* This may refer to geographical distance: those in distant diaspora communities and those in nearby Judah. The Targum understood it in terms of time: "the righteous who have kept my law from of old" and "for the repentant who have returned to my law recently." Interpreting this in terms of keeping the law belongs to the Targum, not to Isaiah. But understanding it in terms of peace to be experienced now which is the same as that offered to early generations is a valid interpretation.

Says Yahweh applies to the entire previous speech. But it cannot close without interjecting: *and I shall heal him.* Persistent grace lives in that phrase.

20 Lest anyone misunderstand, two statements repeat the condemnation of הרשעים "the adversaries." These are the ones who have resisted Yahweh's plan at every step. They can have no place in the Temple unless they repent, and there is no sign of that. They are agitators who are always restless, always spewing out *dirt* and violence.

21 *There can be no peace . . . for the adversaries.* Grace is neither blind nor stupid. *Peace* picks up the references in vv 2 and 18–19 above. This verse recognizes, as 48:22 did, that there is no place for peace in the heart of a zealous rebel agitator, a terrorist. Persons of this kind have existed since Cain and undoubtedly will continue to do so.

Explanation

How can God work in an imperfect world and with an imperfect people? One could be misled by the long account of his judgment on Israel and Jerusalem in chaps. 1–39 to think that he simply gets rid of anyone who will not cooperate with him. But that is not the biblical view, nor is it the case here. The continued existence of adversaries who are pagan at heart and in practice is not allowed to slow the building of the Temple nor to alter God's attitude of grace toward his city and his people. Yet his grace must not blind the reader to his utter abhorrence of sin in any form.

God promised peace to the upright in v 2. He now proclaims it for the approaching pilgrims. But there can be no peace for the adversaries of the project or of Yahweh and his plan.

God offers a place in his house, the Temple, to the contrite, the humble, and the lowly in spirit. There is no other requirement—none of race or creed. Those humble souls who would seek Yahweh are welcomed with a promise of spiritual renewal. How like God to offer a spot in his highest place to persons who have the lowliest stations in life!

Act XI: Zion's Light Shines (Chaps. 58—61)

THE ELEVENTH GENERATION:
ARTAXERXES (465–458 B.C.)

At the end of the reign of Xerxes conditions in Palestine had deteriorated badly. Government control was lax. Lawlessness was rampant. When Artaxerxes came to the throne, there was hope for improvement. He and worshipers in Jerusalem are called to reform and to lead the kind of moral life that makes worship possible. Under strong Persian administration stable government is achieved. The city and its temple are rebuilt. This provides a setting in which humble worshipers may find God.

The act has five scenes:

Scene 1: Yahweh's Kind of Fast (58:1–14)
Scene 2: Troubled Times in Judah (59:1–15a)
Scene 3: Yahweh Decides to Act (59:15b–21)
Scene 4: Zion's Day Dawns (60:1–22)
Scene 5: Yahweh's Agents to Bless Jerusalem (61:1–11)

HISTORICAL BACKGROUND

Bibliography

ANCIENT HISTORIES:

Ctesias. *Patriologiae.* Series Graeca, vols. 103–104. **Esther. Ezra 4:6–24. Herodotus.** Books VII–IX. **Malachi. Thucydides.** *The Peloponnesian War.* Tr. B. Jowett. New York: Bantam Books, 1960.

MODERN HISTORIES:

Bright, J. *HI.* 373–404. **Cook, J. M.** *The Persian Empire.* London: J. M. Dent, 1983. 126–28. **Morgenstern, J.** "Jerusalem—485 B.C." *HUCA* 27 (1956) 101–79; 28 (1957) 15–47; 31 (1960) 1–29. ———. "The Dates of Ezra and Nehemiah." *JSS* 7 (1962) 1–11. **Myers, J. M.** *The World of the Restoration.* Englewood Cliffs, NJ: Prentice-Hall, 1968. 82–105. **Olmstead, A. T.** *History of the Persian Empire.* 234–352. **Smith, R.** *Micah-Malachi.* WBC 32. Waco, TX: Word Books, 1984. 298–99. **Soggin, J. A.** *A History of Ancient Israel.* 271–82. **Widengren, G.** "The Persian Period." *IJH.* 523–32. **Williamson, H. G. M.** *Ezra-Nehemiah.* WBC 16. Waco, TX: Word Books, 1985. 60–61.

Events in the middle years of the fifth century B.C. were decisive for the history of the world for centuries to come: the Persian advance toward Europe was brought to a halt; Athens matured, first as a naval power, and then as a cultural center; and Egypt was confirmed within the Persian orbit. Palestine was obliquely involved in these events beyond her borders. Greek fleets maneuvered near Cyprus just over the horizon. Phoenician fleets, merchantmen and warships alike, sailed in the service of Persia. Mercenaries from the region served in armies fighting in Asia Minor and in Egypt, while Greek mercenaries fought alongside them and against them. Armies and supplies moved over Palestinian roads on the way to Greece. The importance of the area to Persia may be measured by the limited tax burden placed on Syrian and Palestinian regions and the total freedom from taxes accorded the Arabs in this period (cf. J. M. Myers, *The World of the Restoration,* 117).

The reign of Xerxes (485–465B.C.) probably brought major disturbances in Palestine, according to J. Morgenstern. He summarized his position as follows:

> With the approval, and even the encouragement and token support, of the Persian royal administration, the land was overrun by a coalition of ruthless enemies, the nations immediately adjacent to it, the Edomites, Moabites, Ammonites, and Philistines, and with some measure of participation by the Syrians and Sidonians. The Judean community, totally unprepared for actual warfare, could offer no effective resistence. It was conquered completely and speedily. Jerusalem was besieged and captured. Its walls were breached and its gates burned (Pss 79:1–4; 137:7; Isa 64:9f.; Ezek 25:3; Lam 2:5–9). The city itself was depopulated and laid in ruins. The temple too was burned and destroyed (Pss 74:3–8; 79:16; Isa 63:18; 64:10; Ezek 25:3; Lam 1:10; 2:6f., 20b; 5:18). A large section of the people was massacred. Another, apparently large section of them was carried off, and as captives, they were sold in the slave-markets of Tyre, Sidon, and Gaza, and thus came to be scattered throughout the vast Mediterranean world (Joel 4:2b–8; Neh 5:8; Isa 60:4, 8–22). The Jewish community of Judaea which survived this catastrophe was only a tiny, insignificant, pitifully helpless fragment of what it had been previously (*HUCA* 31 [1962] 1).

Aharoni (*Land of the Bible,* 358) supports this view. G. E. Wright (*Shechem* [New York: McGraw-Hill, 1964] 164) cites archeological evidence from Shechem, Bethel, Gibeon, and Tel el-ful of major disturbances during the fifth century B.C. G. Widengren (*IJH,* 526) acknowledges that "there may certainly have been disturbances in Palestine during the first half of the fifth century, for example, during Egyptian periods of revolt in 486–83 B.C.E. and 459 B.C.E.," although he does not agree with Morgenstern's full theory.

Xerxes' concentration on wars with the Greeks led to neglect of his Palestinian and Egyptian territories. When he lost the naval battle at Salamis in 480 B.C. and his army was beaten at Plataea in 479 B.C., he was forced to order a major retreat in Asia Minor. A revolt in Babylon was brutally repressed, resulting in a new satrapal alignment in which Syria and Palestine became a separate satrapy called Beyond the River. Then Xerxes was murdered in 465 B.C.

A period of chaos followed, as claimants for the throne struggled for supremacy. Artaxerxes, the third son of Xerxes, succeeded in overcoming or murdering the others.

Information about events in Palestine in this period is scarce, as Morgenstern's efforts to piece together evidence of destruction show. Jehoezer succeeded Elnathan as Judah's second non-Davidic governor. The high-priestly succession moved from Joshua to Jeoyakim and then to Johanan I (see *Historical Background* to chaps. 52:13–57:21 above).

Photias 20–38b records the account that Ctesias wrote of the succession of Artaxerxes to the throne. A war with Bactria, an eastern satrapy, was a part of that battle for succession. Other than this, little ancient information is available about the period. Herodotus's account does not extend this far and Ctesias had not yet arrived at the Persian court (cf. Cook, *The Persian Empire,* 127). In 463 B.C. a revolt broke out in Egypt led by Inaros, a Lybian. Being a foreigner, he had little Egyptian following and succeeded only in lower Egypt. But in 461 B.C. Pericles came to power in Athens. He revived the old Delian League and built a fleet of two hundred ships to renew the war over Cyprus. Sixty of these ships were sent to Egypt to support Inaros. By 459 B.C. the Greek-Lybian alliance had won most of Egypt.

In 458 B.C. Ezra, a Jewish priest-scribe, was sent to Jerusalem by the Persians, who recognized it as a temple city (see *Excursus: Jerusalem—A Persian Temple City*). He would make the city and Judah, its surrounding district, into a genuine colony. "Persia was tolerant of various ethnic religions but insisted that their cults should be well organized under responsible leadership and that religion should never mask plans for rebellion" (Olmstead, *History of the Persian Empire,* 304). Ezra's mission to organize the cult in Jerusalem met these qualifications and fitted Persia's need for stability on the frontier. "He did not succeed in stopping the activity of the nationalistic party whose dreams of a national kingdom surfaced repeatedly. But he did point the way to the only safe policy for the salvation of Judaism: abandonment of nationalistic hopes, reconciliation to the political rule of foreigners, loyalty to the powers that be, and full acceptance of the unique position of the Jew as the guardian of God's moral law" (Olmstead, *History of the Persian Empire,* 307). Eliashib was high priest at the time (Neh 13:4). He resisted Ezra's reforms. But his son and successor, Johanan I, supported Ezra (Ezra 10:6).

In the chaotic situation in Judah prior to Ezra's appearance which this survey, Zech 9–14, and Malachi portray, the evils pictured in chaps. 57–58 were clearly possible. Chap. 61 appears to hint at the role of Ezra.

MILITARY AND POLITICAL BACKGROUND 480–458 B.C.

Dates B.C.	*Persian Emperor*	*Imperial Events*	*Governor in Judah*	*Priest in Jerusalem*
486	Xerxes		Elnathan	Jeoyakim
480–79		Defeated by Greek Allies		
478		Pausanias liberated Cyprus		
477		Athens assumes leadership of Greek forces under Kimon	Jehoezer	Eliashib
469		Kimon in naval action in Asia Minor; Persian fleet of Phoenician and Cilician ships defeated by Kimon	Ahzai	Johanan I
465		Xerxes dies leaving 3 sons		
	Artaxerxes	Artaxerxes, the youngest, emerges as survivor and victor		
458		Revolt in Bactria	(Ezra in Jerusalem)	

Scene 1: Yahweh's Kind of Fast (58:1–14)

Bibliography

Achtemeier, E. *The Community and Message.* 50–60. **Brongers, H. A.** "Jes 58, 13–14." *ZAW* 87 (1975) 212–16. **Dahood, M.** "The Chiastic Breakup in Isaiah 58,7." *Bib* 57 (1976) 105. **Daris, S.** "Isaia 58:6–9 in uno scritto anonimo P. Med. inv. 71.84 (1) 3 sec." *Aegyptus* 58 (1978) 106–9. **Hanson, P. D.** *The Dawn of Apocalyptic.* 100–112. **Hauret, C.** "Note d'exégèse, Isaïe 58:9." *RSR* 35 (1961) 369–77. **Hoppe, L. J.** "Isaiah 58:1–12: Fasting and Idolatry." *BTB* 13 (1983) 44–47. **Kosmala, H.** "Form and Structure of Isaiah 58." *ASTI* 5 (1967) 69–81. **Lack, R.** *Letture strutturaliste dell'AT* (Isa 58:7–12; 60:18,22; 61:3–11). Rome: Boria, 1978. **Lefevre, A.** "L'épître (de l'ouverture du carême) (Is 58:1–14): Jour de jeune, jour de grace." *AsSeign* 25 (1967) 19–32. **Pauritsch, K.** *Die Neue Gemeinde.* 73–87.

Translation

Yahweh: (to his herald)	1 *Give a loud cry!* [a] *Do not hold back!* *Raise your voice like a trumpet!*	2+1+3
	Announce to my people their rebellion *and to Jacob's house their sin.*	3+3
	2 *Even as they seek me day by day* *and delight to know my ways:*	4+3
	like a nation which [a] *does righteousness* *and does not abandon the justice of its God,*	3+3
	they ask me for righteous judgments. *They delight to approach God.*	3+3
Judean Worshipers:	3 *Why have we fasted* *but you do not see?*	2+2
	Why have we humbled ourselves *but you have not acknowledged us?*	2+2
Heavens:	*See! In the day of your (pl) fast,* *you (pl) find pleasure* *and suppress* [a] *all your pains.* [b]	3+2+2
Earth:	4 *See! For strife and contention you (pl) fast,* *and for hitting an adversary with a fist.*	4+3
	You (pl) may not fast as (you have) today *(if you want) to make your (pl) voice heard on high.*	2+3
Yahweh:	5 *Will the fast that I choose be like this?* *A day for a human being to humble himself?*	4+4
Heavens:	*Is it to bow down his head like a wilting plant?* *Or one in which he spreads sackcloth and ashes?*	3+3

	Is it for this that you (sg) call a fast,	3+3
	a day acceptable to Yahweh?	
Yahweh:	6 *Is not this*[a] *the fast*[b] *I would choose:*[c]	4
	opening the bonds of wickedness,	3
	undoing the bindings of a yoke,	3
	and sending out the oppressed to be free?	3
	You (pl)[d] *shall break every yoke!*	2
Earth:	7 *Is it not sharing your (sg) bread with the poor,*	4+4
(to Judah)	*and that you (sg) bring homeless*[a] *poor persons*[b] *into the house?*[c]	
Heavens:	*When you (sg) see one naked and you cover him,*[d]	3+3
(to Judah)	*and you (sg) do not hide your self from your (sg) own flesh,*	
(to Artaxerxes)	8 *then your (sg) light will break out like the dawn*	4+3
(to Judah)	*and your (sg) healing will spring up in a hurry.*	
Earth:	[a]*Your (sg) legitimacy will walk before you.*	3+3
(to Artaxerxes)	*Yahweh's glory will be your rear guard.*[ab]	
Heavens:	9 *Then you (sg) may call*	2+2
(to each one)	*and Yahweh will answer.*	
Earth:	*You (sg) may cry out*	1+2
	and he will say, "I am here."	
Heavens:	*When you (sg) remove from your (sg) midst*	3+3+2
	a yoke,[a] *pointing*[b] *a finger,*	
	and speaking trouble.	
Earth:	10 *And when you (sg) pour out*[a] *yourself*[b] *(sg) for a hungry one*	3+3
(to Artaxerxes)	*and you (sg) satisfy an afflicted person,*	
	your (sg) light will rise in the darkness	3+2
	and your (sg) gloom (will become)[c] *as noondays.*	
Heavens:	11 *And Yahweh will constantly guide you (sg).*	3+3+2
	He will satisfy your (sg) soul in scorched regions[a]	
	and will strengthen[b] *your (sg) bones.*[c]	
Earth:	*And you (sg) will be like a watered garden*	3+2+3
(to Judah)	*and like a spring water*	
	where waters never fail.	
Heavens:	12 *Age-old ruins will be rebuilt*[a] *by you (sg)*	4+4
(to Artaxerxes)	*and foundations generations old you (sg) will raise up.*	
Earth:	*And you (sg) will be called "Repairer of the Breach,"*	4+3
	"Restorer[b] *of paths*[c] *in which to dwell."*	
Yahweh:	13 *If you (sg) restrain your foot from*[a] *(travel on) the Sabbath,*	3+4
(to Judah)	*(from) doing*[b] *your (sg) pleasure*[c] *on my holy day,*	
	and if you (sg) call the Sabbath a delight	3+3
	and [d]*Yahweh's holy thing*[d] *a thing to be honored,*	
	and you (sg) honor it by not doing your own way	3+2+2
	not seeking your own pleasure	
	or speaking a word,	

Yahweh: (to Artaxerxes and to Judah) [14] *then you (sg) may delight in Yahweh.* 3+3+4
And I[a] *will make you (sg) ride on the heights*[b] *of land*
and I[c] *will make you (sg) eat from the heritage of Jacob, your (sg) father.*
Herald: *Indeed the mouth of Yahweh has spoken!* 4

Notes

1.a. Lit. "cry out in a throat."

2.a. Köhler and Elliger (*Einheit,* 14) suggest that אשר "which" is a prosaic addition and should be dropped, but this is neither necessary nor helpful.

3.a. In context, נגש "press" has "pains" as its object and so is translated "suppress" (BDB, 620).

3.b. MT עצביכם "your toilers" occurs only here as a noun (BDB, 780). The root meaning is "to hurt, be pained." A similar word means "idols." But the meaning here could be "your pains." LXX *τοὺς ὑποχειρίους ὑμῶν ὑπονύσσετε* "you goad your subordinates" apparently reversed the noun and verb (cf. Σ Θ). *BHS* suggests emending to עבטיכם "your articles taken in pledge" (cf. Deut 24:11, 13), which has the support of only Vg *debitores vestros* "your debtors." Keep MT's pointing, but read "your pains" or "your griefs."

6.a. LXX omits הלוא זה "is not this." Pauritsch (*Neue Gemeinde,* 73–74) would drop it. But the formula fits the Heb. style well.

6.b. DDS^{Isa} הצום אשר "the fast which" makes explicit what is implicit in MT, that אבחרהו "I would choose" is a relative clause.

6.c. LXX inserts *λέγει κύριος* "says the Lord."

6.d. MT is pl. LXX Θ Vg read sg to correspond to the following verse.

7.a. LXX (followed by 'A Vg) *ἀστέγους* "ones without a roof," i.e., "homeless." MT מרודים is a noun meaning "wandering" or "homeless" (BDB, 924). Dillmann thought it an old qal pass ptcp; Cheyne emended to a hoph ptcp מורדים; Buhl emended to a hiph ptcp מרידים; while Duhm eliminated *mem* as dittogr to read a qal ptcp. None of these suggestions improves on MT which is supported by the Versions.

7.b. Syr omits.

7.c. LXX *εἰς τὸν οἶκόν σου* "into your (sg) house" adds the poss pron, as do Syr Tg Vg.

7.d. DSS^{Isa} and one MS^{K} add בגד "with a garment" (cf. Ezek 18:7, 16). LXX Syr Tg Vg support MT.

8.a-a. Pauritsch (*Neue Gemeinde,* 74) calls this a redactional addition intended to include the Jews in Babylon.

8.b. יאספך "will gather you" or "be your rear-guard," i.e., "bring up your rear" (BDB, 62). *BHS* suggests reading a piel impf as in 52:12. That is possible, but not necessary.

9.a. MT מוטה "a yoke" (BDB, 557). *BHS* suggests emending to מֻטֶּה "that which is perverted" (BDB, 642; cf. Syr Tg and Ezek 9:9). Let MT stand.

9.b. DSS^{Isa} ושלוח differs from MT שְׁלַח "pointing" only in the vowel of the second syllable. Both are inf abs (BDB, 1018). Cf. Kutscher, *Isaiah Scroll,* 341–42.

10.a. MT ותפק hiph juss "you (sg) pour out" (BDB, 807, II). 'A Σ Θ (OL) *υπερεκχεης* fut ind "you will pour out." *BHS* suggests changing the pointing to impf, but this is hardly necessary.

10.b. MT נפשך "your soul, your self." Several Heb. MSS and Syr read לחמך "your bread." LXX *τὸν ἄρτον ἐκ ψυχῆς σου* "the bread of your soul" has both. MT has the stronger form and the more difficult reading.

10.c. *BHS* suggests possibly inserting תגה "will shine" (BDB, 618). But Heb. may understand the copulative verb without expressing it.

11.a. MT צחצחות is a *hap. leg.* BDB (850) translates "scorched regions" from צחח "be dazzling." *RSV* derives it from Arab *ṣaḥ* "good, healthful." Cf. Whybray.

11.b. MT יחליץ "he will make strong" (BDB, 323). DSS^{Isa} יחליצו "they will become strong" (cf. Kutscher, *Isaiah Scroll,* 394–95). 1QIsa^{b} יחלצו "they will be made strong." The Versions support MT's sg. Read MT.

11.c. MT וְעַצְמֹתֶיךָ "and your bones." A few MSS read וְעָצְמָתְךָ "and your might" (BDB,

782). Cf. 40:29 where it stands parallel to כח "strength." The Versions support MT. Read MT.

12. Note parallel language in 61:4.

12.a. MT וּבָנוּ "and they will build." LXX Vg are pass. Emend MT to read וּבְנוּ "they will be built" (*BHS*).

12.b. MT מְשֹׁבֵב polel ptcp "restorer" (BDB, 996). 1QIsa[b] משיב hiph ptcp. The meaning is the same.

12.c. MT נתיבות "paths" (BDB, 677). *BHS* proposes נתיצות "ruins," presumably from נתץ "tear down" (BDB, 683), parallel to "breach." But no such noun is found in biblical Heb. G. R. Driver ("Linguistic and Textual Problems: Isaiah XL–LXVI," *JTS* 36 [1935] 405) suggests emending לָשָׁבֶת "to dwell" to לְשַׁבֹּת on the analogy of Akk *qaqqara šabātu* "to clear ground," thus "he who restores paths by clearing them." But the idea of "dwelling in paths" is not impossible (see Whybray).

13.a. MT משבת "from the Sabbath." OL presupposes בשבת "on the Sabbath." DSS[Isa] LXX Vg support MT. Keep MT as the more difficult reading.

13.b. DSS[Isa] and LXX add מן, thus "from doing."

13.c. חפציך "your pleasures," pl. 1QIsa[b] Θ Syh Syr Tg Vg read "your pleasures," sg.

13.d-d. MT לקדוש יהוה "to sanctify Yahweh" or "to Yahweh's holy thing." OL *sancta Domino* "holy to the Lord." Keep MT.

14.a. MT is 1st pers sg. DSS[Isa] 1QIsa[b] LXX Syr are 3rd sg. Keep MT, the more difficult reading.

14.b. K בָּמוֹתֵי "heights" (BDB, 119). Q בָּמֳתֵי has the same meaning. See GKC §§ 87*s*, 95*o*.

14.c. MT is 1st pers sg. DSS[Isa] LXX Syr Tg have 3rd sg. Keep MT as the more difficult text.

Form/Structure/Setting

The scene is set on heaven's balcony. Yahweh, Heavens, Earth and a herald are on the balcony. On the lower stage Jerusalemites gather. Regular worship has been observed in Zerubbabel's Temple for half a century. But there has also been an unstable economy (Neh 5:1–8) and high taxes (Neh 5:4, 15). Lax or oppressive government supervision has led to violence and disorder. In Persia Artaxerxes has recently seized control. He is challenged by Yahweh to take up the task assigned previously to Cyrus and Darius.

Note how carefully the opening reference in v 5 is to אדם "a human being" rather than to Israel or Jerusalem. Yahweh's requirements for worship apply to anyone who seeks him. Then in v 6e the address is plural to all those who hear him. Vv 7–14 consistently address individuals in 2nd masc sg. Yet they are clearly not always to the same individual since the content applies appropriately to different persons. These are not spoken to Jerusalem, who is always addressed in the feminine.

Some of the admonitions and promises are suitable to any Judean worshiper. Others are consistent with the kind of promises Yahweh has made to Persian emperors in chaps. 44–45 and 49–52. If the reader assumes that among the listeners are both Judeans and the Persian emperor with his retinue, there is no problem in seeing the words addressed to one and then the other throughout the passage.

Some of the admonitions might well fit either of them (v 7a-c and v 9). Those that apply appropriately to Judah are: v 7d "your own flesh;" v 8b "your healing;" v 11d-f "you will be like a watered garden;" vv 13–14a on Sabbath observance; v 14c "the heritage of Jacob, your father." Those that are fitting to Artaxerxes, the Persian emperor are: v 8a "your light will break forth" (see 45:7, 49:6d); v 8c "your legitimacy" (see *Excursus:* צדק/צדקה *"Righteousness, Legitimacy"*) and "your rear-guard" which fits the military character of the emperor; v 10c "your light will rise" (see v 8a above); v 11a-c "guide, strengthen" which seems to refer to military campaigns; v 12 "Repairer," "Restorer," which fit the edicts spoken to Cyrus, Darius, and Artaxerxes (see Ezra and Isa 44:28cd, 45:13c, and 49:8e); v 14 "ride the heights of land," a metaphor for triumph and conquest which fits the emperor.

The scene has two parts. Vv 1–4 are a dialogue between those on the balcony and those on the lower stage. Vv 5–14 are spoken from the balcony. They are addressed to Israel (cf. v 1) as God's people and to the Persian authority (vv 10–12). The date is about 465 B.C.

A threefold division of the chapter, vv 1–2, 3–12, 13–14, was proposed by H. Kosmala (*ASTI* 5 [1967] 69–81). But a close reading of the chapter shows that vv 1–4 (and 6e) address a group in the plural. Vv 5–14 address individuals in the singular. The scene is unified around the subject of worship, specifically the nature and purpose of "the fast" (צום; cf. BDB, 847) and the will of God. The chapter parallels Zech 7 and 8 in theme and content.

This scene is set a half century later than Zech 7–8. A temple of sorts has been established in Jerusalem. Worship is performed there regularly which includes fasting, "inquiring," and praying for justice. But the result is satisfactory neither to God nor to the worshipers.

The development of the scene turns on the use of חפץ "pleasure" to describe what the people like to do while בחר "choose" and רצון "acceptable" describe what God wants from them. Actions which do not correspond to God's wishes or achieve the results he seeks are useless or worse than useless (cf. 1:11–17).

The scene has an arch structure:

	A Yahweh announces the subject: sins and rebellion (v 1)
pl	B Worship: what they like to do (vv 2–3)
pl	C Worship: occasion for violence, unacceptable (v 4)
sg	D Acceptable worship: helping and freeing (vv 5–8)
sg	KEYSTONE When you get rid of evil, you may pray (v 9)
sg	D′ When you work for the hungry and afflicted, you may be blessed (vv 10–11)
sg	C′ Restorer of order and repairer of walls (v 12)
sg	B′ Worship, as Sabbath restraint, will be blessed (vv 13–14c)
	A′ Yahweh has spoken (v 14d)

The shift in v 5 to singular address coincides with the use of אדם "a human being." What is announced applies to any person seeking Yahweh. This includes the Judean/Israelite worshiper, but it also applies to Yahweh's Persian protégé. A new king named Artaxerxes has taken the throne in Persepolis. For him, this scene performs the same function that 44:24–45:13 did for Cyrus and 49:5–12 did for Darius. All the conditions mentioned here (with the exception of the Sabbath) apply to him, as well as the promised benefits (vv 8–9, 10b–11a, 12, and 14b).

Jerusalem has become a place of violence (cf. 56:9–12; 57:1–10; 59:4). Judean leaders are responsible. Their penchant for rebellion and for obtaining personal gain at the expense of the poor runs counter to God's will that they cooperate with Persian authority. In this the governmental authorities share the blame. So now the appeal is made both to the worshipers in Jerusalem and to the authorities to recover a sense of order and to establish priorities in their policies.

Comment

1 Yahweh orders that his people, *the House of Jacob,* be apprised of פשעם "their rebellion" (cf. 57:4, 59:12, 20) and חטאתם "their sins" (cf. 59:2, 12). *Rebellion* may carry a political meaning. J. Morgenstern ("Jerusalem—485 B.C.," *HUCA* 27 [1956] 101–79, 28 [1957] 15–47, 31 [1960] 1–29; "The Dates of Ezra and Nehemiah," *JSS* 7 [1962] 1–11; cf. F. M. T. de Liagre Böhl, "Die Babylonischen Prätendenten zur Zeit des Xerxes," *BO* 19 [1962] 110–14) thought that Jews, on the death of Xerxes, must have participated in rebellious uprisings which were met by ruthless reprisals from Persian troops and their minions (Neh 1:3 and Ezra 4:23; see H. G. M. Williamson, *Ezra-Nehemiah,* 172; Josephus, *Antiq.* xi.6). *Rebellion* is defined in this scene as doing one's own pleasure or as one wishes in worship or political allegiance (v 3b) rather than as God wishes (vv 5–7, 10, 13). The results of *sin* are: violence and strife (v 4), slavery (a yoke, v 9), spying and accusations (a pointing finger, v 9c) and insolent or libelous talk (speaking trouble, v 9c). Rebellion and sin were a part of Yahweh's accusation against 8th-century Jerusalem (1:17–25 and Mic 3:8).

2 Yahweh insists on this at a time when they are showing signs of being very religious.

3 צמנו "we fasted." Fasting to express mourning or distress had been a part of Israelite piety from earliest times (H. H. Guthrie, Jr., "Fasts, Fasting," *IDB* 2:241–44; F. S. Rothenberg, "Fast," *NIDNTT* 1:611–13; Behm, "*νῆστις* *TDNT* 4:924–35). But they were institutionalized after the Exile into four occasions to memorialize the destruction of Jerusalem: "the 9th day of the 4th month, to commemorate the fall of Jerusalem (2 Kgs 25:3–21), the 10th day of the 5th month, for the destruction of the Temple (Jer 52:12–13), the 2nd day of the 7th month, for the murder of Gedaliah (2 Kgs 25:23–25), and the 10th day of the 10th month for the first attack on Jerusalem" (R. K. Harrison, "Fast," *ISBE* 2:248). The prophetic books discourage emphasis on fasting and ostentation in doing it (Joel 2:13; Jer 14:12). Zech 7–8 proclaims that the day of fasting is past. Fasts should become feasts for joy.

By the time this scene is portrayed fasts had become holidays on which all manner of people gathered. They were popular occasions which had little or nothing to do with worship. Jerusalem in 465 B.C. was not unlike Jerusalem in 740 B.C. (1:11–17). Yahweh's reaction is also similar.

Zech 7 and Neh 8:9–11 join this passage in encouraging worshipers to turn to more positive and profitable pursuits. But the people continue to fast. At Nineveh it had worked a miracle of grace (Jonah 3:5–10). *Humbled themselves* probably means wearing rough clothes and putting ashes on their heads. But they see no sign that God notices them.

The problem is analyzed. The people do not fast because God wants or asks them to. They are finding a particular pleasure in fasting. *You suppress all your pains.* Karl Marx accurately observed that sometimes religious observance is a kind of sedative, an opiate. So it was here. What were their pains? A very unstable social and economic situation, compounded by opportunistic oppression by some in their community and by some of their neighboring peoples, and made worse by heavy taxes and a weak administration. It must have resembled the conditions found by Nehemiah a few years later (Neh 5, 10, 13). It resulted in violence, coercion, and enslavement for many people while perhaps bringing riches and temporary security to a few. Rather than facing their problems, most people simply fasted and prayed. But Yahweh says the Temple was not intended to be a refuge from the challenge to reform. No wonder their prayers were not answered.

4 Their *fast* days were characterized by *strife* and *contention.* They dissolve into physical violence. Such fasting will not make their prayers be *heard on high* where God is present.

5 Having set the scene, the rest of the chapter is a *torah* or lesson on proper worship. The criteria for such turns on what God chooses, not what the people like to do. It is more precise: what God requires of any *human being* (אדם). Does God rejoice in seeing a person *wilt* like a plant without water, as when *he spreads sackcloth and ashes?* Is *the fast* they observe *a day acceptable to Yahweh?* The question is answered by a question, but the implication is: No, it is not.

6 If God chose a fast that would please him, what would he prescribe? He lists three things that related directly to the needs of that time. The people felt enslaved and in bondage (Neh 9:36). Part of that bondage was undoubtedly political. They were a Persian colony. This led to oppression from local officials and from powerful neighbors (Neh 4; 5:15) in the form of heavy taxes, usurious loans and generally unfavorable economic conditions (Neh 5). It also led to enslavement to other Jews when debts could not be repaid (Neh 5:4–5).

God's choice for worship is acts which would remedy these conditions, as indeed the work of leaders like Nehemiah did. He first calls for *opening bonds of wickedness,* breaking the *yoke,* and *setting free the oppressed.* This might have been heard as a call to rebellion. Egypt rose up in revolt against high taxes at about this time. But Nehemiah, a loyal officer of the Persian bureaucracy, perceived the roots of slavery in the greed of fellow Jews and the ambition of corrupt officials. He prohibited the charging of unjust interest on loans (Neh 5:7–8). He set the example by returning fields and homes to people who had lost them for unjust debt (Neh 5:9–12). It was easy to blame the system or the faraway government. God demanded that people clean up their own affairs, their own neighborhood. That was true liberation and the kind of fast that God approved. *You* (*pl*) *shall break every yoke.* There is no excuse for holding a brother or sister in bondage of any kind.

7 A second form of acceptable worship is *sharing your bread with the poor.* Hunger was a basic problem of the day. Nehemiah opened his official table to 150 Jews and officials every day (Neh 5:17).

A third form meets the lack of clothing for the poor. *Covering the naked* was acceptable worship.

It was natural for needy persons to turn to their kin for help. OT law provides for needs to be met by relatives. But such close social ties had been broken by exilic and post-exilic conditions. It was easier to deny kinship and turn away from those who needed aid. But this meant to turn away from God. Acceptable worship meant *not hiding yourself from your own flesh.*

8 These expectations on God's part applied as much to the Persian emperor as to the Judeans around Jerusalem. In order for Artaxerxes' *light to break out* to fulfill the promise made to his grandfather (49:6), he must act to alleviate the oppressive and impoverishing conditions in Judah. For Judah's *healing to spring up in a hurry,* the people need to produce what James would later call "true religion and undefiled" (Jas 1:27).

For Artaxerxes to gain the צדקה "legitimacy" he needs and to have God's protection, he must act to correct these things. *Yahweh's glory* (כבוד) *will be your guard* is reminiscent of the cloud which accompanied and protected Israel in the wilderness (Exod 13:21–22 *et passim,* especially 16:10).

9 *Then*—that is, when actions on such social issues demostrate true worship as Yahweh wants it—*you may call and Yahweh will answer.* There is a proper order to be followed. First, do what is known to be God's will and what one is able to do. Then pray to God with assurance of being heard and answered (cf. Matt 5:23–24).

God's promise to meet and respond to prayer is further conditioned on removing from your midst things that are displeasing to him. These include *a yoke.* All forms of bondage are distasteful to God, whether economic, political, or social. God's people were and are intended to promote freedom. *Pointing a finger* may refer to spying or accusing in an atmosphere of pressure to induce fear. Perhaps the motive was to gain favor from an official or a neighboring political boss. Or it may simply refer to accusation, discrimination, gossip, or character assassination (cf. the frequent NT references to accusations, false and otherwise). The third element to be removed was דבר־און "speaking trouble." This is the vocal parallel to *pointing a finger,* but also much more. Verbal agitation, stirring up trouble, was a constant problem for Nehemiah when it came from neighboring authorities. It was intolerable in his own community.

10 The verse returns to the themes of vv 7–8. The concluding words, *your light will rise,* make this seem applicable to the Persian emperor. His success, too, depends on his *pouring out himself for a hungry one, his satisfying an afflicted person.* The political leader is rare who recognizes that the ultimate measure of a leader's greatness lies in the extent to which he gives himself to and for the very needy of his people. In the end, *satisfying the afflicted* is more important than pleasing the powerful and the rich.

11 The reason lies, not in the influence or power of the poor and afflicted, but in the particular concerns of God. He cares for them and he supports those who do his will in this regard. For Artaxerxes, this meant guidance, sustenance, and power. For Judah, it meant prosperity *like a watered garden,* a permanent *spring of water.*

12 Artaxerxes' destiny to fulfill the assignments first given to Cyrus (44:26; 45:13) and to Darius, his grandfather (49:8b–9a), will come about when he has acted to meet these social and economic needs. *Age-old* ruins in Jerusalem *will be rebuilt* and *foundations* of walls *generations old* will be raised up. His reputation will include the title *Repairer of the Breach* in Jerusalem's walls, as well as *Restorer of paths in which to dwell.* That is, urban development in Jerusalem and in the villages of Judah will be attributed to him. Ezra 4:7–24; 7:1–28; and Neh 2:1–9 attribute the work of Ezra and Nehemiah in part to the support of Artaxerxes.

13 Keeping the Sabbath became in this period a major means of showing one's loyalty to Yahweh and his will (56:2–4; Neh 10:31–33; 13:15–22; Ezek 44–46; J. Morgenstern, "Sabbath," *IDB* 4:135–41). Sabbath observance, like anything else, could become a habit done because one likes to do it (cf. v 3b and frequent references in the Gospels). But here it is seen as a test by which one restrains common desires in order to conform to God's expressed will.

Restrain your feet (תשיב רגלך) refers to restrictions on travel on the Sabbath (Exod 16:29). Unnecessary travel was thought of as a kind of labor that was prohibited on the Sabbath (Exod 20:8–11; Deut 5:12–15). Conforming to Sabbath restrictions was interpreted as symbolic denial of *doing your own pleasure* on the day that is Yahweh's *holy day.*

This does not contradict the earlier call to turn away from mournful fasting. Doing *Yahweh's holy thing* and calling it *a thing to be honored* is thought to be a joyful, festive act, the very opposite of *seeking your own pleasure,* your own will, or speaking your own word. The issue is not joy or mourning. It is rather Yahweh's day or our day, Yahweh's will or our will. Sabbath can be no excuse for not helping others. Here it is ranked with feeding the hungry and clothing the naked as being Yahweh's will.

14 *Delight* or joy is right and blessed in the worshiper. But it is to be *delight in Yahweh* and his ways. Then the king can *ride the heights of land.* That is, when Artaxerxes responds to Yahweh, he can reign in power and success, while the people of God *may eat the heritage of Jacob,* their *father.* They can enjoy the produce of Canaan in peace and prosperity. The closing formula, *the mouth of Yahweh has spoken,* calls for attention to a major issue.

Explanation

The scene addresses a troubled time. The people are pious and the Temple is in use. But violence, dissention, oppression, and trouble testify to a lack of peace and blessing. The people do not understand why their pious acts of worship, which God recognizes, are not rewarded.

The answer is that they worship in ways that seem good to themselves. They do the things they like to do, including fasting, ostentation, self-humiliation (cf. Jesus' words in Matt 6:5, 23:6; Luke 11:42–43, 20:46), in order to forget their troubles and ignore their problems though violence is all around them.

The issue in this scene is the correct view and practice of worship. This was an acute problem both for pre-exilic Israel (1:11–17), for post-exilic Judaism, and indeed for every age. If they want their prayers to be answered, they cannot continue to fast in the way they have been fasting (v 4b).

The kind of worship God will choose and honor (vv 5–14) is not ostentatious self-abnegation in fasting with much beating of breasts, but acts which overcome the problems. (Cf. Nehemiah's acts and programs in Neh 5.) To please God, one should recognize wrongs, stop the ones doing wrong, and aid the victims (vv 6–7). If this is done as an act or prelude to worship, success will follow for ruler and people. God will be present and answer the prayers of worshipers (vv 8–9).

The lessons are repeated in vv 10–11. V 12 assures Artaxerxes success in rebuilding Jerusalem and the Temple if he institutes reforms that help the people. V 13 uses the Sabbath as a symbol of doing God's pleasure instead of one's own pleasure (cf. v 3b) in order to offer acceptable worship. To delight in Yahweh (cf. v 2) is correct, if that means doing God's will. Only in this way can one expect God's blessing and the fulfillment of his promises.

This passage is a major treatment of the spiritual requirement of self-restraint and deliberate submission to God's will. It is an important text for all students of Scripture and for all who want to do God's will. Fasting in sorrowful memory of Jerusalem's great catastrophe and as a symbol of humiliation before God became a problem when it failed to move one to look toward the future (cf. Neh 9). When fasting, accompanied by grief over sin and repentence from sin, leads to new resolve and compensating action, it can be both useful and therapeutic. When it becomes an end in itself, it is sterile and counterproductive.

Scene 2: Troubled Times in Judah (59:1–15a)

Bibliography

Achtemeier, E. *The Community and Message.* 61–71. **Baldacci M.** "Due misconoscuiti parallelismi ad Isaia 59, 10." *BeO* 22 (1980) 237–42. **Hanson, P. D.** *The Dawn of Apocalyptic,* 113–33. **Mendall, D.** "The Use of *Mišpat* in Isaiah 59." *ZAW* 96 (1984) 391–495. **Pauritsch, K.** *Die Neue Gemeinde.* 58–103. **Weissert, D.** "Der Basilisk und das Windei in LXX—Jes. 59,5 Ein textuales und ein folkloristisches Problem." *ZAW* 79 (1967) 315–22.

Translation

Heavens:	1	*See!*	1
(to people in Jerusalem)		*The hand of Yahweh is not too short to save,* *nor his ear too deaf to heed.*	3+3
Earth:	2	*Unless your (pl) iniquities have become separators*	4+3

between yourselves (pl) and your (pl) God
and your (pl) sins have caused a hiding of face[a] 3+2
and from hearing anything from you (pl).[b]
Heavens: 3 *But your (pl) hands have in fact become defiled*[a]
with blood 4+2
and your fingers with iniquity.
[b]*Your (pl) lips have in fact spoken lies*[b] 3+3
Your (pl) tongue mutters calumnies.
Earth: 4 *There is no calling out legitimately.* 3+3
And there is no going to law honestly.
Heavens: *Trusting in empty pleas* 2+2
and speaking lies,
Earth: *thinking up mischief* 2+2
and giving birth to trouble,
Heavens: 5 *they have hatched*[a] *snake-eggs* 3+3
and they have woven spider-webs.[b]
Anyone eating their eggs dies, 3+3
and one that is squashed[c] [d]*hatches a viper.*[d]
Earth: 6 *Their webs*[a] *cannot become clothing* 3+3
and they cannot cover themselves with their products.
Their products are products of trouble 3+3
and deeds of violence are in their hands.
Heavens: 7 *Their feet run to evil* 3+4
and they hurry to shed innocent blood.
Their thoughts are thoughts of trouble, 3+3
while desolation and destruction are on their highways.
Earth: 8 *They have not known a way of peace* 4+3
and there is no justice in their paths.
They have made their roads crooked for themselves 3+3+3
and no one walking on them[a]
will ever know peace.
Chorus: 9 *Because of such, justice has been far from us,* 4+3
and legitimacy does not come to us.
We wait for light. 2+2+3
But see! There is only darkness.
And for brightness, but[a] *we walk in gloom.*
10 *We grope like blind persons by a wall,* 3+3
and as those without eyes we grope.[a]
We stumble at noon as thought it were twilight, 3+2
and at full vigor[b] *as though we were corpses.*
11 *All of us growl like bears.* 3+3
We moan continually like doves.
We wait for justice, but there is none. 3+3
For salvation, but it remains far from us.
12 *Because our rebellions have multiplied*[a] *before*
you (sg) 3+3

and our sins[b] [c]*testify against us.*[c]
Indeed our rebellions are still with us 2+2
and we know our iniquities.
13 *Rebelling (against Persia) and denying against Yahweh,* 3+3
and turning away from following our God.
Speaking oppression and insurrection; 3+3+2
[a]*making up and uttering*[a] *from the heart lying words.*
14 *So justice is turned back* 3+3
and legitimacy stands far off.
Because truth has stumbled in public places, 3+3
candid honesty cannot enter.
15a *So it has come to pass that the truth is absent,* 3+3
and whoever travels is a prey[a] *to evil.*

Notes

2.a. MT פנים "face" is supported by DSS[Isa] Tg. LXX τὸ πρόσωπον αὐτοῦ "his face" is followed by Vg *faciem eius.* Pauritsch (*Neue Gemeinde* 88) and *BHS* emend to פניו "his face," explaining the textual error as dittography. The translation above sees MT as parallel to the first part of the verse. The idiom סור פנים "hiding face" is kept intact. It is usually used of God. Exceptions are found in 50:6 and Exod 3:6. It is never used with מן "from" (see below).

2.b. MT מכם "from you (pl)" is joined in MT's accentuation to the preceding stich, as also in LXX Tg Vg. But this not only creates an unbalanced meter, it places מן with סור פנים in a way never done elsewhere. Following *BHS*'s spacing, divide the line before the word.

3.a. MT נְגֹאֲלוּ "they are defiled" is an unusual niph pf form (BDB, 146, II; GKC § 51*h*). *BHS* suggests emending to a regular niph or pual form. Keep MT as it is. It may be a mixed form.

3.b-b. Omitted by DSS[Isa]. LXX Syr Tg Vg support MT.

5.a. MT בקעו pf "they hatch" (BDB, 31). DSS[Isa] יבקעו makes the same word an impf. Tg has an adj, "poisonous." LXX ἔρρηξαν "they broke." Read MT.

5.b. MT וקורי "webs of" (BDB, 881). Tg וכקוין "as threads" (cocoon?) leads *BHS* to suggest emending to וקוי "lines of." DSS[Isa] LXX Vg support MT.

5.c. MT והזורה qal pass ptcp + article from זור III "press out, squash" (BDB, 266; cf. 1:6), is supported by DSS[Isa] והאזורה (on the spelling, see Kutscher, *Isaiah Scroll,* 161–62). LXX συντρίψας "having crushed." Tg paraphrases with an adj. Vg *confutum est* "being boiled or pressed." *BHS* suggests changing a vowel to the ordinary form (GKC § 80*i*). P. Wernberg-Møller ("A Note on זור 'to stink,'" *VT* 4 [1954] 322–25; "A Note on Isa 41:7," *JSS* 2 [1957] 327–28) translates "the stinking (egg)" as coming from זור II (BDB, 266). This is a viable alternative but the meaning of זור III is better in context.

5.d-d. MT תבקע אפעה "hatches a viper" is supported by DSS[Isa]. LXX οὔριον εὗρε καὶ ἐν αὐτῷ βασιλίσκος "find an egg, and in it a basilisk" translated and expanded the metaphor. A basilisk is a mythical dragon (see Weissert, *ZAW* 79 [1967] 315–22).

6.a. MT קוריהם "their webs" (BDB, 881). DSS[Isa] agress. Tg כקוין "like the threads" presupposes קויהם "their lines or threads" (cf. n. 5.b). LXX ὁ ἱστὸς αὐτῶν "their web." Read MT.

8.a. MT בה "in it" is supported by DSS[Isa]. One Heb. MS, LXX Syh Syr Tg Vg read a pl. *BHS* suggests בהם "in them."

9.a. MT has no conjunction. Syr Vg read "and."

10.a. MT נגששה "Feel with the hand" occurs only in this verse (BDB, 178). Ehrlich (*Randglossen*) and *BHS* suggest emending to the root משש "feel, grope," (BDB, 606) which is similar but occurs several other times. DSS[Isa] supports MT.

10.b. אשמנים "full vigor" is a *hap. leg.* (BDB, 1032). LXX στενάξουσιν "they will groan." Tg paraphrases, Vg *in caliginosis* "in mist, in obscurity." Modern suggestions are equally varied:

"reeling" (T.K. Cheyne, "A Dark Passage in Isaiah," *ZAW* 25 [1905] 22; E. König, *Das Buch Jesaja* [Gütersloh: C. Bertelsmann, 1926]), "in darkness" (Westermann), "over vigorous men" (Ehrlich, *Randglossen*). Cf. Whybray, and Pauritsch, *Neue Gemeinde*, 91.

12.a. MT רבו "have multiplied" is from רבב (BDB, 912, I; GKC § 67*k*). Kissane derived it from ריב "to contest legally."

12.b. Two MSS read חטאתנו sg for MT חטאותינו pl to match the sg verb. But DSS[Isa] LXX Vg support MT's pl.

12.c-c. MT ענתה בנו is usually read as a qal pf 3d fem sg (cf. 3:9; 1 Sam 4:20) followed by a preposition and pronoun, "she testifies against us." But the subject, חטאותינו "our sins," is pl. The discrepancy is often ignored (Tg, Vg, GKC § 145*k*). However, בנו can be read as a qal pf 3d masc pl "they build." DSS[Isa] emends ענתה to ענוא which Kutscher (*Isaiah Scroll*, 175, 191, 395) identifies as an Aram 3d pl form. But emending *taw* to *waw* also suggests the nouns "humility" or "affliction" (BDB, 776). One could then read "our sins build affliction." The evidence of LXX ἀντέστησαν ἡμῖν "risen up against us" is ambiguous. The context, however, points toward the traditional translation which ignores the discrepancy of number to read "our sins testify against us."

13.a-a. MT הרו והגו "making up and uttering" are both poel inf abs. *BHK* suggested reading הָרֹו וְהָגֹו qal inf abs (cf. v 11; BDB, 211; and *BHS*). Pauritsch (*Neue Gemeinde*, 91) would eliminate הרו altogether with DSS[Isa]. The translation above follows MT, which is supported by LXX Syr Tg Vg.

15.a. MT משתולל hithpoel ptcp "is made a prey" from שלל (BDB, 1021). LXX συνιέναι "to understand" leads Whybray to suggest possibly reading השכל "understanding, insight" (BDB, 968) to give "and understanding has departed because of evil." But DSS[Isa] ʼΑ Σ Θ Tg Vg support MT.

Form/Structure/Setting

The mixture of forms has led interpreters to think of this section as a liturgy (see Pauritsch, *Neue Gemeinde*, 100; Elliger, *Einheit*, 15; and Fohrer, 214). The dramatic form of the book is explanation enough for the literary style without further definition of the genre.

This second scene continues the basic theme of the first: "Declare to my people their rebellions!" (58:1). But the situation has become worse. The social fabric has ripped. There is no rule of law. And the people tend to blame God.

Xerxes' wars with Athens sapped Persia's resources and made it much less interested in its Palestinian provinces. Only the Phoenicians and their navy were important to Persia at this time. Corruption and chaos in the entire region were the result of this neglect.

But the Vision blames neither Persia, the war, nor marauding neighbors. It points directly to Judah's own failure to stand up for itself to prevent the decay. The history of the period records no ability in the local community to develop leadership. Neither the high priests Eliashib and Johanan nor the heir apparent of David's house, all of whom are listed in the genealogies, stepped forward to fill the gap. The current governor, Jehoezer or Ahzai, apparently made no move to restore order. The people tended to blame God. The scene opens on that note.

The scene is divided according to the groups addressed:

Vv 1–3 address the people in 2nd person masculine plural.
Vv 5–8 speak of the people in 3rd person masculine plural.
Vv 9–13 have the people speak in 1st person common plural.

Vv 4 and 14–15a assess the situation impersonally.
Vv 8–9 have the people and the observers agree that the situation appears to be hopeless.

The scene pictures troubled times, first from the viewpoint of objective outsiders (vv 1–8) and then from the viewpoint of insiders confessing their situation and its causes. The evils are described in detail:

In general:	iniquities (vv 2a, 12b)
	sins (vv 2b, 12a)
	evil (v 15a)
Specifically:	violent deeds (vv 3a, 6b, 7)
	lying speech (vv 3b, 4b, 13b)
	mischief-making thoughts (vv 4c, 5, 6a, 7b, 13b)
What is lacking:	legitimacy צדקה (vv 4a, 9a, 14a)
	honesty/truth נכחה אמת אמונה (vv 4a, 14b, 15)
	peace/wholeness שלום (vv 8a, 8b)
	justice משפט (vv 8a, 9a, 11b, 14a)
	salvation ישע (vv 1, 11b)
Results:	rebellion (vv 12, 13a)
	oppression (v 13)
	insurrection (v 13)

The situation was bad: no legitimate government, therefore no peace, justice, or protection from violence. There was no honest effort to bring law and order. Conniving conspiracies abounded unchecked leading to violence, lying testimony, and calumnies of character. Political rebellion, oppression and insurrection were everywhere. Prayer was of no avail, for these are sins against God, his law, and his expressed will for the political order. The chaotic scene is framed by noting a lack of relation to God.

The scene also describes what is lacking. This is the other side of the coin. *Salvation,* in terms of military intervention, would impose a government that would earn *legitimacy,* which in turn would impose a system of *justice, peace,* and safety on the roads and in the villages and cities. In this way integrity and *truth* could become a component of social health again. All of these are political conditions.

The scene equates lack of these with religious *sins* and *iniquities,* with *denying* and *turning away from God,* because the Vision ties the two realms together while clearly distinguishing them. Yahweh has delegated political prerogatives and responsibility. When Yahweh does *save* (v 1), it will be through the Persians. At the same time, Persian establishment of legitimate and functional political order in the province, accompanied by safety on the roads, will make possible the function of Jerusalem's Temple and the approach of pilgrims from far places. For this reason revolt against Persia is regarded as sin against Yahweh. The two ideas of mutual recognition/interdependence and separate divine commissions to the Persian king and Jerusalem's Temple are held in delicate balance. Yahweh supports public order *and* free religious expression.

Even as the scene portrays the chaotic situation, it is showing the solution which must cure it. The heart of the *salvation* to come (vv 1, 11) must include *legitimacy* (vv 4, 9, 14), a system of *justice* (vv 8, 9, 11, 14), basic *integrity* (vv 4, 14, 15a) and must produce *peace* (vv 8–9). These are built into the very arch structure of the scene:

A Yahweh can save (v 1)
  B Your sins and iniquities (vv 2–3)
    C No legitimacy or honesty (v 4a)
      D Only conspiracy, trouble, and violence (vv 4b–5b)
KEYSTONE No peace. No Justice. Legitimacy far away (vv 8–9a)
      D′ We wait for light, but only darkness (vv 9b–10)
    C′ We wait in vain for justice, for salvation (v 11)
  B′ Our sins and iniquities, rebellion and apostasy (vv 12–13)
A′ Justice and legitimacy and truth are gone (vv 14–15a)

The problem is clearly defined and the need explained. The people lack legitimate government because of rebellion and apostasy. The implication is that they have thrown off Persian rule. Persia is too busy elsewhere at the moment to bother them. The accusations of neighboring officials in the period of Xerxes and Artaxerxes (Ezra 4:6–23) concur with the way this scene pictures the times.

Comment

1 Chaotic conditions may not be explained simply by God's inability to remedy the situation. Nor can ineffective religious practice be blamed on God's lack of attention.

2 That which *separates* from God is sin. Sin does *cause* a situation in which prayers go unanswered. *A hiding of face* on God's part (8:17; 54:8; 64:6; Deut 31:17; 32:20; Mic 3:4; Jer 33:5; Ezek 39:23, 24, 29; Pss 13:24; 22:25; 27:9; 69:18; 88:15; 102:3; 143:7; Job 13:24; 34:29) is used frequently to describe God's unwillingness to meet his people or hear their prayers at some particular time. 57:17 uses the phrase to describe God's alienation from Israel before the Exile. But this verse (59:2) suggests that the openness which Zerubbabel's temple promised was already nullified by the gross sin and chaos of the next generation just twenty-five to forty years later.

3 *Hands defiled with blood* refers to guilt for violent crimes (cf. 1:15c). *Iniquity* is a broader concept which could well cover all the sins of the mind, of speech, and of action described in this scene. Speech supports acts. Words distort truth and reality. And *calumnies* assassinate character and influence as surely as violence takes innocent life.

4 *Calling out legitimately* and *going to law honestly* describe the integrity of legal processes of justice. But now it has broken down. Claims of *truth* have no more foundations to prove them than *empty pleas* and lies. Intellectual pursuit in most cases turns into *thinking up mischief* and making trouble.

5 This verse is a metaphor comparing the people to snakes and spiders which hatch a poisonous brood. The Septuagint pushed the metaphor to mythical extremes (cf. n. 5.d). *Anyone eating their eggs dies.* The poison of sin and violence destroys anyone who has anything to do with it.

6 The products of criminal behavior cannot serve a useful social purpose. They only produce *trouble* and *violence.*

7 Their criminal tendency results in *desolation and destruction on the highways.* Ancient travel did not run the risk of meeting drunken drivers, but it did suffer from banditry on the way. The Vision is concerned about safety on those roads for the pilgrims who will stream to Zion's temple.

8 The malefactors *know* nothing of either *peace* or *justice.* They have imposed their *crookedness* on the roads. No one *walking on them will ever know peace* as long as they are in charge. No travel means no trade. No trade in Jerusalem means economic depression and poverty. This is the natural result of crime.

9 Jerusalem's people see the truth of the analysis. They exclaim: So that is why *justice* is so *far from us!* That is why *legitimate* government eludes us! *We wait.* Waiting is a legitimate religious exercise. Yet it is sometimes frustrating (cf. 5:2, 4, 7). Sometimes it misses the point altogether. Waiting *for light* without doing something about the violence is hopeless.

10 The people confess their condition and the hopelessness of it.

11 *Growl like bears, moan like doves* are symbols of lamentation and mourning. The fasts of 58:3 were like that. Again the word is *wait for. Justice* is not gained by pious waiting. Justice must be worked out and built up. So it and *salvation* remain far off.

12 But the people do confess that *rebellions, sins, and iniquities . . . have built affliction.* They have created their own troubles.

13 *Rebelling* (פשע) is naturally a political word implying refusal to fulfill a vassal's obligations. That would be a crime against Persia. But the failings that follow, *denying* (כחש) and *turning away* (נסוג) are directed against *Yahweh,* their *God.* Judah's political fealty and religious loyalty are bound together in the Vision's view. They have lost both. *Oppression* against their neighbors and *insurrection* against Persia go hand in hand. How seldom does revolt in the name of social justice actually produce a better society! Especially when it is furthered by lying *words!*

14–15a The theme of v 1 is picked up again. The terrible situation, lacking *justice, honesty, truth and legitimacy,* is not due to Yahweh's inability to save, but to the people's sins. *Whoever travels is a prey* to disaster on the road. No wonder the roads to Jerusalem are empty!

Explanation

Persia has its hands full with wars far away. Palestine is neglected. There is no effective administration. Only the tax collector appears regularly.

Ezra-Nehemiah chronicle the troubles which neighboring officials in Samaria, Ammon, Edom, and Ashdod made for Jerusalem even under the strong leadership of governors officially supported by the emperor. This scene depicts conditions when no such leadership existed and which were therefore much worse.

With no legitimate government which the riffraff of the communities had to recognize, there was no means for establishing justice. Without such support for justice, truth in witness and oath had no basis or support. Without these, there was no order. Without order, no peace.

All this is true because the people of Jerusalem had sinned, having become alienated from God through their iniquities. They had denied Yahweh and turned away from him. Undoubtedly this was true in many ways, but one way was particularly valid in this instance. They had rebelled against Persia and Persian authority. It may have come because of high taxes, as chap. 58 suggests. They were tired of bearing the economic burden of Xerxes' wars against Athens. But rebelling against Persia also meant denying Yahweh's expressed will for them. It left the city and the countryside defenseless against every brigand and ruffian that chose to oppress them.

There is no way to get along without government. The legitimate duty of government is to provide order, safety, peace, and justice in which economic and social life can prosper. God's house needed all these in order to be built, to be supplied, and to receive pilgrims. God provided the government to supply this support. For this service government has a legitimate claim on its citizens' support, even from those who are citizens of the city of God.

Scene 3: Yahweh Decides to Act (59:15b–21)

Bibliography

Achtemeier, E. *The Community and the Message.* 69–73. **Gross, H.** "'Doch für Sion kommt er als Erlöser' (Jes 59:20)." *Conc* 3 (1967) 812–18. **Hanson, P. D.** *The Dawn of Apocalyptic.* 113–34. **Pauritsch, K.** *Die Neue Gemeinde.* 87–103. **Rubinstein, A.** "Word Substitution in Isaiah LXIII, 5 and LIX, 16." *JSS* 8 (1963) 52–55.

Translation

Heavens: 15b *When Yahweh saw,* 2+2+2
[a]*it was wrong in his view*[a]
that there was no justice.
Earth: 16 [a]*When he saw that there was no one,* 3+4
he was appalled that no one intervened.
His own arm wrought victory,[b] 3+3
and his own legitimacy[c] *upheld it.*[a]
Heavens: 17 *So he put on legitimacy as a breastplate* 3+3
and a helmet of victory[a] *on his head.*
Earth: *And he put on clothes of vengeance as his uniform,* 4+3
and draped himself in violent fury as a mantle.
Heavens: 18 *Measured by deeds,*[a] 2+2
so[b] *he repays:*
wrath to his adversaries, 2+2
a deed[c] *to his enemies.*
Earth: [d]*To the coastlands* 1+2

he makes full payment with a deed.[d]
19 *And they from the west fear*[a] *the name Yahweh.* 4+3
And they from the rising sun his glory.
Heavens: *For he comes like a*[b] *rushing stream.* 3+4
The spirit of Yahweh is the driving force in him.
Earth: 20 *But he comes to*[a] *Zion (as) a redeemer* 3+3+2
and [b]*to those repenting of rebellion*[a] *in Jacob.*
[c]*Oracle of Yahweh.*[c]
Yahweh: 21 *On my part,* 1+3+2
this is my covenant with them,[a]
Herald: *says Yahweh.*
Yahweh: *My spirit which is on you (m sg)* 3+4
(to Artaxerxes) *and my words which I have placed in your (m sg) mouth*
will not depart from your mouth, 2+2+3
or from the mouth of your descendant,
or from the mouth of your grandson,
Herald: *says Yahweh,* 2+3
Yahweh: *from now to the age.*[b]

Notes

15b.a-a. MT וירע בעיניו "and it was wrong in his eyes." DSS^{Isa} agrees, as do Tg ובאיש קדמוהי "it was displeasing to him," LXX *καὶ οὐκ ἤρεσεν αὐτῷ* "and it did not please him." Vg *et malum apparuit in oculis eius* "and it appeared evil in his eyes" is even more literal. *BHS,* following Gunkel and Duhm, would reverse the words to read בעיניו וידע "with his eyes and he knew" to make the line read "so Yahweh saw with his eyes and he knew that there was no justice." There seems to be no MSS evidence for this. Read MT and understand as a remark interjected into the speech.

16.a-a. The verse is very similar to 63:5 but with a different person and the substitution of synonymous words. Duhm and Westermann think 63:5 is the earlier reading.

16.b. The Heb. word is תושע which may also mean "save."

16.c. A. Rubinstein ("Word-Substitution in Isaiah LXIII,5 and LIX,16," *JSS* 8 [1963] 52–55) suggests a process by which the different words צדקתו "his legitimacy" (59:16b) and חמתי "my anger" (63:5b) came to be what they are.

17.a. The Heb. word is ישועה which may also mean "salvation."

17.b. MT תלבשת "a uniform" (BDB, 528) is supported by DSS^{Isa}. LXX Syr Vg omit. Tg paraphrases. Follow MT with Ehrlich (*Randglossen*).

18.a. גמול "deed" appears three times and ישלם "repay" twice in this verse, which has led critics to emend, eliminating the duplication. Pauritsch (*Neue Gemeinde,* 93–94) has a summary of the discussion and a suggested shortened text that reads ושלם ישלם המה לצריו גמול לאיביו "he will certainly recompense wrath to his adversaries, a deed to his enemies." But MT's duplication is probably deliberate. Read MT.

18.b. MT כעל begins the verse and occurs here a second time. It is apparently a compound preposition כ "according to" and על "upon." The second occurrence has been challenged because it stands before a verb without a noun which ordinarily a preposition should not do. BDB (758) notes that this is a rare and late form, reading the verb as a contact relative clause without a particle, "the like of their deeds is the like of (that which) he will repay." DSS^{Isa} supports MT. LXX paraphrases. Whybray challenges *BHS*'s claim that emending the second כעל to גמול "deed" is supported by Tg. Vg renders the Heb. more literally, *sicut ad vindictam quasi ad retributionem* "as to claim so to recompense," but changes "he repays" to a parallel noun. If it must be a noun, it should read simply שלם or השלם (piel inf abs) or משלם (piel ptcp) for ישלם. The difference is minor. The translation keeps the verb but adjusts an English equivalent for the prepositions.

18.c. LXX ὄνειδος "a reproach" presupposes כלמה (*BHK*) or חרפה (*BHS*). MT is milder, גמול "a deed." The occurrence of the word in each bistich of the verse is deliberate.

18.d-d. Omitted by LXX, but DSS[Isa] Tg Vg support MT.

19.a. MT וייראו "and they fear" from ירא. Many Heb. MSS read ויראו "and they see" from ראה, followed by Duhm and others. Köhler, Pauritsch (*Neue Gemeinde,* 94), and others follow MT. DSS[Isa] LXX Tg Vg support MT.

19.b. MT points with a definite article, "the." DSS[Isa] Tg are not pointed. The Gr. versions omit the article, ὡς ποταμὸς "like a stream." In spite of the article, MT is not thinking of a specific stream. There is no article on the adj צר "rushing" that follows. Whybray thinks that MT gave צר the meaning "adversary," thus "an adversary will come like a river," though this does not fit the context. Translate with the Gr. versions.

20.a. MT לציון "to Zion" or "for Zion." DSS[Isa] אל ציון "to Zion." LXX ἕνεκεν Σιων "for the sake of Zion" presupposes Heb. למען ציון. Vg supports MT. Rom 11:26 quotes the verse ἐκ Σιών "from Zion," which Duhm held to be the original for the Heb. See Sanday and Headlam on Romans, as well as Cranfield, in ICC. Cf. H. Gross, *Conc* 3 (1967) 813–18. The translation follows MT.

20.b-b. MT ולשבי פשע "to those repenting of rebellion." DSS[Isa] Tg Vg agree. But LXX καὶ ἀποστρέψει ἀσεβείας "and shall turn away ungodliness" has an active verb extending the activity of the redeemer.

20.c-c. Missing in LXX, but supported by DSS[Isa] Tg Vg.

21.a. MT אותם is an awkward form. Read DSS[Isa] אתם "with them" supported by many Heb. MSS LXX Syh Tg Vg.

21.b. The verse has literal similarities with 61:1 and stylistic similarities with 66:22 (cf. Pauritsch, *Neue Gemeinde,* 94).

Form/Structure/Setting

The style has changed to a kind of narrative form. Westermann (278) calls it a kind of epiphany (see Pauritsch, *Neue Gemeinde,* 97–99).

This scene has a problem that is familiar from earlier passages. It contains a number of pronouns without antecedents or with uncertain antecedents. Yahweh is named in v 15b, and "his arm" in v 16b. Presumably, the third person masculine singular subjects of verbs in vv 15b–16a refer to him. "His arm" must be the antecedent through v 18. Who or what is Yahweh's arm? If this passage is like chaps. 44–45 and 49, it refers to the rising Persian emperor, in this case to Artaxerxes I. He, like Darius and Cyrus before him, is a chosen agent to do Yahweh's will. The Vision identifies Yahweh's intention and power with Artaxerxes' military intervention in vv 19 and 20. In v 21 Yahweh addresses Artaxerxes, renewing with him the covenant to make him Yahweh's servant which was made earlier with Cyrus in chaps. 44–45 and with Darius in chap. 49.

Xerxes is dead. Revolt in Phoenicia and in Egypt makes Palestine's situation even worse. Yahweh raises up an unlikely successor to the Persian throne for the third time to accomplish his goals in Judah.

Vv 15b–20 describe the way the newly crowned Artaxerxes enters Palestine as Yahweh's instrument to set right the conditions portrayed in scenes 1 and 2. Vv 18–19 cite the Phoenician and Philistine areas which would have been of primary significance to the Persians. V 20 contrasts the way the invasion will effect Jerusalem, or at least those in Judah who turn away from rebellion.

Comment

15b Yahweh agrees with the complaints of previous scenes and moves to bring judgment.

16 *His own arm* describes the instrument he will use. The pronouns in v 16a refer to Yahweh. The historical setting suggests that his agent is Artaxerxes. He came to power in 465 B.C. Four years later he faced a war with Pericles of Athens over Cyprus. Inarus led a revolt in Egypt and called on Athens for help. The events of this scene fit the kind of move Persia would have made to insure the loyalty and stability of Palestine, especially as it related to Phoenicia and its fleet. Magabyzus was the Persian general responsible for Palestine.

תושע connotes *victory* or "salvation." The effect of a military victory would be resumption of authority over the territory. צדקה means *legitimacy* or "righteousness." In the Vision this has consistently described Yahweh's grant to Persia of the right to rule in Palestine. (Cf. the use of both words concerning Darius in 51:4–8.)

17 The pronouns now turn to Artaxerxes. The metaphor pictures dressing for war in qualities required for victory. *Legitimacy, victory, vengeance, and violent fury* make up his psychological armor.

18 The purpose of the campaign is retribution. The dominant word is גמול *deed* which occurs three times, balanced by words for retribution, *enemies*, and *adversaries*. The time for words is past. Judgment comes through acts of punishment. The crucial Phoenician and Philistine coast is mentioned by name.

19 The geographical positions center on Jerusalem. To the west are *the coastlands*. To the east are the borderlands: Aram, Ammon, Edom, and Arabia. The impetus of the Persian drive is attributed to Yahweh's spirit.

20 The Persian army may have had military objectives. But Yahweh has sent it with another goal in mind, to bring about change in Jerusalem. The Persian appears to Jerusalem as a *redeemer*. He rescues the population from the petty tyrants of the region who had created the chaos pictured in scenes one and two. Persian amnesty will be available in a broader area for those who *repent* by turning against the *rebellion*. *In Jacob* may well speak of Jews in Samaria, Ammon, and surrounding districts which still had substantial Israelite population. Yahweh, as Artaxerxes' patron, seals this with his own word.

21 *My covenant* refers to v 20 and God's promise to Zion. He informs Artaxerxes of this. Then he confirms his promise to him. *My spirit* is the gift which makes rule or service possible. (Cf. 11:2 where it was promised to Ahaz's son to enable him to rule justly, and 42:1 where it was promised to Cyrus so that he could bring "justice to the nations." It will appear again in 61:1.) *My words* refer to decrees for the good of Jerusalem. They could appropriately refer to the letter given to Ezra (Ezra 7:11–26), or those written for Nehemiah (Neh 2:7–9). Yahweh promises support to at least two more generations of Achaemenid rulers. *To the age* means the end of the era.

Explanation

The distressing situation of Scenes 1 and 2 gets God's attention. He doesn't like it, so he sends the Persian to rectify it. He supplies him with the things he needs to bring order to Palestine and redemption to Jerusalem.

A third Persian emperor is chosen to do Yahweh's work in restoring Jerusalem and in building the Temple. Once again God acts through a chosen person to accomplish his purpose. With Artaxerxes I the trilogy of Persian emperors who made possible the restoration of the Temple and the rehabilitation of Jerusalem is complete (Cf. Ezra).

The way God uses his own people to accomplish his will is inspiring enough. But reflection on the mysterious way he uses pagan leaders and peoples within the larger frame of his strategy brings the reader of these verses (as indeed of Ezra-Nehemiah) to recognize with awe a power that is beyond understanding. Yet Israel's dependence on his providence had to assume this control of history. The modern reader can do no less.

Excursus: Jerusalem—A Persian Temple City

Bibliography

Blenkinsopp, J. *A History of Prophecy in Israel.* Philadelphia: Westminster, 1983. 213, 227–34. **Cook, J. M.** *The Persian Empire* 51, 147–57. **Encyclopedia Britannica,** 15th ed., 11:680; 18:913; 20:245; 21:910; 22:355; 27:762. **Olmstead, A. T.** *History of the Persian Empire.* See index on Temple.

Many cities in the ancient world became famous as temple cities, e.g., Memphis (Egypt), Babylon (Mesopotamia), Delphi (Greece), and Ephesus (Asia Minor). Most of these were closely linked to certain royal dynasties who built them and expected devotion to the temple cult to parallel loyalty to the dynasty. In some of them the priests became more powerful than the kings. They used their power to raise up and install rulers as well as to dictate national policy. In any case, as nationalism developed in the ANE, royal dynasties and temple cities became closely related. The temples and their personnel were provided grants of support or given the right to collect tribute or taxes to maintain the cult in return for political support and prayers for the dynastic rulers.

This was true in Jerusalem. Although it was apparently known as a sacred priestly city as early as the time of Melchizedek (Gen 14:18–20), the Temple was planned by David and built by Solomon (1 Kgs 5–9). Several heirs in the Davidic succession are singled out in history as particularly devout supporters of the Temple and its cult including Joash (2 Kgs 12:4–16), Jotham (2 Kgs 15:35c), Hezekiah (2 Kgs 18–19), and Josiah (2 Kgs 22:3–7). With the destruction of Jerusalem in 587 B.C., the Temple was desecrated and the Davidic dynasty lost its throne. Thus the Temple was orphaned.

The same fate befell other temples and temple cities as the great empires replaced local dynasties, taking away their riches and their power to tax. Babylon with its temple for Marduk was a particularly sad case. Nabonidus, the last of the Babylonian emperors, was devoutly religious, but not a devotee of Marduk. He withdrew to a desert monastery and allowed the empire to desintegrate and its temples to languish.

When Cyrus built the Persian empire in the mid-6th century B.C., he found that support of temples and their personnel was a great political asset. When he gained the favor and support of the priests, he also gained the support and loyalty of the adherents of that faith. He applied the policy in Babylon with great success. His successor did the same in Egypt. The policy was applied to numerous Greek cities in Asia Minor and in Greece. In effect, the Persian Achaemenid dynasty became the royal patron of these temple cities and their cults, diverse as they might be. Cyrus I, Darius I, and Artaxerxes I were particularly known for their commitment to these policies.

Blenkinsopp (227) writes: "Judah's was one of several provinces the status of which was determined by its Temple and the cult carried on there. It was the policy of the central government to sponsor, subsidize and, where necessary, restore such cults." This was done for the Marduk cult in Babylon (see the Cyrus cylinder, *ANET*, 315–16), for the moon god Sin at Ur and for the Csagila shrine in Babylon. Cambyses restored the rights of the Sais temple in Memphis, Egypt. Darius I reproved the satrap Gadatas for taxing the Apollo shrine in Magnesia. In action not unlike that for Greek cities on the Ionian seaboard, Yahweh's temple in Jerusalem was granted privileges through royal edict (Ezra 6:8). Cyrus, in effect, succeeded the Davidic dynasty as the dynastic patron of Jerusalem.

The benefits for these temple cities were enormous. They were relieved of paying taxes to the empire and given the right to collect revenues from their districts and from those who came to worship there. The priests were given special status and were in several instances required to produce written codes of law for their adherents. These were administered by the priests but had to be approved by the Persian authorities (see *Excursus: Law Codes under the Persians*). The cities were allowed to draw on the royal treasury of surrounding districts for special building projects. Magistrates and imperial military power insured protection and order.

In return the empire expected prayers to be offered for the sovereign, loyalty to the empire and obedience to the government.

The Persian emperors recognized that temples and their priests formed separate establishments in many countries which were often more lasting, rich, and powerful than the political systems. They had their own tax systems, courts, and codes of law. So they learned to treat them with respect and handle them with care. These policies were instituted by Cyrus and continued by his successors, especially by Darius I and Artaxerxes I.

The Vision of Isaiah and Ezra-Nehemiah teach that Yahweh sanctioned this means of rebuilding the Temple and of maintaining the services to the Temple with its city and district. God is understood to have inspired the imperial policy and its application. He granted the emperors his seal of legitimacy and support in return for their restoration and recognition of the Temple.

The Vision understands that the entire system of empire has Yahweh's approval, indeed that he instigated it. He calls his people to learn how to live and thrive within it. A key feature of this divine strategy lies in welcoming Persian royal patronage and recognition of Jerusalem's temple, as Sheshbazzar, Zerubabbel, Ezra, and Nehemiah did. Jerusalem became a temple city with all the rights and privileges due such a city (see Ezra 1:2–4; 6:3–12; 7:6–28; Neh 2:4–9).

Scene 4: Zion's Day Dawns (60:1–22)

Bibliography

Achtemeier, E. *The Community and Message.* 74–85. **Brayley, I. F. M.** "Yahweh Is the Guardian of His Plantation: A Note on Is. 60,21." *Bib* 41 (1960) 275–86. **Causse, A.**

"Le Mythe de la nouvelle Jérusalem du Deutéro-Esaie à la IIIe Sibylle." *RHPR* (1938) 377–414. ———. "La vision de la nouvelle Jérusalem (Esaïa LX) et la signification sociologique des assemblées de fête et des pèlerinages dans l'orient sémitique." *Mel. Syriens, Dussaud II* (1939) 739–50. **Grelot, P.** "Une Parallèle Babylonienne d'Isaïe LX et du Psaume LXXII." *VT* 7 (1957) 319–21. ———. "L'Épître (de la Fête de l'Épiphanie) Is 60,1–6." *AsSeign* 13 (1962) 19–30. ———. La procession des peuples vers la nouvelle Jérusalem, Is 60,1–6." *AsSeign* 2,12 (1969) 6–10. **Hanson, P. D.** *Dawn of Apocalyptic.* 46–76. **Hessler, B.** "Sion im Glanze der Herrlichkeit Jahwes nach Is 60,1–3." *BK* 16 (1961) 101–3. **Lack, R.** *Letture strutturaliste dell'AT* (Isa 58:7–12; 60:18,22; 61:3–11). Rome: Boria, 1978. **Lipinski, E.** "Garden of abundance, image of Lebanon." *ZAW* 85 (1973) 358–59. **Maertens, I.** "Épiphanie (Mt 2,1–12; Is 60,1–6)." *ParLi* 44 (1962) 716–22. **Mouw, R.** "What Are the Ships of Tarshish Doing Here? (Is 60:9)." *Crux* 17 (1981) 20–26. ———. *When the Kings Come Marching In: Isaiah and the New Jerusalem.* Grand Rapids, MI: Eerdmans, 1983. **Pauritsch, K.** *Die Neue Gemeinde,* 103–4, 119–27, 134–37. **Schildenberger, J.** "Das neue Jerusalem, Isaias 60,1–22." *BenM* 19 (1937) 404–12. ———. "Die Gottesstadt Jerusalem (Is 60:1–6)." *Am Tisch des Wortes* 7 (1965) 21–26. **Wells, R. D. Jr.** *The Statements of Well-Being in Isaiah 60–62: Implications of Form Criticism and the History of Tradition for the Interpretation of Isaiah 56–65.* Diss. Vanderbilt, 1968. *DissAb* 29 (1968/69) 2353-A.

Translation

Heavens: 1 *Rise(fem)! Shine!* 2+3
For your (fem) light comes.
And the glory of Yahweh 2+2
rises on you (fem).
Earth: 2 *Indeed, see! The*[a] *darkness.* 2+2+2
It covers land,
and thick darkness peoples.
But on you (fem) Yahweh dawns 3+3
and his glory appears over you (fem).
Heavens: 3 *And peoples will journey to your (fem) light* 3+3
and kings to the brilliance[a] *of your (fem) dawn.*
Earth: 4 *Raise your (fem) eyes. Look around you.* 4+2+2
All of them are gathered.
They come to you.
Your sons come[a] *from far away,* 3+3
and your daughters are supported[b] *on a hip.*[c]
Heavens: 5 *Now you (fem) see*[a] *and can be radiant.* 3+3
Your (fem) heart thrills[b] *and rejoices.*
Because the sea's riches are turned toward you (fem), 4+4
and the wealth of nations comes[c] *to you (fem).*
Earth: 6 *An entire caravan of camels clothes you (fem).* 3+3+3
Young camels of Midian and Ephah.
All Sheba has come.
They carry gold and frankincense 3+3
[a]*and proclaim Yahweh's praise.*[a]
Heavens: 7 *All the flocks of Kedar are gathered to you (fem).* 4+3
Rams of Negaioth are available for your (fem) service.[a]

Yahweh: *They rise up from my altar* (*a sacrifice*) *for favor*[b] 3+3
when I beautify my beautiful building.
Jerusalem: 8 *Who are those who fly like a cloud* 3+2
and like doves to their windows?
Artaxerxes: 9 *Indeed the coastlands wait*[a] *for me,*[b] 3+3
and ships of Tarshish (*are*) *in the first* (*group*)
to bring your (*fem*) *sons from far off.* 3+3+3
And their silver and their gold is with them
for the name of Yahweh, your (*fem*) *God,*
and for the Holy One of Israel 2+2
because he makes you (*fem*) *beautiful.*
10 *Foreigners build your walls* 3+2
and their kings contribute to you (*fem*) *service.*
Yahweh: *Indeed, in my wrath, I struck you* (*fem*), 3+2
but in my favor, I have compassion on you (*fem*).
Artaxerxes: 11 *Your* (*fem*) *gates are open*[a] *continuously.* 3+3
Day and night they are not shut.
To bring you (*fem*) 2+2+2
the wealth of nations,
and their kings, being led in.[b]
12 *For the nation and the kingdom* 2+3+3
which will not serve you will perish.
Those nations will be completely laid waste.
Yahweh: 13 *The glory of Lebanon*[a] *comes to you:* 4+4
the cypress, the plane tree and the pine together
to beautify the place of my sanctuary 3+3
and the place of my feet I make honorable.
Artaxerxes: 14 *They come to you* (*fem*) *bending low,*[a] 3+2
these[b] *sons of those who were oppressing you,*
[c]*and they bow down on the soles of your* (*fem*) *feet,* 3+2
all those[c] *who were despising you* (*fem*).
And they call you Yahweh's city, 4+3
Zion of the Holy One of Israel.
Yahweh: 15 *Instead of your being forsaken* 3+3
and hated, with no one passing through,[a]
I establish you (*fem*) *for age-long exaltation,* 3+3
a joy generation to generation.
16 *When you* (*fem*) *suckle the milk of nations,* 3+3
and you (*fem*) *suck from the breast*[a] *of kings,*
you (*fem*) *will know that I am Yahweh,* 4+2+2
your (*fem*) *Savior and your* (*fem*) *Redeemer,*
the Mighty One of Jacob.
Artaxerxes: 17 *Instead of the bronze, I bring gold.* 4+4
And instead of the iron, I bring silver.
Instead of the wood, bronze.
And instead of the stones, iron.
Yahweh: *And I establish peace for those determining your fate.* 3+2
and legitimacy for your taskmasters.

Artaxerxes: 18 *Violence is heard in your land no more,* 4+3
nor devastation and destruction within your borders.
You call your (fem) walls "Salvation," 3+2
and your gates "Praise."
Heavens: 19 *The sun is no longer for you* 3+2
a light by day.
Nor for brightness is the moon 2+3
to give you light by night.[a]
But Yahweh (has become) for you 2+2+2
light by day
and your God become your beauty.
Earth: 20 *Your (fem) sun does not set anymore.*[a] 3+3
nor your (fem) moon wane.
But Yahweh will be for you 3+2+3
an age-long light.
And your (fem) days of mourning are ended.
Artaxerxes: 21 *Your (fem) people, all of them, will have citizen's rights.* 3+3
For an age, they inherit land.
Heavens: *Yahweh*[a] *is the Guardian*[b] *of his planting,*[c] 3+3
the work of his hands[d] *for mutual beautification.*[e]
Earth: 22 *The little one becomes a clan* 3+3
and the smallest a mighty nation.
Yahweh: *I am Yahweh!* 2+2
I shall enjoy[a] *her in her time!*

Notes

2.a. LXX omits the article. DSS^{Isa} has it.

3.a. DSS^{Isa} לנגד "in front, before" is supported by Tg, but Kutscher (*Isaiah Scroll,* 263, 536) points out that DSS^{Isa} has been corrected and looks like it originally read לנוגה. MT לנגה "to the brilliance" is supported by Syr ʼA Σ Θ Vg. LXX reads *τῇ λαμπρότητί σου* "to your brilliance" but omits "dawn." Read MT, the less ordinary word.

4.a. MT יָבֹאוּ qal "they come." Westermann emends to יָבִיאוּ hiph "they bring." Unnecessary.

4.b. MT תאמנה "are supported" is niph impf 3d fem pl (BDB, 52, I; GKC § 51*m*). DSS^{Isa} supports MT. 1QIsa^{b} תנשינה "are carried." Tg יתנסבן "are carried." LXX *ἀρθήσονται* "are borne." Vg *surgent* "they get up." Read MT as the less common text. Emendation (see *BHS*) is unnecessary.

4.c. MT על־צד "on a hip" is followed by DSS^{Isa} and Tg. LXX *ἐπ' ὤμων* "on shoulders." Vg *de latere* "on the side."

5.a. So MT. Many MSS read תיראי "you fear." DSS^{Isa} LXX Tg Vg support MT.

5.b. DSS^{Isa} omits ופחד "and thrills" and changes "be radiant" to 3d pers, thus "your heart is radiant and rejoices." LXX omits "be radiant" but reads "and thrills." Syr Tg Θ Vg support MT (see Kutscher, *Isaiah Scroll,* 553). Read MT.

5.c. MT pl with DSS^{Isa}. 1QIsa^{b} Vg read a sg. The difference is academic since the subject may be read collectively. *BHS* suggests a hiph "brought" with Tg.

6.a-a. Many commentators consider this an interpolation (Skinner; Volz; Whybray; Pauritsch, *Neue Gemeinde,* 123), but there is no support for deletion in the sources. Read MT.

7.a. *BHS* suggests deleting ישרתונך "your service" citing its duplication in v 10. DSS^{Isa} Tg Vg support MT. Read MT.

7.b. MT על רצון "upon acceptance" is followed by Vg *super placabili.* But DSS^{Isa} לרצון על "for acceptance on" is supported by LXX Syr Tg. Translation follows DSS^{Isa} (see BDB, 953).

9.a. MT is piel impf from קוה I "wait" (BDB, 874). Feldmann, *BHK*, and *BHS* note a proposal to read niph impf from קוה II "collect" (BDB, 876). MT is supported by LXX Tg Vg. Read MT.

9.b. MT כי־לי "indeed for me." Feldmann, *BHK*, and *BHS* record a suggestion to read כְּלֵי "vessels of," thus "the vessels (i.e. ships) of the coastlands will be assembled." Whybray emends איים "coastlands" to ציים "ships" instead, thus "for me ships will be assembled." But DSS^{Isa} and the Versions support MT.

11.a. MT ופתחו piel pf "are open" is supported by DSS^{Isa}. Tg יתפתחן "be open," LXX ἀνοιχθήσονται "be opened," Vg *aperientur* "be opened" are all passive or reflexive. So Cheyne, GKC § 52*k*, and *BHS* suggest ונפתחו, a niph. Read MT.

11.b. *BHS* suggests reading an act ptcp "leading in" instead of MT's pass ptcp "being led in." MT is satisfactory.

13.a. DSS^{Isa} adds נתן לך ו "is given to you and" (cf. 35:2; Kutscher, *Isaiah Scroll*, 543). LXX Syr Tg Vg support MT.

14.a. *BHS* suggests a vowel change, inf abs instead of inf constr, that makes no difference in translation.

14.b. DSS^{Isa} and two MSS^{K} add כול "all." LXX Syr Tg support MT. Read MT.

14.c-c. Missing in LXX, but present in DSS^{Isa} (corrected) Tg 'A Σ Θ Vg. Kutscher (*Isaiah Scroll*, 544) thinks the original text of DSS^{Isa} was a conflation of MT and LXX, later corrected in line with MT. Read MT.

15.a. MT עובר "passing through" is supported by DSS^{Isa} 'A Σ Θ Vg. LXX ὁ βοηθῶν "one helping" presupposes Heb. עוזר (*BHK*). Read MT.

16.a. שׁד "breast" is an unusual spelling, occurring otherwise only in 66:11 and Job 24:9. The normal pointing is שַׁד (BDB, 994).

19.a. DSS^{Isa} Tg LXX add בלילה "by night." Syr Vg omit with MT. Read with DSS^{Isa}.

20.a. DSS^{Isa} LXX omit עוד "anymore." Tg 'A Σ Θ Vg support MT.

21.a. Insert יהוה "Yahweh" with DSS^{Isa}.

21.b. 1QIsa^{b} and one MS omit. MT נצר may come from נצר I (BDB, 665–66) and mean "keeper, guardian" (as in 27:3, 42:6, 49:8). Or it may come from נצר II and mean "shoot, sprout" (as in 11:1; cf. 14:19). MT points in the latter sense. The translation points as qal act ptcp of the former.

21.c. Q מטעי "my planting" is followed by Syr Tg Vg. K מטעו "his planting" followed by DSS^{Isa} (transcription; but cf. facsimile, *yodh* or *waw?*). 1QIsa^{b} מטעיו "his plantings." LXX has no pronoun. K has the best reading. Cf. I. F. M. Brayley, *Bib* 41 (1960) 275–86.

21.d. MT ידי "my hand." DSS^{Isa} 1QIsa^{b} ידיו "his hands," supported by LXX. Translation assumes the latter form.

21.e. MT להתפאר "for mutual beautification" (BDB, 802, I), reading the hith as reflexive. The word occurs also in 44:23, 49:3, and 61:3.

22.a. אחישנה is niph impf from חוש. There are two meanings: I "hasten," II "enjoy" (BDB, 301–2). The second occurs only in Eccl 2:25, but it is the most appropriate here where the idea of joy has already been expressed in vv 5a and 15b using five different words. Tg reads the chapter in the future and translates איתינה "I will bring it." LXX συνάξω αὐτούς "I will gather them." Vg *subito faciam istud* "I will do that suddenly." Vg is closest to Heb. I, but the others have no clear idea of the meaning. The translation follows root II.

Form/Structure/Setting

Commentators have recognized in this chapter the form of an announcement of salvation (Pauritsch, *Neue Gemeinde*, 134–37). The development is complex and reaches well beyond cultic limitations.

The entire scene addresses Jerusalem at the time of her good fortune. It is a time when light replaces darkness, a time when her people come to her from everywhere (vv 1–5a), and her poverty is replaced by riches (vv 5b–9). Foreigners help to build the city and contribute to sacrificial offerings (v 10).

These events are described from a different viewpoint in Ezra's account of Artaxerxes' decree that allowed Ezra's expedition to Jerusalem (Ezra 7). Those who traveled with him took silver and gold from the king's treasury (v 15) as well as that given by Babylonian Jews (v 17). These were designated to buy offerings. The emperor ordered all the treasurers of Beyond the River to provide for Ezra's needs within broad limits (vv 21–23). Nehemiah 2:8 knows of a letter to the king's forester instructing him to provide timber for the gates and walls of the governor's residence. In the spirit of both of these this scene addresses Jerusalem about her new status and privilege.

The core of the chapter speaks of *beautifying* (פאר) the city (vv 7b, 9, 13, 19, 21). To this end the riches of the nations are gathered (5b–7a, 9b, 10, 13, 16, 17). They will serve to build the temple (7b, 13b), the walls (v 10) and the gates (v 11).

The reestablishment of Persian legitimacy is also clear. Peace and legitimacy for the masters (v 17b) means order and safety within Judah's borders (v 18a) and rights for Jews to own land again (v 21a). It implies Persian authority to uphold Jerusalem's position (v 12) and bring relief from oppressive neighbors (v 14). Yahweh's plan has been to use Persia's wealth and power to accomplish his purpose. When Artaxerxes reestablishes Persia's authority in Jerusalem, Yahweh's presence, his city, and his temple will flourish. What Artaxerxes gives to Yahweh, Yahweh gives to Jerusalem. These include:

Permission for Jews to travel (Isa 60:3–4, 9; Ezra 7:13).
Support for rebuilding the city and the temple (Isa 60:6–7, 11, 17; Ezra 7:15–16, 21; Neh 2:8–9, 13).
Support for operating the temple (Isa 60:3–4, 9; Ezra 7:10, 17).
The threat of imperial reprisal for injury (Isa 60:12, 14; Ezra 7:23, 26).
Rights granted for administration within the law (Ezra 7:25) of order and inheritance (Isa 60:18, 21).

Yahweh gives to Artaxerxes, King of Persia, peace and legitimacy for rule in Palestine (Isa 60:17c).

Thus the scene depicts the effect in Jerusalem of the edict of Artaxerxes that is cited in Ezra 7:1–25. The date is 458 B.C. The scene may be outlined as follows:

Introduction (vv 1–7):
- Jerusalem, your light comes (vv 1–2)
- People journey to your light (v 3)
- These include your sons and daughters (v 4b)
- You may rejoice (v 5a)
- Riches are on the way (vv 5b–6)
- Sacrifices can be abundant (v 7)
- Yahweh: They rise from my alter when I beautify my building (v 7b)

The core of the scene (vv 8–18):
- Who are these? (v 8)
- Artaxerxes: I sent them (vv 9–12)
- Yahweh: Timber for my sanctuary (v 13)
- Artaxerxes: They submit to Jerusalem for Yahweh's sake (v 14)
- Yahweh: I do this. You know I am Yahweh your Savior and your Redeemer (vv 15–16)

Artaxerxes: Instead of bronze I bring gold (v 17a-b)
Yahweh: And I establish peace and legitimacy for him (v 17c)
Artaxerxes: And I establish order and safety in your land (v 18)
Conclusion (vv 19–22):
Yahweh is your light (vv 19–20)
Artaxerxes: Your people are assured inheritance rights (v 21a)
Yahweh is your guardian and joy (vv 21b–22)

The motifs that stand out in the chapter give it structure and flavor. Light is a major motif in vv 1–3, 5a, and 19–20. The reference to beautifying the temple and the city dominates the core in vv 7b, 8, 9, 13, and 21. The call to joy is evident in vv 5a, 15b, and 22.

Comment

1 The use of feminine pronouns in vv 1–7 indicate that Jerusalem is being addressed. The speakers are not identified, so they are presented as Heavens and Earth as is customary in this commentary.

The contrast of dawning *light* against the background of darkness picks up the theme from 58:10b. The light is clearly from Yahweh fulfilling the promise of comfort in 40:5. Its focus is on his use of a new, supportive emperor, continuing the promise of 49:6b.

2 *Darkness covers land and peoples.* The events will not have the same positive effect on all Palestine and its inhabitants as they do on Jerusalem. Artaxerxes' success may have caught many in Palestine backing the wrong persons, thus increasing his anger and reprisal. Perhaps they support the Egyptian revolt. Or they may be involved in the rebellion of the Persian satrap Megabyzus. But no such shadow falls on Jerusalem.

3 *Peoples* and *kings* will be those of surrounding districts in Palestine. They will travel to Jerusalem to be present for her *light,* her dawn—the occasion when she receives the royal favor of the emperor. K. E. Bailey (*Poet and Peasant* [Grand Rapids: Eerdmans, 1983] 58) finds a concentric structure here.

4 Jerusalem is encouraged to look up to see the approaching crowds, including *sons* and *daughters.* Their kinsmen from distant lands return on pilgrimage to the new temple (cf. 2:2–3 and 66:18–23). *Supported on a hip* heightens the metaphor of Jews returning as Zion's children with the encouragement and support of Persian officialdom at imperial command.

5–7a Jerusalem can rejoice because her former poverty is transformed by gifts from Arabia and Phoenicia which support the restoration of the temple and supply clothes, money, perfume, and sacrificial animals (cf. Ezra 7:15–20; Neh 2:7–8). Arabia was the district immediately to the south and west of Judah. It had control of major land trade routes. Phoenicia included the ports of Tyre and Sidon. It had access to commercial wealth from the entire eastern Mediterranean.

7b Yahweh acknowledges the offering and claims credit for the new wealth.

8 Jerusalem is amazed and questions the identity and perhaps the motives of this horde.

9 Artaxerxes enters the scene and the events become understandable. The new emperor is to make an appearance in Jerusalem. His subjects and petty bureaucrats from all over the satrapy Beyond the River hasten to meet him there to assure him of their fealty and support. His expressed interest in Jerusalem and its temple leads them to curry his favor by "contributing to his favorite charity."

Phoenician and Philistine merchants (*the coastlands*) are in the first group. Their ships make possible the journey of Jews from distant places. The religious purpose of the journey and the gifts is expressed: *for the name of Yahweh, your God.* Artaxerxes recognizes Yahweh's inspiration to *make* Jerusalem *beautiful.*

10a *Foreigners* and *their kings* have taken seriously the imperial orders to assist in building *walls* and contributing materials for worship and sacrifice.

10b *In my wrath* summarizes the era of chaps. 1–39 which was epitomized in 6:11–13. *In my favor* describes the era of consolation and blessing portrayed in chaps. 40–66. They are now experiencing that blessing in full measure.

11–12 Artaxerxes orders *open gates* around the clock to receive the flow of goods from *nations* and *kings.* He then explains the threat under which their generosity operates.

13 Yahweh specifies the reason for the gifts. *The glory of Lebanon* lay in its forests which produced the timber for the Temple, as they had for Solomon's temple. The new sanctuary is to be beautiful, a contrast to the simple building among the ruins of the past century. *The place of my feet* is a symbol of Yahweh's presence and authority. It is to be *honorable* in contrast to being despised for so long.

14 Artaxerxes describes Jerusalem's new status, as determined by his decrees and the representatives he has sent. His obvious favor causes neighboring officials who had *oppressed* and *despised* Jerusalem, as Ezra and Nehemiah describe so vividly, Sanballat, Tobiah, and Geshem, to make obeisance and do honor to Jerusalem (at least as long as Artaxerxes is present or is attentive to the situation).

Yahweh's city, Zion of the Holy One of Israel: Jerusalem's importance to Artaxerxes lies in its being a religious center, a temple city (cf. *Excursus: Jerusalem—A Persian Temple City*). Only because of the city's link to Yahweh is it to be privileged.

15 Yahweh notes the change of direction and fortune for Jerusalem. He *establishes* her for this. *Age-long* (see *Excursus:* עולם *"An Age"*) and *generation for generation* (דור ודור) suggest the ongoing status of the city. Neither of these imply "forever." They denote long periods of time. Despite varying fortunes in the following centuries, this and succeeding temples of Yahweh in Jerusalem continued to be the center of Judaism and its pilgrims for half a millennium, until A.D. 70.

16 *Suckle the milk of nations* and *suck from the breast of kings* are metaphors for the support pictured in the previous verses. Yahweh calls on Jerusalem to recognize that he has done this as her *Savior,* and *Redeemer,* her age old covenant God. This moment of joyous fulfillment should be understood in Jerusalem and the diaspora as confirmation of the strategy that used Assyria and Persia for God's own ends. It should lead all Jews to accept his plan and abandon alternative programs.

17a-b Artaxerxes calls for recognition of his gifts that go beyond what is absolutely necessary, upgrading the quality of all materials in the temple.

17c Yahweh calls for him to see what is done for Artaxerxes. God gives him *peace* from *those determining* his *fate.* Even emperors need support and are dependent on the good will of many. Then Yahweh notes his gift to him of that essential necessity that has been emphasized repeatedly in the Vision, *legitimacy* (see *Excursus:* צדק/צדקה *"Righteousness, Legitimacy"*). In the ancient world the perception that deity had granted legitimacy to a ruler was vital to his ability to rule. Yahweh granted that recognition in Palestine.

18 Artaxerxes closes the dialogue by citing Persia's contribution of civil order in the land. *Violence, devastation, and destruction* have been effectively eliminated in Judah. With *walls* and *gates* in place, peace should return. They may be properly named *Salvation* and *Praise.*

19–20 The closing accolades return to exult in *the light* which Yahweh brings to Jerusalem. It is to be an *age-long* (עולם) light that celebrates the end of *mourning* such as that noted in chaps 5, 10, 24 and 31–33. In it *Yahweh,* not the Temple, has become *light by day* (i.e., their sun) and their *beauty.* This direct relation to God is significant. It is not mediated through secondary things, whether Temple or Torah, but direct relationship with God is possible (cf. 57:15; 58:6–9; 66:2b).

21 A final reassurance of *citizen's* and *inheritance rights* from Artaxerxes speaks to the complaints of those who had not been able to settle title claims to their land since they were abrogated by Nebuchadnezzar in 587 B.C.

The people are reminded that it is *Yahweh,* not Artaxerxes, who is the real *Guardian of his planting,* that is his people in Palestine. What Artaxerxes has done, Yahweh inspired him to do. Israel and Jerusalem are *the work of* Yahweh's *hands. For mutual beautification* is an interesting phrase. It picks up the theme of beautifying Jerusalem, but also notes that God beautifies his people and that God, or the knowledge of God, is made beautiful in worship. Cf. "the beauty of holiness" in 1 Chr 16:29; 2 Chr 20:21; Pss 29:2; 96:9; 110:3.

22 *The little one becomes a clan* seems to reflect Judah's growing importance. *The smallest a mighty nation* is hyperbole that contrasts Judah's relative smallness as a kingdom compared to Israel with its present exalted status in relation to neighboring territories.

The scene closes with Yahweh's assertion: *I am Yahweh.* Then the theme of joy returns in his statement that he intends to *enjoy* Jerusalem. Not since Eden has Yahweh truly enjoyed his human creation (Gen 2). *In her time* implies the time of her blessing which is being inaugurated.

Explanation

The "comfort" of 40:1–2 is being fulfilled in this chapter. The "light" promised in 49:6 breaks out here. The restoration of Jerusalem that was ordered in 55:26 and 45:13 and envisioned in 49:8–9, 22–23 moves toward realization. The intervening time has been a long dark period for Jerusalem, whose buildings and social fabric are still largely in ruins.

Ezra 7 and Neh 2 provide the setting. Babylonian Jewry got the attention of the emperor through their remarkable and influential bureaucrats in the Persian administration. Artaxerxes was committed to the same policies regarding cults and temple cities that Cyrus and Darius I had used so successfully before. So he agreed to throw his full support behind Ezra's and Nehemiah's efforts.

Joy, light, and beauty flood the scene because Jerusalem is being rebuilt and rehabilitated as a result of Yahweh's patronage of Artaxerxes, the emperor, and of Artaxerxes' recognition of Yahweh and his city. Jerusalem's rivals, Sanballat in Samaria, Tobiah in Ammon, and Geshem in Arabia, consider this an unholy alliance and do their best to undermine it. Some of Ezra's and Nehemiah's Jewish compatriots oppose this subordination to the empire at every opportunity.

The heart of the chapter speaks of political, economic, and religious decisions that are calculated to change the abandoned chaos of ruins into a bustling center of activity, a busy market for merchants, artisans, and laborers, a place of light, beauty, and joy instead of the dark hopelessness and despairing poverty that it had been. What are these decisions? They involve the return of Jews from Babylon, the influx of foreign capital, and the sudden interest of governments in contributing to Jerusalem's renaissance. When Ezra 7:1–28 is placed alongside this scene, the pieces fall in place.

Artaxerxes specifically empowered Ezra to make Jerusalem's temple function again. He wanted Jerusalem's God to be pleased with him. To this end he sent lavish amounts of royal funds. He ordered other peoples and officials in the satrapy Beyond the River to contribute money, timber, and labor under the threat of imperial reprisal if they refused. He offered Ezra a military guard to see that his orders were obeyed.

The scene in Isaiah picks up the same motifs to picture the results for Jerusalem. Obviously Artaxerxes expects to be rewarded for his generosity and support. This is recognized in v 17c. Poetic imagery exceeds the factual description of Ezra 7. Figures of light, beauty, and joy overflow the passage as the once almost deserted mountain ruin greets the caravans, herds, and crowds that approach it. Under full royal patronage everything in the city will be renovated and rebuilt with quality materials (v 17).

After an opening section summarizes the events and effects (vv 1–7), the heart of the chapter portrays Artaxerxes and Yahweh describing what each is doing for Jerusalem and for each other. It begins with Jerusalem's astonished question, "What are these?" (v 8). Artaxerxes responds (vv 9–12): transport for your people and their wealth because Yahweh, your God, is making you (Jerusalem) beautiful; foreign labor for your restoration; royal gifts for temple sacrifice. He accents a change in imperial attitude toward Jerusalem and closes with a threat against any nation that will not contribute to service in Jerusalem (v 13). The intervening words from Yahweh make sure Jerusalem knows that Yahweh is responsible for every contribution Artaxerxes makes.

This scene points toward the Vision's climax in chap. 66. In this way the new heavens and the new earth are being created.

Scene 5: Yahweh's Agents to Bless Jerusalem (61:1–11)

Bibliography

Caspari, W. "Der Geist des Herrn ist über mir (Jes 61:1)." *NKZ* 40 (1929) 729–47. **Coppens, J.** "L'Oint d'Is 61, 2 et les prêtres d'Is 61,6." *ETL* 53 (1977) 186–87. **Everson, A. J.** "Is 61:1–6." *Int* 32 (1978) 69–73. **Gowen, D. E.** "Isaiah 61:1–3.10–11." *Int* 35 (1981) 404–9. **Lack, R.** *Letture strutturaliste dell'AT* (Isa 58:7–12; 60:18,22; 61:3–11). Rome: Boria, 1978. **Maccagnan, B.** *Isaiah 61:10. Lettura cultuale nella solennita dell'Immacolata.* Rome: Edizioni "Marianum," 1982. **Morgenstern, J.** "Isaiah 61." *HUCA* 40–41 (1969/70) 109–21. **Sanders, J. A.** "From Isaiah 61 to Luke 4." *Christianity, Judaism, and other Greco-Roman Cults.* FS Morton Smith. Ed. J. Neusner. Leiden: E. J. Brill, 1975. 75–106. **Schmitt, J.** "L'oracle d'Isaïe LXI, 1ss et sa relecture par Jésus." *RScRel* 54 (1980) 97–108. **Zimmerli, W.** "Das 'Gnadenjahr des Herrn'." *Archäologie und Altes Testament.* FS K. Galling. Tübingen: J. C. B. Mohr, 1970. 299–319.

Translation

Solo Voice:	1 *The spirit of my Lord*[a] *Yahweh is on me*	4+4
(Ezra ?)	*because Yahweh has anointed me.*	
	To bring good news to poor persons, he has sent me,	3
	to bandage ones with broken hearts,	3
	to proclaim liberty to captives	3+3
	and an opening[b] *to those imprisoned,*[c]	
	2 *to proclaim the year of Yahweh's favor*	4+3
	and[a] *our God's day of vengeance,*[b]	
	to comfort all mourners,	2+3
	3 *to assign (rights) to Zion's mourners.*	
Heavens:	*And to give them*[a]	2+3
	a wreath of flowers [b]*instead of ashes,*[b]	
	oil of gladness instead of mourning,	4+5
	a mantle of praise instead of a spirit of fainting,	
Earth:	*So that one calls them*	2+2+3
	oaks of the legitimate,	
	Yahweh's planting for beautification.	
Artaxerxes:	4 *And they shall build the age-old ruins.*	3+3
	They will raise up former devastations,	
	and they shall repair ruined cities,	3+3
	devastations of generation after generation.[a]	
Earth:	5 *And aliens shall stand*	2+2
(to Jerusalemites)	*and feed your flocks.*	
	And sons of strangers (will be)	2+2
	your ploughmen and your vine-dressers.	
Artaxerxes:	6 *While you shall be called priests of Yahweh.*	4+4
(to priests)	*Ministers of Our God will be your title.*	
	And you will eat the wealth of nations.	3+2

And in their honor you will boast.[a]
7 *Instead*[a] *of your*[b] *shameful little, a double (portion).* 3+3
(to his officials) *and (instead of) dishonor they shall rejoice*[c] *in their lot.*
Therefore they shall possess in their land a double portion 4+4
and age-long joy will be theirs.
Yahweh: 8 *For I am Yahweh,* 2+2+3
one who loves justice
and who hates robbery by injustice.[a]
So I give their recompense[b] *faithfully,* 3+2+2
(to Israel) *but an age-long covenant*
I make with you (pl).
(to Heavens and Earth) 9 *And their*[a] *descendants will be known among the nations,* 3+3
And their[a] *offspring in the midst of peoples.*
All who see them will recognize them, 3+3+2
that they are a seed
whom Yahweh has blessed.
Artaxerxes: 10 *I will rejoice greatly in Yahweh* 3+3
and my soul will exult in my God.
For he has dressed me in clothes of salvation, 4+3
and he has covered me[a] *with a robe of legitimacy.*
As a bridegroom acts as a priest[b] *(with) flowers,* 3+3
and as a bride adorns herself with her bridal dowery,
11 *indeed, as the land sends out its shoots,* 4+3
and a garden makes its seeds sprout,
so my Lord Yahweh will cause legitimacy to spring up 5+4
and praise before all the nations.

Notes

1.a. DSS[Isa] MSS[K] LXX Vg omit אדני "Lord." Syr Tg support MT.

1.b. MT פקח קוח is usually read with DSS[Isa] (see facsimile) as one word פקחקוח, apparently a reduplicated form meaning "opening" or "release" (BDB, 824; cf. 49:9). GKC § 84[b]*n* considers it dittogr and emends to פְּקֹחַ inf constr "to open." Tg אתגלו לניהור "come out to the light" is a paraphrase. LXX *ἀνάβλεψιν* "recovery of sight" (cf. Luke 4:18) follows the usual meaning of פקח "to open eyes." Vg *apertionem* "opening." Both meanings of פקח are plausible. The translation follows DSS[Isa].

1.c. MT לאסורים qal pass ptcp "to those imprisoned." LXX *τυφλοῖς* "to the blind" (Luke 4:18) apparently read עורים or סנורים "blind" (followed by Köhler). But DSS[Isa] Tg Vg support MT. Read MT.

2.a. MT ויום "and the day." DSS[Isa] omits *waw;* LXX Syr Tg have it.

2.b. *BHS* suggests ending the verse here.

3.a. LXX and Syr omit. Read MT.

3.b-b. The Heb. word play, פאר "flowers" instead of אפר "ashes," cannot be reproduced in translation.

4.a. DSS[Isa] adds a second יקוממו "they will raise up." This makes explicit what is implicit in MT.

6.a. BDB (56, 413) locates MT תתימרו as hith impf from אמר meaning "boast, glory in"

(RSV), which is confirmed by DSS[Isa] תתיאמרו, the more conventional spelling. LXX *θαυμασθήσεσθε* "you will be admired." Tg תתפנקין "delight yourselves." Vg *superbietis* "you will pride yourself." For listings of the many proposed emendations, see Whybray or Pauritsch (*Neue Gemeinde,* 112, n. 427). Read DSS[Isa].

7.a. *BHS* suggests inserting כי "for." But this is not needed.

7.b. MT's switch from 2d to 3d pers after the first line has caused great confusion. DSS[Isa] changes חלקם "their lot," יירשו "they possess," and להם "to them" to 2d pers (as does Syr), but otherwise follows MT. LXX omits the first half of the verse. Vg reads 2d pers except for *laudabunt* "they will rejoice." RSV reads 2d pers throughout. *BHS* and Pauritsch (*Neue Gemeinde,* 112) make the first stich 3d pers. Whybray deletes the first משנה "double portion" and makes the first half verse impersonal, "instead of shame and humiliation, rejoicing shall be their lot." Volz would move the sentence to follow "a faint spirit" in v 3. Keep MT and treat it as a deliberate contrast.

7.c. Budde and *BHS* emend ירנו "they rejoice" to ורק "and spittle." This has no support in the sources.

8.a. MT בְּעוֹלָה "in burnt-offering" or "with burnt-offering" (BDB, 750). A few MSS point בְּעַוְלָה "by injustice" (BDB, 732). Tg שקרא ואונסא "falsehood and oppression" apparently reverses the words but follows the second meaning. LXX ἐξ ἀδικίας "of injustice." Vg *in holocausto* "in a burnt-offering." Both meanings are possible. The translation reads "by injustice" because it fits the context best.

8.b. DSS[Isa] Syr make פעלתם "their recompense" and להם "to them" 2d pl. LXX 'Α Σ Θ Tg support MT.

9.a,a. DSS[Isa] Syr make זרעם "their descendent" and צאצאיהם "their offspring" 2d pl. Kutscher (*Isaiah Scroll,* 562) notes that the changes in vv 8–9 stem from the problem in v 7. LXX Tg support MT.

10.a. MT יְעָטָנִי "he has covered me" from יעט (BDB, 418) is a *hap. leg.* But it could be pointed יַעֲטֵנִי from עטה "he wrapped me" (BDB, 742; cf. 59:17). Tg אלבשני "he clothed me." LXX omits. Vg *circumdedit me* "put around me." The two Heb. meanings are virtually indistinguishable.

10.b. MT יכהן "he priests it," "acts as a priest" (BDB, 464). DSS[Isa] ככוהן "like a priest" is a noun (cf. Kutscher, *Isaiah Scroll,* 322). Tg paraphrases in a tristich: "as a bridegroom who is happy in his bride-chamber, and as a high priest that is adorned with his garments, and as a bride who decks herself with her ornaments." LXX *περιέθηκέ μοι μίτραν* "he has put a mitre on me." Vg *decoratum corona* "is adorned by a garland." *BHK* and *BHS* emend to יכין and Duhm and Köhler יכונו, both meaning "fix on." Read MT, the difficult text.

Form/Structure/Setting

The scene begins with a solo speech (vv 1–3a). The rest of v 3 expands on the first line of the verse. Vv 4–5 have another speaker give instructions for the restoration of Jerusalem. Vv 6–7 have the same speaker give instructions concerning the compensation and privileges of priests. Both of these speeches (vv 4–7) are appropriate for a Persian official, perhaps the king himself. Vv 8–9 have Yahweh react to the previous speeches and claim that they result from his blessing. He speaks in the third person plural through most of his speech. But in the second and third stichs of v 8b, he addresses a wider audience, apparently of Jews generally, using second plural. In v 8b "their" represents the priests, while "you" represents the people. V 9 speaks impersonally of Israel as "their." Vv 10–11 form a thanksgiving from one whom Yahweh has saved and given legitimacy. If studies in earlier sections of the Vision are valid, the references to *legitimacy* (צדקה) mark this as a speech by the emperor who credits Yahweh for his successes in Palestine.

The scene has three speakers: a preacher and healer, an administrator, and Yahweh. The position of this scene in the Vision, as well as the characteristics of the speakers, help in identifying who they are. The teacher-preacher is similar in task and gifts with Ezra and with his renewal of covenant and establishment of law in Jerusalem about 458 B.C. (See Ezra 9–10; Neh 8–9.) The ruler-administrator fits the role of Artaxerxes and his renewal of the decree of restoration (Ezra 7:12–28). Yahweh's words are consistent with his purposes presented repeatedly from chap. 40 onward. Those addressed on stage include primarily Jerusalem's priests and temple staff, while at a distance stand representatives of the diaspora. Yahweh's usual escorts accompany him.

The outline is composed of five speeches of two or three verses each:

Vv 1–3: Yahweh's anointed messenger introduces himself as one to proclaim "the year of Yahweh's favor"
Vv 4–5: A program of restoration for Jerusalem to be a temple city supported by pilgrims and devotees
Vv 6–7: Priests are installed and granted the usual privileges
Vv 8–9: Yahweh identifies himself with these developments and with his people
Vv 10–11: A hymn of praise and thanks for salvation and credibility that has come from Yahweh

Many commentators have noted the way this chapter picks up themes from chaps. 40–55. It ties the Vision thematically with the structure of the previous acts. Vv 1–3 are similar to the so-called "Servant Songs." The restoration of fortunes in v 3 is reminiscent of 49:6 and 45:13.

Comment

1 *The spirit of my Lord Yahweh:* compare the similar theme of 11:2. There the king was clearly in view, whether real or ideal. *Has anointed me:* compare 45:1 where the reference is to Cyrus. The anointing here is clearly related more to God's gift of his spirit than to the oil used in ceremonies. In 50:4 where another individual speaks of a divine mission, Yahweh's discipline is the central theme.

Usually only kings and high priests were anointed. However, Elijah was instructed to anoint Elisha as his successor (1 Kgs 19:16). Whybray (241) is undoubtedly correct in viewing the word's use here as figurative for a commissioning for a specific task. The entire paragraph is task-oriented. Note also the close association between anointing and the reception of the spirit in 1 Sam 16:13.

To bring good news picks up a central theme of the Vision from chap. 40 on (cf. 40:9; 41:27). ענוים "poor persons" is used frequently in the Psalms for the faithful who wait on Yahweh in spite of their personal distress (cf. 57:15). It may also be translated "humble" or "afflicted." *Ones with broken hearts* is often used parallel to the "poor" in the Psalms. Here, as in 57:15, it poignantly describes the dispirited Jewish community around the ruins of Jerusalem before Ezra returned.

To proclaim liberty to the captives and an opening to those imprisoned. The words echo the description of 58:6, but they are also metaphors for the Jewish sense of what it means to be exiles and subjects throughout this period (cf. 49:9). לקרא דרור "to proclaim liberty" is used otherwise in the OT for the "year of jubilee" (cf. Lev 25). It calls for a general emancipation of slaves on every fiftieth year. The prophets use it as a symbol for the release from the problems of exile (cf. Jer 34:8, 15, 17). There is no evidence that the Year of Jubilee was ever actually put into effect. But it is a known and very effective metaphor for the freedom which God is providing for his people through his chosen instrument. *And an opening:* the translations have differed over the meaning of the word, "the opening of the prison" (RSV) or "the opening of blind eyes" (LXX and Luke 4:18; see n. 1.b). The parallel position to *liberty* and its grammatical relation to *those imprisoned* determines the translation and meaning here. The new restoration of rights and buildings in Jerusalem will be received as release from a long prison sentence.

2 *To proclaim the year of Yahweh's favor* parallels reference to the Year of Jubilee, but it is closer to the pictures of 40:1–11; chaps. 51–52; and chap. 60. The events predicted and seen dimly in those chapters are now announced as coming to pass. This contrasts in the Vision with the curse of 6:11–13.

The description of the speaker's assignment is in contrast to the anointing of 11:2–5. There the tasks for which the spirit is given are those of a powerful ruler. Here they are simply those of a spokesman, a messenger, and a healer.

יום נקם לאלהינו "our God's day of vengeance" is the complementary element to *the year of God's favor.* It is a familiar phrase in the OT (Prov 6:34) and has appeared in the Vision in 34:8 and will again in 63:4 (but without the explicit relation to Yahweh). The correction of a situation in which abuse and unjust use of force has been an element must involve both freedom for the victims and punishment of the guilty. So it is here.

Comfort has been a central word from chap. 40:1 on. לנחם כל אבלים "to comfort all mourners" sums up and fulfills the commission that was sadly abandoned by those to whom it was originally given (49:1–4). Now an individual is commissioned anew to do the task. The difficult conditions in Palestine, described in chaps. 56–59 and elsewhere, have undoubtedly produced numerous casualties. The individual whose suffering and death is described in chaps. 50 and 53 was certainly not the only one who died and who left families and friends to mourn. They also mourned the loss of possessions and land rights.

3 לשום "to assign (rights)" addresses this problem (see v 7). The speaker offers more than words. He has the authority to establish justice and right wrongs. This brings changes in economic and political conditions which are truly grounds for praise and joy. It provides a basis for calling the Jews in Jerusalem אילי הצדק "oaks of the legitimate," literally, "oaks of the right." (See *Excursus:* צדק/צדקה *"Righteousness, Legitimacy."*) The description credits governmental authorization for their new status. The parallel phrase, *Yahweh's planting for beautification* (cf. 60:21), credits Yahweh's plan and action for the reversal of their fortunes. It is also a reminder that he has done this for a larger purpose involving his use of the city of Jerusalem.

4 The verse repeats the promise of 58:12 and picks up the theme of the restoration of Jerusalem from 49:8 and 60:10. But it goes back even further in reflecting Yahweh's assignment to Cyrus (44:28 and 45:13). Artaxerxes comes to fulfill the decree first given by the founder of the empire (Ezra 7 and 1:2–4).

On עולם "age-old," see *Excursus:* עולם *"An Age."* The sense that the ruins are symbols of a previous age and that restoration is a symbol of the new age pervades these chapters. Most of the fallen stones of Jerusalem's walls and temple had gone untouched for well over a century. With imperial support and a new morale in the city, that will change. *Generation after generation* (cf. 58:12): the *devastation* of Jerusalem had begun as early as the 8th century B.C. (see chaps. 3–4 and 36–39). The *coup de grace* was delivered in 587 B.C. But that is all changing now.

5 The address changes to second person. The developments of this new age will create a labor shortage, especially for skilled builders and experienced farmers. The need will be met by people from neighboring districts (cf. chap. 60).

6 Jerusalem's population was made up substantially of priests and Levites. The imperial decree confirms them in their positions and makes it possible for them to concentrate on their religious duties. They are to live from *the wealth of nations* which is contributed to the temple and its service. The imperial recognition of Jerusalem as a temple city worthy of government support probably gave them freedom from taxes and guaranteed contributions from neighboring district administrations (cf. Ezra 7:21–23).

7 Allotting *a double portion* was sometimes a recognition of status (Deut 21:17). Sometimes it was compensation for damages (Exod 22:4, 7, 9). The rights of Jerusalem's priests are granted both in recognition of their status and to compensate for long neglect.

8 Yahweh supports the provision for the priests. But he then turns his attention away from the priests to his people. He identifies himself with *justice.* He abhors *robbery by injustice,* that is, depriving anyone of his goods or money by unjust judicial action. He provides *recompense faithfully.* (Cf. 49:4 where *justice* and *recompense* occur together.) *Their* seems to refer here to the priests of vv 6–7, while *you* (pl) turns to Israel as a people. With them he makes an *age-long covenant.* His agreement with his people applies to the entire new age (cf. 55:3). The new, beautiful Jerusalem and its temple are symbols of Yahweh's broader commitment to them and theirs to him.

9 The effects of the developments on the diaspora of Jews scattered among the nations is here in view. They will be recognized as those whom *Yahweh has blessed.* The scattered people are not forgotten. They are in Yahweh's purpose. *All who see them* is a reminder of Gen 12:2. As in 41:8 and 51:2 the Vision sees the new developments in light of God's promises to Abraham (Whybray, 244).

10–11 The recipient of *salvation* and *legitimacy* (צדקה) confesses *Yahweh* as *my God.* The decision concerning the identification of the speaker will probably dictate the content of the *salvation* and *legitimacy* for which Yahweh is responsible. The *Translation* takes the speaker to be Artaxerxes. In that case the terms cover his success in stabilizing his regime and in winning full control of Palestine. He confesses that his decision to support Jerusalem's position as a temple-city has been responsible for his success in that area. He expects Yahweh's patronage to continue to support him and his reign.

Sprout (תצמיח) is a word used consistently to speak of the "new thing" that is happening (42:9; 43:19; 45:8; 58:8; see Whybray 246). *Before all the nations* notes the usual gallery of spectators, *the nations* of Palestine (see 52:10; 60:3; etc.).

Explanation

The scene presents three speakers who figure in Jerusalem's renaissance. The first is a preacher, a healer, a messenger (vv 1–3). His message is not for the powerful or the rich, but for the poor, the imprisoned, the broken, and the mourners. He does not come as a strong leader to do something, but as an anointed messenger announcing meaningful things. His message is of freedom, of comfort, and of support. The effect of his words turns all negative conditions into beautiful positive things. The new city requires more than stones and mortar. It needs a new spirit and a new attitude to be truly beautiful. This speaker accomplishes these with his blessed words.

A second speaker is a ruler, an administrator (vv 4–7). He arranges for construction, for herding, for tilling fields and vineyards, for shares of land, and for Temple revenues. He grants priestly titles, privileges, and assignments to administer the affairs of the temple. He confesses that Yahweh has given him salvation and legitimacy as he has restored the temple (vv 10–11).

A third speaker is central to the scene. Yahweh identifies himself (v 8a). He affirms his own dedication to *justice* and his antipathy to *robbery* and *injustice*. He takes credit for *recompense* for the priests, but insists beyond that on his determination to establish an *age-long covenant* with all his people (v 9). His blessing is not for Jerusalem alone. God's purpose encompasses all Jews with the city and its priests and reaches to others beyond that.

The chapter contains a balanced picture of ministries for God's peoples. The spirit-anointed preacher of good news to the disadvantaged and oppressed continues the role of the suffering one of 50:4–9 and 52:13–53:12. He is God's direct line of communication to the outsiders, the needy, and distressed. Jesus identified himself directly with this role and this passage (Luke 4:14–21).

A second essential role is for one who can build, finance, and administer the Temple city. He can bring peace and safety for travelers. He can regulate and compensate Temple priests and staff. Solomon did it first. Jehoshaphat, Hezekiah, and Josiah are cited for their later service. Three Persian emperors are credited in Ezra for such service. Herod the Great built the Temple in which Jesus taught.

But it is God himself who works in and through both of these. Only as his will, his standards, and his blessing move through these human instruments do they have divine sanction and power. Only then do they produce joy, beauty, blessing, and peace for all who worship there.

Act XII: For Zion's Sake: New Heavens and New Land (Chaps. 62—66)

THE TWELFTH GENERATION:
ARTAXERXES (457–CA. 438 B.C.)

Conditions in Palestine and in Judah had improved to some extent. But war continued for almost a decade bringing with it many destabilizing factors. Anxiety was still high in the community and many issues remained open and debated. The lack of a stable economy and government meant the bright hope of chap. 60 had not yet been fulfilled.

The Act has four scenes:

Scene 1: A New Name for Jerusalem (62:1–7)
Scene 2: Yahweh's Oath and a Disturbing Apparition (62:8–63:6)
Scene 3: Sermon/Prayer with Interruptions (63:7–64:11[12])
Scene 4: Yahweh's Great Day: A New Jerusalem (65:1–66:24)
  Episode A: Yahweh Deals with His Opponents (65:1–16)
  Episode B: Yahweh Moves to Finish His New Jerusalem (65:17–66:5)
  Episode C: Yahweh Confirms His Servant in His New City (66:6–24)

Scenes 1 and 3 are expressions of fervent prayer for a change in the direction that things are moving for Jerusalem. The announcement that guards are to be placed on the walls of Jerusalem is reminiscent of Nehemiah's measures (Neh 4–6). This scene is undoubtedly set earlier. But it rings with the same determination to defend the city that is found in Nehemiah. The call for fervent prayer to be made to God in this regard (62:6b–7) is answered by the two long prayers in scene 3.

Scene 2 brings reassurance in Yahweh's oath but great disturbance in the appearance of the bloody warrior. Scene 4, episode A presents Yahweh's direct response to the challenges directed toward his plan. Episodes B and C show him moving resolutely toward its fulfillment.

HISTORICAL BACKGROUND (457–445 B.C.)

(See Bibliography in Act XI.)

The period of thirteen years between Ezra and Nehemiah must have brought considerable problems to the Jews in and around Jerusalem. The report given to Nehemiah in Susa at the end of that period was very bleak (Neh 1:1–3). It was a time of great international changes. At the beginning Athens was an adventurous and ambitious naval and military power. By the end of it she had settled her wars with Persia and was prepared to enjoy two fruitful decades of peaceful and creative life before the outbreak of the

Peloponnesian wars. During this period Egypt rebelled against Persian rule and was brought back under its suzerainty.

Egypt was being led in rebellion against high taxes and other complaints by Inaros, a Lybian, with the help of Greek ships and troops. Artaxerxes countered Athenian aid to Egyptian rebels by helping Sparta defeat Athens at Tanagra in 457 B.C. In 456 B.C. Megabyzus (See *Excursus: Megabyzus*) became satrap of Beyond the River, of which Jerusalem and other Palestinian cities were a loyal part. By 454 B.C. Megabyzus and his fellow general Artabazus were successful in reclaiming Egypt. However, Megabyzus, rebuffed and insulted by palace intrigue, made a show of independence by leading Beyond the River into rebellion against the central government. In at least two battles, Persian armies were unable to subdue him. The locations of these battles are not known, but they must have been in Palestine. They may well provide the background for 63:1–6. Finally Megabyzus again promised loyalty to the crown. He was then restored to favor and his position as satrap.

A strong reason for Artaxerxes to settle matters with Megabyzus lay in the developing conflict with Greece in the eastern Mediterranian. A large Athenian fleet under Kimon attacked Persian installations on Cyprus in 450 B.C. but could not follow through on its initiative, largely because of the strength and wisdom of Megabyzus. The fleet then withdrew and the Peace of Callias that effectively ended major Greek-Persian military confrontations was signed in 449 B.C. This allowed Persia to introduce a period of relative stability in Palestine and Egypt.

It also marked the beginning of the golden age of Greece (i.e., Athens). The fifth century B.C. was probably one of the most eventful and momentous in history. It was then that Herodotus, the father of history, went on his travels in preparation for his great work. The very year that Nehemiah had his first interview about Judah with the Persian king, Herodotus recited his history at Athens. Aeschylus (525–456 B.C.) had just died and Sophocles (495–406 B.C.) and Euripides (480–406) were at the height of their work. Under the direction of Pericles, who was the greatest statesman Athens produced, Phisias was commissioned as director of art and himself built the Propylaea on the Acropolis. He also constructed the magnificant temple of Athena (the famous Parthenon) and a statue of the goddess that was dedicated in 438 B.C., when Nehemiah was building the wall of Jerusalem. It was also the age of Socrates, who was born in 469 B.C. (J. M. Myers, *The World of the Restoration,* 127).

Megabyzus fell from favor again and was banished to exile near the Persian gulf where he stayed for five years. This may be the occasion for Nehemiah's appointment to be governor of Judah in 445 B.C. (Neh 2:1–10).

The events that centered around Megabyzus may have made officials in Palestine particularly nervous about any sign of rebellion. The letter in Ezra 4:8–23 describes one reaction as it related to Judah. The parties that divided Judah when Nehemiah returned were undoubtedly already active in the preceding period. Several of them are dimly visible in the Vision.

Act XII is understood here to portray the time of Ezra and Nehemiah. The intense debate concerning the chronological order of Ezra and Nehemiah has raged for a long time without an end in sight. H. G. M. Williamson

MILITARY AND POLITICAL BACKGROUND 457–445 B.C.

Dates B.C.	*Persian Emperor*	*Imperial Events*	*Governor in Judah*	*Priest in Jerusalem*	*Satrap of Beyond the River*	*Under-officers in Palestine and Egypt*
	Artaxerxes		Ahzai (?)	Johanan I		
457		Sparta defeats Athens at Tanagra				
456		Egypt is invaded by Megabyzus and Artabanus			Megabyzus	Inarus (Egypt)
454		Inarus surrenders; is later murdered in Persia				
ca. 453		The Age of Pericles in Athens			Megabyzus rebels, fights off two armies	
ca. 451					Megabyzus restored to favor and to office	
450		Phoenician ships under Megabyzus defeat Kimon's Athenian fleet off Cyprus; Athens wins at Salamis				
449		The Peace of Kallias			Megabyzus banished to Cyrtae on Persian Gulf	
445			Nehemiah			Geshem (Arabia) Tobiah (Ammon) Sanballet (Samaria) Arsames (Egypt)

(*Ezra-Nehemiah,* WBC 16 [Waco, TX: Word, 1985] xxxix–xliv) has surveyed the debate and concluded that Ezra came first in 458 B.C. This commentary works with that date, in part because the order of passages in Isaiah that seem to portray Ezra and Nehemiah also appear in that order.

Scene 1: A New Name for Jerusalem (62:1–7)

Bibliography

Anderson, T. D. "Renaming and Wedding Imagery in Isaiah 62." *Bib* 67 (1986) 75–80. **Dahood, M.** "The Ugaritic Parallel Pair *qra//qba* in Isaiah 62:2." *Bib* 58 (1977) 527–28. **Hanson, P. D.** *Dawn of Apocalyptic.* 46–47. **Mowinckel, S.** "Der metrische Aufbau von Jes 62:1s und die neuen sogen. 'Kurzverse' (von E. Balla und G. Fohrer)." *ZAW* 66 (1954) 167–87. **Pauritsch, K.** *Neue Gemeinde* 114–19, 130–34. **Rubinstein, A.** "Word-Substitution in Isaiah lxii,5 and lix,16." *JSS* 8 (1963) 52–55.

Translation

Judah's civil administrator: (to a crowd) 1 *For Zion's sake I will not keep quiet!* 4+4
And for the sake of Jerusalem I will not rest
until her legitimacy goes out like a bright light 3+3
and her salvation burns like a torch.

Second Speaker: 2 *And nations see your (fem sg) legitimacy* 3+3
and all kings your glory.

Third Speaker: *And one calls you (fem sg) by a new name* 4+4
which the mouth of Yahweh picks out.

Fourth Speaker: 3 *And you (fem sg) become*[a] *a crown of beauty in Yahweh's hand* 4+4
and a royal turban[b] *in your God's palm.*

Second Speaker: 4 *Until it be no more said of you (fem sg) "forsaken"* 4+4
and of your (fem sg) land [a]*it be said no more*[a] *"desolate."*[b]

Third Speaker: *But you (fem sg) shall be called "Hephzibah"* 4+2
and of your (fem sg) land (it will be said) "Beulah."
Because Yahweh delights in you (fem sg) 3+2
and your (fem sg) land will be fertile.

Fourth Speaker: 5 *Indeed, (as) a choice youth marries*[a] *a maid,* 3+2
[b]*your (fem sg) children would marry you (fem sg)*[b]
and (as) a bridegroom rejoices over a bride, 3+3
your (fem sg) God would rejoice over you (fem sg).

Administrator: 6 *On your (fem sg) walls, Jerusalem,* 2+2
I appoint watchmen.
All day long and all night 2+3
continually,[a] *they will not be silent.*

Second Speaker: *You (pl) who remind Yahweh,* 2+2
do not let quiet[b] *be yours!*
Third Speaker: [7]*Do not let (pl) rest be his* 4+2
[a]*until he establishes*[a]—
Fourth Speaker: *until he makes Jerusalem* 2+2
a praise in the land.

Notes

3.a. L וְהָיִיתְ "and you will become." Many MSS have וְהָיִית. The meaning is the same.

3.b. K and DSS[Isa] צָנוֹף qal inf abs "to wrap." Q צְנִיף "turban," a noun, is supported by all the Versions. Read Q.

4.a-a. *BHS* thinks this is probably an addition to the text. DSS[Isa] LXX Tg Vg all include it.

4.b. MT שְׁמָמָה noun fem sg "devastation" (BDB, 1031), DSS[Isa] שוממה qal act ptcp fem sg "being desolate" from שׁמם, followed by 'A Σ Θ (also in 64:9; but cf. 1:7; 49:8, 19, etc.). Tg צדיא "desolate." Vg *Desolata* "desolate." LXX "Ερημος "desert" is a paraphrase. The difference in translation between the Heb. forms is minimal. See Kutscher, *Isaiah Scroll*, 386.

5.a. MT כִּי־יִבְעַל "for he marries" (BDB, 127). DSS[Isa] כיא כבעול "for as one marries." Tg ארי כמא דמתיתב "for as one dwells with" (= Syr) and LXX *καὶ ὡς συνοικῶν* "for as one lives with" support DSS[Isa]. Vg *habitabit enim* "for (a young man) will live" has read כי as explanatory. Kutscher (*Isaiah Scroll*, 320–21, 348) argues that MT כי here means "like," a meaning unfamiliar to DSS[Isa] which made the same substitution in 55:9. The translation reads MT with an implied comparison.

5.b-b. MT יבעלוך בָּנָיִךְ "your children marry you." *BHS* suggests יבעלוך בֹּנָיִךְ "your builders marry you" or יבעלך בֹּנֵךְ "your Builder (i.e., Yahweh) marries you." Cf. Ps 147:2 בונה ירושלם יהוה "Yahweh builds Jerusalem," but the context does not fit. DSS[Isa] supports MT. Tg כין יתיתבון בגויך בנכי "so your children dwell in your midst." LXX *οὕτως κατοικήσουσιν οἱ υἱοί σου* "so your sons dwell." Vg *et habitabunt in te filii tui* "and your sons will dwell in you." The translation follows MT.

6.a. DSS[Isa] and one MS[K] omit תמיד "continually." LXX Syr Tg Vg support MT.

6.b. MT דֳּמִי is pointed as a noun "quiet, rest" from דמה II "cease" (BDB, 198). LXX *οὐ σιωπήσονται* "they will not be silent," Vg *ne taceatis* "may you not be silent" may suggest a verb, דֹּמִי qal impv fem sg "be silent" from דמם. But the subject is pl. Read MT.

7.a-a. MT עד יכונן "until he establishes." DSS[Isa] עד יכין ועד יכונן "until he makes preparation and until he establishes" adds a hiph form before repeating with a polel form like MT (cf. BDB, 466). LXX Tg Vg support MT. DSS[Isa] is redundant. Follow MT.

Form/Structure/Setting

Westermann (*Das Loben Gottes in den Psalmen*, 108–110) calls these first verses a song of the people in spite of its singular style. Elliger and Fohrer (218) fall back on the term "prophetic liturgy." (See Pauritsch, *Neue Gemeinde*, 130–34.)

A solo speaker opens the scene as in 61:1–3. But the tone conveys angry determination instead of quiet firmness. He announces a speech for the sake of Jerusalem/Zion. The key questions are: Who speaks? How does this relate to what preceded and what follows? If this is Yahweh or the prophet speaking on behalf of Yahweh, one would expect the tone and tenor to continue the development of themes from chaps. 60 and 61.

The content seems to be directed against Yahweh's silence or inaction (see *Comment*). Vv 6c–7a are clearly intended to evoke calls on Yahweh to change his direction in dealing with Jerusalem. Since the contents of the chapter do not continue the earlier themes, the speaker must be someone different, perhaps an administrator who leads a group in Jerusalem in a demonstration against Yahweh's announced policies of having an open city and of depending on Persian defense. Yahweh does not speak until v 8.

The scene creates a tension in the drama, standing opposed to the views of chaps. 60 and 61, indeed of the whole Vision to this point. It is in tune with 63:7–19 and chap. 64. Legitimacy and salvation are sought for the city as in other passages. But they are sought for Jerusalem in her own right. Until now these were promised to the Persian who in turn would restore, rebuild, and protect the city. Here, the prayers call for Jerusalem to be allowed to do this herself, as the guards on the walls (v 6) attest. They close her off from those around, while the Vision has presented its view of an open city ready to receive worshipers and artisans of all nations. The prayers contain the request for riches and blessing as the others have done. But their hope is unrealistic in spurning the help of Jerusalem's neighbors.

What was the occasion for the panicky attempts to set up defenses? During the first two decades of Artaxerxes' reign, his brother-in-law Megabyzus was governor of the satrapy Beyond the River. Megabyzus was a remarkable military figure who won great battles in Babylon and Egypt before this time and would do so later against Greek naval forces off Cyprus. After the Egyptian campaign he fell out with the royal court (see *Excursus: Megabyzus*) and withdrew his entire satrapy from fealty to the Persian throne. For two years he held out against all attempts to force his submission. He then returned to favor and to cooperation in time to lead Persian naval forces against the Greeks.

This series of events may be the historical background that would account for the events in chaps. 62–64. With the satrap in rebellion against the emperor, who will be responsible for the safety of Jerusalem? The local leaders panic and call for self-defense and prayer.

Vv 1–4 string out conditions introduced by "I will not rest until." The determination to act culminates in the appointment of watchmen in v 6ab. It then presses on in a prayer that Yahweh should not be allowed to rest until he has answered their plea.

Comment

1 *For Zion's sake* announces the commitment of the speaker. His urgency and restless agitation for his purpose is unmistakable. חשה "keep quiet" is parallel to שקט "rest" and shares the semantic field of דמה II "to be silent" (*TDOT* 2:279). It also suggests passivity and inactivity. It is used of stilling the waves (Ps 107:29), of the disciplined silence of a distraught person (Ps 39:3), but also of God's perceived failure to act in response to a prayer of one distressed (Ps 28:1).

The word is used six times in Isa 40–66, two of them in this passage (vv 1 and 6). All the others have Yahweh as subject. Twice he concedes that he has long "been silent, or inactive" in the face of Israel's needs and prayers (42:14; 57:11). 64:11(12) asks plaintively: "O Yahweh, will you keep silent?" while 65:6 asserts: "I will not keep silent (or remain inactive)."

62:1 and 6 have usually been understood as words from God parallel to other uses in Isaiah. But if they are not spoken by God (see the argument in *Form/Structure/Setting*), the word points in a very different direction. Rather than waiting for God to break his silence, the speaker forces the issue, in effect acting for God or as God. Since the Vision has portrayed Yahweh speaking in specific detail about Jerusalem as recently as 60:10, 22, and 61:8, the implied accusation that he is silent means that he is not saying or doing what the speaker wants him to do. Because the speaker disagrees with God's announced actions, he ignores them and accuses God of total silence and inaction on the issues. He then announces that he will take matters into his own hands while the crowd is urged to pray unceasingly that God will make his response conform with what the speaker has already done (vv 6c–7).

The speaker calls for *legitimacy* (צדקה) and *salvation* (ישועה) for the city. That is, he seeks the right for the city to exist as a city and to be recognized. He insists on relief from oppression and attack. *Burns like a torch* picks up the imagery of 60:2 and 58:8. The objectives appear to be very nearly the same as those mentioned there.

2 He will not cease to speak and pray until *nations* on all sides recognize Jerusalem's *legitimacy* and *all their kings* her *glory,* that is, her restored and prosperous state. This is parallel to 60:2 but with a reverse twist. There these characteristics were promised to the emperor. Here they are claimed for Jerusalem alone. There, Jerusalem was to receive Yahweh's benefactions through the Empire and from her neighbors. Here, she sets out to get them for herself.

Another goal is to have *a new name* that *Yahweh* himself will choose. Zion or Jerusalem is not enough. Perhaps those names had come to remind the people of destruction, judgment, and ruin. The Bible has several instances where the giving of a new name was appropriate to recognize a new status or character (e.g., Israel instead of Jacob, Gen 32:28; Mara instead of Naomi, Ruth 1:20; Paul instead of Saul, Acts 13:9). The issue of a new name for Jerusalem was broached in 60:14, 18 where the city was now to be called "The City of Yahweh" or "Zion of the Holy One of Israel." Her walls were to be renamed "Salvation" and her gates "Praise." These all have strong religious connotations. The need for a new name is also mentioned in 1:26, Jer 33:16, and Ezek 48:35. The new name will be given in v 4 below.

3 A speaker prays for Jerusalem's beauty as chap. 60 had done, but insists that it must come directly from *Yahweh's hand* (see chap. 64), that is, not be mediated by the Persians or Jerusalem's neighbors. The terms עטרת "crown" and צנוף מלוכה "royal turban" reveal the royalist ambitions of the speaker. He wants Zion to become Yahweh's royal ornament again. It had been the headquarters of Yahweh's rule on earth during the United Monarchy. That ideology was continued in the temple and Davidic monarchy in Jerusalem until 587 B.C. (see works on the kingship of Yahweh in the Psalms). There were those in post-exilic Judaism that hoped for a future return to power of a descendant of David. In that case, Jerusalem should be the capital of his kingdom. There is an anomaly in this verse, however. Instead of being the crown on Yahweh's head, the city is to be *in* his *hand.* A Babylonian inscription provides the model that one would have expected here: "Borsippa is Bel-Marduk's crown." V 3 avoids the obvious. It draws back from an overly ambitious claim for the city. In any case, Jerusalem's significance as the symbol and seat of Yahweh's kingly rule should be displayed. But this insistence runs counter to the whole thrust of chaps. 40–66 of the Vision where Yahweh's rule of the world is demonstrated in his choice of Cyrus and successive Persian rulers. The roles assigned to Israel and Jerusalem have been significantly changed for the post-exilic age.

4 Inhabitants of the city must have been deeply hurt by derisive remarks that Jerusalem had been *forsaken* by Yahweh. עזובה "forsaken" usually refers to being forsaken by a husband (54:6 and 60:15; see also 1 Kgs 22:42). שממה "desolate" means to be without children as in 54:1. That God would marry the land is an appropriation of Baʿal imagery. The speakers call for new names that will demonstrate their change of fortunes.

חפצי־בה "Hepzibah" means "My delight is in her" (cf. 2 Kgs. 21:1). בעולה "Beulah" means "Married." The cutting remarks, like those to an abandoned wife or an unmarried woman, are silenced as she proudly wears her wedding ring and married name. A comparison with the other new names mentioned in the *Comment* to v 2 above shows the crass emphasis on status and material prosperity that dominates here. There is no hint of praise to Yahweh or recognition of his lordship.

5 The prayer would see Jerusalem *married to her children.* The metaphor is mixed. It undoubtedly calls for Jews to be united, in spirit at least, with Jerusalem. The second figure calls for Yahweh, her God, to *rejoice* over her as a *bridegroom* over his bride. Again the language is tightly limited to divine action for Israel with no room left for Yahweh to act through third parties.

6ab Measures are announced for the physical defense of the city. It will include a 24-hour watch which will call its stations throughout the night, as was the custom in antiquity. The sound of their calls should reassure the population. The need for a watch could certainly be demonstrated (see 49:16–17 and Neh 4:7–9). One might see this as a hint that the speaker is Nehemiah. It certainly points to someone who, like Nehemiah, thinks in the practical terms of a government administrator concerned for the safety of the city.

6c המזכרים את־יהוה "you who remind Yahweh." Whybray (249) notes the close connection with 49:16 where Yahweh assures Jerusalem that the problem of her walls is before him constantly. In the monarchy one of the principal court officials was called a *Mazkir* "reminder." In 36:3 Joah has this title, translated "recorder" (NIV). (See also 2 Sam 8:16 and 1 Kgs 4:3.) Whybray suggests that both the watchmen and the reminders were members of the heavenly court of Yahweh, which makes this passage the equivalent of praying to angels to intercede on Jerusalem's behalf. This commentary takes the view that both terms refer to persons in Jerusalem. The *watchmen* follow their rounds as constant reminders to the community itself of its need for safety. *The ones who remind Yahweh* are those who pray unceasingly for the full restoration of Jerusalem. Both groups are urged to intensify their activities, in no case letting their voices or their efforts be stilled.

7 The goal of these intense efforts lies beyond what they can accomplish. They are not to let Yahweh *rest until he establishes.* The object is left unspoken, but it must be understood to resume the wishes in vv 1–6. *Until he makes Jerusalem a praise in the land* states the aims of the group most precisely: a restoration of Jerusalem's reputation to one of *praise* and glory (v 2a). It also shows that the building and defense of the walls is a program at this stage, not an accomplished reality. The goal of establishing Jerusalem again is in line with the Vision's view of Yahweh's strategy which has been voiced repeatedly from chap. 40 on. The dissonance of these verses is due to the means, the methods, and the goals which differ sharply from those presented in chaps. 40, 44–45, 49–54, 60–61, and 65–66. This scene, with 63:7–64:12, presents an opposition view of what God's plan and action ought to be.

Explanation

The call to commitment and prayer are admirable as far as they go. (See Jesus' parable in Luke 11:5–10.) The goals requested for Jerusalem overlap with those offered and promised in the mainstream of the Vision: *legitimacy* and *salvation*. Even prosperity, safety, and blessing cover much of the same ground.

But significant omissions flaw the fervor. There is no mention of God's goals or what he will gain through answering this prayer. There is no hint of the Temple or Jerusalem's purpose as a Temple city. The prayers are narrowly selfish and defensive. The speakers want to close off the city from attack. They want no help or fellowship from neighbors or foreigners. They want walls guarded by their own people under their authority and command.

Ezra-Nehemiah tells a story that shows leaders acting in this way repeatedly. Zerubbabel refused the offered participation of neighboring districts (Ezra 4:1–4). This undoubtedly increased their suspicion and determined opposition. Ezra insisted on a division of families on ethnic lines (Ezra 9–10) and created enmities with the Samaritans that continued over centuries. Nehemiah built a wall that would make self-determination possible, at least in terms of resisting the leadership of neighboring areas.

The thrust of the Vision has been very different. 2:1–4 envisioned a Temple-city, open to pilgrims from any land. Chap. 55 extended the invitation and chap. 56 made it include eunuchs and foreigners. The Temple should become "a house of prayer for all nations." Chap. 60 pictured a realistic way in which the decree of Artaxerxes (Ezra 7:13–26) would insure imperial support and participation from neighboring nations.

Now this scene turns its back on that to appeal to God in very selfish terms to let Jerusalem stand on its own feet, isolated and alone. Prayers in 63:7–19 and in chap. 64 will continue and expand this counter program that is laid before God to allow a narrow Jewish isolationism to replace his call for openness and dependence.

Scene 2: Yahweh's Oath and a Disturbing Apparition (62:8—63:6)

Bibliography

Achtemeier, E. *The Community and Message.* 100–109. **Buse, I.** "The Markan Account of the Baptism of Jesus and Isaiah 63." *JTS* 7 (1956) 74–75. **Giglioli, A.** "Nuova versione di 'sql' in Is 5,2; 62,10." *RivB* 15 (1967) 385–92. **Grelot, P.** "L'exegese messianique d'Isaie lxiii, 1–6." *RB* 70 (1963) 371–80. **Hanson, P. D.** *Dawn of Apocalyptic.* 203. **Holmgren, F.** "Yahweh the Avenger: Isaiah 63:1–6." *Rhetorical Criticism.* Ed.- J. J. Jackson and M. Kessler. Pittsburgh: Pickwick Press, 1974. 133–48. **Maier, J.** "Ergänzend zu Jes 62:9." *ZAW* 91 (1979) 126. **Nebe, G.** "Noch Einmal zu Jes 62:9." *ZAW* 90 (1978) 106–11. **Pauritsch, K.** *Neue Gemeinde.* 138–44. **Robinson, T. H.** "Note on the Text and Interpretation of Isaiah lxiii, 3,11." *ExpTim* 71 (1960) 383. **Rudolph, W.** "Zu Jes 62:9." *ZAW* 88 (1976) 282. **Schult, H.** "Jes 63,1: *mi za ba'.*" *Dielheimer Blätter zum AT* 6 (1974) 31–32. **Schwarz, G.** "'. . . trinken in meinen heiligen Vorhofen'? Eine Emendation (Jes 62:9)." *ZAW* 87 (1975) 216–17.

Translation

Herald:	8 *Yahweh swears with his right hand*	3+2
	and with his mighty[a] *arm:*	
Yahweh:	*I will not give your (fem sg) grain again*	3+2
	to become food for your (fem sg) enemies.	
	Foreigners shall not drink your (fem sg) wine	3+2
	for which you (fem sg) have labored.	
Heavens:	9 *But*[a] *those who reap it will eat it,*	3+2
	and they will praise Yahweh.[b]	
Yahweh:	*And those who gather it will drink it*	2+2
	in my holy courts.[c]	
Earth:	10 *Pass through!*[a] *(pl) Pass through (pl) the gates.*	3+3
(to workers)	*Prepare (pl) a way for the people!*	
	Build up! (pl) Build up (pl) the highway!	3+2+3
	Clear away (pl) the rock![b]	
	[c]*Raise a flag (pl) over the peoples!*[c]	
Herald:	11 *See! Yahweh has let it be heard*[a]	3+2
	as far as the border of the land.	
Heavens:	*Say (pl) to daughter Zion:*	2+2
(to the peoples)	*See! Your (fem sg) savior has come!*	
Earth:	*See! His recompense is with him*	3+2
	and his reward before him.	
Heavens:	12 *And they call them:*	2+2+2
	People of the Holy One,	
	Yahweh's Redeemed.	
Earth:	*Of you (fem sg) it is said: "One Sought Out,*	3+3
	A City Not Forsaken."	
Heavens:	63:1 *Who is this?*	2+2+2
	He comes from Edom,[a]	
	with crimsoned clothes from Bozrah.[a]	
Earth:	*This is one glorious in his dress,*	3+3
	stooping[b] *under the weight of his armor.*	
Military Officer:	*I myself am speaking with legitimacy*	3+2
	ample to save.	
Heavens:	2 *Why the red color of*[a] *your clothes?*	3+3
	And why are your garments like someone who treads a wine-press?[b]	

Officer: 3 *I have tread a wine-press*[a] *alone.* 3+3
And no one from the peoples[b] *was with me.*
[c]*I trod them in my anger* 2+2
and trampled them in my wrath.
Their eminence[d] *spurted*[e] *onto my garments,*[c] 3+3
and I have polluted[f] *all my clothes.*
4 *For a day of vengeance was in my mind,* 4+3
and the year of my redemption had come.
5 *When*[a] *I looked, there was no helper.* 3+3
When I was appalled, there was no support.[b]
So my arm accomplished salvation for me, 3+3
and, as for my wrath,[c] *it sustained me,*
6 *When I walked over peoples in my anger,* 3+2+3
and when I made them drunk[a] *in my wrath,*
and when I poured out their eminence[b] *on the land.*

Notes

8.a. MT עזו "his mighty." Cairo Geniza fragment קדשו "his holy." DSS^{Isa} LXX Tg Vg support MT.

9.a. DSS^{Isa} LXX Syr add אם "if."

9.b. DSS^{Isa} inserts שם, "the name of Yahweh." LXX Vg support MT. Tg inserts קדם, "before Yahweh." Read MT.

9.c. The mix of themes has prompted considerable rearrangement of the verse (see *Comment*). It is unnecessary. The verse makes sense as it stands.

10.a. DSS^{Isa} has עברו "pass through" only once, as does LXX. Read MT.

10.b. MT מאבן "away the rock." DSS^{Isa} אבן הנגף "rock of stumbling" (cf. 8:14) is supported by Tg (cf. Kutscher, *Isaiah Scroll,* 544). LXX τοὺς λίθους τοὺς ἐκ τῆς ὁδοῦ "the rocks from the road." Read MT.

10.c-c. MT הרימו נס על־העמים "raise a flag over the peoples." DSS^{Isa} אמורו בעמים "his words against the peoples." LXX Syr Vg support MT. Read MT.

11.a. MT השמיע pf "he let it be heard." DSS^{Isa} השמיעו impv "announce!" LXX Tg Vg support MT. Read MT.

63:1.a,a. Lagarde (*Semitica I*), followed by many, including *BHS,* emended מֶאֱדוֹם "from Edom" to מְאָדָּם pual ptcp "reddened" (cf. Exod 25:5; 26:14; 35:7, 23; 36:19; 39:34; Nah 2:4; hiph in Isa 1:18) and מִבָּצְרָה "from Bozrah" to מִבֹּצֵר qal act ptcp "than a grape-cutter, grape gatherer," thus "with crimson clothes redder than a grape-cutter's." This has no support in the ancient sources and translations. With Whybray, read MT.

1.b. MT צעה "bending, stooping" (BDB, 858) is supported by DSS^{Isa}. LXX omits. Σ βαινων "walking" and Vg *gradiens* "stepping" lead BDB (857) and *BHS* to follow Lowth and others in emending to צעד "marching." This is unnecessary. Read MT.

2.a. LXX Syr Vg omit the preposition. But it is needed. Read MT.

2.b. MT בגת could be either "in a wine-press" or "in Gath" (BDB, 387). DSS^{Isa} reads בגד, mistaking the similar sounding *daleth* for *taw* (Kutscher, *Isaiah Scroll,* 227). LXX ληνοῦ "wine-vat." Tg במעצרא "in the press." Vg *in torculari* "in a wine-press."

3.a. The meaning of פורה is uncertain (BDB, 807). The word occurs otherwise only in Hag 2:16. LXX omits. Tg במעצרא "in the wine-press," 'A κεραμυλλιον "small jar," Σ ληνον "wine-vat," Vg *torcular* "wine-press."

3.b. MT מעמים "from peoples." DSS^{Isa} מעמי "from my people" is supported by Syr. LXX 'A Σ follow MT. Read MT.

3.c-c. Omitted by DSS^{Isa}.

3.d. נצח is usually translated here "juice, blood, gore," though everywhere else it means "eminence." Perhaps it should be translated according to its normal meaning.

3.e. ויז "and spurted" (BDB, 633). *BHS* suggests pointing as a *waw* consec.

3.f. MT אגאלתי "I have polluted" (BDB, 146) is an unusual hiph form, perhaps due to Aramaic influence (cf. GKC § 53*p*). DSS[Isa] 1QIsa[b] Σ Θ Syh Syr Vg read piel גאלתי followed by many modern commentators. The meaning is the same.

5.a. MT has a simple *waw* conjunction that may introduce a dependent clause. LXX 'A Syr Tg presuppose a *waw* consec to be translated "and then." Read MT.

5.b. MT סומך "support" (BDB, 701). DSS[Isa] תומך "support" (BDB, 1069) but follows MT's סמכתני "it supported me." Kutscher (*Isaiah Scroll,* 295–96) considers DSS[Isa]'s reading preferable, noting that LXX 'A Σ also use two different roots.

5.c. MT וחמתי "and my wrath" is supported by LXX Vg. Tg paraphrases. *BHS* suggests אמתי "my forearm," citing Ps 91:4. But Isa 59:16 is a better parallel. Keep MT.

6.a. MT אשכרם "I made them drunk." Several MSS read אשברם "I broke them." LXX omits. Tg אדושינון "I trample them." DSS[Isa] Σ Θ Vg support MT. Read MT.

6.b. See n. 3.d above.

Form/Structure/Setting

The scene answers the challenge posed in 62:1–7 in two ways. First, Yahweh responds by reviewing the situation: in vv 8–9 Yahweh swears that the fields will not be pillaged again; in v 10 he calls for the work on roads to continue; in v 11a–d the fact is cited that news is out that Zion has a patron; and in vv 11e–12c one notes that everyone knows that restoration is funded and that Jerusalem's functioning sanctuary is a reality.

The second answer is acted out. A huge figure of a bloody warrior appears and is challenged (63:1–6). He claims *legitimacy* (i.e., authority) and *ample* strength *to save* (that is, to punish rebellion and thus make the area safe again) (v 1). He reports a battle (vv 3–6) in which he fought without aid from *the peoples* (that is, without support from Persian vassals in the area). This answers the charge that Yahweh has done nothing to defend Jerusalem (62:1–7) and implies that significant and effective military force has been used to keep peace and order for Jerusalem and its neighbors.

The two answers show that Yahweh is using the second (Persian military force) to fulfill his promise of security and restoration given in the first. The scene supports the Vision's main line of argument that the Persian emperor is Yahweh's servant entrusted with the tasks of restoring Jerusalem and keeping peace in the area.

During most of the first decade and a half of Artaxerxes' rule, the general named Megabyzus, satrap of Beyond the River (see *Excursus: Megabyzus*), won significant victories in Egypt and major naval engagements off the island of Cyprus. He also was in rebellion against the central government for several years, repulsing two armies sent to subdue him. He is the most likely identification for the bloody uniformed figure. There is no indication of what battle is described.

The first answer summarizes what the Vision has presented repeatedly as Yahweh's plan and action on behalf of Jerusalem. The oath includes his promise of security. V 10 reiterates his encouragement to restore access and transportation for pilgrims. V 11 speaks of the message heard throughout Palestine of the emperor's patronage of the temple in Jerusalem. V 12 tells of funds available which make the city known as favored by her God and which make its people known as *Yahweh's redeemed.*

The second answer is symbolic and metaphoric. The words bear connotations of color (red) and of war. They can be heard as references to nearby areas of conflict: Edom, Bozrah, Gath. They also conjure up pictures of vineyards and the gathering and pressing of grapes. Towering above and within these is an impressive and mysterious military figure, obviously victorious, who claims authority and success, but who also complains of lack of support in the battle. (Is Judah perhaps one of *the peoples* who failed to rally to his aid?) He had acted to requite rebellion (*vengeance*) and also to restore order and safety (*to save*).

The horrible scene portrays a victory won without Jewish participation which nonetheless secured safety and order for her prosperity and restoration. Without Persian troops and administration, the victory over vandals and intruders would have had to be bought with Jewish blood as it had been from the days of Deborah through those of Josiah. What historical data there is suggests that Megabyzus did not allow his differences with the emperor in Suza or Persepolis to interfere with his administration of the satrapy. He continued to be in control there and to exercise authority there while he carried out his rebellion against Artaxerxes. This would make the scene historically credible. The fears of Jerusalem's leaders proved groundless.

Excursus: Megabyzus

Bibliography

Cook, J. M. *The Persian Empire.* 127–28. ***Encyclopedia Britannica,*** 15th ed. 1:598; 7:1010. **Olmstead, A. T.** *History of the Persian Empire,* 237–345.

Megabyzus was a remarkable person in the Persian court of the 5th century B.C. The son of Zoprus, he became the son-in-law of Xerxes I. In 482 B.C. he was sent to put down an uprising in Babylon. He devastated the city and removed the gold statue of Bel-Marduk that was the city's pride. He then had it melted down to prevent any future ruler from legitimizing his position by "taking the hand of Bel" in the New Year festival.

He traveled with Xerxes on his campaigns to Greece. But in 465 B.C. he was part of the conspiracy that murdered Xerxes and gave the throne to Artaxerxes I. By 456 B.C. he was satrap of the province Beyond the River that included Palestine. He was sent to Egypt to subdue a rebellion there which he did partially through superior military force and partially through diplomacy. He gave Inaros his word that he and the Greek officers would be sent home safely. But when he brought them first to Susa, his mother-in-law, the queen mother Amestris, demanded their execution and eventually got it.

Megabyzus subsequently led a rebellion in his province against Artaxerxes. Two different Persian armies failed to defeat him. Battles were undoubtedly fought in Palestine during this time. Finally, he reached an understanding with the central government in time for him to take command of all Persian forces, including the Phoenician fleet, in order to stop the aggressive advance of an Athenian fleet off Cyprus in 550 B.C.

His career took another bizarre turn when he offended Artaxerxes during a hunt. His sentence of execution was commuted to banishment to Cyrtae on the

Persian gulf where he stayed for five years. He then made his way back to court and was forgiven by the king. He died at age seventy-six. He was a most effective general whose marriage into the inner circle of the court saved his life and prolonged his career under a very fickle emperor.

Megabyzus is not named in the Bible. But he was satrap of Palestine during an important period of its history and undoubtedly left his mark on events of the period. Ezra and Nehemiah would undoubtedly have known him and may well have owed some of their influence to him.

Comment

8 *Yahweh swears . . . not . . . not.* The Hebrew formula אם . . . אם is literally "if . . . if . . ." asserting that God puts himself at risk of bearing a heavy penalty if these things do happen in spite of his oath. This does not make good English sense, so it is rendered in the form that one would speak of taking an oath in English.

His right hand and his mighty arm (see 40:10–11; 48:14; 51:5,9; 59:1; 60:21) may refer to his arm raised in taking the oath. But they also refer to his chosen instruments of military strength, the emperor and his armies. The Vision from 41:25 on has proclaimed that they had been chosen to achieve God's goals for order and safety in Palestine. *Your grain again* and *your wine:* the villages and field have for so long lain defenseless and open to any thief or ruffian passing by. This is always true when there is no authority to maintain order, without which the peasants and their villages are helpless. E. Achtemeier (*The Community and Message,* 99) cites the covenant ceremonies in Israel which promised blessings for those who keep covenant and curses for those breaking it (Deut 28; Lev 26). One curse included having enemies consume the harvests for which Israel had labored (Deut 28:30–33; Lev 26:16). Yahweh's oath confirms that the time of living under curse is past (40:1–2). Whybray thinks of taxation which claimed the harvests of fields and of vineyards under imperial rule. But imperial orders for the restoration of Judah included clear orders that they were not to be taxed (Ezra 7:24), which was consistent with Persian practice regarding recognized temple cities.

9 *Those who reap it will eat it.* Justice will be served. Persian authority will make it possible, but *they* (Jewish villagers) *will praise Yahweh* when they recognize the Vision's claim that Yahweh has sent the Persian armies and administrators. *In my holy courts* moves beyond the promise of material prosperity to include the restoration of worship in the temple. Whybray correctly relates this verse to the practice of bringing first-born cattle and first-fruits of grain and wine to be offered to God in the festivals (Deut 12:17–18; 14:22–27; 16:9–17). They were to be an offering of praise (Lev 19:24). G. Schwarz (*ZAW* 87 [1975] 216–17) sought to separate the two themes by rearranging the stichs to read:

> But those who reap it will eat it,
>   and those who gather it will drink it.
> And they will praise Yahweh
>   in his holy courts.

His suggestion aroused spirited responses from Rudolph, Nebe, and Maier (see *Bibliography*). Rearrangement is not necessary to make the point that prosperity should bring the recognition that Yahweh has made it possible and call out the appropriate response in worship.

10 The workers are called back to the task at hand, instead of guarding the walls and engaging in continuous prayer (62:6–7) for something that is not in God's plan. They are called rather to implement a faith in Yahweh's plan which had appeared in 48:20, 52:11 and 57:14. The workers are summoned to get on with *building up the highway* and *raising a flag over the peoples.* References to *the highway* have appeared in 11:16, 19:23, 33:8, 40:3 and 49:11. The opening of the renovated temple draws near. The importance of having passable roads and safety in travel in this age when Jews are scattered and must travel long distances to reach Jerusalem cannot be overemphasized. The imperatives of this verse exhort workers to continue in the tasks already begun. They must not allow the calls for self-defense of vv 1–7 to impede construction! Nehemiah in a similar situation accomplished both by having workers take their weapons with them to the workplace (Neh 4:16–18).

11 הנה "see" is a device that calls attention. The verse is directed to the speakers of vv 1–7. Their perception is that Yahweh has been inactive and unresponsive to their needs. The neighbors continue to revile and despise them. But they are reminded that Yahweh had *let it be heard as far as the borders of the land* (that is, throughout Palestine) that Jerusalem's *savior had come.* The direct reference is to 60:9 and the edict of Artaxerxes (Ezra 7:13–26). But it also picks up earlier announcements made to the coastlands (Phoenicia and Philistia) and to the border areas (see 41:1–9; 42:10–15; 43:6; 45:22; 48:20; 49:1–6; 51:5; 52:10; 59:18). The Vision pictures Yahweh's work as something that had had ample publicity in all Palestine. But these speakers, like their forebears in Babylon, are blind to this work (42:18–20; 43:8). The raising of *the flag* would be the signal that Jerusalem and its temple are prepared to receive the pilgrims (see 49:22).

The Persians came to the task of restoring Zion with ample funds for the project. *Recompense* and *reward* for the city and for the builders are available in full supply (see Ezra 2:68–69; 3:7; 6:8–10; Neh 2:8–9). The emperor's decree included provision for all their needs (chap. 60).

12 *They* refers to the surrounding peoples who reviled the survivors in the ruins of Jerusalem and who opposed all attempts to rebuild the temple and the city. They are those against whom the speaker in vv 1–7 wanted to organize a defensive force. These peoples already call Jerusalem's inhabitants *People of the Holy One* and *Yahweh's redeemed.* The plea for a new name (in vv 2 and 4) has been anticipated. But note the difference. Here there is a strong testimony to Yahweh's role in the renaissance of Jerusalem which was missing in the demands of vv 2 and 4. The prosperity of having their own food and their city restored leads, as God had intended, to a restored reputation. The neighbors are witnesses (43:10), just as the Jerusalemites bear witness by their very existence, to Yahweh's faithfulness. The common gossip about Jerusalem has changed although the inhabitants still cringe under the unkind cries of "Deserted," and "Forsaken" (v 4). But they are assured that their reputation has improved. The names are now: *One Sought Out* by divine favor, *A City Not Forsaken* by its ancient Deity. The promises extended in chap. 54 are being fulfilled.

63:1 The scene is suddenly dominated by an awesome figure in a uniform splattered with red spots. *Who is this?* is answered in three ways.

He comes from Edom . . . from Bozrah. מאדום is usually understood to mean "from Edom." The name's root means "to be red." Perhaps the country derived its name from the red rock formations found there. Edom was no longer a nation (cf. Obadiah). It had been overrun a generation earlier by Arab-like peoples from the desert (see J. R. Bartlett, "The Moabites and Edomites." *POTT* 229–38). But the territory to the south and east of Judah would still bear that name. *Bozrah* was a major town in that region. Both Edom and Bozrah bear meanings related to "red" and to the grape harvest as well, meanings that will be exploited in the following verses. *Crimsoned clothes from Bozrah* may well have described a common sight as workers who pressed the grapes of that region returned to villages in Judah (see n. 1.a).

The second part of the answer to *Who is this?* dispels the idea that this is a worker from the grape harvest in Bozrah. It points to his military uniform. *Glorious* describes an officer's dress complete with badge of rank and medals of honor. *Stooping* describes the peculiar posture required by *the weight of his armor.* He is a soldier, an officer, still in battle attire stained with evidence of recent carnage.

The third part of the answer is in the first person. The officer shows his credentials and claims that he has ample forces to handle the situation. He speaks to calm the people. *Legitimacy* claims that his authority derives from the imperial government. *Ample to save* claims that his troop strength is sufficient to carry out his mandate to restore order, put down rebellion, and rescue the oppressed. The two words appear regularly in the Vision to describe Yahweh's patronage of Persian rulers to accomplish his goals for Jerusalem: of Cyrus 45:8–24; 46:13; of Darius 49:6–8; 51:5–8; of Artaxerxes 59:16; 60:17–18; 61:10–11. They are used of Yahweh himself in 56:1 and 64:4–5 and claimed for Jerusalem in 62:1–2.

Most interpreters have identified the bloody warrior as Yahweh himself, but the text does not so identify him. He is more likely a symbol of Persian imperial power fighting Jerusalem's and Yahweh's battles for them. Perhaps he is best thought of as Megabyzus, the redoubtable Persian general who served as satrap of Beyond the River during this period (see *Excursus: Megabyzus*). The bloodied figure claims the right to rule and the power to rescue from any danger.

So the answer to the question *Who is it?* is: he is a warrior who has legitimately fought a bloody battle to save Jerusalem and others from dangerous enemies. His appearance suggests that the fears voiced in vv 62:1–7, that Jerusalem needs to organize a vigilante-style self-defense, are groundless. The Persian army has things well in hand.

2 But the Jerusalemites are still curious about *the red color of his clothes.* Why should a uniformed soldier look *like someone who treads a wine-press?* The first answer had settled the question of identification: he is a soldier. It had not answered the question about the strange condition of his attire. Again there is the possibility for double meaning. בגת "wine-press" may also mean "in Gath" which is another neighboring city, one of the Philistine cities.

3 The officer answers candidly. He uses the metaphor to give his report, making it a gory figure for the carnage of battle. He has indeed been *treading a wine-press.* That is, he has been engaged in violent conflict. Then he adds a significant word: לבדי "alone." He complains, *No one from the peoples was with me!* Normally an imperial army could compel vassal peoples to provide military support and provisions. This was apparently not possible in this instance. If the suggestion that the figure was Megabyzus is correct, the fact that he was in rebellion at about this time against Artaxerxes, his brother-in-law, because of a personal rebuff in the royal court by his mother-in-law could mean that Palestinian peoples had been reluctant to recognize him as the legitimate governor of Beyond the River and as the representative of the Persian governor. The officer then claims to have responded to this insubordination by *treading* and *trampling* them (like grapes) in *anger* and *wrath,* the emotions of battle. The evidence of the bloody battles is on his clothes. *Their eminence* (see n. 3.b) implies that the battles reduced the peoples in importance and vitality.

4 *Vengeance* implies retaliation for previous wrongs. *Redemption* suggests the restoration of order that had previously existed. The word-pair is appropriate to putting down rebellion. It may imply that those who refused to join in suppressing the original rebels were treated just as the rebels themselves were treated.

5–6 The verses repeat the account, stressing that the warrior acted alone in gaining victory. *My arm* means that his own forces *accomplished salvation,* that is, succeeded in establishing order and putting down the rebellion. *My wrath* refers to his own emotional motivation.

Explanation

The previous scene consisted of shrill patriotic calls for a vigilante-style force to meet a crisis of self-defense. The Vision has previously insisted that God is in control of the situation and that his plan is being implemented on schedule. But these activists panicked because of some current events. They refused to allow God to meet their needs in his own way.

This scene meets their challenge. It appeals to faith in citing Yahweh's oath concerning their safety (62:8–9). Faith should lead to continuing the work that had begun to build the roads leading up to Jerusalem (v 10). These roads are essential for the Vision's program to become a reality. If Jerusalem is to become a center for pilgrimage, the people have to be able to travel.

E. Achtemeier (*Community and Message,* 99–100) links this assurance that Israel can eat their own food in the sacred courts with the assurance experienced by Christians when the Lord's Supper is celebrated (1 Cor 11:23–25) that their labor will not be in vain (1 Cor 15:58). God speaks to the anxiety of all times that the uncertainties of the future will rob us of the product of our labor and thus make all planning and labor fruitless. And Paul, like the Vision, summons believers back to the task at hand in making the will of God become reality in the world.

The second response turns to the complaint that Jerusalem's reputation has suffered so badly. It insists that God has already changed their status and reputation, but the people were so concerned about their hurt feelings that they have not noticed. Their prayers were already answered, but they did not know it.

The challenge in 62:1–7 reacts to a military threat at their very door. In 63:1 this threat materializes as a bloody officer who appears at Jerusalem's gates. Is he a laborer from the vineyards? Or is that human blood on his clothes? He indicates that he is not threatening Jerusalem. The battle is over. He identifies himself as a soldier and claims to have acted legitimately to save something (or someone) precious. He is then challenged to explain why or how this evidence of violence is to be justified.

The evidence is clear. The blood-spattered clothes are unmistakable. First comes the confession: "I did it, alone and in anger." Then comes the justification: it was an act of vengeance. That is, the enemy had done something first which created an unjust situation. This had to be answered and put right. So this was done to redeem something or someone. It freed someone from bondage and it allowed healthy progress and life to return to the communities and societies of the land. Then the speech returns to the confession: "Yes, I did it, alone and in anger."

Violence in the service of justice, to repress tyranny or oppression and to create a secure and free society, is the proper justification for the use of military or police force in any time. That is the case here ex post facto.

The purpose of the scene is not to justify the action. It does suggest that God has provided for the forceful enforcement of order and that activist self-help measures for Jerusalem, like those proposed in the previous scene (62:1–7), are not necessary.

Scene 3: Sermon and Prayers (63:7—64:11[12])

Bibliography

Achtemeier, E. *The Community and Message.* 109–21. **Beek, M. A.** "Das Mitleiden Gottes. Eine masoretische Interpretation von Jes 63,9." *Symbolae F. M. T. de Liagre Böhl.* Leiden: E. J. Brill. 1963. 23–30. **Blank, S. H.** "'And All Our Virtues.' An Interpretation of Is 64:4b–5a." *JBL* 71 (1952) 149–54. **Botterweck, G. J.** "Sehnsucht nach dem Heil: Is 64:1–7." *BibLeb* 6 (1965) 280–85. **Buse, I.** "The Markan Account of the Baptism of Jesus and Isaiah 63." *JTS* 7 (1956) 74–75. **Conrad, D.** "Zu Jes 64,3b." *ZAW* 80 (1968) 332–34. **Hanson, P. D.** *Dawn of Apocalyptic.* 81–100. **Kuntzmann, R.** "Le vocabulaire de salut en Is 63,7–14." *RScRel* 51 (1977) 22–39. **Morgenstern, J.** "Is 63,7–14." *HUCA* 23 (1950) 187–203. **Pauritsch, K.** *Die neue Gemeinde.* 144–71.

Translation

Levitical Preacher:

7 *Yahweh's acts of covenant loyalty* — 2+1
I will bring to remembrance,
Yahweh's praises — 2+4
according to all that Yahweh has dealt out to us
and much[a] *goodness*[b] [c]*to the house of Israel*[c] — 3+3+2
which he dealt out to them[d] *according to his compassion*
and according to the greatness of his acts of covenant loyalty.
8 *Then he said: surely, they are my people,* — 3+3+3
children who will not deal falsely.
So he became their savior.
9 *In all their affliction*[a] — 2+2+3
he did not[b] *afflict.*[c]
And the angel[d] *of his face saved them.*
By his love and by his pity — 2+2
he himself redeemed them.
Thus he lifted and carried them. — 2+2
all the days of (that) age.
10 *But they rebelled* — 2+3
and offended his holy spirit.
So he turned around (to become) an enemy to them. — 3+3
He himself fought against them.
11 *Then he remembered days of (that) age:* — 2+2
[a]*Moses,* [b]*his people.*[a]
Where was the one bringing them[c] *from a sea?*[d] — 3+3
[e]*The shepherds*[f] *of his flock?*
Where was the one who established them in his presence? — 3+2
(Where) was His holy spirit?
12 *(Where) was the One sending his glorious arm* — 3+2
to be Moses' right hand?
(Where) was the One dividing waters before them — 3+4
to make a name for himself[a] *(for that) age?*[b]
13 *(Where) was the One leading them in the ocean depths?*[a] — 2+2+2
Like the horse in the wilderness[b]
they would not be tripped up.
14 *Like the cattle when they go down into the valley* — 3+3
Yahweh's spirit gave us rest.[a]
Thus you led your people — 3+2+2

to make for yourself
a glorious name!
Zadokites: 15 *Look from heaven and see* 3+3
from your holy and glorious dwelling!
Nationalist: *Where is your zeal and your valor*[a] *(now)?* 3+3+2
(Where) is the yearning of your heart and your compassion
[b]*which have been withheld from me?*[b]
People of the land: 16 *For you are our father (too)!* 2+4+3
Even if Abraham did not know us
and Israel does not recognize us![a]
Israelites: *You are*[b] *our father, Yahweh,* 3+3
Our redeemer, from (that) age, that is your name!
Jerusalemites: 17 *Why, O Yahweh, did you make us stray from your ways?* 4+3
(Why) did you harden our hearts so as not to fear you?[a]
Israelites: *Return, for the sake of your servants,* 3+2
the tribes of your inheritance.
Jerusalemites: 18 [a]*It has become a matter of no consequence that your holy people secure their inheritance*[a] 3+3
since our adversaries have trod down your holy place.
Israelites: 19 *We are from (that) age.*[a] 2+2+3
Jerusalemites: *You have never ruled over them.*
Israelites: *Your name has never been pronounced over them.*[b]
Zadokites: [64:1][c] *If only you would cleave the heavens!* 3+1+3
(If only) you would come down,
from facing you, mountains would quake![d]
Nationalists: 64:1[2] *As fire kindles dry bushes,*[a] 3+3
or fire makes water boil,[b]
to make your name known to your adversaries, 3+3
(to make) nations tremble before you.
Zadokites: 2[3] *When you did awesome things* 2+2
that we did not[a] *expect,*
[b]*you came down!* 1+3
From facing you, mountains quaked![b]
The Preacher: 3[4] *From (that) age (until now) no one has heard of*[a]*—* 2+2+2
no one has attended[b]*—*
no eye has seen
any God except[c] *you* 2+2
who works for one who waits[d] *for him.*
4[5] [a]*You meet*[b] *with* [c]*the joyful* 2+2
and (with) the one doing[c] *right*
[d]*who remember you in your ways.*[d]

Look! [e]When you, yourself, were angry, and we sinned 3+3
[f]in those ancient times, we could still be saved![ef]
5[6]*And even if all of us are as one unclean,* 3+3
and all our right deeds are like soiled underclothes,
even if all of us are faded[a] *like a leaf,* 3+3
our iniquity[b] *can be lifted*[c] *like the wind.*
6[7]*And even if no one is calling your name,* 3+3
bestirring himself to take hold of you,
because you have hidden your face from us 3+2
and melted[a] *us down by means of our iniquities,*
7[8]*now,*[a] *Yahweh,* 2+2
you are still our father!
We are the clay, 2+2+2
and you are our potter.
All of us are the work of your hand![b]
8[9]*Do not be angry, Yahweh, to excess!* 3+3+4
Do not remember iniquity forever!
Look! Consider all of us your people, we pray!
Zadokite: 9[10]*Your holy cities*[a] *have become wilderness!* 4+3+2
Zion has become a wilderness!
Jerusalem (is) a desolation[b]
10[11]*Our holy and beautiful building* 3+3
where our fathers praised you
has become[a] *a place burned by fire* 3+3
and all our pleasant places[b] *have become*[a] *devastations.*
11[12]*Will you restrain yourself concerning these, Yahweh?* 3+3
Will you be silent while you afflict us so much?

Notes

7.a. MT רַב "much" is an adj (BDB, 912) LXX *κριτὴς* "a judge" read רָב qal ptcp from ריב (BDB, 936). Vg *multitudinem* read רֹב "abundance," a noun (BDB, 913). MT is best in context.

7.b. MT טוּב "goodness." LXX *ἀγαθὸς* and Vg *bonorum* presuppose טוֹב "good." Tg Syr support MT but add a pronoun, "his goodness." Σ *αγαθωσυνης* "goodness." Read MT.

7.c-c. *BHS* considers this an addition. But it fits the meter and the sense. Keep it.

7.d. MT גמלם "he dealt out to them." LXX *ἡμῖν* "to us" parallels גמלנו "he dealt out to us" earlier in the verse. DSS[Isa] Tg Σ Vg support MT.

9.a. *BHS* and Whybray (257) suggest breaking the verse at this point. But none of the Versions or MSS do this. We follow MT by making both v 8 and 9a tristich units.

9.b. K לא "not." Q לו "to him." AV RSV NIV follow Q. LXX Σ Tg Vg support K. DSS[Isa] לוא could be either. Read K.

9.c. LXX *πρέσβυς* "ambassador" reads צר "affliction" as ציר "envoy" (BDB, 851).

9.d. MT ומלאך פניו "and angel of his presence/face" is pointed as a construct relation. LXX makes "angel" absolute, adds *ἀλλ'* "but," and reads "his face" as *αὐτὸς* "himself." Tg keeps the connection but expands by adding שליח "sent from" to deal with the unusual Heb. phrase. DSS[Isa] Θ Vg support MT. Whybray follows LXX and emends to read "it was no messenger or angel, but his presence which saved them" (cf. Exod 33:14–15). But this requires a *waw* before "presence." The translation follows MT, reading literally.

11.a-a. Omitted in LXX, but present in DSS^Isa Tg Vg.

11.b. Vg Syr add "and." A few MSS of Syr presuppose עבדו "his servant." Stay with MT.

11.c. MT המעלם "the one bringing them" is supported by Tg 'A Σ. DSS^Isa and MS^K המעלה "the one bringing" omit the suffix (as do LXX Θ Syr) taking "shepherds" as the object. Keep MT as the difficult reading.

11.d. LXX γῆς "land." But MT ים "sea" is supported by DSS^Isa and the other Versions.

11.e. MT את, the sign of the direct object. Tg אן "where." MT has two extended questions. Tg has three.

11.f. MT רעי "shepherds of" pl. LXX τὸν ποιμένα "the shepherd" sg. Tg כרעיא "as the shepherd of" sg. Read MT with DSS^Isa Vg.

12.a. DSS^Isa and MS^K omit לו "for himself." But LXX Σ Syr Tg Vg support MT.

12.b. *BHS* suggests deleting עולם on metrical grounds. Not necessary.

13.a. Heb. בתהמות "in the chaotic primeval oceans."

13.b. MT במדבר "in the wilderness." *BHS* suggests כמדבר "like the desert" and moving it prior to "like the horse." But MT makes sense as it stands.

14.a. MT תניחנו "he gave us rest" hiph impf from נוח (BDB, 628). LXX ὡδήγησεν "he led," Vg *ductor* "guide" presuppose the Heb. root נחה (BDB, 634; cf. *BHS*). But Whybray notes correctly that the context and the parallel in Exod 33:14 support MT's derivation.

15.a. MT גְּבוּרֹתֶךָ "your mighty deeds" pl (BDB, 150). LXX Vg read a sg, Heb. גְּבוּרָתֶךָ "your might" (*BHS*). The unpointed DSS^Isa text could be either, since it contains defective as well as *plene* spellings (Kutscher, *Isaiah Scroll,* 134–35). There is little difference in meaning.

15.b-b. אלי התאפקו, lit., "they have restrained themselves to me." The awkward phrase and 1st sg pronoun have prompted various emendations (see *BHS*). LXX ὅτι ἀνέσχου ἡμῶν "because you withheld (them) from us" is followed by many interpreters. But DSS^Isa 'A Σ Θ Vg support MT. MT makes sense and should be kept.

16.a. MT יכירנו impf "recognize us." DSS^Isa הכירנו is pf to match ידענו pf "know us" (Kutscher, *Isaiah Scroll* 352). Read MT.

16.b. DSS^Isa adds הואה "he," thus "you are he." LXX Syr Tg Vg support MT.

17.a. Lit., "from fearing you."

18.a-a. The line is usually considered corrupt and emended in various ways (see *BHS,* Whybray). The problem originated in למצער which is here usually translated "for a little while," though this temporal meaning appears nowhere else (BDB, 859). If translated in its normal meaning, "for a little or insignificant thing," the verse may be read as it stands with an implicit contrast between the lines. See *Comment.*

19.a. MT מעולם "from an age" is supported by DSS^Isa. Vg *quasi in principio* "as in the beginning" presupposes כעולם "as an age." LXX Σ conflate both readings. Read MT.

19.b. *BHS* suggests ending the verse here.

19.c. MT 63:19b–64:11 = EVV (LXX) 64:1–12.

19.d. MT נָזֹלּוּ "they quake" niph from זלל I (BDB, 272). LXX τακήσονται "they will be melted down" and Vg *defluerent* "they flow down" presuppose Heb. נָזְלוּ "they flow down" qal from נזל (BDB, 633). זלל I occurs only here and in 64:2, though Whybray observes that LXX presupposes זלל in Judg 5:5 where MT has נזל! Stay with MT.

64:1.a. המסים is a *hap. leg.* LXX κηρὸς "wax" may have derived it from מסס "melt" (BDB, 587). Σ Θ εκκαυσις "burning heat." Tg רגזך "your anger." Vg *exustio* "conflagration." BDB (243) suggests "brushwood" from a hypothetical root המס. DSS^Isa has עמסים which A. Guillaume ("Some Readings in the Dead Sea Scroll of Isaiah," *JBL* 76 [1957] 42) translates "brushwood" on the basis of Arab *ghamīs* and considers original. Kutscher (*Isaiah Scroll,* 506) prefers MT, noting the frequent confusion of gutturals in DSS^Isa. The meaning of the word remains uncertain.

1.b. DSS^Isa LXX Syr Tg read לצריך "to your adversaries" twice, once with MT and once at the end of the first stich. Σ Θ Vg support MT (Kutscher, *Isaiah Scroll,* 544).

2.a. DSS^Isa omits לא "not." LXX Vg omit the entire phrase.

2.b-b. The second stich is identical to 63:19b and is considered by most interpreters a gloss and deleted. Keep MT. Repetition is common in the Vision.

3.a. MT שמעו "they heard." LXX ἠκούσαμεν "we heard." Tg לא שמעת אודן "ear has not heard" (cf. 1 Cor 2:9). DSS^Isa Vg support MT. *BHS* and other interpreters follow LXX to read שמענו "we heard." Keep MT.

3.b. MT לא האזינו "they did not listen." LXX omits. Tg לא אציתת "nor listened" (but see previous note). Vg *neque auribus perceperunt* "nor did they perceive with ears" and 1 Cor 2:9 οὖς οὐκ ἤκουσεν "ear did not hear" led Duhm, Marti, and *BHS* to suggest לא האזינה אזן "no ear listened" (Pauritsch, *Neue Gemeinde,* 156). But it is not certain that Paul is quoting this verse (see H. Conzelmann, *1 Corinthians,* Hermeneia, tr. J. W. Leitsch [Philadelphia: Fortress, 1975] 63–64). Read MT.

3.c. MT זולתך "except you." The noun זולה means "removal." In constr it acts like a prep "except, only, save that" (BDB, 265).

3.d. MT למחכה sg "for the one waiting." *BHS* follows two Heb. MSS LXX Vg to read למחכי pl "for those waiting." DSS[Isa] supports MT. Read MT.

4.a. *BHS* mentions Grätz's suggestion that לו "if, O that" has fallen out by haplogr.

4.b. MT פגעת "you meet" has led to a variety of translations and emendations (see Pauritsch, *Neue Gemeinde,* 156).

4.c-c. MT את־שש ועשה "the one rejoicing and doing" is supported by DSS[Isa] Vg. LXX τοῖς ποιοῦσι "those doing" leads *BHS* to delete שש "the one rejoicing" and read עשי pl "those doing." Read MT. (Cf. n. 3.d.)

4.d-d. MT בדרכיך יזכרוך "those remembering you in your ways" is supported by DSS[Isa] Vg. LXX καὶ τῶν ὁδῶν σου μνησθήσονται "and they will remember your ways" led *BHS* to read ודרכיך יזכרו. Stay with MT.

4.e-e. Taking הן + pf followed by *waw* consecutives as protasis of conditions "taken-for-granted" (see Watts, *Syntax,* 134), and the following impf as the apodosis. The conditional sentences continue through v 7.

4.f-f. MT בהם עולם ונושע "in them for an age and we will be saved" (= DSS[Isa] Σ Vg). LXX διὰ τοῦτο ἐπλανήθημεν "because of it we strayed." Volz and *BHS* suggest בהעלמך ונרשע "when you hid yourself we behaved wickedly"; Cheyne, Köhler, and Westermann במעלנו ונושע "in our treachery and we will be saved"; Elliger ויחם לבך ונרשה "and your heart became hot and we were guilty." RSV follows MT, but makes the last word a question. MT remains the best.

5.a. MT וַנָּבֶל is a strange form which could be derived from נבל "sink, fade" (so BDB, 615), or בלל "mingle, confuse" (so Whybray), or בול (?). DSS[Isa] ונבולה is from נבל. Though the Versions support DSS[Isa]'s meaning, Kutscher (*Isaiah Scroll,* 262) discounts their evidence since the context forces this meaning anyway. *BHS* follows DSS[Isa] to point וַנִּבֹּל "we fade." Translate "fade" with the context.

5.b. MT עווננו "our iniquity" appears to be sg, though BDB (730) locates as pl (but BDB has added a *yodh*). DSS[Isa] עוונותינו is obviously pl, but in v 6 it duplicates MT's sg. It apparently changed the number here to match the pl verb (see below).

5.c. MT יִשָּׂאֻנוּ "they take us away" qal impf from נשא is supported by DSS[Isa] ישאונו. LXX οἴσει ἡμᾶς "it will take us away" sg. *BHS* suggests יִשָּׂאֵנוּ sg for consistency. DSS[Isa] made the opposite change (see above). In both cases, MT seems the difficult reading. Keep it.

6.a. MT ותמוגנו qal impf "and you melted us" from מוג. DSS[Isa] ותמגדנו from מגד "give as a gift" (so Kutscher, *Isaiah Scroll,* 252, on the basis of an Arab cognate root). LXX Syr Tg Vg all translate with meanings similar to "give," but Kutscher wonders if this is due to their text or the context. BDB (556), GKC § 72*cc,* and *BHS* suggest ותמגננו piel from מגן "deliver" (BDB, 171). Keep MT as the difficult reading.

7.a. MT עתה, DSS[Isa] אתה: Kutscher points out "laryngeals and pharyngeals were indistinguishable in the dialect of the scribe of the Scr." (*Isaiah Scroll,* 508; see 507). The same exchange occurs in 5:5; 28:22.

7.b. MT ידך "your hand." DSS[Isa] LXX Vg read pl, "your hands."

9.a. ערי קדשך pl "your holy cities" is unusual. LXX πόλις τοῦ ἁγίου σου "city of your holy one," also Vg. DSS[Isa] supports MT.

9.b. MT שממה "desolation." DSS[Isa] שוממה "being desolate." See n. 62:4.b above.

10.a,a. MT היה sg "it has become." DSS[Isa] reads both היו pl, perhaps because of מחמדינו "our pleasant places."

10.b. MT מחמדינו pl "our pleasant places" followed by a sg היה "it has become." DSS[Isa] LXX also pl. Syr Tg Eth Arab make the noun sg.

Form/Structure/Setting

The scene is a formal unity but contains a mixture of genres. The most frequently identified genre is that of Communal Lament (Hanson, Pauritsch,

Westermann, et al). Signs of this genre are present, particularly in 63:15–64:1, 9–11). However, the controlling genre is that of the sermon-prayer which is well known from Deuteronomy and Chronicles. This shows itself in 63:7–14, 64:3[4]–8[9].

The scene begins with a recital introduced by אזכיר "I will bring to remembrance." Remembering, both on God's part and on that of his people, is a major element in worship, religious education, and exhortation in the OT (see *Comment*). The recital will speak of things from a previous age (ימי עולם). Deut 32:7 provides a key statement for this part of the genre in combining the two words: "memorialize days of (that) age." The two words are repeated in this scene: זכר in 63:7, 11; 64:4(5), 8(9); עולם in 63:9, 11, 12, 16, 19; 64:3(4), 4(5).

The recital in 63:7–9 is positive throughout. It speaks of חסדי יהוה "Yahweh's acts of covenant loyalty," of תהלת יהוה "Yahweh's praises," of "goodness" and of "compassion." It continues the positive recital with "my people," "sons," and "Savior." It recognizes periods of "affliction" but insists that God shared them with his people and eventually "saved them."

An outline of the scene which shows the two genres looks like this (the sermon/prayer on the outer margin and the lament indented):

The Recital (63:7–14)
- A. God's compassionate acts of "that age" (vv 7–9)
- B. But they rebelled (v 10)
- C. Then he remembered "that age" (vv 11–14)

Complaints that interrupt (63:15–64:11[12])
1. Look down from heaven and see! (v 15a)
2. Where is your zeal and valor now? (v 15b)
3. You are our father (too)! (v 16a)
4. And ours, too, from that age on! (v 16b)
5. Why did you make us stray? (v 17a)
6. Return the tribes of your inheritance! (v 17b)
7. Our adversaries trod down your holy place! (v 18)
8. We are from that age—but not they! (v 19a)
9. If only you would come down (v 19b [1])
10. To make nations tremble before you (v 1 [2])
11. When you did come down, mountains quaked (v 2 [3])

The Recital continued (64:3–8[4–9])
- D. From that age until now—no God except you (vv 3–4a [4–5a])
- E. If you have been angry and we have sinned, you are still our father; regard us all as your people (vv 4b–8 [5b–9])

12. Your city is destroyed. Can you restrain yourself? (vv 9–11 [10–12])

At first glance, the sermon appears to be a conventional deuteronomic sermon. But key phrases, on closer scrutiny, turn out to be new and unique formulations of deuteronomic themes. These include: "the angel of his presence saved them"; "offended his holy spirit"; "shepherds of his flock"; "established them in his presence"; "his holy spirit"; "Yahweh's spirit gave them rest"; and "to make himself a glorious name." The sermon is composed in a style apparently intended to reflect levitical preaching, but it does so with the inimitable originality that is typical of the Vision.

The sermon/prayer (63:7–14 and 64:3–8) follows the style and manner of the levitical sermons and prayers in Deut 4–11, in DtH and in Chronicles, Ezra-Nehemiah (see G. von Rad, "The Levitical Sermon in I and II Chronicles," *The Problem of the Hexateuch and Other Essays* [London: SCM, 1966] 267–80; N. Lohfink, *Das Hauptgebot,* AnBib 20 [Rome: Pont. Bib. Inst., 1963]). Israel's psalms provide a number of parallel uses of history (Pss 44, 74, 79, 106; Exod 15; Deut 32). Prayers in 1 Kgs 8:12–21, 23–53, 56–61; 1 Chr 17:16–27; 29:10–19; 2 Chr 6:14–42; 20:6–12; 30:6–9; Ezra 9:6–15; Neh 1:4–11; 9:5–37; and Dan 9:4–19 show similar format and deal with similar themes. In particular, Deut 32:7 "remember days of old" sets the same theme. The sermon/prayer cites God's actions and attitudes in the age of salvation (of Moses and the Exodus) as a model for current faith and prayer. It cites God's gracious acts of that age and then notes that there was rebellion and sin, even in that time (the wilderness period). It then goes on to remind them that in repenting, remembrance of that age of salvation paved the way for forgiveness and renewal. The prayer confesses that there is no other god who does this, before closing with an appeal that urges God in the present moment to accept them all as his people. The sermon/prayer appeals to an "all Israel" tradition (Deuteronomy-2 Kings) to present a prayer for unity as well as for forgiveness.

But interruptions (63:15–64:2[3] and 64:9–11[10–12]) try to turn the occasion into one of accusations against God and of sectarian complaints. (The genre of "lament" is usually attributed to the entire section. See Westermann, and Hanson, *Dawn of Apocalyptic,* 81–100. Pauritsch [*Neue Gemeinde*] calls vv 7–14 a historical psalm.) In some of them the perspective has changed from God who works in history to God who comes down from heaven (63:15a and 19b–64:2 [64:1–3]), from a concern for all to sectarian appeals on behalf of various segments of the community. Various phrases from the sermon, such as people, father-children, that age, etc., are twisted to serve their interests. The complaints illustrate the fragmented nature of the Jerusalem community of this period.

The setting for the scene is the same as in Scene 1 (62:1–7) when there was a call for continuous prayer for the safety of Jerusalem. A levitical preacher recites God's saving acts from of old and the way in which reminders of those times become a basis for repentance and forgiveness that is acceptable to God. But the crowd is in no mood for spiritual sermons, breaking into the prayer with complaints, claims, and demands in prayer form to state their own sectarian views.

Perhaps Zadokite priests speak out of their Zionist views in 63:15 and 19b–64:2 (64:1–3) when they say that Yahweh descends on Zion. Are they also the ones who claim Yahweh as father through David's use of them as priests in Jerusalem in spite of their non-Israelite origin although "Abraham did not know them, or Israel recognize them"; or are these the people of the land? (See 2 Sam 15:24–37, 1 Kgs 1:22–39; 2:35; R. W. Corney, "Zadok the Priest," *IDB* 4:928–29. See also Ezek 40–48 and P. D. Hanson, *Dawn of Apocalyptic* 148–49, *et passim.*) Perhaps Zadokites, too, should be credited with the particular plea for Jerusalem and the temple in 64:9–11[10–12]. Levites who are proud of their roots in Abrahamic lineage protest that they especially are Yahweh's concern in 63:16b and 19a. Someone representing the concerns of Israelites other than Judeans and Levites prays for God to return the tribes of Yahweh's inheritance (63:17b). Someone else identifies himself with Yahweh's people and complains that their "adversaries" have trodden down his holy place (63:18). The terms are vague. It is not clear whether the "holy place" is Palestine or Zion and whether the "adversaries" are Zadokites or others. A political activist appeals for God to make "the nations to tremble before you" (64:1[2]). There are evident signs of disunity and of rivalry between groups for exclusive recognition as Yahweh's people. This contrasts with the concern of the preacher for "all of us."

The references to the burnt ruins of the Temple (64:10[11]) have usually led interpreters to date this chapter before the rebuilding of the Temple in 515 B.C. The possibility that the Temple buildings lie destroyed and charred late in the following century is opened by the report given to Nehemiah (Neh 1:3) in 445 B.C., although the Temple is not specifically mentioned. J. Morgenstern has contended for one or more desolations of Zion and the Temple in numerous writings (see above). The worshipers may be exaggerating the conditions, since they do not recognize any of the work that Yahweh has had done there in the post-exilic period.

Comment

7 *Yahweh's acts of covenant loyalty* (חסדי יהוה) serves as a title to the sermon. The nature of the sermon is more clearly noted by אזכיר "I will bring to remembrance" or "I will memorialize" (for this same form see Pss 45:18; 71:16; and 77:12). זכר "remember" and חסד "covenant loyalty" appear together also in Pss 25:6 and 98:3. The root זכר "remember" is important in the OT and has received renewed attention from P. A. H. de Boer, *Gedenken und Gedächtnis in der Welt des Alten Testaments*, Franz Delitzsch Lectures (1960; Stuttgart: Kohlhammer, 1962); G. Rinaldi, "Zakar," *BeO* 5 (1963) 112–14; and W. Schottroff, *"Gedenken" im Alten Orient und in AT,* WMANT 15 (Neukirchen-Vluyn: Neukirchener Verlag, 1964). Remembering what God has done was an important religious exercise and aid to faith. חסד "covenant loyalty" is also an important word in the OT. In the plural it must refer to specific instances or acts. The root has also had its share of attention (see Zobel, "חסד hesed," *TWAT* 3:48–71, for a review of literature and the range of possible meanings). In this context it is parallel to תהלת יהוה "Yahweh's praises" which in unique in the OT and to טוב "goodness." The word is repeated at the end of the verse.

These are understood to have been done *to us.* The speaker identifies himself and his audience with the recipients of those gracious acts, although they were performed in an earlier age. He further identifies the recipients of God's goodness as *the house of Israel.* In some contexts this may refer to the royal dynasty of Northern Israel. But here it can only be a synonym for "the children of Israel." It serves to narrow the focus of his review of God's acts in salvation history to Israel and its origins. A further word describes these acts: רחמים "compassion." The review stresses the positive aspects of God's relation to his people.

8 *Surely, they are my people.* God identified himself with them expecting only good responses from them: they are *children who will not deal falsely. So he became their savior.* The precise events are not yet defined. These may cover the themes of the Exodus and of Sinai. A great portion of the ensuing discussion will try to determine who are the legitimate heirs of the designation as Yahweh's *people* and *children,* and recipients of his *salvation.*

9 This verse describes a honeymoon period in God's relation to Israel. They had afflictions, but not from Yahweh. This may refer to the wilderness journey. Hosea also saw this period as a honeymoon (Hos 2:14–20). *The angel of his face* (or "of his presence") is unique. The more usual term is "the angel (or messenger) of Yahweh." "The presence of Yahweh" is used in the accounts of the wilderness journey.

God's providential care is reflected in the words *saved, redeemed,* and *carried. The days of that age* sets that ancient time apart from the present of the speaker. עולם "that age" is used repeatedly in the scene. It designates that period of salvation history as an example for doctrine and faith. It will also be used to separate those whose ancestry can be traced to that time from those who have been grafted onto the tree of Israel's life at a later time. Memorializing that age is a typical device of Deuteronomy and the Pentateuch for teaching and for eliciting faith.

10 *But they rebelled* introduces the second part of Deuteronomy's theology of sacred history. God's goodness is met with Israel's stiff-necked refusal. *His holy spirit,* like *the angel of his face,* is evidence of God's presence and his agent of providential leading, salvation, and redemption. But Israel even in that ancient age rebuffed them.

So God *turned around.* Instead of being their supporter and protector he became their *enemy. He fought against them.* The deuteronomic doctrine of retribution is evident here. God's personal involvement with his people is evident positively in his leading and negatively in his judgment.

11 *Then he remembered.* Memory is a regular motivation attributed to God. When he remembers Abraham, he moves to get Israel out of Egypt (Exod 2:24). In this case he remembers the age of *Moses* and *his people.* From the time of Josiah (2 Kgs 23:25) Moses' relation to the Torah and the Covenant caused his name to become more familiar and more important as the Torah, especially Deuteronomy, had become more important. By this time both the adherents to Deuteronomy (Levites and others) and the ones that depended upon Leviticus (the priests) revered Moses and his age.

Who asks the questions beginning with *where?* Apparently it is a rhetorical device used by the preacher. Repeatedly in Israel's history these questions had been asked. If God remembers, why doesn't he do it again. *The one bringing them from the sea* could refer to Moses or to Yahweh. *The shepherds* must refer to all those leaders of the Exodus generation. *Establishing them in his presence* seems to refer to Sinai and the making of covenant. *His holy spirit* is a rare phrase in the OT, but it appeared above in v 10 as the one *offended* by rebellious Israelites.

12 The attention then turns unambiguously to Yahweh. Where is he who supported Moses, *dividing the waters . . . to make a name for himself in that age?* The use of עשה "make" with God's name appears only here and in v 14 below. It declares that God's purpose in saving Israel went beyond his concern for her per se. He expected his deeds on Israel's behalf to be a witness for him to others, that is, to build his reputation among the nations.

13 *One leading them in the ocean depths* appears to still refer to the crossing of the sea. תהמות "ocean depths" is used as a parallel to "sea" in Exod 15:5. The reference to *the wilderness* extends the metaphor of providential leading in the wilderness experience.

14 The metaphor for entry into the land of Canaan is *like cattle when they go down into the valley. Rest* is the result, as it is in Josh 23:1, of Yahweh's gift, this time through his *spirit.* The sermon has covered the period when Yahweh had led Israel out of Egypt, to Sinai, through the wilderness, and into Canaan.

The sermon becomes a prayer when in second person he says: *Thus you led your people.* The third-person references to God had been accompanied in vv 7–14a with first person plural identification of the worshiping community with the age of salvation. Now, in prayer, the near reference is impersonal. Again God's motive in salvation *to make a glorious name* for himself comes to the fore.

15 *Look from heaven!* The perspective changes. Thus far God is seen as moving within the continuum of history. Now the perspective is vertical. He is in heaven looking down or coming down to his people. This first response to the sermon reflects a sense that God has not been a part of their experience but has simply looked on from his *holy* and *glorious dwelling.*

Where is picks up the cry of the sermon's illustration from Israel's earlier experience to express the sense of lacking divine presence and intervention in the current scene. קנאתך "your zeal" and גבורתך "your valor" are terms of war and violence. They imply that God has not unleashed the spectacular forces of heaven and nature or his fiery divine violence to aid Judah and Jerusalem. The respondent misses evidence of God's *yearning heart* and his *compassion* from his own experience. In this he has picked up the references to Yahweh's compassion for his people in the times of Moses (v 7) but has no testimony to a similar experience in his own day. He accuses God in saying these *have been withheld* from him.

16 *For you are our father* picks up the theme of the sermon from v 8 which has God speak of ancient Israel as his "children." The anguished cry wants to claim that the relation to ancient Israel should apply to them also across all the intervening centuries. It is the cry of one who represents a group not normally identified with ancient Israel of twelve tribes, as the following qualifying clauses show. *Abraham does not know us* confesses that they cannot claim to be descended from Abraham. Who, in Jerusalem *ca.* 440 B.C. could this be? Is it one of "the people of the land," persons brought to occupy sections of northern Israel under the empires (2 Kgs 17:24–28) who learned to worship at Yahweh sanctuaries (cf. Zech 7:1–3)? The Zadokite priests would also fit this classification, but not the one that follows. *Israel does not recognize us* complains of a current disenfranchisement. This points to the people of the land (see Zech 7:4–14, Ezra 4:1–3) who Ezra and Nehemiah also excluded from cooperation or marriage with Israelites. The verse shows the diversity of persons seeking to work and worship in Jerusalem at this time. The Vision calls for openness toward them. Other leaders suspected them and refused cooperation.

A group of direct descendants of Israel from the Exodus on claims Yahweh as their *redeemer from that age.* They want God to recognize that he is *their father,* perhaps implying "only theirs."

17 *Why . . . did you make us stray* represents still another view. This response recognizes no guilt for sin. Yahweh is responsible for their errant ways, not they. He must be the reason their *hearts were hardened.* He caused them *not to fear him.* This view stands in direct contradiction to the sermon and to deuteronomist theology as well as that of the Vision. The meeting has gotten out of hand. All kinds of wrong views are being expressed.

As long as anything goes in this prayer, a worshiper presents the case for returning all Palestine to the descendants of the original tribes: *Return the tribes of your inheritance.* There have been references in the Vision to settling land right claims in Judah and in the surroundings of Jerusalem. But this brings up excessive issues of rights to land.

For the sake of your servants. Who are these who claim to be Yahweh's servants? עבדים "servants" has been used in the vision from 54:17b where it also appeared in connection with "inheritance." This stands in contrast to the use of the singular form "servant" in chaps. 40–54. But the question in these latter chapters has been: who are the legitimate "servants of Yahweh?" These prayers demonstrate the problem of getting an answer to that issue and chap. 65 will turn to deal with it directly. These claimants to being Yahweh's servants are apparently also the ones who plead for a *return* of *the tribes of his inheritance.* Perhaps they are best seen as those who belonged to Northern Israel and who went into Assyrian exile in 732 and 721 B.C.

18 למצער "a matter of no consequence" is a word that stresses something insignificant or small. This is the only instance in which BDB and most translations think it is used of time, translating "for a little while." The verse is controlled by the two second personal pronouns related to the word קדש "holy": "your holy people" and "your holy place." Two statements are juxtaposed: "your holy people inherit (or possess)" and "our adversaries tread down your holy place." And למצער "a matter of no consequence" is prefixed to the first. In either a questioning or accusing tone someone compares the two issues with the implication that the first is being trivialized. Jerusalemites are insisting that their issue relating to the Temple be given priority over claims to inheritances in all of Palestine. The pronoun *our* identifies the speakers as Jerusalemites.

19 *We are from (that) age.* The *age* in question is that of Moses. The Israelites assert their rights in terms of their lineage.

You have never ruled over them. The implication is that they were never subjects to Yahweh's kingship. Whether this refers to the kind of kingship that Samuel claimed for the tribal confederacy (1 Sam 8:7; 12:12) or whether this refers to Yahweh's rule through David and in the Temple service as the Psalms present it is not clear. Here it is taken as the latter and thus understood as a retort of Jerusalemites against the Israelites.

Your name has never been pronounced over them. This appears to be a reference to covenant-making and its conclusion which sealed the relation between

Yahweh and his people Israel. The taunt continues the accusations and claims being made in prayers. It is spoken by Israelites claiming the priority of covenant privilege over Zion's claims.

19b[64:1] The pleas turn again to those who think in the vertical dimension. *If only you would cleave the heavens and come down.* They see the problem in God's transcendence. They sense nothing of his work and presence in the current scene. They think only of spectacular supernatural happenings as signs of his presence. *Mountains* are metaphors for all that they sense as great, imposing, and oppressive. As at Sinai and later in Zion's ritual, the signs of God's presence will cause all powers and authorities *to quake.*

64:1[2] *Fire* becomes the second metaphor for God's direct intervention. *Fire* makes things happen. *Bushes* burn and *water boils.* This is interpreted for their times: *to make your name known to your adversaries.* This touches a legitimate issue in the Vision and elsewhere in prophecy. But the major concern had been for Israel and Judah to recognize Yahweh and his work so that they could become witnesses to his name and his will. Here they are pleading for a new revelation which will particularly impress their adversaries.

To make nations tremble before you. Nationalists yearn for renewed political power through Yahweh's acts and the acknowledgment of his name. The Vision is more concerned with people from the nations appearing in his Temple as worshiping pilgrims.

2[3] *When you did* is a nostalgic reference to the "mighty acts of old." In those days *you came down.* The prayer asks, why not again? In those days *mountains quaked,* meaning Pharaoh and the Palestinian cities.

3[4] The preacher regains control of the tumultous prayer. He puts the relation between *that age* and the present into perspective. In that time there was no competing revelation. Israel's attention turned to God alone. But there was a clear focus on those to whom he is available. He *works for one who waits for him.* The negative implication is: not for the impatient activist. *You meet with the joyful.* The negative implication is: not with the sorrowful and lamenting (see 58:1–9; Zech 7:1–19). *With one who is doing right.* The negative implication is: not with those doing evil. *Who remember your ways.* That is what this sermon was supposed to do (see 63:7), but instead of *remembering* in praise and thanks they let their memories lead to recrimination, accusation, lament, and rivalry.

4b[5b] Having claimed God's attention on behalf of these acceptable worshipers, the liturgist uses the memory of sacred history to make his point. *In those ancient times* the people who were under judgment for sin *could still be saved.*

5[6] A confession of sin and guilt that has left the people like a dried leaf or *soiled underclothes* still leaves the door open to forgiveness, to *our iniquities being lifted like the wind.*

6[7] The confession broadens to include indifference to worship and to God in face of God's having *hidden his face* from them. The verse recognizes the circular interaction of sin that leads to judgment that leads to further sin. But it also recognizes another effect of God's withdrawal of himself from the stubborn and rebellious people. He has thus *melted us down by means of our iniquities.* He implies that the burden of judgment prepares them to be less resilient in rebellion, more prepared to finally recognize and accept God.

7[8] The climax is introduced with ועתה "now." (See A. Laurentine, "*Weattah—kai nun.* Formule caracteristique des textes juridiques [a propos de Jean 17,5]," *Bib* 45 (1964) 168–97; H. A. Brongers, "Bemerkungen zum Gebrauch des adverbialen we'attah im Alten Testament," *VT* 15 [1965] 269–99.) This marks the critical point in the prayer. It claims: *You are still our father.* The words are the same as those in 63:16, but the intention is very different. The identity of those praying is comprehensive as the "all of us" in v 5[6] and at the end of this verse show. The prayer picks up the theme from the sermon on the age of salvation (63:7) to claim identity with the chosen and saved people for the entire diverse congregation in Jerusalem of the 5th century. It confesses and claims: *All of us are the work of your hand.* The theme of *clay* and *potter* draws on Jer 18 as well as earlier references in the Vision (29:16; 30:14; 41:25).

8[9] The plea for mercy brings the prayer to its climax on the theme with which the sermon began: *Consider all of us to be your people!* To that end he pleads for God to end his anger and judgment of their iniquity.

9[10] The prayer is properly ended. But an activist for Jerusalem and the temple adds a second prayer in a very different spirit. His concern is not the spiritual condition of God's people, but the physical and political condition of Jerusalem. *Your holy cities* is clearly plural, probably including other places in Palestine where Yahweh's presence had been known like Bethel and Shechem. But then it focuses specifically on the desolate condition of *Zion/Jerusalem.*

10[11] *Our holy and beautiful building where our fathers praised you.* This provides a precise description. But which building and which fathers? Is this a reference to Solomon's temple with the *fathers* referring to those of the united monarchy and the kingdom of Judah from the 10th to the 6th centuries? No temple of post-exilic age matched the extent of Solomon's temple and undoubtedly portions of the old temple were still in ruins at this time. Or does this refer to Zerubbabel's reconstruction and to the worship under Joshua, the high priest, and the prophets, Zechariah and Haggai? If so, this would imply a recent devastation and burning as Morgenstern and others have suggested. In either case, the appeal senses a lack in Jerusalem that demands God's intervention.

11[12] He cries with great emotion: *Will you restrain yourself concerning these, Yahweh?* A second question in accusation follows: *Will you be silent while you afflict us so much?* With these the series of questions following the model of the sermon in 63:11 and continuing in vv 15 and 17 is brought to an end.

Explanation

The scene presents a beautiful and theologically meaningful sermon/prayer in the style of levitical preaching of that period. Memorializing the great deeds of salvation in that ancient age of Moses provides a theological basis for a prayer which acknowledges the state of sin and judgment and yet pleads for God's mercy that will allow all of the diverse elements of the community to be recognized by God as his people and eligible for his mercy.

However, the prayer is preempted by those with special sectarian concerns which eventually lead to accusations within their prayers against other factions. There are those who would pray exclusively for Jerusalem. There are others that would pray for redemption for all the twelve tribes in Israel. There are those whose sole concern is the Temple and their rights there. There are others who feel that only descendants of the original covenant community should receive God's attention and blessing. There are activists that demand a return to political power and military strength that will win the respect of the nations. The scene closes with the shouted prayers of Zionists that claim God's attention to a restoration of Zion.

All the parties ignore God's work with the people in the post-exilic period which has been the center of the Vision's concern from chap. 40 onward. There is no willingness to recognize the Persian policies toward Jerusalem as the work of Yahweh. There is no hint that Yahweh has shown his concern for his people in the work of Zerubbabel and Ezra, or in the prophecies of Haggai and Zechariah, or in the presence of teachers and preachers of Torah. They all think only in terms of what God did once long ago and pray for a return to that kind of action as they imagine it.

Scene 4: Yahweh's Great Day: A New Jerusalem (65:1—66:24)

Bibliography

Achtemeier, E. *The Community and Message,* 121–51. **Aus, R. D.** "God's Plan and God's Power: Isaiah 66 and the Restraining Factors of 2 Thess 2, 6–7." *JBL* 96 (1977) 537–53. **Baldacci, M.** "Due antecedente storici in Is. 65." *BeO* 20 (1978) 198–91. **Bouma, H.** *De droom van Jesaja* (*65:17–25*). Kampen: J. H. Kok. **Causse, A.** "Le Myth de la nouvelle Jerusalem du Deutero-Esaie a la IIIe Sibylle." *RHPR* 18 (1938) 377–414. **Esaman, C. M.** "The Body and Eternal Life (Jes. 66, 7–8)." *Horae Soederblomianae* (1946) 33–104. **Hanson, P. D.** *The Dawn of Apocalyptic.* 134–85. **Heerboth, L. A.** " 'New Creation' According to Is. 65." *CTM* 5 (1934) 29–37. **Jefferson, G. H.** "Notes on the Authorship of Isaiah 65 and 66." *JBL* 68 (1949) 225–30. **Lü Ch'ang-ch'üen.** "Yelusaleng te lienching ho huanghsin" (Is 66:1–16). *ColcTFujen* 830 (1976) 465–74. **Lupieri, E.** "Agostino e Ireneo." *VC* 15 (1978) 113–15. **Martin-Achard, R.** "L'espérance des croyants d'Israël face à la mort selon Esaïe 65, 16c–25 et selon Daniel 12:1–4." *RHPR* 59 (1979) 439–51. **Mauser, U.** "Isaiah 65:17–25." *Int* 36 (1982) 181–86. **Monaci Castagno, A.** " 'Un nuovo cielo ed una nuova terra'. L'esegesi di Is 65, 17 e 66, 22 nei Padri." *Augustinianum* 22 (1982) 337–48. **Pauritsch, K.** *Die Neue Gemeinde.* 171–218. **Pythian-Adams, W. J.** "The Mystery of the New Creation." *CQR* 142 (1946) 61–77. **Rinaldi, G.** "Gli 'scampati' di Is. 66, 18–22." *À la recontre de Dieu: Memorial A. Gelin.* Le Puy: X. Mappus (1961) 109–18. **Rofé, A.** "Isaiah 66:1–4: Judean Sects in the Persian Period According to Trito-Isaiah." *Esel Beer-Sheba,* peraqim 2. Beersheba: Ben Gurion Negev University, 1980, 27–37 = *Biblical and Related Studies.* FS Iwry.

Winona Lake, IN: Eisenbrauns, 1985. 205–18. **Sasson, J. M.** "Isaiah lxvi 3–4a." *VT* 26 (1976) 199–207. **Sehmsdorf, E.** "Studien zur Redaktionsgeschichte von Jesaja 55–66 (I): Jes 65, 16b–25; 66, 1–4; 56, 1–8; (II): Jes 66, 17–24." *ZAW* 84 (1972) 517–76. **Smart, J. D.** "A New Interpretation of Isaiah 66, 1–6." *ExpTim* 46 (1934/35) 420–24. **Viret, P.** *Quatre sermons français sur Es 65.* Ed. H. Meylan. Lausanne: Payot, 1961. **Watts, J. D. W.** "The Heavenlies of Isaiah." Diss. Louisville: Southern Baptist Theological Seminary, 1948.

Form/Structure/Setting

Chaps. 65–66 form a thematic unity. They are set in the great hall of the heavenly king with Jerusalem and its struggling parties visible alongside it. A number of Yahweh's speeches are introduced with the formulas of the court. In other books these might imply a prophet's presentation of Yahweh's words. But there is no prophet here. These are to be seen as the formal signs that the heavenly court is in session and that Yahweh's pronouncements are being delivered in a formal manner.

Yahweh presents a progress report on the Jerusalem project and announces its completion. He also reports on how he is dealing with the complaining rebels in Jerusalem.

Although the unity of the chapters is evident, there are inner shifts in emphasis. In 65:1–16 Yahweh addresses his court and those in Jerusalem who have opposed his Vision. In 65:17–66:5 he speaks impersonally about his goals for Jerusalem without reference to either his opponents or his servants. In 66:6–24 the reality of his accomplished Vision moves into the foreground. There are no "gardens" for the idolatrous. There are no "sacrifices" for the priests. There is uproar as Yahweh deals with his enemies (vv 2b–6, 14d–16, 17, 24). Zion gives birth to her children of the new age (vv 7–14c). Zion's purpose is achieved: worshipers from all nations and tongues may gather, some become priests, and all worship Yahweh (vv 18–24). For the purpose of making the size of the unit manageable, these will be treated as three episodes of this great final scene.

Episode A: Yahweh Deals with His Opponents (65:1–16). His court is prominent. The adversaries are "on stage" and clearly visible as they are addressed. Yahweh's servants are in the background and are not addressed. (Note that neither Persia nor any historical leaders appear. Whereas many parties were evident in the last scene, here there are only two groups in Jerusalem: Yahweh's foes and Yahweh's servants.)

Episode B: Yahweh Moves to Finish His New Jerusalem (65:17–66:5). Yahweh's court is at the center of this part. The skyline of the new city is clear in the background, but the groups of persons who vie for control of the city fade into insignificance. It is a new world in which this new city comes to life. Yahweh's ideals echo the thoughts of 11:6–9 and 35:1–10.

Episode C: Yahweh Confirms His Servants in His New City (66:6–24). The realities of the rebuilt city return to view. The radical departures from the past are stressed in the uproar that results from Yahweh's dealing with his foes (vv 14d–16, 17, 24). But Zion gives birth (vv 7–14c) just as had been promised in chap. 54. And Yahweh gathers all nations to Jerusalem, chooses some of them as priests, to worship before him (vv 18–24) to fulfill the purpose he stated in 2:1–4. With this the Vision is complete.

Episode A:
Yahweh Deals with His Opponents (65:1–16)

Translation

Yahweh: (to the heavenly court)	1 *I let myself be consulted*[a] *by those who have not asked*[b] *(to do so).*	3+3
	I let myself be found[a] *by those who have not looked for me.*	
	I say: Here I am! Here I am!	3+3
	to a nation that has not called[c] *me by my name.*	
	2 *I spread out my hand all day*	3+2
	toward a rebellious[a] *people*	
	who are walking in ways that are not good	3+2
	after their own thoughts:	
	3 *the people who are provoking me*	3+2
	to my face, continually,	
	[a]*sacrificing in the gardens,*	2+2
	[b]*burning incense on the tiles,*[b]	
	4 *sitting in the tombs*	2+2
	and lodging between rocks,[a]	
	eating swine's flesh	3+3
	and who have a broth[b] *of polluted things in their vessels,*[c]	
	5 *saying, "Go, be by yourself.*	3+3+2
	Do not come near[a] *me.*	
	I am set apart from you.[b]*"*	
	These are smoke in my nostrils,	3+3
	a fire burning all day.	
	6 *See! It is written before me.*	3
	I will not keep silent.[a]	2+2+2
	Rather I will repay.[b]	
	[c]*Yes, I will repay on their bodies.*[c]	
	7 *Your iniquities*[a] *and the iniquities of your fathers*[a] *together,*	4+2
Herald:	*says Yahweh,*	
Yahweh:	*which they burned as incense on the mountains*	3+2
	and on the hills they reproached me,	
	[b]*I measure their earlier doing on their bodies.*[b]	4
Herald:	8 *Thus says Yahweh:*	3
Yahweh:	*As the wine is found in the cluster*	4+3+3

and one says, Do not destroy it
for there may be a blessing in it,
so I will do for my servants' sake 4+3
in order not to destroy the whole (lot).
9 *I will being out a seed from Jacob* 3+3
and from Judah an heir to my mountains.
And my chosen will inherit it[a] 2+3
and my servants will live there.
10 *And the Sharon will become a sheep-pasture* 4+4+3
and the Achor valley for cattle to lie down
for my people who seek me out.
(to those in Jerusalem who prayed) 11 *But you who are forsaking Yahweh,* 3+3
who are forgetting the mount of my holiness,
who are arranging[a] *a table for Fortune* 3+3
and who are filling cups of wine for Fate,
12 *I assign you*[a] *to the sword* 3+3
and all of you will bow for the slaughter.
Because I called, but you (pl) did not answer. 4+3
I spoke, but you (pl) did not listen.
So you (pl) did evil in my eyes 3+3
and you (pl) chose that in which I took no pleasure.
Herald: 13 *Therefore, thus says my Lord Yahweh:*[a] 4
Yahweh: *See! My servants will eat,* 3+2
but you (pl) will be hungry.
See! My servants will drink, 3+2
but you (pl) will be thirsty.
See! My servants will rejoice, 3+2
but you (pl) will be put to shame.
14 *See! My servants will sing* 3+2
from a glad heart,
but you (pl) will cry because of a pained heart 4+3
and because of an anguished[a] *spirit you will wail.*
15 *And you (pl) will leave your (pl) name* 2+2
for a curse to my chosen.
Earth: *When my Lord Yahweh kills you (sg)* 3+4
and [a]*calls his servants*[a] *another name,*[b]
Heavens: 16 *which one who blesses himself in the land (will use)* 3+3
(when) he blesses himself by the God of truth,[a]
Earth: *and (which) the one who swears in the land (will use)* 2+3
(when) he swears by the God of truth.
Yahweh: *For the former troubles will be forgotten* 4+3
when they are hid from my eyes.

Notes

1.a-a. On this use of niph, see GKC § 51*c*.

1.b. MT שאלו "they ask." DSS^{Isa} שאלוני "they ask for me," supported by LXX Syr Tg and Rom 10:20, makes explicit what MT implies.

1.c. MT לֹא קֹרָא pual pf "it is not called." LXX *οἱ οὐκ ἐκάλεσαν* "who did not call." Vg *quae non invocabat* "who did not call." *BHS* correctly suggests לֹא קָרָא qal pf "has not called."

2.a. MT סוֹרֵר "rebellious." DSS^{Isa} סורה (?), less likely מורה "disobedient" though Kutscher (*Isaiah Scroll,* 269–70) wonders if the former reading is a combination of MT and the latter, which appear together in Deut 21:18, 20; Jer 5:23; Ps 78:8. LXX in fact conflates the two: *ἀπειθοῦντα καὶ ἀντιλέγοντα* "rebellious and disobedient." Whybray would therefore add ומורה for a better meter. Keep MT.

3.a. DSS^{Isa} LXX add המה "they." Syr Tg omit with MT.

3.b-b. MT ומקטרים על הלבנים "and burning incense on the tiles." DSS^{Isa} וינקו ידים על האבנים "they suck (from ינק) hands upon the rocks" (maybe "they clean" from נקה, but nowhere else in qal; cf. BDB, 667). Kutscher postulates a long series of corruptions to explain DSS^{Isa}'s reading, but still calls it "not understandable" (*Isaiah Scroll,* 216, 243). LXX adds *τοῖς δαιμονίοις ἃ οὐκ ἔστι* "to the demons who do not exist," but otherwise follows MT. Tg Vg (cf. Syr) support MT.

4.a. MT בנצורים "in guarded places" qal pass ptcp from נצר (BDB, 665 I). LXX *ἐν τοῖς σπηλαίοις* "in caves." M. Dahood ("Textual Problems in Isaiah," *CBQ* 22 [1960] 408–9) divides the word to read בן צורים "in between rocks" (so *BHS*) which fits the context best.

4.b. K פרק "a fragment" is a *hap. leg.* (BDB, 830). Q מרק "a broth" (BDB, 600 II; cf. Judg 6:19, 20) is supported by DSS^{Isa} LXX Tg Vg. Read Q.

4.c. MT כליהם "their vessels." DSS^{Isa} בכליהמה "in their vessels," followed by Tg Vg.

5.a. MT תגש is from נגש "come near" (BDB, 620). DSS^{Isa} תגע is from נגע "touch" (BDB, 619). Kutscher (*Isaiah Scroll,* 263; cf. 553) explains DSS^{Isa}'s substitution as the clear meaning in context. The Versions support MT (though see Kutscher, 263). Read MT.

5.b. MT קְדַשְׁתִּיךָ qal "I am set apart from you." *BHS* and others point קִדַּשְׁתִּיךָ piel "I set you apart" (see Whybray). Both meanings are ambiguous. See *Comment.*

6.a. L אחשה is obscure. Can it be related to יחש "genealogy" (BDB, 405)? Many MSS have a *shin,* אחשה "I will be silent, inactive" (BDB, 364; see 64:11[12]) which is presupposed by LXX Tg Vg and appears appropriate.

6.b. LXX Syr Eth delete. DSS^{Isa} supports MT as do Vg's synonyms, *sed reddam et retribuam* "but I will give back and return." Tg paraphrases. Keep MT.

6.c-c. *BHS* recommends deleting because the sentence is continued in v 7. But the ancient witnesses have it.

7.a-a. MT has 2d pl suffs. LXX Syr have 3d pl. DSS^{Isa} Tg Vg support MT.

7.b-b. *BHS,* Whybray, and others have proposed various emendations, but without textual support. Keep MT.

9.a. *BHS* emends to וירשום "and they will inherit them." LXX omits the pron. Tg Vg support MT's sg pron. Keep MT.

11.a. MT הַעֹרְכִים "arranging." A Cairo Geniza fragment has the usual pointing, הָעוֹרְכִים (GKC § 35*g*). The meaning is the same.

12.a. MT וּמָנִיתִי qal "I assign" (BDB, 584), though everywhere else the qal means "count, number." So *BHS* prefers to point וּמִנֵּיתִי piel "I assign." The play on the name מְנִי (v 11) may account for MT's vocalization (see *Comment*).

13.a. One MS^{K} omits אדני "Lord," as did DSS^{Isa} which then added it above the line. LXX has *κύριος* "Lord" only once. But Σ Θ Syr Tg Vg support MT. Read MT.

14.a. MT שבר and DSS^{Isa} שברון both mean "crushing, breaking" (BDB, 991), thus "anguished." But the latter form occurs elsewhere only twice (Jer 17:18; Ezek 21:11) which leads Kutscher to consider it original (*Isaiah Scroll,* 385). Translation is not affected.

15.a-a. MT לעבדיו יקרא "he will call to his servants." LXX *τοῖς δὲ δουλεύουσιν αὐτῷ* (some MSS: *μοι*) *κληθήσεται* "but (a new name) will be called to his (my) servants." 'A Σ Tg Vg support MT. Read MT.

15.b. DSS^{Isa} replaces the line with תמיד "continually" followed by a space of half a line. In v 16, it omits the first line and begins the second והיה הנשבע "and it will be the one who swears." Kutscher (*Isaiah Scroll,* 289) suggests that the scribe was copying from an illegible or defective text. All the Versions support MT.

16.a. MT אָמֵן is an adverb "truly, verily," so *BHS* suggests אֵמוּן or אֹמֶן both meaning "faithfulness." LXX *ἀληθινόν* "true," 'A *πεπιστωμενως* "faithfully." Σ Θ transliterate *αμην* as does Vg *amen.* The title is unique in the OT (see *Comment*).

Form/Structure/Setting

The episode is structured around three formal edicts relating to the rebels in Jerusalem. Each of them contains a formula that describes its nature. The first (v 7) announces that Yahweh will lump their guilt with that of their fathers in assessing their punishment. The second (v 8) limits the effect of the judgment "for my servants' sake." The third (vv 13–15a) announces a clear separation of the rebels from "my servants" in assessing curses to the former and blessings to the latter.

These are preceded by Yahweh's introduction of the issues (vv 1–6) which contains a number of themes from earlier sections in the Vision, particularly chaps. 63–64. A second speech follows the second formal edict and explains his decision to distinguish between those in Israel/Judah who are to be considered his obedient servants and those who will not heed or listen to instruction (vv 9–12). A closing dialogue by supporting speakers interprets the events. These produce this outline:

- Yahweh's opening speech to the court about his rebellious people (vv 1–6)
  - First formal edict: Judgment on the sinners (v 7)
  - Second formal edict: Limitation of the judgment (v 8)
- Yahweh's speech:
    - Promise of hope for his "chosen" (vv 9–10)
    - Judgment on the sinners (vv 11–12)
  - Third formal edict: Separation of sinners from servants (vv 13–15a)
- Speeches interpreting the meaning of the separation (vv 15b–16)

See the parallel to this passage in 57:1–13. Achtemeier (*The Community and Message,* 122) understands that it "spells failure of the Levitical-prophetic efforts to intercede for the Judean community as a whole." Its prayers had not been answered. The opposition had not repented. There was nothing left but separation.

There are no historical references in the episode to provide it with a specific setting. A date can only be deduced from its position in the Vision and the references in the scenes that precede it.

Comment

1 This word from God seems strange since it follows the extended prayers of chaps. 63–64. It clearly draws a distinction between prayers in the sense of asking for something the worshiper wants and true worship in the sense of *asking* to *consult* with God or *looking for* him to inquire what his will is. This true kind of worship is summed up in the phrase *calling by my name.* To pray in God's name means to submit to him and to pray in terms of his revealed character and will. This the worshipers of chaps. 63–64 had not done. It is a pitiful scene: worshipers praying earnestly with their backs toward God who is reaching out to them with open hands.

2 *Spread out my hands* is usually a description of prayer. But here God is the one reaching out to his people (see Rom 10:21). *A rebellious* (סורר) *people* is a description like those in 1:23 and 30:1. It appears here as there with synonyms to sum up God's problem with his people who are deliberately blind and deaf to his words and call. The judgment on their rebellion defines it. They *walk in ways that are not good.* That is reason enough for judgment because these ways are fashioned *after their own thoughts,* that is not after God's ways revealed to them (see 56:11; 57:17; 58:13; 59:8; Ps 81:13[12]). As Achtemeier (*The Community and Message,* 123) notes, the Bible teaches that man cannot find God by searching for him. God must take the initiative. Only by prior revelation is faith possible. Here Yahweh proclaims his efforts to reveal himself to Judeans despite their refusal to seek or ask for him (see Ps 81:11[10]; Rom 10:20 understands v 1 to refer to the gentiles).

3 These include rites of pagan worship which are a direct affront to Yahweh. *Provoking* God is a deuteronomic word (Deut 32; Jer 7:18; 11:17). Fertility rites *in the gardens* (see 1:29) and *incense on the tiles* (see 2 Kgs 23:12; Jer 19:13; Zeph 1:5) are very similar to the Canaanite rituals for which Israel was exiled (see 1:29). They belong to the popular paganism that had dominated that area for centuries.

4 *Sitting in the tombs and lodging between the rocks* appear to be rituals of the cult of the dead, that is, necromancy in which one contacts the spirits of the dead by spending the night in the cemeteries. This ancient Palestinian cult was there long before the Israelites first entered the country. *Eating swine's flesh* was, of course, forbidden in the Torah (Lev 11:7; Deut 14:8), probably because it was used in pagan worship. *Broth of polluted things* is food from other creatures forbidden in Lev 11 and Deut 14. These are breeches of laws defining the difference between what is "clean" and "unclean" for Israelites to eat.

5 The rebellious ones claim for themselves a special and separate status. Hanson (*Dawn of Apocalyptic* 148–49) and Achtemeier (*Community and Message* 124) take them to be Zadokite priests. The language is priestly and found frequently in the priestly code of the Pentateuch. קדשתיך "I am set apart from you" is from the verb "be holy." With a slightly different pointing (in piel) it would mean "for I should communicate holiness to you" (Whybray, 270). By their priestly status they consider themselves to have received a special quality of holiness that sets them apart or that gives them special powers. These are priestly words that would be fitting to a priest. Hanson cites Ezek 40–48 to document the Zadokite claim to the priesthood. The references in Ezek 44:5, 13, 15 use exactly the same verbs as those used here to define the special rights of the Zadokites and restrictions on Levites in the sanctuary. But Isa 60:21 and 61:6 claimed the priesthood for all God's people.

Yahweh's aversion to these practices is expressed by *these are smoke in my nostrils* (see Deut 32:22; Jer 17:4). It has been continual and provocative. He reverses their claim to exclusive access to his presence.

6 *See! It is written before me* announces the first of the edicts or official statements in these chapters which are marked by "says Yahweh" or a similar formula. But first Yahweh introduces it. *I will not keep silent* picks up the plea that ended the prayers in 64:11 [12] (cf. 62:1). But the word Yahweh speaks is very different from what they expected. *I will repay* fits the expectation of those who prayed (see 58:18; 61:8; 62:11). But they expected it to be on their enemies. They thought they had been punished enough. Instead God says of them *Yes, I will repay on their bodies.* The presence of the same pagan practices in Jerusalem of the 5th century which had been condemned in Jerusalem of the 8th century shows that exile and punishment had been no catharsis for the people.

7 The edict proclaims that *the iniquities* of the current generation will be added to the guilt of their *fathers* (chaps. 1–3) who had done the same things in the past (see Ezek 20:27–28). The guilt of both will be assessed in their punishment. This, in effect, means that the amnesty announced in 40:2 is revoked for those who have opened the old wounds by continued pagan worship.

8 A second edict begins *Thus says Yahweh* and limits the application of this revocation. It will not apply to all. Yahweh quotes a proverb from the vineyard to justify the distinction being made for *my servants' sake.* Israel is seen as a bunch of grapes. 5:1–7 pictured Israel as a vineyard. Achtemeier (*Community and Message,* 13) thinks of the first fruits (Jer 2:3) which were to be set apart as an offering to Yahweh (Exod 23:19). The first grapes cut were never the best for making wine. Yet some of them were kept for Yahweh as a sign of life and blessing. She also notes the phrase *Do not destroy* in the superscriptions of Pss 57–59 as the title of a tune. Perhaps the phrase belonged to a harvest ritual. Here it is said of Israel: *do not destroy.* The whole is preserved from deserved destruction for the sake of the few faithful *servants* and the potential life and blessing inherent in them. This chapter is characterized by the division between Yahweh's servants and the pagans who are coming under judgment here. The judgment is designed to get rid of the rebellious group, but is carefully administered *not to destroy the whole.* The process by which a remnant is preserved in which God's promised destiny can be fulfilled is being put into effect.

9 Yahweh comments on his edict restricting punishment: *I will bring out a seed from Jacob.* The confirmation refers to the promises to Abraham that his children will inherit the land, here called *my mountains,* the hill country of Palestine. The later history as well as a part of that ancient promise is recognized in *and from Judah an heir.* Yahweh stresses continuity with the past at this point, even in the very new creation that is being announced. *My chosen will inherit it.* He deliberately uses the language of election. *And my servants will live there.* Yahweh's servants will include the elect, and presumably faithful, of the northern tribes as well as Judeans and Jerusalemites. The inclusive views of the Vision are enforced again. There is to be a division here, but not between north and south or between Judah and the other tribes or between priest and people. It will be between true servants of Yahweh and those who rebel by insisting on their own ways of worship and politics.

10 Favorite places in Palestine, *Sharon* and *the Achor valley,* are mentioned as places that will be returned to Israel. *My people who seek me* defines the servants mentioned before. Note the contrast to v 1.

11 Yahweh's commentary turns back to the judgments of vv 6–7. He addresses those involved. Their crimes are laid out: *forsaking Yahweh* is a breech of covenant which requires "remembering" and "being faithful" to Yahweh. *Forgetting* parallels *forsaking* as capital crimes. *The mount of my holiness* is often translated "my holy mountain," but that translation fails to convey the Hebrew emphasis that "holy" applies to God, not in the first place to the mountain.

The crimes are further detailed. *Fortune* (גד) is a god's name who stood for good fortune. He was apparently a Syrian deity known from Phoenicia to Palmyra and in Palestine (see Josh 11:17; 12:7; 15:37). *Fate* (מני) also was a god's name, a god of destiny. *Preparing the table* and *filling the cups of wine* seem to refer to cultic meals eaten in honor of these deities.

12 מניתי "I assign" uses a Hebrew word with the same letters of the name of the god of fate just mentioned. It is a grim reminder that Yahweh assigns fate, not some pagan deity. *Sword* and *slaughter* define their bleak prospects of sudden death. *Because I called, but you (pl) did not answer* reminds one of vv 1–2 above and will be repeated in 66:4. The condemnation sums up God's complaint against his people through the Vision. Far more important than specific acts that were immoral or pagan was their unresponsiveness to God (see 50:2). Other prophets had the same complaint (Jer 7:13). *You did what was evil in my eyes* reflects phraseology found frequently in Deuteronomy and DtH. *You chose that in which I took no delight* reverses the recommendation of 56:4. The self-will that was determined to make God do what they wanted him to do is apparent throughout.

13 The distinction to be drawn between the two groups is presented as a formal written announcement. Yahweh's servants are destined to obtain the blessing, first announced in chap. 40 and now presented, while the rebellious and pagan group being addressed is cut out of these benefits. Yahweh's servants are those who have heeded God's call to respect the empire, to go to Jerusalem to aid in building the temple, and to worship there. They are the humble who tremble at his word. They are the ones who welcome those from the nations who seek God in Jerusalem. Those who are excommunicated from all the benefits of the new blessings are represented by the prayers of chaps. 63–64. They include those who see God's future only in terms of Israel's past, whether that of Moses and the tribes, or that of David and the kingdom. They include zealots who foment rebellion against Persia and priests who exclude Levites from temple service and foreigners from its worship. They include those who practice the pagan rites mentioned in this chapter. They have been present in some measure from chap. 40 onward, but there always seemed a chance that they would see the error of their ways and turn to Yahweh. They have not. And now their destiny is sealed. (Luke 6:20–26 and Matt 25:31–46 make a similar distinction between two groups.)

14 The contrast in the fate of the two groups is shown by their responses. Yahweh *servants will sing.* The others will *wail* in their *anguished spirit.*

15 The old and the new are shown by names for the groups. The judged group's *name* is to become an *oath* or *curse* for the servants (see Jer 29:22 for the use of a name in a curse). The text does not reveal that name. Is it "Israel"? *My chosen* is a synonym for Yahweh's servants which gives that group the sanction of election. They are to be called by *another name.* (See the discussion of a new name in 62:2–4, 12.) Is this new name "Jew" which comes into prominence after the Exile?

16 *One who blesses himself* refers to the oath formula and the use of the old name to contrast with the blessing prayed for. *In the land* fixes the group as well as the place. It means Jews returned to Palestine. *The God of Truth* (or "of faithfulness"—Whybray, 275) is a phrase used nowhere else in the OT. It stresses his faithfulness to his word which is now revealed anew in the new city and its temple.

The former troubles refers to the judgments on pre-exilic Israel which were the subject of chaps. 1–39 in the Vision. *Forgotten* stands in contrast to the deliberate "remembering" in chaps. 63–64 where these were thrown into God's face either as models for what they want him to do or as wrongs done to Israel. *Hid from my eyes.* God has turned to the future. The past is done with now and hidden. The stress for God is on what is new and real in the present and the future. (See 43:18–19 for the earlier distinction between the "former things" and "the new thing.")

Explanation

The context calls for Yahweh's response to the intense prayers offered in the previous scene. First Yahweh talks about them (vv 1–10) explaining why he has made the decisions concerning them that he has. Their appeals for mercy and compassion are denied (v 7). The passage is a classic explanation for unanswered prayer.

God points out that he has been available to them constantly and without interruption (vv 1–2). Why then had they not made connection? He charges that they had "not asked for him." They had "not looked for him." In the preceding prayers the people had been called to "remember" what God had done in the past. Then they had presented their intense requests in terms of asking him to do it again in the present. Apparently that does not count with God as "asking" or "looking" for him. He speaks of himself as actively presenting himself to them in the present. But they were not interested in seeking out the living God as he presented himself to them. They were "not calling by his name." This means that they were not submitting themselves to him in the usual covenant forms which prescribed confession of sins, submission to Yahweh's will in renewing covenant, and asking for his direction.

Abraham's question is appropriate here: "Will you destroy the righteous with the wicked?" (Gen 18:23; see Achtemeier, *Community and Message,* 125.) Matt 13:24–30 notes that wheat and weeds grow together. But justice requires distinction and separation. The dilemma is deep-rooted (see Hab 1; Jer 31:29; Ezek 18; John 9:2). V 8 suggests that the evil are spared temporarily on the chance that the good will survive and emerge from them with life and blessing. Later the process of separation is inevitable. Achtemeier (128–29) correctly notes a new development in biblical teaching at this point. Vv 8–10 deal with Israel as a whole in the manner usual in the OT and in the Vision to this point. In this wholeness sinners corrupt the whole, while the righteous sanctify the whole. But in the verses that follow, in a manner that extends the distinctions made in Ezek 18, the servants of Yahweh are separated from the rebels in the roles they will play in Yahweh's plan.

The need for this separation has been shown in 1:9, 10:20–23, *et passim.* (See Zech 8:11–13; Jer 24:4–7.) But before this the view of the future regularly returned to salvation for a single, whole community (2:2–4; Ezek 37; Jer 31:31–34; Zeph 3:14–20). Achtemeier (129) notes that "Paul stands in this prophetic tradition when he writes of 'all Israel' in Rom 11:26."

But in this scene the procedure changes. It breaks from the whole covenant community concept. An earlier picture had related the return from Babylon to the Exodus (43:14–21; 51:9–11; 52:11–12). But this scene sees the future, not in terms of the Sinai covenant with all twelve tribes, but in terms of volunteer servants, Yahweh's chosen who have been singled out from the Israelite community. They are the "meek, the humble, and those who tremble at Yahweh's word" (57:13b–15). They are the only ones out of this deaf and blind people (42:18–20; 43:8) who seem able to hear and to see. This division has become increasingly evident since chap. 55. Here it is complete.

The picture of a divided future has influenced Jews and Christians in their view of a future in which the righteous and the unrighteous would have separate existences. Believers and unbelievers will go separate ways into their separate destinies (see the Manual of Discipline of the Qumran community and Matt 25:31–46). This passage marks an important stage in the development of those doctrines.

They are called "a rebellious people." They were determined not to do the things that had been revealed to them of God's will as chaps. 40–62 of the Vision have presented it. God had reached out to them through the favorable edicts of Cyrus, Darius, and Artaxerxes to restore the temple. He had provided leaders like Zerubbabel, Haggai, Zechariah, Ezra, and Nehemiah. The position of Jews in Mesopotamia, Egypt, and other places was tolerable and sometimes pleasant. But they demanded divine action according to their prescription. Like those in Jesus' day, they demanded a sign from God (Mark 8:11–12; Matt 12:38–42; Luke 11:29–30). Here, as in the Gospels, their demand is denied. They do not want to take God on his own terms. They want to write the script themselves. This is rebellion against the sovereign plan of God. Their ways are "not good." They are limited by the range of their own interests and want to draw the plans "after their own thoughts." Of course they are rejected.

Beyond that, they are pagan in their worship. They do all the things which have been specifically forbidden to Yahweh's people to do and then have the nerve to think of themselves as "holier than thou." Their prayers are not only not acceptable, they are a provocation to Yahweh (vv 3–5).

This leads up to the first formal edict placed before the heavenly court. Yahweh introduces it with a reference to the close of the prayer in 64:11 (12) where he was asked, "Will you keep silent and punish us beyond measure?" They hoped that he would break his silence to speak judgment against their enemies. Instead, he breaks his silence to announce judgment against them (v 6). He recognizes that the pagan practices still being performed as a provocation against him are the same ones practiced by their ancestors before the exile and for which they had been judged by earlier prophets. For these people in Jerusalem the judgments on Jerusalem and Judah that brought on the exile had been neither a lesson nor a catharsis. They were just like their "fathers." Yahweh's judgment lumps them together with their ancestors and charges them all together. The amnesty announced in chap. 40 is repealed as far as they are concerned. The continued punishment that they protested in 64:11 (12) is judged to be justly apportioned and understood. Here the children have not just inherited the sensitive teeth caused by their parents' sins (Ezek 18:2); they continue to feast on the bad grapes.

But the marvelous grace of God is shown in his patient continuance of his efforts to provide for his servants the inheritance he had promised (vv 8–9). Thus the story of salvation is continued. Although one or another of the "heirs," from Esau to the wilderness generation to the kingdoms of Israel and Judah, falls by the wayside, God patiently cultivates those who can be his servants in spirit and in truth, from Jacob to Moses to Samuel to Ezra with all of those who stood with them, minority though they may be. At the very moment when the failure and rebellion is recognized and judged, hope is rekindled for those who seek Yahweh in order to serve him.

The scene then turns to address the rebellious ones. Their sins are listed. "Forsaking" and "forgetting," failing to "answer" or to "listen" stand at the head of the list. The capital crimes are those that flaunt God's offer of a personal relation with himself (vv 11–12). They are accompanied by a preoccupation with pagan practices and with choosing "evil" things in which God has "no pleasure" (vv 11–12). The self-centered life that makes decisions purely in terms of self-interest has left God out of its priorities. So that life will be left out of God's priorities. "Doing things my way" can at most achieve goals within that person's capabilities. Doing things God's way opens the way to achieving goals that lie within God's capabilities.

The consequences of this division between those addressed as rebels and Yahweh's servants are spelled out in the third edict of this episode (vv 13–14). The servants participate in all that God had been working to bring about for his people. The rebels will have no part in this. They could have, but they chose not to participate. So there is prosperity and gladness on one side, but only bitterness on the other.

This judgment has consequences which are discussed in vv 15–16. Much of the hope for a return to Palestine and Jerusalem centered on reestablishing a link to their heritage. They wanted their children's generation to have the chance to enter their heritage in a way that their generation had not been able to do. The wish is universal. But the rebels have violated that privilege. Their actions and inactions have made their name fitting for curses rather than blessings. God will go on, even if under another name. The rebels will leave a legacy all right, but not the one that they had intended.

God is determined to press on. To that end he will forget the "former troubles" with which the rebels by their practices have identified themselves. These edicts have settled those things and God wants to put them behind him (v 16c). The very last verse of the Vision will show that this is not fully possible. The bitterness of the continued rebellion will have a smoldering memorial all its own.

Episode B: *Yahweh Moves to Finish His New Jerusalem (65:17—66:5)*

Translation

Yahweh:	[17] *Indeed, look at me;* *creating a new heaven* *and a new land.*	2+3+2
	The first are not remembered, *nor do they come to mind,*	3+3
	[18] *but rather they rejoice and find continuing gladness* *(in) what*[a] *I am creating.*	3+3
	For look at me: *creating Jerusalem (to be) a rejoicing* *and her people a joy.*	2+3+2
	[19] *And I rejoice in Jerusalem* *and am glad in my people.*	2+2
	And there is not heard in her any more *a sound of crying* *or a sound of distress.*	3+2+2
Heavens:	[20] *From there does not come any more* [a]*an infant (who only lives a few) days*[a]	3+2
	or an old person *who does not fill out his (quota) of days.*	1+3
	For the child *dies a hundred years old,*	2+3
	and [b]*the one who fails* *to live to be a hundred* *is thought accursed.*[b]	1+2+1
Earth:	[21] *And they build houses and live in them.* *And they plant vineyards* *and eat (their) fruit.*	3+2+2
	[22] *They do not build* *and have another live (in them).*	2+2
	They do not plant *and have someone else eat (the fruit).*	2+2
Yahweh:	*For my people's days are* *like the days of the tree.*	2+2
	And my chosen ones wear out by their own use *the thing made by their hands.*	2+2
Heavens:	[23] *They do not work for nothing* *and they do not bear children*[a] *for sudden terror.*	3+3
	But they are the seed of Yahweh's blessed ones, *and their offspring are with them.*	5+2
Yahweh:	[24] *And it is so that*	1+2+2

before they call
I answer.
And while they are still speaking 2+2
I myself hear (them).
25 *A wolf and a lamb feed together,* 4+4+3
and a lion eats straw like an ox,
and a snake has dust as his food.
They do no harm— 2+2+3
they do not destroy
in all of the mountain of my holiness,
Herald: *says Yahweh.* 2
66:1 *Thus says Yahweh:* 3
Yahweh: *The heavens are my throne* 2+3
and the land is my footstool.
What[a] *is this?* 2+3
A house that you build for me?
What[a] *is this?* 2+3
The place of my rest?
2 *My own hand has made all these* 3+3+2
so that all these came into being![a]
Herald: *Oracle of Yahweh.*
Yahweh: *I pay attention to this (one):* 3+3+3
to a humble and contrite[b] *spirit*
who trembles at my word.
Heavens: 3 *One who slaughters an ox* 2+2
(is just like) one who strikes down a person.
Earth: *One who sacrifices a lamb* 2+2
(is just like) one who breaks a dog's neck.
Heavens: *One who presents a cereal offering* 2+2
(is just like) swine's blood.[a]
Earth: *One who makes a memorial with frankincense* 2+2
(is just like) one who blesses an idol.
Yahweh: *Even as these have fixed their choice on their own ways* 3+3
and their soul delights in their abominations,
4 *so I have fixed my choice on their afflictions* 3+3
and bring their worst fears to reality for them.
Because, when I called, 2+2
no one answered.
When I spoke, 1+2
no one heard (me).
Thus they did (what was) evil in my sight, 3+3
and they fixed their choice on that in which I took no delight.
Herald: 5 *Hear (pl) the word of Yahweh,* 3+2
you (pl) who tremble at his word!
Yahweh: *Your brothers who hate you say,* 3+3
those who threw you out for my name's sake,

"Let Yahweh be glorified[a] 3+2
that we may see[b] *your joy,"*
when (it is) they who will be shamed. 2

Notes

18.a. *BHS* suggests adding על "on account of" to אשר "which." But the implication is plain enough in MT.

20.a-a. עול ימים, lit., "an infant of days" has caused some interpreters to think a verb is missing or to emend ימים to ימות "he dies" (see Whybray). But a substantive can be used to express age (GKC § 118*q*).

20.b-b. The line is usually translated "the sinner who lives to be a hundred is thought accursed" which seems strange in the context of the previous line. *BHS* emends MT יְקֻלָּל piel "he is accursed" to יֵקַל qal "he is of little account," i.e., not unusual. But it is more effective to simply translate החוטא "sinner" as "one who fails" (BDB, 306), following NEB and Whybray.

23.a. MT יֵלְדוּ qal "bear children." *BHS* suggests יולדו hiph "beget children," but LXX *τεκνοποιήσουσιν* and Vg *generabunt* can have either meaning. Read MT.

66:1.a-a. MT אי זה, lit., "where is it? which is it?" LXX *ποῖον* "what?" and Vg *quae* "what?" correctly translate the meaning in context.

2.a. MT ויהיו impf "and they came to be." DSS[Isa] והיו is pf, due perhaps to the preceding verb (Kutscher, *Isaiah Scroll*, 354). LXX *καὶ ἔστιν ἐμὰ* "and they are mine." Tg הלא הואה "have they not come to be?" turns it into a negative question. Vg *et facta sunt universa ista* "and they are making that whole world." MT is the least likely to have evolved from the context and should be kept.

2.b. MT ונכה "and contrite, stricken" occurs only here and 2 Sam 4:4, 9:3 (BDB, 646). DSS[Isa] ונכאי, 1QIsa[b] ונכאה, MSS[K] ונכא all seem derived from נכא "stricken" (BDB, 644; cf. Prov 15:13; 17:22; 18:14), though Kutscher (*Isaiah Scroll*, 265–66) suggests the Scrolls' readings derive from niph of כאה "disheartened" (BDB, 456; cf. *BHS*). LXX *ἡσύχιον* "meek" omitting "spirit." Tg מכיך "contrite," Vg *contritum* "contrite." Read MT supported by LXX Tg Vg.

3.a. Volz and *BHS* suggest emending MT דם "blood" to חֹמֵד "one enjoying" to parallel the other ptcps. This has no MS support.

5.a. MT יִכְבַּד qal impf of a stative verb "be honored." LXX Syr Vg, lacking an equivalent stative verb, read a passive, as one must do in English for the same reason. It is not necessary to change MT.

5.b. MT ונראה "that we may see." DSS[Isa] יראה "he may see." LXX *καὶ ὀφθῇ* "and he may see." 'A Σ Θ Tg Vg support MT. Read MT.

Form/Structure/Setting

The limits of this episode are marked by the exclamatory כי הנני "Indeed, look at me!" in v 17 which introduces a change of mood and pace as the scene turns to a description of Yahweh's new world for his new city. It continues through 66:5 where the radical newness of the city is contrasted with the opponents who will be "shamed" when the new city becomes reality.

Like the first episode, this one is structured around two formal edicts. The first (vv 24–25) announces that "before they call I will answer." This reverses Yahweh's reaction to the rebels in v 1 and reflects the different character of the inhabitants of the city to come. The second edict reacts to the announcement that the rebels are about to put in a temple (v 1–2a): "What sort of house will you build?"

These are framed by speeches by Yahweh and his courtiers in vv 17–23 describing the new creation and in 66:2b–5 confirming his rejection of the old priestly ways and his installation of a more direct spirituality for the meek who tremble at his word. This suggests an outline like this:

Yahweh's speech and courtier's support: "Look at me creating new heavens and new earth" (65:17–23)
  First formal edict: "Before they call I will answer" (65:24–25)
  Second formal edict: "What sort of house will you build?" (66:1–2a)
Yahweh's speech and courtier's support: "I heed the humble" (66:2b–5)

The issue of the nature of worship in the new temple helps to place the passage historically. The nature of worship and the status of the priests were major concerns in the restoration of Jerusalem from 520 through the reforms of Ezra and Nehemiah in the latter 5th century B.C. They were still burning issues at the end of that period. The Vision does not support the rising power of the priesthood that Ezra is installing with the intention of continuing the sacrifices of Leviticus.

The reference in 66:1 to "a house built for" Yahweh brings the passage back to an historical issue. The episode challenges plans for building the temple. It does not reject the practice of worship, as v 2b makes plain. V 3 shows that the issue turns on the kind of house and the nature of that worship (see *Comment*). This position is consonant with that of the Vision throughout, opposing sacrifice (1:11–14), urging commitment to justice (1:16–17) and supporting a view of religion as pilgrimage to experience God's presence and hear his teaching that will lead to peace (2:1–4).

This view is apparently set against a doctrine of temple worship that is exclusive in the claim that God is only present there (not in the rest of the city) and that only certain priests may practice because they are the only ones authorized to sacrifice. These issues are emphasized in Leviticus and portions of Numbers dealing with priestly privileges. Interpreters correctly find many of these issues present in Haggai and in Ezra's description of the building of the temple under Zerubbabel and Joshua. E. Sellin (*Geschichte des israelitisch-jüdischen Volkes* II [Leipzig: Quelle U. Meyer, 1932] 15) and K. Elliger (*Einheit,* 107–8) date this passage to that period (520–515 B.C.). They are followed in current commentaries by Westermann and Whybray. P. Hanson (*Dawn of Apocalyptic,* 168–82) agrees with this dating but identifies the adversaries more precisely as the prophetic party and the priestly party. E. Achtemeier (*Community and Message,* 139–40) identifies the parties as a prophetic-Levitical party opposing a Zadokite priestly party.

The structure of the Vision presented in this commentary supports identification with a situation in the latter 5th century B.C. as Duhm and Marti (406) argued. However, their identification of the temple mentioned here with that built at Mount Gerizim by the Samaritans can no longer be maintained. It does not fit the requirements of the context. The date for this scene comes after Ezra and Nehemiah have arrived. Zerubbabel's building is almost a hundred years old. Under the best of conditions it would have been in need of repair and renovation. That building was not particularly well built or spacious to begin with. So Nehemiah's rebuilding program in Jerusalem may have involved more than just the walls of the city.

Of more pertinent concern to this passage is Ezra's introduction of the Mosaic Torah to Jerusalem (Neh 8–9) and the description of worship on the occasion of the rededication of the walls (Neh 12:27–47). The roles of singers and Levites were very prominent on that occasion, but there is no reference to sacrifice. The priests are called "sons of Aaron" (Neh 12:47). This is very different from the position of the Zadokite high priest, Joshua, in Malachi or in the projected reform of Ezek 40–48, which is often seen as the inspiration of Zerubbabel's temple.

The setting for 66:1–3 is best understood in the complicated interactions of multiple parties in Jerusalem where Zadokite priests wielded authority over all sacrifice and the temple area. The Vision opposes both the view that the sacred area should be limited to the temple and the view that worship is primarily a matter of sacrifice. It equally disputes the claim that one priestly family should have exclusive priestly privileges in Jerusalem (see 66:21). The Vision is much more at home with the kind of worship described in Neh 12:27–47 with broad participation in songs, prayers, and processions. It argues that the entire city, not just the temple, comprises Yahweh's sacred mountain. This debate is understandable in the late 5th century.

The specific application of 66:1–3 may be even more clearly defined. Nehemiah was determined to concentrate first on the building of the city (its walls, etc.) rather than on repairs and extension of the temple (Neh 2–6). This was opposed by people in Jerusalem as well as by their neighbors (Neh 4 and 6). The policy from the time of Zerubbabel on had been to concentrate only on the temple. The Vision supports Nehemiah but goes beyond him in seeing the entire city as sacred, a place for Jews and other worshipers of Yahweh to gather from all over the known world.

Comment

17 בורא "creating" is a word used only with God as subject. It appears in the early chapters of Genesis (nine times) and in Isa 40–66 (nineteen times). There is a concentration of uses in chap. 45 (six times) and here in 65:17–18 (three times). The emphasis is on Yahweh, as the personal pronoun indicates. He calls attention to himself in the process of creating. This process sums up what he has been doing since he began to bring Cyrus to power (chap. 42).

חדש "new" may mean several different things. It may be temporal in describing something that has never existed before and therefore is unknown to this time. It may distinguish what is different from what has already existed. Or it may mean "to be fresh, pure, young . . . or sharp, polished, bright" (J. Fürst, *Hebrew and Chaldee Lexicon,* 3d ed., tr. S. Davidson [London: Williams & Norgate, 1867] 1404; R. North, "חדש," *TDOT* 4:225–44; J. D. W. Watts, *The Heavenlies of Isaiah,* 92–96). The word is contrasted here with הראשנות "the first," which is already familiar from earlier uses in Isaiah (see *Excursus: The Former and the New*). Westermann understands these eschatologically. Only after the old present order has gone can a new age be created. But the references in chaps. 40–66 presumed a position in which the former age is already gone and a new age with Cyrus and his successors has begun. Here, too, the new order that is being created is (like chap. 45) the one in which Persia holds sway over the entire area so that Jerusalem can be rebuilt.

שמים "heavens." The word is based on a Hebrew biliteral root שם which is found in a number of words relating to height and brilliance, but also to awe and to breath (J. D. W. Watts, *The Heavenlies of Isaiah,* 82–88). *Heavens* refers to the sky or to God's dwelling place. When used with הארץ "the land" (or "the earth") it gives a description of totality, the universe including the divine realm, or the land and all that stands above it. Job 38:33 and Jer 33:25 speak of the "ordinances of heaven." Jer 10:2 speaks of the "signs of heaven." And Dan 4:26 even refers to heaven as embodying God. The *new heavens* may well represent the new order, divinely instituted, which chaps. 40–66 have revealed and in which the Persian Empire has Yahweh's sanction and Israel is called to be a worshiping and a pilgrim people with Jerusalem as its focus.

הארץ has been translated in this commentary consistently as "the land" and understood as referring to Palestine. *Creating* it *new* may refer to regaining agricultural fertility (27:2–5; 35:2–3; 41:18–20; 43:19–21; 44:3–4; 49:9–10; 55:9–13; 62:8–9; 65:9–10). Or it may refer to a new political and social reality under the empire. The land, which in chap. 24 stood under the curse of blood and death, is now recreated for blessing and joy as Yahweh's proclamation in 26:19 decreed. But this is not an eschatological picture of the distant future. It portrays the goal of Yahweh's plans as they are fulfilled in these chapters. Jerusalem is being rebuilt and made ready for the pilgrims who come throughout the following centuries.

הראשנות "the first" things are the past kingdoms of Israel under curse and judgment that were pictured in chaps. 1–39. (See *Excursus: The Former and the New.*) These are to be eliminated from memory and attention. This command is understandable, but the Vision will show that this was not totally possible with contemporary rebels reviving dreams of the past in their current paganism and rebellion.

18 The new creation is intended to be enjoyed. This contrasts with the sadness of chaps. 1–39. The building of *Jerusalem,* the focal point of God's creative action is intended to be *a rejoicing. Her people* are to become *a joy* in themselves and for Yahweh's scattered people everywhere.

19 God himself will *rejoice in Jerusalem* and *be glad in* his *people.* Undoubtedly God's tears had flowed for both the city and his people many times during the previous four centuries. Finally this can be reversed.

A series of contrasts between the two ages is spelled out in vv 19b–25.

"Not any more"	*"But"*
Crying, distress	Rejoicing
An infant dying a few days old	A child living to be a hundred
An elderly person dying prematurely	One hundred deemed an early age to die
Build and another live there	Build houses and live in them
Plant for another to eat	Plant vineyards and eat their fruit
Work for nothing	Be like a tree
Bear children for terror	Wear out their own things
(Build houses for others to take)	Build for their children to live in
(Receive answers to prayer)	Before they call, God answers
(Constant violence)	Not harm or destroy in all God's mountain

24 The verse recalls the motif of 65:1 which promises a satisfying kind of worship in which reciprocal participation is experienced.

25 *A wolf and a lamb* are proverbial opposites. The first is aggressive and voracious, the latter weak and helpless, the wolf's natural food. *A lion* is known to be carnivorous, but here will placidly munch straw. *A snake has dust for its food* recalls the curse placed upon him (Gen 3:14), but the context of the verse calls for understanding this, not as a parallel to enmity with humankind, but as a peaceful element of the newly created order. *They do no harm—they do not destroy in all the mountain of my holiness* summarizes the absence of violence. It is a literal duplication of 11:9a. *Mount of my holiness* is a special phrase in Isaiah which pictures the new Zion as that earthly spot where the reality of God's presence, his peace and joy, may be experienced. It occurs in 11:9; 27:13; 56:7; 57:13; 65:11, 25, and 66:20. Outside of Isaiah it is found in Jer 31:23; Joel 2:1; 4:17; Zech 8:3; Pss 3:5; 43:3; 48:2; Dan 9:16, 20. See Talmon, *TWAT* 2:482.

66:1 *Heavens are my throne.* The Vision has consistently portrayed Yahweh's courtroom (6:1–8) from which he and his aides view and direct events in Jerusalem and the world. *The land is my footstool.* The place that demonstrates Yahweh's sovereignty to humankind is Palestine: promised to Abraham, given through Moses and Joshua, secured through David and Solomon. The Vision has seen *the land* as the arena for Yahweh's actions. To this place he summoned first the Assyrian to destroy and then the Persian to rebuild.

Yahweh expresses surprise: *A house you will build for me?* Building a temple always brings up basic questions like those put to David in 2 Sam 7 and those to Zerubbabel in Haggai and in Ezra 4. Issues related to the temple set off the Maccabean wars and lay at the heart of the division with the Samaritans. Herod's temple was still controversial in Jesus' day. Architecture and function may be at issue. Will it be a building for sacrifice centered around a high altar? A place for priests to parade and officiate? Or will it be a place for singing and for worshipers to meditate? What kind of house should one build for the ruler of heaven and earth who himself builds worlds and establishes dynasties?

My rest in Ps 95:11 refers to Canaan which was denied to the wilderness generation. This passage presents the same tension between a rebellious generation and God's sovereign rule over heavens and earth (see vv 3–4). Ps 132:8 relates the term to Zion to stress the permanency of his presence there. But the total phrase here seems to be unique in linking Yahweh to a "place." Yahweh's objection lies precisely in that emphasis on a *place* which can claim exclusive rights to Yahweh's presence, when he is the one who has made all things and presumably goes wherever he chooses.

2 In contrast to his objections to a house and a place, Yahweh affirms his attention to a particular kind of person: one who is *humble* and is a *contrite spirit.* This phrase is familiar from 57:15 and Ps 34:18 (see also Matt 5:3 and Luke 18:13–14). *Who trembles at my word* is new here. It picks up an element from the original statement of the Vision's goals, that "the word of Yahweh will go out of Zion" (2:3). The *word* rather than the place or the sacrifice is significant (see Ezra 9:4; 10:3).

3 A series of legitimate sacrifices, as far as the Torah is concerned, is then identified with some that are prohibited:

Acceptable	*Unacceptable*
slaughtering an ox (Lev 17:3–4)	striking a person (Lev 24:17–21; Deut 19:6; 27:24–25)
sacrificing a lamb (Lev 14:10–24)	breaking a dog's neck (Exod 34:20, of a donkey)
presenting a cereal offering (Lev 2:1, 13)	swine's blood (Lev 11:7; Deut 14:8; Isa 65:4; 66:17; cf. R. de Vaux, "Les sacrifices de porcs en Palestine et dans l'Ancient Orient," FS O. Eissfeldt, BZAW 77 [Berlin: de Gruyter, 1958] 250–65)
a memorial with frankincense (Lev 2:2, 16; 6:8 [15]; see G. R. Driver, *JSS* 1 [1956] 99–100)	blessing a vain thing (see below)

און "a vain thing" appears frequently in the Vision (1:13; 10:1; 29:20; 31:2; 32:6; 41:29; 55:7; 58:9; 59:4, 6, 7). But these usually refer to deeds of vanity or words of vanity. The phrase used here, *blessing a vanity,* is unique. The word is used in other contexts for idols. But whether this means heaping blessings on an idol or a blessing using an idol's name is not clear.

The emphasis in using these participles is on the one doing these things. Either the pairs express identification (the one doing this also does that) making these an accusation of syncretism (which is not really credible here) or the one doing legal sacrifices is portrayed as no more acceptable to God than one who is doing the illegal and abhorrent things. The latter seems most fitting: a heavy insult heaped on the practicing priests. And it is also a claim that the ancient sacrifices are no longer valid in the new age. The priests have *fixed their choice on their own ways* without seeking to know Yahweh's decisions for his own house. This is a familiar complaint (56:11; 57:10, 17, 18; 58:13; 59:7, 8). They *delight in their abominations,* that is their unacceptable pagan practices (57:8; 58:2, 13; 65:12). They continue practices from older times, pagan and legal, without regard to Yahweh's will for his new age. The charge may well apply to remnants of the old Zadokite priesthood who were fighting to maintain their grip on Zion's ritual. (See Rofé, *Biblical and Related Studies,* FS Iwry, 207–12).

4 As they have chosen, so Yahweh has *fixed his choice.* Since their choices were at variance with Yahweh's will, so he chooses *affliction* for them in place of the support they sought from him. He confirms *their worst fears.* The punishment will fit the crime, as Gilbert and Sullivan sang it. Their crime lay in ignoring Yahweh's calling. That in itself was rebellion against God. But, beyond that *they fixed their choice* on things that meant nothing to God. V 4b-d duplicates 65:12b-d and obviously refers to the same group. If these are priests, then Achtemeier (*Community and Message,* 141) is right in saying that this speech is about the freedom of the sovereign God who "is never coerced by ritual."

5 A speech directed to the faithful says they *hear the word* and *tremble at the word.* The measure of piety, instead of being related to temple and sacrifice, is said to relate to God's word and the response to that word. (See 2:3.) *Your brothers* is a remarkably generous designation for those elsewhere called rebels. *Brothers* is used for fellow members of covenant in Deut 1:16; 2:4; 3:18; Jer 7:15; 29:16. This shows how the division between servants and enemies cuts through the heart of the community, perhaps even through families. *Who hate you* accents the bitterness of the fraternal struggle which had occasioned their previous expulsion. E. Achtemeier (*Community and Message,* 142) thinks this refers to the Zadokites who expelled the Levites on the charge of idolatry (Ezek 44:10), heaped scorn on them (59:4; 58:9), segregated them (63:16; 65:5), and condemned them to death (57:1–2). *For my name's sake.* The faithful had defended the honor of Yahweh's name against the derisive taunt: *Let Yahweh be glorified!* (Cf. the taunts against idols in 41:21–24.) In this simply a taunt that suggests that God cannot do anything? Or is it, as Achtemeier suggests, a call for God to be glorified in their project of a rebuilt temple (see Hag 1:8, Zech 2:10) and for the faithful group to lend their joyful support?

Things have gone too far for reconciliation. Yahweh assures the faithful that their enemies will *be shamed* and their work shattered.

Explanation

The Vision moves toward its climax, but there is no release of tension yet. It has come a long way from the announcement in chap. 40 and the song in 43:9–10. But the full glory of Yahweh (40:5) is still only seen by the eye of faith. The enemies "who rage" (41:11) have not disappeared, although they are no longer the same persons or parties referred to back then. The promise concerning them is still the same: "they will be shamed" (41:11 and 66:5). The contrast between the "former things" and the "new things" continues. But in 41:22 the idols are challenged to interpret them. In 42:9 only "the former things" are open to them while Yahweh alone "declares new things." 43:18–19 called on Israel to forget "the former things" in order to concentrate on Yahweh's "new thing." Now in chap. 65 the "new thing" is an accomplished fact. "Former things are not remembered."

The new order promises security and longevity in contrast to the history of some three centuries past. It promises a receptive religious climate. Then, for at least the third time in the Vision, a picture of an idyllic existence is given which has no violence of any kind. The picture should be read against a background which pictures only partial or intermediate stages in the achievement of God's purpose. But these idyllic passages (11:6–9; 35:1–2, 5–7; 65:25) point to a perfection of nature like that in the Garden of Eden before the expulsion of Adam and Eve. They point to God's original and ultimate plan for humanity in a totally nonviolent and innocent creation. But each is set in a context that, while it speaks of ideals, nevertheless is realistic in terms of rulers, of worship, or of Israel's return to Palestine. 11:1–5 speaks of a spirit-anointed ruler while vv 10–16 promise a gathering of the people from the far corners of the empire. 35:3–4 and 8–10 reflect a people on the way to Zion and in need of salvation. 65:19–24 speaks of changes in living conditions while 66:1–2 speaks of a building project in Jerusalem. A highway for the people is pictured in 11:16 and 35:8 and is recalled by the great pilgrimage in 66:18–21.

References to God's "holy mountain" are regularly linked to pilgrimage. God's holiness and presence are very real to the pilgrims there. A later age would say that this gives a preview of what God has in store for his saints beyond the present life. In the sanctuary the awareness of God's holy presence would overpower all sense of the fallen world around. There the pilgrim could sense God and his purpose purely and without interruption.

Jerusalem is called to rejoice. But the bitterness of continuing struggle overshadows the new creation. There is hatred between brothers. No hope of reconciliation remains, for one group is unalterably set against Yahweh and his plans. Anyone so set against God can only be shamed and destroyed.

Yahweh presses on toward the completion of the new city. But opponents insist that the Temple must be built first, a Temple designed for sacrifice. Their stubborn insistence is so bitter that Yahweh seems to say: the city will be built, but no Temple and no sacrifice. They are not essential.

Those things that are essential in the new city are clearly shown: Yahweh's creative power, direction, and presence with humble worshipers who are hungry for Yahweh's word in the city open to all who want to come. In Yahweh's new creation that is enough.

Episode C: Yahweh Confirms His Servants in His New City (66:6–24)

Translation

Heavens: 6 *A sound of an uproar from a city—* 3+2
a sound from a temple—
Earth: *A sound of Yahweh* 2+3
making full payment to his enemies—
Heavens: 7 *Before she*[a] *is in labor* 2+1
she gives birth![b]
Earth: *Before her pain comes on her* 4+2
she delivers a male child!
Heavens: 8 *Who ever heard of such a thing as this?* 3+3
Earth: *Who ever saw things like these?*
Heavens: *Can a land*[a] *be in labor only one day* 4+4
or a nation be born in one moment?
Earth: *But Zion has gone into labor* 2+2
and already birthed her children!
Yahweh: 9 *Would I rupture* (*the membrane*) 2+2+2
and not cause birth to follow?
Herald: *says Yahweh.*
Yahweh: *If I am the one who brings to birth, shall I hinder it?* 3+2

Herald: *says your God.*
Heavens: 10 *Rejoice (pl) with*[a] *Jerusalem* 2+2+2
and be glad (pl) with her,
all of you who love her.
Earth: *Exult an exultation with her,* 3+2
all of you who were mourning over her (until now),
Heavens: 11 *so that you (pl) may suck and be satisfied* 3+2
from the breast of her consolations,
so that you may drink and take satisfaction 3+2
from the abundance of her glory.
Herald: 12 *For thus says Yahweh:* 3
Yahweh: *Look at me extending to her* 3+2
(prosperous) peace like a river
and the glory (wealth) of nations 2+3
like an overflowing stream (from which) you (pl) may suckle.[a]
Heavens: *You (pl) may be carried*[b] *on a hip (like a baby)* 2+2
and you may play[c] *on her knees (like a toddler).*
Yahweh: 13 *Like a person whose mother comforts (him),* 4+3+3
so I myself will comfort you (pl)
and with Jerusalem you (pl) may (now) be comforted.[a]
Earth: 14 *And you (pl) will see and your (pl) heart will rejoice* 3+3
and your (pl) bones will flourish like the grass.
Heavens: *And it is known* 1+2+2
that Yahweh's hand (is) with his servants
and indignation[a] *(is) with his enemies.*
Earth: 15 *For see, Yahweh comes in*[a] *a fire* 4+2
and his chariots (are) like the storm wind
to bring back his anger[b] *with fury* 3+3
and his rebuke with flames of fire.
Heavens: 16 *For Yahweh enters into judgment*[a] *by fire* 4+2+3
and with all flesh[b] *by his sword*[c]
and Yahweh's[d] *wounded will be many.*[e]
Yahweh: 17 *Those who sanctify and purify themselves for the gardens,* 3+3
after one[a] *in the middle,*
eating pork 3+2
and the abomination[b] *and the mice,*
will be terminated together! 2+2
Herald: *Oracle of Yahweh.*
Yahweh: 18 *And I (despite)* [a]*their deeds and their thoughts,*[a] 3+4+4
am coming[b] *to gather all the nations and the language groups*
that they may come and see my glory.
19 *And I shall establish a sign in them.* 3+4
And I shall send some of their survivors to the nations:

Tarshish, Pul[a] *and Lud,* 3+2
drawers[b] *of a bow,*[c]
Tubal and Javan, 2+2+3
the coastlands afar off
which have not heard my announcements
and those who have not seen my glory 2+3
will make known my glory among the nations.
20 *And they will bring all your brothers from all the nations* 3+2
as an offering to Yahweh
on horses and in wagons, 2+3
in litters and on mules and on camels,[a]
upon my holy mountain, Jerusalem, 4+2
Herald: *says Yahweh,*
Yahweh: *just as Israelites bring the grain offering* 5+4
to the house of Yahweh in a clean vessel.
21 *And from them also I will take (some)*[a] 2+2+2
for priests, for Levites,[b]
Herald: *says Yahweh.*
Yahweh: 22 *Indeed, just as the new*[a] *heavens* 4+4+2
and the new land which I am making
are standing before me,
Herald: *oracle of Yahweh,* 2
Yahweh: *so your (pl) seed and your (pl) name will stand before me.* 4
23 *And it will be* 1+3+3
from a new moon to its (following) new moon,
and from a sabbath to its[a] *(following) sabbath,*
all flesh will come 2+2+2
to worship before me,
Herald: *says Yahweh.*
Yahweh: 24 *When they go out, they will look* 2+2+2
at the corpses of persons
who were rebelling against me.
Heavens: *For their worm will not die,* 4+3+3
and their fire will not go out.
But they will continue to be an abhorrence[a] *to all flesh.*

Notes

7.a. *BHS* suggests providing a subj ילדה "the one giving birth." But this is not necessary. The subj, of course, is Jerusalem.

7.b. *BHS* again inserts an obj, בן "son." Again unnecessary and pedantic.

8.a. היוחל ארץ "can a land be in labor?" consists of a masc verb and a fem subject. *BHS* cites a proposal to expand the subject עם ארץ "people of the land" to create agreement. But disagreement is common in an impersonal passive construction (Whybray; GKC § 121*a*).

10.a. את "with" is used with שמח "rejoice" only here (BDB, 970). Y. Yadin ("A Note on the Title of the Verse of the Genizah MS 1134," *HUCA* 49 [1978] 82–83, 51 [1980] 61) supports the reading.

12.a. MT וינקתם qal pf "and you will suckle" (BDB, 413). The Masoretic accentuation places this in the preceding stich, as translated here. LXX omits and inserts *τὰ παιδία* "their children" as subject for the following verbs, which leads *BHS* to emend to וינקתה "and her sucklings" (collective). DSS^{Isa} is missing about three letters but what remains, -תיהמה, is clearly different from MT. Tg ותתפנקון "and you will delight yourself." Vg *sugetis* "you suck." Follow MT. The conjunction ties it to the preceding stich. The lack of a following conjunction implies a new sentence.

12.b. MT תנשאו "you (pl) will be carried." DSS^{Isa} תנשינה 2 fem sg. LXX *ἀρθήσονται* "they will be carried." 'A Σ Θ Tg Vg support MT. Read MT.

12.c. MT תשעשעו reduplicated piel "you may play" (BDB, 1044). DSS^{Isa} תשתעשעו reduplicated hithp. LXX *παρακληθήσονται* "they will be comforted." Vg *blandientur vobis* "they will be pleasing to you." Read MT.

13.a. MT תְּנֻחָמוּ pual "you may be comforted." DSS^{Isa} תתנחמו is the more common hithp form (Kutscher, *Isaiah Scroll,* 362).

14.a. MT has a verb, וְזָעַם "and he is indignant" (BDB, 276). A slight change in pointing makes it a noun, וְזַעַם "and indignation," which parallels the previous stich. *BHS* suggests וְזַעְמוֹ "and his indignation."

15.a. MT באש "in fire." Two Heb. MSS כאש and LXX *ὡς πῦρ* read "like fire." DSS^{Isa} 'A Σ Θ Tg Vg support MT. Read MT.

15.b. DSS^{Isa} has אפו "his anger" twice, due to dittogr (Kutscher, *Isaiah Scroll,* 545). The Versions support MT.

16.a. נִשְׁפָּט niph "enter into judgment" (BDB, 1047). DSS^{Isa} יבוא לשפוט "will come to judge" (cf. Pss 96:13; 98:9; 1 Chr 16:33; Kutscher, *Isaiah Scroll,* 545). LXX adds *πᾶσα ἡ γῆ* "all the land (or earth)." MT makes sense as it is and is the less common expression.

16.b. *BHS* would insert two words from v 18. But there is no need for this.

16.c. *BHS* notes a proposal to make this a verb. But the Versions support MT.

16.d. DSS^{Isa} omits יהוה "Yahweh." The Versions support MT.

16.e. MT ורבו "they will be many" is supported by DSS^{Isa}. Tg reverses noun and verb, וסגיאין קטיליא "many will be slain." LXX *πολλοὶ τραυματίαι ἔσονται* "many will be wounded." Read MT.

17.a. K אחד masc "one." Q DSS^{Isa} and other MSS אחת fem "one."

17.b. MT והשקץ "and the abomination" (BDB, 1054) occurs elsewhere only in Leviticus and Ezek 8:10. DSS^{Isa} והשקוץ is the more common form (Kutscher, *Isaiah Scroll,* 386). Syr *wšrṣ'* "swarming things." LXX Tg Vg support MT. Read MT.

18.a-a. The phrase is difficult to place in context. LXX adds *ἐπίσταμαι* "I know," as does Syr. Tg adds וקדמי גלן "before me are revealed." DSS^{Isa} Vg follow MT. *BHS* suggests transferring to v 16. See Whybray (289).

18.b. MT בָּאָה fem sg "she comes." DSS^{Isa} באו pl "they come" makes "their deeds and thoughts" the subject. LXX *ἔρχομαι* "I come" and Vg *venio* "I come" lead *BHS* to recommend qal act ptcp בָּא "coming." This is the best solution.

19.a. MT פול "Pul" is followed by DSS^{Isa} Tg. LXX *καὶ Φουδ* "and Phud" presupposes פוט "Put" as in Jer 46:9. Vg *in Africam* "in Africa."

19.b. MT משכי "drawers" (BDB, 604). DSS^{Isa} is illegible. Tg דנגדין ושדן "draw and shoot." LXX Μοσοχ "Mosoch" = Akk *Muški* (cf. Gen 10:2). Vg *tendentes* "drawing."

19.c. קשת "bow" is omitted in some Heb. MSS and LXX, which probably follow the same text tradition as Jeremiah (*BHS*).

20.a. כרכרות "camels, dromedaries" is a *hap. leg.* (BDB, 503). LXX omits. Σ *φορείοις* "litters." Tg תשבחן "songs of praise." Vg *carrucis* "in chariots." The meaning is uncertain.

21.a. DSS^{Isa} LXX add "for myself." Syr Tg Vg support MT.

21.b. MT ללוים "for the Levites." Many Heb. MSS, Syh and Syr add a *waw* "and." LXX Tg Vg omit the articles on both "priests" and "Levites." Read with LXX.

22.a. L הַחֲדשים. Many other MSS הַחֲדָשִׁים. There is no difference in meaning.

23.a. MT בשבתו "with its (masc) Sabbath." DSS^{Isa} בשבתה "with its (fem) Sabbath." שבת "Sabbath" can be either masc or fem (BDB, 992).

24.a. MT דראון "an abhorrence" (BDB, 201) occurs only here and in Dan 12:2.

Form/Structure/Setting

Vv 6–16 are thought by Westermann (332) to be colored by an apocalyptic frame, while von Waldow sees the passage as a judgment speech against the heathen peoples (*Anlass*, 46–53). Pauritsch (*Neue Gemeinde*, 217–18) finds the closing verses (18–24) to be cast in the form of an announcement of salvation, but admits that the present form is of a literary nature intended not so much for the Jerusalem congregation as for diaspora Jews and proselytes.

The limits of this episode are set at the beginning by the uproarious recognition that the decisive moment in Jerusalem's renaissance is occurring (vv 6–8) and at the end by the sad recognition of the fate of the rebels (v 24).

Again formal edicts determine the structure. The first (v 9) acknowledges Yahweh's role in the new birth of the city. The second (v 12a-b) announces the new peace that Yahweh is extending to the city. The third (v 17) confirms that the rebellious sinners have come to their end. Four formal decrees establish the ways that Jerusalem is going to function in its new status. People from the nations will facilitate the return of Jews (v 20). Some of these will become priests and Levites (v 21). Jewish successors in blood and name are assured for the period of the new creation (v 22). And all humanity may come to worship in the new city (v 23). Thus the episode ties up the loose ends from the Vision and establishes the ground rules for the new era.

The edicts are framed by excited speeches that note the tumultuous events in the city (vv 6–8) and by reactions from Yahweh and courtiers to the edicts (vv 10–11, 12c–16, 18–19). A final word from Yahweh and a supporter notes the bitter reminder that not all Israel or Judah or Jerusalem are participants in the celebration. God's victorious joy cannot be complete without a mixture of pain.

The episode yields this outline:

- Notice of events in Jerusalem (vv 6–8)
  - Formal edict: "Would I rupture and not bring to birth?" (v 9)
- Reactions (vv 10–11)
  - Formal edict: "I am extending peace to Jerusalem" (v 12a-b)
- Reactions (vv 12c–16) A Yahweh speech
  - Formal edict: The sinners are brought to their end (v 17)
- Yahweh speech (vv 18–19)
  - Formal edict: "They will bring your brothers to Jerusalem" (v 20)
  - Formal edict: "I will take priests and Levites from them" (v 21)
  - Formal edict: "Your seed and your name shall stand before me" (v 22)
  - Formal edict: "All flesh will come and worship" (v 23)
- Yahweh speech: A reminder of the rebels now judged (v 24)

The Vision closes as it began with a scene in the heavenly court of God. It is vitally related to the happenings in Jerusalem's temple and the people who worship there. But, in these scenes at least, the point relates more to that worship and the attitudes of the worshipers than to any historical issues. The Vision has come full circle.

Note that this scene has three "closures" for openings earlier in the Vision. The city on a hill to which all people would flow (2:1–4) finds its fulfillment here in vv 18–20. The great announcement of good news for Jerusalem (40:1–9) is fulfilled in this scene. The promises of the restoration of Jerusalem in chaps. 45, 49, and 54 and especially chaps. 60–62 are picked up and closed here. It is a grand finale indeed.

Comment

6 Tumultuous sounds are noted "offstage." They derive *from a city.* Earlier one might have expected the opposition to instigate such a fight. But Yahweh is fully in charge of this scene. He is *making full payment to his enemies.* Even this final scene is marked by opposition to Yahweh's plan. But his patience is exhausted.

7 The next eight verses use birth and child imagery to describe the emergence of the new city. The suddenness of the events is portrayed in this verse: *Before . . . labor, she gives birth.* Jerusalem's destruction in 587 B.C. had left marks on the city which were not removed until Nehemiah rebuilt the walls in 437 B.C. (see Bright, *HI,* 381). After that long wait of well over a century, it took only two years for Nehemiah to complete the wall. It was an unbelievable feat. The metaphor picks up imagery from 49:20–21 (see Rev 12:5).

8 *Who ever heard of such a thing? . . . Zion has gone into labor and birthed her children.* The achievements of Ezra and Nehemiah were memorable. They accomplished more in a short period than anyone else in the century before and the century after them. *The children of Zion* are the new covenant community of faithful servants of Yahweh. This passage develops the theme of 65:8–10, 13–25. The picture of Yahweh's Israel as a "son" is common (1:2; Exod 4:22–23; Deut 8:5; Jer 31:20; Hos 11:1). The reference to children could also be to the new inhabitants (see Neh 11).

9 Yahweh pictures the stages of birth. He is the midwife. The process of birth will be carried through. *If I am the one who brings to birth.* He has claimed from chap. 40 on that he had initiated all the things that had happened. All of them pointed to this moment when Jerusalem would resume its functions and open its gates to believing pilgrims. *Shall I hinder it?* After having brought this project this far, it is unthinkable that God would turn back now.

10 It is time for Jerusalem to rejoice. Mourning for Jerusalem had been a Jewish preoccupation for a long time (see the Book of Lamentations and 60:20; 61:2–3). Later centuries would revive the laments at "the wailing wall." But in 438 B.C. Yahweh finds that mourning indicates lack of faith in his plans. It is no longer appropriate. *Rejoice with Jerusalem, you who love her* (see Pss 26:8; 122:6; 137:6).

11 *You may drink . . . from the abundance of her glory.* The people of the dispersion may join the rejoicing. They love Jerusalem. The restoration of the city gives them a focus for their faith and hope. They can visit it on pilgrimage. They can all take *satisfaction* and *consolation* from the knowledge that she is well and prosperous. In that hope they can live out their faith where they are.

12 שלום "peace" means much more than absence of conflict. Its completeness includes health and prosperity. *Like a river* pictures this *extending* as a constant flowing (see 48:18). כבוד גוים "glory of nations" continues the picture of prosperity as the wealth of nations converge on the city (see 60:5–7, 11, 13; 61:6). The figure pictures Jerusalem nurturing the faithful as a mother nurtures a baby or a toddler.

13 Yahweh is the ultimate source of *comfort. With Jerusalem* the faithful everywhere are comforted as 12:1 had sung. This would not apply to the opposition, of course (57:6, 21). But the comforts are for his *elect* (see Hos 11:1–4). In this Yahweh fulfills his word (40:1–11; 2 Cor 1:3–5).

14 The address to all who love Jerusalem continues. They can *see, rejoice,* and *flourish* in the sight of what is happening there. *Heart* and *bones* (58:11; Ezek 37) point to the very center and structure of their being. *Like the grass* is a metaphor which reverses the intention of 40:6–8. Here it pictures its ubiquitous presence.

It is known. The Vision has insisted that God's work be known among the nations (40:5; 44:23; 60:3, 14; 61:6, 9, 11; 62:2). Now the content of that knowledge points to the separation between *servants* and *enemies.* That separation, pictured in chap. 65, is now complete. Yahweh's *hand,* that is his power to save, is *with his servants.* His *indignation,* that is his fury and wrath, and his *punishment* is *with his enemies.*

15 Yahweh appears as the Divine Warrior (F. M. Cross, *Canaanite Myth and Hebrew Epic* [Cambridge: Harvard University Press, 1973] 91–111; D. L. Christensen, *Transformations of the War Oracle in OT Prophecy* [Missoula: Scholars Press, 1975]; P. D. Miller, *The Divine Warrior in Early Israel* [Cambridge: Harvard U. P., 1973]) to execute judgment and the sword. The two verses draw on imagery that is very old in Israel. *He comes in a fire and his chariots are like the storm wind* is a quotation from Jer 4:13 (see also Ps 68:17 and Hab 3:8).

16 *Fire* in judgment is also found in 5:24; 9:5, 18; 10:16; 26:11; 30:27; 33:14; 47:14; 64:1[2]; 65:5. The sword appeared in 65:12 (see 34:6). Yahweh's intervention to "bring to birth" also involves settlement of issues relating to his enemies.

17 This verse includes another description of pagan rites: *the gardens* (1:29; 65:3), eating pork (65:4; Lev 11:7), *abomination* and *mice* (Lev 11:29). Those who practice them will be *terminated* (יסֻפו "come to an end") *together* (see 1:28, 31). Their communal judgment stresses the horrible and social nature of their sins. It will be a mass judgment and a mass execution as it had been a mass provocation against God.

18 *Their deeds and their thoughts* are two Hebrew words which many interpreters think to be out of order. However, *their* has a clear antecedent in the pagans of v 17. If the words are understood antithetically in this position (*despite*), they fit the context. *I am coming* (אנכי בא) is also a problem (see n. 18.b). The idea of God's coming is pervasive in the Bible (*TWAT* 1:549–61; E. Jenni, " 'Kommen' im theologischer Sprachgebrauch des AT," *Wort, Gebot, Glaube,* FS W. Eichrodt, ATANT 59 [Zürich: Zwingli Verlag, 1970] 251–61; J. Jeremias, *Theophanie: Die Geschichte einer alttestamentlichen Gattung,* WMANT 10, [Neukirchen-Vluyn: Neukirchener-Verlag, 1965]; S. Mowinckel, *He That Cometh,* tr. G. W. Anderson [Oxford: Blackwell, 1959]; G. Pidoux, *Le Dieu qui vient* [Neuchatel/Paris: Delachaux & Niestlé, 1947]; F. Schutenhaus, "Das Kommen und Erscheinen Gottes im AT," *ZAW* 76 [1964] 1–21). The purpose of God's appearance is *to gather all the nations and the language groups* (see 55:1–8; Zech 8:23). He wants them all to *see his glory* (see 40:5; 59:19; 60:1) in fulfillment of his earlier words. This will occur in Judah (60:1–3). And his presence will bring salvation for his people (62:11).

19 אות "a sign" (*TWAT* 1:182–204). In 7:14 the sign was a child yet to be born. In 19:20 it was a monument on Egypt's border. In 55:13 the joyful return and the land's renewal was the sign. Here the sign is not defined. It is *in them,* that is in the nations and *established* by Yahweh. In context *their survivors* refers to those who survive among the nations, although the antecedent for *their* is not defined. Or does it refer to survivors who are among the group in Jerusalem? Some of these Yahweh *will send to the nations.* These ancient missionaries ("sent ones" or "apostles") are sent to distant lands. The Vision has given most attention so far to the nations in Palestine or immediately adjacent to it. But here the list reaches far afield in distance and in time (see Gen 10). *Tarshish* is a distant port city, perhaps in Spain or on the Black Sea (see 2:16; 23:1, 6, 10, 14; Ezek 27:12). *Pul* (LXX calls it Put) may be in Africa and *Lud* in Asia Minor (see Gen 10:6, 13; Ezek 27:10, 30:5); Heb. *drawers of a bow* is rendered in Greek "Meshek," which is unknown; *Tubal* (see *MBA* 146) may be in Asia Minor; while *Javan* is in Greece. The list uses ancient names and makes no effort to put them in current forms. It is intended symbolically. They go out to those who *have not heard* God's *announcements* (like that in 40:1–9), *those who have not seen* what is going on in Jerusalem. These may be Jews or other believers who have not yet been to Jerusalem. *My glory* is a reference to the renovated city of Zion. The messengers will spread the news.

20 The believers in the diaspora *will bring your brothers* in covenant and faith from all the nations. They do this as *an offering to Yahweh* which is obviously far more acceptable than the ox or lamb in v 3 above. The vision of 2:2–3 is coming true. (See also 11:9; 56:7; 57:13; 65:1, 25.) This effort to transport the pilgrims to Zion joins the efforts of believers in Jerusalem to restore the city and it will be blessed.

21 *From them also* means from the diaspora and the believers that come from everywhere. Yahweh will *take some to be Levites and priests.* The new openness will keep nothing reserved for special groups. Leadership in worship may be accorded to the pilgrims (see 56:3–8). *Levites* here refers to persons who perform a function. It is not a tribal designation. The temple, instead of being a place where privileged priests perform sacrifices, will have truly become "a house of prayer for all nations" (56:7).

22 This verse addresses the faithful pilgrims by picking up references in 65:17 to *the new heavens and the new land.* Yahweh promises the worshipers permanence. Their children and their name will last as long as the new order and they will have their place before Yahweh in worship (56:5). This does not promise them eternal life in the NT sense (John 10:27–29; 1 Pet 1:23; see E. Achtemeier, *Community and Message,* 150), but it does promise permanence through a remembered name and line of children (51:11; 61:9; 65:9, 23).

22 *From a new moon to its (following) new moon* means every month. *Sabbath to . . . sabbath* means weekly. *All flesh* is a term used three times in chap. 40 and three times in chap. 66 to describe Zion's congregation representing all mankind. *All come to worship before me.* The goal of restoration has been achieved. *Worship* here is "bowing down." It assumes Yahweh's presence and the purpose of worship found in seeking his presence.

24 *When they go out* from the city, the pilgrims cannot avoid seeing *the corpses of persons who were rebelling* against God. Complete separation of servants and enemies allowed the restoration to be completed and the pilgrims to come for worship. But the memory of the bitter opposition cannot be forgotten. Their bodies have been thrown out on the city's dump. E. Achtemeier (*Community and Message,* 150) explains: "their bodies feed worm (14:11; 15:8) and fire." And they, too, have become a kind of permanent facet of the city, *an abhorrence to all flesh* who worship there, a reminder of the stubborn group in Israel who resisted God to the very end.

Explanation

The great Vision shows God's strategy successfully concluded. But he had to execute determined opposition to get there. And even then their corpses remain as a grim reminder of Israel's rebellion.

Is this a realistic reminder that Israel survived the exile but was never united again? Schisms continued to wrack her being between Samaritans, Pharisees, Sadducees, Essenes, and others. Finally the Christians went out from her.

Jerusalem does become the rallying point for all the Jewish diaspora. She went through other bad times and had to be rebuilt again and again before she reached her glorious position with Herod's temple under the Romans. Pilgrims came by the thousands. In the twentieth century they still do, though there is no longer a temple there, and Jews make room for Moslems and Christians around the sacred places. In a remarkable way "all flesh" does come to marvel at the glory of God.

What are the important things the Vision of Isaiah has said? Yahweh's new age needed a symbol, a crown, a gathering place. Jerusalem became that place. God's people needed a sign that God was alive and in charge, that he was still present on the earth where people could meet with him. Jerusalem became that sign. The world needed a forum where persons of every race could be assured of a place in God's plan. Jerusalem is that place. Jerusalem yields her treasures of meaning and worship still, not to the mighty of the earth, but to "the meek and mild who tremble at his word."

The destruction of Jerusalem in A.D. 90 brought that era to a close. But the city had a secure place as "a city foursquare in the heavens" (Rev 21) and as the focus of love and devotion for the multitudes who love her Lord.

The Vision has affirmed God and his purpose as revealed in his original creation. It has recognized the persistence of sin as rebellion and its terrible consequences. It has affirmed God's continuing efforts to establish a new order. It has recognized divisions, even in Israel, between believers and unbelievers. It has affirmed God's commitment to resist the rebels and support the humble, meek believer. The Vision has recognized the rebels as the religious conservatives of that day: the priests and the teachers of Torah who looked for God in the past. The Vision has affirmed that God is to be found in the new. He is out front in the future turning his back on the old ways. The Vision affirms his opposition to institutions and authorities, be they kingdom or temple, sacrifice, priesthood, or king. It affirms his commitment to open his city to "all flesh" who want to worship and to meet him there.

Bibliography

Abramowski, R. "Zum literarischen Problem des Tritojesaja." *TSK* 96/97 (1925) 90–143. **Achtemeier, E.** *The Community and Message of Isaiah 56–66.* Minneapolis: Augsburg Press, 1982. **Blenkinsopp, J.** *A History of Prophecy in Israel.* Philadelphia: Westminster, 1983. 242–51. **Carroll, R. P.** *When Prophecy Failed.* New York: Seabury, 1979. 150–56. **Cramer, K.** *Der geschichtliche Hintergrund der c. 56–66 im Buche Jes.* Dorpat, 1905. **Elliger, K.** *Die Einheit des Tritojesaja.* BWANT 45. Stuttgart: Kohlhammer, 1928. ———. "Der Prophet Tritojesaja." *ZAW* 49 (1931) 112–40. ———. *Deuterojesaja in seinem Verhältnis zu Tritojesaja.* BWANT 63. Stuttgart: Kohlhammer, 1933. **Gressmann, H.** *Ueber die in Jes lvi–lxvi vorausgesetzten zeitgeschichtlichen Verhältnisse.* Göttingen: 1898. **Hanson, P. D.** *The Dawn of Apocalyptic.* Philadelphia: Fortress, 1975. 32–208. **Jones, D. R.** "The Cessation of Sacrifice after the Destruction of the Temple in 586 B.C." *JTS* 14 (1963) 12–31. **Kessler, K.** "Zur Auslegung von Jesaja lvi–lxvi." *TLZ* 81 (1956) 335–58. ———. "Studien zur religiösen Situation im ersten nachexilischen Jahrhundert und sur Auslegung von Jes 56–66." *Wissenschaftliche Zeitschrift* 6 (1956–57) 41–74. ———. *Gott geht es um das Ganze: Jesaja 56–66 und Jesaja 24–27 übersetzt und ausgelegt.* Stuttgart: Calwer Verlag, 1960. **Kraus, H.-J.** "Die ausgebliebene Endtheophanie: Eine Studie zu Jes 56–66." *ZAW* 78 (1966) 317–32. **Lindblom, J.** *Prophecy in Ancient Israel.* Philadelphia: Muhlenberg Press, 1962. 403–22. **Littmann. E.** *Über die Abfassungszeit von Trito-jesaja.* Freiburg i.Br.: 1899. **Maass, F.** "Tritojesaja." *Das ferne und nahe Wort.* FS L. Rost. BZAW 105. Berlin: Töpelmann, 1967. 151–63. **Marty, J.** *Les chapîtres 56–66 du livre d'Esaie, étude critique.* Paris: 1924. **McCullough, W. S.** "A Re-Examination of Isaiah 56–66." *JBL* 67 (1948) 27–36. **Michel, D.** "Zur Eigenart Tritojesajas." *TViat* 10 (1966) 213–30. **Odeberg, H.** *Trito-Isaiah (Isaiah lvi–lxvi): A Literary and Linguistic Analysis.* Uppsala: 1931. **Pauritsch, K.** *Die Neue Gemeinde: Gott Sammelt Ausgestossene und Arme.* AB 47. Rome: Biblical Institute Press, 1971. **Praetorius, F.** "Zum Text des Tritojesaia." *ZAW* 33 (1913) 89–91. **Renaud, B.** "La confession dans le livret d'Isa 56–66." *RevDrCan* 34 (1984) 185–207. **Scullion, J. J.** "Some Difficult Texts in Isa cc. 56–66 in the Light of Modern Scholarship." *UF* 4 (1973) 105–28. **Sehmsdorf, E.** "Studien zur Redaktionsgeschte von Jesaja 56–66." *ZAW* 84 (1972) 517–76. **Wallis, G.** "Gott und seine Gemeinde: Eine Betrachtung zum Trito-jesaja-Buch." *TZ* 27 (1971) 182–200. **Wodecki, B.** "Der Heilsuniversalismus bei Trito-Jesaja." *VT* 32 (1982) 248–52. **Zimmerli, W.** "Zur Sprache Tritojesajas." *STU* 20 (1950) 110–22 = *Gottes Offenbarung. Gesammelte Aufsetze zum Alten Testament.* ThB 19. Munich: Kaiser, 1963. 217–33.

The same book that established the separation of the Servant Poems in Deutero-Isaiah (B. Duhm, *Das Buch Jesaja,* HKAT, Göttingen: Vandenhoeck & Ruprecht, 1892) suggested that chaps. 56–66 should be treated as a separate unit written by a prophet to be called Trito-Isaiah who lived in Jerusalem before the time of Nehemiah (about 450 B.C.). Duhm thought the chapters to be a unity roughly contemporary with the time of Malachi. The question of literary independence has found general acceptance, but questions of date, provenience, and unity have been contested throughout the intervening period.

Most interpreters place the chapters either around 520 B.C. or about 450 B.C. They see a tumultuous period reflected in the chapters where the issue of building (or rebuilding) the temple is prominent. See current introductions to the OT and the commentaries for details.

This commentary relates the final chapters to a date past the middle of the fifth century as Duhm did. But it differs in the structural analysis and the historical settings of the rest. Instead of two collections (chaps. 40–55 and 56–66), it sees a division into six acts using the signals at the end of chaps. 48, 57, and 66 as significant marks of that structure. Instead of historical settings of *ca.* 540 B.C. in chaps. 40–55 and *ca.* 450 B.C. for chaps. 56–66, it suggests a structure that depicts periods in Jewish history from *ca.* 545 to *ca.* 450 B.C. It views the entire work, including chaps. 1–39, as a single composition intended to depict Yahweh's relation to Israel from the reign of Uzziah in Judah to that of Artaxerxes in Persia. Many themes in the final chapters hark back to parallels in the first chapters.

This view accounts for the similarities through the book in terms of a single composition and purpose. It accounts for the difference in terms of the complex historical changes from one generation to the next, and it accounts for the major change between chaps. 1–39 and 40–66 in terms of a new age in which God offers blessing, replacing the old which had fallen under judgment and curse.

Chaps. 58–66 are seen as representative of the author's (and the first readers') generation. They represent the reign of Artaxerxes in which first Ezra and then Nehemiah bring renewal and new hope for Jerusalem. They fulfill the promise of 2:2–4 and project a form of religious life for Jews under imperial rule that becomes the norm for Judaism.

Index of Authors Cited

Abel, F. M. 12
Abramowski, R. 367
Achtemeier, E. R. 133, 198, 268, 277, 284, 289, 314, 319, 322, 323, 337, 342, 343, 344, 346, 352, 356, 357, 365, 366, 367
Ackroyd, P. R. 18, 62, 73, 201, 219
Adams, L. xxvii
Aharoni, Y. xvi, 73, 266
Ahlström, G. W. 222
Ahuviah, A. xxvii
Airoldi, N. 53
Aistleitner, J. xix, 87, 100
Akpunonu, P. xxvii
Albertz, R. 93
Albright, W. F. 47, 226
Allegro, J. M. 140
Allen, L. C. 62, 113, 222
Allis, O. T. 70
Alonso, A. 222
Alonso, N. 115
Alonso-Schökel, L. 72
Alt, A. xvi
Altmann, P. xxvii, 13
Amir, Y. xxvii
Amirtham, S. xxvii
Amsler, S. xxvii
Anderson, B. W. 80, 81
Anderson, T. D. 309
Ap-Thomas, D. R. 97
Arragon, G. J. van xxvii
Aus, R. D. 337
Auvray, P. xxvi, 40, 148
Avaux, M. 30
Avi-Yonah, M. xiv, xvi, 73, 219
Avigad, N. 201, 219, 221

Baars, W. 222
Bachl, G. 222
Bachmann, J. 196
Bailey, K. E. 295
Baldacci, M. 277, 337
Balentine, S. E. 196
Baltzer, K. xxvii, 115
Balzer, D. 69
Banwell, B. O. 69
Bardtke, H. xxvii
Barr, J. 82, 237, 238
Barrois, G. xxvii
Barstad, H. M. xxvii
Barstadt, N. M. 115
Bartlett, J. R. 10, 321
Battenfield, J. R. 222
Bauer, H. and P. Leander xiii, 141, 142
Bauer, W., W. F. Arndt, and F. W. Gingrich xiii
Baumgartner, W. xv, 21, 47, 56, 63
Beaucamp, E. 109, 121
Beaudet, R. 81
Becker, J. P. 38, 104
Bedenbough, B. xxvii
Beecher, W. J. 115
Beek, M. A. 240, 323
Beeston, A. F. L. 167
Begrich, J. 26, 53, 55, 56, 58, 71, 72, 79, 101, 105, 109, 127, 129, 143, 154, 186, 197, 198, 244
Behler, G. M. 109, 115
Behm, J. 273
Behr, J. W. xxvii
Bentzen, A. 120
Bergmeier, R. 172, 222
Bergstrasser, G. 99, 141
Bernhardt, K.-H. 93
Betram, R. W. 109
Beuken, W. A. M. 109, 158, 181, 193, 233, 240
Bickel, G. 5
Bilik, E. 207
Bjornard, R. B. xxvii
Blank, S. H. xxvii, 214, 323
Blau, J. 81
Blenkinsopp, J. xxvii, 70, 81, 198, 204, 288, 289, 367
Blocher, H. 115
Blythin, I. 181, 222
Boadt, L. 97
Boecker, H. J. 26, 101
Boer, P. A. H. de xxvii, 53, 55, 56, 69, 77, 88, 153, 177, 331
Bogaert, M. 153
Böhl, F. 93
Boman, T. 93
Bongers, H. A. 251
Bonnard, P. E. xxvi, 69, 72, 106, 120, 131, 132, 133, 134, 142
Booij, T. 136
Borchardt, L. 52
Botterweck, G. J. xviii, xix, 75, 323
Bouma, H. 337
Boutflower, C. xxvi
Brawer, A. J. 172
Brayley, I. F. M. 289, 293
Breasted, J. H. 147
Bredenkamp, C. J. 33, 55, 56, 57
Briggs, C. A. xxvii
Bright, J. xv, xxvii, 73, 147, 180, 201, 219, 265, 363
Brockelmann, C. xiii, xix
Bromiley, G. W. xv
Brongers, H. A. 172, 268, 336
Brown, C. xvi, 59
Brown, F., S. R. Driver, and C. A. Briggs xiii, 6, 7, 9, 21, 27, 34, 40, 41, 49, 52, 55–57, 64, 77, 86–88, 99, 100, 102, 112, 113, 125–28, 140–42, 151–53, 160, 165, 170, 175, 176, 184, 185, 191, 192, 195–97, 209, 210, 215, 225, 226, 235, 236, 243, 244, 254, 255, 261, 262, 270, 271, 272, 279, 280, 285, 292, 293, 300, 301, 310, 316, 317, 326–28, 334, 341, 351, 360, 361
Brownlee, W. H. 100
Bruce, F. F. 237
Budde, K. F. R. xvi, xxvi, 301
Buhl, F. P. W. xv, 41, 254, 270
Bundy, D. D. 222
Buri, F. 227
Burke, D. G. 249
Burney, C. F. 18
Burrows, M. 185
Buse, I. 314, 323
Butler, T. C. xxvi
Buttrick, G. A. xv

Calderone, P. S. 40, 53, 55
Calvin, J. 103
Canellas, G. 69, 115
Cannon, W. W. 260
Caquot, A. 240
Carmignac, J. xxvii
Carroll, R. P. xxvii, 367
Caspari, W. 2, 72
Cassuto, U. xxvii
Castellino, G. R. 53
Causse, A. xxvii, 289, 337
Cazelles, H. 115, 120, 227
Charbel, A. 115
Charles, R. H. xii
Chary, T. xxvii
Chavasse, C. 227
Cheyne, T. K. 22, 41, 55, 57, 185, 195, 196, 255, 270, 280, 293, 328
Chiesa, B. xxvii, 75, 240
Childs, B. S. xv, 18, 130
Chilton, B. D. 133
Christensen, D. L. 364
Chrysostom 225
Clark, K. C. 71
Clements, R. E. xxvi, 18
Clifford, R. J. 83, 240
Clines, D. J. A. 222, 227
Cobb, W. C. xxvii
Cohen, C. 167
Collins, J. J. 222
Conrad, D. 323
Conrad, E. W. xxvii, 69, 75, 79, 80, 83, 97, 101, 121, 129, 143
Constantinescu, A. N. xxvii
Contenau, G. 13
Conzelmann, H. 328
Cook, J. M. 219, 265, 267, 288, 318
Cook, S. A. 201, 219
Coppens, J. 109, 115, 222, 299
Cornaly, W. A. 38
Corney, R. W. 193, 330
Couroyer, B. 83
Cowley, A. xv, 20
Cox, J. M.
Cramer, K. 367
Cranfield, C. E. B. 286
Crim, K. xv
Crosby, C. E. 101
Cross, F. M. xxvii, 9, 78, 219, 221, 364
Crown, A. D. 26, 63
Crüsemann, F. xxvii, 154
Ctesias 147, 180, 181, 265, 267
Culican, W. 147, 180, 219

Daabe, P. R. 222
Dahl, G. xxvii
Dahlberg, B. T. 147, 180, 201
Dahms, J. V. 240
Dahood, M. xxvii, 53, 55, 64, 77, 83,

148, 190, 193, 196, 207, 222, 226, 233, 255, 268, 309, 341
Dalmon, G. H. xii
Daris, S. 268
Daube, E. 81
Davidson, R. xxvii
Day, J. 222
Delitzsch, F. J. 64, 141
Deming, L. xxvii
Denton, R. C. 106
Deutsch, R. R. 23
DeVries, S. J. 82, 127, 238
Dietrich, E. K. xxvii
Diettrich, G. 78
Diez-Macho, A. 113
Dijk, H. J. van 75
Dijkstra, M. xxvii, 109, 158
Dillmann, A. 235, 270
Dion, H. M. xxviii, 148, 154, 158
Dion, P. E. xxviii
Döderlein, J. C. 70
Driver, G. R. xxviii, 5, 6, 55, 56, 57, 100, 126, 128, 141, 152, 165, 170, 175, 184, 196, 197, 209, 215, 226, 243, 271
Duarte Lourenco, J. 227
Dubshani, M. xxviii
Duhm, B. 5, 6, 7, 32, 55, 86, 105, 116, 127, 153, 175, 209, 210, 227, 235, 236, 243, 253, 254, 270, 285, 286, 301, 328, 352, 367
Dünner, A. xxviii, 133

Eakins, J. xxviii
Eaton, J. H. xxviii, 118
Ehrlich, A. B. xxviii, 6, 7, 21, 32, 33, 35, 40, 56, 63, 128, 279, 280, 285
Eichhorn, J. G. 70
Eichrodt, W. xxvi, xxviii
Eisenbeis, W. xxviii, 12
Eissfeldt, O. xxviii, 70, 240, 256
Eldridge, V. xxviii
Elliger, K. xiii, xxvi, xxviii, 2, 69, 71, 72, 77, 78, 79, 82, 83, 86, 87, 88, 97, 99, 100, 102, 104, 105, 109, 112, 113, 125–28, 130, 131, 139–42, 151–53, 175, 196, 197, 209, 223, 226, 236, 243, 270, 280, 310, 328, 352, 367
Ellul, J. 18
Emerton, J. A. 2
Engnell, I. xxviii
Esaman, C. M. 337
Ettore, F. 75
Everson, A. J. 299
Ewald, H. 128, 235

Fahlgren, K. H. 133
Falk, Z. W. 191
Feldmann, F. 7, 32, 120, 293
Feuillet, A. xxviii, 115
Fichtner, J. 18, 214
Fieldner, M. J. 133
Fillerton, K. 48
Fischer, G. 75, 81
Fischer, L. R. 93
Fishbane, M. 24
Fisher, R. W. 75, 79
Fohrer, G. xxvi, xxviii, 86, 97, 102, 128, 176, 198, 223, 251, 256, 280, 310
Fokkelman, J. P. 75
France, R. T. 233
Franco, E. xxviii
Fredriksson, H. 130
Freedman, D. N. 109, 121, 125, 167
Frezza, F. 109
Friedrich, G. xviii
Frye, R. N. 73, 147, 180, 219
Fullerton, K. 30
Fürst, J. 353

Galbiati, G. 75
Galland, C. 223
Galling, K. xiii, xvii, xxviii, 131, 201
Gamper, A. xxviii, 69
Garofalo, S. xxviii, 75
Gaster, T. H. 13
Gelston, A. xxviii, 136
Gerhardt, P. 136
Gerleman, G. xxviii, 7, 115
Gesenius, W. xv, 52, 141
Gesenius, W., and F. P. W. Buhl xv, 6, 21, 100
Gesenius, W., E. Kautzsch, and A. E. Cowley xv, 6, 7, 21, 55, 56, 77, 78, 86, 88, 100, 112, 113, 142, 152, 175, 185, 209, 215, 225, 226, 235, 236, 243, 244, 261, 271, 279, 280, 292, 293, 300, 317, 328, 340, 341, 351, 360
Geyer, J. xxviii
Giglioli, A. 314
Gileadi, A. 71
Ginsburg, C. D. xx, xxviii
Gispen, W. H. 223
Gitay, Y. xxviii, xxix, 69
Glahn, L. xxix
Glueck, N. 81
Goethe, W. 14
Goldingay, J. 71, 97
Golebiewski, M. 240
Gordis, R. 83, 141
Gordon, R. P. 223
Gorion, M. J. bin 14
Goshen-Gottstein, M. H. 181
Gosker, R. 223
Gottwald, N. K. 9, 45
Gowen, D. E. 299
Gozzo, S. xxix
Graffy, A. xxiii, 83, 181
Grätz, H. 2, 41, 86, 254, 328
Gray, G. B. xxvi
Gray, J. 35
Greenfield, J. C. 251
Grelot, P. 115–16, 290, 314
Gressmann, H. xii, 71, 72, 73, 198, 367
Grether, H. G. 190
Grimm, W. xxix, 121
Grindel, J. A. 75
Gross, H. xxix, 177, 284, 286
Gruber, M. I. 181
Guillaume, A. 112, 140, 327
Guillet, J. xxix
Gunkel, H. 285
Gunn, D. M. xxix, 233
Guthrie, H. H. 273

Haag, E. 93, 109
Haag, H. xiii, 116, 149, 223
Habel, N. C. 93
Haller, M. 109, 149
Hallo, W. W. 54
Hamel, J. A. van xxix
Hamlin, E. J. xxix, 97, 107
Hänel, J. xxix
Hanson, P. D. 198, 199, 201, 214, 240, 251, 260, 268, 277, 284, 290, 309, 315, 323, 328, 330, 337, 343, 352, 367
Haran, M. xxix, 69, 71, 120
Harner, P. B. 72, 93
Harrison, R. K. 273
Harvey, J. xxix, 81
Hauret, C. 268
Havelock, E. A. 133
Hayes, J. H. xv, xvii, 198
Headlam, A. C. 286
Heerboth, L. A. 337
Heintz, J.-G. 158
Helberg, J. L. 207
Herbert, A. S. xxvi, 69
Hergesel, A. T. 75
Hermisson, H. J. xxix, 72, 116, 149
Herodotus 52, 73, 148, 180, 181, 219, 265
Herrmann, S. xxix
Hertzberg, H.-P. 223
Hessler, B. 290
Hessler, E. xxix, 71, 93, 97, 107
Hillyer, N. xxix
Hobbs, T. R. 35
Höffken, P. 12
Hoffmann, A. 149, 152
Hoffmann, H. W. xxix
Hofheinz, W. C. xxix
Hoftijzer, J. xiv, 100
Holladay, W. L. xiv, xxix, 100, 112
Hollenberg, D. E. xxix
Holmes, I. V. 75
Holmgren, F. 69, 106, 193, 315
Homer 59
Homerski, J. 227
Hommel, F. 6
Hoppe, L. J. 268
Horn, S. H. 18
Horst, F. 133, 177
Houbigant, C. F. 56, 152
Hubmann, F. D. 2
Huey, F. B., Jr. xxix
Humbert, P. xxix, 93
Hurst, J. C. xxix
Hurwitz, S. 13
Hyatt, J. P. 93

Ibn Ezra 7, 70, 103
Illman, K. J. 48
Irons, L. 72
Irwin, W. H. 251
Iwry, S. 38, 41, 48, 50, 52

Jackson, R. S. xxix
Jacobs, L. 134
Japhet, S. 201
Jastrow, M. 88
Jean, C. F. xiv, 100
Jefferson, G. H. 337
Jenni, E. xviii, xxix, 82, 145, 149, 238, 364
Jeppesen, K. xxix
Jepsen, A. xxix, 51, 106, 133
Jeremias, C. 48
Jerome 77, 100
Johl, C. H. 56
Johns, A. F. 149
Johnson, A. R. 106
Jones, D. R. 367
Jones, H. J. 133
Josephus 5, 11, 64, 180, 201, 202, 273
Joüon, P. P. xvi, 7, 97
Junker, H. xxix
Justesen, J. P. 134

Kahmann, J. xxix
Kaiser, O. xxvi, 18, 32, 41, 64, 186, 197, 256

Kaminka, A. xxix
Kapelrud, A. S. xxix, 69, 116, 227
Kaufmann, Y. xxix
Kautzsch, E. xv
Keane, D. P. 93
Keller, B. 116
Kellermann, U. 10
Kelley, P. H. xxvi
Kennett, R. H. xxix
Kennicott, B. xx, 63
Kessler, K. 367
Kida, J. 227
Kiesour, K. 81
Kiesow, K. xxix
Kilian, R. 75
Killen, A. M. 13
Kim, J. C. xxix
Kimchi, D. 7
Kingsbury, E. C. 78
Kirchschläger, W. 93
Kissane, E. J. xxvi, 32, 77, 103, 128, 153, 175, 280
Kitchen, K. A. 30
Kittel, G. xviii
Kittel, R. xiii
Klein, H. xxix–xxx
Klein, R. W. 69
Klostermann, A. 99, 195
Knight, G. A. F. xxvi, 69
Koch, K. xxx, 131, 149, 223
Koch, R. xxx, 69
Koenig, J. 109
Koeverden, W. van 6
Köhler, L. 56, 71, 72, 86, 104, 125, 128, 141, 198, 209, 236, 270, 286, 300, 301, 328
Köhler, L., and W. Baumgartner xvi, 6, 33, 56, 63, 100
Komlosh, J. 223, 240
König, E. 280
König, F. W. 73
Koole, J. L. xxx, 75, 149
Kosmala, H. 77, 268, 272
Kosters, W. H. A. xxx
Krasovec, J. 121
Kraus, H.-J. xxx, 2, 93, 367
Krause, G. xix
Krebs, W. 13, 14
Krinetski, L. 75
Krupp, K. xxx
Kruse, C. G. 116
Kselman, J. S. 260
Kuntz, J. K. 193
Kuntzmann, R. 323
Kutsch, E. xxx, 136
Kutscher, E. Y. xxx, 5, 6, 7, 20, 41, 50, 55, 64, 87, 185, 191, 196, 209, 210, 215, 225, 226, 235, 236, 243, 244, 254, 261, 262, 270, 271, 279, 280, 292, 293, 301, 310, 316, 317, 327, 328, 341, 351, 361
Kuyper, L. J. 75, 78

Laan, J. H. van der 75
Labuschagne, C. J. xxx, 90, 145
Lack, R. 71, 149, 268, 290, 299
Lagarde, P. A. de 165, 316
Lambert, G. 93
Lambert, W. G. 18
Landy, D. 48
Langdon, R. 116
Langsdon, S. H. 13
Laperrousaz, E. M. 201
LaPointe, R. 101
Lau, G. 116
Lauha, A. xxx, 109
Laurentine, A. 336
Leene, H. 121, 149, 163, 172, 193
Leeuwen, C. van 75
Lefevre, A. 268
Legrand, L. 93
Lehmann, H. 93
Lehmann, M. R. 41
Leslie, E. A. xxvi
Levonian, L. 5
Levy, R. xxvi, 88, 113
Ley, J. xxx
Liagre Böhl, F. M. T. de 273
Liao Yong-hsiang 227
Lidzbarski, M. 14
Liebreich, L. J. 71
Limburg, J. 75
Lind, M. C. xxx
Lindblom, J. xxx, 367
Lindsey, F. D. 116, 181, 193, 223
Lipinski, E. 241, 290
Littmann, E. 367
Ljung, I. 116
Lofthouse, W. F. 134
Lohfink, N. 181, 330
Long, B. O. 75
Loretz, O. 75
Löw, I. xvi
Löwinger, D. S. 125, 140
Lowth, R. 113, 125, 316
Lü Ch'ang-ch'üen 337
Lubsczyk, H. 81
Ludwig, T. M. xxx, 93, 120
Lugt, P. van der 193
Lupieri, E. 83, 337
Luther, M. 103, 195

Maalstad, K. 121, 127
Maass, F. 367
Maccagnan, B. 299
MacRae, A. A. 116, 238
Maertens, I. 290
Maggioni, B. 193
Maier, J. 315, 320
Mailland, A. 2, 5
Manahan, R. E. 149
Mansoor, M. 99
March, W. E. 43
Marcheselli-Casale, C. 223
Marcil, M. 116
Marcus, R. 109
Margalioth, R. xxx
Marti, K. 55, 57, 77, 196, 253, 328, 352
Martin, W. C. 207
Martin-Achard, R. 131, 167, 223, 233, 337
Marty, J. 367
Matthews, A. D. 93
Mauch, T. M. xxx, 93
Mauser, U. 337
Mayer, R. xxx
McCarthy, D. J. 75
McCullough, W. S. 367
McEleney, N. J. 109
McEvenue, S. 219
McKenzie, J. L. xxvi, 69, 86, 128, 152, 153
Melugin, R. F. 68, 69, 71, 72, 78, 79, 83, 89, 90, 101, 114, 128–29, 130, 143, 153, 167, 169, 170, 176, 186, 192, 197, 198, 210, 214, 215, 228, 236, 244, 245
Mendall, D. 277
Mendenhall, G. E. xxx, 131
Merendino, R. P. xxx, 72, 75, 77, 83, 97, 102, 109, 121, 136, 143, 149, 154, 158, 163, 167, 169, 170, 172, 175, 181
Merwe, B. J. van der xxx, 136
Mesters, C. 116
Mettinger, T. N. D. 83, 116
Meyers, E. M. 198, 202, 219, 221
Michaelis, J. D. 185
Michel, D. xxx, 367
Miegge, G. 75
Mihelic, J. L. xxx
Millard, A. R. 83
Miller, J. M. xxx, 198
Miller, J. W. xxx
Miller, P. D. 364
Mitchell, H. G. 62
Monaci Castagno, A. 337
Monloubou, L. 116
Montgomery, J. A. 14
Moor, J. C. de 116
Morgenstern, J. xxx, 2, 6, 109, 125, 140, 181, 193, 207, 241, 251, 256, 265, 266, 273, 276, 299, 324, 331, 336
Moriarty, F. L. 62
Mouw, R. 290
Mowinckel, S. xxx, 69, 71, 72, 99, 198, 309, 364
Moye, J. E. M. xxx
Moyne, J. le 18
Muilenberg, J. xxvi, 2–3, 69, 72, 77, 78, 99, 102, 105, 128, 141, 142
Mulder, M. J. 109
Müller, G. xix
Müller, H. P. xxx, 223
Murphy, R. T. xxx
Murray, H. 223
Murtonen, A. 21
Myers, J. M. 265, 266, 307

Naidoff, B. D. xxx, 83, 149
Nakazawa, K. 116, 223
Nandrasky, K. 238
Napier, B. D. 93
Nebe, G. 315, 320
Nelis, J. 26
Neyrey, J. H. 109
Nielsen, E. xxx, 69
Nijen, A. J. van 121
North, C. R. xxvi, xxx, 69, 77, 102, 112, 113, 120, 128, 142, 153, 227, 235
North, R. 120, 353
Noth, M. 126
Nunez Regodon, J. 116
Nyberg, H. S. 54, 55, 56, 57

Odeberg, H. 367
Oded, B. 73
Odendaal, D. H. xxx, 69, 120
Ogden, G. S. xxxi, 149
Olley, J. W. 134, 158, 162
Olmstead, A. T. 114, 147, 155, 156, 180, 188, 198, 204, 205, 219, 221, 265, 267, 288, 318
Oort, H. 127, 210
Oosterhoff, B. J. 109
Orelli, C. von 238
Orlinsky, H. M. xxxi, 18, 86, 114, 126–28
Oswalt, J. T. xxvi

Patai, R. 13
Paul, S. 69
Pauritsch, K. 241, 252, 253, 256, 260, 262, 268, 270, 277, 279, 280, 284, 285, 286, 290, 292, 293, 301, 309,

310, 315, 324, 328, 330, 337, 362, 367
Pavan, V. 233
Payne, D. F. xxxi, 223
Payne, J. B. xxxi, 23
Penna, A. xxxi, 128
Perlitt, L. xxxi
Peterson, D. L. xxxi, 198, 199, 202
Phillips, A. 75, 116
Phillips, M. L. xxxi
Photeus of Constantinople 147
Pidoux, G. 364
Pilch, J. J. 48
Pipal, B. 116
Plamadeala, A. 116
Plamondon, P.-H. xxxi
Ploeg, J. S. van der 93, 116
Plöger, O. 199
Pope, M. 3
Porubcan, S. xxxi
Praetorius, F. 367
Preuss, H. D. xxxi, 104
Pritchard, J. B. xii, 29, 33, 47, 50, 104, 114, 115, 118, 148, 205, 289
Procksch, O. xxvi, 6, 33, 40, 41, 106
Pythian-Adams, W. J. 337

Rabban, N. 120
Raberger, W. 93, 149
Rabinowitz, J. J. 163
Rad, G. von xv, xvii, xxxi, 9, 75, 89, 93, 330
Radai, Y. T. 70
Rainey, A. 219
Ravasi, G. 241
Ravenna, A. 77, 121
Reicke, B. xiii
Reider, J. 87
Reisel, M. 93, 121
Reiterer, F. V. 109, 134, 223
Rembaum, J. E. 223
Renaud, B. 252, 367
Rendtorff, R. xxxi, 94
Renkema, J. 109
Reventlow, H. Graf 26, 134
Reyse, K. M. 202
Ribichini, A. 13
Richter, A. xxxi
Riciardi, A. 116
Ridderbos, J. xxvi
Riesel, M. 149
Rignell, L. G. xxxi, 70, 77, 87
Rinaldi, G. 63, 177, 331, 337
Ringgren, H. xviii, xix, xxxi, 106, 182
Robinson, G. 241
Robinson, H. W. 78
Robinson, T. H. 315
Rofe, A. 199, 337, 356
Rölig, W. 26
Roodenburg, P. C. xxxi, 116
Rose, M. 10
Rosenrauch, H. 182
Rossi, J. B. de xx
Rost, L. xiii
Rothenberg, F. S. 273
Rowley, H. H. 131
Rubinstein, A. 122, 260, 284, 285, 309
Rudolph, W. xiii, 315, 320
Rüger, H. P. 113
Ruiz, G. xxxi
Ruppert, L. 227
Ruprecht, E. xxxi

Sacon, K. K. 75
Saggs, H. W. F. xxxi, 109
Sanday, W. 286
Sanders, J. A. 241, 299
Sasson, J. M. 338
Sauer, G. xxxi, 12, 202
Saydon, P. P. xxxi
Schaeffer, C. F. A. 52
Scharbert, J. 21
Scheiber, A. xxxi, 70
Schildenberger, J. 290
Schmidt, H. 105, 134
Schmidt, J. J. xxxi
Schmidt, K. L. xxxi
Schmitt, H. C. xxxi, 70, 172
Schmitt, J. 299
Scholem, G. 13
Schoors, A. xxxi, 70, 72, 83, 89, 109, 120, 136, 149, 153, 154
Schottroff, W. 26, 202
Schreiner, J. xxxi
Schroten, E. N. P. xxxi
Schult, H. 315
Schunck, K. D. xxxi
Schüpphaus, J. 72
Schutenhaus, F. xxxi, 364
Schwabl, H. 94
Schwarz, G. 109, 193–94, 223, 233, 315, 319
Schweizer, H. 109
Scoggin, E. B. xxxi
Scott, M. 3
Scott, R. B. Y. xxvi, 3
Scullion, J. J. xxvi, 134, 367
Seebass, H. 131
Seeligmann, I. L. xxxi
Sehmsdorf, E. 338, 367
Seidl, T. 207
Sekine, S. 227
Sellin, E. xxxii, 202, 352
Sen, F. 109
Seters, A. van 75
Seybold, K. xxxii, 54, 58, 116
Shargel, D. xxxii
Sicre, J. L. xxxii, 116
Sievi, J. xxxii
Simcox, C. R. 149
Simian-Yofre, H. xxxii, 81
Simon, M. 199
Simon, U. xxxii, 149
Simons, J. xv
Skehan, P. W. xxxii
Skinner, J. 292
Sklba, R. J. xxxii
Sloley, R. W. 52
Smart, J. D. xxvi, 69, 338
Smelik, K. A. D. 22
Smith, B. L. 136
Smith, J. M. P. 132
Smith, M. S. xxxii, 110, 180, 199
Smith, R. L. 261, 265
Smith, S. xxxii, 73, 147
Smitten, W. T. in der 48
Snaith, N. H. xxxi, xxxii, 76, 77, 83, 106, 134, 160, 182
Snodgrass, K. R. 76
Soggin, J. A. 54, 73, 202, 219, 223, 265
Southwood, C. H. 149, 152
Spykerboer, H. C. 70, 71
Squillaci, D. xxxii
Stachowiak, L. 76
Staerk, W. xxxii, 132
Stähli, H.-B. 35
Stamm, J. J. 16, 20, 106, 182
Steck, O. H. xxxii, 116, 199, 223
Steinmann, J. xxvi, xxxii, 86, 102, 128
Stendahl, K. 76
Stern, E. 202, 219
Stoebe, H. J. 76
Stramare, P. T. xxxii
Stuhlmacher, P. xxxii
Stuhlmueller, C. xxxii, 70, 72, 81, 94, 106, 120, 128, 129, 130, 132, 145, 146, 153, 158
Stummer, F. xxxii, 76, 83, 110, 122, 149
Swartzentruber, A. O. xxxii
Szczurek, T. 110
Szlaga, J. 110
Szubin, Z. H. 134

Tadmor, H. 220
Talmon, S. 30, 32, 33, 199, 355
Talstra, E. xxxii
Tannert, W. xxxii
Tawil, H. 38
Terrien, S. xxxii
Thomas, D. W. xiv, 84, 87, 136
Thompson, R. C. 52
Thucydides 265
Tidwell, N. 76, 84, 110
Tom, W. 76
Torczyner, B. 149
Torrey, C. C. xxxii, 3, 6, 70, 103, 185, 244, 255
Trembelas, P. xxxii
Trever, J. C. 113
Treves, M. 223
Troadec, H. G. 241
Trudinger, P. 84, 87

Uchelen, N. A. van 194
Uffenheimer, B. xxxii
Ungnad, A. 47

Vasholz, R. 70, 110
Vaux, R. de 18, 26
Vincent, J. M. xxxii
Viret, P. 338
Virgulin, S. 116, 158
Voeltzel, R. 116
Vogt, E. xxxii, 132
Volz, P. xxvi, xxxii, 69, 77, 105, 113, 128, 165, 292, 301, 328
Vriezen, T. C. 132

Wada, M. 110
Wagner, M. 57
Waldman, N. M. 76
Waldow, H. E. von xxxii, 71, 72, 89, 100, 101, 122, 129, 136, 153, 154, 198, 227, 244, 362
Wallis, G. xxxii, 367
Ward, J. M. xxxii
Watson, N. M. 134
Watson, W. G. R. xxxii
Watts, J. D. W. 10, 120, 131, 338, 353
Watts, J. W. xxxii, 100, 175, 185, 186, 328
Weinfeld, M. xxxii, 94, 149
Weippert, M. xxxiii, 10
Weise, M. 252, 254
Weiss, R. 54, 56
Weissert, D. 277, 279
Wellens, A. 116
Wells, R. D. xxxiii, 290
Welshman, H. 223
Welton, P. 52
Wernberg-Møller, P. 3, 7, 125, 255, 279
Westermann, C. xviii, xxvi, xxxiii, 69, 70, 71, 72, 77, 94, 101, 120, 127, 128, 129, 131, 143, 149, 153, 154, 172, 176, 186, 187, 197, 243, 256,

280, 285, 286, 292, 310, 328, 329, 330, 352, 353, 361
Whitcomb, J. C., Jr. 149
Whitley, C. F. xxxiii, 110, 122, 134, 136, 153, 163, 165, 172
Whybray, R. N. xxvi, 69, 70, 84, 86, 91, 175, 191, 196, 215, 223, 227, 235, 236, 243, 261, 271, 280, 285, 286, 292, 293, 301, 302, 304, 305, 313, 316, 319, 326–28, 341, 343, 346, 351, 352, 360, 361
Widengren, G. 182, 202, 220, 265, 266
Wiener, H. M. 18
Wijngaards, J. N. M. 110
Wildberger, H. xxvi, xxxiii, 5, 6, 7, 10, 11, 12, 13, 14, 16, 18, 20, 21, 26, 27, 32, 33, 35, 40, 41, 47, 49, 50, 52, 55, 56, 57, 59, 60, 63, 64, 118, 132
Williams, D. L. xxxiii
Williams, P. xxxiii, 116
Williamson, H. G. M. 84, 87, 122, 223, 241, 265, 273, 307
Wilshire, L. E. xxxiii, 116
Wiseman, D. J. xvii
Wissowa, G. xvii
Wodecki, B. xxxiii, 367
Wolf, C. U. 249
Wolff, H. W. 116, 199
Worthing, M. 129
Woude, A. S. van der xxxiii
Wright, G. E. 266
Wyatt, R. J. 145
Wypych, S. 97

Yadin, Y. 52, 360
Yalon, H. 194
Young, E. J. xxvi, 3, 70

Zakowitcz, Y. 49
Zenger, E. 241
Ziegler, J. xxxiii, 32, 77, 125, 128, 140, 141, 152
Zillessen, A. xxxiii, 81
Zimmerli, W. xxxiii, 18, 81, 101, 104, 149, 223, 299, 36
Zobel, H.-J. 331
Zurro Rodriguez, E. xxxiii

Index of Principal Subjects

Adversaries 179, 263
Age 95, 237–39, 287, 297, 329, 332
Arm of Yahweh 211
Artaxerxes 265–70, 276, 286, 290–97, 306–9, 311, 314, 317

Babylon 62–67, 167–179

Cambyses 180–81
Coastlands 187, 206
Comfort 303
Court of Yahweh 78
Create/Creator 93, 130, 132, 237, 263
Cyrus 74, 147–48, 156, 160–63, 178

Darius 180–81, 187, 204, 210, 219–33
David 46, 241
Deutero-Isaiah 69–71
Double portion 304

Edom 2, 10, 321
Elect 131–32
Exodus typology 80–81
Ezra 276, 306–9, 314, 352

Fast 273–74
Favor 303
Formation of chaps. 40–46, 72–73
Form-critical Categories 72–73
Former and new 120

Heritage 320
Hezekiah 22, 67 ff. *passim*
Highway 15–16, 80, 320
Holy One of Israel 237

Isaiah 38–67 *passim*

Jacob/Israel 94
Judgment scene 102, 135
Justice 248

Landrights 188, 256
Law codes under Persians 204
Legitimacy 133, 158, 304, 317, 321
Lilith 13

Married 313
Martyr 227–28
Megabyzus 307, 317–19
Merodach-Baladan 63–67
Moses 332

Name 312, 345
Nebuchadnezzar 74
Nehemiah 276, 306, 314, 352
New 120

Parties 198–201
Prayer 335–37
Prayer, house of 249
Provoke 343

Rebellion 283, 287, 332
Redeemer 130, 171, 287
Remembered 332
Righteousness 102, 133, 157, 204, 205–6, 227–28

Sabbath 242–43, 248–49, 276, 365
Salvation 304, 321
Seedbed for Vision 23
Sennacherib 1–48 *passim*
Separation 347
Servant of Yahweh 115–18, 189, 201
Servants 241
Shepherd 90
Sufferer 227–28
Sundial 52
Survivors 45–46

Temple City 288–89
Trito-Isaiah 240–42

Wolf 355

Xerxes 355

Zerubbabel 181, 201–3, 204, 220–33, 314, 352–53

Index of Biblical Texts

A. The Old Testament

Genesis

1–2 94
1–9 238
1:2 12
1:2–10 211
1:6 155
1:21 211
2 297
2:17 61
2:25 165
3:4 61
3:14 355
7:11 155
9:11 237
10 365
10:6 365
10:7 133
10:13 365
10:14 64
11:1–9 172
12:2 304
14:18–20 204, 208
15:1 129
15:4 175
15:5 178
15:7 101
15:18 237
16:13 59
17:1 101
17:6 64
18:2 142
18:23 346
19 47
19:11 42
19:15 176
19:24 12
21:17 129
22:17 178
25:29–34 249
26:24 129
32:28 312
32:31 59
36:9–43 13
36:33 12
41:6 41
41:23 41
41:27 41
43:31 131
46–47 216
46:3 129
48:16 105

Exodus

2:3 12
2:24 332
3:6 101, 279
3:9 280
3:12 104
4 79
4:11 90
4:22–23 363
6:6 16, 106
7:9 211
7:10 211
7:12 211
12:11 215
12:12 44
12:29–30 44
13 106
13:13 16
13:15 16, 44
13:21–22 275
14:19 47
14:21 211
15 330
15:1–15 211
15:5 333
15:13 16, 106
15:16 211
16:10 275
16:29 276
17 179
19:1–20:21 249
19:5 133, 248
19:6 107
20 247
20:2 101, 104
20:2–4 145
20:3–4 143
20:8–11 248, 276
22:4, 7, 9 304
23:19 344
25:5 316
25:18–22 36
26:14 316
32:1–6 144
32:9–14 178
33:14 327
33:23 61
34:20 356
35:7, 23 316
36:19 316
39:34 316

Leviticus

2:1, 2, 13, 16 356
4 156
6 156
6:8 356
11:7 343, 356, 364
11:14 6
11:29 364
14:10–24 356
16 231
17:3–4 356
18:21 258
19:24 319
20:2–5 258
21:20 249
24:17–21 356
25 106, 303
25:25–49 146
26 319
26:16 319
26:17 320

Numbers

1:46 47
6:24–26 13
12 144
20:1–13 144
20:16 47
21:34 101
23:2 11
24:8 60
24:18 11

Deuteronomy

1:16 357
2:4 357
2:8 15
3:2 101
3:18 357
4–11 330
4:34 211
5:6 101, 104
5:12–15 248, 276
6 145
6:4, 5, 9 258
7:8 16
7:19 211
8:5 363
9:26 16
9:29 211
11:2 211
11:20 258
11:24 237
12:17–18 319
14:8 343, 356
14:22–27 319
15:16 175
16:9–17 319
16:13 215
19:6 356
21:17, 18, 20 340
23:1–2 249
24:11, 13 270
26:8 211
27:24–25 356
28 319
28:30–33 319
29:22 12
31:17 282
32 330, 343
32:4 145
32:7 329, 330
32:15 144
32:20 282
32:22 343
32:33 211
33:5 144
33:17 11
33:26 144
33:27 211
34:7 209

Joshua

1:4 237
6:18 9

8:1–2 101
10:1 9
10:8 101
10:12–14 52
10:28 9
10:35 9
11:6 101
11:17 345
12:7 345
15:37 345
15:61–62 14
23:1 333
24 249

Judges

5:5 327
5:19–20 341
6:11 47
6:23 104

Ruth

1:20 312

1 Samuel

4:4 36
4:20 280
5:3–4 104
8:5 135
8:7 334
8:20 135
12:12 334
13:12 131
15:3, 8, 9 9
16:1–5 11
16:13 302
24 156
26 156
28:23 210

2 Samuel

1 156
4:4 351
6:2 36
7 355
7:12 175
7:12–16 47, 246
7:16 35
8:16 26, 313
9:3 351
15:11 175
15:24–37 330
17:29 56
18:19–23 79
19:9 210
20:24 26
22:11 36
24:9, 16 47

1 Kings

1:22–39 330
2:35 330
4:3 26, 313
4:21 287
5–9 288
6:23–28 36
8:6 36
8:12–21 330
8:23–53 330
8:27–30 249
8:42 211
8:56–61 330
11:7 258
13:24, 25, 28 9
15:19 153
18–20 1, 24
21:29 51
22:5 34
22:42 313
23:12 343

2 Kings

3:8 15
12:4–16 288
12:11 26
15:35 288
16:8 153
17:24–28 333
17:31 47
17:36 211
18 27
18–19 44, 288
18–20 22, 23, 29, 53, 65
18:1–12 12
18:2 51
18:3–6 62
18:4–10 25
18:5 28
18:5–7 22
18:7 29
18:8 22
18:9–12 22
18:13 20, 22, 51
18:14–15 22, 23
18:14–16 20, 52
18:17 20
18:17–32 22
18:18 20
18:20, 21, 23 20
18:25, 26–32 21
18:34 21, 22
18:35 22, 90
18:36, 37 22
19 35
19–20 22
19:2, 4 32
19:5 47
19:6 32, 47
19:9, 10, 11 32
19:12 32, 33
19:13 21, 33
19:15 33, 36
19:16 33, 302
19:17, 18 33
19:19 33, 36
19:20, 22–25 40
19:26, 29 41
19:31–35 41
20 50, 51, 58, 65
20:2 49
20:3–5 50
20:6 50, 53
20:7 50
20:7–8 50
20:8 50
20:8–11 53
20:9 50
20:10 64
20:11 50
20:12, 13 63
20:16 64
21 43, 65
21:1 313
21:27–29 51
22:3 26
22:3–7 288
22:8 26
22:12 34
22:19–22 78
23:10 258
23:12 50
23:25 332
23:34–35 2
24–25 23
24:1, 7 2
24:10–16 65
24:17 2
25 37, 44
25:3–21 273
25:23–25 273
25:27–30 74

1 Chronicles

1:12 64
3:19 202
13:6 36
16:29 297
16:33 361
17:16–27 330
18:15 26
29:10–19 330

2 Chronicles

6:14–42 330
6:32 211
20:6–12 330
20:21 297
29–30 28
29:2–31:21 62
30:6–9 330
32:5–8 29
32:23 29
32:32 78
34:8 26, 27
35:26 78

Ezra

1–6 229
1:1–8 189
1:1–14 148
1:2–4 289
1:2–8 178
1:4 192
1:5–8 148
1:8 147
2–6 181
2:2 198, 202
2:68–69 320
3:1–5 230, 240
3:1–13 222
3:2 198, 201
3:3 198
3:7 192, 320
3:8 202
4 355
4:1–2 255
4:1–3 231, 248, 333
4:1–4 188, 189, 201, 213, 217, 218, 314
4:1–5 198, 220, 222
4:2–3 202, 203
4:4–6 221
4:5 187
4:6–17 229
4:6–23 282
4:7–24 276
4:8–23 307

4:23 273
4:24 220, 222
5–6 218
5:1–2 216, 220, 222
5:2 202
5:2–5 203
5:3 220
5:3–4 222, 230
5:3–17 240
5:4 220, 231
5:8–17 230
5:10 203
6:1–12 228, 230
6:1–13 222
6:1–19 232
6:3–12 289
6:6–10 220
6:8 289
6:8–10 320
6:13 220
6:13–15 229
7 294, 298, 304
7:1–28 276, 298
7:6–28 289
7:10 294
7:11–26 287
7:12–28 302
7:13 294
7:13–26 314, 320
7:15–16 294
7:15–20 295
7:17 294
7:21 294
7:21–23 304
7:23 294
7:24 319
7:25 294
7:26 205, 294
9–10 248, 249, 302, 314
9:3 196
9:4 355
9:6–15 330
10:3 355
10:6 267

Nehemiah

1:1–3 306
1:3 273, 331
1:4–11 330
2 298
2–6 353
2:1–9 276
2:1–10 307
2:4–9 289
2:7–8 295
2:7–9 287
2:8–9 294, 320
2:13 211, 294
2:19 11
3:16 16
4 274
4–6 306, 353
4:7–9 313
4:16–18 320
5 274, 277
5:1–8 271
5:4 271
5:4–5 274
5:7–8 274
5:8 266
5:9–12 274
5:13 191
5:15 221, 271, 274
5:17 275
6:1 11
7:7 202
8–9 302, 352
8:9–11 274
9 277
9:5–37 330
9:14 248
9:36 275
10 274
10:31 248
10:31–33 276
11 363
12:1 202
12:27–47 352, 353
12:47 353
13 274
13:4 267
13:15–21 248
13:15–22 276
13:25 196

Esther

1 249
1:8 205
1:13–15 205
1:19 205
2:8, 12 205
5:10 131

Job

1:6 78
6–12 78
7:12 211
8:12 79
9:13 211
11:20 56
13:24 282
15:11 261
16:20 56
17:3 60
17:5 56
18:15 13
21:2 261
24:9 293
26:12 209, 211
28:28 259
34:29 282
38–42 89, 101
38:17 59
38:33 354
39:9 11
40:25–41:3 89

Psalms

1:1 248
1:2 245
3:5 355
5:9 152
13:24 282
16 55
18:3 145
18:11 36
18:47 145
19:5 145
20:2 34
21:6 15
22 161
22:7 105
22:22 11
22:25 282
23:1–3 90
23:6 245
25:6 331
25:8 90
26:8 363
27:4 59
27:9 282
28:1 145, 311
29:2 297
31:3 145
31:21 77
31:23 57
32:3 131
33:21 262
34:18 355
35:1 6, 191
35:5 47
37:2 79
39:3 311
41:5 57
43:3 355
44 330
45:4 15
45:18 331
48:2 355
50:15 34
50:21 131
55:24 55
56–60 55
57–59 344
59:17 78
62:6, 7 55
62:12–13 78
63:3, 7 145
68:17 364
69:4 56
69:18 282
71:16 331
72:9 191
73:26 145
74 330
74:2 16
74:3–8 266
74:12–17 36
74:13 211
76:6 165
77 130
77:2 16
77:3 34
77:12 331
78:8 341
78:49 47
79 330
79:1–4 266
79:16 266
80:2 36
81:11 343
81:13 343
82 118
83:2 55
84:7 16
84:10 245
86:7 34
88:15 282
89:9 36
89:11 211
91:1 145
91:4 317
91:13 211
93 118
93:1 104
93:1–4 9
93:5 104, 216
94:3–5 9
94:19 261
95:10–13 9
95:11 355

96 118
96:6 15
96:9 297
96:10 104
96:13 361
98:3 331
98:7–9 9
98:9 361
99 118
99:1 36
102:3 282
102:13 90
102:25 55
102:26 36
103 153
103:1 262
103:15 79
104:1 15
104:2 9
106 330
106:10 16
107:18 59
107:29 311
107:33–37 131
110:3 297
111:3 15
111:10 259
116:5 185
116:11 57
119:82 56
119:122 60
115:17 55
120–134 17
122:7 363
123 56
129:6 79
129:7 191
131:2 56
132:8 355
136:12 211
137:6 363
137:7 11, 266
141:4 225
141:7 60
143:7 282
145:5 15
145:12 15
145:21 262
147:2 310
149:7 34

Proverbs

1:7 259
3:4 89
6:13 255
8:4 225
11:15 60
15:13 351
17:22 351
18:14 351
20:16 60
27:13 60

Ecclesiastes

2:25 165, 293

Song of Solomon

1:10 216

Isaiah

1 xxiv, 78, 19, 101, 171
1–3 344
1–4 72
1–24 24
1–33 xxiii, 72, 163, 166
1–39 xxiv, xxvi, 72, 108, 132, 247, 264, 296, 346, 354
1:1 24
1:1–7 94
1:2 78, 103, 188, 257, 363
1:2–3 249
1:2–4 304
1:2–7 xxiv
1:3 108
1:7 310
1:9–31 xxiv
1:11–14 352
1:11–17 91
1:13 356
1:15 282
1:16–17 352
1:17–25 273, 274, 277
1:18 316
1:19 132, 249
1:20 6
1:21–23 257, 258
1:23 343
1:24–25 80
1:25 177
1:26 312
1:27 16
1:28 364
1:29 343, 364
1:31 12, 364
2 145
2:1 24
2:1–4 18, 25, 72, 81, 133, 314, 339, 352, 362
2:2 16
2:2–3 46, 295, 365
2:2–4 xxiv, 16, 24, 188, 232, 250
2:3 131, 239, 355, 356
2:3–4 135
2:4 34
2:6–9 94
2:9 171
2:11 171
2:11–12 45
2:11–22 42
2:16 365
2:17 171
2:18 13
2:22 171
3 xxiv, 80, 171, 257, 258
3–4 304
3:3 153
3:9 280
4 46
4:1–6 25
4:2 43
4:2–4 24
4:2–5 xxiv
4:3 43, 45
4:5 15
4:5–6 46
5 xxiv, 94, 157, 162, 297
5:1–7 94, 344
5:2 283
5:4 283
5:5 328
5:5–10 135
5:6 247
5:7 283
5:8 152
5:13 135
5:24 364
5:26 29, 192
6 72, 79, 82, 177, 213, 246, 263
6–65:12 131
6:2 21, 78
6:9 15, 108
6:9–10 133
6:9–13 16, 68, 146
6:11 135
6:11–13 xxiv, 15, 133, 162, 213, 247, 296, 303
6:12 135
6:13 45
7 35, 51, 66, 77, 80, 258
7–8 24, 25, 66
7–10 25, 103, 108
7:1–8 24
7:1–9 30
7:3 15, 43
7:10–17 45
7:14 42, 264
7:17 27
7:17–25 23, 29, 239
7:18 192
7:22–25 247
8:6–8 29
8:7–8 23
8:10 30
8:14 316
8:17 23, 282
8:19 60
9 47
9:5 27, 364
9:6 41, 46
9:18 364
10 xxiv, 94, 157, 297
10:1 356
10:5 27, 28, 45, 189
10:5–6 156
10:5–19 23, 25, 30
10:12–19 42
10:13–19 42
10:14 60
10:16 364
10:20 43
10:21–22 46
10:24 81
10:24–27 25
10:26 81
10:27–32 80
11 47
11:1 293
11:1–15 357
11:1–9 247
11:2 27, 178, 287, 302
11:2–5 91, 303
11:3, 4 34
11:6–9 338, 357
11:9 355, 365
11:10 15
11:11 43
11:12–16 46
11:14 11
11:16 15, 43, 320, 357
11:16–18 81
12 17
12:1–6 247
12:2 27
13 xxiv, 10, 12, 24, 170, 239
13–14 67–172
13:2 192
13:9–13 42
13:10 9
13:21 6
14 xxiv, 24, 26, 64, 170, 259
14–22 119

14:1 132
14:4–23 42
14:11 366
14:19 9, 293
14:24–27 25, 30, 166
14:25 42
14:26–27 30, 41
14:28 22
14:28–32 22, 103
14:30 27
15 79
15–16 103
15–22 22
15–23 24
15:8 366
17:1–3 103
17:6 43
17:9 153
18 67
18:7 243
19 67
19:12–17 166
19:20 365
19:23 15, 16, 320
20 24, 30, 35, 66, 177
20:1–6 24
21 xxiv, 21, 24, 26, 172
21:11–12 103
21:13–17 103
22 22, 26, 43, 46, 58, 66, 80
22:15 24, 26
22:15–19 26
22:22 24
23 67, 103
23–28 43, 48
23:1 365
23:6, 10, 14 365
24 9, 17, 92, 119, 162, 297, 354
24:14 13
24:21–23 9
24:23 9
25 9, 119, 245
25:6 245
25:6–8 9
25:9 107
26–27 80
26:4 27, 145
26:11 364
26:13–14 42
26:15 127
26:16–18 34
26:19 354
27:1 211
27:2–5 354
27:3 184, 293
27:4 247
27:13 355
28–33 46
28:1 130
28:15 257, 259
28:16 87
28:17 259
28:22 328
28:24 153
29 239
29:4 60
29:16 336
29:16–19 193
29:18 153
29:19 107
29:20 356
29:21 34
29:22 16, 238
30–31 25
30–33 67
30:1 343
30:2–5 28
30:7 28, 211
30:12 27
30:14 336
30:15 27
30:27 364
30:31–33 30, 42
30:33 12
31–33 297
31:1 27
31:1–3 28
31:2 356
31:8–9 30–42
31:9 196
32 37, 134
32:6 356
32:9, 10, 11 27
32:13 247
32:15 178
32:17 262
33:2 34
33:8 15, 320
33:9 15
33:14 364
33:16 261
34 8, 16, 80, 103, 119
34–35 15, 71
34–39 vii, 22
34–66 xxiii, 71
34:1 103
34:1–4 7
34:1–17 11
34:1–35:10 vii, 1, 2
34:2, 3, 4 5
34:5–8 7
34:6 5, 364
34:7 5
34:8 5, 7, 15, 303
34:9–15 7
34:13 7
34:14 13, 14
34:15 13
34:16–17 7
35 8
35:1–2 8, 357
35:1–10 247, 358
35:2 293
35:3–4 8, 357
35:4 7
35:5 153
35:5–7 357
35:5–10 8
35:8 16, 357
35:8–10 357
35:10 209
36 24, 33, 35, 37
36–37 53, 67
36–39 23, 24, 29, 41, 42, 66, 71, 73, 79, 304
36:1 22, 44
36:1–22 vii, 1, 18
36:2 15, 44
36:2–22 22
36:3 63, 313
36:4 35
36:4–10 23, 34, 45
36:5 37
36:6 29
36:7 29, 35
36:8 42
36:8–9 29
36:10 29, 30, 42, 45
36:11 43, 44
36:11–37:13 25
36:12 30
36:13–20 45
36:13–21 30
36:14 30
36:16–17 30
36:18–20 30
36:20 90
37 25, 67
37–39 22
37:1–20 vii, 1, 30, 37
37:2 63
37:3 44
37:4 23, 44
37:9 24
37:10–13 42, 45
37:13 21
37:15–20 51
37:16 23, 37
37:17 37
37:17–20 44
37:18, 19 37
37:20 24, 33, 37
37:21 44, 51
37:21–38 viii, 38, 42
37:22–29 41
37:23 23
37:31–32 23
37:32 43
37:33–34 43
37:35 23, 24, 43, 50, 246
37:36–38 44
37:38 44
38 67
38:1 63
38:1–8 vii, 1, 48
38:6 43, 46
38:7 45
38:7–8 42
38:9–20 vii, 1, 53
38:21–22 vii, 1, 48
39 xxiv, 24, 26, 67, 172, 258
39:1–8 vii, 2, 62
39:5 24
39:8 50, 51
40 71, 178, 211, 239, 244, 302, 313, 314, 337, 345, 348, 357, 363, 365
40–44 199
40–48 xxiv, 24, 36, 42, 46, 68, 72, 79, 120, 187
40–53 24, 71
40–55 70, 71, 78, 81, 102, 116, 302
40–57 xxiv
40–62 347
40–66 xxv, xxvi, 70, 72, 92, 106, 120, 132, 134, 153, 239, 296, 311, 312, 353, 354
40:1 82, 303
40:1–2 xxiv, 68, 119, 244, 263, 297, 319
40:1–5 100, 104, 119
40:1–8 78
40:1–9 vii, 68, 72, 75, 121, 155, 178, 216, 245, 246, 263, 361, 365
40:1–11 189, 190, 303, 363
40:1–12 62
40:1–44:23 vii, 68, 72
40:1–49:4 117
40:2 68, 133, 218, 344
40:2–5 107
40:3 15, 16, 131, 320
40:3–4 262
40:3–5 81, 90, 244
40:3–8 68
40:5 6, 15, 295, 357, 364
40:6 100

40:6–7 89, 94, 95, 96, 100, 105, 108
40:6–8 244, 364
40:7 94
40:7–8 95
40:8 94, 245
40:9 78, 104, 216, 226, 302
40:9–10 119
40:9–11 68, 232
40:10 187
40:10–11 118, 319
40:10–31 vii, 68, 83, 87, 88
40:11 156, 188, 211
40:12–17 89
40:12–26 245
40:12–29 89
40:12–44:12 79
40:13 93
40:14 95
40:16 107
40:17 113
40:18–20 166
40:20 132, 142
40:22 9, 108, 209
40:25–26 166
40:26 94
40:27 68, 91, 100, 108, 158
40:28 94, 127, 196
40:28–29 201
40:29 196, 271
40:30 132, 196
40:31 99
41 239
41–48 xxv
41:1 120
41:1–9 320
41:1–20 vii, 68, 97, 100, 101
41:2 102, 108, 118
41:4 105
41:5 77
41:8 132, 238, 304
41:8–9 119
41:8–10 186
41:9 127, 132
41:10 104, 105, 112
41:11 102, 160, 357
41:12 113
41:13 104, 105
41:14 16, 104, 105
41:15 120
41:17 105
41:17–20 81
41:18–20 131, 354
41:20 94
41:21–24 114, 357
41:21–29 102, 114
41:21–42:12 vii, 68, 109
41:22 120, 357
41:23 77
41:24 91, 113
41:25 xxv, 121, 319, 336
41:25–26 187
41:25–27 114
41:25–29 114
41:25–42:9 117
41:27 302
41:28–29 114
41:29 91, 356
42 353
42:1 117, 132, 178, 287
42:1–4 xxv, 70, 114, 116, 186, 187, 204
42:3 121
42:5 94, 114, 209
42:5–9 102
42:6 102, 105, 121, 156, 184, 186, 293
42:6–7 114
42:8 105
42:8–9 114
42:9 105, 120, 305, 357
42:9–14 120
42:10 86, 114, 120
42:10–15 320
42:11 14
42:12 128, 129
42:13 118, 129
42:13–25 128
42:13–43:21 viii, 68
42:14 131, 311
42:14–16 81
42:14–25 129
42:16 129, 260
42:18 153
41:18–20 320, 347
42:18–25 68
42:19 153
42:21 102
42:21–25 129
42:22 82
42:24 131
43:1 94, 155
43:1–3 81
43:1–7 128, 129, 136, 186
43:2–5 105
43:3 156, 161
43:3–4 145
43:6 320
43:7 94
43:8 82, 320, 347
43:8–13 128, 129
43:9 120
43:9–10 357
43:10 105, 132, 320
43:11 105
43:12 105, 142
43:12–13 105
43:14 16, 155
43:14–15 128, 129
43:14–21 347
43:15 94, 105, 118
43:16 86, 131
43:16–21 128, 130
43:17 128, 130
43:17 82
43:18 120
43:18–19 346, 357
43:19 120, 304, 305
43:19–21 354
43:20 82, 132
43:21 82
43:22–24 68, 143
43:22–28 143
43:22–44:23 viii, 68, 136, 144
43:25 105, 143
43:27–28 143
43:28 146
44–45 70, 114, 271, 286, 314
44:1–2 132
44:1–5 143, 186
44:2 104
44:3–4 354
44:6 105, 118, 155
44:6–8 143
44:7 166
44:8 104
44:9–10 178
44:9–11 91
44:9–20 166
44:11 170
44:12 184
44:13 156
44:16 196
44:21–22 143
44:22 155
44:23 143, 155, 247, 293, 364
44:24 105, 154, 209
44:24–28 102
44:24–45:13 viii, 147, 148, 273
44:24–47:15 170, 172
44:24–48:22 viii, 72, 147
44:25–26 154
44:25–28 154
44:26 82, 276
44:27 131, 154
44:28 xxv, 56, 117, 154, 189, 204, 213, 232, 272, 303
44:28–45:7 146
45 353, 362
45–48 199
45:1 117, 154, 160, 302
45:1–6 186
45:1–7 102, 160, 162
45:1–8 xxv
45:2 105
45:2–3 154
45:3 105, 157, 160, 161
45:3–5 118
45:3–7 154
45:4 132, 187
45:5 177
45:5–8 105
45:6 157
45:7 94, 272
45:8 102, 154, 305
45:8–24 321
45:9–11 102, 154
45:10 131
45:11–13 157
45:12 94, 105, 154, 209
45:13 xxv, 102, 105, 131, 154, 186, 187, 189, 204, 213, 232, 272, 276, 297, 302, 303
45:14 160
45:14–25 viii, 147, 158
45:15–18 160
45:17 239
45:18 105
45:18–19 161
45:19 102, 105
45:20 43, 161, 170
45:20–21 161
45:21 105
45:22 105, 161, 320
45:22–23 161
45:23–24 161
45:24 xxv
45:24–26 161
45:25 107
46 xxiv, 24, 171
46–47 24
46:1–2 91, 165, 170
46:1–13 viii, 147, 163
46:3 43
46:3–7 165
46:4 105
46:5 91
46:5–11 90
46:8–11 166
46:9 105, 120
46:10 156
46:10b–13 xxv
46:12 177
46:12–13 166
46:13 177, 321

46:15 131
46:17 131
47 xxiv, 18, 24, 65, 67
47:1–15 viii, 147, 167, 170
47:4 140
47:12 178
47:14 196, 364
48 24, 199
48:1–11 176
48:1–22 viii, 147, 172
48:2, 3 120
48:3–11 176
48:6 120
48:7 94
48:10 132
48:12 105
48:12–15 102, 176
48:12–16 176
48:13 105
48:14 156, 319
48:14–15 xxv
48:15–17 105
48:16 xxiv, 176, 197, 203
48:16–20 117
48:16–21 147
48:17–19 176
48:18 86, 363
48:18–19 176
48:20 127, 189, 197, 217, 262, 320
48:20–21 16, 81, 176, 203, 147
48:21–22 176
48:22 72, 176, 219, 262, 264
49 79, 156, 286, 362
49–52 199, 271
49–54 43, 46, 202, 314
49–57 xxv, 72, 202
49–60 120
49:1 103, 175
49:1–4 185, 189, 199, 201, 303
49:1–6 70, 116, 320
49:1–13 189
49:1–21 viii, 180, 181
49:1–52:12 viii, 72, 180
49:3 185, 293
49:4 189, 201, 304
49:5 185, 186
49:5–6 117
49:5–7 201, 204
49:5–8 xxv
49:5–9 217, 227
49:5–12 186, 189, 273
49:6 82, 127, 204, 213, 272, 275, 295, 297, 302
49:6–8 185, 321
49:6–9 246
49:7 77, 82, 132, 186, 226
49:8 186, 213, 245, 259, 272, 293, 303, 310
49:8–9 232, 276, 297
49:8–12 81, 186
49:9 131, 300, 302
49:9–10 354
49:9–11 186
49:9–12 185
49:11 15, 320
49:12 86
49:13 82, 107, 185, 186, 247
49:14 193, 213, 236
49:14–21 185, 186, 187
49:15 105
49:15–16 187
49:16 313
49:16–17 313
49:17 187
49:18 77, 105, 187, 236
49:18–21 193
49:19 187, 215, 217, 310
49:19–21 187
49:20–21 363
49:21 131
49:22 195, 320
49:22–23 192, 297
49:22–50:3 viii, 180, 190, 192
49:23 105
49:24 213
49:24–25 192
49:25 6
49:26 105
50 303
50:1–3 192
50:2 16, 86, 345
50:2–5 203
50:4 302
50:4–6 197
50:4–9 viii, xxiv, 70, 116, 117, 197, 201, 203, 227, 228, 231, 305
50:4–51:8 viii, 180, 193, 197
50:6 206, 279
50:9 206
50:10 126, 227, 246
50:10–11 197
51 156, 239
51–52 303
51:1 102, 198, 239
51:1–3 198
51:1–8 198
51:2 238, 304
51:4–5 198
51:4–8 xxv, 287
51:5 102, 319, 320
51:5–8 321
51:6 198, 206
51:7 82, 102, 104
51:7–8 198
51:8 198, 200
51:9 319
51:9–10 81
51:9–11 347
51:9–52:2 viii, 180, 207, 210, 211
51:10 86, 131
51:11 7, 365
51:12 105
51:13 128, 209
51:15 86, 105, 140, 196
51:16, 17 82
51:17–52:2 209
51:18 131
51:22 82
52–53 25
52:1 xxv
52:2 82
52:3–12 viii, 180, 214, 216, 217
52:4, 5 82
52:6 xxv, 82, 105
52:7 226
52:7–10 230, 232, 247
52:9 215
52:10 77, 230, 305, 320
52:11 176, 203, 216, 320
52:11–12 81, 176, 197, 201, 262, 347
52:12–15 xxv, 228
52:12 216, 270
52:13 117, 178, 226, 228, 230, 232
52:13–53:12 viii, 70, 116, 201, 203, 219, 222, 229, 305
52:13–57:21 viii, 72, 219, 267
52:14 203, 226, 230
52:14–15 232
52:15 226
53 viii, xxiv, 24, 220, 227, 228, 236, 246, 247, 251, 303
53–57 200
53:1 226
53:1–6 226
53:1–11 117
53:1–12 197
53:2 225
53:4–6 233
53:4–12 203
53:5 226
53:6 131, 257
53:7 243
53:7–8 226
53:7–9 227
53:8, 9 226
53:10 xxv, 156
53:10–12 226, 233
53:11 117, 226, 228
53:11–12 230
53:12 227
54 200, 220, 239, 244, 246, 321, 338, 362
54–55 255
54:1 131
54:1–17b viii, 219, 233, 236
54:3 245
54:4 104
54:5 140
54:6 313
54:8 282
54:9 238, 239, 247
54:11 105
54:11–15 xxv
54:16 92, 105
54:17b 331, 334
54:17c 82, 117, 249
54:17c–56:8 viii, 200, 219, 236, 240, 244, 245
55 162, 163, 200, 244, 245, 314, 347
55:1 248
55:1–5 244
55:1–8 250, 364
55:3 304
55:3–5 244
55:6–7 244
55:6–11 245
55:6–13 244
55:7 356
55:8 131
55:8–9 244
55:9 131, 310
55:9–13 354
55:10 131
55:10–11 244
55:11 xxv, 156, 178
55:12–13 81, 244
55:13 186, 365
55:26 297
56 314
56–59 303
56–66 81
56:1 xxv, 321
56:1–8 245, 250
56:2–4 276
56:3–8 365
56:4 132, 156, 345
56:5 365
56:7 355, 365
56:8 xxv, 253
56:9–12 255, 256, 257, 273
56:9–57:13 viii, 219, 251, 255, 256
56:10 254
56:10–57:22 254
56:11 343, 356

57–58 267
57:1 xxv
57:1–2 357
57:1–10 273
57:1–13 256, 342
57:3–10 200
57:4 273
57:6 364
57:8 356
57:10 356
57:11 xxv, 311
57:12 178
57:13 265, 355
57:13–15 347
57:14 197, 320
57:14–21 viii, 219, 260
57:15 58, 297, 302, 355
57:17 282, 343, 356
57:18 356
57:19 94
57:21 72, 176, 179, 364
58 284
58–61 viii
58–62 200
58–63 xxv
58–66 72
58:1 200, 280
58:1–9 335
58:1–14 viii, xxv, 265, 268, 271, 272, 273, 277
58:1–62:12 72
58:2 356
58:2–12 200
58:3 283
58:5–6 132
58:5–14 277
58:6 302
58:6–9 297
58:8 305, 312
58:9 357
58:10 260, 295
58:10–11 277
58:11 364
58:12 303, 304
58:13 200, 343, 356
58:14 16
58:18 344
59 200
59:1–15a viii, 265, 277, 280, 281, 282
59:2 273, 282
59:4 273, 356, 357
59:4–15 xxv
59:6 356
59:7 356
59:8 343, 356
59:9 260
59:11 60
59:12 273
59:15b–21 ix, 265, 284, 286
59:16 285, 317, 321
59:17 301
59:18 320
59:19 364
59:20 273
60 117, 156, 239, 303, 304, 306, 310, 311, 312, 314, 320
60–61 239, 314
60–62 362
60–64 239
60–66 24, 43
60:1 xxv, 15, 364
60:1–3 364
60:1–7 298
60:1–22 ix, 265, 289, 293, 294, 295
60:2 312
60:3 305, 364
60:3–4 294
60:5–7 363
60:8 298
60:8–22 266
60:9 320
60:9–12 298
60:10 303, 312
60:11 363
60:13 298, 262
60:14 312, 364
60:15 239, 313
60:16 16
60:17–18 321
60:17–21 xxv
60:18 312
60:19 239
60:20 239, 363
60:21 239, 303, 319, 343
60:22 312
61 239, 267, 310, 311
61:1 286, 287
61:1–3 117, 203, 310
61:1–4 xxiv
61:1–11 ix, 265, 299, 301, 302
61:2 15
61:2–3 363
61:3 xxv, 293
61:4 120, 239, 271
61:4–8 120
61:6 343, 363, 364
61:7 239
61:7–11 xxv
61:8 239, 312, 344
61:9 364, 365
61:10 107
61:10–11 321
61:11 364
62 200
62–64 311
62–66 ix, 306
62:1 311, 343
62:1–2 321
62:1–3 197
62:1–7 ix, 306, 309, 310, 314, 320, 321, 323, 330
62:2 120, 320, 364
62:2–4 364
62:4 320
62:5 132
62:6 311
62:6–7 306, 320
62:6–9 xxiv
62:6–11 197
62:6–12 117
62:8–9 322, 354
62:8–63:6 ix, 306, 314, 317
62:10 15
62:10–12 176
62:11 344, 364
62:12 346
63 166, 239
63–64 200, 239, 342, 345, 346
63–65 244
63–66 200
63:1 10, 321
63:1–3 16
63:1–4 18
63:1–5 xxv
63:1–6 80, 307, 317
63:1–8 10
63:1–66:24 72
63:4 15, 303
63:5 285
63:7 329, 335, 336
63:7–14 329, 330
63:7–19 311, 314
63:7–64:11[12] ix, 211, 306, 314, 323, 329
63:9 16, 239, 329
63:11 239, 329, 336
63:11–12 238
63:12 239, 329
63:15 131, 330
63:15–64:1 329
63:16 16, 238, 239, 329, 330, 336, 337
63:17 330
63:18 266
63:19 239, 327, 329, 330
63:19–64:1 10
64 166, 311, 312, 314
64:1 364
64:1–3 330
64:2 327
64:3 239, 329
64:3–7 329
64:3–8 330
64:4 239, 329
64:4–5 321
64:6 282
64:8 329
64:9 266, 310
64:9–11 329, 330
64:10 266
64:11 130, 131, 311, 340, 343, 347, 348
65 334, 357, 364
65–66 xxiv, 166, 314, 338
65:1 355, 367
65:1–2 345
65:1–16 ix, 306, 338, 339, 342
65–66:24 ix, 306, 337
65:2–4 200
65:3 364
65:4 356, 364
65:5 357, 364
65:6 311
65:7 120, 200
65:8–10 363
65:9 132, 275, 365
65:9–10 354
65:11 355
65:11–12 200, 348
65:12 132, 356, 264
65:13–14 348
65:13–16 46, 117, 244
65:13–25 363
65:15 132
65:15–16 348
65:16 120, 348
65:17 35, 94, 120
65:17–18 353
65:17–25 135
65:17–66:5 ix, 306, 338, 349, 351, 352
65:17–66:24 24, 81
65:18 94
65:19 107
65:19–24 357
65:19–25 354
65:22 132
65:23 365
65:24–25 351
65:25 255, 257, 265
66 16, 25, 71, 145, 162, 163, 298, 365
66:1 352
66:1–2 351, 357
66:1–3 91, 353

66:1–8 355
66:1–24 72
66:2 46, 58, 297
66:2–5 351
66:3 132, 352
66:3–4 200
66:4 132, 345
66:5 351, 357
66:5–6 200
66:6–16 361
66:6–24 ix, 306, 338, 358, 362
66:7–9 35
66:10 107
66:11 261, 293
66:17 356
66:18 15, 46
66:18–20 362
66:18–21 133, 188, 257
66:18–23 295
66:18–24 339, 362
66:19 43
66:20 335
66:21 249, 353
66:22 120, 286
66:24 12, 71, 200, 262

Jeremiah

1:6 79
2:3 344
2:6–7 81
2:20–3:18 255
4:4 12
4:9 165
4:13 364
5:8 87
5:23 341
6:6 60
7:13 345
7:15 357
7:18 343
7:22, 25 81
8:7 56
9:25 11
10:2 354
10:14 257
10:25 197
11:4, 7 81
11:17 343
14:6 56
14:12 273
16:7 261
16:19 34
17:4 343
17:11 55
17:18 341
17:27 12
18 336
18:19 191
19:13 343
20:6 64
22:17 60
23:9–40 48
23:18, 22 78
24:1 64
24:4–7 347
25:15–25 11
27:5 211
28:3 64
28:15–16 143
29:16 357
29:22 345
31:11 17
31:20 363
31:23 355
31:29 346
31:35 209
32:17, 21 211
32:35 258
33:5 282
33:16 312
33:25 354
34:4–5 143
34:8, 15, 17 303
36:5 11
36:12, 20 26
36:30 9
37:15, 20 26
46:10 11
48:24 11
49:7–22 11
50:17 60
50:34 196
50:36 151
51:17 257
51:34 211
52:12–13 273

Lamentations

1:10 266
2:5–9 266
2:11 56
3:4 60
4:17 56
4:21 11
4:21–22 11
5:18 266

Ezekiel

1:4–14 35
5:2 196
9–11 80
9:9 270
10:1–2 36
14:8 32
16 178, 255
16:5 9
18 346, 347
18:2 348
20:27–28 344
20:33–34 211
21:3–5 143
21:4 12
21:11 341
22:8 248
23 178, 255
23:38 248
25:3 266
25:12–14 11
27:10 365
27:25 254
29:3 211
30:5 365
32:2 211
32:14–15 326
34:1–10 256
35 11
35:1–15 11
35:9 152
37 364
37:12 365
38:22 12
39:23, 24, 29 282
40–48 330, 343, 353
44–46 276
44:5 343
44:10 357
44:13, 15 343
46:1 248
48:35 312

Daniel

1–6 145
1:3–18 249
4:27, 33 15
5:18 15
8:1 74
9:4–19 330
9:16, 20 355
12:2 361

Hosea

1–3 106, 178, 255
2:14–20 332
2:16–17 81
5:9 34
6:5 209
11:1 81, 363
11:1–4 364
11:8 261
12:2–4 144
12:10, 14 81
13:4–5 81

Joel

2:1 355
2:13 273
2:22 14
4:2–8 266
4:17 355
4:19 11

Amos

1:11–12 11
1:12 12
2:9–10 81
3:1–2 81
7:16–17 143
9:7 81

Obadiah

1 213
1:5 189
1:8–15 11
1:11 11
1:12, 14 34

Jonah

3:5–10 274

Micah

1:3 10
1:4 5
3:3 60
3:4 282
3:8 273
4:1–3 24
6:4 81
6:8 248
7:17 191

Nahum

1:7 34
2:4 316

Habakkuk

1 346
3:8 364

Zephaniah

1:5 343
1:7 11
1:14 125
3:14–20 82

Haggai

1:1 202
1:1–2:9 231
1:1–2:23 220
1:8 357
1:12, 14 202
1:10–23 231
2:2, 4 202
2:16 316
2:21, 23 202

Zechariah

1–8 228
1:13 261
2:10 357
2:13, 15 176
3–4 220
3:8–10 143
4 202
4:6 192
4:9 176
4:10 79, 214, 218
6:15 176
7 274
7–8 272
7–9 273
7:1–3 255, 333
7:1–19 335
7:2 47
7:4–14 333
8:3 355
8:3–18 217
8:11–13 347
8:23 364
9–14 267
9:9 82
10:2–3 156
11:3–9 156
11:16–17 156
12:1 9
12:7 156

Malachi

1:4 11
1:6–9 255
1:12 261

B. Old Testament Apocrypha and Pseudepigrapha

1 Esdras

3:13–4:63 202

Wisdom of Solomon

16:13 59

1 Maccabees

5:26 11

3 Maccabees

5:51 59

C. The New Testament

Matthew

1:21 46
3:3 77
4:17 250
5:2–12 248
5:3 355
5:23–24 275
6:5 277
10:16–23 251
12:18, 20 113
13:24–30 346
13:38–42 347
16:18 260
17:20 192
18:28–30 60
20:28 253
22:1–14 250
22:8–10 246
23:6 277
23:37–39 250
25:31–46 345, 347
26:28 233
28:20 104

Mark

1:2 250
8:11–12 347
9:48 12
10:45 233
13:25 9
14:24 233
15 250

Luke

4:14–21 305
4:17–21 250
4:18 300, 303
6:20–26 345
11:5–10 314
11:29–30 347
11:42–43 277
14:15–24 250
14:16–24 246
17:6 192
18:8 193
18:13–14 355
20:46 277
22:20, 37 233

John

1:5 260
7:6 96
9:2 346
10:27–29 365
17:20–21 250

Acts

8:27–37 249
8:34 117, 227
10:34–35 250
10:43 250
11:38 250
13:9 312
20:38–39 250

Romans

1:21–32 257
2:24 216
6:4 62
9–11 250
10:20 340, 343
10:21 343
11:26 286
13:1 121

1 Corinthians

2:9 327
11:23–25 322
15:58 322

2 Corinthians

1:3–5 364
12:9 109

Philippians

2:6–9 62
2:6–11 163

Hebrews

13:14 109

James

1:27 275

1 Peter

1:23 365
1:24 78

1 John

1:5 260
2:8 260

Revelation

6:14 9
7:9–17 61
12:5 363
14 109
16:19 172
17:5 172
18:10, 21 172
21 366

Index of Key Hebrew Words

אבלים 303
אדם 271–74
און 356
אות 365
אחרון 103, 120
איים 103
אמת 51, 66, 119
אני/אנכי 105
ארץ 92, 188, 354

בחר/בחיר 131–32, 272
בטח 23–25, 27–28
ברא 93–94, 120, 130, 132, 263, 353
ברית 188

גאל 16, 105–7, 130, 132, 146
גד 345

דרור 303

זכר 331

ישע 43–44, 134, 205–6, 287, 312

חדל 55, 59
חדש 120, 353
חזק 103–5
חטאת 273
חסד 78, 81
חסדי יהוה 331
חפץ 272
חפצי בה 313

חרבות 215–16
חשה 130, 311

טוב 51

לילית 13–14

מבשר 216
מזכיר 26, 313
מכתם 59
מלך 26–27
מנה 345
מצער 327, 334
משפט 114, 119, 204, 206

נאצה
נחלה 188, 244, 245
נחם 303
נקם 303

ספר 26

עבד 46, 115–18, 117, 119, 125, 144, 201, 227–28, 244, 334
עבדים 244, 334
עווים 302
עולם 82, 120, 237–39, 247, 304, 332
עם 82, 188
ענוים 302
עצה 23–25, 27, 42, 166
ערב 60
עשקה 60

פדה 16–17
פליטה 42–3
פקד 59
פשע 273, 283

צדק/צדקה 102, 105, 133–34, 162, 204, 205–6, 248, 257, 275, 287, 301, 303–4, 312
צום 273–74
צור 145
צמח 305

קדש 343
קום 82
קדוש ישראל 42
קצות הארץ 103

ראשון 103, 120, 353, 354
רעים 255–56
רשע 179, 263–64

שארית 42–43
שלם/שלום 51, 60, 102, 363
שמים 353–54
שממה 313
שקר 257

תוכחה 34
תורה 119, 204
תצמיח 305